The Life of Muhammad

Muhammad Husayn Haykal

Translated from the 8th Edition
of *Hayat Muhammad* by
Isma'il Ragi A. al Faruqi

American Trust Publications

© American Trust Publications 1397/1976

First Print 1976
Second Print 1993
Third Print 1995
Fourth Print 2005

Library of Congress cataloging in publication data
A catalog record for this book is available from the Library of Congress

ISBN 0-89259-137-4

American Trust Publications

Printed in the United States of America

Dedication

To Those Who Seek the Truth
for the Sake of the Truth

Contents

List of Illustrations

Foreword to the English Edition

The book, *Hayat Muhammad,* by Dr. Muhammad Husayn Haykal is well known to the Arabic reader. It is a biography of the Holy Prophet, *salla Allahu 'alayhi wa sallam,* written in light of all the rules and requirements of modern, exacting scholarship. As its author has said, it is a renewed effort to establish the historical truth of the details of the Prophet's life in accordance with these rules, as well as to refute, by the same means, the false allegations against Islam and its Apostle. It has derived its materials from genuine sources and treated them with a mind unshackled by *parti pris* or superstition, by ignorance or false hopes. We trust that it will be followed by the research works of many other scholars; for the English readers stand in great need for books to enlighten them in the nature and history of Islam.

Fortunately, Islamic sanity has persistently resisted all attempts at deifying the Prophet's person. Despite the fact that no human being has ever commanded as much respect, and none has ever been object of so much affection by his followers, Muslims have rejected every suggestion imputing to the Prophet superhuman power or characteristics. By itself, and when compared with the conceptions of the careers of charismatic founders and leaders of other religions in history, the Muslims' insistence on Muhammad's humanity remains a miracle, a genuine triumph of the Muslim's historical sense. This book is a tribute to the Muslims' critical attitude in religious matters.

This is the fact which makes the quest of the historical Muhammad not only possible, but certain of achieving its objectives. It underlies this book and blesses its findings, as it invites further research and offers greater promise. Biography was never a critical science (it may even be contended that it ever existed!) before the Muslims began to sift the oral and written traditions concerning the Prophet. They undertook this task with a mind unwaveringly committed to Muhammad's humanity, absolutely convinced of his fulfillment of his mission under the full light of history.

It was these Muslim endeavors that produced the science of textual criticism. Firstly, the language, style, form, redaction and vocabulary of every reported tradition was subjected to the most complete analysis. Secondly, the ideational content of every tradition was subjected to critical tests of internal and external coherence *(i.e.,* with itself, with the Holy Qur'an, with other traditions, with other established historical data). That content was further tested for historical relevance and relationality, and for reasonableness or systematic correspondence with reality. Finally, every *isnad* (or chain of reporters) was subjected to the most exacting tests of historicity and verification, giving birth to *'Ilm al Rijal,* or the critical establishment of the minutest details of the personal lives of thousands of Muhammad's companions and contemporaries. This was Islamic "Criticism" — a whole millennium ago! It was objective and scientific textual research such as the world has never seen nor probably ever will, despite the tremendous advances the science of criticism has made in modern times. This academic sophistication has made of Islam the scholarly, modernist, critical religion long before the priesthood, not to speak of the laity, of other religions achieved the minimum standards of literacy. Unfortunately for humanity as a whole, this critical and scientific spirit was lost to the Muslims with their decline.

How refreshing it is to see in this book evidence of awakening and reactivation of this spirit which Islam, the foremost champion of natural religion, of reasonableness in religion, has nurtured through the centuries! Great as the achievements of our ancestors are, it is our duty to make ourselves worthy of them. Benefit from their achievement, we certainly must. Indeed, inspired by their example, we ought to move and aspire to match and surpass them. Muhammad Husayn Haykal's *Hayat Muhammad* is a fair step in that direction.

This book has another value. For centuries, the English reader has been presented with prejudiced literature about Islam and the Prophet.

Such polemics has prevented the non-Muslim from appreciating the genuine light of revelation, the beneficial contribution Islam can make to the solution of humanity's spiritual and social ills in modern times. It is certainly high time for the voice of Islam to be raised against the forces of atheism and materialism which have blinded modern man and dissipated his effort at finding the truth. Allah, *subhanahu wa ta'ala*, does not wish man to be lost in skepticism, to be corrupted by injustice, alienation and ethnocentrism. On the contrary, He wishes him to realize universal brotherhood through justice, truth, dignity and mercy; to restore to him his lost poise and equilibrium; to guide him towards peace, well-being and happiness. It is He Who said in His Holy Book:

يَٰٓأَيُّهَا ٱلنَّاسُ إِنَّا خَلَقْنَٰكُم مِّن ذَكَرٍ وَأُنثَىٰ وَجَعَلْنَٰكُمْ شُعُوبًا وَقَبَآئِلَ لِتَعَارَفُوٓا۟

"0 mankind! We created you from a single (pair) of male and female, and made you into nations and tribes, that ye may know and cooperate with one another" (49: 13).

يَٰٓأَيُّهَا ٱلنَّاسُ ٱتَّقُوا۟ رَبَّكُمُ ٱلَّذِى خَلَقَكُم مِّن نَّفْسٍ وَٰحِدَةٍ وَخَلَقَ مِنْهَا زَوْجَهَا وَبَثَّ مِنْهُمَا رِجَالًا كَثِيرًا وَنِسَآءً وَٱتَّقُوا۟ ٱللَّهَ ٱلَّذِى تَسَآءَلُونَ بِهِۦ وَٱلْأَرْحَامَ إِنَّ ٱللَّهَ كَانَ عَلَيْكُمْ رَقِيبًا ۝

"0 mankind! Reverence your Guardian Lord, Who created you from a single person; Who created the first person's mate of like nature; Who created from them twain all men and women on earth" (4:1).

إِنَّمَا ٱلْمُؤْمِنُونَ إِخْوَةٌ

"The believers are but a single brotherhood" (49:9).

$$\text{إِنَّ اللهَ يَأْمُرُ بِالْعَدْلِ وَالْإِحْسَانِ وَإِيتَآئِ ذِى الْقُرْبَى وَيَنْهَى عَنِ الْفَحْشَآءِ وَالْمُنْكَرِ وَالْبَغْيِ يَعِظُكُمْ لَعَلَّكُمْ تَذَكَّرُونَ}$$

"God commands justice, the doing of the good, and liberality to kith and kin. He forbids all shameful deeds, injustice and rebellion. Thus does He instruct you, that you may receive admonition" (16 :90).

The Prophet of Islam *(salla Allahu 'alayhi wa sallam)* has said:

$$\text{النَّاسُ سَوَاسِيَةٌ كَأَسْنَانِ الْمُشْطِ}$$

"All Muslims are equal like the teeth of a comb."

$$\text{الْمُسْلِمُ لِلْمُسْلِمِ كَالْبُنْيَانِ يَشُدُّ بَعْضُهُ بَعْضًا}$$

"In relation to one another, the Muslims are like a building: every unit reinforces and is reinforced by all others."

These values of Islam are indeed the only ones capable of saving humanity from its certain collapse. The life of the Prophet is the guide and key. His conduct is the example for everyone to follow at all times and places.

It is of the essence of rational religion, as it is of the truth, to convince and to persuade its audience by mere presentation. But presentation must be honest and critical, thorough and substantiated, as well as alive and appealing. It is by Allah's grace that Professor Isma'il Ragi al Faruqi completed translation of this volume. He is a Muslim scholar of great renown, gifted with deep Islamic knowledge and commitment.

Recognition is equally due to the World Assembly of Muslim Youth and to the Muslim Students Association of the United States and Canada for their part in bringing this project to fulfillment. We pray that Allah may continue to guide them as well as all other organizations and Islamic academic establishments dedicated to Islam, and assist them in their work for the salvation of mankind.

Allah alone is our help! He alone is Witness of our commitment and Judge of our deed!

— Hasan ibn ʿAbdullah Al al Shaykh
   Riyad, Dhu al Hijjah 1395

Translator's Preface

Haykal's *Hayat Muhammad* has a long and strange story. Its translation into English and publication by the University of Chicago Press was discussed by numerous western experts in the forties and early fifties. Obvious as the need for a scholarly sympathetic biography of the Prophet may be, negotiations took years to complete. Agreement, however, was not reached until 1964. When in 1968 the translation was completed, approved by the Supreme Council of Islamic Affairs, Cairo, Egypt, and the University of Chicago Press, the manuscript copy edited, and its actual production begun, mysterious forces intervened and the University of Chicago Press unilaterally withdrew from its agreement.

Another agreement was negotiated *de novo* between the same parties and Temple University Press, on practically the same terms as Chicago, in 1969. Five years passed with little or no action. Then, mysterious forces again intervened and resulted in the unilateral withdrawal of Temple University Press from its agreement.

This Determined opposition to the publication of the work did not dissuade the translator from preparing this new translation with the encouragement of the Muslim Students' Association of the United States and Canada, an agency interested in the promotion of Islamic scholarship.

— Isma'il Ragi al Faruqi
  Temple University, Philadelphia
  Safar 1396 / February 1976

Translator's Acknowledgments

The assistance of the Supreme Council of Islamic Affairs, Arab Republic of Egypt, in making the translation of this work possible; of Professor Roger Parsell in copy editing; of Professor Erdogan Gurmen, Sr. Freda Shamma, Miss Andrée Coers, Mrs. Margaret Peirce, Dr. Lois Lamiya' al Faruqi, and Dr. Kaukab Siddique in proofreading; of Sr. Anmar al Faruqi in preparing the index; of Dr. Lois Lamiya' al Faruqi in preparing the maps and illustrations; and of the North American Islamic Trust in the production of this book is gratefully acknowledged.

I wish to acknowledge with thanks the financial help and encouragement extended to this work by the World Assembly of Muslim Youth, Saudi Arabia.

Foreword to the First Edition

Ever since man appeared on earth he has been anxious to penetrate the universe and discover its laws and secrets. The more he came to know, the more he wondered at its greatness, the weaker he appeared to himself and the less reason he saw for vanity, The Prophet of Islam — may God's peace be upon him — is very much like the universe. From the very beginning, scholars worked hard to uncover various aspects of his great humanity, to grasp the realization of the divine attributes in his mind, character and wisdom. Certainly they achieved a fair measure of Knowledge. Much however has escaped them; and there still lies ahead a long and indeed infinite road.

Prophethood is a gift which cannot be acquired. In His wisdom God grants it to whosoever stands prepared for it and is capable of carrying it. He knows best when and where it will be of most benefit. Muhammad — may God's peace and blessing be upon him — was indeed prepared to carry the prophetic message unto all the races of mankind. He was equipped to carry the message of the most perfect religion, to be the final conclusion of prophethood, the unique light of guidance for ever and ever.

The infallibility of the prophets in the conveyance of their message and the performance of their divine trust is a matter on which the scholars have agreed for a long time. Once they are chosen for their task, the prophets' conveyance of their message and their performance of the duties entrusted to them carry no reward. Their work is a necessary consequence of such divine revelation. Like all men, prophets are truly fallible; their distinction lies in that God does not leave them in their error. He corrects them and often even blames them therefor.

Muhammad — may God's peace and blessing be upon him — was commanded to convey a divine message. But he was not shown how to carry it out nor how to protect the fruits of his work. It was left to him as any rational and sentient being to conduct his affairs as his intelligence and wisdom might dictate. The revelation which he received was absolutely precise and clear in all that concerns the essence, unity, attributes and worship of God. But this was not the case as regards the social institutions of family, village and city, the state in its relations with the said institutions and with other states. There is hence wide scope for research on the Prophet's greatness before his commission as prophet, as there is after his commission had taken place. He became a messenger for his Lord, calling men unto Him, protecting the new faith and guaranteeing the freedom and security of its preachers. He became the ruler of the *Ummah* of Islam,[1] its commander in war and teacher, the judge and organizer of all its internal and foreign affairs. Throughout his career he established justice and reconciled hopelessly disparate and hostile nations and groups. His wisdom, farsightedness, perspicacity, presence of mind and resoluteness are evident in all that he said or did. From him streams of knowledge have sprung and heights of eloquence have arisen to which the great bend their heads in awe and wonder. He departed from this world satisfied with his work, assured of God's pleasure and crowned with the gratitude of men.

All these aspects of the Prophet's life deserve special study and research. It is not possible for anyone scholar to give them their due; nor to exhaust the meanings inherent in anyone of them.

Like that of any other great man, the biography of Muhammad — may God's blessing be upon him and upon his house — has been expanded by many an imaginary story, whether innocently or with ulterior motive, deliberately or accidentally. Unlike all other biographies, however, a great portion of it has been included in the divine revelation and has thus been preserved forever in the pure Qur'an. Another fair portion has been safely preserved for us by trustworthy narrators. From these unmistakable sources the biography of the Prophet should be constructed, and on their basis its hidden meanings and complicated problems should be investigated, and its moral established. Its constitutive materials should be subjected to objective and scholarly analysis taking well into consideration the circumstances of time and environment as well as the prevalent beliefs, institutions and customs.

In his book, *The Life of Muhammad,* Dr. Haykal gave us the biography of the Prophet — may God's peace and blessings be upon him — which I have had the pleasure of reading in part before printing. Dr. Haykal is well known to the Arabic reader; his many books obviate the need for an introduction. He studied law and familiarized himself with logic and philosophy. His personal circumstances and career enabled him to study ancient as well as modern culture and to learn a great deal from both. He lectured on and debated, attacked and defended many questions of belief, of social organization and politics. The maturity of his mind is matched by the perfection of his knowledge, and the wide range of his readings. He debates with powerful, convincing arguments and he treats his subject with sound logic and a style all his own. Such preparation stands behind Dr. Haykal's book. In his Preface, Dr. Haykal wrote: "No one should think that research in the life of Muhammad is completed with this work; and I am far from making any such claim. It is closer to the truth for me to say that my work is really only the beginning of scientific research in this field in Arabic."[2] The reader might be surprised if the strong resemblance of the modern scientific method to the call of Muhammad is pointed out. The former demands that the investigator suspend his own beliefs and refrain from prejudgment, to begin his investigation with observation of the data, and then to proceed to experimentation, comparison, classification and finally to conclusion based upon these objective steps. A conclusion thus arrived at is scientific in that it is itself subject to further testing and critical analysis. It is reliable only as long as further scientific investigations do not disprove any of the premises on which it is based. True, the scientific method is the highest achievement of the human race in its effort to liberate man's thought, but it is precisely the method of Muhammad and the foundation of his call.

Dr. Haykal's new method is truly Qur'anic. For he has made reason the judge, and evidence the foundation, of knowledge. He has repudiated conservatism and castigated the conservatives. Agreeing with the Qur'anic principle "opinion and speculation are no substitute for true knowledge" (Qur'an, 53 :28), Dr. Haykal has chastised those who speculate without evidence; who regard the old purely for its age, as sacred. He has imposed the teaching of the truth upon all those who have the capacity to grasp it. "Muhammad — may God's peace and blessing be upon him — had only one irresistible miracle — the Qur'an. But it is not irrational. How eloquent is the verse of al Busayri: 'God did not try us with anything irrational. Thus, we fell under neither doubt nor illusion.'"

xxii   The Life of Muhammad

As for Dr. Haykal's claim that this method is a modern method, that is rather questionable. In holding such a claim, Dr. Haykal was reconciling the scholars who are his would-be critics. He himself has acknowledged that this method was the method of the Qur'an. It is also the method of Muslim scholars of the past. Consider the books of *kalam*.[3] Some of them insisted that the first duty of the adult is to know God. Others held that the first incumbent duty is to doubt; for there is no knowledge except by means of proof and argument. Although the process of verification is a kind of deduction, the premises of such reasoning must be either self evident, mediately or immediately given to sense, or dependent upon unmistaken experimentation and generalization, following the rules of logic. The slightest error in any premise or in the form of reasoning vitiates the whole proof.

Al Ghazzali, the great teacher, followed exactly the same method. In one of his books, he reported that he had decided to strip his mind bare of all former opinions, to think and to consider, to compare and to contrast, then to rethink all the proofs and all the evidence step by step. After all this reconstruction he reached the conclusion that Islam is true, and thus established a number of views and arguments regarding its nature. He did all this in order to avoid conservatism, to achieve faith with certitude, founded upon truth and argument. It is this kind of faith arising from rational conviction which, all Muslims agree, cannot but be true and bring about salvation.

The same method or deliberate repudiation of all creeds, as a preliminary to investigation and scholarly study, is found in most books of *kalam*. Doubt is indeed an old method; and so is experimentation and generalization. The latter is founded upon observation; and it is not new with us at all. Neglected and forgotten in the orient since it took to conservatism and irrationalism, this old method was taken up by the West, purged clean, and used with great benefit to science and industry. We are now taking it back from the West thinking that we are adopting a new method of scientific research.

This method then is both old and new. However, to know a method is easy; to apply it is difficult; Men do not differ much in their knowledge of a certain law; but they stand widely apart in their application of it.

To suspend all prejudices, to observe, to experiment, to compare, to deduct and to extrapolate are all easy words. But for man standing under an inheritance of heavy biological and mental burdens, struggling against an oppressive environment of home, village, school, city and country, suffering under the tremendous weight of conditioning by temperament, health, disease and passion — how could it be easy for him to apply the law? That is the question, whether in the past or in the present. That is the reason for the proliferation of views and doctrines. That is the reason for the movement and change of these views from country to country and people to people. With every generation, philosophy and literature don new robes very much like women do. Hardly any theory or principle stands beyond attack, and none is an impregnable fortress. Change has even attacked the theories of knowledge which were venerated during long ages. The theory of relativity brought a whirlwind to accepted scientific principles. But soon, it too was put under attack. Likewise, the theories of nourishment and disease, of their causes and cures, are undergoing continual change. A closer look, therefore, will convince us that there is no security for the productions of our minds unless they are supported by convincing proofs. But what is the proportion of such secure productions of the mind to the long parade of theories which are produced by fancy, projected by sick minds, imposed by politics, or created by scientists who simply love to differ from their peers? This thought may perhaps sober such men of knowledge and science who are too proud of reason and depend on it alone. Such a thought may yet guide them one day toward the truth, to take shelter under the absolute conviction which it provides, the conviction of true revelation, of the holy Qur'an and the veritable *Sunnah*.[4]

Let us now turn to Dr. Haykal and his book. A number of *mutakallimun*[5] have held that the knowledge which astronomy and the dissection of the human body provide clearly points to the fact that divine knowledge includes the most minute details of existence. I concur that the discovery and establishment of the laws and secrets of nature will, besides helping the human mind to penetrate what was incomprehensible before, finally support religion. In this vein, God said, "We shall show them Our signs in the horizons as well as within themselves, and We shall continue to do so until they realize that Our revelation is the truth. Is it not sufficient that your Lord witnesses everything?" (Qur'an, 41 :53). The discovery of electricity and all the theories and inventions to which it has led has made it possible for us to understand how matter may be transformed into energy and energy into matter. Spiritualism has helped us to understand the transcendent nature of the soul and shed light on the possibility of its separate existence, of its capacity to travel through space and time. It has helped explain many matters on which men differed in ignorance. Dr.

Haykal has used this new knowledge in his novel explanation of the story of Muhammad's *Isra*.[6]

To list the good points which Dr. Haykal has made in his book would take many long pages. Suffice it then to point to these contributions in a general way. Undoubtedly, the reader will realize the worth of this work and will learn much from Dr. Haykal's well documented arguments, fine logic, and penetrating insight. The reader will realize that Dr. Haykal's whole devotion has been to the truth alone, and that he has approached his task with a heart replete with the light and guidance of the revelation of Muhammad, as well as with great awe for the beauty, majesty, greatness, and moral height of the life of Muhammad — may God's peace and blessing be upon him. Dr. Haykal is fully convinced that this religion of Muhammad will surely deliver mankind from doubt, from dark materialism, and will open their eyes to the light of conviction, guide them to the divine light with which they will come to know God's infinite mercy. Dr. Haykal is confident that men will thereby come sooner or later to acknowledge the glory of God as heaven and earth already do, and praise the divine might before which all beings become humble. Indeed, he writes: "Indeed, I would even go further. I would assert that such a study may show the road to mankind as a whole to the new civilization to which it is currently groping. If western Christendom is too proud to find the new light in Islam and in its Prophet but willingly accepts it from Indian theosophy and other religions of the Far East then it devolves upon the Orientals themselves, Muslims, Jews or Christians, to undertake this study in all objectivity and fairness in order to reach and establish the truth. Islamic thought rests on a methodology that is scientific and modern as regards all that relates man to nature. In this respect it is perfectly realistic.

But it becomes personalist the moment it leaves nature to consider the relationship of man to the cosmos as a whole and to his creator."[7] Dr. Haykal goes on to say that "the pioneer fighters against this all-embracing paganism of modern times, however, are clearly distinguishable under close observance of the current flow of events. Perhaps, these pioneer forces will grow and become surer of themselves when scholarship has found answers to these spiritual problems through the study of the life of Muhammad, of his teachings, of his age, and of the spiritual world revolution which he incepted."[8]

Dr. Haykal's firm conviction is corroborated by real events. What we have witnessed today of the West's concern for the study of our heritage and the care with which western scholars study the legacy of Islam, its various contents, its ancient and modern history and peoples, of the fair treatment that some of them give to the career of the Prophet — may God's peace and blessing be upon him — and finally, what we know by experience of the necessary final victory of truth — all this leads to the consideration that Islam will spread all over the world. In this process, the strongest protagonists of Islam may well be its strongest enemies whereas its present alien antagonists may be Islam's adherents and defenders. As in the early period the strangers have supported Islam, strangers may yet help it achieve its final victory. It is said that "Islam began as a stranger and will return as a stranger. God bless the strangers!"

Since the Prophet — may God's peace and blessing be upon him — was the last of the prophets, and the world is to have no prophet after him, and since, as the revealed text has said, his religion is the most perfect, it is not possible that the *status quo* of Islam will last. Its light must necessarily eclipse all other lights as the rays of the sun eclipse those of the stars.

Dr. Haykal related the events of the Prophet's life closely to one another. His book therefore presents a closely knit argument. In every case, he has elaborated strong evidence and articulated it clearly and convincingly. His work is not only persuasive; it is pleasant reading and it moves the reader to keep on reading to the very end.

Furthermore, the book contains many studies which do not properly belong to the biography of the Prophet but are necessitated by the author's pursuit of questions related thereto. Finally, let me conclude this prefatory note with the prayer of the master of all men — may God's peace and blessing be upon him, his house, and his followers: "God, I take shelter under the light of Your face before Whom darkness became light, by Whose command this world and the next were firmly established. Save me from Your wrath and displeasure. To You alone belongs the judgment, harsh as it may be when You are not pleased. There is neither power nor strength except in You."

— Muhammad Mustafa al Maraghi
Former Grand Shaykh of al Azhar
15 February, 1935

"God and His angels bless the Prophet. O men who have believed:
Invoke God's peace and blessing upon him"

Qur'an, 33 :56

In the name of God, the Merciful, the Compassionate
Praise be to God, Lord of the universe,
The Gracious, the Merciful,
Master of the Day of Judgment.
You alone we worship; You alone we implore for help.

Guide us unto the straight path —
The path of those whom You have blessed,
Those who have not incurred Your displeasure,
Those who have not gone astray.

Amen

Qur'an, 1 :1-7

Preface to the First Edition

Muhammad, God's peace and blessing be upon him! This noble name has been on the lips of countless millions of men. For almost fourteen centuries, millions of hearts have palpitated with deep emotion at the pronouncement of it. Many more millions of people for a period as long as time, will pronounce it, and will be deeply moved thereby. Every day, as soon as the black thread becomes distinguishable from the white, the muezzin will call men to prayer. He will call them to the worship of God and the invocation of blessing upon His Prophet, a task the fulfillment of which is better for them than their sleep. Thousands and millions of men in every corner of the globe will undoubtedly respond to the muezzin's call, springing to honor through their prayers God's mercy and bounty, richly evidenced for them with the break of every new day. At high noon, the muezzin will call again for the noon prayer; then at mid-afternoon, at sunset, and after sunset. On each of these daily occasions Muslims remember Muhammad, the servant of God and His Prophet, with all reverence and piety. Even in between these prayers the Muslims never hear the name of Muhammad but they hasten to praise God and His chosen one. Thus they have been, and thus they will be until God vindicates His true religion and completes His bounty to all.

Muhammad did not have to wait long for his religion to become known, or for his dominion to spread. God has seen fit to complete the religion of Islam even before his death. It was he who laid down the plans for the propagation of this religion. He had sent to Chosroes, to Heraclius and other princes and kings of the world inviting them to join the new faith. No more than a hundred and fifty years passed from then until the flags of Islam were flying high between Spain in the west and India, Turkestan and indeed China in the east. Thus by joining Islam, the territories of al Sham[1] Iraq, Persia, and Afghanistan have linked the Arabian Peninsula with the kingdom of "the Son of Heaven."[2] On the other hand, the Islamization of Egypt, Burqah, Tunisia, Algeria and Morocco have linked the native land of Muhammad — may God's peace and blessing be upon him — with Europe and Africa. From that time until our day Islam remains supreme throughout all these territories. It withdrew from Spain only under the attack of Christendom which inflicted upon the people of Spain all kinds of suffering and persecution. As the people could not bear these tragedies, some of them returned to Africa. Others under the threats of fear and panic apostasized, withdrew from the religion of their ancestors, and entered into that of the tyrants and conquerors.

What Islam had lost in Spain and in western Europe was regained when the Ottomans conquered Constantinople and established the religion of Muhammad therein. From there, Islam spread throughout the Balkans into Russia and Poland and spread over territories many times wider than Spain. From the day of its initial conquest until now, no religion has ever conquered Islam despite the fact that its people have fallen under all kinds of tyrannies and unjust governments. Indeed, reduction of their worldly power has made the Muslims more strongly attached to their faith, to their Islamic way of life, and to their Islamic hope.

Islam and Christianity

The power with which Islam quickly spread brought it face to face with Christianity and involved the two religions in a *guerre à outrance.* Muhammad vanquished paganism and eliminated it from Arabia just as his early successors pursued it across Persia, Afghanistan and a good portion of India and eliminated it from these territories. Later on the successors of Muhammad conquered Christianity in Hirah, Yaman, Syria, Egypt, and even in the capital of the Christian empire, Constantinople. Was Christianity then to receive the same fate of extinction which befell paganism despite the fact that Muhammad had praised it and confirmed the prophethood of its founder? Were the Arabs, coming out of their arid desert peninsula, destined to conquer the gardens of Spain, of Byzantium, and all Christendom? "No! Death rather than such a fate!" Thus the fight continued for many centuries between the followers of Jesus and the followers of Muhammad. The war was not limited to swords and guns. It spread out to the fields of debate and controversy where the contenders contended in the names of Muhammad and Jesus. No means were spared to sway the community, to arouse the populace and to stir the passions of the people.

The Muslims and Jesus

Islam, however, prevented the Muslims from attacking the person of Jesus. It held that Jesus was a servant of God endowed with scripture and appointed as prophet. It also held that Jesus was always blessed; that he was enjoined as long as he lived to hold prayer and to give *zakat*;[3] that his mother was innocent and that he was neither unjust nor unfortunate. It asserted that Jesus was blessed on the day of his birth, on the day of his future death as well as on the day of his resurrection. Many Christians, on the other hand, have attacked the person of Muhammad and attributed to him the most unbecoming epithets — thereby giving vent to their resentment and sowing the seeds of hatred and hostility. Despite the commonly held view that the Crusades have long been finished and forgotten, fanatic Christian antagonism still continues to rage against Muhammad. The present situation has not changed except perhaps for the worse. Moved by the same fanaticism, the missionaries resort to immoral and depraved means in their struggle against Islam. This fanaticism was never exclusive to the Church. It stirred and inspired many writers and philosophers in Europe and America who are not related to the Church.

Christian Fanatics and Muhammad

One may wonder why Christian fanaticism against Islam continues to rage with such power in an age which is claimed to be the age of light and science, of tolerance and *largeur de coeur*. This fanaticism is all the more surprising when one remembers that the early Muslims were overjoyed at the news of the victory of Christianity over Zoroastrianism, when the armies of Heraclius carried the day against those of Chosroes. Persia had a dominant influence in South Arabia ever since the Persians expelled the Abyssinians from Yaman. Chosroes had sent his army in 614 C.E. under the command of his general named Shahrbaraz[4] to conquer Byzantium. When their armies met in Adhri'at and Busra, territories of al Sham close to Arabia, the Persians inflicted upon the Byzantines heavy losses in lives and destroyed their cities and orchards. The Arabs, especially the people of Makkah, used to follow the news of this war with great anxiety. At the time, the two hostile powers were the greatest on earth. The Arabs adjoined both powers and had territories which fell under the suzerainty of both. The Makkan idolaters rejoiced at the defeat of the Christians and celebrated the event. They regarded them as people with a scripture, very much like the Muslims, and they even attempted to attribute their defeat to their religion. For the Muslims, it was hard to believe the defeat of the Byzantines for the same reason, namely that like them they were a people with scripture. Muhammad and his companions especially hated to see the Zoroastrians victorious. This difference in the views of the Muslims and the idolaters of Makkah led to open contention between the two groups. The Muslims were ridiculed for holding such opinions. One of them was so bold in his show of joy in front of Abu Bakr that the latter, known for his great calm and friendliness, was prompted to say: "Don't take to joy too soon. The Byzantines will avenge themselves." When the idolater rejoined, "This is a lie," Abu Bakr became angry and said: "You are the liar, O Enemy of God: I wager ten camels that the Byzantines will win against the Zoroastrians within the scope of a year." When this came to the notice of Muhammad, he advised Abu Bakr to increase the amount of the wager and to extend its term. Abu Bakr then raised the wager to one hundred camels and extended the time to nine years. In 625 C.E. Heraclius was victorious. He defeated Persia and wrenched from it the territory of Syria as well as the cross of Christ. Abu Bakr won his wager and the prophesying of Muhammad was confirmed in the following Qur'anic revelation: "The Byzantines have been defeated in the land nearby. However, they shall win in a few years. To God belongs the command before and after. Then will the believers rejoice at the victory which God has sent. God, the Mighty and Merciful, gives His victory to whomsoever He wishes, He never fails in His promise. Most men however do not know."[5]

The First Principles of the Two Religions

Muslim rejoicing at the victory of Heraclius and his Christian armies was great. Despite the many controversies that had taken place between the followers of Muhammad and those who believed in Jesus, their friendly and fraternal relationships continued to be strong throughout the life of the Prophet. It was otherwise with the relationships of Muslims and Jews. There had been an armistice followed by alienation and war with consequences so disastrous and bloody that the Jews had to be moved out of the Arabian Peninsula altogether. The Qur'an confirms the bond of friendship between Muslims and Christians and denounces the enmity of the Jews. It advises the Muslims, "You will find greater enmity to the believers among those who are Jews and idolaters; but you will find greater friendliness among those who say, 'We are Christians.' For they, especially the monks and priests among them, do not take to false pride."[6]

Indeed Christianity and Islam entertain the same view of life and ethics. Their view of mankind and of creation is one and the same. Both religions believe that God created Adam and Eve, placed them in paradise and commanded them not to listen to Satan, and that eating of the tree thereby caused them to be discharged. Both religions believe that Satan is the enemy of mankind who, according to the Qur'an, refused to prostrate himself to Adam when commanded to do so by God and, according to Christian scripture, refused to honor the word of God. Satan whispered to Eve and deceived her, and she in turn deceived Adam. They ate from the tree of eternal life, discovered their nakedness, and then pleaded to God to forgive them. God sent them to earth, their descendants enemies of one another, forever open to the deception of Satan, some of them liable to fall under this deception and others capable of resisting it to the end. In order to transcend man's war against this deception, God sent Noah, Abraham, Moses, Jesus and the other prophets, commissioning every one of them to convey in the tongue of his people a book which confirms, elaborates, and makes evident the revelations received from his predecessor-prophet. As Satan is assisted by his helpers among the evil spirits, the angels praise the Lord and adore Him. Both the good and the evil powers therefore compete to win mankind until the Day of Judgment when every soul will receive that which it has earned and when everyone will be responsible for himself alone.

The Difference between Them

Not only has the Qur'an mentioned Jesus and Mary, but it has honored them and presented them in such light that the readers cannot but feel this fraternal feeling towards Christianity when they read its verses. It is all the more perplexing, therefore, that the Muslims and Christians have continued to fight each other century after century. The confusion disappears however, when we learn that Islam has differed from Christianity in many fundamental matters which were subjects of strong controversy, without ever leading to hatred and hostility. Christianity does not acknowledge the prophethood of Muhammad as Islam acknowledges the prophethood of Jesus. Moreover, Christianity upholds trinitarianism whereas Islam strongly rejects anything but the strictest monotheism. The Christians apotheosize Jesus and, in their argument with Muslims, seek confirmation of his divinity in the Qur'anic assertion that he spoke out in the cradle (19 :29-34) and in the many miracles which he alone had been favored by God to perform. During the early days of Islam, the Christians used to dispute with the Muslims in the following vein: Doesn't the Qur'an itself, which was revealed to Muhammad, confirm our view when it says:

إِذْ قَالَتِ الْمَلَائِكَةُ يَا مَرْيَمُ إِنَّ اللَّهَ يُبَشِّرُكِ بِكَلِمَةٍ مِّنْهُ اسْمُهُ الْمَسِيحُ عِيسَى ابْنُ مَرْيَمَ وَجِيهًا فِي الدُّنْيَا وَ الْآخِرَةِ وَ مِنَ الْمُقَرَّبِينَ ۞ وَيُكَلِّمُ النَّاسَ فِي الْمَهْدِ وَ كَهْلًا وَّ مِنَ الصَّالِحِينَ ۞ قَالَتْ رَبِّ أَنَّى يَكُونُ لِي وَلَدٌ وَّ لَمْ يَمْسَسْنِي بَشَرٌ قَالَ كَذَلِكِ اللَّهُ يَخْلُقُ مَا يَشَاءُ إِذَا قَضَى أَمْرًا فَإِنَّمَا يَقُولُ لَهُ كُنْ فَيَكُونُ ۞ وَيُعَلِّمُهُ الْكِتَابَ وَالْحِكْمَةَ وَالتَّوْرَاةَ وَالْإِنْجِيلَ ۞ وَرَسُولًا إِلَى بَنِي إِسْرَائِيلَ ۞ أَنِّي قَدْ جِئْتُكُمْ بِآيَةٍ مِّنْ رَّبِّكُمْ أَنِّي أَخْلُقُ لَكُمْ مِّنَ الطِّينِ كَهَيْئَةِ الطَّيْرِ فَأَنْفُخُ فِيهِ فَيَكُونُ طَيْرًا بِإِذْنِ اللَّهِ وَ أُبْرِئُ الْأَكْمَهَ وَ الْأَبْرَصَ وَ أُحْيِ الْمَوْتَى بِإِذْنِ اللَّهِ وَ أُنَبِّئُكُمْ بِمَا تَأْكُلُونَ وَ مَا تَدَّخِرُونَ فِي بُيُوتِكُمْ إِنَّ فِي ذَلِكَ لَآيَةً لَّكُمْ إِنْ كُنْتُمْ مُّؤْمِنِينَ

"The angels said, 'O Mary, God announces to you His command that a son will be born to you whose name shall be the Messiah, Jesus, Son of Mary, and who will be honored in this world and in the next and be close to God. He will speak as a baby in the cradle and he will be righteous throughout his long age.' Mary asked: 'How can I have a son when no human has touched me?' The angel answered: 'Thus God creates whatever He wills. He commands a thing to be and it is.' God will teach Jesus the scripture, wisdom, the Torah and the Evangel. He will send him a prophet of Israel, and charge him with the conveyance of a new revelation from God. He will confirm him by giving him the power to blow life into birds which he could fashion out of clay, to give vision to the blind, to heal the leper, to resurrect the dead, and to prophesy about what the Jews eat and what they hide in their houses — all with God's permission — that the Jews may believe in him and thereby prove their faith."[7]

The Qur'an then did declare that Jesus would resurrect the dead and give vision to the blind and heal the leper, create birds out of clay and prophesy — all of which are divine prerogatives. Such was the view of the Christians who, at the time of the Prophet, were disputing and arguing with him that Jesus was a god besides God. Another group of them apotheosized Mary on the grounds that she had been the recipient of God's command. The Christian adherents to this view regarded Mary as a member of a trinity which included the Father, the Son and the Holy Ghost.[8] However, those who held that Jesus and his mother were divine were but one of the many sects into which Christianity was divided in those days.

Debate of the Christians with the Prophet

The Christians of the Arabian Peninsula debated with Muhammad on the basis of their diverse views. They argued that Jesus was God, that Jesus was the Son of God, that Jesus was the third person of the trinity. The apotheosizers of Jesus had recourse to the foregoing argument. Those who held the view that Jesus was the Son of God argued that he had no known father, that he had spoken out in the cradle as no other human had ever done. Those who held that he was the third person of the trinity argued that God referred to Himself as "We" in His acts of creation, of commanding and providing, and that this was evidence for his plurality — for otherwise He would have referred to Himself as "I." Muhammad used to listen to all these arguments and debate with them in kindness. He never showed in his debates the hardness and severities which characterized his debates with the associationists[9] and the worshipers of idols. Rather, he argued with them on the basis of revealed scripture and based himself on what could be deduced therefrom. God said: "Blasphemous are those who claim that God is Jesus, the son of Mary. Say, 'Who is capable of anything should God desire to destroy Jesus, the son of Mary, as well as his mother and all that is on the face of the earth? To Him alone belongs the dominion of heaven and earth and all that is in between. He, the Omnipotent, creates what He wills.' Both Jews and Christians claim that they are the sons of God and His favorite people. Say, 'Why does He then punish you for your sins? Rather, you are all humans, on a par with all other men He has created. God forgives whomsoever He wills and punishes whomsoever He wills.'"[10]

God said: "Blasphemous are those who claim that God is Jesus, the son of Mary. Jesus said: 'O Children of Israel, worship God alone, your

Lord and my Lord. Whoever associates aught with God, God will exclude
from paradise and punish in hell. Such unjust people will have no helper.'
Blasphemous are those who claim that God is the third person of a trinity. There is no God other than God, the One. Unless they stop this blasphemy, God will inflict upon them a painful punishment."[11] He, to
Whom is the glory, also said: "God asked Jesus, son of Mary: 'Did you ask
the people to take you and your mother as two gods beside God?' Jesus
answered: 'Praise be to You alone, I had not said but that which I was
commanded to say. You surely know whether I am guilty of such blasphemy, for You know all that is in my thoughts, and I know none of what is
in Yours. You alone are omniscient. I did convey to them that which You
commanded me to convey, namely, that they ought to worship God alone,
my Lord and their Lord. In their midst, I have been a witness unto You
throughout my life. And when You caused me to die, knowledge of what
they did was Yours for You are the witness of everything. If You punish
them, they are Your creatures and servants: if You choose to forgive them,
You are the Mighty and Wise.'"[12]

Christianity upholds the trinitarian view and claims that Jesus is the
Son of God. Islam, on the other hand, categorically denies that God could
possibly have a son. "Say," God commands Muhammad, "God is one. God
is eternal. He has neither progeny nor ancestry. He is absolutely without
parallel."[13] "It is not possible for God — may He be praised — to take
unto Himself a son."[14] "Jesus is to God as Adam was to Him, a creature
made out of dust that had come to be at God's command."[15] Islam is
monotheistic *par excellence;* the unity of God it teaches is the most cate-
gorical, the clearest, the simplest, and therefore the strongest. Whatever
casts the slightest doubt upon the unity of God is strongly rejected by
Islam and declared blasphemous. "God does not forgive that He be associated with anyone, but He will forgive anything lesser than that to
whomsoever He Wills."[16] Whatever connection Christianity may have
had with ancient religions as far as its trinitarian doctrine is concerned
furnished no justification at all in the eye of Muhammad. The truth is that
God is one and unique, that He has no associates, that He has neither
progeny nor ancestry and that He is absolutely without parallel. It is no
wonder therefore that controversy arose between Muhammad and the
Christians of his time, that he debated with them in kindness, and that
revelation confirmed Muhammad with the foregoing Qur'anic corrobora-
tions.

The Question of Jesus' Crucifixion

Another problem in which Islam differed from Christianity and which aroused controversy at the time of the Prophet is that of the crucifixion of Jesus as atonement for the sins of mankind. The Qur'an clearly denies that the Jews had killed or crucified the Messiah. It says: "As for the Jews' claim that they killed the Messiah, Jesus, son of Mary, the Prophet of God, the truth is that they have not killed him, nor have they crucified him, but that that appeared to them to be the case; whereas those who contend concerning this matter have no certain knowledge at all but merely conjecture. None of them is absolutely certain that they killed Jesus. Rather, God the Mighty and Wise raised Jesus unto Himself."[17]

Despite the fact that the idea of the Messiah's sacrifice and his atonement for the sins of mankind with his own blood is undoubtedly beautiful and the writings it had inspired are worthy of poetical, moral, and psychological analysis, Islam founded :itself upon the principle that moral guilt is non-transferable and that on the Day of Judgment justice shall be meted out to each according to his due. This fact rules out any logical rapprochement between the two doctrines. The *logique* of Islam is so precise on this matter and so clear and distinct that the difference between it and Christianity cannot be composed. The doctrine of sacrificial atonement runs diametrically counter to that of personal justice. "No father may bear the guilt of his son, and no son may earn anything for his father."[18]

Byzantines and Muslims

Did any Christians at the time consider this new religion and ponder the possibility of harmonizing its "unization"[19] of God and their revelation of Jesus? Indeed! And many of them joined it as a result. The Byzantines, however, whose victory the Muslims had celebrated and regarded as the victory of the scriptural religions, did not take the trouble to investigate this new religion. Rather, they looked at it from a political angle, and worried about their dominion should the new religion carry the day. They therefore began to attack it and its people and sent an army of a hundred thousand soldiers (or of two hundred thousand according to another report) against it. This led to the conquest of Tabuk by the Muslims and the retreat of the Byzantines in front of the army which rallied around Muhammad to repulse the aggression with such power and determination as it deserved.

Ever since then, Muslims and Christians have followed a policy of hostility towards each other; for many centuries victory was on the side of the Muslims, enabling them to extend their empire from Spain in the west to India and China in the east. Most of the inhabitants of this empire joined the new faith and adopted its Arabic language. When history came full cycle, the Christians forced the Muslims from Spain, launched the Crusades against them, and began to attack their religion and Prophet with falsehoods, lies, and forgeries. In their prejudice, they forgot the great respect and honor accorded to Jesus — may God's blessing be upon him — by Muhammad — may God's blessing be upon him — as the tradition has reported and the Qur'an, the revelation to Muhammad, has stated.

Christian Scholars and Muhammad

In presenting the views Christian scholars had of Muhammad during the first half of the nineteenth century, the French *Encyclopédie Larousse* stated: "Muhammad remained in his moral corruption and debauchery a camel thief, a cardinal who failed to reach the throne of the papacy and win it for himself. He therefore invented a new religion with which to avenge himself against his colleagues. Many fanciful and immoral tales dominated his mind and conduct. The *Life of Muhammad* by Bahomet is an example of this kind of literature. Other books on Muhammad, such as those published by Renault and François Michel in 1831, illustrate the idea of Muhammad prevalent in the Middle Ages. In the seventeenth century, Peel looked at the Qur'an from a historian's point of view. But he refused to divulge his conclusions to his readers though he acknowledged that the ethical and social system of Muhammad does not differ from the Christian system except in the theory of punishment and polygamy."

Emil Dermenghem, the French writer, was one of the few orientalists who investigated the life of Muhammad with some objectivity. Quoting some of the writings of his colleagues, he wrote: "After the war between Islam and Christianity had been going on for centuries, the misunderstanding naturally increased and we are forced to admit the most serious ones were on the side of the Occidentals. Numerous were the Byzantine polemists who covered Islam with their contempt without taking the trouble to study it (with perhaps the exception of St. John of Damascus), as well as the writers and minstrels who fought the Saracens with only ridiculous calumnies. They portrayed Mahomet as a camel-thief, a rake, sorcerer, a brigand chief, and even as a Roman cardinal furious at not having been elected pope. . . they showed him as a false god to whom the faithful made human sacrifices.

"The worthy Guibert de Nogent himself tells us that he (Muhammad) died through excessive drunkenness and that his corpse was eaten by pigs on a dunghill, explaining why the flesh of this animal and wine are prohibited. . . .

"The opposition of the two religions had not, in the main, any more serious foundations than the affirmations of heroic songs portraying Mahomet, the iconoclast, as a golden-idol, and Mussulman mosques as pantheons filled with images! The *Song of Antioch* describes, as if the author had seen it, a massive idol, Mahom, in gold and silver enthroned on the mosaic seat of an elephant. The *Song of Roland*, which shows Charlemagne's horsemen throwing down Mussulman idols, tells us that the Saracens worshiped a Trinity composed of Termagant, Mahom and Apollo. The *Roman de Mahomet* asserts the Islam permitted polyandry. . .

Hate and prejudice were tenacious of life. From the time of Rudolph de Ludheim (620) until the present, Nicholas de Cuse, Vives, Maracci, Hottinger, Bibliander, Prideaux, etc. present Mohamet as an impostor, Islam as the cluster of all the heresies and the work of the devil, the Mussulmans as brutes, and the Koran as a tissue of absurdities. They declined to treat such a ridiculous subject seriously. However, Pierre le Vénérable, author of the first Occidental treatise against. Islam, made a Latin translation of the Koran in the twelfth century. Innocent III once called Mahomet Antichrist, while in the Middle Ages he was nearly always merely looked upon as a heretic. Raymond Lull in the fourteenth century, Guillaume Postel in the sixteenth, Roland and Gagnier in the eighteenth, the Abbe de Broglie and Renan in the nineteenth give rather varied opinions. Voltaire, afterwards, amended in several places the hasty judgment expressed in his famous tragedy. Montesquieu, like Pascal and Malebranche, committed serious blunders on the religion, but his views of the manners and customs of the Mussulmans are well-considered and often reasonable. Le Comte de Boulainvilliers, Scholl, Caussin de Perceval, Dozy, Sprenger, Barthélemy, Saint-Hilaire de Castries, Carlyle, etc., are generally favorable to Islam and its Prophet and sometimes vindicate him. In 1876 Doughty nonetheless called

Mahomet 'a dirty and perfidious nomad,' while in 1822 Foster declared that 'Mahomet was Daniel's little goat's horn while the Pope was the large one.' Islam still has many ardent detractors."[20]

What a nether world of degradation have the writers of the West sunk to! What chronic, centuries-old obstinacy to go astray and to stir hatred and hostility between men! Many of the aforementioned men belonged to the Age of Enlightenment, the century of science, of free thought and research, and of the establishment of brotherhood between man and man. Perhaps the gravity of this unfortunate chronicle is somewhat attenuated by the fact that a number of objective scholars, mentioned by Dermenghem, have accepted the truthfulness of Muhammad's faith in the message which God had revealed to him, have commended the spiritual and moral greatness of Muhammad, his nobility and virtue, or have written about all these matters in literary and eloquent style. On the whole, however, the West continued to attack Islam and its prophet in the harshest possible terms. Indeed, western impertinence has gone so far as to spread Christian missionaries throughout the Muslim World, to urge them to dig their claws into its body, to dissuade the Muslims from their religion and to convert them to Christianity.

The Cause of Hostility between Islam and Christianity

We must search for the cause of this stormy hostility and fierce war which Christianity has been waging against Islam. We believe that western ignorance of the truth of Islam and of the life of its Prophet constitutes the first cause of this hostility. Without a doubt, ignorance is one of the most chronic causes of lethargy, conservatism and prejudice; and it is the most difficult to correct.

Ignorance and Fanaticism

This ignorance is centuries old. Over the years it has set up in the souls of generations idols of its own whose destruction will require a spiritual strength as great as that which characterized Islam when it first made its appearance. However, it is our opinion that there is yet another cause behind this fanaticism of the West and the terrible war it has waged and still wages against the Muslims, century after century. We are not here referring to political ambitions, or to the will of states to subjugate people for the purpose of exploiting them. In our opinion this is the result and not the cause of the fanaticism which goes beyond science and all its researches.

Christianity Does Not Accord with the Nature of Western Man

This deeper lying cause, we think, is the fact that Christianity — with its call for asceticism, other-worldliness, forgiveness, and the high personalist values — does not accord with the nature of western man whose religious life had for thousands of years been determined by polytheism and whose geographic position had imposed upon him the struggle against extreme cold and inclement nature. When historical circumstances brought about his Christianization, it was necessary for him to interpret it as a religion of struggle and to alter its tolerant and gentle nature. Thereby western man spoiled the spiritual sequence, completed by Islam, in which Christianity stood as a link in the chain. This spiritual continuum reconciles the claims of the body with those of the spirit; it synthesizes in harmony emotion and reason. It is a system which integrates the individual, indeed mankind, as a natural part of the cosmos and co-existent with it in its infinity of space and time. In our view, this spoiling is the cause of the fanaticism of the West *vis-a-vis* Islam and the cause of an attitude which Christian Abyssinia found beneath its dignity to adopt when the Muslims sought its protection at the beginning of the Prophet's career.

It is with reference to this cause that we can explain the exaggerated religiosity of western man as well as his extremist irreligiosity. For here too western fanaticism and hostility know neither tolerance nor temperance. Admittedly, history has known many saints among western men who in their lives have followed the example of Jesus and his disciples. But it cannot be denied that this same history affirms the life of the western people to be one of struggle, power, antagonism, and bloody war in the name of politics or religion. Nor can it be denied that the popes of the Church as well as the secular rulers have always engaged one another in strife: that one or the other was one day conqueror and the other vanquished. As secular power emerged victorious in the nineteenth century, it sought to stamp out the life of the spirit in the name of science, claiming that the latter should replace religious faith in human spirituality. Nowadays, after a long struggle, the West has come to realize its error and the impossibility of what it sought to achieve. Voices are now being heard from all sides demanding to regain the lost spirituality by looking for it in the new theo-

The Life of Muhammad

sophic and other schools.[21] Had Christianity accorded with the instinct of strife which among westerners is the law of life, they would have realized the bankruptcy of materialism to furnish them with the needed spiritual power. They then would have returned to the noble Christian religion of Jesus, son of Mary, unless God were to guide them toward Islam. They would not have needed to emigrate to India and other places to obtain a necessary spiritual life. Such spirituality is of the essence of the religion of Jesus, indeed its very nature and being.

Colonialism and Christian Mission against Islam

Western colonialism helped the West to continue its war against Islam and Muhammad. It encouraged the West to proclaim that Islam is the cause of the decadence of its adherents and their subjugation by others. Many western scholars still subscribe to this claim unaware that by doing so they cede the point to the Makkans who proclaimed thirteen centuries ago that Christianity is responsible for the shameful defeat of Heraclius and Byzantium by Persia, as well as to anyone who wishes to make use of the argument to explain Christendom's retreat under the blows of the Muslims. One fact alone is sufficient to refute such an obvious piece of falsehood. That is the fact that the civilization of Islam was dominant in, and its people sovereign over, the whole known world for many centuries; that in the Muslim world arose greater men of science and knowledge who lived and worked in an atmosphere of freedom which the West was not to know until very recently. If it were at all possible to attribute to a religion the decay of its adherents, no such imputation is possible in the case of Islam which aroused the Bedouins of the Arabian Peninsula and enabled them to dominate the world.

Islam and the Present State of the Islamic Peoples

Those who impute to Islam responsibility for the decay of the Islamic peoples are partially right in the fact that there was added to the religion of God much which neither God nor His Prophet would have approved of. Such additions soon became integral to the religion, and whoever denied them was declared a heretic. Apart from the doctrine itself, let us take a close look at the biography of the Prophet of Islam — may God's blessing be upon him. Most of his biographies have narrated stories which no reason would accept and which no confirmation of Muhammad's prophethood needed. It was from such additions that the western orientalists and critics of Islam, of its Prophet and of the Muslim peoples, drew their conclusions and formed their unjust and revolting attacks. After basing themselves on these incoherent assumptions, they launched further attacks and claimed for what they wrote the status of modern scientific research. The scientific method demands that events, people, and heroes be presented objectively, that the author's judgment be given only in light of the given evidence. The writings of these authors, however, were dictated by their passion for controversy and vituperation. They were aptly cast in expressions which deluded their co-religionists into believing that they were scientific, and that they were made in seeking after truth alone. Nonetheless, God did grant His peace to a number of contented souls, for among them there were men of letters, men of science, and other free thinkers who carne closer to justice and fairness.

Conservatism and Ijtihad among the Muslims

A number of 'ulama'[23] in different circumstances responded to the claims of these western fanatics. The name of Muhammad 'Abduh shines most in this regard. But they have not observed the scientific method which the European writers and historians claim to have observed. Their argument would not have the same power as that of their opponents. Moreover, the same Muslim scholars — Muhammad 'Abduh above all others — were accused of heresy and blasphemy — a fact which weakened their argument before the opponents of Islam. Such accusations as were directed at them left deep impressions in the hearts of educated Muslim youths. These young men felt that for a group of Muslim 'ulama' adjudication by reason and logic amounts to heresy, that heresy is the twin of *ijtihad*, and that *iman*[24] is the twin of conservatism. Hence their minds panicked, and they rushed to the books of the West seeking to learn the truth which they believed was not to be found in the books of Muslim authors. They did not at all consider the books of Christianity and of Christian history. Instead, they turned to the books of philosophy to quench their burning thirst for the truth. In western logic and scientific method they sought the light with which to illuminate their human souls, and the means by which to communicate with the universe. In the western products of pure philosophy, literature, and allied fields, these men found many great ideas by which they were deeply impressed. The methods of their presentation, the precision of their logic and their authors' candidness in the search for the truth added all the more to their attractiveness. That is why our youths' thinking was drawn away from all the religions in general and from the methods of Islam and its carriers in particular. They were anxious not to stir a war with conservatism which they were not confident they could win, and they did not realize that spiritual intercourse with the universe is the necessary requisite of any human realization of perfection, of that moral power which is strong enough to withstand the storms.

Western Science and Literature

Our young men were thus drawn away from serious confrontation with the Islamic message and its carriers. In this they were encouraged by what they observed of positive science and positivist philosophy, ruling for them that religious questions are not subject to logic, that they do not fall within the realm of scientific thinking, and that the metaphysical assumptions implied in those questions fall outside the realm of the scientific method. Our men have also observed the clear separation of state and church in the western countries. They learned that despite the fact that the constitutions of these countries prescribe that their kings are the protectors of Protestantism or Catholicism, or that the official religion of the state is Christianity, the Western states do not mean any more than to subscribe to the public observance of the feasts and other occasions of the Christian calendar. Hence they were encouraged to enter into this line of scientific thinking and to derive therefrom, as well as from the related philosophy, literature and art, all the inspiration possible. When the time came to transfer their attention from study to practical life, their occupations pulled them away further from those problems which they could not solve even at the time of their study. Their minds, therefore, continued to run in their original courses. They looked at conservatism with contempt and pity and drew their nourishment from the lifeline of western thought and philosophy. Remembering this lifeline as the source from which they obtained their nourishment in their youth, they continued to find therein their intellectual pleasure; their admiration for it was always growing.

Nevertheless, the Orient stands today in great need of learning from western thought, literature and art. The present of the Orient is separated from its past by centuries of lethargy and conservatism which have locked its old healthy mind in ignorance and suspicion of anything new.

Anyone who seeks to dissolve this thick curtain must needs be assisted by the most modern thinking in the world if he is to forge anew the link between the live present and the great legacy of the past.

Efforts of Islamic Reform

It is undeniable that we must acknowledge the worthy western achievements in Islamic and Oriental studies. These have prepared the road for Muslims as well as Orientals to enter these fields of research with greater promise than was open to their western colleagues. The Muslims and Orientals are naturally closer to the spirit of Islam and the Orient which they are seeking to penetrate. As long as the new leadership in this field has come from the West, it is the Muslim's and Oriental's duty to look into the products of the West, to correct their mistakes, and to give to the discipline the proper orientation which will re-establish the unity of the old and the new. This should not be done merely on paper, for it is a living legacy, spiritual and mental, which the heirs ought to represent to themselves, to add thereto, and to illumine with their own vision and understanding of the central realities.

Many of our young men have succeeded in their undertaking of scientific researches on these lines. The orientalists have often appreciated their work and complimented them on their contributions to scholarship.

Western Missionaries and Muslim Conservatives

Scientific cooperation in Islamics between Muslim and Oriental scholars on one hand, and western scholars on the others, is worthy of great promise. Although it has just begun to make progress, we yet notice that the Christian missionaries continue their attacks against Islam and Muhammad with the same ferocity as their predecessors to whom we nave alluded earlier. In this they are encouraged and supported by the western colonialist powers in the name of freedom of opinion. These very missionaries were themselves thrown out of their countries by their own governments because they were not trusted by them to implant true faith in the hearts of their own co-religionists at home.[25] Moreover this colonialism assists the leaders of conservatism among the Muslims. Colonialism in fact has brought about a coalescence of the two tendencies; on the one hand it confirms the infusion of Islam with that which is not Islamic, such as the irrational and unrefined superstitions added to the life of the

Prophet; on the other hand, it confirms the antagonists of Islam in their attacks against these forgeries.

The Idea and Plan of This Book

The circumstances of my life have enabled me to observe all these maneuvers in the various countries of the Islamic East, indeed throughout the Muslim World, and to discover their final purpose. The objective of colonialism is to destroy in these countries the freedom of opinion, the freedom to seek the truth. I have come to feel that I stand under the duty to foil these maneuvers and spoil their purpose, for they are certainly harmful to the whole of mankind, not only to Islam and the Orient. What greater damage could befall humanity than to have its greater half, the half which has throughout history been the carrier of civilization, to wallow in sterility and conservatism? It was this consideration which led me at the end of the road of life to the study of the life of Muhammad, the carrier of the message of Islam and the target of Christian attacks on one side and of Muslim conservatives on the other. But I have resolved that this will be a scientific study, developed on the western modern method, and written for the sake of truth alone.

I began to study the history of Muhammad and to look more closely into the *Sirah* of Ibn Hisham, the *Tabaqat* of Ibn Sa'd, the *Maghazi* of Waqidi, and *The Spirit of Islam* of Sayyid Ameer Ali. Then I took care to study what some orientalists have written on the subject such as the work of Dermenghem, and also that of Washington Irving. The winter of 1932 at Luxor provided me with the occasion to begin my writing. At that time I was quite hesitant to publish my thoughts because I feared the storm which the conservatives and their followers who believe in superstitions might raise. But I was encouraged by a number of professors in the Islamic institutions of learning, many of whom took such care in studying my writing and making pertinent observations on it that I resolved to follow my scientific treatment of the life of Muhammad to a conclusion. It was the encouragement of these men that stirred me to search for the best means by which to analyze the biography of the Prophet.

The Qur'an as the Most Reliable Source

I discovered that the most reliable source of information for the biography of Muhammad is the Holy Qur'an. It contains a reference to every event in the life of the Arab Prophet which can serve the investigator as a standard norm and as a guiding light in his analysis of the reports of the various biographies and of the *Sunnah*. As I sought to understand all the Qur'anic references to the life of the Prophet, Professor Ahmad Lutfi al Sayyid, of Dar al Kutub al Misriyyah, offered me great assistance by letting me use a topically arranged collection of all the verses of the Qur'an. While analyzing these verses, I began to realize that it was necessary to discover the causes and occasions of their revelation. I acknowledge that despite all the effort I put in that direction I was not always successful. The books of exegesis sometimes refer to these relations but often overlook them. Al Wahidi's *Asbab al Nuzul,* and Ibn Salamah's *al Nasikh Wa al Mansukh* treat this matter very precisely but, unfortunately, very briefly. In these as well as other books of exegesis, I discovered many facts which helped me in my analysis of the claims various biographies have made as well as the many other facts worthy of being considered and investigated by all scholars of the Qur'an and *Sunnah*.

Candid Advice

As my research progressed I found candid advice coming to me from all directions, especially from the professors of Islam and the learned men of religion. Dar al Kutub al Misriyyah and its officers were responsible for the greatest assistance. No expression of appreciation of their work is adequate. Suffice it here to mention that, encouraged by his director and other senior officers, Professor 'Abd al Rahim Mahmud, Editor in the Division of Literature, used often to save me from great trouble by borrowing for me all the needed books. Whenever I did manage to go to Dar al Kutub, all the employees were delightfully ready to assist me in my search. Some of these men were personally known to me and others were not. I referred many a question which was opaque or presented difficulties to those of my friends whom I knew would shed some light thereon; and more often than not the confusion or opaqueness was cleared. This was many times the case with the Grand Shaykh Muhammad Mustafa al Maraghi, along with my expert friend, Ja'far Pasha Waliy, who lent me several of his books, such as the *Sahih of Muslim* and the histories of Makkah, and who guided me in many problems. Makram 'Ubayd Pasha, another friend of mine, lent me Sir William Muir's *The Life of Muhammad* and Father Lammens's *Islam*. This valuable assistance is all in addition to that which I found in the writings of the contemporary authors such as

Fajr al Islam by Ahmad Amin, *Qisas al Anbiya'* by 'Abd al Wahhab al Najjar, *Fi al Adab al Jahili* by Taha Husayn, *The Jews in Arabia* by Israel Wolfenson, and many other contemporary works mentioned in my list of old and new references used in the preparation of this book.

As I progressed in my research more and more complicated problems emerged which overtaxed my powers. Throughout, the biographies of Muhammad and the books of exegeses as well as the works of the orientalists have assisted me in achieving a measure of certainty of purpose. I found myself compelled to limit my investigation to the events in the life of Muhammad and to refrain from tackling a number of side issues connected therewith. Had I allowed myself to indulge in the discussion of all these problems, I would have needed to write many volumes of this size or larger. Let me mention in passing that Caussin de Perceval wrote three volumes under the title *Study in Arab History,* of which he devoted the first two to the history and life of the Arab tribes and the third to the history of Muhammad and his first two successors, Abu Bakr and 'Umar. Likewise, the *Tabaqat of Ibn Sa'd* devoted one of its many volumes to the life of Muhammad and all the others to the lives of his companions. My purpose in this work has never gone beyond the investigation of the life of Muhammad itself; therefore, I did not allow myself the liberty to investigate the other problems involved.

Restriction to the Life of Muhammad

Another consideration restricted me to the frontiers of the life of Muhammad — the greatness, majesty, and brilliance which make his life unique among all others. How great was Abu Bakr! And how great was 'Umar! Each was a great sun eclipsing all others around him. How great, too, were the first Muslims, the companions of Muhammad, who are remembered from generation to generation with the greatest pride. All these men, however, stood beneath Muhammad, reflecting his light and his glory. It is not easy therefore for the investigator to restrict himself to the life of Muhammad alone. This is all the more so if the investigation is to follow the modern scientific method, and thereby present the greatness of that life with all its strength and moving appeal in a manner which both Muslims and non-Muslims may accept and admire.

If we were to disregard those foolish fanatics, such as the missionaries and their like, whose purpose never goes beyond vituperation of Muhammad, we could still find a clear and distinct respect for greatness in the life of Muhammad in the works of the western orientalists. In his *On Heroes and Hero Worship,* Thomas Carlyle devoted a chapter to Muhammad in which he described the revelation of Muhammad as issuing from a spark that is divine and holy. He understood Muhammad's greatness and portrayed it in its whole strength. Likewise, Muir, Irving, Sprenger, and Weil, among other orientalists, eloquently described the greatness of Muhammad. A lack of vision, penetration, and critical skill prevented some of them from regarding one point or another of Muhammad's life as other than blameworthy. It is probable that they had relied in their investigation on unreliable biographies and books of exegesis of the Prophet, forgetting that the earliest biography was not written down until two centuries after Muhammad's death, and that during this time a great number of Israelitisms and other forgeries were forced into his biography and into his teachings. Generally, western orientalists acknowledge this fact even though they attribute to the Prophet materials which the least investigation would reject as superfluous. The cases of the goddesses of Makkah, of Zayd and Zaynab, of the wives of the Prophet, constitute examples of such superfluous materials as I have had the occasion to investigate in this book.

This Book as Mere Beginning of Research

No one should think that research in the life of Muhammad is completed with this work. It is closer to the truth for me to say that my work is really only the beginning of scientific research in this field in Arabic and that all my efforts in this regard do not make my work any more than a mere beginning in the scientific as well as Islamic undertaking of this grave subject. As many scholars have devoted all their energies to the study of one period of history, even as Aulard has specialized in the study of the French Revolution, some scholars and historians ought to devote themselves to the study of the Age of Muhammad. The life of Muhammad is certainly worthy of being studied in a scientific and academic manner by more than one specialist or by more than one competent scholar. I have no doubt that any efforts spent on such scientific study of this brief period in the history of Arabia and on investigating the relations of Arabia to other countries during that age will prove beneficial to mankind as a whole, not merely to Islam or the Muslims. Such a study will clear many psychological and spiritual problems and prepare them for scholarly research. It will shed great light on the social moral and legislative life of Arabia and thus illuminate areas which so far science has been unable to penetrate on account of the religious conflict between Islam and Christianity. Such a study would dissipate the futile attempt at westernizing the Orientals or Christianizing the Muslims in a way that history has proven to be impossible and harmful to the relations of the various parts of mankind with one another.

Universal Benefits of the Study

Indeed, I would even go further. I would assert that such a study may show the road to mankind as a whole to the new civilization to which it is currently groping. If western Christendom is too proud to find the new light in Islam and in its Prophet but willingly accepts it from Indian theosophy and other religions of the Far East, then it devolves upon the Orientals themselves, Muslims, Jews or Christians, to undertake this study in all objectivity and fairness in order to reach and establish the truth. Islamic thought rests on a methodology that is scientific and modern as regards all that relates man to nature. In this respect it is perfectly realistic. But it becomes personalist the moment it leaves nature to consider the relationship of man to the cosmos as a whole and to his creator. Moreover, in the psychological and spiritual fields Islamic thought made contributions which science has not yet been able either to confirm or to deny. Although science may not regard these discoveries as facts in the scientific sense of the terms, they still remain the constituents of man's happiness and the determinants of his conduct in the world. What then is life? And what is man's relation to this world? How shall we explain his concern for life? What is the common faith which inspires human groups and by which their morale is raised to high pitch or dissolved? What is being? And what is the unity of being? What is the place of man in this being and in its unity? These are problems of metaphysics and a whole literature has arisen around them. Answers far nearer human understanding and implementation than are usually found in the literature of metaphysics are found in the life of Muhammad and his teachings. Ever since the 'Abbasi period, Muslim thinkers have spent centuries looking for metaphysical answers.

Likewise western thinkers have spent three centuries, from the sixteenth through the nineteenth, to lead the West to modern science in the same manner as the Muslims have done in the past. Once more, science stands today as it stood in the past as failing to realize human happiness on earth. Such happiness is impossible to realize unless we resume research for a correct understanding of the personal relationship of man to the cosmos and to the creator of the cosmos, and unless such understanding is sought on the basis of a divine unity, which is eternal and immutable, and with regard to space and time in relation to our short life. The life of Muhammad provides us with the best example of personalist communion with being, as well as the best materials for a scientific study of this relationship. The same materials may equally be the object of practical study for those who are endowed therefore but naturally removed from achieving such communion with God as the Prophet had achieved. It is most likely that the scientific study, and the practical study, if felicitously undertaken, may yet shake our world loose from the paganism into which it has fallen in spite of its religious creeds and scientific doctrines. It may yet save the world from its present monolatry of wealth that has made all science, art, and ethics its servants and conscripted all man's powers to do its bidding and sing its praises. Such hopes may still be far from realization. However, the beginning of the end of this all-embracing paganism of modern times is clearly distinguishable under close observance of the current flow of events. Perhaps, these humble beginnings will grow and become surer of themselves when scholarship has found answers to these spiritual problems through the study of the life of Muhammad, of his teachings, of his age, and of the spiritual world revolution which he incepted. Should such scientific and scholarly research uncover for man his stronger bonds with the higher reality of the world, it would have then provided the new civilization with its first foundation.

As I said already, this book is only a mere beginning on this road. It will prove sufficient reward for me if it should succeed in convincing the reader of the validity of its assertions, and the scholars and researchers of the need for dedication and specialization if the final end of the study is to be reached. God will surely reward the good doers.

— Muhammad Husayn Haykal

Preface to the Second Edition

The speed with which the first edition of this work was exhausted has exceeded all expectations. Ten thousand copies were printed, of which one-third were sold before the book came off the press. The remaining copies were sold during the first three months following its publication. If this is any indication, the reader must have been quite interested in its contents. A second printing, therefore, is as imperative as the reconsideration of those contents.

An Observation

Without a doubt, the title of the book attracted the reader most. The attraction may also have been due to the method with which the subject was treated. Whatever the reason, the thought of a second edition has occasioned the question of whether or not I should allow the book to be reprinted without change or have it corrected, considering that a need for correction, clarification, or addition has in the meantime seemed to me evident. Some, whose counsel I certainly value, have advised me to make the second edition an exact copy of the first in order to achieve equality between the earlier and later buyers and to allow myself longer time for revision thereafter. This view almost convinced me. Had I followed it, this second edition would have been put in the hands of the readers many months ago. But I hesitated to accept this advice and finally decided in favor of revisions which many considerations had made necessary. The first of such considerations concerned a number of observations which Muhammad Mustafa al Maraghi, Grand Shaykh of al Azhar, had kindly made when he read the first parts of the book as they came from the press, and kindly decided to write the foreword. When the book made its appearance, a number of 'ulama' and other scholars spoke and wrote about it. Their observations were all preceded by numerous compliments for the achievement of this work, indeed more than the book actually deserved. These observations were based upon the understanding that a book about the Arab Prophet, which is so well written that it has won their approval and appreciation, ought to be absolutely free of all shortcomings. It is therefore necessary for me to take them into account and give them the consideration due.

It was perhaps this very approval and appreciation of the readers which moved them to make observations on incidental matters related neither to the essence of the book nor to its main themes. Some of them, for instance, pleaded for further clarification of certain points. Others called for closer scrutiny of my use of prepositions. Still others suggested different words better to express the meanings I intended. A number of them did focus on the themes of the book and therefore caused me to review what I have written. I certainly wish that this second edition will come closer to satisfying all these writers and scholars. All this notwithstanding, I still believe that this book provides no more than a mere beginning in the Arabic language of such studies using the modern scientific method.

A further consideration caused me to review the first edition. Having read the many observations made, most of which were not new, I became convinced as I read my work again that I ought to add, where relevant, a discussion of the points to which the observations referred in order at least to convince their authors of my point of view and of the veracity of my arguments. My reconsideration of some of these points opened new vistas which any student of the biography of the Arab Prophet will have to study. Although I am proud that the first edition did in fact deal with the points raised in the reviews, I am more proud yet today to present to the reader this second edition in which the same points have been treated more fully. No study, however, can be full or perfect which undertakes the investigation of the life of the greatest man history has known — the Seal of the Prophets and of the Messengers from on high — may God's peace and blessing be upon him.

In this edition, I have tried to address myself to a number of observations made regarding my method of investigation. I have added to the book two new chapters in which I have dealt with matters which have been only slightly referred to toward the end of the preface of the first edition. I have also re-edited the work wherever it needed editing, and added to its various sections and paragraphs such points as my rethinking has made necessary.

Answering the Followers of Western Orientalists

I want first to address myself to a letter I received from an Egyptian writer. He claimed that his letter is an Arabic translation of an article he wrote for a German Orientalist magazine in criticism of this book. I have not published this letter in the Arabic press because it contains many unfounded attacks; and I thought that its author had better bear the responsibility of publishing it if he wished to. Nor will I mention his name here because I believe he will repudiate his old views when he reads the critical analysis that follows. The substance of the letter is that my *The Life of Muhammad* is not a scientific one in the modern sense. He argues that I have depended upon Arabic sources alone and have not consulted the studies of German orientalists such as Weil, Goldziher, Nöldeke, and others, and have not adopted their conclusions. The letter also blames me for regarding the Qur'an as a certain historical document, whereas the investigations of the foregoing orientalists have proven that it has been tampered with and been changed after the death of Muhammad in the first century A.H. It reported that these investigations have discovered that the name of the Prophet is a case in point; that having once been "Qutham" or "Quthamah," it was later changed to "Muhammad" in order to accord with the verse, "Jesus said: O Children of Israel, I am the Prophet of God sent to you to confirm the scripture that is already in my hand and to announce to you the advent of a prophet after me whose name shall be Ahmad."[1] This fabrication was deemed desirable in order to forge a link between the Prophet and the Evangel's announcement of a prophet coming after Jesus. Moreover, the letter added, the researches of the orientalists have revealed that the Prophet suffered from epilepsy, that his so-called revelations were really effects of his epileptic attacks; that the symptoms of epilepsy — loss of consciousness, perspiration, convulsion, foam around the mouth — were all apparent in his case. It was after he recovered from these fits that he claimed that the revelation had come to him, recited it to the believers, and claimed that it had come from God.

By itself, this letter is not worthy of attention or investigation. Its author, however, is a Muslim and an Egyptian. Had he been an orientalist or a missionary, I would have let him alone to rave as he pleased. What I have said in the preface to the first edition in this regard is sufficient refutation for such people and views. The author of this letter, however, is an example of a class of young Muslims who are too ready to accept what the orientalists say and regard it as true knowledge. It is precisely to this class of people that I want now to address myself and warn them of the errors in which the orientalists fall. Some of these orientalists are candid and scholarly despite their errors. Error nonetheless finds its way into their conclusions either because of their lack of mastery of the nuances of the Arabic language, or of their prejudice against religion as such, or Islam in particular, which, in turn, conditions them to seek to destroy the fundamental basis of religion. Both shortcomings are unworthy of scholars and it behooves them to seek a remedy therefor. We have seen Christian thinkers who, moved by this same antagonism, denied that Jesus ever existed in history; and we have seen others who have gone further and have even written about the madness of Jesus. The western thinker's innate antagonism to religion was generated by the struggle between the Church and the state and this led both the men of science and the men of religion to pull in different directions in order to wrench power from the other side and seize it for themselves. Islam, on the other hand, is free of such strife; Muslim scholars, therefore, should not be affected by it as their western colleagues have been. In most cases, to fall under such a complexus would vitiate the research. Muslim readers, therefore, should watch out more carefully when they read a religious study by a westerner. They should scrutinize every claim these studies make for the truth. A large measure of their researches are deeply affected by this past strife which the men of religion and the men of science had waged against one another during long centuries.

Dependence upon the Muslim Biographers

The case of the letter from the Egyptian Muslim colleague clearly points to the need for such care. His first criticism concerned my dependence upon Arabic and Islamic sources. Of course this is not denied. But I have also consulted the books of the orientalists mentioned in my list of references. The Arabic sources, however, constituted my primary sources as they constituted the primary sources for orientalists before me. That is natural. For these sources, and the Qur'an above all, were the first ones ever to discuss the life of the Arab Prophet. There is nothing objectionable if such early historical documents are taken as primary sources for any modern and scientific biographical study of the Prophet. Nöldeke, Goldziher, Weil, Sprenger, Muir, and other orientalists have all taken the same works as primary sources for their studies, just as I have done. I have also allowed myself as much liberty in scrutinizing the reports of these works as they did. And I have also not omitted to consult some of the early Christian books which the orientalists had consulted despite the fact that they were products of Christian fanaticism rather than of scholarly research and criticism. If anybody were to criticize my work on the grounds that I have allowed myself to differ from some orientalists and have arrived at conclusions other than their own, he would in fact be calling for intellectual stagnation — a conservatism not less reactionary or retrogressive than any other conservatism we have known. It is unlikely that any of the orientalists themselves agree with such call; for to do so implies approval of religious stagnation. Neither for me nor for any scholarly student of history is such a stand viable. Rather, I should ask myself, as well as any other scholar, to scrutinize the work of his colleagues. Unless he is convinced by clear evidence and incontestable proofs, he should seek other ways to the truth. To this task I call those of us, particularly the youth, who admire the researches of the Orientalists. This has also been my task. Mine is the reward where I have in fact arrived at the truth; and mine is the apology where I have erred despite my good intentions.

The Orientalists and the Bases of Religion

The aforesaid Muslim Egyptian's letter gives evidence of the western orientalists' extreme care to destroy the basis of religion. They claim that their researches have established that the Qur'an is not a historical document devoid of doubt but that it has been tampered with and edited, and many verses added to it for religious or political ulterior purposes in the first century after the death of the Prophet of Islam. I am not questioning the author of the letter from an Islamic point of view but arguing with him, as it were, as a fellow Muslim, the veracity or otherwise of the Islamic conviction that the Qur'an is the work of God and that it is impossible for it to be forged. The stand from which he wrote his letter is clearly that of the orientalists who hold that the Qur'an is a book written by Muhammad. According to a number of orientalists, Muhammad wrote the Qur'an in the belief that it was God's revelation to him; according to others, Muhammad claimed that the Qur'an was the revelation of God merely in order to prove the genuineness of his message. Let me then address the author of this letter in his own language assuming that he is one of those free thinkers who refuse to be convinced except by scientific, apodeictic proof.

The False Charge of Forgery

Our young author depends upon the western orientalists and their views. A number of these do think of the Qur'an in the manner this young author exemplified. Their claim is based upon flagrant motives which stand at the farthest possible remove from science and the scientific method. Suffice it to expose the incoherence of their arguments that the phrase, "and announcing the advent of a prophet after me whose name shall be Ahmad"[2] was added to the Qur'an after the death of the Prophet in order to establish proof of Muhammad's prophethood based upon the scriptures preceding the Qur'an. Had these orientalists who make this claim truly sought to serve the purpose of science, they would not have recoursed to this cheap propaganda that the Torah and the Evangel are truly revealed books. Had they honored science for its own sake, they would have treated the Qur'an on a par with the scriptures antecedent to it. Either they would have regarded the Qur'an as sacred as these scriptures — in which case it would have been natural for it to refer to its antecedents — or, they would have regarded all these books as they did the Qur'an and imputed to them the same kind of doubtful nature as they did to it, holding as well their authors to have forged or written them in satisfaction of ulterior religious or political purposes. Had the orientalists held such a view, logic would rule out their claim that the Qur'an had been tampered with and forged for political and religious purposes. It is inadmissible that the Muslims would have sought such confirmation of Muhammad's claim to prophethood from these scriptures after Muslim dominion had been established, the Christian empire vanquished, so many other peoples of the earth subjugated and, indeed, after the Christians themselves had entered into Islam *en masse*. The inadmissibility of these orientalists' claims is demanded by genuine scientific thought. Furthermore, the claim that the Torah and the Evangel are sacred whereas the Qur'an is not is devoid of scientific support. Therefore, the claim that the Qur'an had been tampered with and forged in order to seek confirmation of Muhammad's prophet-hood on the basis of the Torah and the Evangel is a piece of sheer nonsense unacceptable to either logic or history.

Those western orientalists who have made this false claim are very few and belong to the more fanatic group. The majority of them do believe that the Qur'an which is in our hands today is precisely the Qur'an which Muhammad had recited to the Muslims during his lifetime; that it has neither been tampered with nor forged. They admit this explicitly in their writings while criticizing the method by which the verses of the Qur'an were collected and its chapters arranged — a matter of discussion which does not belong here. The Muslim students of the Qur'an did in fact study these criticisms and exposed their errors. As for our purpose here, suffice it to look at some orientalists' writing on this subject. Perhaps our young Muslim Egyptian author would thereby be convinced and, per-haps, he would convince those of his fellows who think like him.

Muir Rejects the Forgery of the Qur'an

The orientalists have written a great deal on this subject. We can select a passage by Sir William Muir from his book, *The Life of Mahomet*, in the hope that those who claim that the Qur'an has been forged will realize wherein they have erred, to the detriment of both the truth and their own scholarship. It should be remembered that our author, Muir, is a Christian, an *engage* and proud Christian, as well as a missionary who never misses occasion to criticize the Prophet of Islam or its scripture.

When he came to speak of the Qur'an and the veracity and precision of its text, he wrote:

> "The divine revelation was the corner-stone of Islam. The recital of a passage from it formed an essential part of daily prayer public and private; and its perusal and repetition were enforced as a duty and a privilege fraught with religious merit. This is the universal voice of early tradition, and may be gathered also from the revelation itself. The Coran was accordingly committed to memory more or less by every adherent of Islam, and the extent to which it could be recited was one of the chief distinctions of nobility in the early Moslem empire. The custom of Arabia favoured the task. Passionately fond of poetry, yet possessed of but

limited means and skill in committing to writing the effusions of
their bards, the Arabs had long been habituated to imprint these,
as well as the tradition of genealogical and other tribal events, on
the living tablets of their hearts. The recollective faculty was thus
cultivated to the highest pitch; and it was applied, with all the
ardour of an awakened spirit, to the Coran. Such was the tenacity of their memory, and so great their power of application, that
several of Mahomet's followers, according to early tradition,
could, during his lifetime, repeat with scrupulous accuracy the
entire revelation.

"However retentive the Arab memory, we should still have
regarded with distrust a transcript made entirely from that source.
But there is good reason for believing that many fragmentary
copies, embracing amongst them the whole Coran, or nearly the
whole, were made by Mahomet's followers during his life.
Writing was without doubt generally known at Mecca long before
Mahomet assumed the prophetical office. Many of his followers
are expressly mentioned as employed by the Prophet at Medina in
writing his letters or despatches. . . Some of the poorer Meccan
captives taken at Bedr were offered their release on condition that
they would teach a certain number of the ignorant citizens of
Medina to write. And although the people of Medina were not so
generally educated as those of Mecca, yet many are distinctly
noticed as having been able to write before Islam. The ability thus
existing, it may be safely inferred that the verses which were so
indefatigably committed to memory, would be likewise committed carefully to writing.

"We also know that when a tribe first joined Islam, Mahomet
was in the habit of deputing one or more of his followers to teach
them the Coran and the requirements of the faith. We are frequently informed that they carried written instructions with them
on the latter point, and they would naturally provide themselves
also with transcripts of the more important parts of the
Revelation, especially those upon which the ceremonies of Islam
were founded, and such as were usually recited at the public
prayers. Besides the reference in the Coran to its own existence in
a written form, we have express mention made in the authentic
traditions of Omar's conversion, of a copy of the 20th Sura being

used by his sister's family for social and private devotional reading. This refers to a period preceding, by three or four years, the emigration to Medina. If transcripts of the revelations were made, and in common use, at that early time when the followers of Islam were few and oppressed, it is certain that they must have multiplied exceedingly when the Prophet came to power, and his Book formed the law of the greater part of Arabia.

"Such was the condition of the text of the Coran during Mahomet's lifetime, and such it remained for about a year after his death, imprinted upon the hearts of his people, and fragmentary transcripts increasing daily. The two sources would correspond closely with each other; for the Coran, even while the Prophet was yet alive, was regarded with a superstitious awe as containing the very words of God; so that any variations would be reconciled by a direct reference to Mahomet himself, and after his death to the originals where they existed, or copies from the same, and to the memory of the Prophet's confidential friends and amanuenses.

"It was not till the overthrow of Moseilama, when a great carnage took place amongst the Moslems at Yemama, and large numbers of the best reciters of the Coran were slain, that a misgiving arose in Omar's mind as to the uncertainty which would be experienced regarding the text, when all those who had received it from the original source, and thence stored it in their memories, should have passed away. 'I fear,' said he, addressing the Caliph Abu Bakr, 'that slaughter may again wax hot amongst the reciters of the Coran, in other fields of battle; and that much may be lost therefrom. Now, therefore, my advice is, that thou shouldest give speedy orders for the collection of the Coran.' Abu Bakr agreed, and thus made known his wishes to Zeid ibn Thabit, a citizen of Medina, and the Prophet's chief amanuensis: 'Thou art a young man, and wise; against whom no one amongst us can cast an imputation; and thou wert wont to write down the inspired revelations of the Prophet of the Lord. Wherefore now search out the Coran, and bring it together.' So new and unexpected was the enterprise that Zeid at first shrank from it, and doubted the propriety, or even lawfulness, of attempting that which Mahomet had neither himself done nor commanded to be done. At last he yield-

ed to the joint entreaties of Abu Bakr and Omar, and seeking out
the fragments of the Coran from every quarter, 'gathered it
together, from date leaves, and tablets of white stone, and from
the breasts of men.' By the labours of Zeid, these scattered and
confused materials were reduced to the order and sequence in
which we now find them, and in which it is said that Zeid used
to repeat the Coran in the presence of Mahomet. The original
copy prepared by Zeid was probably kept by Abu Bakr during the
short remainder of his reign. It then came into the possession of
Omar who. . . committed it to the custody of his daughter
Haphsa, the Prophet's widow. The compilation of Zeid, as
embodied in this exemplar, continued during Omar's ten years'
Caliphate to be the standard and authoritative text.

"But variety of expression either prevailed in the previous
transcripts and modes of recitation, or soon crept into the copies
which were made from Zeid's edition. Mussulmans were scan-
dalised. The Coran sent down from heaven was ONE, but where
was now its unity? Hodzeifa, who had warred both in Armenia
and Adzerbaijan and had observed the different readings of the
Syrians and of the men of Irac, alarmed at the number and extent
of the variations, warned Othman to interpose, and 'stop the people, before they should differ regarding their Scripture, as did the
Jews and Christians.' The Caliph was persuaded, and to remedy
the evil had recourse again to Zeid, with whom he associated a
syndicate of three Coreish. The original copy of the first edition
was obtained from Haphsa's depository, the various readings were
sought out from the different provinces, and a careful recension of
the whole set on foot. In case of difference between Zeid and his
coadjutors, the voice of the latter, as conclusive of the Coreishite
idiom, was to preponderate; and the new collation was thus
assimilated exclusively to the Meccan dialect, in which the
Prophet had given utterance to his inspiration. Transcripts were
multiplied and forwarded to the chief cities in the empire, and the
previously existing copies were all, by the Caliph's command,
committed to the flames. The old original was returned to
Haphsa's custody.

"The recension of Othman had been handed down to us
unaltered. So carefully, indeed, has it been preserved, that there
are no variations of importance — we might almost say no varia-

tions at all — among the innumerable copies of the Coran scattered throughout the vast bounds of the empire of Islam. Contending and embittered factions, taking their rise in the murder of Othman himself within a quarter of a century from the death of Mahomet, have ever since rent the Mahometan world. Yet but ONE CORAN has been current amongst them; and the consentaneous use by them all in every age up to the present day of the same Scripture, is an irrefragable proof that we have now before us the very text prepared by command of the unfortunate Caliph. There is probably in the world no other work which has remained twelve centuries with so pure a text. The various readings are wonderfully few in number, and are chiefly confined to differences in the vowel points and diacritical signs. But these marks were invented at a later date. They did not exist at all in the early copies, and can hardly be said to affect the text of Othman.

"Since, then, we possess the undoubted text of Othman's recension, it remains to be enquired whether that text was an honest reproduction of Abu Bakr's edition, with the simple reconcilement of unimportant variations. There is the fullest ground for believing that it was so. No early or trustworthy traditions throw suspicion upon Othman of tampering with the Coran in order to support his own claims. The Sheeahs of later times, indeed, pretend that Othman left out certain Suras or passages which favoured Ali. But this is incredible. . . .

"When Othman's edition was prepared, no open breach had taken place between the Omeyads and the Alyites. The unity of Islam was still complete and unthreatened. Ali's pretensions were as yet undeveloped. No sufficient object can, therefore, be assigned for the perpetration by Othman of an offence which Moslems regard as one of the blackest dye. . . At the time of the recension, there were still multitudes alive who had the Coran, as originally delivered, by heart; and of the supposed passages favouring Ali — had any ever existed — there would have been numerous transcripts in the hands of his family and followers. Both of these sources must have proved an effectual check upon any attempt at suppression. Fourth: The party of Ali shortly after assumed an independent attitude, and he himself succeeded to the Caliphate. Is it conceivable that either Ali, or his party, when thus arrived at power, would have tolerated a mutilated Coran —

mutilated expressly to destroy his claims? Yet we find that they
used the same Coran as their opponents, and raised no shadow of
an objection against it. The insurgents are indeed said to have
made it one of their complaints against Othman that he had
caused a new edition to be made, and had committed the old
copies of the sacred volume to the flames; but these proceedings
were objected to simply as unauthorised and sacrilegious. No hint
was dropped of alteration or omission. Such a supposition, palpa-
bly absurd at the time, is altogether an after-thought of the modern Sheeas.

"We may then safely conclude that Othman's recension was,
what it professed to be, namely, the reproduction of Abu Bakr's
edition, with a more perfect conformity to the dialect of Mecca,
and possibly a more uniform arrangement of the component parts
— but still a faithful reproduction. The most important question
yet remains, viz., Whether Abu Bakr's edition was itself an
authentic and complete collection of Mahomet's Revelations. The
following considerations warrant the belief that it was authentic
and in the main as complete as at the time was possible.

"First. — We have no reason to doubt that Abu Bakr was a
sincere follower of Mahomet, and an earnest believer in the divine
origin of the Coran. His faithful attachment to the Prophet's person, conspicuous for the last twenty years of his life, and his simple, consistent, and unambitious deportment as Caliph, admit no
other supposition. Firmly believing the revelations of his friend to
be the revelations of God himself, his first object would be to
secure a pure and complete transcript of them. A similar argument applies with almost equal force to Omar and the other
agents in the revision. The great mass of Mussulmans were
undoubtedly sincere in their belief. From the scribes themselves,
employed in the compilation, down to the humblest Believer who
brought his little store of writing on stones or palm-leaves, all
would be influenced by the same earnest desire to reproduce the
very words which their Prophet had declared as his message from
the Lord. And a similar guarantee existed in the feelings of the
people at large, in whose soul no principle was more deeply rooted than an awful reverence for the supposed word of God. The
Coran itself contains frequent denunciations against those who
should presume to 'fabricate anything in the name of the Lord,' or

conceal any part of that which He had revealed. Such an action, represented as the very worst description of crime, we cannot believe that the first Moslems, in the early ardour of their faith and love, would have dared to contemplate.

"Second. — The compilation was made within two years of Mahomet's death. We have seen that several of his followers had the entire revelation. . . by heart; that every Moslem treasured up more or less some portions in his memory; and that there were official Reciters of it, for public worship and tuition, in all countries to which Islam extended. These formed a living link between the Revelation fresh from Mahomet's lips, and the edition of it by Zeid. Thus the people were not only sincere and fervent in wishing for a faithful copy of the Coran: they were also in possession of ample means for realising their desire, and for testing the accuracy and completeness of the volume placed in their hands by Abu Bakr.

"Third. — A still greater security would be obtained from the fragmentary transcripts which existed in Mahomet's lifetime, and which must have greatly multiplied before the Coran was compiled. These were in the possession, probably, of all who could read. And as we know that the compilation of Abu Bakr came into immediate and unquestioned use, it is reasonable to conclude that it embraced and corresponded with every extant fragment; and therefore, by common consent, superseded them. We hear of no fragments, sentences, or word intentionally omitted by the compilers, nor of any that differed from the received edition. Had any such been discoverable, they would undoubtedly have been preserved and noticed in those traditional repositories which treasured up the minutest and most trivial acts and sayings of the Prophet.

"Fourth. — The contents and the arrangement of the Coran speak forcibly for its authenticity. All the fragments that could be obtained have, with artless simplicity, been joined together. The patchwork bears no marks of a designing genius or moulding hand. It testifies to the faith and reverence of the compilers, and proves that they dared no more than simply collect the sacred fragments and place them in juxtaposition.

"The conclusion, which we may now with confidence draw, is that the editions of Abu Bakr and of Othman were not only faith-

ful, but, so far as the materials went, complete; and that whatever
omissions there may have been, were not on the part of the compilers intentional. . . we may upon the strongest presumption
affirm that every verse in the Coran is the genuine and unaltered
composition[3] of Mahomet himself."[4]

The Slanderers of Islam

We have quoted Sir William Muir at length. Hence, we do not need
to bring further quotations from the work of Father Lammens, Von
Hammer, and other orientalists who hold this view. All these are absolutely certain that the Qur'an which we recite today contains all that
Muhammad reported in all candidness as having been revealed to him
from his Lord. If a certain group of orientalists do not agree and insist that
the Qur'an is forged without regard to these rational proofs which Muir
had listed and which most orientalists had in fact taken from Muslim historians and scholars, it is in order to slander Islam and its Prophet. Such
is the dictate of hate and resentment. However clever and adept such orientalists may be in formulating their slander, they will never be able to
pass it as genuine scientific research; nor will they ever be able to fool any
Muslims, except perhaps those young men deluded enough to think that
free research demands of them the denial of their tradition and the naive
acceptance of any nicely presented falsehood and attacks against their
legacy, regardless of the validity or falsity of its premises and assumptions.
We could have quoted these same arguments of Sir William Muir and
other orientalists directly from their primary Muslim sources as written by
the scholars of Islam. But we have preferred to quote them in the words
of an orientalist in order to show those of our youths who are spellbound
by western works that precision in scientific research and a candid desire
to seek the truth are sufficient to lead anyone to the ultimate facts of history. It was also our intention to show that the investigator ought to be
very exact and precise in his investigation if he is to arrive at an understanding of his objective unaffected by ulterior motives or prejudice. Some
orientalists undoubtedly arrive at the truth in some cases; others have not
been as fortunate. The research which we have conducted in the writing
of this book has convinced us that as regards the problem which the life
of the Prophet poses to the scholar most of the orientalists have indeed
erred.

Proper Methodology

It behooves us here to remember that the researcher should never assert or deny a thesis until his research and analysis have led him to perfect conviction that he has actually grasped all there is to know concerning the given problem. Here, the historian stands in the same predicament as his colleague researcher in the natural sciences. Such is his duty regardless of whether the material he analyzes is the work of an orientalist or that of a Muslim scholar. If we sincerely seek the truth, our duty is to scrutinize critically all that the Arab and the Muslim scholars have written in the fields of medicine, astronomy, chemistry and other sciences, and to reject all that does not hold its ground before the tribunal of science and to confirm that which does. The search for truth imposes upon us such exactitude in historical matters even though they may be related to the life of the Prophet — may God's peace and blessing be upon him. The historian is not a mere reporter. He is also a critic of what he reports, analyzing it and ascertaining the truth that it contains. There is no criticism without analytic scrutiny; and science and knowledge constitute the foundation of such criticism and analysis.

The exacting analysis which we have quoted in the foregoing pages regarding the Qur'an is not enough. It does not obviate the need to respond to the letter of that Egyptian Muslim who naively believes all the writings of the orientalists, more particularly their claim that verses have been added to the Qur'an regarding the name of the Prophet, that it was once "Qutham" or "Quthamah." This claim is false, and it is motivated by the same ulterior motive that stands behind the charge of the forgery of the Qur'an.

Let us then return to the last point in the letter of our young Muslim Egyptian author. He says that the investigations of the orientalists have established that the Prophet suffered from epilepsy, that the symptoms of the disease were all present in him and that he used to lose consciousness, perspire, fall into convulsions and sputter. After recovering from such seizures, the claim continues, Muhammad would recite to the believers what he then claimed to be a revelation from God, whereas that was only an aftereffect of the epileptic fits which he suffered.

The Slander of Epilepsy

To represent the phenomenon of Muhammad's revelations in these terms is, from the standpoint of scientific research, the gravest nonsense.

The fit of epilepsy leaves the patient utterly without memory of what has taken place. In fact, the patient completely forgets that period of his life and can recollect nothing that has happened to him in the meantime because the processes of sensing and thinking come to a complete stop during the fit. Such are the symptoms of epilepsy as science has established them. This was not the case at all with the Prophet at the moment of revelation, for his cognitive faculties used to be strengthened — rather than weakened — and do so to a superlative degree hitherto unknown by the people who knew him most. Muhammad used to remember with utmost precision what he received by way of revelation and recited it to his companions without a flaw. Moreover, revelation was not always accompanied by paroxysms of the body. Much of it took place while the Prophet was perfectly conscious, during his usual wakefulness. We have advanced sufficient evidence for this in our discussion of the revelation of the *Surah* "al Fath" upon return of the Muslims from Makkah to Yathrib after signing the Pact of Hudaybiyah.[5]

Scientific investigation therefore reveals that the case of Muhammad was not one of epilepsy. For this reason very few orientalists have upheld this claim and these turn out to be the same authors who upheld the charge of forgery against the Qur'an. Obviously, in charging Muhammad with epilepsy, their motivation was not the establishment of historical fact but the derogation of the Prophet in the eyes of his Muslim followers. Perhaps, they thought, propagation of such views would cast some suspicion upon his revelation, for it was precisely the revelation that came as a result of the so-called epileptic fits. This, of course, makes them all the more blameworthy and, from the standpoint of science, positively in error.

Return to Science

Had these western orientalists been candid, they would not have presented their non-scientific claims in the name of science. They did so in order to delude the ignorant who, ignorant though they be of the symptoms of the epileptic disease, are prevented by their own naïveté from checking the orientalists' claims against the writings and opinions of the men of the medical sciences. A consultation of medical literature would have quickly exposed the errors of the orientalists, deliberate or accidental, and convinced them that in an epileptic fit all the intellectual and spiritual processes come to an absolute stop. When in a fit, the epileptic patient is either in a ridiculously mechanical state of motion or on a rampage injurious to his fellow men. He is utterly unconscious, unknowing of what he himself does, or of what happens to him, very much like the somnambulant who has no control over his movements during his sleep and who cannot remember them when he wakes up. A very great difference separates an epileptic fit from a revelation in which an intense and penetrating consciousness establishes, in full knowledge and conviction, a contact with the supernal plenum that enables the prophet to report and convey his revelation. Epilepsy, on the other hand, stops cognition. It reduces its patient to a mechanical state devoid of either feeling or sensation. Revelation is a spiritual heightening with which God prepares His prophet to receive from Him the highest and apodeictic cosmic truths that he may convey them to mankind. Science may eventually reach some of these truths and discover the secrets and laws of the universe. The rest may never become object of human knowledge until existence on this earth has come to an end. Nonetheless, these truths are apodeictically certain, furnishing true guidance to the earnest believer though they remain opaque to the ignorant whose hearts are locked and whose vision is dim.

Incapacity of Science in Some Fields

We would have understood and appreciated the western orientalists having said: "Revelation is a strange psychic phenomenon inexplicable in terms of contemporary science." Such a statement would mean that despite its wide scope and penetration, our science is still unable to explain many spiritual and psychic phenomena of which revelation is one. This statement is neither objectionable nor strange. Science is still unable to explain many natural, cosmic phenomena. The nature of the sun, moon, stars, and planets is still largely a matter for hypothesis. These heavenly bodies are only some of what the human eye, whether naked or through the telescope, reveals to us of the cosmos. Many of the inventions of the twentieth century that we presently take for granted were regarded by our predecessors in the nineteenth century as pure fiction. Psychic and spiritual phenomena are now subject to careful scientific study. But they have not yet been subject to the dominion of science so that it could be made to reveal their permanent role. We have often read about phenomena witnessed by the men of science and ascertained by them without explanation in terms coherent with scientific knowledge. Psychology, for instance, is a science which is not yet certain of the structures of many areas of psychic life. If this uncertainty is true of everyday phenomena, the demand to explain all the phenomena of life scientifically must be a shameful and futile exaggeration.

The revelations of Muhammad were phenomena witnessed by his Muslim contemporaries. The more they heard the Qur'an, the more convinced they became of the truth of these revelations. Among these contemporaries were many of extreme intelligence. Others were Jews and Christians who had argued with the Prophet for a long time before, and they believed in his mission and trusted his revelation in every detail. Some men of Quraysh had accused Muhammad of magic and madness. Later, convinced that he was neither a magician nor a madman, they believed in and followed him. Since all these facts are certain, it is as unscientific to deny the phenomenon of revelation as it is unworthy of the men of science to speak of it in derogative terms. The man of science candid in his search for the truth will not go beyond asserting that his discipline is unable to explain the phenomenon of revelation according to the materialistic theory. But he will never deny the factuality of revelation as reported by the companions of the Prophet and the historians of the first century of Islam. To do otherwise would be to fall under prejudice and betray the spirit of science.

Slander against Muhammad Is *Argumentum ad Hominem*

Such obstinate prejudice only proves the determined concern of its author to arouse suspicion in Islam itself. Such people have been incapable of arguing against Islam because they had found it sublimely noble, simple, and easy to understand, and realized that these qualities are the sources of its strength. They hence resort to the trick of the impotent who shifts attention from the great idea beyond his reach to the person advocating it. That is the *argumentum ad hominem* fallacy which every scholar should seek to avoid. It is natural for men to concern themselves with ideas and not with the personal circumstances of their authors and advocates. Men do not give themselves the trouble to investigate the roots of a tree whose fruits they had found delectable, nor the fertilizer which had helped it to grow, as long as their purpose is not to plant a similar or better tree. When they analyze the philosophy of Plato, the plays of Shakespeare, or the paintings of Raphael, and find nothing objectionable in them, they do not look for blameworthy aspects in the lives of these great men who constitute humanity's glory and pride. And if they try to fabricate charges against these persons, they will never succeed in convincing anyone. They only succeed in betraying themselves and exposing their ulterior motives. Casting resentment in the form of scientific research does not alter it from being what it is: namely resentment. Resentment refuses to recognize the truth; and the truth will always be too proud to allow resentment to be its source or associate. Such is the case of the orientalists' charges against the person of the Arab Prophet Muhammad, Seal of the Prophets; and that is why their charges fall to the ground.

That is all I have to say by way of response to those orientalists to whom the letter of the Egyptian Muslim had referred. Having thus refuted their views, let me now direct my attention to a number of observations made on the first edition of this book by the Islamicists at home.

It is my earnest hope that such base charges unworthy of science and unacceptable to scholars will never be repeated again. Perhaps, hitherto, the orientalists felt themselves excused on the grounds that they were writing for the consumption of their fellow Christians and Europeans and that they were actually discharging a national or religious duty imposed upon them by a patriotism or faith which requires scholarly form to make its propaganda palatable. Our day, however, is different. Communication between the various corners of the globe by means of radio broadcasting and the press has made it possible for anything said or published in Europe or America today to become known throughout the Orient in that same day or even the same hour. It is therefore the duty of those who assume the scholarly profession and the pursuit of truth to tear away from their hearts and eyes every curtain of national, racial, or religious isolation. They should realize that whatever they say or write will soon reach the ears of all men throughout the world and will be subject to universal criticism and scrutiny. The absolute and unconditional truth should be the objective of every one of us; and let us all take due care to connect the present reality of mankind with its past, to regard humanity as one great unit undivided by nationality, race or religion. Let such connection be the bond of free fraternity in the pursuit of truth, goodness, and beauty, and the noblest ideal that humanity has ever known. Such a bond is alone capable of guiding humanity in its quick march toward happiness and perfection.

Observations of Muslim Islamicists

Whereas the naive believers in the exaggerations of the orientalists blame us for having recourse to the Arabic sources and depending upon them, a number of Muslim Islamicists blame us for turning to the writings of the orientalists rather than limiting ourselves to the Islamic biographies and books of Hadith. The latter have also criticized us for not following the same method as these ancient books.

It was on this basis that some of them made friendly observations in hope of reaching the fact of the matter in question. Others made observations which betray such ignorance or prejudice as no scholar would wish to associate himself with. The former took note of the fact that we have not reported the miracles of Muhammad as the biographies and Hadith have done. In this regard we wrote in the conclusion of our first edition: "The Life of Muhammad, therefore, has realized the highest ideals possible to man. Muhammad — may God's peace and blessing be upon him — was very careful that the Muslims should think of him as a human to whom revelation came. He never accepted that any miracle be attributed to him other than his association with the advent of the Qur'an, and actually told this much to his companions." As regards the story of the splitting of Muhammad's chest we wrote: "Orientalists as well as Muslim scholars take their attitude towards this event in the life of Muhammad on the grounds that Muhammad's whole life was all too human and noble and that he never resorted to miracles as previous prophets had done, in order to prove the veracity of his revelation. In taking this attitude, the above-mentioned thinkers rely upon the Arab and Muslim historians who share their view and who deny any place in the biography of the Arab Prophet to all that is irrational. They regard their stand as being in perfect accord with the Qur'an's call to man to study the creation of God and discover therein His immutable laws. They find the claim for miracles incoherent with the Qur'an's condemnation of the associationists as men who do not reason, as men who have no faculties with which to reason." Other more considerate critics criticized us for having mentioned at all the orientalists' attacks upon the Prophet, though we did so but to refute them. In their opinion, this procedure does not accord with the veneration due to the person of the Prophet — may God's blessing be upon him. Lastly, there is the class of prejudiced critics who were known even before the first edition of this book had appeared and, indeed, even before my researches had been collected in book form. Their strongest criticism was that I have given my work the title, "The Life of Muhammad," without joining it to an invocation of peace and blessing upon him. Such invocations occur frequently in the course of the book. I had thought, nonetheless, that they would discover their prejudice once the title page of the first edition came out decorated, as it was, with the verse: "God and his angels bless the Prophet. O you who believe, invoke God's peace and blessing upon him and salute him with the salutation of peace."[6] I had also thought that the method used in this book would itself dissolve their prejudice. By insisting as they did, however, they betrayed their ignorance of Islamic truths and their satisfaction with the imitation of their ancestors.

Let us begin by answering their false criticism in the hope that neither they nor any others will repeat it regarding this or any other book. We shall refuse their criticism by turning to the books of the classical leaders of Islamic knowledge. Everyone will then realize the free stand Islam has taken *vis-a-vis* all verbal restrictions and will then appreciate the *hadith*, "This religion is indeed sound. Analyze it as you wish, but gently. You will never find a flaw therein." Abu al Baqa' wrote in his book, *Al Kulliyyat:* "Writing the invocation of peace and blessing on Muhammad at the beginning of a book occurred during the 'Abbasi period. That is why the *Sahih* of al Bukhari and others are devoid of it."[7] The majority of the great men of Islamic knowledge agree that the invocation of peace and blessing upon the Prophet need not be made by the Muslim more than once in his lifetime. In his book *Al Bahr al Ra'iq*, ibn Nujaym wrote: "The religious imperative implied in the divine command, 'Invoke upon him God's peace and blessing,' is that it should be made at least once in a lifetime whether during or outside the prayer. For no command by itself implies repetition. On this there is no disagreement." Likewise, al Shafi'i contended with his colleagues on "whether or not the invocation of God's peace and blessing on the Prophet is imperative during the prayer or outside of it. Prayer is itself invocation. As it stands in the above mentioned verse, to invoke God's peace and blessing upon the Prophet simply means that one should ask God to bless the Prophet and to salute him the salutation of peace." That is the lesson which the Muslim men of knowledge and their leaders have taught in this regard. It proves that those who claim that this invocation is imperative whenever the name of the Prophet is mentioned or written are simply exaggerating. Had they known the foregoing facts, and that the greatest traditionists had not written such an invocation regarding the Prophet on the title pages or beginnings of their collections of *hadiths*, they would perhaps have avoided falling into their present error.

Refutation of the Orientalists and Its Method

As to those who claim that it does not become a Muslim scholar to repeat the attacks of the Orientalists and the missionaries against the Prophet even in order to refute them, they have really nothing to stand upon except an Islamic emotion which we salute. From the religious as well as scholarly points of view, they simply have no argument at all. The Holy Qur'an itself reported much of what the associationists of Makkah used to say about the Prophet and refuted them with clear and eloquent argument. The Arabic style of the Qur'an is the highest and its morals the noblest.[8] It mentioned the accusation of the Quraysh that Muhammad was either possessed or a magician. It said: "We do know that they say that it is only a man who teaches Muhammad the Qur'an. But the tongue of him to whom they refer by this insinuation is foreign whereas this Qur'an is in the Arabic tongue, plain and clear."[9] There are many such statements in the Qur'an. Moreover, an argument is not scientifically refuted unless it is honestly and precisely stated. In writing this book, my purpose has been to reach objective truth by means of scholarly research. And I have written my book so that both Muslims and non-Muslims may read it and be convinced of this objective truth. Such a purpose cannot be achieved unless the scholar be honest in his pursuit. He should never hesitate to acknowledge the truth whencesoever it may come.

Biographies and Hadith Books

Let us return to the first criticism the Muslim students of Islam have kindly directed to our work, namely, that we have not taken into consideration the Islamic biographies and Hadith books and that we have not followed the same methodology as these ancient works. It should suffice to say in reply to this criticism that I have resolved to follow the modern scientific method and to write in the style of the century and that I have taken this resolution because it is the only proper one in the eyes of the contemporary world, whether for historiography or any other discipline. This being the case, ancient methods are ruled out *a priori*. Between these and the methods of our ago there is great difference, the most obvious of which is the freedom to criticise. Most of the ancient works were written for a religious purpose and as devotional exercises, whereas contemporary writers are interested only in scientific analysis and criticism. To say this much concerning my method and work should be sufficient answer to their criticism. But I see the need for a more detailed treatment in order to show the reasons why our classical scholars of the past did not, and those of the present should not, assume in wholesale fashion the veracity of all that the books of biography and Hadith have brought. It is also my intention to clarify the reasons why we ought to observe the rules of scientific criticism as closely as possible in order to guard against all possible errors.

The Difference between These Books

The first of these reasons is the difference of these books in their reporting of events supposed to have taken place in the life of the Arab Prophet. Those who studied these books have observed that the miracles and extraordinary events reported increased or decreased for no reason other than the change in the time when they were written. The earlier report fewer miracles than the later; and the miracles they do report are less unreasonable than those reported in later books. The oldest known biography, namely, that of ibn Hisham for example, has far less material than the *Tarikh* of Abu al Fida', than *Al Shifa'* of Qadi 'Ayyad and of most later writings. The same is true of the books of the Hadith. Some of them tell a story and others omit it, or they report it and point out that it is not trustworthy. The objective researcher investigating these books must therefore have a standard by which he can evaluate the various claims. That which agrees with the standard he would find acceptable and that which does not, he would subject to closer scrutiny wherever possible.

Our ancestors have followed this method in their investigations at times, and they have omitted doing so at others. An example of their omission is the story of "the daughters of God." It is told that when the Prophet, under ever-increasing oppression of Quraysh, recited the Qur'anic *surah* "al Najm" and arrived at the verse: "Consider al Lat and al 'Uzza; and Manat, the third goddess,"[10] he added: "Those are the goddesses on high; their intercession with God is worthy of our prayers." He then went on reciting the *surah* to its end and when he finished, he prostrated himself in worship, and Muslims and associationists joined him and did likewise. This story was reported by ibn Sa'd in his *Al Tabaqat al Kubra* without criticism. It also occurs with little variation in some books of Hadith. Ibn Ishaq, however, reported the story and judged it as being the fabrication of *zindiqs*.[11] In his *Al Bidayah wa al Nihayah fi al Tarikh*, ibn Kathir wrote: "They mentioned the story of the goddesses of Makkah, whereas we have decided to omit it for fear that the uninstructed may naively accept it as truth. The story was first reported in the books of Hadith." He then reported a tradition from Bukhari in this regard and qualified it as being "unique to Bukhari, rejected by Muslim." As for me, I did not hesitate to reject the story altogether and to agree with ibn Ishaq that it was the fabrication of *zindiqs*. In analyzing it I brought together several pieces of evidence. In addition to its denial of the infallibility of the Prophets in their conveyance of their divine messages, this story must also be subject to modern scientific criticism.

The Age of These Books

The books of the ancestors should be closely scrutinized and criticised in a scientific manner because the most ancient of them was written a hundred or more years after the death of the Prophet. At that time, many political and religious movements were spreading throughout the Islamic Empire, each of which fabricated all kinds of stories and *hadiths* to justify its own cause. The later books, written during even more turbulent and unsettled times, are more vulnerable. Political struggles caused a great deal of trouble to the collectors of Hadith because they took utmost care in scrutinizing these various reports, rejecting the suspicious, and confirming only those which passed the severest tests. It is sufficient to remember here the travails of al Bukhari in his travels throughout the Muslim World undertaken for this purpose. He told us that he had found some six hundred thousand *hadiths* current, of which only 4,000 he could confirm as true. The ratio is that of one to 150 *hadiths*. As for Abu Dawud, he could confirm 4,800 *hadiths* out of half a million. Such was the task of all collectors of *hadiths*. Nonetheless, many of the *hadiths* which they had found true after criticism were found untrue by a number of other scholars under further criticism. Such was the case of the goddesses. If such is the case of Hadith, despite all the efforts spent by the early collectors, how trustworthy can the later biographies of the Prophet be? How can their reports be taken without scientific scrutiny?

Effects of Islamic Political Strife

In fact, the political struggles of the first century of Islam caused the various parties to invent, and press into their service, a great number of stories and *hadiths*. No Hadith has been committed to writing until the last years of the Umawi period. It was 'Umar ibn 'Abd al 'Aziz who ordered its collection for the first time. The job, however, was not completed until the reign of al Ma'mun, the time when "the true *hadith* was as discernible from the false as a white hair is in the fur of a black bull," to borrow the phrase of Daraqutni. The Hadith was not collected in the first century of

Islam perhaps because of the reported command of the Prophet: "Do not write down anything I say except the Qur'an. Whoever has written something other than the Qur'an, let him destroy it." Nonetheless, the *hadiths* of the Prophet were current in those days and must have been varied. During his caliphate, 'Umar ibn al Khattab once tried to deal with the problem by committing the Hadith to writing. The companions of the Prophet whom he consulted encouraged him, but he was not quite sure whether he should proceed. One day, moved by God's inspiration, he made up his mind and announced: "I wanted to have the traditions of the Prophet written down, but I fear that the Book of God might be encroached upon. Hence I shall not permit this to happen."

He therefore changed his mind and instructed the Muslims throughout the provinces: "Whoever has a document bearing a prophetic tradition shall destroy it." The Hadith therefore continued to be transmitted orally and was not collected and written down until the period of al Ma'mun.

The Standard of Hadith Criticism

Despite the great care and precision of the Hadith scholars, much of what they regarded as true was later proved to be spurious. In his commentary on the collection of Muslim, al Nawawi wrote: "A number of scholars discovered many *hadiths* in the collections of Muslim and Bukhari which do not fulfill the conditions of verification assumed by these men." The collectors attached the greater weight to the trustworthiness of the narrators. Their criterion was certainly valuable, but it was not sufficient. In our opinion, the criterion for the Hadith criticism, as well as standard for materials concerning the Prophet's life, is the one which the Prophet himself gave. He said: "After I am gone differences will arise among you. Compare whatever is reported to be mine with the Book of God; that which agrees therewith you may accept as having come from me; that which disagrees you will reject as a fabrication." This valid standard is observed by the great men of Islam right from the very beginning. It continues to be the standard of thinkers today. Ibn Khaldun wrote: "I do not believe any *hadith* or report of a companion of the Prophet to be true which differs from the common sense meaning of the Qur'an, no matter how trustworthy the narrators may have been. It is not impossible that a narrator appears to be trustworthy though he may be moved by ulterior motive. If the *hadiths* were criticised for their textual contents as they were for the narrators who transmitted them a great number would have had to be rejected. It is a recognized principle that a *hadith* could be declared spurious if it departs from the common sense meaning of the Qur'an from the recognized principles of the Shari'ah,[12] the rules of logic, the evidence of sense, or any other self-evident truth." This criterion, as given by the Prophet as well as ibn Khaldun, perfectly accords with modern scientific criticism.

True, after Muhammad's death the Muslims differed, and they fabricated thousands of *hadiths* and reports to support their various causes. From the day Abu Lu'lu'ah, the servant of al Mughirah, killed 'Umar ibn al Khattab and 'Uthman ibn 'Affan assumed the caliphate, the old pre-Islamic enmity of Banu Hashim and Banu Umayyah reappeared. When, upon the murder of 'Uthman, civil war broke out between the Muslims, 'A'ishah fought against 'Ali and 'Ali's supporters consolidated themselves into a party, the fabrication of *hadiths* spread to the point where 'Ali ibn Abu Talib himself had to reject the practice and warn against it. He reportedly said: "We have no book and no writing to read to you except the Qur'an and this sheet which I have received from the Prophet of God in which he specified the duties prescribed by charity." Apparently, this exhortation did not stop the Hadith narrators from fabricating their stories either in support of a cause they advocated, or of a virtue or practice to which they exhorted the Muslims and which they thought would have more appeal if vested with prophetic authority. When the Banu Umayyah firmly established themselves in power, their protagonists among the Hadith narrators deprecated the prophetic traditions reported by the party of 'Ali ibn Abu Talib, and the latter defended those traditions and propagated them with all the means at their disposal. Undoubtedly they also deprecated the traditions reported by 'A'ishah, "Mother of the Faithful." A humorous piece of reportage was given us by ibn 'Asakir who wrote: "Abu Sa'd Isma'il ibn al Muthanna al Istrabadhi was giving a sermon one day in Damascus when a man stood up and asked him what he thought of the *hadith* of the Prophet: 'I am the city of knowledge and 'Ali is its gate.' Abu Sa'd pondered the question for a while and then replied: 'Indeed! No one knows this *hadith* of the Prophet except those who lived in the first century of Islam. What the Prophet had said, he continued, was, rather, "I am the city of knowledge; Abu Bakr is its foundation; 'Umar, its walls; 'Uthman its ceiling; and 'Ali its gate.' The audience was quite pleased with his reply and asked him to furnish them with its chain of narrators. Abu Sa'd could not furnish any chain and was terribly embarrassed." Thus *hadiths* were fabricated for political and other purposes. This wanton multiplication alarmed the Muslims because many ran counter to the Book of God. The attempts to stop this wave of fabrication under the Umawis did not succeed. When the 'Abbasis took over, and al Ma'mun assumed the caliphate almost two centuries after the death of the Prophet, the fabricated *hadiths* numbered in the thousands and hundreds of thousands and contained an unimaginable amount of contradiction and variety. It was then that the collectors applied themselves to the task of putting the Hadith together and the biographers of the Prophet wrote their biographies. Al Waqidi, ibn Hisham and al Mada'ini lived and wrote their books in the days of al Ma'mun. They could not afford to contradict the caliphate and hence could not apply with the precision due the Prophet's criterion that his traditions ought to be checked against the Qur'an and accepted only if they accorded therewith.

Had this criterion, which does not differ from the modern method of scientific criticism, been applied with precision, the ancient masters would have altered much of their writing. Circumstances of history imposed upon them the application of it to some of their writings but not to others. The later generations inherited their method of treating the biography of the Prophet without questioning it. Had they been true to history, they would have applied this criterion in general as well as in detail. No reported events disagreeing with the Qur'an would have been spared, and none would have been confirmed but those which agreed with the Book of God as well as the laws of nature. Even so, these *hadiths* would have been subject to strict analysis and established only with valid proof and incontestable evidence. This stand was taken by the greatest Muslim scholars of the past as well as of the present. The grand Shaykh of al Azhar, Muhammad Mustafa al Maraghi, wrote in his foreword to this book: "Muhammad — may God's peace and blessing be upon him — had only one irresistible miracle — the Qur'an. But it is not irrational. How eloquent is the verse of al Busayri: 'God did not try us with anything irrational. Thus, we fell under neither doubt nor illusion.'"[13]

The late Muhammad Rashid Rida, editor of *al Manar*, wrote in answer to our critics: "The most important objection which the Azharis and the Sufis raise against Haykal concerns the problem of the miracles. In my book, *Al Wahy al Muhammadi*, I have analyzed the problem from all aspects in the second chapter and the second section of the fifth chapter. I have established there that the Qur'an alone is the conclusive proof of the prophethood of Muhammad — may God's peace and blessing be upon him — as well as of the other prophets of their messages and prophecies regarding him. In our age it is impossible to prove any work of the Prophet except by the Qur'an. From its standpoint, supernatural events are *ipso facto* doubtful. Besides the ubiquitous reports of their occurrence in all ages and places, they are believed in by the superstitious of all faiths. I have also analyzed the causes of this predilection for belief in miracles and distinguished the miraculous from the spiritual and shown the relationship of both to cosmic laws."[14]

In his book, *Al Islam wa al Nasraniyyah,* Muhammad 'Abduh, the great scholar and leader, wrote: "Islam, therefore, and its demand for faith in God and in His unity, depend only on rational proof and common sense human thinking. Islam does not overwhelm the mind with the supernatural, confuse the understanding with the extraordinary, impose acquiescent silence by resorting to heavenly intervention, nor does it impede the movement of thought by any sudden cry of divinity. All the Muslims are agreed, except those whose opinion is insignificant, that faith in God is prior to faith in prophethood and that it is not possible to believe in a prophet except after one has come to believe in God. It is unreasonable to demand faith in God on the ground that the prophets or the revealed books had mid so, for it is unreasonable to believe that any book had been revealed by God unless one already believed that God exists and that it is possible for Him to reveal a book or send a messenger."

I am inclined to think that those who wrote biographies of the Prophet agreed with this view. The earlier generation of them could not apply it because of the historical circumstances in which they lived. The later generation of them suspended the principle deliberately on account of their belief that the more miraculous their portrayal of the Prophet, the more faith this would engender among their audience. They assumed, quite naively, that the inclusion of these extraneous matters into his biography achieved a good purpose. Had they lived to our day and seen how the enemies of Islam had taken their writings as an argument against Islam and its people, they would have followed the Qur'an more closely and agreed with al Ghazzali, Muhammad 'Abduh, al Maraghi, and all other objective scholars. And had they lived in our day and age, and witnessed how their stories have alienated many Muslim minds and hearts instead of confirming their faith, they would have been satisfied with the indubitable proofs and arguments of the Book of God.

Reports Condemned by Reason and Science

Now that the defect of reports condemned by reason and science has become obvious, scientific and critical analysis of the materials involved is demanded. This is equally the demand of Islam and a service to it as well as to the history of the Arab Prophet. It is a necessary requisite if that history is to illuminate the road of mankind towards high culture and civilization.

The Qur'an and Miracles

We will quickly agree with the views of the objective Muslim scholars as soon as we compare a number of narratives from the biography and Hadith books with the Qur'an. The latter told us that the Makkans had asked the Prophet to perform some miracles if they were to believe in him; it mentioned specifically their demands, and refuted them. God said:

إِذْ قَالَتِ الْمَلَائِكَةُ يَمَرْيَمُ إِنَّ اللَّهَ يُبَشِّرُكِ بِكَلِمَةٍ مِنْهُ اسْمُهُ الْمَسِيحُ عِيسَى ابْنُ مَرْيَمَ وَجِيهًا فِي الدُّنْيَا وَالْآخِرَةِ وَمِنَ الْمُقَرَّبِينَ۞ وَيُكَلِّمُ النَّاسَ فِي الْمَهْدِ وَكَهْلًا وَمِنَ الصَّالِحِينَ۞ قَالَتْ رَبِّ أَنَّى يَكُونُ لِي وَلَدٌ وَلَمْ يَمْسَسْنِي بَشَرٌ قَالَ كَذَلِكِ اللَّهُ يَخْلُقُ مَا يَشَاءُ إِذَا قَضَى أَمْرًا فَإِنَّمَا يَقُولُ لَهُ كُنْ فَيَكُونُ۞ وَيُعَلِّمُهُ الْكِتَابَ وَالْحِكْمَةَ وَالتَّوْرَاةَ وَالْإِنْجِيلَ۞ وَرَسُولًا إِلَى بَنِي إِسْرَائِيلَ ۞ أَنِّي قَدْ جِئْتُكُمْ بِآيَةٍ مِنْ رَبِّكُمْ أَنِّي أَخْلُقُ لَكُمْ مِنَ الطِّينِ كَهَيْئَةِ الطَّيْرِ فَأَنْفُخُ فِيهِ فَيَكُونُ طَيْرًا بِإِذْنِ اللَّهِ وَأُبْرِئُ الْأَكْمَهَ وَالْأَبْرَصَ وَأُحْيِي الْمَوْتَى بِإِذْنِ اللَّهِ وَأُنَبِّئُكُمْ بِمَا تَأْكُلُونَ وَمَا تَدَّخِرُونَ فِي بُيُوتِكُمْ إِنَّ فِي ذَلِكَ لَآيَةً لَكُمْ إِنْ كُنْتُمْ مُؤْمِنِينَ

"They said that they will never believe in you unless you cause a fountain to spring forth from the earth; or create for yourself a garden of big trees and vines and cause abundant streams of water to run from one side of it to the other, or cause heaven to fall upon them in pieces as you had claimed, or bring God and His angels before them face to face, or create for yourself a beauteous palace, or ascend to heaven in front of them. 'Nay,' they said to Muhammad, 'we will not believe in your ascension unless you send down upon us a book confirming that you have done all these things clearly and unequivocally.' Answer: 'Praised be my Lord: Have I ever claimed to be anything but a human and a messenger?'"[15]

God also said: "They swore their strongest oaths that if they could witness a miracle they would believe. Answer: 'Miracles are God's prerogative, not mine.' But what would convince you [Muhammad] that they will not believe even if such miracles were to take place? Let their mind and understanding remain as confused as ever. Let them wander aimlessly in their misguidance. Indeed, unless of course God wills for them to believe, they will not believe even if We sent them the angels, caused the dead to speak to them, and placed everything squarely before them. But most of them are ignorant."[16] There is no mention in the whole Qur'an of any miracle intended to support the prophethood of Muhammad except the Qur'an, notwithstanding its acknowledgment of many of the miracles performed with God's permission by the prophets preceding Muhammad and description of the many other favors which God has bestowed upon him. What the Qur'an did report about the Arab Prophet does not violate any of the laws of nature in the least degree.

The Greatest Miracle

Since this is the logic of the Book of God and is demanded by the advent of His Prophet, what reason could have caused some of the Muslims of the past, and still cause some of them in the present, to attribute miracles to Muhammad? It must be their reading in the Qur'an of miracles performed by prophets preceding Muhammad and their jumping to the conclusion that such supernatural occurrences are necessary for prophethood. They thus believed the stories circulating about Muhammad's miracles despite the fact that they could not find any confirmation of them in the Qur'an. They mistakenly believed that the more of them they could muster the more convinced they and their audiences would be of their faith. To compare the Arab Prophet with his predecessor prophets is to compare the incomparable. For he was the last of the prophets and the first one sent by God unto all mankind rather than unto any specific people alone. That is why God desired that the "miracle" of Muhammad be human and rational, though unmatchable by any humans or genii. This miracle is the Qur'an itself, the greatest that God permitted. He — may His glory be praised — willed that His Prophet's mission be established by rational argument and clear proof. He willed that His religion achieve victory in the life of His prophet and that men might see in his victory the might and dominion of God. Had God willed that a material miracle force the conversion of Makkah, the miracle would have occurred and would have been mentioned in the Qur'an. But some men do not believe except in that which their reason understands and corroborates. The proper way to convince them would be to appeal to their understanding and reason. God made the Qur'an Muhammad's convincing argument, a miracle of the "illiterate Prophet." He willed that men's entry into Islam and the sense of their faith in Him be dependent upon true conviction and apodeictic evidence. A religion thus founded would be worthy of the faith of all men in all times whatever their race or language.

Should a people convert to Islam today who did not need any miracle beside the Qur'an, this fact would neither detract from their faith nor from the worth of their conversion. As long as a people is not itself recipient of a revelation, it is perfectly legitimate to subject all the reports of such revelation to the closest scrutiny. That which unquestionable proof confirms is acceptable; the rest may validly be put to question. To believe in God alone without associate does not need recourse to a miracle. Nor does it need more than consideration of the nature of this universe which God created. On the other hand, to believe in the Prophethood of Muhammad who, by command of God, called men precisely unto such faith, does not need any miracles other than the Qur'an. Nor does it need any more than the presentation of the revealed text to consciousness.

Were a people to believe today in this religion without the benefit of any miracle other than the Qur'an, its faithful would belong to one of the following kinds: the man whose mind and heart does not oscillate but is guided by God directly to the object of his faith, as was the case with Abu Bakr who believed without hesitation; and, the man who does not seek his faith in the miraculous but in the natural (i.e., the created world, unlimited in space or time and running perfectly in accordance with eternal and immutable laws), and whose reason guides him from these laws of nature to the creator and fashioner thereof. Even if miracles did exist, they would constitute no problem for either kind of believer who regards them as mere signs of divine mercy. Many leaders of Islamic knowledge regard this kind of faith as indeed the highest. Some of them even prescribe that faith should not stand on a foundation of fear of God's punishment or ambition to win His reward. They insist that it should be held purely for the sake of God and involve an actual annihilation of self in God. To Him all things belong; and so do we. To Him, we and all things shall return.

The Believers during the Life of the Prophet

Those who believe today in God and in His Prophet and whose faith does not rest on miracles are in the same position as those who believed during the life of the Prophet. History has not reported to us that anyone of those early companions had entered the faith because of a miracle he witnessed. Rather, it was the conclusive divine argument conveyed through revelation and the superlatively noble life of the Prophet himself which conduced those men to their faith. In fact, all biographies mention that a number of those who believed in Muhammad before the *Isra'* abandoned their faith when the Prophet reported to them that he had been transported during the night from the Mosque of Makkah to the Blessed One of Jerusalem. Even Suraqah ibn Ju'shum, who pursued Muhammad on the latter's flight to Madinah in order to capture him dead or alive and win the prize the Makkans had placed on his head, did not believe despite the miracle which the biographers have reported to have taken place on his way there. History has not reported a single case of an associationist who believed in Muhammad because of a miracle performed. Islam has no parallel to the case of the magicians of Pharaoh whose rods were swallowed up by that of Moses.[17]

The Goddesses and Tabuk

The classical biographies are not unanimous in their reportage of the so-called miracles. Many a time their narratives were subject to strong criticism despite their corroboration by the books of Hadith. We have already referred to the question of the goddesses in this preface, and we have also treated the problem in detail in the course of this work. The story of the opening of Muhammad's chest as reported by Halimah, Muhammad's wet nurse, is equally inconclusive.[18] There is a difference of opinion concerning Halimah's reports as well as the age of Muhammad at which the story has supposedly taken place. Likewise, the reports of the biographies and of the Hadith concerning Zayd and Zaynab are devoid of foundation, as we shall have occasion to see later.[19] Similar disagreement exists as regards the story of the military expedition to Tabuk (Jaysh al 'Usrah). In his *Sahih*, Muslim reported from Mu'adh ibn Jabal that "the Prophet told ibn Jabal and his companions who were marching to Tabuk: 'Tomorrow, but not before mid-day, you will, with God's leave, reach the spring of Tabuk. You will not, however, touch its waters until I come.'

When we arrived, we found that two of our men had reached it before us and the spring had very little water. The Prophet asked the two men whether they had touched the water of the spring, and they confessed. He — may God's peace and blessing be upon him criticized and scolded them as he should. They then filled a container with water from the spring. Mu'adh said: 'The Prophet of God — may God's peace and blessing be upon him — washed his face and his hands and poured the water back into the spring whereupon the spring gushed forth abundantly (he might have said 'profusely') until all men drank and were satisfied. The Prophet then said: 'If you were to live long enough, O Mu'adh, you would see this place full of gardens.'"[20]

In the biographies, on the other hand, the story of Tabuk is told in a different way without mention of any miracles. Thus we read in Ibn Hisham's *The Life of Muhammad:* "When, in the morning, the men discovered they had no water, they complained to the Prophet — may God's peace and blessing be upon him. He prayed to God, who then sent a rain cloud. So much rain fell that everybody drank his fill and filled his skin. Ibn Ishaq said: 'Asim ibn 'Umar ibn Qatadah, reporting from Mahmud ibn Labid, who in turn was reporting what he heard from some men of the Banu 'Abd al Ashhal tribe, said: 'I said to Mahmud, 'Did these Muslims know that some hypocrites were among them'? He answered, 'Yes. Sometimes a man would tell a hypocrite even if he were his brother, father, uncle or fellow tribesman; at other times he would not be able to differentiate between them.' Mahmud continued: 'A fellow tribesman told me of a well-known hypocrite who used to accompany the Prophet of God — may God's peace and blessing be upon him wherever he went, and who was present at this expedition. After the miracle had taken place, we went to him and asked: 'Are you still in doubt after what you saw with your own eyes?' He answered, 'It was but a passing cloud.' "

Such a wide range of difference as separates the classical accounts of this story makes it impossible for us to affirm it conclusively. Those who apply themselves to the study of it should not stop at probable solutions which neither confirm nor deny the classical reports. Whenever they are confronted by a story not supported by positive evidence, the least they can do is to discard it. Should other investigators later on discover the required evidence, the duty of presenting the story with its proof-claims would devolve upon them.

My Methodology

This is the method which I have followed in my study of the life of Muhammad, the Prophet of the Islamic mission to mankind. It characterizes my work throughout; for ever since I decided to undertake this study I resolved that it would be conducted in accordance with the modern scientific method in all sincerity and for the sake of truth alone. That is what I announced in the preface of this book and prayed, in the conclusion of its first edition, that I may have accomplished, thereby paving the way for deeper and wiser investigations. I had hoped that this and similar studies would clear for science a number of psychic and spiritual problems and establish facts which would guide mankind to the new civilization for which it is groping. There is no doubt that deepening of analysis and extending the scope of the investigation would unlock many secrets which many people have thought for a long time to lie beyond scientific explanation. The clearer the understanding mankind achieves of the psychological and spiritual secrets of the world, the stronger man's relation to the world will become and, hence, the greater his happiness. Man will then be better able to rehabilitate himself in the world when he knows its secrets, just as he became better able to enjoy it when he understood the latent forces of electricity and radio.

It therefore behooves any scholar applying himself to such a study to address his work not only to the Muslims but to mankind as a whole. The final purpose of such work is not, as some of them think, purely religious. Rather, it is, following the example of Muhammad, that all mankind may better learn the way to perfection. Fulfillment of this purpose is not possible without the guidance of reason and heart, and the conviction and certainty they bring when founded on true perception and knowledge. Speculative thinking based upon imprecise knowledge which is not conditioned by the scientific method is likely to go astray and point to conclusions far removed from the truth. By nature, our thinking is deeply influenced by temperament. Men with equal training and knowledge, common purpose and resolution, often differ from one another for no reason other than their difference in temperament. Some are passionate, deeply perceptive, over-hasty in their conclusions, mystical, stoic, ascetic, inclined towards matter, or utterly conditioned by it. Others are different, and their views of the world naturally separate them from one another. As far as artistic expression and practical living are concerned, this variety of the human kind is a great blessing. It is, however, a curse in the field of scientific endeavor which seeks to serve the higher benefit of mankind as a whole. The study of history should search for high ideals within the facts of human life. Anyone who applies himself to this search should therefore be free from passion and prejudice. No method succeeds as well in avoiding these pitfalls as the scientific method, and no method will more surely lead to error than that which uses the materials of history to propagate a certain view or bends them to corroborate a certain prejudice.

The Works of Orientalists

Many western Orientalists have been affected in their so-called scientific research by their preconceptions and passions. The same is true of many Muslim authors as well. More surprising in both is the fact that each had taken the passionate and prejudiced propaganda of the other as basic sourcework, and each had claimed for his writing the objectivity which belongs to a research done for the sake of truth alone. Neither realized how deeply affected he was by his own vehement reaction to the propaganda of the other. Had either party taken the trouble to analyze objectively the work of the other, the respective claims would have dissolved and crumbled. Had any author kept his own predilections at bay, immunizing himself against them by applying scientific principles, his writings would have had a more lasting effect on his readers. In this preface I have attempted to expose as briefly as possible some of the errors of both parties; I hope I have done so with fairness and objectivity.

It is not possible to expect the western Orientalists to carry out their researches in Islamic matters with such precision and fairness, however sincere and scientific they may be. It is especially difficult for them to master the secrets of the Arabic language and to know its usage, its nuances and rules. Moreover, they are inevitably affected by the history of western Christianity which makes them regard all other religions with suspicion. The history of the struggle between Christianity and science affects equally the very few Orientalists who are still Christians. It causes them in their Islamic studies to fall under the same prejudice which generally characterizes all their Christian or religious research: namely, that one or the other party's line must be vindicated against its opposite. The candid Orientalists, however, cannot be blamed for this. For no man can completely escape the conditioning of his time and place. Nonetheless, this conditioning vitiates their Islamic researches and clouds their vision of the truth. All this imposes upon the Muslim scholars, whether in the religious or other fields of Islamic research, the very grave burden of studying their legacy with precision and exactitude, according to the scientific method. Assisted as they are by their mastery of the Arabic language and understanding of Arab life in general, their researches should convince all or some Orientalists of their errors; these researchers should also persuade them to accept the new results readily and with intellectual satisfaction.

The Muslims and Research

Such results will not be easy to achieve, nor are they impossible or altogether difficult. Patience, perseverance in study and research, sound judgment, and free thinking are all required. Moreover, this is an extremely grave matter, grave in its promise for or threat to the future of Islam, as well as mankind. It seems to me that to undertake it well, one must distinguish between two periods of Muslim history: the first begins with Muhammad and ends with the murder of 'Uthman; the second begins with the murder of 'Uthman and ends with the closing of the gates of *ijtihad*. In the first period, Muslim agreement was complete. It stood unaffected by the conquest of foreign lands, the War of Apostasy, the so-called "differences over the caliphate." After the murder of 'Uthman, disagreement spread among the Muslims; civil war was declared between 'Ali and Mu'awiyah; insurgence and rebellion continued; and politics played a serious role even in the religious life itself. In order to help the reader appreciate this difference, let us compare the principles implied in the accession speeches of Abu Bakr and al Mansur al 'Abbasi. The former said: "O men! Here I have been assigned the job of ruling over you while I am not the best among you. If I do well in my job, help me. If I do wrong, redress me. Truthfulness is fidelity, and lying is treason. The weak shall be strong in my eye until I restore to them their right, and the strong shall be weak in my eye until I have dispossessed them of that right. No people give up fighting for the cause of God but He inflicts upon them abject subjection; and no people give themselves to lewdness but He envelops them with misery. Obey me as long as I obey God and His Prophet. But if I disobey God's command or His Prophet, then no obedience is incumbent upon you. Rise to your prayer so he may have mercy on you." The other said: "O men! I am the power of God on His earth. I rule you with His guidance and confirmation. I am the guardian over His wealth and I manage it by His will and in accordance with His pattern. I disburse from it with His permission, for He has made me the lock. If He chooses to open me so that you may receive therefrom and be provided for, He will. And if He chooses to keep me locked, He will. . . ." A comparison of these two speeches is sufficient to realize the great change which had taken place in the basic rules of Muslim life in less than two centuries. It was a change from the rule of *shura*[21] to that of absolute power derived from divine right.

Revolts and successive changes of government and political principles were the cause of the retrogression and decay of the Islamic state. Despite the fact that Islam and the civilization to which it gave birth continued to blossom two centuries after the murder of 'Uthman, and despite the fact that after the first decay the Islamic state was energized again to conquer many provinces and kingdoms first by the Saljuqs and then by the Moghuls, it was during the first period which came to an end with the murder of 'Uthman that the true principles of Islamic public life were established and crystallized. Therefore, one must look to that period alone if he seeks certitude regarding these principles. Later on, despite the blossoming of knowledge and science during the Umawi and especially the 'Abbasi periods, these normative principles were tampered with and often replaced by others which did not accord with the spirit of Islam. For the most part, this was done in pursuit of political *shu'ubi* reasons.[22] It was the insincere converts from Judaism and Christianity as well as the Persians who propagated these new principles. They had no inhibition against the fabrication of *hadiths* and their attribution to the Prophet — may God's peace be upon him — nor against the fabrication of tales about the early caliphs contrary to what is known of their biographies and temperament.

None of the materials which have come to us from this late period can be depended upon without the strictest scrutiny and criticism; none may be scientifically accredited without subjection to impersonal analysis, absolutely free of prejudice. The first requirement consists of referring all controversial material concerning the Arab Prophet to the Qur'an and of discarding all that disagrees therewith. As for the rest of the period ending with the murder of 'Uthman, scientific and critical analysis should accredit the materials that have come to us and thus enable us to use them as reference in our analysis of later materials. If we do this with scientific precision, we may gain a true picture of the genuine principles of Islam and of early Islamic life. We will grasp the mind and spirit of Islam which achieved such heights of power and vision that the Arab Bedouins who were caught by it sallied forth into the world to spread in a few decades the noblest humanism that history has ever known. Success in this task

would lay bare for the benefit of humanity new horizons capable of leading it to communion with the realm of soul and spirit and the achievement
of happiness and felicity, just as man's knowledge of electricity and radio
and his resultant communion with the forces of nature have led to his
greater enjoyment of his life on earth. Furthermore, our success in this
undertaking would bring to Islam the same honor which belonged to it in
its early history when the Arabs carried forth its high principles from the
Peninsula to the farthest reaches of the earth. If we are to serve truth, science and humanity, one of our foremost requirements is to deepen our
study of the biography of the Arab Prophet in order to uncover therein the
guidance mankind seeks. The Qur'an is unquestionably the truest and
most reliable source for such a study. It is the book which is absolutely free
of error and which no doubt can penetrate. It is the only book whose text
has remained for thirteen centuries, and will remain for the rest of time,
absolutely pure and unadulterated. The purity of the Qur'anic text is and
will forever remain the greatest miracle of all history. God said of it: "It is
We who have revealed it and it is We who will guard it."[23] The Qur'an
will always remain as it once was, the only miracle of Muhammad. Of all
that concerns his life, that is true which accords with the Qur'an, and that
is false which does not. I have attempted to heed this principle in this elementary study as precisely as I could. In going over the first edition of this
work I praise God and thank Him for His guidance and pray that He will
guide and provide for the continuation of the scientific study of the life of
the Prophet.

"Oh God! It is upon You that we depend, to You that we have
recourse, and to You that we shall return."[24]

Preface to the Third Edition

This edition does not differ from the second except in a few words and phrases as demanded by clarity or syntactical precision. The changes are unnoticeable except in *verbatim* comparison. Hence, there is no need to mention them.

My reticence to undertake more serious emendation of the text is not due to any judgment on my part that in its second edition the book is perfect. I do not tire of repeating here what I said in the preface to the first edition, namely, that this book is merely the beginning of scientific Islamic research in an important field. I have discussed many problems attendant upon such research in my book *Fi Manzil al Wahy* ["At the Locus of Revelation"] written after my pilgrimage and following the traces of the Prophet through Hijaz and Tihamah. I therefore refer the reader to it. Preoccupied with other things during the last eight years I have not been able to pursue my study of the life of the Prophet, of his teaching, and the careers of his companions, nor to analyze in detail the general assertions of the concluding chapters of the second edition. But I hope God will grant me the power to do so in a separate book devoted entirely to the subject. Perhaps, after reading the conclusion of the present edition, the reader might even share this hope with me.

Finally, I thank God for the appreciation with which this book has been met by Muslim as well as non-Muslim readers, and for the reviews and announcements of it in the publications of East and West. I pray Him to guide those who undertake the continuation of this research that they may be capable of bringing it to its ultimate purpose of service to the truth.

The Life of Muhammad

1

Arabia Before Islam

The Cradle of Human Civilization

The problem of the origin and development of human civilization continues to baffle the student in modern times. Scholars have long thought that Egypt was the cradle of civilization six thousand years ago and that the earlier ages consisted of a proto-history of which no scientific knowledge was possible. Today, however, archeologists have been at work in Iraq and Syria in the hope of discovering clues regarding the origins of the Mesopotamian and Phoenician civilizations, of establishing whether they are anterior or posterior to Egyptian civilization, and of determining the influence of one upon the other. Whatever the results of archeological research on this period of history, one fact has never been challenged by any archeological find in China or the Far East: that is the fact that the cradle of the earliest human civilization, whether in Egypt, Phoenicia, or Mesopotamia, was connected with the Mediterranean Sea. It is equally indubitable that Egypt was the first to export its civilization to Greece and Rome, and that modern civilization is very closely related to that antiquity. Whatever archeological study of the Far East may reveal concerning the civilizations of that region, it can hardly establish that any determining relationship existed between those civilizations and Egypt, Mesopotamia, and Greece. It is no more questioned whether these ancient civilizations of the Near East were influenced by the civilization of Islam. Indeed, the latter was the only civilization which has altered its course as

1

soon as it came into contact with them. The world civilization of the present which is dominating the four corners of the globe is a result of the influences of the civilizations of the ancient Near East and that of Islam upon one another.

The Mediterranean and Red Sea Basins

The civilizations which sprang up several thousand years ago on the shores of the Mediterranean Sea or in proximity thereto — in Egypt, Mesopotamia and Greece — reached heights of achievement which elicit our wonder and admiration today, whether in the fields of science, industry, agriculture, trade, war, or any other human activity. The mainspring of all these civilizations which gave them their strength is religion. True, the figurations of this mainspring changed from the trinitarianism of ancient Egypt expressed in the myth of Osiris, Isis and Horus, and representing the continuity of life in death and resurrection and permanence through generation, to the paganism of Hellas expressed in the sensory representation of truth, goodness, and beauty. It changed, likewise, in the succeeding periods of decay and dissolution to levels where the sensory representations of Hellas became gross. Regardless of these variants, religion has remained the source which has fashioned the destiny of the world; and it plays the same role in our age. Present civilization has sometimes opposed religion, or sought to get rid of and discard it; and yet from time to time, it has inclined towards religion. On the other hand, religion has continued to court our civilization and, perhaps, one day, may even assimilate it.

In this environment where civilization has rested for thousands of years on a religious base, three well known world religions arose. Egypt saw the appearance of Moses. He was brought up and disciplined in Pharaoh's house, instructed in the unity of divine being and taught the secrets of the universe by Pharaoh's priesthood. When God permitted Moses to proclaim His religion to the people, Pharaoh was proclaiming to them: "I am your Lord supreme" (Qur'an, 79 :24). Moses contended with Pharaoh and his priesthood until he finally had to emigrate with the children of Israel to Palestine. In Palestine there appeared Jesus, the spirit and word of God given unto Mary. When God raised Jesus unto Himself,[1] his disciples preached his religion and met in the process the strongest prejudice and opposition. When God permitted Christianity to spread, the Emperor of Rome,[2] then sovereign of the world, converted to the new faith and adopted its cause. The Roman Empire followed, and the religion of Jesus spread through Egypt, Syria, and Greece. From Egypt it spread to Abyssinia, and for centuries it continued to grow. Whoever sought Roman protection or friendship joined the ranks of the new faith.

Christianity and Zoroastrianism

Facing this Christian religion which spread by Roman influence and power, stood the religion of Persia supported by the moral power of India and the Far East. The civilization of Egypt, extending to Phoenicia, and that of Mesopotamia had for many ages separated the East from the West and prevented any grave confrontation of their ideologies and civilizations. The entry of Egypt and Phoenicia into Christianity dissolved this barrier and brought the Christianity of the West and the Zoroastrianism of the East face to face. For centuries East and West confronted each other without intermingling between their religions. Each felt such fear of the other party's religion that a moral barrier came to replace the old barrier provided by the ancient Near Eastern civilizations. Each was thus compelled to direct its religious expansion to its own hinterland, away from the other's territory. Despite the numerous wars they fought, each exhausted its power without being able to confront the other on the religious or civilizational level. Although Persia conquered and ruled Syria and Egypt and the approaches of Byzantium, its kings never thought of spreading their religion or of converting the Christians. On the contrary, the conquerors respected the religions of the conquered and assisted them in reconstructing the temples which war had ravished. They granted them the liberty of upholding their religious rituals. The farthest the Persians had gone in infringing on their subjects' religion was to seize the "Holy Cross" and to keep it in Persia. When the tables were turned and the Byzantines won, they took the cross back. Thus the spiritual conquests of the West were restricted to the West, and those of the East were restricted to the East. The moral barrier separated them as decisively as the geographic civilizational one had done. Spiritually speaking, the two paths were equivalent and their equivalence prevented any clash between them.

Byzantium, the Heir of Rome

This situation remained without significant change until the sixth century of the Christian Era. In the meantime, competition between the

East and West Roman empires was intensified. Rome, which had ruled the West as far as Gaul and England for many generations, and which looked proudly back to the age of Julius Caesar, began to lose its glory gradually. The glory of Byzantium was increasing and, after the dissolution of Roman power following the raids of the Vandals and their conquest of Rome itself,[3] it became in fact the only heir of the wide Roman World. Naturally, these events were not without influence on Christianity, which arose in the lap of Rome where the believers in Jesus had suffered tyranny.

Christian Sects

Christianity began to divide into various sects, and every sect began in turn to divide into factions, each of which held a different opinion concerning the religion and its principles and bases. In the absence of commonly held principles, in terms of which these differences could be composed, the various sects became antagonistic toward one another. Their moral and mental backwardness transformed the opposing doctrines into personal antagonisms protected by blind prejudice and deadening conservatism. Some of them denied that Jesus ever had a body other than a ghostly shadow by which he appeared to men. Others regarded the person and soul of Jesus as related to each other with such extraordinary ties that only the most fastidious imagination could grasp what they meant. While some worshiped Mary, others denied that she remained a virgin after the birth of Christ. Thus the controversies dividing the followers of Jesus were typical of the dissolution and decadence affecting any nation or age; that is to say, they were merely verbal disputes arising from the assignment to words of secret and esoteric meanings removed from their commonsense connotations, oppugn ant to reason and tolerated only by futile sophistry.

One of the monks of the Church wrote describing the situation of his day: "The city and all its precincts were full of controversy — in the market place, in the shops of apparel, at the changers, in the grocery stores. You ask for a piece of gold to be changed at the changer's and you find yourself questioned about that which in the person of Jesus was created and that which was not created. You stop at the bakery to buy a loaf of bread and ask concerning the price, only to find the baker answer: 'Will you agree that the Father is greater than the Son and the Son is subordinate to the Father?' You ask your servant about your bath, whether or not the water is warm, and your servant answers you: 'The Son was created from nothing.'"

The decay which befell Christianity and caused it to split into factions and sects did not shake the political foundations of the Imperium Romanum. The Empire remained strong and closely knit while the sects disputed their differences with one another and with the councils which were called from time to time to resolve them. For some time at least no sect had enough power to coerce the others into agreement. The Empire protected them all and granted them the freedom to argue their doctrines with one another, a measure which increased the civil power of the Emperor without reducing his religious prestige. Each faction sought his sympathy and encouragement; indeed, each claimed that the emperor was its patron and advocate. It was the cohesion of the Empire which enabled Christianity to spread to the farthest reaches of imperial authority. From its base in Roman Egypt, Christianity thus reached to independent Abyssinia and thence to the Red Sea which it then invested with the same importance as the Mediterranean. The same imperial cohesion also enabled Christianity to move from Syria and Palestine once it had converted their people to the adjoining Arab tribe of Ghassan and the shores of the Euphrates. There it converted the Arabs of Hirah, the Banu Lakhm, and Banu Mundhir who had migrated thence from the desert but whose history has been divided between independence and Persian tutelage.

The Decay of Zoroastrianism

In Persia, Zoroastrianism was attacked by the same kind of decay. Although fire worship continued to give the various factions a semblance of unity, the religion and its followers divided into sects which contended with one another. Apparently unaffected by the religious controversy around the divine personifications and the meanings behind them, the political structure of the land remained strong. All sects sought the protection of the Persian emperor, and the latter readily gave it to them if only to increase his own power and to use them one against the other wherever a political gain for him was to be made or a political threat from anyone section was to be avoided. The two powers, Christianity and Zoroastrianism, the West and the East, each allied with a number of smaller states which it held under its influence, surrounded the Arabian Peninsula at the beginning of the sixth century C.E. Each entertained its own ideas of colonialism and expansion. In each camp, the men of religion exerted great efforts to spread the faith and doctrine in which they believed. This proselytizing notwithstanding, the Arabian Peninsula remained secure against conquest except at the fringes. Like a strong fortress it was secure against the spread of any religious call, whether Christian or Zoroastrian. Only very few of its tribes had answered the call, and they did so in insignificant numbers — a surprising phenomenon in history. To understand it we must grasp the situation and nature of Arabia and the influence that nature had exerted upon the lives, morals and thought of its people.

The Geographic Position of the Peninsula

The Arabian Peninsula has the shape of an irregular rectangle. On the north it is bounded by Palestine and the Syrian desert; on the east by the kingdom of al Hirah, the Euphrates and Tigris and the Persian Gulf; on the south by the Indian Ocean and the Gulf of 'Adan; and to the west by the Red Sea. The natural isolation of the Peninsula combined with its size to protect it against invasion. The Peninsula is over a thousand kilometers long and as wide. Moreover, this vast expanse is utterly uncultivable. It does not have a single river nor a dependable rainy season around which any agriculture could be organized. With the exception of fertile and rainy Yaman in the southwest, the Peninsula consists of plateaus, valleys and deserts devoid of vegetation and an atmosphere so inclement that no civilization could prosper therein. The Arabian Peninsula allows only desert life; and desert life demands continuous movement, adoption of the camel as means of transportation, and the pursuit of thin pasture which is no sooner discovered than it is exhausted and another movement becomes imperative. These well sought-after pastures grow around springs whose waters have collected from rainfall on the surrounding rocky terrain, allowing a scarce vegetation to grow in the immediate vicinity.

Except Yaman the Arabian Peninsula Is Unknown

In a country such as this, or such as the Sahara of Africa, it is natural that no people would seek to dwell and that it have a scarce population. It is equally natural that whoever settles in such a desert has done so for the sake of the refuge the desert provides and that he entertains no purpose beyond survival. The inhabitants of the oasis, on the other hand, may envision a different purpose. But the oases themselves remain unknown to

any but the most daring adventurer prepared to venture into the desert at
the risk of his own life. Except for Yaman, the Arabian Peninsula was literally unknown to the ancient world.

The geographic position of the Peninsula saved it from depopulation.
In those ancient times, men had not yet mastered navigation and had not
yet learned to cross the sea with the confidence requisite for travel or commerce. The Arabic proverbs which have come down to us betray the fact
that men feared the sea as they feared death. Trade and commerce had to
find another road less dangerous than the sea. The most important trade
route was that which extended from the Roman Empire and other territories in the west to India and other territories in the east. The Arabian
Peninsula stood astride the two roads connecting East and West, whether
by way of Egypt or by way of the Persian Gulf. Its inhabitants and masters, namely the Bedouins, naturally became princes of the desert routes
just as the maritime people became princes of the sea lanes when sea communications replaced land communications. It was equally natural that the
princes of the desert would plan the roads of caravans so as to guarantee
the maximum degree of safety, just as the sea navigators were to plan the
course of ships away from tempests, and other sea dangers. "The course of
the caravan," says Heeren, "was not a matter of free choice, but of established custom. In the vast steppes of sandy desert which the caravans had
to cross, nature had sparingly allotted to the traveler a few scattered places
of rest where, under the shade of palm trees and beside cool fountains, the
merchant and his beast of burden might refresh themselves. Such places
of repose became *entrepots* of commerce and, not infrequently, sites of
temples and sanctuaries under the protection of which the merchant pursued his trade and to which the pilgrim resorted."[4]

The Two Caravan Routes

The Arabian Peninsula was criss-crossed with caravan routes. Of
these, two were important. The first ran alongside the Persian Gulf, then
alongside the Tigris[5] and then crossed the Syrian desert towards
Palestine. It was properly called "the eastern route." The other route ran
along the shore of the Red Sea and was properly called "the western
route." On these two main routes, world trade ran between East and West
carrying products and goods in both directions. These two routes provided the desert with income and prosperity. The peoples of the West, however, lived in total ignorance of the routes which their own trade took.

None of them, or of their eastern neighbors, ever penetrated the desert territory — unless it be the case of an adventurer who had no concern for his own life. A number of adventurers perished in trying the desert labyrinth in vain. The hardships which such travel entailed were unbearable except to those who had been accustomed to desert life from a tender age. A man accustomed to the luxuries of town living cannot be expected to bear the discomfort of these barren mountains separated from the Red Sea only by the narrow passages of Tihamah,[6] and leading through naked rocks to the apparently infinite expanse of most arid and desolate desert. A man accustomed to a political order guaranteeing the security of all inhabitants at all times cannot be expected to bear the terror and lawlessness of the desert, devoid as it is of political order, and whose inhabitants live as utterly independent tribes, clans — nay individuals — except where their relations to one another come under the jurisdiction of tribal law, or some *ad hoc* convention of a strong protector. The desert had never known any urban order such as we enjoy in our modern cities. Its people lived in the shadow of retributive justice. They repelled attack by attack, and they sought to prevent aggression by the fear of counter aggressions. The weak had no chance unless somebody took them under protection. Such a life does not encourage anyone to try it, nor does it invite anyone to learn of it in any detail. That is why the Arabian Peninsula remained an unknown continent throughout the world until the circumstances of history permitted its people, after the advent of Muhammad — may God's peace and blessing be upon him — to migrate and thus tell about their country and give the world the information it lacked.

The Civilization of Yaman

The only exception to this universal ignorance of the Arabian Peninsula concerns Yaman and the coastline of the Persian Gulf and Arabian Sea. This exception is not due merely to their near location to the sea and ocean but to their radical difference from the rest of the Arabian Peninsula. Rather than being a barren desert profitless to befriend, explore, or colonize, these lands were fertile and had well-defined seasons with a fait amount of rainfall. They had an established civilization with many urban centers and long-lasting temples. Its people, the Banu Himyar, were well-endowed and intelligent. They were clever enough to think of ways of saving rain water from running down to the sea and of making good use of it. They built the dam of Ma'rib and thereby changed the course which water would have naturally followed to courses such as settled life and intensive agriculture required. Falling on high mountains, rainwater would gather in a 400 meters wide valley flanked by two mountains east of the city of Ma'rib. It would then divide into many streams and spread over a wide plain that is very much like the Nile in the dam area in upper Egypt. As their technological and administrative skill developed, the people of Yaman constructed a dam at the narrowest point between the two mountains with gates which allowed controlled distribution of water. By putting the resources of their country to good use, they increased the fertility of the land and the prosperity of the people. What has so far been discovered and is still being discovered — by way of remains of this Himyari civilization in Yaman, proves that it had reached an impressive height and was strong enough to withstand not only a number of great political storms but even war.

Judaism and Christianity in Yaman

This civilization, founded upon agricultural prosperity and settled life, brought upon Yaman great misfortune, unlike the desert whose barrenness was for it a sort of protector. Sovereigns in their own land, Banu Himyar ruled Yaman generation after generation. One of their kings, Dhu Nuwas, disliked the paganism of his people and inclined toward the Mosaic religion. In time, he was converted to this faith by the Jews who had migrated to Yaman. Historians agree that it was to this Himyari king that the Qur'an referred in the "story of the trench," reported in the following verses:

قُتِلَ أَصْحَابُ الْأُخْدُودِ ۞ النَّارِ ذَاتِ الْوَقُودِ ۞ إِذْ هُمْ عَلَيْهَا قُعُودٌ ۞ وَهُمْ عَلَىٰ مَا يَفْعَلُونَ بِالْمُؤْمِنِينَ شُهُودٌ ۞ وَمَا نَقَمُوا مِنْهُمْ إِلَّا أَن يُؤْمِنُوا بِاللَّهِ الْعَزِيزِ الْحَمِيدِ

"Cursed be the fellows of the trench who fed the fire with fury, sat by it and witnessed the burning of the believers whom they threw therein. They executed the believers only because the latter believed in God, the Almighty, the Praiseworthy."[7]

The story is that of a pious Christian, Qaymiyun by name, who emigrated from Byzantium, settled in Najran, and converted the people of that city by his piety, virtue, and good example. When the news of the increasing converts and widening influence of Christianity reached Dhu Nuwas, he went to Najran and solemnly warned its people that they must either convert to Judaism or be killed. Upon their refusal to apostasize, the king dug a wide trench, set it on fire, and threw them in. Whoever escaped from the fire was killed by the sword. According to the biographies, twenty thousand of them perished in this manner. Some nonetheless escaped, sought the Byzantine Emperor Justinian and asked for his help against Dhu Nuwas. Byzantium was too far from Yaman to send any effective assistance. Its emperor therefore wrote to the Negus of Abyssinia to avenge the Christians of Yaman. At the time — the sixth century C.E. — Abyssinia was at the height of its power, commanding a wide sea trade protected by a strong maritime fleet and imposing its influence upon the neighboring countries.[8] The Abyssinian kingdom was the ally of the Byzantine Empire and the protagonist of Christianity on the Red Sea just as the Byzantine Empire was its protagonist on the Mediterranean. When the Negus received the message of the Byzantine emperor, he sent with the Yamani, who carried the emperor's message to him, an Abyssinian army under the command of Aryat. One of the officers of this expeditionary force was Abraha al Ashram.[9] Aryat conquered Yaman and ruled it in the name of the negus of Abyssinia. Later on he was killed and succeeded by Abraha, "the general with the elephant," who sought to conquer Makkah and destroy the Ka'bah but failed, as we shall see in the next chapter.[10]

The successors of Abraha ruled Yaman tyrannically. Seeking relief from the yoke the Himyari Sayf ibn Dhu Yazan approached the Byzantine emperor complaining against the Abyssinians and pleading for a Byzantine governor to be sent to establish justice. He was turned down because of the alliance between Byzantium and Abyssinia. Disappointed, he stopped on his way back at the court of Nu'man ibn al Mundhir, Viceroy of Chosroes for al Hirah and surrounding lands of Iraq.

Conquest and Rule of Yaman by Persia

When al Nu'man entered the audience hall of Chosroes, he was accompanied by Sayf ibn Dhu Yazan. Chosroes received them at his winter residence, sitting on the throne of Darius in the great *iwan* decorated with the pictures of the Zodiac. The throne was surrounded with a curtain made of the most precious furs which served as background for golden and silver chandeliers filled with warm water and for his golden and silver crown filled with rubies, beryls and pearls which, being too heavy to rest on his head, was attached to the ceiling by a golden chain. His clothes were of a golden weave, and he decorated himself with gold. So brilliant was this spectacle that any person was seized with awe at the mere sight of it. Surely, such was the case of Sayf ibn Dhu Yazan. When he came back to himself and felt reassured, he was asked by Chosroes about his mission and told the emperor the story of Abyssinia's conquest and tyrannous rule. Chosroes hesitated at the beginning, but then decided to send to Yaman an army under the command of Wahriz, one of the noblest and bravest commanders of Persia. The Persian army arrived in Yaman, vanquished the Abyssinians and expelled them after a rule of seventy-two years. Yaman remained under Persian rule until the advent of Islam and the succeeding entry of all Arab countries into the religion of God as well as into the Islamic Empire.

Cyrus's Rule of Persia

The Persians who ruled Yaman did not come directly under the authority of the Persian Emperor, particularly after Cyrus had killed his father Chosroes and succeeded to his throne. The new emperor seemed to think that the whole world ran according to his wishes and that the kingdoms of the world existed only to fill his treasury and to increase his affluence and luxury. Because he was a young man, he neglected most of the affairs of state in order to devote himself to his pleasures and pastimes. The pageantry of his hunting trips was greater than any imagination could possibly conceive. He used to go out surrounded by a whole troop of youthful princes clad in red, yellow, and violet; carriers of falcons and servants held back their muzzled panthers, perfume-carrying slaves, fly-fighters and musicians. In order to give himself a feeling of spring in the midst of winter, he used to sit surrounded by the members of his house on an immense carpet on which were drawn the roads and highways of the kingdom, the orchards, and gardens full of flowers, the forests and greenwoods and the silvery rivers — all in a state of blossoming spring. Despite Cyrus's extravagance and addiction to pleasure, Persia maintained its glory and strong resistance to Byzantium and prevented the spread of Christianity further east. It was clear, however, that the accession of Cyrus to the throne was the beginning of the decline of this empire and a preparation for its conquest by the Muslims and the spread of Islam therein.

Destruction of the Dam of Ma'rib

The conflict of which Yaman had been the theatre ever since the fourth century C.E. influenced the distribution of population in the Arabian Peninsula. It is told that the dam of Ma'rib, by means of which the Himyaris changed the course of nature to benefit their country, was destroyed by the great flood, *"Sayl al 'Arim,"* with the result that large sections of the inhabitants had to migrate. Apparently the continuing political conflicts so distracted men and governments from attending to the repair and maintenance of the dam that when the flood came it was incapable of holding the water. It is also told that the shift in population was due to the fact that the Byzantine emperor, realizing the threat to his trade by the conflict with Persia over Yaman, built a fleet of ships to ply the Red Sea and thereby avoid the caravan routes of Arabia. Historians agree on the historicity of the immigration of the Azd tribes from Yaman to the north but disagree in explaining it. Some attribute it to the loss of trade, and others to the destruction of the dam of Ma'rib and the resultant loss in food production. Whatever the explanation, the historicity of the event is beyond doubt. It was at the root of the blood relation of the Yamanis with the northern Arabs and their involvement in the history of the north. Even today the problem is still far from solved.

The Social Order of the Peninsula

As we have just seen, the political order of Yaman was disturbed because of the geographic circumstances of that country and the political wars of conquest of which it had been the object. *Per contra,* the Arabian Peninsula was free from any such disturbances. Indeed, the political system known in Yaman, as well as any other political system — whatever the term may mean or may have meant to the civilized peoples of old — was literally unknown in the areas of Tihamah, Hijaz, Najd, and other wide spaces constituting the Arabian Peninsula. The sons of the desert were then, as most of them are today, nomads who had no taste for settled life and who knew no kind of permanence other than perpetual movement in search of pasture and satisfaction of the wish of the moment. In the desert, the basic unit of life is not the state but the tribe. Moreover, a tribe which is always on the move does not know of any universal law nor does it ever subject itself to any general political order. To the nomad, nothing is acceptable that falls short of total freedom for the individual, for the family, and for the tribe as a whole. Settled land farmers, on the other hand, agree to give up part of their freedom, whether to the group as a whole or to an absolute ruler, in exchange for peace, security, and the prosperity which order brings. But the desert man who disdains the prosperity and security of settled life and derides the comforts of urban living cannot give any of his freedom for such "gains." Neither does he accept anything short of absolute equality with all the members of his tribe as well as between his tribe and other tribes. Naturally, he is moved like all other men by the will to survive and to defend himself, but such will must accord with the principles of honor and integrity demanded by the free life of the desert. Therefore, the desert people have never suffered with patience any injustice inflicted upon them but resisted it with all their strength. If they cannot throw off the injustice imposed upon them, they give up the pasture and move out into the wide expanse of the desert. Nothing is easier for them than recourse to the sword whenever a conflict seems insoluble under the conventional desert rules of honor, nobility, and integrity. It was these very conditions of desert living which led to the cultivation and growth of the virtues of hospitality, bravery, mutual assistance, neighbor protection, and magnanimity. It is not by accident that these virtues are stronger and more popular in the desert and weaker and more scarce in the cities. For the abovementioned economic reasons neither Byzantium nor Persia entertained any ideas of conquering the Arabian Peninsula with the exception of Yaman. For they know that the people of the Peninsula would prefer emigration to the life of subjection and that they would never yield to any established authority or order.

These nomadic characteristics influenced in large measure the few small towns which grew up in the Peninsula along the caravan routes. To these centers the traders used to come in order to rest. In them they found temples wherein to give thanks to the gods for bringing them safely through their travels and for safe-guarding their goods while in transit. Such were Makkah, Ta'if, Yathrib, and others scattered between the mountains of the west coastland and the desert sands. In their order and organization these towns followed the pattern and laws of the desert. Indeed, their being closer to the desert than they were to civilized life was reflected in the system of their tribes and clans, in their morals and customs, and in their strong resistance to any imposition upon their freedom, despite the fact that settled life had somewhat restricted their movements in comparison with their desert cousins. We shall witness more of this in the coming chapters when we talk about Makkah and Yathrib.

Arab Paganism and Its Causes

This state of nature and the moral, political, and social order it implied were equally consequential for religion. Was Yaman influenced by Byzantine Christianity or Persian Zoroastrianism, and did it influence in turn the Arabian Peninsula? It would seem so, especially in the case of Christianity. The missionaries of Christianity were as active in those days as they are today. Moreover, unlike the life of the city, desert life is especially conducive to the rise of religious consciousness. In the desert, man is in constant touch with the universe as a whole. He senses the infinity of existence in all its forms and is thereby prompted to order his relationship with the infinite. The city man, on the other hand, is distracted from the consciousness of infinity by his constant occupation. He is protected from the *angst* and dread such consciousness of the infinite brings by the group to which he gave up part of his freedom. His submission to political authority and the consequent security arising from this submission prevent him from establishing a direct contact, beyond the civil power, with the spiritual powers of the world, and weaken his speculative thinking about them. In the case of the desert man, on the other hand, nothing impedes his speculation over religious meanings and problems to which the life of the desert naturally leads.

And now we may ask, did Christianity, with all its missionary activity, benefit from these circumstances to spread and propagate itself? Perhaps it would have done so had it not been that other factors went into play and enabled the Peninsula as a whole to preserve its paganism, the religion of its ancestors. Only a very few tribes therefore responded favorably to the Christian call.

Christianity and Judaism

The greatest civilization of the day stood in the basins of the Mediterranean and the Red Sea. The religions of Christianity and Judaism divided this civilization, and though they were not at war with each other, they were surely not friendly to each other. The Jews then remembered, as they still do, the rebellion Jesus had launched against their religion. As much as they could, therefore, they worked secretly to stop the flow of Christianity, the religion which forced them out of the promised land and assumed the Roman color as its own throughout the Empire. There were large communities of Jews living in Arabia, and a good number of them had settled in Yaman and in Yathrib. Zoroastrianism, on the other hand, was anxious to prevent Christianity from crossing the Euphrates. Hence, it lent its moral support to paganism while overlooking, or being mindful of, its spiritual and moral degradation. The fall of Rome and the passing of its power under all forms of dissolution encouraged the multiplication of sects in Christianity. These were not only becoming numerous and varied but were also fighting desperately with one another. Indeed, the Christian sects fell from the high level of faith to that of controversy regarding forms, figures, and words which related to the holiness of Mary and her priority to her son, the Christ. The sectarian controversies of Christianity betray the level of degradation and decay to which Christian thought and practice had sunk. It takes a truly decadent mind to discard content in favor of external form, to attach so much importance to externalities that the essence disappears under their opaque weight. And that is precisely what the Christian sects did.

The subjects under controversy varied from place to place; the Christians of al Sham[11] disputed other questions than those of Hirah or Abyssinia. In their contact with the Christians, the Jews did nothing to calm the raging controversies or to temper the generated antagonism. The Arabs, on the other hand, were on good terms with the Christians of Damascus and Yaman with whom they came into contact during the winter and summer caravan trips, as well as with the Abyssinian Christians who visited them from time to time. It was natural for them to refrain from taking sides with any Christian party against another. The Arabs were happy with their paganism, contented to follow in the footsteps of their ancestors, and prepared to leave both Christians and Jews alone as long as these were not interfering with their religion. Thus, idol worship continued to flourish among them and even spread to the centers inhabited by their Christian and Jewish neighbors, namely Najran and Yathrib. The Jews of Yathrib tolerated idol worship, co-existed with it, and finally befriended it as the trade routes linked them to the pagan Arabs with mutually beneficial relations.

The Spread of Paganism

Perhaps the desperate struggle of the Christian sects against one another was not the sole cause of why the Arabs remained pagan. Varieties of paganism were still adhered to even by the people who had converted to Christianity. Egyptian and Greek paganism was quite apparent in the ideologies and practices of many Christian sects. Indeed, they were apparent in some of the views of orthodox Christianity itself. The school of Alexandria and its philosophy still enjoyed a measure of influence, though it was naturally reduced from that which it enjoyed during the time of the Ptolemies, at the beginning of the Christian Era. At any rate, this influence was deeply imbedded in the consciousness of the people, and its brilliant logic, though sophistic in nature, still exercised appeal for a polytheistic paganism of human deities so close and lovable to man. It seems to me that polytheism has been the strongest appeal of paganism to weak souls in all times and places. The weak soul is by nature incapable of rising high enough to establish a contact with total being and, in a supreme moment of consciousness, to grasp the unity of total being represented in that which is greater than all that exists, in God, the Lord of Majesty. The weak soul therefore stops at one of the differentiated phenomena of total being, like the sun or the moon or the fire, and awkwardly withdraws from rising beyond it to the unity of being itself.

What poverty of spirit characterizes those souls who, arrested by their grasp of a confused, insignificant little meaning of total being in an idol, commune with that object and wrap it with a halo of sanctity! We still witness this phenomenon in many countries of the world despite all the claims this modern world makes for its advances in science and civilization. Such is what the visitors see at St. Peter's cathedral in Rome where the foot of a statue of a certain saint is physically worn out by the kisses which the saint's worshipers proffer to it, so that the church has to change it for a new foot every now and then. If we could keep this in mind, we would excuse those Arabs whom God had not yet guided to the true faith. We would be less quick to condemn them for their continued idolatry and following in the footsteps of their ancestors when we remember that they were the witnesses of a desperate struggle of Christian neighbors against one another who had not yet liberated themselves completely from paganism. How can we not excuse them when pagan conditions are still with us and seem to be inextricably rooted in the world? How can we not excuse the pre-Islamic Arabs when paganism is still evident in the idolatrous practices of so many Muslims of the present world despite the fact that Islam, the one unflinching enemy of paganism that had once succeeded in sweeping away every other worship besides that of God, the Lord of majesty, is their professed religion?

Idol Worship

In their worship of idols, the Arabs followed many ways difficult for the modern researcher to discover and understand. The Prophet destroyed the idols of the Ka'bah and commanded his companions to destroy all idols wherever they might be. After they destroyed the idols' physical existence, the Muslims launched a campaign against the very mention of idols and sought to wipe them out from history, literature, and, indeed, from consciousness itself. The evidence the Qur'an gives for the existence of idolatry in pre-Islamic times as well as the stories which circulated in the second century A.H. concerning idolatrous practices, prove that idolatry once enjoyed a position of tremendous importance. The same evidence proves that it was of many kinds, that idolatrous practices were of great variety and that idols differed widely in the degree of sacralization conferred upon them. Every tribe had a different idol which it worshiped. Generally, objects of worship belonged to three genres: metal and wooden statues, stone statues, and shapeless masses of stone which one tribe or another consecrated because its origin was thought to be heavenly, whereas in reality it was only a piece of volcanic or meteoric rock. The most finely made statues were those which belonged to Yaman. No wonder, for the Yamanis were more advanced in technology than the people of Hijaz, Najd, or Kindah. The classical works on pre-Islamic idols, however, did not report to us that any fine statues existed anywhere, except perhaps what they reported concerning Hubal, namely that it was made out of carnelian in the likeness of man, that its arm once broke off and was replaced by another contributed by Quraysh and made of solid gold. Hubal was the greatest member of the Arab pantheon and resided in Makkah, inside the Ka'bah. Pilgrims came to its shrine from all corners. Still unsatisfied by these great idols to which they prayed and offered sacrifices, the Arabs used to adopt other statues or sacred stones for domestic worship and devotion. They used to circumambulate the "holy" precincts of these gods both before leaving on a trip and upon returning home. They often carried their idols with them when they traveled, presuming that the idol had permitted its worshiper to travel. All these statues, whether in the Ka'bah, around it or scattered around the tribes or the provinces, were regarded as intermediaries between their worshipers and the supreme god. They regarded the worship of them as a means of rapprochement with God even though in reality that same worship had caused them to forget the true worship of God.

Makkah's Place in Arabia

Despite the fact that Yaman was the most advanced province in the Arabian Peninsula and the most civilized on account of its fertility and the sound administration of its water resources, its religious practices never commanded the respect of the inhabitants of the desert. Its temples never constituted a single center of pilgrimage. Makkah, on the other hand, and its Ka'bah, the house of Isma'il, was the object of pilgrimage ever since Arab history began. Every Arab sought to travel to it. In it the holy months were observed with far more ado than anywhere else. For this reason, as well as for its distinguished position in the trade of the Peninsula as a whole, it was regarded as the capital. Further, it was to be the birthplace of Muhammad, the Arab Prophet, and became the object of the yearning of the world throughout the centuries. Its ancient house was to remain holy forever. The tribe of Quraysh was to continue to enjoy a distinguished and sovereign position. All this was to remain so forever despite the fact that the Makkans and their city continued to lead a life closer to the hardness of bedouin existence which had been their custom for many tens of centuries.

2

Makkah, the Ka'bah, and the Quraysh

Geographic Position of Makkah

About eighty kilometers east of the shore of the Red Sea a number of mountain chains run from north to south paralleling the shoreline and dovetailing with the caravan route between Yaman and Palestine. These chains would completely enclose a small plain, were it not for three main outlets connecting it with the road to Yaman, the road to the Red Sea close to the port town of Juddah and the road leading to Palestine. In this plain surrounded by mountains on all sides stands Makkah. It is difficult to trace its origins. In all likelihood these origins lie thousands of years in the past. It is certain that even before Makkah was built the valley on which it stands must have been used as a resting point for the caravan routes. Its number of water springs made it a natural stopping point for the caravans going south to Yaman as well as for those going north to Palestine. Isma'il, son of Ibrahim, was probably the first one to dwell there permanently and establish it as a permanent settlement after it had long been a resting station for transient caravans and a marketplace in which the north-bound and south-bound travelers exchanged their goods.

Ibrahim — May God's Peace be upon Him

Granted that Isma'il was the first to make of Makkah a permanent habitat, the history of the city before Isma'il is rather obscure. Perhaps it

can be said that Makkah was used as a place of worship even before Isma'il
had migrated there. The story of the latter's migration to Makkah
demands that we summarize the story of his father, Ibrahim — may God's
peace be upon him. Ibrahim was born in Iraq to a father whose occupation was carpentry and the making and selling of statues for worship. As
Ibrahim grew up and observed his father making these statues out of
pieces of wood, he was struck by his people's worship and consecration of
them. He doubted these deities and was troubled by his doubt. One day
he asked his father to explain how he could worship that which his hand
had wrought. Unsatisfied by his father's answer, Ibrahim talked about his
doubts to his friends, and soon the father began to fear the consequences
for the security of his son as well as for his own trade. Ibrahim, however,
respected his own reason too much to silence its voice. Accordingly, he
sought to convince his people of the futility of idol worship with argument
and proof. Once he seized the opportunity of the absence of worshipers
from the temple and destroyed all the statues of the gods but that of the
principal deity. When he was accused in public of this crime he was asked:
"Was it you, Ibrahim, who destroyed our gods?" He answered: "No, rather,
it was the principal god who destroyed the other gods. Ask them, for they
would speak, wouldn't they?"[1] Ibrahim's destruction of the idols came
after he had long pondered the error of idol worship and searched earnest-
ly for a worthier object of devotion.

فَلَمَّا جَنَّ عَلَيْهِ الَّيْلُ رَأَىٰ كَوْكَبًا قَالَ هَـٰذَا رَبِّى فَلَمَّآ أَفَلَ قَالَ لَآ أُحِبُّ الْآفِلِينَ ۞ فَلَمَّا رَأَى الْقَمَرَ بَازِغًا قَالَ
هَـٰذَا رَبِّى فَلَمَّآ أَفَلَ قَالَ لَئِن لَّمْ يَهْدِنِى رَبِّى لَأَكُونَنَّ مِنَ الْقَوْمِ الضَّآلِّينَ ۞ فَلَمَّا رَأَى الشَّمْسَ بَازِغَةً
قَالَ هَـٰذَا رَبِّى هَـٰذَآ أَكْبَرُ فَلَمَّآ أَفَلَتْ قَالَ يَـٰقَوْمِ إِنِّى بَرِىٓءٌ مِّمَّا تُشْرِكُونَ ۞ إِنِّى وَجَّهْتُ وَجْهِىَ لِلَّذِى فَطَرَ
السَّمَـٰوَٰتِ وَ الْأَرْضَ حَنِيفًا وَمَآ أَنَا مِنَ الْمُشْرِكِينَ

"When the night came, and Ibrahim saw the star rise, he took it to be
the true God. Soon, however, the star set and Ibrahim was disappointed.
'How could a veritable God set and disappear?' he asked himself. He then
observed the moon shining brilliantly and thought: 'That is my Lord.' But
when it too set, he was all the more disappointed and thought: 'Unless
God guides me truly, I shall certainly go astray.' Later on Ibrahim
observed the sun in its brilliant and dazzling glory and he thought: 'This
finally must be my Lord, for it is the greatest of all.' But then it too set and
disappeared. Ibrahim was thus cured of the star worship common among

his people. 'I shall devote myself,' he therefore resolved, 'to Him Who has created the heavens and the earth, I shall dedicate myself as a *hanif* and not be an idol worshiper.'"[2]

Ibrahim and Sarah in Egypt

Ibrahim did not succeed in liberating his people from paganism. On the contrary, they punished him by throwing him into the fire. God rescued him by allowing him to run away to Palestine together with his wife, Sarah. From Palestine he moved on to Egypt, which was then ruled by the Hyksos or Amalekite kings. Sarah was a beautiful lady, and as the Hyksos kings were in the habit of taking into their households any beautiful married women they met, Ibrahim therefore pretended that Sarah was his sister and hence unmarried so that the king might not take her away and kill him in the process. The king, however, did take her and later realized that she was married. He returned her to Ibrahim, blamed him for his lie, and gave him a number of gifts, one of which was a slave girl by the name of Hagar.[3] As Sarah remained barren after many years of married life, she urged her husband to go into Hagar. After Ibrahim did so, Hagar soon bore him his son Isma'il. Later on, after Isma'il became a youth, Sarah bore a son who was called Ishaq.

Who Was the Sacrificial Son?

Historians of this period disagree on the matter of Ibrahim's sacrifice of Isma'il. Did the event take place before the birth of Ishaq or thereafter? Did it take place in Palestine or in the Hijaz? Jewish historians insist that the sacrificial son was Ishaq, not Isma'il. This is not the place to analyze this issue. In his book *Qisas al Anbiya'*, Shaykh 'Abd al Wahhab al Najjar concluded that the sacrificial son was Isma'il. His evidence was drawn from the Qur'an itself where the sacrificial son is described as being Ibrahim's unique son, which could only be Isma'il, and only as long as Ishaq was not yet born.[4] For with the birth of Ishaq, Ibrahim would have no "unique" son but two, Isma'il and Ishaq. But to accede to this evidence implies that the sacrifice should have taken place in Palestine.[5] This would equally be true in case the sacrificial son was Ishaq, for the latter remained with his mother Sarah in Palestine and never left for the Hijaz. On the other hand, the report which makes the sacrifice take place on the mountain of Mina near Makkah identifies the sacrificial son as Isma'il.

The Qur'an did not mention the name of the sacrificial son, and hence Muslim historians disagree in this regard.

The Qur'anic Version of the Sacrifice

The story of the sacrifice is that Ibrahim saw in a dream God commanding him to sacrifice his son to Him. In the morning he took his son and went out to fulfill the command. "When they reached the destination Ibrahim said to his son: 'My son, I saw in a dream God commanding me to sacrifice you. What will you say?' His son answered: 'Fulfill whatever you have been commanded; by God's will you will find me patient.' When Ibrahim threw his son on the ground for the sacrifice and both had acquiesced to the commandment, God called out to him: 'O Ibrahim, you have fulfilled the commandment. We shall reward you as We reward the virtuous. You have manifestly succeeded in your travail.' We ransomed him with a worthy animal to sacrifice."[6]

The Historians' Version

Some historians tell this story in more dramatic way. The beauty of some versions justifies a brief pause despite the fact that the story itself does not belong in this *aperçu* of Makkan history. It is told, for instance, that when Ibrahim saw in his dream that he should sacrifice his son and ascertained that that was God's commandment, he asked his son to take a rope and a knife and to go ahead of him to a nearby hill in order to collect some wood for fuel. The boy complied with his father's request. Satan took the guise of a man, came to Isma'il's mother and said: "Do you know where Ibrahim is taking your son?" She answered: "Yes, they both went to collect some wood." Satan said: "By God, he did not take him except to sacrifice him." The mother answered, "Not at all! His father is even more loving and gentler to him than me." Satan said: "But he claims that God has commanded him to do so." The mother answered: "If God has thus commanded him then so let it be." Thus Satan lost the first round. He ran to the son as he was following his father and repeated to him the same temptations he offered to his mother. But the son answered in exactly the same way as his mother did. Satan then approached Ibrahim and told him that what he saw in his dream was only a Satanic illusion that he may kill his son and grieve thereat the rest of his days. Ibrahim dismissed him and cursed him. Iblis (Satan) returned maddened and frustrated at his failure to dissuade Ibrahim, his wife, and his son from fulfillment of God's command. The same story tellers also report that Ibrahim divulged his dream to his son and asked for his opinion. They report the son as answering: "O Father, do what you are commanded to do." A still more fanciful version of the story reports the son as saying: "O Father, if you want to kill me, then bind me tight that I may not move and splatter you with my blood and thus reduce my own reward for the fulfillment of God's command. I know that death is hard, and I am not certain I will stay still when it comes. Therefore sharpen your blade that you may finish me quickly. Lay me face down rather than on my side, for I fear that if you were to witness my face as you cut my throat you would be moved by compassion for me and fail to complete that which God had asked you to do. And if you see fit to return my shirt to my mother that she may remember me therewith and, perhaps, find some consolation, please do so.' Ibrahim answered: 'My son, you are the best help in the fulfillment of God's command.' As he prepared for the sacrifice, bound the child, and laid him down, Ibrahim was called to stop. For he had given evidence of his obedience to God's command, and the son was ransomed with a sheep which Ibrahim found close by and which he killed and burnt."

That is the story of the sacrifice. It is the story of submission to God and His decree as well as of the fulfillment of His commandment.

Ibrahim, Isma'il, and Hagar's Trip to the Valley of Makkah

Ishaq grew up in the company of his brother Isma'il. The father loved both equally, but Sarah was not pleased with this equation of her son with the son of the slave girl Hagar. Once, upon seeing Isma'il chastising his younger brother, she swore that she would not live with Hagar nor her son. Ibrahim realized that happiness was not possible as long as the two women lived in the same household; hence, he took Hagar and her son and traveled south until they arrived to the valley of Makkah. As we said earlier, the valley was a midway place of rest for caravans on the road between Yaman and al Sham. The caravans came in season, and the place was empty at all or most other times. Ibrahim deposited Isma'il and his mother there and left them some sustenance. Hagar built a little hut in which she settled with her son and whereto Ibrahim returned when he came. When water and provisions were exhausted, Hagar set out to look for food, but she could not find any. As the storytellers put it, she ran towards the valley seeking water and, not finding any, would run in another direction. After running to and fro seven times between Safa and Marwah, she returned in despair to her son. But what surprise when she found him! Having scratched the surface of the earth with his foot, he uncovered a water fountain which sprung under his feet. Hagar drank and gave Isma'il to drink until they were both satisfied. She then closed in the spring that its water might not be lost in the sand. Thereafter the child and his mother lived in Makkah. Arab travelers continued to use the place as a rest stop, and in exchange for services they rendered to the travelers who came with one caravan after another, Hagar and Isma'il were sufficiently provided for.

Subsequently a number of tribes liked the fountain water of Zamzam sufficiently to settle nearby. Jurhum was the first such tribe to settle in Makkah. Some versions assert that Jurhum was already settled in Makkah even before Hagar and her son arrived there. According to other reports, no tribes settled in Makkah until Zamzam had sprung forth and made life possible in this otherwise barren valley and hence, after Isma'il's advent. Isma'il grew up, married a girl from the tribe of Jurhum and lived with this tribe in the same area where he built the holy temple. Thereafter, the city of Makkah arose around the temple. It is also told that Ibrahim once took leave of Sarah to visit Isma'il and his mother. When he inquired about the house of Isma'il and found it, he asked Isma'il 's wife, "Where is your husband?" She answered, "He went out to hunt." He then asked her whether she had any food or drink to give him. She answered in the negative. Before he turned back, Ibrahim asked her to convey to her husband a message. "Give him my greetings," he said, "and tell him that he should change the threshold of his house." When Isma'il's wife related to her husband his father's message, he divorced her and married a girl from the Jurhum tribe, the daughter of Mudad ibn 'Amr. This second wife knew well how to entertain Ibrahim when he came to visit his son a second time later. At the end of his second visit, Ibrahim asked Isma'il's wife to greet her husband for him and to tell him, "Now the threshold of your house is straight." Twelve sons were born to Isma'il from this marriage with the Jurhum girl. These were the ancestors of the twelve tribes of Arabized or Northern Arabs. On their mother's side these were related through Jurhum to the Arabizing Arabs, the sons of Ya'rub ibn Qahtan. They were also related to Egypt through their grandmother on their father's side, Hagar, which was a close relation indeed. Through their grandfather Ibrahim, they were related to Iraq and to Palestine, his old and new abodes.

Discussion of the Story

Despite disagreement on details, the main theme of this story which history had brought down to us, namely the emigration of Ibrahim and Isma'il to Makkah, is backed by an almost complete consensus on the part of the historians. The differences center on whether, when Hagar arrived with Isma'il in the valley of Makkah, the springs were already there and whether the tribe of Jurhum had already occupied the place and had welcomed Hagar when Ibrahim brought her and her son to live in their midst. When Isma'il grew up, he married a Jurhum girl and had several sons from her. It was this mixture of Hebrew, Egyptian and

Arab blood that gave to Isma'il's descendants resoluteness, courage, and all the virtues of the native Arabs, the Hebrews, and the Egyptians combined. As for the detail regarding Hagar's difficulty when she ran out of water, and of her running to and fro between Safa and Marwah and the way in which Zamzam sprang forth, all these are subject to debate.

Sir William Muir, for instance, doubts the whole story of Ibrahim and Isma'il's trip to Hijaz and denies it altogether. He claims that it is one of the Israelitisms which the Jews had invented long before Islam in order to strike a link with the Arabs by making them descendents of Ibrahim, now father of all. Since the Jews regarded themselves as descendants of Ishaq, they would become the cousins of the Arabs and therefore entitled to Arab hospitality if the Arabs were declared the sons of Ishaq 's brother, namely Isma'il. Such a theme, if properly advocated, was probably thought to help establish Jewish trade in the Peninsula. In making this claim, Muir assumed that the religious situation in Arabia was far removed from the religion of Abraham. The former was pagan whereas Ibrahim was a Hanif and a Muslim. For our part, we do not think that this is sufficient reason to deny a historical truth. Our evidence for the paganism of the Arabs is centuries later than the arrival of Ibrahim and Isma'il to the scene. It cannot therefore constitute any proof that at the time of Ibrahim's arrival to Hijaz and his building of the Ka'bah with his son Isma'il that the Arabs were pagan. Neither would Sir William's claims be corroborated had the religion of the Arabs been pagan at the time. Ibrahim's own people, whom he tried to bring forth to monotheism without success, were also idol worshipers. Had Ibrahim called the Arabs to monotheism, as he did his own people earlier, and not succeeded, and the Arabs remained idol worshipers, they would not have acquiesced to Ibrahim's coming to Makkah nor in his son's settlement there. Rather, logic would here corroborate the report of history. Ibrahim, the man who left Iraq to escape from his peo-

ple and traveled to Palestine and to Egypt, was a man who knew how to
travel and was familiar with desert crossing. The road between Palestine
and Makkah was one trodden by the caravans for ages. There is, therefore,
no reason to doubt a historical event which consensus has confirmed, at
least in its general themes.

Sir William Muir and others who shared his view claim that it is possible that a number of the descendants of Ibrahim and Isma'il had moved
to the Arabian Peninsula after they had settled in Palestine and that the
blood relationship had developed after their arrival to Arabia. That is a
fine opinion indeed! But if it is possible for the sons of Ibrahim and Isma'il
to do such a thing, why should it not have been possible for the two men,
Ibrahim and Isma'il personally, only a generation or two earlier? How can
we deny a confirmed historical tradition? And how can we doubt an event
which the Qur'an, as well as a number of other old scriptures, has mentioned?

Ibrahim and Isma'il's Construction of the Ka'bah

Together Ibrahim and Isma'il laid down the foundations and built the
holy temple. "It was the first house built for public worship in Makkah. It
still stands as a blessing and guidance to mankind. In it are manifest signs;
that is the house of Ibrahim. Whoever enters it shall be secure."[7] God also
says: "For We made the house a refuge and a place of security for the people. We commanded them to take the house of Ibrahim as a place of worship and We have commanded Ibrahim and Isma'il to purify My house for
pilgrims and men in retreat, for those who kneel and prostrate themselves
in prayer. When Ibrahim prayed, 'O Lord, make this town a place of security and give its people of Your bounty, those of them who have believed
in God and in the day of judgment,' God answered: 'Yea, even those who
do not believe will enjoy my security and bounty for a while before I inflict
upon them the punishment of fire and the sad fate they deserve.' As
Ibrahim and Isma'il laid the foundations and raised the walls of the house,
they prayed: 'O Lord, bless our work; for You alone are all-hearing and all-
knowing.'"[8]

Religious Development in Arabia

How did it happen that Ibrahim built the house as a place of refuge
and security for the people so that the believers in God alone might use it

for prayer, and then it became a pantheon full of statues for idol worship? What were the conditions of worship after Ibrahim and Isma'il? In what form and with what ritual was worship conducted in the holy house? When were these conditions and forms superceded by paganism? In vain do we turn the pages of history books looking for answers to these questions. All we find therein are presumptions which their authors think are reports of facts. The Sabeans were star worshipers, and they enjoyed great popularity and prestige in Arabia. As the reports go, the Sabeans did not always worship the stars for their own sake. At one time it is said that they had worshiped God alone and venerated the stars as signs of His creation and power. Since the majority of people were neither endowed nor cultivated enough to understand the transcendent nature of the Godhead, they confused the stars with God and took them as gods. Some of the volcanic or meteoric stones appeared to men to have fallen from heaven and therefore to be astral in nature. Consequently, they were taken as hierophanies of the astral divinities and sanctified as such. Later on they were venerated for their own sake, and then worshipped as divinities. In fact, the Arabs venerated these stones so much that not only did they worship the black stone in the Ka'bah, but they would take one of the stones of the Ka'bah as a holy object in their travels, praying to it and asking it to bless every move they made. Thus all the veneration and worship due to the stars, or to the creator of the stars, were now conferred upon these stones. It was in a development similar to this that paganism was established in Arabia, that the statues were sanctified, and that sacrifices were made to them.

This is the picture which some historians give of religious development in Arabia after Ibrahim dedicated the Ka'bah to the worship of God. Herodotus, father of written history, mentions the worship of al Lat in Arabia; and Diodorus, the Sicilian, mentions the house of Makkah venerated by the Arabs. Their two witnesses point to the antiquity of paganism in the Peninsula and therefore to the fact that the religion of Ibrahim was not always observed there.

The Arab Prophets

During these long centuries many prophets called their tribes to the worship of God alone. The Arabs gave them little hearing and continued with their paganism. Hud was one of those prophets sent to the tribe of 'Ad which lived in the north of Hadramawt. Few tribesmen responded to his call. The majority were too proud to relinquish their old ways and they answered, "O Hud! You brought us no sign. We cannot relinquish our gods just because you tell us to. We shall not believe."[9] Hud kept on calling for years, but the more he called the more obstinate they became. Similarly, Salih arose in the tribe of Thamud who lived in al Hijr between Hijaz and al Sham, this side of Wadi al Qura and to the southeast of the land of Madyan, close to the Gulf of 'Aqabah. His call bore no more fruit than Hud's. Shu'ayb arose among the people of Madyan who then lived in the Hijaz. He called them to the worship of God alone, but they refused to hear and they perished as the people of 'Ad and Thamud before them. The Qur'anic narratives told us about the stories and missions of other prophets who called men unto God alone, and of their peoples' obstinacy and pride, their continued paganism, their worship of the idols of the Ka'bah, and their pilgrimage to the Ka'bah from every corner of the Arabian Peninsula. All this is implied in God's statement, "And We inflict no punishment on anyone until We have sent them a prophet to warn them."[10]

Offices of the Ka'bah

Ever since its establishment, the Ka'bah gave rise to a number of offices such as those which were held by Qusayy ibn Kilab when he took over the kingship of Makkah, in the middle of the fifth century C.E. His offices included *hijabah, siqayah, rifadah, nadwah, liwa'* and *qiyadah. Hijabah* implied maintenance of the house and guardianship over its keys. *Siqayah* implied the provision of fresh water — which was scarce in Makkah — as well as date wine to all the pilgrims. *Rifadah* implied the provision of food to the pilgrims. *Nadwah* implied the chairmanship of all convocations held. *Qiyadah* implied the leadership of the army at war. *Liwa'* was the flag which, hoisted on a spear, accompanied the army whenever it went out to meet the enemy and, hence, it meant a secondary command in times of war. All these offices were recognized as belonging to Makkah, indeed to the Ka'bah, to which all Arabs looked when in worship. It is more likely that not all of these offices developed at the time when the house was constructed but rather that they arose one after the other independently of the Ka'bah and its religious position, though some may have had to do with the Ka'bah by nature.

At the building of the Ka'bah, Makkah could not have consisted, even at best, of more than a few tribes of 'Amaliq and Jurhumis. A long time must have lapsed between Ibrahim and Isma'il's advent to Makkah and their building of the Ka'bah on the one hand, and the development of Makkah as a town or quasi-urban center on the other. Indeed, as long as any vestiges of their early nomadism lingered in the mind and customs of the Makkans, we cannot speak of Makkah as urban. Some historians would rather agree that Makkah had remained nomadic until the kingship of Qusayy in the middle of the fifth century C.E. On the other hand, it is difficult to imagine a town like Makkah remaining nomadic while her ancient house is venerated by the whole surrounding country. It is historically certain that the guardianship of the house remained in the hands of Jurhum, Isma'il's in-laws, for continuous generations. This implies continuous residence near the Ka'bah — a fact not possible for nomads bent on movement from pasture to pasture. Moreover, the well established fact that Makkah was the rendezvous of the caravans traveling between Yaman, Hirah, al Sham and Najd, that it was connected to the Red Sea close by and therefrom to the trade routes of the world, further refutes the claim that Makkah was merely a nomad's campsite. We are therefore compelled to acknowledge that Makkah, which Ibrahim called "a town" and which he prayed God to bless, had known the life of settlement many generations before Qusayy.

Ascendency of Quraysh

After their conquest of the 'Amaliq, the tribe of Jurhum ruled Makkah until the regime of Mudad ibn 'Amr ibn al Harith. During these generations, trade had prospered so well that the tribe of Jurhum waxed fat and forgot that they were really living in a desolate place and that they ought to work very hard to keep their position. Their neglect led to the drying up of the Zamzam spring; furthermore, the tribe of Khuza'ah had even thought of conquering Makkah and establishing their authority over its whole precinct.

Mudad's warning to his people did not stop their indulgence and carelessness. Realizing that his and his tribe's power was on the decline and would soon be lost, he dug a deep hole within the well of Zamzam in which he buried two golden gazelles and the treasure of the holy house, with the hope that he would return some day to power and reclaim the treasure. Together with the Jurhum tribe and the descendants of Isma'il he withdrew from Makkah in favor of the tribe of Khuza'ah, who ruled it from generation to generation until the advent of Qusayy ibn Kilab, the fifth grandfather of the Prophet.

Qusayy ibn Kilab (circa 480 C.E.)

Fatimah, daughter of Sa'd ibn Sayl, mother of Qusayy, married Kilab and gave him two sons, Zuhrah and Qusayy. Kilab died when Qusayy was an infant. Fatimah then married Rabi'ah ibn Haram who took her with him to al Sham where she gave birth to a son called Darraj. Qusayy grew up knowing no other father than Rabi'ah. When a quarrel broke out between Qusayy and some members of the Rabi'ah tribe, they reproached him as they would a foreigner and betrayed the fact that they never regarded him as one of their own. Qusayy complained to his mother and related to her the reproach he heard. Her answer was as defiant as it was proud. "O my son," she said, "your descendance is nobler than theirs, you are the son of Kilab ibn Murrah, and your people live in the proximity of the holy house in Makkah."

This was the cause of Qusayy's departure from al Sham and return to Makkah. His seriousness and wisdom soon won him the respect of the Makkans. At the time, the guardianship of the holy house was in the hands of a man of the Khuza'ah tribe called Hulayl ibn Hubshiyyah, a very wise man with deep insight. Soon Qusayy asked for and married Hubba, daughter of Hulayl. He continued to work hard at his trade and acquired much affluence, great respect, and many children. When his father-in-law died, he committed the keys of the Ka'bah to Hubba, wife of Qusayy. But the latter apologized and committed the keys to Abu Ghibshan, a man from Khuza'ah. Abu Ghibshan, however, was a drunkard and one day he exchanged the keys of the Ka'bah for a jug of wine from Qusayy. The Khuza'ah tribe realized that it was in danger should the guardianship of the Ka'bah remain in the hands of Qusayy whose wealth and influence were always increasing and around whom the tribe of Quraysh was now rallying. They therefore thought to dispossess him of his guardianship. Qusayy called upon the Quraysh tribe to help him and, with the concurrence of a number of tribes from the surrounding area, he was judged the wisest and the mightiest and confirmed in his guardianship. When the tribe of Khuza'ah had to evacuate, Qusayy combined in his person all the offices associated with the holy house and became king over the Quraysh.

Construction of Permanent Residences in Makkah

Some historians claim that Makkah had no constructed houses other than the Ka'bah until Qusayy became its king because neither Khuza'ah nor Jurhum wanted to raise any other construction besides the holy house and neither one spent his life outside of the holy area in the open desert. They added that upon his assumption of the kingship of Makkah, Qusayy commanded his people, the Quraysh tribe, to build their residences in the vicinity of the holy house. They also explained that it was Qusayy who built the house of Nadwah where the elders of Makkah met under his chairmanship in order to run the affairs of their city, for it was their custom not to allow anything to happen without their unanimous approval. No man or woman of Makkah married except in the Nadwah and with the approval of the Quraysh elders. According to this view, it was the Quraysh that built, at the command of Qusayy, their houses around the Ka'bah, leaving sufficient space for circumambulation of the holy house. Their residences in the vicinity were spaced so as to leave a narrow passage to the holy house between every two houses.

The Descendants of Qusayy

Although 'Abd al Dar was the eldest of Qusayy's children, his brother 'Abd Manaf was more famous and more respected by the people. As Qusayy grew old and weak and became unable to carry out the duties of his position, he delegated the *hijabah* to 'Abd al Dar and handed over to him the keys of the holy house. He also delegated to him the *siqayah*, the *liwa'*, and the *rifadah*.[11] The *rifadah* implied a contribution the tribe of Quraysh used to levy from every member to help Qusayy in the provision of food for pilgrims incapable of procuring nourishment on their own. Qusayy was the first to impose the *rifadah* on the Quraysh tribe; and he incepted this practice after he rallied the Quraysh and dislodged the tribe of Khuza'ah from Makkah. At the time the *rifadah* was imposed, Qusayy said, "O people of Quraysh! You are the neighbors of God and the people of His house and temple. The pilgrim is the guest of God and visitor of His house. Of all guests that you receive during the year, the pilgrim is the most worthy of your hospitality. Provide for him food and drink during the days of pilgrimage."

The Descendants of 'Abd Manaf

'Abd al Dar discharged the new duties incumbent upon him as his father had directed. His sons did likewise after him but could not match the sons of 'Abd Manaf in honor and popular esteem. Hence, Hashim,

'Abd Shams, al Muttalib and Nawfal, the sons of 'Abd Manaf, resolved to take over these privileges from their cousins. The tribe of Quraysh stood divided into two factions, each supporting one of the contestants. The descendants of 'Abd Manaf concluded the *Hilf al Mutayyibin*, a treaty so called because the covenantors dipped their hands in perfume as they swore allegiance to its new terms. The descendants of 'Abd al Dar, for their part, entered into another treaty called *Hilf al Ahlaf* [literally, the alliance of the allies—Tr.], and the stage was set for a civil war which could have dissolved the Quraysh tribe. A peace was reached, however, under which the descendants of 'Abd Manaf were granted the *siqayah* and *rifadah*, and the descendents of 'Abd al Dar kept the *hijabah*, the *liwa'*, and the *nadwah*.[12] Thereafter the two parties lived in peace until the advent of Islam.

Hashim (646 C.E.)

Hashim was the leader of his people and a prosperous man. He was in charge of the *siqayah* and the *rifadah*. In the discharge of his duties he called upon every member of the Quraysh to make a contribution for use in providing food for the pilgrims. Like his grandfather Qusayy, he argued with his contemporaries that the pilgrims and visitors to the house of God are God's guests and, therefore, worthy of their hospitality. He discharged his duties well and provided for all the pilgrims during the time of their pilgrimage in Makkah.

Makkan Affluence and Prosperity

Hashim did for the people of Makkah more than his duty demanded. In a year of drought he was generous enough to provide food for the whole population and turned the occasion into one of joy. It was he who regulated and standardized the two main caravan trips of the Makkan traders, the winter trip to Yaman, and the summer trip to al Sham. Under his good ordering and wise leadership Makkah prospered and its position rose throughout the Peninsula. It soon became the acknowledged capital of Arabia. From this position of influence the descendents of 'Abd Manaf concluded peace treaties with their neighbors. Hashim went in person to Byzantium and to the neighboring tribe of Ghassan to sign a treaty of friendship and good neighborliness. He obtained from Byzantium permission for the tribe of Quraysh to move anywhere in the territories of al Sham in peace and security. 'Abd Shams, on the other hand, concluded a treaty of trade with the Negus of Abyssinia and Nawfal and al Muttalib, both a treaty of friendship with Persia and a trade treaty with the Himyaris of Yaman. The glory of Makkah increased with its prosperity. The Makkans became so adept in trade that nobody could compete with them. The caravans came to Makkah from all directions, and the goods were exported in two big convoys in summer and winter. Surrounding Makkah all kinds of markets were built to deal with all the attendant business. This experience developed in the Makkans competence in business affairs as well as adeptness in the administration of the calendar and interest in financing.

Hashim remained the uncontested chief of Makkah throughout his life. Nobody thought of competing with him in this regard. His nephew, however, Umayyah ibn 'Abd Shams, did entertain such ideas but he lost and chose to live in exile in al Sham for ten full years. On one of his trips to al Sham, Hashim stopped in Yathrib where he saw a woman of noble birth engaging in business with some of her agents. That was Salma, daughter of 'Amr of the Khazraj tribe. Hashim fell in love with her and inquired whether she was married. When he learned that she was a divorced woman, but a very independent person, he asked her directly to marry him. As his position and prestige were known to her, she accepted. She lived with him in Makkah for a while before she returned to Madinah where she gave birth to a son called Shaybah, whom she kept with her in Yathrib.[13]

Al Muttalib

Several years later Hashim died on one of his trips and was buried in Gaza. His brother, al Muttalib, succeeded him in his posts. Though al Muttalib was younger than 'Abd Shams, he was well esteemed by the people. The Quraysh used to call him "Mr. Abundance" for his generosity and goodness. Naturally, with such competence and prestige as al Muttalib enjoyed, the situation in Makkah continued to be prosperous and peaceful.

One day al Muttalib thought of his nephew Shaybah. He went to Yathrib and asked Salma to hand the child over now that he had become fully grown. On return to Makkah, al Muttalib allowed the young man to precede him on his camel. The Quraysh thought that he was a servant of al Muttalib and called him so, namely 'Abd al Muttalib. When al Muttalib heard of this he said, "Hold it, Fellow Tribesmen. This man is not my ser-

vant but my nephew, son of Hashim, whom I brought back from Yathrib."
The title 'Abd al Muttalib was so popular, however, that the young man's
old name, Shaybah, was forgotten.

'Abd al Muttalib (495 C.E.)

When al Muttalib sought to return to his nephew the wealth which
Hashim left behind, Nawfal objected and seized the wealth. 'Abd al
Muttalib waited until he grew and then asked for the support of his uncles
in Yathrib against his uncles in Makkah. Eighty Khazraj horsemen arrived
from Yathrib ready to give him the military support he needed in order to
reclaim his rights. Nawfal refused to fight and returned the seized wealth.
'Abd al Muttalib then was assigned the offices which Hashim occupied,
namely the *siqayah* and the *rifadah,* after al Muttalib passed away. He
experienced no little difficulty in discharging the requisite duties because
at that time he had only one son, al Harith. As the well of Zamzam had
been destroyed, water had to be brought in from a number of subsidiary
wells in the outskirts of Makkah and placed in smaller reservoirs near the
Ka'bah. Plurality of descendants was an asset in the execution of such a
task as this but 'Abd al Muttalib had only one son, and the task nearly
exhausted him. Naturally, he gave the matter a good deal of thought.

The Redigging of Zamzam

The Makkans still had memories of the Zamzam well which was
filled with dirt by Mudad ibn 'Amr of the Jurhum tribe a few hundred
years back and wished that it could be reactivated. This matter concerned
'Abd al Muttalib more than anyone else, and he gave it all his attention.
Suffering under his duties, he thought so much about the matter that he
even saw in his dreams a spirit calling him to re-dig the well whose waters
sprang under the feet of his ancestor, Isma'il. But no one knew where the
old well stood. Finally, after much investigation, 'Abd al Muttalib was
inspired to try the place between the two idols, Isaf and Na'ilah. Helped
by his second son al Mughirah, he dug at the place until water sprang
forth and the two golden gazelles and swords of Mudad of the Jurhum
tribe appeared. The Quraysh wanted to share his find with 'Abd al
Muttalib. After objecting, he finally came to an agreement with them to
determine the rightful ownership of the treasure by the drawing of lots
among three equal partners, namely the Ka'bah, the Quraysh, and himself.

The divinatory arrows were drawn near the idol Hubal within the Ka'bah, and the result was that the Quraysh lost completely, 'Abd al Muttalib won the swords, and the Ka'bah won the two gazelles. 'Abd al Muttalib ordered his part, namely the swords, reforged as a door for the Ka'bah, and placed the two golden gazelles within the holy house as a decoration. Now that the Zamzam water was close by, 'Abd al Muttalib performed his *siqayah* duties with ease.

The Vow and Its Fulfillment

'Abd al Muttalib realized the limitations which his lack of children imposed upon him. He vowed that should he be given ten sons to grow to maturity, and to help him in his task he would sacrifice one of them to God near the Ka'bah. 'Abd al Muttalib's wish was to be fulfilled: he had ten fully grown sons. When he called them to assist him in the fulfillment of his vow, they accepted. It was agreed that the name of each one of them would be written on a divinatory arrow, that the arrows would be drawn near Hubal within the Ka'bah and that he whose name appeared on the drawn arrow would be sacrificed. It was then customary among the Arabs whenever they faced an insoluble problem to resort to divination by means of arrows at the foot of the greatest idol in the area. When the arrows were drawn it was the arrow of 'Abdullah, the youngest son of 'Abd al Muttalib and the most beloved, that came out. Without hesitation 'Abd al Muttalib took the young man by the hand and prepared to sacrifice him by the well of Zamzam between the idols of Isaf and Na'ilah. 'Abd al Muttalib insisted upon the sacrifice, but the whole of Quraysh insisted that 'Abdullah be spared and that some kind of indulgence be sought from the god Hubal. Finally, in answer to 'Abd al Muttalib's inquiry as to what should be done to please the gods, al Mughirah ibn 'Abdullah al Makhzumi volunteered the answer, "Perhaps the youth can be ransomed with wealth; in that case, we shall be pleased to give up all the necessary wealth to save him." After consultation with one another, they decided to consult a divineress in Yathrib renowned for her good insight. When they came to her, she asked them to wait until the morrow; upon their return she asked, "What, in your custom, is the amount of a man's blood wit?" "Ten camels," they answered. She said, "Return then to your country and draw near your god two arrows, one with the name of the youth and the other with the term 'ten camels.' If the arrow drawn is that of the youth, then multiply the number of camels and draw again until your god is satisfied. They accept-

ed her solution and drew the divinatory arrows which they found to con-
verge on 'Abdullah. They kept multiplying the number of camels until the
number reached one hundred. It was then that the camels' arrow was
drawn. The people were satisfied and told 'Abd al Muttalib, who stood
nearby in terror, "Thus did your god decide, O 'Abd al Muttalib." But he
answered, "Not at all! I shall not be convinced that this is my god's wish
until the same result comes out three times consecutively." The arrows
were drawn three times, and in all three it was the camels' arrow that came
out. 'Abd al Muttalib then felt sure that his god was contented, and he sacrificed the one hundred camels.

In this way the books of biography have reported to us some of the
customs of the Arabs and of their religious doctrines. In this way they
have informed us of the Arabs' adherence to these doctrines and of their
loyalty and devotion to their holy house. In confirming this custom al
Tabari reports that a Muslim woman had once vowed to sacrifice one of
her sons. She sought the advice of 'Abdullah ibn 'Umar without much
avail. She went to 'Abdullah ibn al 'Abbas who advised her to sacrifice one
hundred camels after the example of 'Abd al Muttalib. But when Marwan,
the governor of Madinah, knew of what she was about, he forbade her to
do it, holding to the Islamic principle that no vow is valid whose object is
illegitimate.

The Year of the Elephant (570 C.E.)

The respect and esteem which Makkah and her holy house enjoyed
suggested to some distant provinces in Arabia that they should construct
holy houses in order to attract some of the people away from Makkah.
The Ghassanis built such a house at al Hirah. Abraha al Ashram built
another in Yaman. Neither of them succeeded, however, in drawing the
Arabs away from Makkah and its holy house. Indeed, Abraha took a special care to decorate the house in Yaman and filled it with such beautiful
furniture and statues that he thought that he could draw thereto not only
the Arabs but the Makkans themselves. When later he found out that the
Arabs were still going to the ancient house, that the inhabitants of Yaman
were leaving behind the newly built house in their own territory and did
not regard the pilgrimage valid except in Makkah, he came to the conclusion that there was no escape from destroying the house of Ibrahim and
Isma'il. The viceroy of the Negus therefore prepared for war and brought
a great army for that purpose from Abyssinia equipped with a great ele-

phant on which he rode. When the Arabs heard of his war preparations, they became quite upset and feared the impending doom of Makkah, the Ka'bah, its statues, and the institution of pilgrimage. Dhu Nafar, a nobleman from Yaman, appealed to his fellow countrymen to revolt and fight Abraha and thus prevent him from the destruction of God's house. Abraha, however, was too strong to be fought with such tactics: Dhu Nafar as well as Nufayl ibn Habib al Khath'ami, leader of the two tribes of Shahran and Nahis, were taken prisoners after a brief but gallant fight. On the other hand, the people of al Ta'if, when they learned that it was not their house that he intended to destroy, cooperated with Abraha and sent a guide with him to show him the way to Makkah.

Abraha and the Ka'bah

Upon approaching Makkah, Abraha sent a number of horsemen to seize whatever there was of Quraysh's animal wealth in the outskirts. The horsemen returned with some cattle and a hundred camels belonging to 'Abd al Muttalib. The Quraysh and other Makkans first thought of holding their ground and fighting Abraha, but they soon realized that his power was far superior to theirs. Abraha sent one of his men, Hunatah al Himyari to inform 'Abd al Muttalib, chief of Makkah, that Abraha had not come to make war against the Makkans but only to destroy the house and that should the Makkans not stand in his way, he would not fight them at all. When 'Abd al Muttalib declared the intention of Makkah not to fight Abraha, Hunatah invited 'Abd al Muttalib and his sons and some of the leaders of Makkah to Abraha's encampment in order to talk to Abraha directly. Abraha received 'Abd al Muttalib well and returned his seized camels. But he refused to entertain any suggestion of saving the Ka'bah from destruction as well as the Makkans' offer to pay him one-third of the yearly crop of the Tihamah province. The conference therefore came to no conclusion, and 'Abd al Muttalib returned to Makkah. He immediately advised the Makkans to evacuate the city and withdraw to the mountains and thus save their own persons.

It was certainly a grave day on which the Makkans decided to evacuate their town and leave it an open city for destruction by Abraha. 'Abd al Muttalib and the leaders of the Quraysh grasped the lock of the door of the Ka'bah and prayed to their gods to stop this aggression against the house of God. As they left Makkah, and Abraha prepared to send his terrifying and formidable army into the city to destroy the house, small-pox

spread within its ranks and began to take its toll. The epidemic attacked
the army with unheard of fury. Perhaps the microbes of the disease were
carried there by the wind from the west. Abraha himself was not spared;
and terrified by what he saw, he ordered the army to return to Yaman.
Attacked by death and desertion, Abraha's army dwindled to almost nothing, and, by the time he reached San'a', his capital in Yaman, he himself
succumbed to the disease. This phenomenon was so extraordinary that the
Makkans reckoned time with it by calling that year "The Year of the
Elephant." The Qur'an had made this event immortal when it said,

$$\text{اَلَمۡ تَرَ كَيۡفَ فَعَلَ رَبُّكَ بِأَصۡحَٰبِ الۡفِيۡلِ ۝ اَلَمۡ يَجۡعَلۡ كَيۡدَهُمۡ فِىۡ تَضۡلِيۡلٍ ۝ وَّاَرۡسَلَ عَلَيۡهِمۡ طَيۡرًا اَبَابِيۡلَ ۝ تَرۡمِيۡهِمۡ بِحِجَارَةٍ مِّنۡ سِجِّيۡلٍ ۝ فَجَعَلَهُمۡ كَعَصۡفٍ مَّاۡكُوۡلٍ ۝}$$

"Consider what your Lord had done to the people of the elephant.
Did he not undo their evil plotting? And send upon them wave after wave
of flying stones of fire? And made their ranks like a harvested corn field
trodden by herds of hungry cattle ?"[14]

The Position of Makkah after the Year of the Elephant

This extraordinary event enhanced the religious position of Makkah
as well as her trade. Her people became more committed than ever to the
preservation of their exalted city and to resist every attempt at reducing it.

Makkan Luxury

The prosperity, affluence, and luxury which Makkah provided for its
citizens, like an island in a large barren desert, confirmed the Makkans in
their parochial zeal. The Makkans loved their wine and the revelry it
brought. It helped them satisfy their passionate search for pleasure and to
find that pleasure in the slave girls with which they traded and who invited them to ever increasing indulgence. Their pursuit of pleasure, on the
other hand, confirmed their personal freedom and the freedom of their
city which they were prepared to protect against any aggressor at any cost.
They loved to hold their celebrations and their drinking parties right in
the center of the city around the Ka'bah. There, in the proximity of three
hundred or more statues belonging to about three hundred Arab tribes,

the elders of the Quraysh and the aristocracy of Makkah held their *salons* and told one another tales of trips across desert or fertile land, tales of the kings of Hirah on the east or of Ghassan on the west, which the caravans and the nomads brought back and forth. The tribes carried these tales and customs throughout their areas with great speed, efficiency, and application. Makkan pastimes consisted of telling these stories to neighbors and friends and of hearing others, of drinking wine, and of preparing for a big night around the Ka'bah or in recovering from such a night. The idols must have witnessed with their stone eyes all this revelry around them. The revelers were certain of protection since the idols had conferred upon the Ka'bah a halo of sanctity and peace. The protection, however, was mutual, for it was the obligation of the Makkans never to allow a scripturist,[15] *i.e.*, Christian or Jew, to enter Makkah except in the capacity of a servant and under the binding covenant that he would not speak in Makkah either of his religion or of his scripture. Consequently, there were neither Jewish nor Christian communities in Makkah, as was the case in Yathrib and Najran. The Ka'bah was then the holy of holies of paganism and securely protected against any attack against its authorities or sanctity. Thus Makkah was as independent as the Arab tribes were, ever unyielding in its protection of that independence which the Makkans regarded as worthier than life. No tribe ever thought of rallying with another or more tribes in order to form a union with superior strength to Makkah, and none ever entertained any idea of conquering her. The tribes remained separated, leading a pastoral nomadic existence but enjoying to the full the independence, freedom, pride, and chivalry, as well as the individualism which the life of the desert implied.

The Residences of Makkah

The houses of the Makkans surrounded the Ka'bah and stood at a distance from it proportionate to the social position, descendance, and prestige these inhabitants enjoyed. The Qurayshis were the closest to the Ka'bah and the most related to it on account of the offices of *sidanah* and *siqayah*[16] which they held. On this account no honorific title was withheld from them, and it was for the sake of these titles that wars were fought, pacts concluded, and treaties covenanted. The texts of all Makkan treaties and pacts were kept in the Ka'bah so that the gods who undoubtedly were taken as witnesses thereto might punish those covenanters who violated their promises. Beyond these stood the houses of the less important tribes, and further still stood the houses of the slaves, servants and

those without honor. In Makkah the Jews and Christians were slaves, as
we said earlier. They were therefore allowed to live only in these far away
houses on the edge of the desert. Whatever religious stories they could tell
regarding Christianity or Judaism would be too far removed from the ears
of the lords and nobles of Quraysh and Makkah. This distance permitted
the latter to stop their ears as well as their conscience against all serious
concern. Whatever they heard of Judaism or Christianity they obtained
from a monastery or a hermitage recluse in the desert which lay on some
road of the caravans.

Even so, the rumors circulating at the time about the possible rise of
a prophet among the Arabs caused them great worry. Abu Sufyan one day
strongly criticized Umayyah ibn Abu al Salt for repeating such Messianic
stories as the monks circulated. One can imagine Abu Sufyan addressing
Umayyah in some such words as these, "Those monks in the desert expect
a Messiah because of their ignorance of their own religion. Surely they
need a prophet to guide them thereto. As for us, we have the idols right
here close by, and they do bring us close to God. We do not need any
prophet, and we ought to combat any such suggestion." Fanatically committed to his native city as well as to its paganism, it was apparently
impossible for Abu Sufyan to realize that the hour of guidance was just
about to strike, that the prophethood of Muhammad — may God's blessing be upon him — had drawn near, and that from these pagan Arab lands
a light was to shine over the whole world to illuminate it with monotheism and truth.

'Abdullah ibn 'Abd al Muttalib

'Abdullah ibn 'Abd al Muttalib was a handsome young man admired
by the unmarried women of his town. They were fascinated by the story
of ransom and the hundred camels which the god Hubal insisted on
receiving in his stead. But fate had already prepared 'Abdullah for the
noblest fatherhood that history had known, just as it had prepared
Aminah, daughter of Wahb, to be mother to the son of 'Abdullah. The
couple were married and, a few months after their marriage, 'Abdullah
passed away. None could ransom him from this later fate. Aminah survived him, gave birth to Muhammad, and joined her husband while
Muhammad was still an infant.

Following is a genealogical tree of the Prophet with approximate birth
dates.

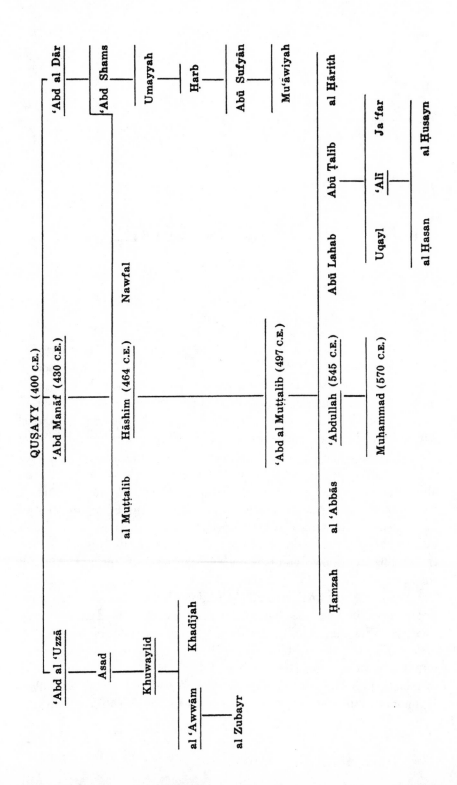

3

Muhammad:
From Birth to Marriage

The Marriage of 'Abdullah and Aminah

'Abd al Muttalib was seventy years old or more when Abraha arrived
in Makkah to destroy the ancient house. His son 'Abdullah was twenty-
four years of age and was hence ready for marriage. His father chose for
him Aminah, daughter of Wahb ibn 'Abd Manaf ibn Zuhrah, the chief of
the tribe of Zuhrah as well as its eldest and noblest member. 'Abd al
Muttalib took his son and went with him to the quarter of the tribe of
Zuhrah. There, he sought the residence of Wahb and went in to ask for
the hand of Wahb's daughter for his son. Some historians claim that 'Abd
al Muttalib went to the residence of Uhayb, uncle of Aminah, assuming
that her father had passed away and that she was under the protection of
her uncle. On the same day that 'Abdullah married Aminah, his father
'Abd al Muttalib married a cousin of hers named Halah. It was thus that
the Prophet could have an uncle on his father's side, namely Hamzah, of
the same age as he.

As was the custom in those days, 'Abdullah lived with Aminah among
her relatives the first three days of the marriage. Afterwards, they moved
together to the quarter of 'Abd al Muttalib, and soon he was to be called
on a trading trip to al Sham. When he left, Aminah was pregnant. A
number of stories circulated telling of 'Abdullah's marriage with other
women besides Aminah and of many women's seeking to marry 'Abdullah.
It is not possible to ascertain the truth of such tales. What is certainly true

is that 'Abdullah was a very handsome and strong young man; and it is not at all surprising that other women besides Aminah had wished to marry him. Such women would have at least temporarily given up hope once 'Abdullah's marriage to Aminah was announced. But who knows! It is not impossible that they may have waited for his return from al Sham hoping that they might still become his wives along with Aminah. 'Abdullah was absent for several months in Gaza. On his way back he stopped for a longer rest at Madinah, where his uncles on his mother's side lived, and was preparing to join a caravan to Makkah when he fell ill. When the caravan reached Makkah his father was alerted to 'Abdullah's absence and disease. 'Abd al Muttalib immediately sent his eldest son al Harith to Madinah in order to accompany 'Abdullah on the trip back to Makkah after his recovery. Upon arriving at Madinah, however, al Harith learned that 'Abdullah had died and that he had been buried in Madinah a month after the start of that same caravan to Makkah. Al Harith returned to Makkah to announce the death of 'Abdullah to his aged father and his bereaved wife Aminah. The shock was tremendous, for 'Abd al Muttalib loved his son so much as to have ransomed him with a hundred camels, a ransom never equaled before.

'Abdullah left five camels, a herd of sheep, and a slave nurse, called Umm Ayman, who was to take care of the Prophet. This patrimony does not prove that 'Abdullah was wealthy, but at the same time it does not prove that he was poor. Furthermore, 'Abdullah was still a young man capable of working and of amassing a fortune. His father was still alive and none of his wealth had as yet been transferred to his sons.

The Birth of Muhammad (570 C.E.)

There was nothing unusual about Aminah's pregnancy or delivery. As soon as she delivered her baby, she sent to 'Abd al Muttalib, who was then at the Ka'bah, announcing to him the birth of a grandson. The old man was overjoyed at the news and must have remembered on this occasion his loved one 'Abdullah. He rushed to his daughter-in-law, took her newborn in his hands, went into the Ka'bah and there called him "Muhammad." This name was not familiar among the Arabs, but it was known. He then returned the infant to his mother and awaited by her side for the arrival of wet nurses from the tribe of Banu Sa'd in order to arrange for one of them to take care of the newborn, as was the practice of Makkan nobility.

Historians have disagreed about the year of Muhammad's birth. Most of them hold that it took place in "the Year of the Elephant," *i.e.* 570 C.E. Ibn 'Abbas claims that Muhammad was born on "the Day of the Elephant." Others claim that he was born fifteen years earlier. Still others claim that he was born a few days, months, or years after "the Year of the Elephant." Some even assert that Muhammad was born thirty years and others seventy years later than "the Year of the Elephant." Historians have also differed concerning the month of Muhammad's birth although the majority of them agree that it was Rabi' al Awwal, the third month of the lunar year. It has also been claimed that he was born in Muharram, in Safar, in Rajab, or in Ramadan. Furthermore, historians have differed as to the day of the month on which Muhammad was born. Some claim that the birth took place on the third of Rabi' al Awwal; others, on the ninth; and others on the tenth. The majority, however, agree that Muhammad was born on the twelfth of Rabi' al Awwal, the claim of ibn Ishaq and other biographers. Moreover, historians disagreed as to the time of day at which Muhammad was born, as well as to the place of birth. Caussin de Perceval wrote in his book on the Arabs that after weighing the evidence, it is most probable that Muhammad was born in August, 570 C.E., *i.e.* "the Year of the Elephant," and that he was born in the house of his grandfather 'Abd al Muttalib in Makkah. On the seventh day after Muhammad's birth, 'Abd al Muttalib gave a banquet in honor of his grandson to which he invited a number of Quraysh tribesmen and peers. When they inquired from him why he had chosen to name the child Muhammad, thus changing the practise of using the ancestors' names, 'Abd al Muttalib answered: "I did so with the wish that my grandson would be praised by God in heaven and on earth by men."

Muhammad's Nurses

Aminah waited for the arrival of the wet nurses from the tribe of Banu Sa'd to choose one for Muhammad, as was the practise of the nobles of Makkah. This custom is still practiced today among Makkan aristocracy. They send their children to the desert on the eighth day of their birth to remain there until the age of eight or ten. Some of the tribes of the desert have a reputation as providers of excellent wet nurses, especially the tribe of Banu Sa'd. At that time, Aminah gave her infant to Thuwaybah, servant of Muhammad's uncle Abu Lahab, who nursed him for a while as she did his uncle Hamzah later on, making the two brothers-in-nursing.

Although Thuwaybah nursed Muhammad but a few days, he kept for her great affection and respect as long as she lived. When she died in 7 A.H., Muhammad remembered to inquire about her son who was also his brother-in-nursing, but found out that he had died before her.

The wet nurses of the tribe of Banu Sa'd finally arrived at Makkah to seek infants to nurse. The prospect of an orphan child did not much attract them since they hoped to be well rewarded by the father. The infants of widows, such as Muhammad, were not attractive at all. Not one of them accepted Muhammad into her care, preferring the infants of the living and of the affluent.

Halimah, Daughter of Aba Dhu'ayb

Having spurned him at first as her colleagues had done before her, Halimah al Sa'diyyah, daughter of Abu Dhu'ayb, accepted Muhammad into her charge because she had found no other. Thin and rather poor looking, she did not appeal to the ladies of Makkah. When her people prepared to leave Makkah for the desert, Halimah pleaded to her husband al Harith ibn 'Abd al 'Uzza, "By God it is oppressive to me to return with my friends without a new infant to nurse. Surely, I should go back to that orphan and accept him." Her husband answered, "There would be no blame if you did. Perhaps God may even bless us for your doing so." Halimah therefore took Muhammad and carried him with her to the desert. She related that after she took him, she found all kinds of blessings. Her herd became fat and multiplied, and everything around her seemed to prosper.

In the desert Halimah nursed Muhammad for two whole years while her daughter Shayma' cuddled him. The purity of desert air and the hardness of desert living agreed with Muhammad's physical disposition and contributed to his quick growth, sound formation, and discipline. At the completion of the two years, which was also the occasion of his weaning, Halimah took the child to his mother but brought him back with her to the desert to grow up away from Makkah and her epidemics. Biographers disagree whether Halimah 's new lease on her charge was arranged after her own or Aminah's wishes. The child lived in the desert for two more years playing freely in the vast expanse under the clear sky and growing unfettered by anything physical or spiritual.

The Story of Splitting Muhammad's Chest

It was in this period and before Muhammad reached the age of three that the following event is said to have happened. It is told that Muhammad was playing in a yard behind the encampment of the tribe with Halimah's son when the latter ran back to his parents and said, "Two men dressed in white took my Qurayshi brother, laid him down, opened his abdomen, and turned him around." It is also reported that Halimah said, "My husband and I ran towards the boy and found him standing up and pale. When we asked what happened to him, the boy answered, "Two men dressed in white came up to me, laid me down, opened my abdomen and took something I know not what away." The parents returned to their tent fearing that the child had become possessed. They therefore returned him to Makkah to his mother. Ibn Ishaq reported a *hadith* issuing from the Prophet after his commission confirming this incident. But he was careful enough to warn the reader that the real reason for Muhammad's return to his mother was not the story of the two angels but, as Halimah was to report to Muhammad's mother later on, the fact that a number of Abyssinian Christians wanted to take Muhammad away with them once they had seen him after his weaning. According to Halimah's report, the Abyssinians had said to one another, "Let us take this child with us to our country and our king, for we know he is going to be of consequence." Halimah could barely disengage herself from them and run away with her protégé. This story is also told by al Tabari, but he casts suspicion on it by reporting it first at this early year of Muhammad's age as well as later, just before the Prophet's commission at the age of forty.

Orientalists and many Muslim scholars do not trust the story and find the evidence therefore spurious. The biographies agree that the two men dressed in white were seen by children hardly beyond their second year of age — which constitutes no witness at all — and that Muhammad lived with the tribe of Banu Sa'd in the desert until he was five. The claim that this event had taken place while Muhammad was two and a half years old and that Halimah and her husband returned the child to his mother immediately thereafter, contradicts this general consensus. Consequently, some writers have even asserted that Muhammad returned with Halimah for the third time. The Orientalist, Sir William Muir, refuses even to mention the story of the two men in white clothes. He wrote that if Halimah and her husband had become aware of something that had befallen the child, it must have been a sort of nervous breakdown which could not at all have hurt Muhammad's healthy constitution. Others claim that Muhammad stood in no need of any such surgery as God had prepared him at birth for receiving the divine message. Dermenghem believes that this whole story has no foundation other than the speculative interpretations of the following Qur'anic verses:

أَلَمْ نَشْرَحْ لَكَ صَدْرَكَ ۞ وَوَضَعْنَا عَنكَ وِزْرَكَ ۞ الَّذِىٓ أَنقَضَ ظَهْرَكَ

"Had we not revived your spirit [literally, "opened your chest"] and dissipated your burden which was galling your back."[1]

Certainly, in these verses the Qur'an is pointing to something purely spiritual. It means to describe a purification of the heart as preparation for receipt of the divine message and to stress Muhammad's over-taxing burden of prophethood.

Those orientalists and Muslim thinkers who take this position *vis-a-vis* the foregoing tradition do so in consideration of the fact that the life of Muhammad was human through and through and that in order to prove his prophethood the Prophet never had recourse to miracle-mongering as previous prophets had done. This finding is corroborated by Arab and Muslim historians who consistently assert that the life of the Arab Prophet is free of anything irrational or mysterious and who regard the contrary as inconsistent with the Qur'anic position that God's creation is rationally analyzable, that His laws are immutable, and that the pagans are blameworthy because they do not reason.

Muhammad in the Desert

Until the fifth year of his life Muhammad remained with the tribe of Banu Sa'd inhaling with the pure air of the desert the spirit of personal freedom and independence. From this tribe he learned the Arabic language in its purest and most classical form. Justifiably, Muhammad used to tell his companions, "I am the most Arab among you, for I am of the tribe of Quraysh and I have been brought up among the tribe of Banu Sa'd ben Bakr."[2]

These five years exerted upon Muhammad a most beautiful and lasting influence, as Halimah and her people remained the object of his love and admiration all the length of his life. When, following his marriage

with Khadijah a drought occurred and Halimah came to visit
Muhammad, she returned with a camel loaded with water and forty heads
of cattle. Whenever Halimah visited Muhammad, he stretched out his
mantle for her to sit on as a sign of the respect he felt he owed her.
Shayma', Halimah's daughter, was taken captive by the Muslim forces
along with Banu Hawazin after the siege of Ta'if. When she was brought
before Muhammad, he recognized her, treated her well, and sent her back
to her people as she wished.

The young Muhammad returned to his mother after five years of
desert life. It is related that when Halimah brought the boy into Makkah,
she lost him in the outskirts of the city. 'Abd al Muttalib sent his scouts to
look for him and he was found with Waraqah ibn Nawfal.[3] 'Abd al
Muttalib took his grandson under his protection, and made him the object
of great love and affection. As lord of Quraysh and master of the whole of
Makkah, the aged leader used to sit on a cushion laid out in the shade of
the Ka'bah. His children would sit around that cushion, not on it, in deference to their father. But whenever Muhammad joined the group, 'Abd
al Muttalib would bring him close to him and ask him to sit on the cushion. He would pat the boy's back and show off his pronounced affection
for him so that Muhammad's uncles could never stop him from moving
ahead of them to his grandfather's side.

Orphanhood

The grandson was to become the object of yet greater endearment to
his grandfather. His mother, Aminah, took him to Madinah in order to
acquaint him with her uncles, the Banu al Najjar. She took with her on
that trip Umm Ayman, the servant left behind by her husband 'Abdullah.
In Madinah, Aminah must have shown her little boy the house where his
father died as well as the grave where he was buried. It was then that the
boy must have first learned what it means to be an orphan. His mother
must have talked much to him about his beloved father who had left her
a few days after their marriage, and who had met his death among his
uncles in Madinah. After his emigration to that city the Prophet used to
tell his companions about this first trip to Madinah in his mother's company. The traditions have preserved for us a number of sayings which
could have come only from a man full of love for Madinah and full of grief
for the loss of those who were buried in its graves. After a stay of a month
in Yathrib, Aminah prepared to return to Makkah with her son and set out

on the same two camels which carried them thither. On the road, at the village of Abwa'[4] Aminah became ill, died, and was buried. It was Umm Ayman that brought the lonely and bereaved child to Makkah, henceforth doubly confirmed in orphanhood. A few days earlier he must have shared his mother's grief as she told him of her bereavement while he was yet unborn. Now he was to see with his own eyes the loss of his mother and add to his experience of shared grief that of a grief henceforth to be borne by him alone.

The Death of 'Abd al Muttalib

The doubled orphanhood of Muhammad increased 'Abd al Muttalib's affection for him. Nonetheless, his orphanhood cut deeply into Muhammad's soul. Even the Qur'an had to console the Prophet reminding him, as it were, "Did God not find you an orphan and give you shelter and protection? Did He not find you erring and guide you to the truth ?"[5] It would have been somewhat easier on the orphaned boy had 'Abd al Muttalib lived longer than he did, to the ripe age of eighty when Muhammad was still only eight years old. The boy must have felt the loss just as strongly as he had felt that of his mother. At the funeral Muhammad cried continuously; thereafter, the memory of his grandfather was ever present to his mind despite all the care and protection which his uncle Abu Talib gave him before and after his commission to prophethood. The truth is that the passing of 'Abd al Muttalib was a hard blow to the whole clan of Banu Hashim, for none of his children had ever come to enjoy the respect and position, the power, wisdom, generosity, and influence among all Arabs as he had. 'Abd al Muttalib fed the pilgrim, gave him to drink, and came to the rescue of any Makkan in his hour of need. His children, on the other hand, never achieved that much. The poor among them were unable to give because they had little or nothing, and the rich were too stingy to match their father's generosity. Consequently, the clan of Banu Umayyah prepared to take over the leadership of Makkah, till then enjoyed by Banu Hashim, undaunted by any opposition the latter might put forth.

Under Abu Talib's Protection

The protection of Muhammad now fell to Abu Talib, his uncle. Abu Talib was not the eldest of the brothers. Al Harith was the eldest but he was not prosperous enough to expand his household responsibilities. Al 'Abbas, on the other hand, was the richest but he was not hospitable: he undertook the *siqayah* alone and refused to assume responsibility for the *rifadah*. Despite his poverty, Abu Talib was the noblest and the most hospitable and, therefore, the most respected among the Quraysh. No wonder that the protection of Muhammad devolved upon him.

The First Trip to al Sham

Abu Talib loved his nephew just as 'Abd al Muttalib had done before him. He loved him so much that he gave him precedence over his own children. The uprightness, intelligence, charity, and good disposition of Muhammad strengthened the uncle's attachment to him. Even when Muhammad was twelve years old, Abu Talib did not take him along on his trade trips thinking that he was too young to bear the hardship of desert travel. It was only after Muhammad's strong insistence that Abu Talib permitted the child to accompany him and join the trip to al Sham. In connection with this trip which he took at an early age, the biographers relate Muhammad's encounter with the monk Bahirah at Busra, in the southern region of al Sham. They tell how the monk recognized in Muhammad the signs of prophethood as told in Christian books. Other traditions relate that the monk had advised Abu Talib not to take his nephew too far within al Sham for fear that the Jews would recognize the signs and harm the boy.

On this trip Muhammad must have learned to appreciate the vast expanse of the desert and the brilliance of the stars shining in its clear atmosphere. He must have passed through Madyan, Wadi al Qura, the lands of Thamud, and his attentive ears must have listened to the conversation of the Arabs and desert nomads about the cities and their history. On this trip, too, Muhammad must have witnessed the luscious green gardens of al Sham which far surpassed those of Ta'if back at home. These gardens must have struck his imagination all the more strongly as he compared them with the barren dryness of the desert and of the mountains surrounding Makkah. It was in al Sham that he came to know of Byzantine and Christian history and heard of the Christians' scriptures and of their struggle against the fire-worshipping Persians. True, he was only at the tender age of twelve, but his great soul, intelligence, maturity, power of observation, memory and all the other qualities with which he was endowed in preparation for his prophethood enabled him at an early age to listen perceptively and to observe details. Later on he would review in memory all that he had seen or heard and he would investigate it all in solitude, asking himself, "What, of all he has seen and heard, is the truth?"

In all likelihood, Aba Talib's trip to al Sham did not bring in much income. He never undertook another trip and was satisfied to remain in Makkah living within his means and taking care of his many children. Muhammad lived with his uncle, satisfied with his lot. There, Muhammad grew like any other child would in the city of Makkah. During the holy months he would either remain with his relatives or accompany them to the neighboring markets at 'Ukaz, Majannah, and Dhu al Majaz. There he would listen to the recitations of the *Mudhahhabat* and Mu'allaqat[6] poems and be enchanted by their eloquence, their erotic lyricism, the pride and noble lineage of their heroes, their conquests, hospitality, and magnanimity. All that the visits to these market places presented to his consciousness, he would later review, approve of, and admire or disapprove of and condemn. There, too, he would listen to the speeches of Christian and Jewish Arabs who strongly criticized the paganism of their fellow countrymen, who told about the scriptures of Jesus and Moses, and called men to what they believed to be the truth. Muhammad would review and weigh these views, preferring them to the paganism of his people, though not quite convinced of their claims to the truth. Thus Muhammad's circumstances exposed him at a tender age to what might prepare him for the great day, the day of the first revelation, when God called him to convey His message of truth and guidance to all mankind.

The Fijar War

Just as Muhammad learned the routes of the caravans in the desert from his uncle Abu Talib, and just as he listened to the poets and the orators in the markets around Makkah during the holy months, he learned how to bear arms. In the Fijar War[7] he stood on the side of his uncle. The war was so-called because, unlike other wars, it was fought during the holy months. Arabia stood then under the convention that during the holy months no tribe should undertake any hostile activity against another; the general peace permitted the markets of 'Ukaz between Ta'if and Makkah, of Majannah and Dhu al Majaz in the proximity of 'Arafat, to be held and to prosper. On these market occasions, men were not restricted to trade. They competed with one another in poetry and debated, and they performed a pilgrimage to their gods in the Ka'bah. The market at 'Ukaz was the most famous in Arabia. There, the authors of the Mu'allaqat poems recited their poetry. Quss exercized his oratory,[8] and Jews, Christians and pagans spoke freely each about his faith in the peace and security that the holy months provided.

In violation of the holiness of such months, al Barrad ibn Qays al Kinani stealthily attacked 'Urwah al Rahhal ibn 'Utbah al Hawazini and killed him. Every year at this time, al Nu'man ibn al Mundhir, King of Hirah, used to send a caravan to 'Ukaz to bring thither a load of musk and to take hence a load of hides, ropes, and brocade from Yaman. Al Barrad al Kinani offered his services to guide the caravan as it passed through the lands of his tribe, namely Kinanah. 'Urwah al Hawazini did likewise and offered to guide the caravan through the Hijaz on the road of Najd. King al Nu'man chose 'Urwah and rejected the offer of al Barrad. The latter, enraged with jealously, followed the caravan, committed his crime, and ran away with the caravan itself. Al Barrad then informed Bishr ibn Abu Hazim that the tribe of Hawazin would avenge the murder of 'Urwah from Quraysh because the crime took place within the area under Quraysh jurisdiction. Indeed, members of the tribe of Hawazin followed members of the tribe of Quraysh and caught up with them before the latter entered the holy sanctuary. Hawazin, not yet satisfied, warned that they would make war next year at 'Ukaz. This war continued to rage between the two parties for four consecutive years. It ended in reconciliation and a peace treaty, very much the kind of arrangement usually met with in the desert. The tribe with the lesser number of casualties would pay the other tribe the bloodwit of the victims making up the difference. In the arrangement between Quraysh and Hawazin, the former paid the latter the blood wit of twenty men. Henceforth, al Barrad became the exemplar of mischief. History has not established the age of Muhammad during the Fijar War. Reports that he was fifteen and twenty years old have circulated. Perhaps the difference is due to the fact that the Fijar War lasted at least four years. If Muhammad saw its beginning at the age of fifteen, he must have been close to twenty at the conclusion of the peace.

There is apparent consensus as to the kind of participation that Muhammad had in this war. Some people claim that he was charged with collecting the arrows falling within the Makkan camp and bringing them over to his uncle for re-use against the enemy. Others claim that he himself participated in the shooting of these arrows. Since the said War lasted four years, it is not improbable that both claims are true. Years after his commission to prophethood, Muhammad said, "I had witnessed that war with my uncle and shot a few arrows therein. How I wish I had never done so!"

The Alliance of Fudul

Following the Fijar War, the Quraysh realized that their tragedy and deterioration as well as all the loss of Makkah's prestige in Arabia which they entailed ever since the death of Hisham and 'Abd al Muttalib were largely due to their disagreement and internal division. They realized that once they were the unquestioned leaders of Arabia, immune to all attacks, but that every tribe was now anxious to pick a fight with them and deprive them of what was left of their prestige and authority. With this recognition, al Zubayr ibn 'Abd al Muttalib called together the houses of Hashim, Zuhrah, and Taym and entertained them at the residence of 'Abdullah ibn Jud'an. At his request and appeal, they covenanted together, making God their witness, that they will henceforth and forever stand on the side of the victim of injustice. Muhammad attended the conclusion of this pact, which the Arabs called the Alliance of Fudul,[9] and said, "I uphold the pact concluded in my presence when ibn Jud'an gave us a great banquet. Should it ever be invoked, I shall immediately rise to answer the call."

In the Fijar War, hostilities were waged only during a few days every year. During the rest of the year the Arabs returned to their normal occupations. Neither losses in property nor in life were grave enough to change the Makkans' daily routines of trade, usury, wine, women, and other kinds of entertainment. Was this Muhammad's daily routine as well? Or did his poverty and dependence upon his uncle for protection force him to stay away from the luxury and extravagance of his contemporaries? That he kept away from these indulgences is historically certain. That he did so not on account of his poverty is equally certain. The debauchees of Makkah who were hardly capable of providing for themselves the immediate needs of the day could still afford their life of turpitude. Indeed, some of the poorest among them could outdo the nobles of Makkah and the lords of Quraysh. Rather, the soul of Muhammad was far too possessed by his will to learn, to discover, and to know, to incline towards any such depravities. His having been deprived as a boy of the learning which was the privilege of the rich made him all the more anxious to learn on his own. His great soul whose light was later to fill the world and whose influence was to fashion history was so involved in its will to perfection that Muhammad could only turn away from the recreative pursuits of his fellow Makkans.

As one already guided by the truth, Muhammad's mind was always turning towards the light of life evident in everyone of its manifestations in the world. His constant preoccupation was with the discovery of the underlying truth of life, the perfection of its inner meaning. Ever since he was a youth his conduct was so perfect, manly, and truthful that all the people of Makkah agreed to call him" al Amin", or "the truthful," "the loyal."

Muhammad as Herdsman

Muhammad's occupation as herdsman during the years of his youth provided him with plenty of leisure to ponder and to contemplate. He took care of his family's and neighbors' herds. Later, he used to recall these early days with joy, and say proudly that "God sent no prophet who was not a herdsman. . . Moses was a herdsman; David was also a herdsman; I, too, was commissioned to prophethood while I grazed my family's cattle at Ajyad." The intelligent, sensitive herdsman would surely find in the vastness of the atmosphere during the day and in the brilliance of the stars during the night fair enticement to thinking and contemplation. He would try to penetrate the skies, to seek an explanation for the manifestations of nature around him. If he were profound enough, his thoughts would bring him to realize that the world around him is not quite separate from the world within him. He would ponder the fact that he takes the atmosphere into his lungs, that without it he would die. He would realize that the light of the sun revives him, that that of the moon guides him, and that he is not without relation to the heavenly bodies of the high and immense firmament. He would ponder the fact that these heavenly bodies are well ordered together in a precise system in which neither sun overtakes the moon nor night overtakes the day. If the security of this herd of animals demanded his complete and constant attention, if it were to be safeguarded against attack by the wolf and loss in the desert dunes, what supreme attention and what perseverance were needed to guard the order of the universe in all its detail! Such speculative thought can indeed divert man from preoccupation with worldly cares and passions; it can pull him beyond their apparent persuasiveness and appeal. Thus, in all his deeds, Muhammad never allowed anything to detract from his reputation, but answered to every expectation to which his nickname "al Amin" gave rise.

Further evidence to this effect may be found in the reports Muhammad made about this early period of his life. It is said that while he was a herdsman he had a companion whom he asked to take over his duties while he spent the night in town in some recreation as other youths were wont to do in those days. Before he reached his destination, however, Muhammad's attention was arrested by a wedding in one of the houses on the way. He stopped there to listen to the sounds emanating from the house and fell asleep. He came back to Makkah on another occasion for the same purpose, and again on the way his attention was arrested by the sound of beautiful music. He sat down on the street to listen, and again fell asleep. The temptations of Makkah had no power over the disciplined soul of Muhammad whose prime concern was contemplation. This is not surprising. Far lesser men than Muhammad have also overcome these temptations. He led a life far removed from vice and immorality, and found his pleasures in immersing himself in thought and contemplation.

The Life of Thought and Contemplation

The life of thought is satisfied with very little of the world's wealth and pleasure. Herding cattle and goats never brings much material return, anyway. Material return, however, did not concern Muhammad, for he regarded the world stoically and avoided, often with ascetic detachment, pursuing anything beyond the barest needs of survival. Did he not say, "We are a people who do not eat until we become hungry, a people who when sitting to eat would never eat their fill?" Was he not known throughout his life to call men to a life of hardness and himself to lead a life of stoic self-denial? Those who long after wealth and strive hard to obtain it satisfy passions which Muhammad never knew. Muhammad's greatest spiritual pleasure was that of beholding the beauty of the universe and responding to its invitation to ponder and to admire. Such pleasure is known only to the very few, but it was Muhammad's nourishment ever since he was a young child, and it was his only consolation when life began to try him with the unforgettably cruel misfortunes of the death of his father, of his mother, and of his grandfather. Spiritual and intellectual pleasures are free. Their pursuit demands no wealth but requires the moral tautness to direct one's gaze inward, to penetrate one's very essence. Even if Muhammad had never been called to prophethood, his soul would never have allowed him to waste his energy in the pursuit of wealth. He would have been happy to remain as he was — namely, a herdsman — but he would have been a herdsman whose soul encompassed the whole universe and was in turn encompassed by that universe as if he were the very center of it.

Khadijah

As we have said earlier, Muhammad's uncle, Abu Talib, was poor and had many mouths to feed. It was necessary that he find for his nephew a higher paying job than herdsmanship. One day he heard that Khadijah, daughter of Khuwaylid, was hiring men of the Quraysh tribe to work for her in her trade. Khadijah was a tradeswoman of honor and great wealth. She used to hire men to bid and compete in the market on her behalf and rewarded them with a share of the profits. Being of the tribe of Banu Asad and having married twice within the tribe of Banu Makhzum, she had become very rich. Her father Khuwaylid and other people whom she trusted used to help her administer her large wealth. She had turned down several noblemen of Quraysh who asked for her hand, believing that they were after her wealth. Bound to a life of solitude, she had given all her energy to the development of her business. When Abu Talib learned that she was preparing a caravan to send to al Sham, he called his nephew, who was then twenty-five years of age, and said to him, "My nephew, I am a man devoid of wealth and possessions. The times have been hard on us. I have heard that Khadijah has hired a man to do her trade for a remuneration of two young camels. We shall not accept for you a remuneration as little as that. Do you wish that I talk to her in this regard?" Muhammad answered, "Let it be as you say, my uncle." Abu Talib went to Khadijah and said, "O Khadijah, would you hire Muhammad? We have heard that you have hired a man for the remuneration of two young camels, but we would not accept for Muhammad any less than four." Khadijah answered: "Had you asked this for an alien or a hateful man, I would have granted your request. How then can I turn you down when your request is in favor of a dear relative?" Abu Talib returned to Muhammad and told him the news, adding, "That is a true grace from God."

Muhammad in the Employ of Khadijah

On his first trip in the employ of Khadijah, Muhammad was accompanied by Maysarah, her slave, who was also recommended to Muhammad by his uncle. The caravan made its way to al Sham, passing through Wadi al Zahran, Madyan and Thamud as well as those spots through which Muhammad had passed once before with his uncle Abu Talib when he was twelve years old. This trip must have recalled to Muhammad the memory of his first trip in that area. It furnished more grist for his thinking and contemplating as he came to know more of the doctrines and rituals of the people of al Sham. When he arrived at Busrah, he came into contact with Syrian Christianity and talked to the monks and priests, some of whom were Nestorians. Perhaps those very priests or some others discussed with him the religion of Jesus which had by then divided itself into several sects and parties. Muhammad's adeptness and loyalty enabled him to make great gains for Khadijah — indeed more than any one had done before! — and his loyalty and gentleness had won for him the love and admiration of the slave, Maysarah. When the time came for them to return, Muhammad bought on behalf of Khadijah all that she had asked him to buy of the products of al Sham.

When the caravan had returned to al Zahran near Makkah, Maysarah said to Muhammad, "Run to Khadijah, O Muhammad, and bring to her the news of your success. She will reward you well." Muhammad galloped on his camel toward the residence of his employer and arrived there about noon. Khadijah happened to be in an upper story of her house, saw Muhammad coming, and prepared to receive him. She listened to his report — which he must have rendered in his very eloquent style — about his trip, the successes he achieved in his trade, and the goods he had imported from al Sham. She must have been well pleased with her new employee. Later on, Maysarah arrived and reported to her about Muhammad, his gentle treatment of him, and his loyalty to her that confirmed what she had already known of Muhammad's virtue and superiority over the other youths of Makkah. Shortly, despite her forty years of age and the indifference with which she rejected the offers of the noblest of Quraysh, her satisfaction with her employee was to turn into love. She desired to marry this youth whose eloquence and looks had made such a profound impression upon her. According to one version, she intimated her desire to her sister, and according to another, to her friend Nufaysah, daughter of Munyah. Nufaysah approached Muhammad and said, "What prevents you from getting married?" Muhammad answered, "I have no means with which to afford it." She said, "What if you were excused from providing such means and were called by a person of beauty, wealth, status and honor; what would be your response?" He answered, "Who can such a person be?" She said, "Khadijah." Muhammad wondered, "How could that be?" He too had felt inclined toward Khadijah but he never allowed himself to entertain the idea of marrying her. He knew of her rejection of the noblest and wealthiest men of Quraysh. When, therefore, Nufaysah reported to him in answer to his question, "I shall arrange it," he hastened to declare his acceptance. Soon Khadijah appointed the hour at which the uncles of Muhammad could find her people at her home and thus arrange for the completion of the marriage. It was her uncle, 'Umar ibn Asad, who gave her away as her father Khuwaylid had died before the Fijar War. This fact disproves the claim that Khadijah's father did not agree to the marriage and that his daughter had given him wine in order to extract such agreement from him.

Here a new page in the life of Muhammad begins. It is the page of married and family life which had brought great happiness to him as well as to Khadijah. It was also a page of fatherhood in which he was to suffer the loss of children even as Muhammad had in his childhood suffered the loss of parents.

4

From Marriage to Prophethood

Muhammad married Khadijah and gave her a dowry of twenty young camels. He moved to her house and thus began a new chapter in the life of both. Muhammad offered Khadijah the love of a man of twenty-five, though not the raging passion of youth which is as quickly kindled as cooled or put off. Khadijah gave him sons as well as daughters. The sons, namely al Qasim and 'Abdullah, died in childhood to the great grief of their father. The daughters survived and constantly remained the object of Muhammad's love and compassion just as he was the object of their love and devotion.[1]

Muhammad's Qualities

Muhammad was handsome of face and of medium build, and neither conspicuously tall nor inconspicuously short. He had a large head, very black thick hair, wide forehead, heavy eyebrows, and large black eyes with a slight redness on their sides and long eyelashes to add to their attractiveness. He had a fine nose, well spaced teeth, a thick beard, a long handsome neck, wide chest and shoulders, light colored skin, and thick palms and feet. He walked resolutely with firm steps. His appearance was always one of deep thought and contemplation. In his eyes there lurked the authority of a commander of men. It is no wonder that Khadijah combined love for him with obedience to his wishes or that she soon excused him from having to administer her trade and took over its reins as she had done before marriage in order to give him leisure to pursue a life of contemplation.

Aided by a marriage which complemented his genealogical honor and provided amply for his needs, Muhammad spent his days respected and loved by all the people of Makkah. His family life, numerous offspring, along with the ample provisions he now enjoyed, kept him from falling in public esteem. On the other hand, Muhammad had not withdrawn from society, from participating in the public life of Makkah as he did before. His new status added to his prestige among his peers as well as strengthened his already great modesty. Despite his great intelligence and outstanding ability, he listened well and attentively to anyone who spoke to him, never turning his face away from his interlocutor. Whosoever addressed him, Muhammad was never satisfied to lend his ear alone but turned to him with all his being. He spoke little, listened much, and inclined only to serious conversation though he did not refuse to share a joke.

He always spoke the truth. Sometimes he would laugh until one could see his molars, but his anger could never be recognized except by perspiration between his eyebrows. His anger and fury were always sublimated, and his magnanimity, candidness, and loyalty knew no bounds. He loved to do the good, and was charitable, hospitable, and friendly, as well as resolved and strong willed. Once resolved on a course of action, he was persevering and knew no hesitancy. Whoever came into contact with him was deeply impressed by all these qualities; whoever saw him would immediately fear him; and whoever had anything to do with him, loved him. All these qualities helped strengthen the bond of loyalty, truthfulness, and love which united him to Khadijah.

Reconstruction of the Ka'bah

We have said that Muhammad did not withdraw from the people of Makkah or from participating in the public life of the city. At the time, the Makkans were preoccupied with the rebuilding of the Ka'bah after a sudden flood had shaken its foundation and cracked its walls. The Ka'bah had for some time been the concern of the Quraysh. It had no ceiling and the treasures it housed were exposed to robbery. The Makkans were afraid, however, that a rebuilding of the Ka'bah with doors and ceilings might bring upon them a curse. The Ka'bah was girded by a series of superstitions designed to frighten the people from ever altering anything that pertained to it. Any such change would have been regarded as forbidden innovation and anathema. When the floods cracked its walls, it was imperative to do something about it despite fear and hesitancy. Coincidentally, a ship coming from Egypt belonging to a Byzantine trader called Pachomius was washed ashore. Pachomius was a builder by trade and knew something of carpentry. When Quraysh heard of him, al Walid ibn al Mughirah headed a delegation of Makkans to Juddah to negotiate with him. They bought from him the ship and commissioned him to come with them to Makkah and help them in the building of the Ka'bah. Pachomius accepted. In Makkah, there resided another Coptic man who knew something of carpentry. They asked him to assist Pachomius and the work began.

Wrecking and Rebuilding the Ka'bah

To every one of the four clans of Makkah fell the duty of wrecking and rebuilding one of the four walls of the Ka'bah. No one, however, volunteered to begin the work of wrecking for fear of punishment by its gods. Al Walid ibn al Mughirah, approaching his task with strong premonitions, prayed to the gods before pulling down part of the Yamani wall assigned to his tribe. The rest waited in order to see what would befall al Walid as a result of his deed. When the morning came and nothing had happened to him, they took courage and began their work. Like the rest, Muhammad carried stones back and forth, and the wrecking continued until the Ka'bah was leveled. Below the walls green stones were found which the Makkans were unable to shake loose. They decided to use them as foundation on which to build the new walls. From the neighboring mountains, they carried stones of blue granite. As the walls rose from the ground and the time came to place the sacred black stone in its place in the east wall, they differed as to who would have the honor of laying it in place. Competition was so keen that it almost led to a new civil war. The descendents of 'Abd al Dar and of 'Adiyy allied themselves together and swore that none would rob them of this honor. They were so serious in their resolution that members of the clan of Banu 'Abd al Dar brought a bowl full of blood in which they dipped their hands in confirmation of their solemn oath. For this act they were later called "the bloodmongers." When Abu Umayyah, son of Mughirah al Makhzumi saw what happened, he took advantage of his power and prestige and said to the

Makkans, "While we are all standing here, let the first one to pass through the gate of al Suffah be our arbitrator in this dispute." The first one to pass through the gate was Muhammad. When they beheld him they said, "There goes al Amin. We shall agree with his verdict." Realizing, as he listened to them, that the contenders had worked themselves up into a passion, Muhammad thought for a moment and said, "Bring me a robe." He took the robe they brought, spread it on the ground, and placed the black stone on it and then said, "Let the elders of each clan hold onto one edge of the robe." They all complied and together carried the stone to the site of construction. There, Muhammad picked up the stone and laid it in its place by himself. Bloodshed was thus averted and the dispute was solved. The Quraysh completed the building of the Ka'bah, raising its walls to a height of eighteen cubits. In order to make it more defensible, they raised its entrance above ground level. Inside the Ka'bah, they erected two parallel rows of three pillars each to support the ceiling and built a stairway on its north side leading to the roof. Hubal, the idol, was placed inside the Ka'bah together with all the treasures whose security concerned the Makkans.

There is disagreement about the age of Muhammad at the time of the rebuilding of the Ka'bah and of his arbitration between the Quraysh clans concerning the black stone. While some claimed that he was twenty-five years old, Ibn Ishaq reported him to be thirty-five. Regardless which of the two claims is true, the acceptance by the Quraysh of his arbitration and verdict — as well as his taking over the stone with his own hands and laying it down first on the robe and then in its place in the wall — all this proves the very high prestige Muhammad enjoyed among all Makkans as well as appreciation by his fellow countrymen for his objectivity and candidness of purpose.

Dissolution of Authority in Makkah and Its Effects

The foregoing dispute between the clans, the alliance of "the bloodmongers," and the recourse to arbitration by the first man to pass through the gates of al Suffah, all proved that public power and authority in Makkah had by that time dissolved and that none of the absolute power of Qusayy, Hashim, or 'Abd al Muttalib had passed to any Makkan. Undoubtedly, this dissolution was furthered by the power struggle between Banu Hashim and Banu Umayyah after the death of 'Abd al Muttalib. Such dissolution of public power and authority was bound to harm the city sooner or later were it not for the sanctified status of the ancient house and the awe and reverence it commanded in the hearts of all Arabs. Nonetheless, a natural consequence of political dissolution was the noticeable increase in the liberty of many to speak out their religious and other views. It was equally evident in the boldness of Jews and Christians, hitherto living in fear, publicly to criticise Arab idolatry. This dissolution of public power also contributed to the gradual disappearance among large numbers of Qurayshis of their old veneration of the idols, though their elders continued at least to appear to respect them. Anxious to safeguard the old ways, the elders held that to stabilize the situation and to prevent further deterioration of Makkan unity, idol worship in the Ka'bah might preserve for Makkah its place in the trade relations and religious life of Arabia. In fact, Makkah continued to benefit from this position of religious eminence, and its commerce continued to prosper. In the hearts of the Makkans themselves, however, Makkan prosperity could not for long impede the deterioration and final disappearance of idol worship.

Dissolution of Idol Worship

It is reported that one day the Quraysh tribe convened at a place called Nakhlah to celebrate the day of the goddess al 'Uzza. Four Qurayshis failed to show up and participate in this sacrament: namely, Zayd ibn 'Amr, 'Uthman ibn al Huwayrith, 'Ubayd Allah ibn Jahsh and Waraqah ibn Nawfal. They are reported to have addressed one another in these words, "Mark well these words! By God, the people are unworthy and surely misguided. As for us, we shall circumambulate no stone which neither hears nor sees, which is capable of neither harm nor good and on which the blood of sacrifice runs. O people, seek for yourselves a religion other than this!" Waraqah joined Christianity, and it is reported that he translated into Arabic some of the contents of the Evangels. 'Ubayd Allah ibn Jahsh remained a man without religion until he joined Islam and emigrated with his fellow Muslims to Abyssinia. There it is reported that he joined Christianity and died a Christian. His wife Umm Habibah, daughter of Abu Sufyan, remained a Muslim. She returned to Madinah and became one of the wives of the Prophet and a "Mother of the Faithful."[2] As for Zayd ibn 'Amr, he separated himself from his wife and from his uncle al Khattab, lived for a while in al Sham and Iraq and returned to Arabia without ever joining either Judaism or Christianity. He also separated himself from Makkan religion and avoided the idols. Leaning on the walls of the Ka'bah he used to pray, "O God! If I knew in which form you preferred to be worshipped, I would surely worship you in that form." Finally, as for 'Uthman ibn al Huwayrith, a relative of Khadijah, he traveled to Byzantium, became a Christian and, for some time, achieved a position of eminence in the imperial court. It is said that he sought to subjugate Makkah to Byzantium and to get himself appointed as the emperor's viceroy. The Makkans finally banished him from Makkah. He joined the Ghassanis in al Sham. From there he sought to cut off the trade route of Makkah, but the Makkans undid his schemes by sending all sorts of gifts to the Ghassani court. There, ibn al Huwayrith died by being poisoned.

Muhammad's Sons

The years passed while Muhammad participated in the public life of Makkah and found in Khadijah, the loving woman who gave him many children, the best of all woman companions. She gave him two sons, al Qasim and 'Abdullah — the last of whom was nicknamed al Tahir and al Tayyib — and four daughters, Zaynab, Ruqayyah, Umm Kulthum and Fatimah. Hardly anything is known of al Qasim and 'Abdullah except that they died before the coming of Islam, while still infants. Undoubtedly their loss caused their parents great grief and affected them deeply. As their mother, Khadijah must have received a permanent wound at their loss. She must have turned to her idols, inquisitively asking why the gods did not have mercy on her, and why they did not prevent her happiness from repeated shipwreck by the loss of her children. Certainly, Muhammad must have shared her grief and unhappiness. It is not difficult for us to imagine the depth of their tragedy in an age when daughters used to be buried alive and male descendants were sought after as the substance of life itself — indeed more. Sufficient proof of this grief is the fact that Muhammad could not last long without a male heir. When he saw Zayd ibn Harithah offered for sale, he asked Khadijah to buy him; no sooner was the new slave bought than Muhammad manumitted and adopted him as a son. He was called Zayd ibn Muhammad, lived under his protection, and became one of his best followers and companions. There was yet more grief ahead for Muhammad when his third son Ibrahim passed away in the Islamic period, after Islam had prohibited the burial of live daughters and declared paradise to stand under the feet of mothers. It is not surprising, therefore, that Muhammad's losses in his children should leave their deep mark upon his life and thought. He must have been quite shocked when on each of these tragic occasions, Khadijah turned to the idols of the Ka'bah, and sacrificed to Hubal, to al Lat, al 'Uzza, and Manat in the hope that these deities would intercede on her behalf and prevent the loss of her children. But Muhammad must have then realized the vanity and futility of these hopes and efforts in his tragic bereavement and great sorrow.

Muhammad's Daughters

Muhammad took care to marry his daughters to good husbands. He married Zaynab, the eldest, to Abu al 'Asi ibn al Rabi' ibn 'Abd Shams, whose mother was Khadijah's sister, and who was an upright and successful citizen. This marriage proved a happy one despite the separation of the two spouses following Zaynab's emigration to Madinah after Islam; as we shall see later.[3] He married Ruqayyah and Umm Kulthum to 'Utbah and 'Utaybah, the sons of his uncle Abu Lahab. These marriages did not last, for soon after the advent of Islam, Abu Lahab ordered his two sons to divorce their wives. It was 'Uthman that married both of them one after the other. Fatimah, who was still a child, did not marry 'Ali until after Islam.

Still, Muhammad's life during these years was one of well being, peace, and security. Were it not for the loss of his sons, it would have been a very happy one blessed with progeny and Khadijah's constant love and loyalty. During this period it was natural for Muhammad to allow his soul to wander, his mind and imagination to contemplate and to listen to the Makkan dialogue concerning their religion, to Jews and Christians concerning theirs, as well as to the latter's critique of Makkan religion. He could afford to give these problems his time and energy and to concern himself with them far more than could his compatriots. Endowed with such penetrating insight and prepared for conveying the divine message to mankind and ready for guiding their spiritual life to the true path, Muhammad could not enjoy his peace and security while men sank in misguidance and untruth. It was necessary for such a soul as he had to seek the truth perennially and everywhere, for only by such seeking and soul searching would it receive that which God was about to reveal. Despite this keen and noble obsession with the spiritual, this natural impulsion to religion, Muhammad never sought to become a priest nor a wise counsellor, such as Waraqah ibn Nawfal and others were, to whom men ran for advice. Rather he sought first to convince himself of the truth, not to pass it on to others. Consequently, he spent long intervals alone, completely absorbed in his thoughts and meditation, and hardly ever given to communicating his ideas to anyone.

The Arabs' Annual Retreat

It was Arabia's custom at the time for the pious and thoughtful to devote a period of each year to a retreat of worship, asceticism, and prayer. They would seek an empty place far away from their people where they could concentrate on their prayers and genuinely seek a new level of seriousness, wisdom, and ethical goodness through meditation. This practice was called *tahannuth* or *tahannuf.* Therein Muhammad found the best means of satisfying his will to thinking and meditating. In its solitude he could find a measure of spiritual detachment and peace that would enable his consciousness to screen the whole universe for inspiration and to pursue his thought wherever it might lead. At the head of Mount Hira', two miles north of Makkah, Muhammad discovered a cave whose perfect silence and total separation from Makkah made of it a perfect place for retreat. In that cave Muhammad used to spend the whole month of Ramadan. He would satisfy himself with the least provisions, carried to him from time to time by a servant, while devoting himself uninterruptedly to his spiritual pursuits in peace, solitude and tranquility. His devotion often caused him to forget himself, to forget his food, and, indeed, to forget the whole world around him. At these moments the very world and existence must have appeared to him like a dream. Through his mind he would turn the pages of all that he had heard and learned, and his search could only whet his appetite for the truth.

Groping after Truth

Muhammad did not hope to find the truth he sought in the narratives of the rabbis or the scriptures of the monks but in the very world surrounding him, in the sky and its stars, moon, and sun, and in the desert with its burning air under the brilliant sun — its impeccable purity enclosed by the light of the moon or that of the stars in the balmy night, in the sea with its countless waves, and in all that which underlies this existence and constitutes its unity of being. It was in the world that Muhammad sought to discover the supreme truth. He sought to unite his soul to it, to penetrate it, and to grasp the secret of its being. He did not take much thought to realize that his peoples' understanding of the nature of this world, of their religiosity and devotion, was all false. Their idols were mere stones — speechless, thoughtless, and powerless. Hubal, al Lat, and al 'Uzza, as well as every one of these idols and statues inside or around the Ka'bah, had never created even so much as a fly and never did Makkah any good. Where was to be found the truth in this vast universe of infinite skies and stars? Is it in the brilliant stars which give men their light and warmth and sends them rain? Is it in their water, the light and warmth as sources of life to all mankind throughout the world? No! For all these are creatures like the earth itself. Is the truth then behind the sky and their stars, in the boundless space beyond? But what is space? And what is this life which is today and is gone tomorrow? What is its origin and source? Is this world and our presence therein all a mere accident? The world and its life have, however, immutable laws which cannot be the product of circumstances. Men do good and they do evil. But do they do it willingly and deliberately, or is their action a mere instinct which they are powerless to control? It was of such spiritual and psychological problems that Muhammad thought during his solitary retreat in the cave of Hira', and it was in the totality of spirit and life that he sought to discover the truth. His ideas filled his soul, his heart, his consciousness, indeed all his being. This paramount occupation diverted him from the commonplace problems of everyday. When at the end of Ramadan, Muhammad returned to Khadijah, his perturbed thoughts showed on his face and caused Khadijah to inquire whether he was well.

In his devotions during that retreat, did Muhammad follow anyone of the known religious schools? That is a question on which scholars disagree. In his *Al Kamil fi al Tarikh,* ibn Kathir reported some of the current views in answer to this question. Some claimed that Muhammad followed the law of Noah; others, the law of Ibrahim; others, the law of Moses; others the law of Jesus. Others claimed that Muhammad had followed every known law and observed it. Perhaps this last claim is nearer to the truth than the others, for it agrees with what we know of Muhammad's constant search for answers and for ways to the truth.

The True Vision

Whenever the year revolved and the month of Ramadan arrived, Muhammad would return to the cave of Hira' for meditation with a soul yet more ripe and more concerned. After years of preoccupation with such problems, Muhammad began to see in his dreams visions of the truth he sought. Contrasted with these visions, the illusory character of this life and the vanity of its ornaments became especially apparent. He had become perfectly convinced that his people had gone utterly astray and that their spiritual lives had been corrupted by their idols and the false beliefs associated with them. He was also convinced that neither the Jews nor the Christians had anything to offer that would save his people from their misguidance. Some truth there certainly was in the claims of both Judaism and Christianity, but there was also a fair measure of falsehood and illusion, of outright paganism, which could not possibly agree with the simple absolute truth beyond all the barren dialectics and futile controversies in which Christians as well as Jews indulged. This simple absolute truth is God, Creator of the universe, other than Whom there is no God. The truth is that God is Lord of the universe, that He is the Compassionate and the Merciful, and that men are responsible for their deeds. "Whoever will do an atom's weight of good, will be rewarded therefor on the Day of Judgment; and whoever does an atom's weight of evil, will likewise be punished therefor."[4] The truth is that paradise and hell are true; that those who worship other gods than God shall dwell in hell and suffer eternal punishment.

When Muhammad retreated into the cave of Hira' as he approached the fortieth year of his age, his soul was fully convinced of the vision of truth he had seen. His mind was cleansed of all illusion and falsehood. His soul was well disciplined by the search for truth and devotion to it. His whole being was now oriented toward the eternal truth, and his whole life was devoted to the pursuit of its path. He had prayed with all his power that God might deliver his people from their misguidance and error. In his retreat he prayed day and night and fasted long periods. He would come down from the cave for a stroll on the desert highway and then return to his retreat, always rethinking, contemplating and reconsidering. This continued for six whole months while Muhammad was unable to tear himself away. Naturally he was scared, and intimated to his wife, Khadijah, the fear that he might even be possessed by an evil spirit. His loving and loyal wife reassured him, reminding that he was al Amin" [i.e., the faithful], that evil spirits could not approach him precisely because of his faith and strong morality. It had never occurred to either that God was preparing His chosen one by means of all these spiritual exercises for a truly great day, the day of the great news, the day of the first revelation. It did not occur to them that God was preparing His Prophet for prophethood.

The Beginning of Revelation (610 C.E.)

One day, while Muhammad was asleep in the cave, an angel approached with a sheet in his hand. The angel said to Muhammad, "Read." Muhammad answered in surprise, "What shall I read?" He felt as if the angel had strangled and then released him and heard once more the command, "Read." Muhammad's reply was, "What shall I read?" Once more he felt the angel strangling and then releasing him, and he heard him repeat the command, "Read." For the third time Muhammad answered, "What shall I read?" fearful that this time the strangling would be stronger. The angel replied, "Read in the name of your Lord, the Creator, Who created man of a clot of blood. Read! Your Lord is most gracious. It is He who taught man by the pen that which he does not know.'" Muhammad recited these verses, repeating them after the angel who withdrew after they were permanently carved upon his memory.[6] Thus the earliest of the biographies reported, and so did ibn Ishaq. Many of the Muhaddithan [*i.e.*, "reporters of the Prophet's traditions"—Tr.] have reported likewise. Some of them have claimed that the beginning of revelation was in the hours of wakefulness, and they mention a *hadith* to the effect that Gabriel first said words of reassurance to assuage Muhammad's fear at his appearance. In his *Al Kamil fi al Tarikh*, Ibn Kathir gave a quotation from the book, *Dala'il al Nubuwwah* by Abu Na'im al Isbahani, in which the latter reported that 'Alqamah ibn Qays had said, "The first revelations come to the prophets in their sleep until their hearts are reassured. Thereafter, revelation comes any time of the day or night." To this report Abu Na'im added, "This report comes to me from 'Alqamah ibn Qays in person. It is sound and reasonable, and it is corroborated by that which comes before and after it."

Muhammad's Fear

Stricken with panic, Muhammad arose and asked himself, "What did I see? Did possession of the devil which I feared all along come to pass?" Muhammad looked to his right and his left but saw nothing. For a while he stood there trembling with fear and stricken with awe. He feared the cave might be haunted and that he might run away still unable to explain what he saw. He walked in the area around the mountain asking himself who could have commanded him to read. Until that day in his retreat, Muhammad used to have visions of the truth dawning upon him after his meditation and filling his consciousness with great light. In these visions, Muhammad was guided to the truth, his doubts were dissolved, and the darkness which had enveloped the Quraysh in their idol worship was exposed. This light that illuminated the way in front of him was that of the truth which provided him with true guidance. It was the One and only God. But who was this who came to remind Muhammad of Him, that He had created man, and that He was the most gracious who taught man by the pen that which he does not know? Pursued by his own questioning and still trembling in fear of what he had seen and heard in the cave, Muhammad stopped in the middle of the road when the same voice called to him from above. Mesmerized in his place, Muhammad lifted his head toward heaven. He saw the angel in the form of a human giant across the sky. For a moment he sought to escape, but wherever he looked or ran, the angel stood right there before him. In his absence from the cave a messenger from Khadijah looked for him and could not find him. Filled with what he had seen, Muhammad returned home once the angel disappeared. His state was one of extreme dread. He had literally experienced the *Mysterium Tremendum et Fascinans*.

Khadijah, the Faithful

As Muhammad entered his house he asked Khadijah to wrap him in blankets. She could see that her husband was shivering as if struck with high fever. When he calmed down, he cast toward his wife the glance of a man in need of rescue and said, "O Khadijah, what has happened to me?" He told her of his experience and intimated to her his fear that his mind had finally betrayed him, and that he was becoming a seer or a man possessed. Khadijah was still the same angel of mercy, peace, and reassurance she had always been. As she did on earlier occasions when Muhammad feared possession by the devil, she now stood firm by her husband and devoid of the slightest doubt. Respectfully, indeed reverently, she said to him, "Joy to my cousin! Be firm. By him who dominates Khadijah's soul I pray and hope that you will be the Prophet of this nation. By God, He will not let you down. You will be kind to your kin; your speech will all be true; you will rescue the weary; entertain the guest and help the truth to prevail."

Reassured, Muhammad thanked Khadijah and was grateful for her faith. Exhausted, he fell asleep. This sleep was to be followed by a spiritual life of utmost strength, a life whose sublimity and beauty was to confront each and every mind. His life was to be dedicated purely to God, to truth, and to humanity. He was being commissioned to convey to man the message of His lord. He was to carry out his charge not by force, but by argument yet more gentle, sound and more convincing than any man has known. Despite every unbeliever, the light of God and His guidance will yet fill the world.

5

From the Beginning
of Revelation to the
Conversion of ‘Umar

Muhammad lapsed into perfect sleep while Khadijah's eyes, full of compassion and hope, were pinned on him. She withdrew from his room pensive and restless at what she had just heard. She looked to the morrow hoping that her husband would become the Prophet of this Arab nation long lost in error. She wished her husband could bring his people to the religion of truth and blaze for them the path of goodness and virtue. But she was very apprehensive of that morrow, fearful for the good of her loving and faithful husband. She reviewed in her mind the events he had reported to her, and imagined the beautiful angel appearing to her husband across the sky after conveying to him the words of His Lord. She tried to imagine the angel perched in the sky so that, following Muhammad's description, wherever one looked one could not lose sight of him, and she recalled the holy words which Muhammad recited to her after they had been carved on his memory. As she reviewed all this she may have at one moment smiled with hope and conviction and later frowned with fear for what might have befallen her husband. She could not bear her solitude long, and the alternation of sweet hope and bitter fear overpowered her. She therefore thought to divulge what she knew to someone sure of insight and wisdom who could give her some advice and good counsel.

The Conversation of Waraqah and Khadijah

Khadijah ran to her cousin Waraqah ibn Nawfal who, as we saw earlier, had already become a Christian and had translated part of the Evangel into Arabic. When she finished telling him what Muhammad had seen and heard and of her compassionate and hopeful response to her husband, Waraqah broke into these words: "Holy, Holy! By Him who dominates Waraqah's soul, if your report is true, O Khadijah, this must be the great spirit that spoke to Moses. Muhammad must be the Prophet of this nation. Tell him that he must be firm." Khadijah returned home and found Muhammad still asleep. For a while, she stared at him lovingly, faithfully, and hopefully. Suddenly she noticed that he was shivering, breathing deeply and perspiring. As he opened his eyes, he heard the angel say, "O you who lie wrapped in your mantle. Arise and warn. Glorify your Lord. Purify yourself. Shun uncleanliness. Give not in order to have more in return. For the sake of your Lord endure patiently."[1] Seeing him in this state, Khadijah pleaded that he return to his bed and resume his rest. But Muhammad sprang to his feet and said to her, "The time of slumber and rest is past, O Khadijah. Gabriel has commanded me to warn men and to call them to God and to His worship. But whom shall I call? And who will listen to me?" Khadijah tried to appease and reassure him, to encourage him with predictions of success. She told him what she had heard from Waraqah and declared to him her *Islam, i.e.,* her faith in his prophethood.

It was natural for Khadijah to be the first one to believe in Muhammad. For many long years she had known him to be the exemplar of truthfulness, fidelity, honesty, charity, and compassion. In his many retreats during the last few years, she had noticed how he had been constantly preoccupied with the search for the truth, with the truth alone; how he had sought that truth with his heart, mind, and spirit beyond the idolatrous superstitions of the people and their sacrifices, and beyond the deities that are capable of neither good nor evil but which the people venerated without avail. She had witnessed his great doubt and utter perplexity on his return from the cave of Hira' after the first revelation. She asked him to tell her when the angel would come. When he did she seized Muhammad and placed him on her left leg, then on her right leg, then in her lap, always asking him whether he was still seeing the angel and Muhammad answering in the affirmative. She then uncovered herself and threw off her clothes and asked Muhammad whether he still saw the angel, but the angel then disappeared. At this her doubt that the appear-

ance was that of the devil rather than of the angel was dissolved once and
for all.

Waraqah and Muhammad

One day Muhammad went to the Ka'bah for circumambulation. He
was met by Waraqah ibn Nawfal, who asked him about himself.
Muhammad related the events as they had happened. When he finished,
Waraqah said, "By Him Who dominates my soul I swear that you are the
Prophet of this nation. The great spirit that has come to Moses has now
come to you. You will be denied and you will be hurt. You will be abused
and you will be pursued. If I should ever live to see that day I shall surely
help the cause of God. God knows that I will." Waraqah then approached
Muhammad, kissed his forehead and went away. Muhammad realized the
faithfulness of Waraqah, and at the same time felt the burden weighing on
his shoulder. Waraqah's warning that the struggle ahead would be hard
only confirmed Muhammad's fears that the Quraysh were so attached to
their false beliefs that they would fight to death for them. How could he
fight them when they were his very people, his nearest relatives?

Surely the Makkans were mistaken. Just as surely, it was to the truth
that Muhammad was now calling them. He was calling them to transcend
themselves, to commune with the God Who created them as well as their
parents, and to worship Him alone in purity and faith. He called them to
bring themselves near to God with good works, to give the neighbor and
the wayfarer his due, and to reject the worship of those idols which they
had taken as gods who overlooked their vices and immorality, their usury
and robbery of orphans. But in doing all this, Muhammad was calling
men whose minds and hearts were petrified and hardened beyond the
stones to which their idol worship oriented them. Muhammad called men
to consider the sky and the earth and all therein which God created, to
perceive all this in its sublimity and gravity and grasp the laws by which
heaven and earth exist. Muhammad called men to rise, through their worship of the sole Creator of all existence, beyond all that is mean and
unworthy, to treat the misguided lovingly and to help him achieve proper
guidance, to bring charity and goodness to every orphan, to the weak, the
oppressed, and the poor. Yes, to all this did God command Muhammad
to call men. But these obstinate souls, these coarse hearts, had committed
themselves to remain forever loyal to the religion of the ancestors. Around
this religion they had built trade relations which gave Makkah its emi-

nence and centrality as a center of pilgrimage. Would the Makkans abjure the religion of their ancestors and expose their city to loss of prestige, a loss which would surely follow if all idol worship were to stop? Even if such a renunciation were possible, how could their hearts be purified of their chronic passion for every pleasure? How could they be lifted above the animal satisfaction of these passions? Muhammad called men to rise above their passions and above their idols. But what if they didn't respond to his call and refused to believe in him? What would he do?

Subsiding of the Revelations

Muhammad expected the revelations to guide his path from day to day, but they subsided. Gabriel did not appear for some time, and all around him there was nothing but silence. Muhammad fell into solitude, separated from himself as well as from the people. His old fears recurred. It is told that even Khadijah said to him, "Does it not seem that your Lord is displeased with you?" Dismayed and frightened, he returned to the mountain and the cave of Hira'. There, he prayed for God fervently, seeking assiduously to reach Him. Particularly, he wanted to ask God about the cause of this divine displeasure. Khadijah did not dread these days any less than Muhammad, nor was she any less fearful. Often Muhammad wished to die, but he would again feel the call and the command of his Lord which dispelled such ideas. It was also told that he once thought of throwing himself down from the top of Mount Hira' or Mount Abu Qubays, thinking what good was this life if his greatest hope therein was to be frustrated and destroyed? Torn between these fears on one hand and despair on the other, revelation came to him after a long interval. The word of God was as clear as it was reassuring:

وَالضُّحَىٰ ۝ وَالَّيْلِ إِذَا سَجَىٰ ۝ مَا وَدَّعَكَ رَبُّكَ وَمَا قَلَىٰ ۝ وَلَلْآخِرَةُ خَيْرٌ لَّكَ مِنَ الْأُولَىٰ ۝ وَ لَسَوْفَ يُعْطِيكَ رَبُّكَ فَتَرْضَىٰ ۝ أَلَمْ يَجِدْكَ يَتِيمًا فَآوَىٰ ۝ وَوَجَدَكَ ضَآلًّا فَهَدَىٰ ۝ وَوَجَدَكَ عَآئِلًا فَأَغْنَىٰ ۝ فَأَمَّا الْيَتِيمَ فَلَا تَقْهَرْ ۝ وَ أَمَّا السَّآئِلَ فَلَا تَنْهَرْ ۝ وَ أَمَّا بِنِعْمَةِ رَبِّكَ فَحَدِّثْ ۝

"By the forenoon, and by the night as it spreads its wings over the world in peace, your Lord has not forsaken you; nor is He displeased with you. Surely, the end shall be better for you than the beginning. Your Lord will soon give you of His bounty and you will be well pleased. Did He not find you an orphan and give you shelter? Did He not find you erring and guide you to the truth? Did He not find you in want and provide for you? Do not, therefore, oppress the orphan nor turn away whosoever seeks your help. And the bounty of your Lord, always proclaim."[2]

The Call to Truth Alone

Oh, what divine majesty, what peace of mind, what joy of heart and exaltation to the soul! Muhammad's fears dissolved and his dread was dissipated. He was overjoyed with this fresh evidence of his Lord's blessing and fell down in worship to God and praise of Him. There was no more reason to fear, as Khadijah had done, that God was displeased with him, and there was no cause for his dread. God had now taken him under His protection and removed from him every doubt and fear. Henceforth there was to be no thought of suicide but only of a life dedicated to calling men unto God and unto God alone. To the Almighty God on High shall all men bend their brows. To Him shall all that is in heaven and earth prostrate themselves. He alone is the True, and all that they worship besides him is false. To Him alone the heart should turn, on Him alone the soul should depend, and in Him alone the spirit should find its confirmation. The other realm is better for man than this realm. In the other realm, the soul becomes aware of all being as well as the unity of being; and in this unity space and time disappear and the needs and considerations of this realm are forgotten. It is in the other realm that the forenoon with its brilliant and dazzling sun, the night with its widespread darkness, the heavens and the stars, and the earth and the mountains all become one; and the spirit which enters into awareness of this unity is happy and felicitous. That is the life which is the objective of this life. And that is the truth which illuminated with its light the soul of Muhammad. When revelation subsided for a while, it was this truth which inspired him anew to solicit and think of his Lord and to call men unto Him. The calling of men unto God demands the purification of oneself, the shunning of evil, and the bearing with patience all the harm and injury with which the caller may meet. It demands that he illumine the path of true knowledge for the benefit of ignorant mankind, that he never rebuke the inquisitive, and that he never reject the man in need or oppress the orphan. Sufficient unto him must be the fact that God had chosen him to convey His message to mankind. Let this message then be the permanent subject of his conversation. Sufficient unto him must be the fact that God had found him an orphan and given him shelter under the protection of his grandfather, 'Abd al Muttalib, and his uncle, Abu Talib. Sufficient unto him must be the fact that God had found him in want and provided for him through his trustworthiness, and had shown him His favor by granting to him Khadijah, the companion of his youth, of his solitude and retreat, of his prophetic mission, and of love and kindness. Sufficient unto him must be the fact that God had found him erring and had guided him to the truth through His message. All this must be sufficient unto him. Let him now call to the truth and exert himself as heartily as he could. Such was the command of God to His Prophet whom He had chosen, whom He had not forsaken, and with whom He was not displeased.

Salat [Islamic Worship]

God taught His prophet how to worship. In turn Muhammad taught Khadijah, and both worshipped together. Besides their own daughters, 'Ali ibn Abu Talib, who was still a boy, lived with them in the same house. 'Ali's residence with Muhammad dated from the time that Makkah suffered from economic depression. Since Abu Talib had a very large family, Muhammad approached his uncle al 'Abbas, who was the richest member of the Banu Hashim clan, saying, "Your brother Abu Talib has a very large family, and he is in a state of want as a result of this depression. Let us together lighten his burden and take into our homes some of his children." Al 'Abbas agreed and took into his care Ja'far, and Muhammad took 'Ali. One day while Muhammad and Khadijah were worshipping together, 'Ali entered their room suddenly and found them kneeling and prostrating themselves and reciting together some of the Qur'anic revelations. Surprised at this behavior, the youth stood still at the door until the pair finished their prayer. To his question, "To whom did you prostrate your-selves?" Muhammad answered, "We have prostrated ourselves to God Who has sent me a prophet and Who has commanded me to call men unto Him." Muhammad then invited his nephew to worship God alone without associates, and to enter into the religion that He had revealed to His Prophet. He asked him to repudiate the idols, like al Lat and al 'Uzza, and recited to him something from the Qur'an. 'Ali was overwhelmed. The beauty and sublimity of the verses he heard gripped him. He plead-ed for time to consult his father. After a tempestuous night, 'Ali rushed to Muhammad and Khadijah and declared to them his conversion without consulting his father. The youth said, "God created me without consulting

Abu Talib, my father. Why should I now consult him in order to worship God?" 'Ali was then the first youth to enter Islam. He was followed by Zayd ibn Harithah, Muhammad's client.[3] Islam remained limited to one house. Besides Muhammad himself, the converts of the new faith were his wife, his cousin, and his client. The problem of how to call Quraysh to the new faith continued to press for a solution. Considering how attached the Makkans were to the religion of their ancestors and to their idols, and how fiercely they resisted any innovation, there was no easy solution in sight.

The Conversion of Abu Bakr

Abu Bakr ibn Abu Quhafah al Taymi was a very close friend to Muhammad. He trusted Muhammad, whom he knew to be worthy of this trust, and whose truthfulness was, as far as Abu Bakr was concerned, beyond doubt. Outside Muhammad 's own household, Abu Bakr was the first man to be called to the worship of God alone and to the repudiation of idols. He was the first outsider to whom Muhammad confided the vision he had seen and the revelations he had heard. Abu Bakr did not hesitate to respond favorably to the call of Muhammad and to believe therein. But what soul would hesitate to leave idol worship for the worship of God alone if it were open at all to the voice of truth? What soul would prefer the worship of stones to the worship of God if it were endowed with any kind of nobility and transcendent awareness? What soul would resist self-purification, giving of one's bounty and doing good to the orphan, if it had any degree of innate purity and goodness? Abu Bakr broadcast his conversion and new faith in God and in His Prophet among his companions. He was "a good man and a noble character, friendly to his people, and amiable and gentle. He enjoyed the noblest lineage in Quraysh and was the most knowledgeable of its clans and genealogies and its past and present history. Better than any other member of the tribe, he knew its strengths and weaknesses. By profession he was a trader, well known and honest. His people loved him and respected him for his knowledge, his honesty and his entertaining conversation."[4] Abu Bakr began to call unto Islam those of his people whom he trusted, and a number of them were converted. 'Uthman ibn 'Affan, 'Abd al Rahman ibn 'Awf, Talhah ibn 'Ubayd Allah, Sa'd ibn Abu Waqqas, and al Zubayr ibn al 'Awwam were the first to respond favorably to his cause. Thereafter Abu 'Ubaydah ibn al Jarrah was converted as well as a number of other Makkans. Whenever a man converted to Islam, he would seek the

Prophet and declare his Islam to him and receive from him his instruction. Fearful of arousing the enmity and antagonism of Quraysh for their departure from idol worship, the new Muslims used to hide the fact of their conversion. They would go to the outskirts of Makkah in order to hold their prayers. For three years while Islam continued to spread among the Makkans, the Muslims continued to hide. In the meantime, the Qur'an was continually being revealed to Muhammad and this fortified the Muslims in their faith and confirmed them in it.

The personal example of Muhammad was the best support for the spread of his cause. He was merciful and charitable, humble yet manly, sweet of word yet just, giving to each his due yet full of compassion and sympathy for the weak, the orphan, the deprived, and the oppressed. In his nightwatch and prayer, in his chanting the Qur'an revealed to him, in his constant scrutinizing of the heavens and of the earth, he looked for the meaning of their existence and that of everything they contain; in his permanent orientation toward God alone, in his search for the meaning of existence and quintessence of life, deep within his own soul, he provided such an example for his followers that they became ever more convinced of their faith and ever more anxious to adhere to its precepts. The new Muslims did so notwithstanding the fact that they were repudiating the religion and practice of their ancestors as well as exposing themselves to injury by those who believed otherwise. Many noblemen and tradesmen from Makkah believed in Muhammad, but all were already known for their purity, honesty, kindness, and mercy. In addition, Muslim ranks included many converts from the weak, deprived, and oppressed classes of Makkah. The cause of God and His Prophet spread as men and women entered the faith wave after wave.

The Muslims and Quraysh

People talked about Muhammad and his message. The obdurate and hard-hearted among the Makkans did not pay much attention to him, thinking that his cause would not go beyond what they had known of the causes of Quss, Umayyah, Waraqah, and others among the wise men and priests. They were certain men will eventually return to the religion of their ancestors, and that victory would finally belong to Hubal, al Lat, al 'Uzza, Isaf, and Na'ilah. But they forgot that candid faith is invincible and that the truth must someday prevail.

Muhammad's Nearest Relatives

Three years after the revelation began, God commanded the Prophet to proclaim Islam openly and to bring His revelation to the public. The following verses were revealed: "Warn, O Muhammad, your nearest relatives. Extend your gentle protection to all those believers who follow in your footsteps and obey you. As for those who disobey, proclaim your repudiation of their doings. . . . Proclaim what you are commanded and turn away from the associationists."[5]

Muhammad invited his kinsmen to a banquet in his home at which he tried to talk to them about Islam and to call them unto God. His uncle, Abu Lahab, interrupted his speech and asked the guests to stand up and leave. Muhammad invited them again on the morrow. After they had eaten he said, "I do not know of any man in Arab history who served his people better than I have served you. I have brought you the best of this world as well as of the next. My Lord has commanded me to call you unto Him. Who of you then would stand by me on this matter"? To this appeal, his kinsmen were unsympathetic and prepared to leave." 'Ali, however, though only a boy, arose and said, "Prophet of God: I shall be your helper. Whosoever opposes you, I shall fight as mortal enemy." The Banu Hashim smiled at this; others laughed loudly. All present looked once at 'Ali, once at Abu Talib, his father, and left full of ridicule for what they beheld.

After addressing his kinsmen, Muhammad now directed his call to the Makkans as a whole. One day he climbed to the top of al Safa and called, "O People of Quraysh!" Hearing his call, the Quraysh assembled around him and asked what was the matter. Muhammad answered, "Tell me, O Men of Quraysh, if I were to tell you that I see a cavalry on the other side of the mountain, would you believe me?" They answered, "Indeed, for we trust you, and we have never known you to tell a lie." Muhammad said, "Know then that I am a warner and that I warn you of a severe punishment. O Banu 'Abd al Muttalib! O Banu 'Abd Manaf! O Banu Zuhrah! O Banu Taym! O Banu Makhzam! O Banu Asad! God has commanded me to warn you, my nearest kinsmen, that I can guarantee to you no good on earth or in heaven unless you witness that there is no God but God." Abu Lahab, fat but quick of temper as he was, arose and said, "Woe to you on this day! Did you assemble us for this ?"

Severely shocked, Muhammad looked toward his uncle for a moment. Soon the following verses were revealed: "Accursed be the hands of Abu

Lahab and accursed may he be. Neither his property nor his wealth will save him. He shall burn in the flames of hell."[6]

Islam and Freedom

Neither the rancor of Abu Lahab nor the antagonism of other opponents in Quraysh prevented the spread of the Islamic call among the people of Makkah. Hardly a day passed without some new person joining the faith. Those inclined toward asceticism accepted Islam more readily, as neither trade nor vested interest could prejudice their consideration of the call. Such men had observed that Muhammad depended upon Khadijah's wealth, but that he never allowed wealth to influence his religious judgment. The material considerations were always rejected wherever they ran counter to the dictates of love, compassion, friendship, and forgiveness. Indeed, revelation itself commanded that the will to wealth is a curse upon the spirit. Did it not say, "The pursuit of wealth has exhausted all your energies and preoccupied your life to the very end? But you will surely come to know — and you will surely come to know it well! — that your wealth will not avail a thing. Had you known it with certainty, you would have known of hell and you would have convinced yourselves of it. But it is on the Day of Judgment that you will be questioned concerning the moral worth of your deeds."[7] What is better than that to which Muhammad calls? He calls to freedom, to absolute and limitless freedom, to that freedom which is as dear to the Arab as his very life. Does he not liberate men from the bondage which the worship of other gods besides God imposes? Has he not destroyed all the obstacles that have once stood between man and God? Neither Hubal, al Lat, nor al 'Uzza, neither the fire of the Zoroastrians nor the sun of the Egyptians, neither the astral bodies of the star worshippers, the apostles of Christ as princes of the church, nor any other human, angel or genii could stand between man and God. Before God and before Him alone is man responsible for his good and evil works. Man's works alone are his intercessor. On earth man's conscience alone is the final judge of his deeds, as it is its sole subject. Upon its everyday verdicts depends the last judgment of the person. What liberty is wider than this liberty to which Muhammad called men? Did Abu Lahab and his companions call to anything like it? Do they not call men to remain enslaved under superstitions so great that the light of truth and guidance can hardly penetrate and reach through them?

The Poets of Quraysh

Abu Lahab and Abu Sufyan, noblemen of Quraysh and lords of its commerce and entertainment, began to feel the threat which the call of Muhammad presented. They therefore decided to begin by ridiculing him and belying his prophethood. Their first act was to tempt their poet friends to attack Muhammad in their poetry. It was then that Abu Sufyan ibn al Harith, 'Amr ibn al 'As, and 'Abdullah ibn al Zib'ari launched their vituperative attacks in verse. A number of Muslim poets undertook to answer these attacks in kind, despite the fact that Muhammad hardly needed their efforts. Besides the poets, others advanced and asked Muhammad to perform some miracles with which to prove his prophethood. They challenged him to do as much as Moses or Jesus had done. They asked, "Why don't you change Mount Safa and Mount Marwah into gold? Why don't you cause the book of which you speak so much to fall down from heaven already written? Why don't you cause Gabriel to appear to all of us and speak to us as he spoke to you? Why don't you resurrect the dead and remove these mountains which bound and enclose the city of Makkah? Why don't you cause a water fountain to spring whose water is sweeter than that of Zamzam, knowing how badly your town needs the additional water supply?" The unbelievers did not stop at these demands for miracles. In ridicule, they asked, "Why doesn't your God inform you of the market prices of the future in order to help you and us in the trade of the morrow?" Whether serious or in ridicule, all these questions and demands were answered once and for all by revelation. God commanded Muhammad, "Say: 'I have no power whatever to bring advantage or avoid disadvantage. What God wills, that will happen. If it were given me to tell the future I would have used such knowledge to my own advantage. But I am only a man sent to warn you, and a messenger to convey a divine message that you may believe."[8]

Indeed: Muhammad was only a warner and a messenger. How could they demand of him that which reason denies while he demanded of them only that which reason commends — nay, dictates and imposes? How could they demand of him that which no morality can tolerate, whereas he called them to goodness and genuine virtue? How could they ask him to perform miracles when the Book that was being revealed to him, which was his guide to the truth, was the end of all miracles? How could they ask him to prove his prophethood with miracles that they might then see whether or not they would follow him, while their so — called gods were dead and cold, utterly devoid of power to do anything, whether miracle or nonmiracle? How could they ask him to prove himself with miracles when they worshipped their stone and wooden gods without ever asking them to prove their divinity? If they had only once asked their gods to prove their divinity, they would have seen through their wood and stone and convinced themselves that they were no gods at all but dead, immobile, and unable to defend themselves against anyone.

Muhammad's Attack against the Idols

Muhammad did take the initiative of attacking their gods. Hitherto he had not mentioned them at all. Now, he attacked them directly. To the Quraysh this was so serious that it aroused deep hatred. This man had become a threatening problem to them demanding definite solution. Until then they had not taken him seriously but had ridiculed him. When they assembled in Dar al Nadwah or around the Ka'bah and its idols and happened to mention him, they would speak lightly of him and ridicule his cause. Now that he had directly attacked their gods, ridiculed their worship as well as their ancestors', severely condemned Hubal, al Lat, al 'Uzza and all other idols, the matter called for something more than ridicule. It called for a fight-plan and serious thinking of how to combat and counter-attack. If this man were to succeed in converting the people of Makkah and in turning them against their old worship, what would happen to Makkan trade? What would remain of Makkah's religious eminence? These and like thoughts were ominous and called for the most careful strategy.

Abu Talib, Muhammad's uncle, had not joined the faith, but he continued to protect his nephew and let everyone know of his preparation to fight for him. Led by Abu Sufyan ibn Harb, some noblemen of Quraysh went to Abu Talib and addressed him in these words: "O Abu Talib, your nephew has blasphemed our gods, attacked our religion, ridiculed our ideals and condemned our fathers for unbelief. Either you stop him or you relinquish your protection of him. Our faith which he attacks is equally your faith. Why don't you let us take care of him for you?" Abu Talib talked to them gently and discharged them. Muhammad continued his preaching and intensified his missionary activity. His followers multiplied. Once more Quraysh plotted against him. They went to Abu Talib and brought with them 'Umarah ibn al Walid ibn al Mughirah, the most handsome youth in Quraysh. They asked Abu Talib to adopt 'Umarah as his son and to let them handle Muhammad. Once more they were turned down. As Muhammad continued his missionary activities, they continued to plot. Finally, they went to Abu Talib for a third time saying, "O Abu Talib, you are an honorable elder among us. We have asked you to stop your nephew but you have not. By God, we cannot permit him to insult our fathers, to ridicule our ideals, and to castigate our gods. Either you stop him or we shall fight both you and him until one of us perishes in the process." To alienate them and to arouse their enmity was too much for Abu Talib, and yet he was neither prepared to join the faith of his nephew nor to betray him. What would he do? He called Muhammad and told him what had happened and pleaded with him: "Save me as well as yourself, and do not cause me to carry a burden I cannot bear."

The Logic of History

For a while Muhammad stood motionless in his place. It was a moment in which the history of being itself stopped without knowing which course to take. Whichever word this one man was about to say, would be a judgment of mankind. Should the world continue to wallow in its darkness? Should Zoroastrianism triumph over a corrupt and lifeless Christianity? Should paganism be allowed to raise its superstitious, rotten head? Or should he, Muhammad, proclaim to this world the unity of God, enlightening it with the light of truth, liberating the minds of men from the bondage of superstition, and raising the souls for communion with the Supernal Plenum? There was his uncle — weakened by the people's opposition, unable to help or protect — indeed, likely to betray him. And there were the Muslims, few and weak, unable to wage war or to resist a strong and well equipped army such as Quraysh had. There was none to lend him support in this hour of dire need. Only the truth which he proclaimed and of which he was the advocate could console or rescue him. Nothing was left to count upon except his own faith and conviction of that truth. That alone was his whole force. Well, let it be. The other realm is better than this one. Let him then discharge his duty and convey his message. It is better to die faithful to the truth than to betray it or stammer in its cause. Refreshened and energized by the strength and determination of new resolution, he turned to his uncle and said, "O uncle! By God Almighty I swear, even if they should put the sun in my right hand and the moon in my left that I abjure this cause, I shall not do so until God has vindicated it or caused me to perish in the process."

How great is the truth! And how sublime is faith in the truth! The old man was shaken to his depths when he heard the answer of Muhammad. It was his turn to stand motionless and speechless in front of this holy power and great will which had just spoken on behalf of a life above life. Choked with emotion at his uncle's request as well as at his own certainty of the course he was to follow, Muhammad got up to leave. For but a moment Abu Talib hesitated between the enmity of his people and the cause of his nephew. Immediately, he called Muhammad back. "Go forth, my nephew," he said, "and say what you will. By the same God I swear I shall never betray you to your enemies."

Banu Hashim Protects Muhammad against Quraysh

Abu Talib communicated his resolution to Banu Hashim and Banu al Muttalib and spoke to them about his nephew with great admiration and deep appreciation of the sublimity of Muhammad's position. He asked them all to protect Muhammad against the Quraysh. All of them pledged to do so except Abu Lahab, who declared openly his enmity to him and his withdrawal to the opposite camp. Undoubtedly, the tribal bond they shared with Muhammad and their traditional enmity with Banu Umayyah influenced their decision to stand by Muhammad. Tribal solidarity and politics, however, do not completely explain their new opposition to all Quraysh in a matter so grave as to require them to repudiate the faith and beliefs inherited from the fathers. The attitude of Muhammad toward them, his firm conviction, his calling them in kindness to the worship of God alone, and their awareness that among the tribes of Arabia there were certainly other religions besides their own — all these factors caused them to realize that to their nephew and fellow tribesman belonged the right to speak out his views, just as Umayyah ibn Abu al Salt and Waraqah ibn Nawfal and others had done before him. If Muhammad were saying the truth — and they did not think that that was the case — truth will certainly prevail, and they stand to share in the glory of its victory. If, on the other hand, Muhammad was not telling the truth, then people would pass his claim by as they had other claims before. In this case it would not destroy their traditions, and there was, therefore, no reason why they should betray him to his enemies and allow them to kill him.

Persecution of the Muslims by Quraysh

From whatever harm might come from Quraysh Muhammad took
refuge behind his people. From the worries he generated within himself
he took refuge in the person of Khadijah. With her faith and great love
she was for him a refreshing source of joy. She supported him against
every symptom of weakness or despondency generated by the harm his
enemies had inflicted against him or against his followers. In fact, ever
since Muhammad made public cause of his revelations, Quraysh knew no
peace, and the tranquility of earlier days vanished. Instigated by the
Quraysh, every clan and tribe began to attack its Muslim members to dissuade them from their faith. One unbeliever threw his Abyssinian slave,
Bilal, onto the sand under the burning sun, laid a heavy stone on his chest
and left him there to die, for no reason except his insistence upon Islam.
Bearing himself gallantly under this torture, Bilal kept on repeating, "God
is one, God is one." Abu Bakr saw him, bought him from his master and
set him free. Indeed, Abu Bakr bought many of the slaves and clients who
were being thus tortured by the unbelievers. Among these there was even
a slave woman whom Abu Bakr had bought from 'Umar ibn al Khattab
before the latter's conversion. One woman is known to have been tortured
to death because of her attachment to Islam and her refusal to return to
the old faith. Muslims of pure Arab blood were beaten and subjected to
all sorts of maltreatment and contemptuous humiliation. Even
Muhammad did not escape, despite the protection of Banu Hashim and
Banu al Muttalib. Umm Jamil, Abu Lahab's wife, used to throw the refuse
from her house onto Muhammad's door. All Muhammad could do was
simply to remove it. While Muhammad was praying near the Ka'bah, Abu
Lahab threw on him the entrails of a goat sacrificed to one of the gods;
and Muhammad could only go to his daughter Fatimah for her to clean
him and wash the dirt off his clothes. This abuse was all in addition to the
terrible vituperation and vile calumnies the unbelievers directed against
the Muslims on every occasion and in every quarter. Such persecution
continued for a long time, but it only confirmed the Muslims in their faith
and challenged them to sacrifice everything for the sake of their convictions.

Muslim Patience

This period of Muhammad's life is one of the noblest and greatest
pages of human history. Neither he nor his followers sought wealth or rep-

utation, power or sovereignty. Rather, they were seekers after the truth and believers therein. To those who did harm him, Muhammad prayed for guidance, for liberation from the yoke of vile paganism and from its immorality and villainy. It was for this noble spiritual objective that Muhammad suffered persecution. The poets insulted him; the tribe plotted against him, threw stones at his house, threatened his folks and followers, and came close to killing him near the Ka'bah. The more they persecuted, the more patience and resolve Muhammad showed in his mission. The believers repeated and were encouraged by Muhammad's pledge that he would not abjure this cause even if given both sun and moon. Great sacrifices became small, and death itself became a welcome alternative. One must appreciate the strength of these men's faith and the depth of their commitment at a time when the new religion was not even complete and the Qur'an was not yet fully revealed. No doubt Muhammad's gentleness, good character, truthfulness, resoluteness, strength of will, and conviction were contributing factors. But there were other factors besides.

Muhammad lived in a free country very much like a republic. As far as social eminence and nobility of lineage, he ranked among the highest and best. Muhammad did not have much wealth, but he had all he needed, and so did Banu Hashim. To them belonged the *sidanah* of the Ka'bah and the *siqayah* and all that they wished by way of religious titles. Therefore, Muhammad stood in no need of money, prestige, political power, or religious eminence. In this respect, Muhammad was quite different from the prophets that preceded him. Moses, for instance, was born in Egypt when Pharaoh was worshipped by its people as God. It was he who called to them, "I am your supreme God."[9] The priesthood assisted Pharaoh in tyrannizing over the people and in exploiting them. The revolution that Moses led by command of his Lord was a revolution against the political as well as the religious order. Did Moses not seek to reduce Pharaoh to the equal of the most ordinary peasant in front of God, even though that peasant was of the meanest class who drew their water from the Nile with the *shadoof*? Pharaoh's divinity, Moses thought, as well as the social order on which it stood, must all be destroyed. The revolution must first be political. Consequently, from the very beginning the Mosaic call was met by Pharaoh with all-out war, and miracles were necessary that the Mosaic call might be believed by the rank and file. When, for instance, Moses threw his stick on the ground, it became a living serpent devouring what Pharaoh's magicians had created. These miracles, however, turned out to be futile, for Moses had to flee from his country of birth. His flight was assisted by another miracle, that of the splitting of the waters of the sea. As for

Jesus, he was born in Nazareth, in Palestine, a province under the yoke of Roman colonialism. He called men to patience in their suffering of injustice, to forgiveness after repentance and to forms of love and mercy which the rulers regarded as tantamount to rebellion against their tyranny. The miracles of resurrecting the dead, healing the sick, and all that Jesus did with the support of the Holy Spirit were necessary for the success of his cause. In their essence, the doctrines of Jesus and Muhammad were built on the same premises and led to the same conclusions, with differences in detail not relevant for our present discussion. The point is that these various factors, especially the political among them gave to the call of Jesus the orientation it took. As for Muhammad, since his circumstances were what we have just seen, his message was spiritual and rational. At every stage of its development, it rested on a foundation of truth, goodness, and beauty for their own sakes. Because of its distance from any political struggle, Muhammad's message did not disturb the republican regime of Makkah in the least, nor was it disturbed thereby.

The Call of Muhammad and Modern Scientific Inquiry

The reader may be surprised by our emphasis on the similarity of Muhammad's teaching to the methods of modern science. The scientific method demands that were one to undertake an investigation, he should suspend his personal views, beliefs and doctrines. It demands that he begin his study by observation, classification, comparison, experimentation, and then draw his conclusions from these scientific observations as premises. A conclusion reached through this method is scientific and, by the same token, it remains susceptible to further scrutiny and investigation. It remains valid as long as further scientific study has not disproved anyone of the premises on which it is based. This scientific method is the highest human achievement in the cause of free thought. And yet this very method is none other than that of Muhammad, the very foundation of his cause. How did his followers become convinced of it? They repudiated all their previous beliefs and began to concentrate their thoughts on what lay before them. But what was before them? What were the facts of religious life in Arabia? Every one of the Arab tribes had its own idols; but which one was true and which false? Besides, within Arabia as well as in the surrounding countries, there were Christians, Jews, Sabeans, Zoroastrian fire-worshippers, and others who worshipped the sun. Whose faith was true and whose false?

The Essence of Muhammad's Call

Suppose we lay all this aside and completely avoid its influence upon our minds and hearts. Suppose we cut ourselves loose from every view and every doctrine we have previously entertained. And suppose we observe and consider. The first truth to stand out is that every being is somehow connected with all other beings. In the case of man, the clans, the tribes, and nations are obviously interconnected. Man is also connected with the animals and the world of things. This earth of ours is connected with the sun, the moon, and all the heavenly bodies.

Necessary and immutable laws regulate and govern all these interconnections. Neither may the sun overtake the moon nor the night overtake the day. If anyone being in the universe were to alter or change these laws, the cosmos itself would change and would no more be what it is. If the sun, for instance, failed to provide the earth with light and heat and thus violate the laws by which nature has been running for millions of years, the earth and the sky would not be what they are. As long as this does not happen it is not possible for the totality of the cosmos to hold itself together except by a moving spirit,
a spirit from which it has arisen and has developed and to which it must return. This spirit alone is that to which man should be subject. Everything else in this universe is subject to that spirit just as man is. Man, the cosmos, space, and time are therefore a unity; and this spirit is the origin and substance of this unity. To this spirit alone therefore belongs worship. To this spirit alone all minds and hearts should be oriented. Everywhere in this universe we should be able by reason and meditation to discover this spirit's eternal laws. Hence, whatever men worship besides God — be it idols, kings, Pharaohs, fire, or sun — is a falsehood and an illusion unworthy of man, of human reason, of the human capacity to discover the laws of God through examination of the creation with which God has endowed man.

That is the essence of the message of Muhammad as the early Muslims knew it. It was conveyed to them by Muhammad as a revelation cast into such sublime form that it is still regarded as a miracle. This revelation has combined the truth of content with the perfection of form. Upon contact with it, the souls of the Muslims became ennobled, and their hearts were moved to seek communion with the noble spirit of Muhammad. Muhammad led them to the realization that good works constitute the road of felicity and that men shall be rewarded for their works on the day they complete in piety their duties in this world, *i.e.*

when every soul shall receive its due. "And whosoever does an atom's weight of good shall be rewarded therefor, and whosoever does an atom's weight of evil shall be punished therefor."[10]

What great and ennobling respect for human reason! What sweeping destruction of all the impediments that stand in the way of human reason! Sufficient is it to man to understand this for him to appreciate it, to believe in it, and to realize what it demands of him to rise to the highest level of humanity. As long as one takes his stand on the side of reason, every sacrifice demanded by such heights seems easy.

The Conversion of Hamzah

The majestic stand of Muhammad and of his followers convinced Banu Hashim and Banu al Muttalib to strengthen their protection of him. Once, on encountering Muhammad on the road, Abu Jahl insulted him and abused his new religion. Muhammad did not answer him and walked away. Hamzah, Muhammad's uncle and brother-in-nursing, still followed the religion of Quraysh and was very strong and fear-inspiring. He was an addicted hunter who would circumambulate the Ka'bah every time he returned from a hunting trip and before he entered his home. As he entered the city on the day that Abu Jahl insulted Muhammad and learned of what had happened to his nephew, he became furious, and went straight to the Ka'bah. Upon entering the Mosque, he did not greet anyone as he used to do. Rather, he went straight to Abu Jahl and hit him very hard with his bow. Some members of Banu Makhzum rose to the help of Abu Jahl, but Abu Jahl pushed them aside. He acknowledged that he had insulted Muhammad and then decided that the dispute had better be cut short rather than allowed to spread. Hamzah then declared his conversion to Islam, took the oath of allegiance to Muhammad and promised to sacrifice everything for the sake of God.

Delegation of 'Utbah ibn Rabi'ah

Undaunted by any harm or injury that befell them, their faith unshaken, the Muslims kept on increasing in numbers and strength. They proclaimed their faith loudly and performed their prayers publicly — all to the alarm of Quraysh, who were at a loss what to do next. For a moment they thought that they could get rid of Muhammad by satisfying what they took to be his personal ambitions. Obviously they forgot the greatness of the Islamic call, the purity of its spiritual essence, and its noble transcendence of any political partisanship. 'Utbah ibn Rabi'ah, one of the distinguished leaders of Arabia, convinced the Quraysh at one of their community meetings to delegate him to approach Muhammad with a number of alternative offerings of which, he thought, Muhammad would surely accept one. He therefore went to Muhammad and said, "O Nephew, you certainly enjoy among us great eminence and noble lineage, and you have brought about a great issue and divided your people. Listen to me for I am about to make several offers to you, certain as I am that one of them will prove satisfactory to you. If by bringing about the conflict you did, you have sought to achieve some wealth, know that we are prepared to give you of our wealth until you become the richest man among us. If, on the other hand, you desired honor and power, we would make you our chief and endow you with such power that nothing could be done without your consent. Even if you wanted to be a king, we should not hesitate to crown you king over us. Finally, if you are unable to cure yourself of the visions that you have been seeing, we shall be happy to seek for you at our expense all the medical service possible until your health is perfectly restored." When he finished, Muhammad recited to him the *surah* "al Sajdah."[11] 'Utbah listened attentively to the divine recitation. Facing him was a man devoid of all ambition for wealth, prestige, honor, power, or sovereignty. Neither was he sick. Facing him was indeed a man telling the truth, calling to the good, answering him with arguments yet more soundly and sublimely expressed than any he had ever heard. When Muhammad finished, 'Utbah returned to Quraysh spellbound by the beauty and sublimity of what he had seen and heard and by the greatness of this man and his eloquence. The Quraysh were obviously not happy with this turn, nor did they agree with 'Utbah's opinion that they should leave Muhammad for all the Arabs together to deal with; they would thereby reap a harvest of pride in the event that Muhammad wins, or enjoy an effortless victory in the event he loses. In fact, Quraysh resumed their attacks upon Muhammad and his followers, intensified their aggression, and inflicted upon his companions all sorts of injuries from which Muhammad was saved only through the protection of Abu Talib, Banu Hashim, and Banu al Muttalib.

Emigration to Abyssinia

Makkan persecution of the Muslims increased in intensity. Many Muslims now became so subject to torture and murder that Muhammad instructed them to disperse throughout the world. When they asked where they should go, he advised them to escape to Abyssinia, the Christian kingdom — where "a king rules without injustice, a land of truthfulness — until God leads us to a way out of our difficulty." Fearful of Makkan persecution and desirous of worshipping God in peace and freedom, a number of Muslims emigrated to Abyssinia at Muhammad's advice. The first group to emigrate included eleven men and four women. After secretly leaving Makkah, they arrived in Abyssinia where they lived under the protection of the Negus until they heard that the Muslims in Makkah had become secure against Quraysh's attacks, as we shall see a little later. When upon return they found the Quraysh's persecution stronger than it ever was before, they emigrated once more to Abyssinia, this time about eighty men strong, not counting women and children. This larger group of Muslims lived in Abyssinia until after the Prophet's emigration to Yathrib. Their emigration to Abyssinia is usually referred to as "the first emigration in Islam."

Quraysh's Delegation to the Negus

It is perfectly appropriate for the biographer of Muhammad to ask whether the purpose of this emigration undertaken by the Muslims at the advice and command of Muhammad was merely to escape from the pagans of Makkah and their persecution and harm. Or was it dictated by an Islamic political strategy by which Muhammad sought to realize a higher objective? These questions are indeed proper when we consider that the whole history of the Arab Prophet confirms ever more clearly that he was a profound and far-sighted statesman in addition to being the carrier of the divine message and a man of unrivaled discipline and magnanimity. What makes this matter especially questionable is the report that the Makkans were so upset at this exodus of the Muslims to Abyssinia that they immediately sent a delegation to the Negus carrying precious gifts in order to bring about the emigrants' extradition and return to Makkah. Abyssinia, as well as its Negus, were all Christians and, therefore, there was no fear that they might follow the religion of Muhammad. Did the Makkans then fear that the Negus' protection of the Muslims might provide support for the cause of Muhammad's religion within Arabia? Or did they think that the Muslim emigrants would one day return greater in numbers, wealth, and power in order to wage a retaliatory war against them?

The two ambassadors, 'Amr ibn al 'As and 'Abdullah ibn Abu Rabi'ah, presented to the Negus and his patriarch their precious gifts and asked for permission to have the Muslim emigrants extradited and sent back to Makkah. They said to the Negus, "O King! A number of ignoble plebeians from Makkah have taken refuge in your county. They have apostasized from the religion of their people and have not joined your religion. They follow a new religion, known neither to us nor to you, which they created. The leading noblemen of Makkah, who are their parents, uncles, and relatives, have sent us to you to ask for their return. Their elders at home are better judges of the differences between them" The two ambassadors had already obtained the approval of the patriarch for extradition without prior reference of the matter to the Negus. Apparently, the Makkan gifts to the patriarch were instrumental in obtaining this summary decision. The Negus, however, refused to concur in the judgment of his patriarch until he had had a chance to hear the refugees plead their own case. He sent after them and asked, "What is this new religion which caused you to separate yourselves from your people, a religion which is different from mine as well as from any other of the known religions?"

The Muslims' Answer to the Ambassadors' Claims

Ja'far ibn Abu Talib rose and said in answer, "O King! We were in a state of ignorance and immorality, worshipping idols, eating carrion, committing all sorts of iniquity. We honored no relative and assisted no neighbor. The strong among us exploited the weak. Then God sent us a prophet, one of our own people, whose lineage, truthfulness, loyalty, and purity were well known to us. He called us to worship God alone and to repudiate all the stones and idols which we and our ancestors used to worship. He commanded us always to tell the truth, to remain true to trust and promise, to assist the relative, to be good neighbors, to abstain from blood and things forbidden, and to avoid fornication, perjury, and false witness. He commanded us not to rob the wealth of the orphan or falsely to accuse the married woman. He ordered us to worship God alone and never to associate any other being with Him, to hold prayers, to fast, and to pay the zakat (the five pillars of Islam were here enumerated and explained). We believed in him and what he brought to us from God and followed him in what he enjoined and forbade. Our people, however, tried to sway us away from our religion and persecuted us and inflicted upon us great suffering that we might re-enter into the immoral practices of old.

As they vanquished and berated us unjustly and made life intolerable for
us in Makkah, we chose you and your country and came thither to live
under your protection in justice and peace." Thereupon the Negus asked,
"Will you show me some of the revelation which your Prophet claims to
have come to him from God?" Ja'far answered, "Yes!" and recited to the
Negus the *surah* of Mary from its beginning until the following verses:

فَأَشَارَتْ إِلَيْهِ ۖ قَالُوا كَيْفَ نُكَلِّمُ مَنْ كَانَ فِي الْمَهْدِ صَبِيًّا ۝ قَالَ إِنِّي عَبْدُ اللَّهِ ۖ أَتَانِيَ الْكِتَٰبَ
وَجَعَلَنِي نَبِيًّا ۝ وَجَعَلَنِي مُبَارَكًا أَيْنَ مَا كُنْتُ وَأَوْصَانِي بِالصَّلَوٰةِ وَالزَّكَوٰةِ مَا دُمْتُ حَيًّا ۝
وَبَرًّا بِوَالِدَتِي وَلَمْ يَجْعَلْنِي جَبَّارًا شَقِيًّا ۝ وَالسَّلَامُ عَلَيَّ يَوْمَ وُلِدْتُ وَيَوْمَ أَمُوتُ وَيَوْمَ
أُبْعَثُ حَيًّا

"Mary, therefore, pointed to the child as her only answer. Her people
asked, 'How can we inquire of an infant in the cradle?' At this, Jesus spoke,
'I am the servant of God to whom He has given the Book and whom He
has blessed and commissioned with prophethood; whom He has enjoined
with holding the prayer and giving the *zakat* as long as he lives. My mother is innocent and I am neither unjust nor evil. Peace be upon me on the
day I was born, on the day I shall die, and on the day I shall be resurrected."[12]

Answers of the Negus and the Patriarchs

When the patriarchs heard this statement confirming as it did the
message of the Evangel, they were pleasantly surprised and said: "These
words must have sprung from the same fountainhead from which the
words of our master Jesus Christ have sprung." The Negus then said,
"What you have just recited and that which was revealed to Moses must
have both issued from the same source. Go forth into my kingdom; I shall
not extradite you at all." On the following day, 'Amr ibn al 'As returned to
the Negus and pleaded, "There is another side to the Muslims' new religion in which they judge Jesus, Son of Mary, in totally different but con-
demnable terms." The Negus sent after the Muslims, brought them back
into his presence and asked them to tell him more about Jesus. The same
Ja'far ibn Abu Talib answered for them, "Our judgment of Jesus is exactly
the same as that which was revealed to our Prophet; namely, that Jesus is
the servant of God, His Prophet, His spirit, His command given unto
Mary, the innocent virgin." The Negus drew a line on the floor with his

cane and said with great joy, "Between your religion and ours there is really no more difference than this line." Thus the Negus was convinced, after hearing the two parties, that the Muslims not only acknowledged Jesus and Christianity as true religion but worshipped the same God as well. The Muslims found under his protection the peace and tranquility they sought, and lived in his country until they found cause to return while Muhammad was still in Makkah. Apparently they had been misinformed that Quraysh's antagonism to the Muslims had subsided. When they discovered that the Makkans were still persecuting Muhammad and his followers, they returned to Abyssinia, this time eighty strong besides women and children. The question remains, however, whether these two emigrations were merely for escape from injury or were, at least in the foresight of Muhammad alone, devised for a political motive which the historian ought to investigate and clarify.

The Muslims and Abyssinian Christianity

The historian may certainly ask why Muhammad trusted that his companions and followers would go to a country whose religion was Christianity, a scriptural religion, and whose prophet was Jesus, whom Islam acknowledged as prophet and in whose message it concurred, without fearing that they might be exposed to abjuring their faith even though in favor of one different from that of Quraysh. How did he trust that his followers would remain faithful and loyal when Abyssinia was a far more fertile and affluent country than that of Quraysh? One of the Muslims that emigrated to Abyssinia did, in fact convert to Christianity, thus establishing that the danger was real. It was natural for Muhammad to have felt such fears, especially since Muhammad, himself, was still weak and his old followers were still in great doubt as to his ability to protect them or to come to their rescue. Assuming, therefore, Muhammad's great intelligence and foresight, his charity, kindness and compassion, it is most likely that such fears must have stirred within his soul. But he felt absolutely secure in this regard. Islam was on that day, as it was to remain throughout the Prophet's life, absolutely pure and unspoiled by internal doubts, divisions, and deviations. On the other hand, Abyssinian Christianity, like the Christianity of Najran, al Hirah, and al Sham, was mixed up with devious doctrines brought into the faith by the apotheosizers of Mary, the apotheosizers of Jesus, and the opponents of both. The Muslims, drawing directly from the pure fountainhead of prophetic revelation, could not possibly stand in any danger of being swayed by any such confusion.

The Spirit in Islam

In actual fact, most religions did not survive for a number of generations without becoming polluted by some kind of idolatry. Even if it were not of the same ignoble kind prevalent in early days in the Arabian Peninsula, it was still some form of idolatry. Islam is diametrically opposed to idolatry in any form or kind. From the earliest days of church history Christianity has accorded to the priesthood a special status in the religion itself; Islam has never given such position to anyone. On the contrary, Islam both condemned the priesthood and transcended it. Then as now, Islam has remained precisely the religion which enables the human soul to rise to the greatest heights. It has not tolerated any link between man and God except a person's own piety and good works and his wishing for his fellow men that which he wishes for himself. Nothing — neither idols nor priesthood, diviners nor officiators — could prevent the human soul from rising to a consciousness of unity with ultimate reality and to a unity of good will and good works, and, thereby, from winning its great reward with God. The human soul! That spirit which is from God! That spirit which is connected to eternal time! That spirit, which as long as it does the good, is not separated from God by anything whatever and is subject to no being whatever other than God. The rich, the mighty, and the evil can all lay hold upon the body. They can torture it and prevent it from realizing its passions and pleasures. They can even destroy it and rob it of its life. But they can never reach the soul as long as that person wants the soul to rise above matter, above power, and above time to link itself with ultimate, total reality! Only on the Day of Judgment will the human soul receive the punishment or reward that is its due. On that Day no father may take the place of his son, and no son may replace his father. On that Day neither the wealth of the rich, the strength of the mighty, nor the argument of the eloquent will avail them. Good works will be the only witness and the only defense for or against their author. On that Day, all being — its eternal past as well as its eternal future — will stand as one integral unit. On that Day none will be done an injustice, and none will receive aught except his due.

How could Muhammad fear that his companions would abjure the spiritual meaning and values which he had so well inculcated upon their hearts? Why should he fear that they might be diverted from this conviction and faith when his example was ever present to them in his own person, so beloved of them that they cherished him more than themselves, their families and people? How could there be any chance of their deviation from the faith when Muhammad's resolution not to abjure the cause even if they should place the sun in his right hand and the moon in his left hand is a living reality, ever present to their minds? How could they abjure their faith when the spirit of Muhammad filled their being with the light of conviction, wisdom, justice, goodness, truth, and beauty; when their character and ethos had been molded by Muhammad's humility, charity, loving kindness, and compassion? Muhammad felt at ease toward the emigration of his companions to Abyssinia. The religious freedom and security the emigrants enjoyed under the Negus had caused the Quraysh no little embarrassment. That the Muslims were free among total strangers but persecuted by their own relatives, despite the closest bonds of family and tribe, must have been an annoying spectacle for Quraysh. It must have hurt their tribal pride to see their fellow tribesmen enjoy security and peace after having been subjected to all kinds of injustice and injury. After the victims had suffered much despair and helplessness, they began to see in suffering and patience, although this view runs counter to the logic of Islam, a very rapprochement to God, an attunement of themselves to His mercy.

The Conversion of 'Umar ibn al Khattab

At that time, 'Umar ibn al Khattab was a mature man of thirty to thirty-five years of age. Physically he was well built and strong of muscle. Temperamentally he was capable of strong passion. He loved wine and amusement, and despite his very harshness of character, he was gentle and compassionate toward his people. As for the Muslims, he was one of their strongest opponents, a merciless aggressor upon their peace, security and religion. Their emigration to Abyssinia and the Negus's protection of them caused him no little resentment. His pride as a national of Makkah was wounded by the fact that a foreign king and country were protecting Makkans who can find neither security nor peace in their own homes. Muhammad was meeting one day with his own companions in a house in al Safa quarter of Makkah. Among those present were his uncle Hamzah, his cousin, 'Ali ibn Abu Talib, Abu Bakr ibn Abu Quhafah, and other Muslims. 'Umar learned of their meeting and went there resolved to kill Muhammad and thus relieve the Quraysh of its burden, restore its ravaged unity, and re-establish respect for the gods that Muhammad had castigated. On the road to Makkah he was met by Nu'aym ibn 'Abdullah. Upon learning what 'Umar was about, Nu'aym said, "By God, you have deceived yourself, O 'Umar! Do you think that Banu 'Abd Manaf would let you run around alive once you had killed their son Muhammad? Why don't you return to your own house and at least set it straight?" When 'Umar learned that Fatimah, his sister, and her husband, Sa'id ibn Zayd, had already been converted to Islam, he turned around and went straight to their house. Upon entering the house without knocking, he found them listening to a third person reciting the Qur'an. They, too, having heard him approach, had hid their visitor and put away the manuscript of the Qur'an from which they were reading. 'Umar asked, "What is this cantillation that I have heard as I walked in?" The pair denied hearing anything.

Flying into a rage, 'Umar told them that he knew that they had foresworn their faith and entered into that of Muhammad. He chastised them and delivered a strong blow to his brother-in-law, Sa'id. Fatimah rose to protect her husband. As she came between the two men, 'Umar hit her on the head and caused her to bleed. At this, the pair lost their fear entirely and said together, "Yes, indeed! We have become Muslims. Do what you will!" At this surge of courage, as well as upon seeing the blood of his sister flow, 'Umar was moved. After calming down a little, he asked his sister to let him see the manuscript which she and her husband had been reading together. After she surrendered the manuscript to him, he read it and his face changed to an expression of regret for what he had just done. As for what he had just read, he was deeply shaken by its beauty, its majesty, the nobility of its call, and the magnanimity of its message. In short, 'Umar's good side got the better of him. He left the house of his sister, his heart mellow and his soul reassured by the new certainty which he had just discovered. He went straight to al Safa, where Muhammad was meeting with his companions, sought permission to enter, and declared his conversion to Islam in front of the Prophet. The Muslims acclaimed his conversion and found therein, as they did in the conversion of Hamzah, new security for the community as a whole.

The conversion of 'Umar divided the Quraysh further. It reduced their power and caused them to reconsider their strategy. In fact, it increased Muslim power so greatly and so significantly that both they and the Quraysh had to change their positions *vis-a-vis* each other. Moreover, it triggered a whole line of events in inspiring new levels of sacrifices and stirring new forces which, together, led to the emigration of Muhammad and to the inception of the political side of his career.

Courtyard of Qarawiyyin Mosque, Fez, Morocco.

6

The Story of the Goddesses

The Emigrants Return from Abyssinia

The emigrants resided in Abyssinia three months during which 'Umar ibn al Khattab converted to Islam. In their exile, they heard that upon 'Umar's conversion the Quraysh had stopped their persecution of Muhammad and his followers. According to one report a number of them had returned to Makkah, according to another, all. On reaching Makkah they realized that the Quraysh had resumed persecution of the Muslims with stronger hatred and renewed vigor. Unable to resist, a number of them returned to Abyssinia while others entered Makkah under the cover of night and hid themselves away. It is also reported that those who returned took with them a number of new converts to Abyssinia where they were to stay until after the emigration to Madinah and the establishment of Muslim political power.

We may ask what incited the Muslims of Abyssinia to return to Makkah three months after their emigration. It is at this stage that the story of the goddesses is told by ibn Sa'd in his *Al Tabaqat al Kubra*, by al Tabari in his *Tarikh al Rusul wa al Muluk*, as well as by a number of Muslim exegetes and biographers. This story arrested the attention of the western Orientalists who took it as true and repeated it *ad nauseam*. This story tells that realizing how alienated the Quraysh had become and how intensely they had persecuted his companions, Muhammad expressed the wish that a revelation might come that would reconcile his people rather

100

than further alienate them. When, one day, he was sitting with the Quraysh in one of their club houses around the Ka'bah, he recited to them *surah* "al Najm." After reading the verses, "Would you consider al Lat and al 'Uzzil? as well as Manat, the third goddess?"[1] he continued the recitation with the statement, "They are the goddesses on high. Their intercession is worthy of being sought." He then proceeded with his reading of the *surah* as we know it. When he finished he prostrated himself, and all the Quraysh likewise followed him. At this moment, the Quraysh proclaimed its satisfaction with what the Prophet had read and said, "We have always known that God creates and gives life, gives food, and resuscitates. But our gods intercede for us with Him. Now that you have allowed for them a place in your new religion, we are all with you." Thus the difference between Muhammad and the Quraysh was dissolved. When the news of this reconciliation reached Abyssinia, the Muslims there decided to return to their beloved country and people. As they reached the approaches of Makkah, they met some Kinanah tribesmen who informed them that Muhammad allowed the gods a good position in his religion, reconciled the Quraysh, and was now followed by everyone. The story then relates how Muhammad reverted by blaspheming those gods and the Quraysh reverted to persecution. It further adds that the returnees stopped to consider what their next course should be. They longed so much to see their relatives and next of kin that they went ahead and entered Makkah.

Other versions of the same story give detailed descriptions of Muhammad's attitude toward the gods of Quraysh. They claimed that Quraysh's plea that if he but grant their gods a share in his religion the Makkans would all support him, troubled the Prophet. They relate how Muhammad one evening reviewed *surah* "al Najm" with Gabriel when the latter made a timely appearance. When he arrived at the sentence in question, Gabriel asked where it came from. Muhammad answered, "I must have attributed to God that which He did not say." God then revealed the following verses: "They have almost succeeded in inducing you, under promise of their friendship, to attribute to Us, against Our command, that which We did not reveal to you. Had We not confirmed you in your faith, you might have been tempted and hence fallen under the inescapable punishment."[2] Thereafter, Muhammad returned to his condemnation of the gods, and Quraysh returned to their persecution.

Incoherence of the Story

Such is the story of the goddesses reported by more than one biographer, pointed to by more than one exegete of the Qur'an, and singled out and repeated by a number of western Orientalists. It is a story whose incoherence is evident upon the least scrutiny. It contradicts the infallibility of every prophet in conveying the message of his Lord. All the more wonder, therefore, that some Muslim scholars have accepted it as true. Ibn Ishaq, for his part, did not hesitate at all to declare it a fabrication by the *zindiqs*.[3] Those who were taken in by it rationalized it further with the verse, "Every prophet We sent before you was such that whenever he pressed for revelation to come, Satan would hasten to inspire him with something satisfying his wish and thus necessitate God's abrogation of it if scripture is to be kept absolutely pure and true. God is all-wise and all-knowing. That which Satan had given is a lure for those who are sick of mind and hard of heart. Surely the unjust are deep in error."[4] Some explain the word *"tamanna"* in the foregoing verse as meaning "to read;" others give it the usual meaning of "to press wishfully." Muslim and Western scholars who accept the story explain that the Prophet suffered heavily from the persecution the unbelievers directed at his companions. They tell how the unbelievers killed some Muslims, exposed others to burning by the sun while pinned down to the ground with heavy stones (as was the case with Bilal), and how these sufferings pressured Muhammad to permit his companions to migrate to Abyssinia. They underscore Quraysh's alienation and the psychological effect of their boycott upon the Prophet. Since Muhammad was very anxious to convert them to Islam and to save them from idol worship, they claim that his thinking of reconciling them by adding a few verses to *surah* "al Najm" is not farfetched. Finally, they allege that Muhammad's jubilation was all too natural when, coming to the end of his recitation and prostrating himself, the Quraysh joined in, showing their preparation to follow him now that he had given a share to their gods with God.

To these tales of some books of biography and exegesis, Sir William Muir adds what he thinks is a final and conclusive proof. He says that the emigrants to Abyssinia had hardly spent three months there during which the Negus had tolerated as well as protected them when they decided to return to Makkah. Had they not heard news of a reconciliation between Muhammad and Quraysh nothing would have caused them to return so soon. But, reasons Muir, how could there be reconciliation between Muhammad and Quraysh without a determined effort to that effect on the part of Muhammad? In Makkah, the Muslims had then been far fewer and weaker than the Quraysh. They were still incapable of protecting themselves against the injuries which the Quraysh had been inflicting upon them. Why, then, should the Quraysh have taken the initiative in such reconciliation?

Refutation of These Arguments

These are the arguments on which stands the claim for veracity of the story of the goddesses. They are all false, incapable of standing any scrutiny or analysis. Let us begin with the argument of the Orientalist Muir. The Muslims who returned from Abyssinia did so for two reasons. First, 'Umar ibn al Khattab was converted to Islam shortly after their emigration. With him, he brought to the Muslim camp the same boldness, determination, and the tribal standing with which he had been fighting the Muslims before. He never concealed his conversion nor did he ever shun the Quraysh opponents. On the contrary, he proclaimed his conversion publicly and challenged the Quraysh openly. He did not approve the Muslim's concealment of themselves, their secret movement from one end of Makkah to the other, and their holding of prayers at a safe distance from any Quraysh attack. 'Umar began to fight the Quraysh as soon as he entered the faith of Islam, constantly pressed his way close to the Ka'bah, and performed his prayer there in company with whatever Muslims that decided to join him. It was at this new challenging turn of events that the Quraysh came to the realization that any further injury inflicted upon Muhammad or his companions would henceforth create a civil war of which nobody knew the consequences. By this time, a great number of men from the various clans of Quraysh had joined Islam. To kill anyone of these would necessarily imply the rise to war not only of his fellow Muslims but of all the clans of which the various Muslims or allies were members, even though the rest of the clan or the tribe were still of a different religion. After the conversion of 'Umar and the entry of so many members of other clans into the faith, it became impossible to fight Muhammad in the same way as before. Such a course could easily expose the whole of Quraysh to terrible peril. It was necessary to find a new way which did not incur such risks, and until such way was found, the Quraysh thought it advantageous to enter into an armistice with Muhammad and the Muslims. It was this news which reached the emigrants in Makkah and prompted them to return home.

Two Revolutions in Abyssinia

The emigrants would have hesitated to return to Makkah were it not for another reason. A revolution broke out against the Negus in which his personal faith as well as his protection of the Muslims were under attack. For their part, the Muslims had prayed and wished that God would give the Negus victory over his enemies. But they could not participate in such a conflict since they were foreigners who arrived there too recently. When, at the same time, they heard of the news of an armistice between Muhammad and Quraysh favorable to the Muslims and protecting them from injury, they decided to escape from the Abyssinian revolution and return home. That is exactly what all or some of them did. They hardly reached Makkah, however, when Quraysh decided upon a course of action against the Muslims and entered into a pact with their allies to boycott Banu Hashim completely in order to prevent any intermarriage with them and to stop any purchase by or sale to them. As soon as this new alliance was concluded, open war broke out again. The returning Muslims sought immediately to re-emigrate and take with them all those who could manage to go. These were to meet greater difficulties as the Quraysh sought to impede their move. What caused the Muslims to return from Abyssinia, therefore, was not, as Orientalist Muir claims, the reconciliation of Muhammad with Quraysh. Rather, it was the armistice to which the Quraysh was compelled to resort following the conversion of 'Umar and his bold support of the religion of God with his tribal relations. The so-called reconciliation, therefore, constitutes no evidence for the story of the goddesses.

Inverted Evidence of the Qur'anic Text

As for the argument of some biographers and exegetes that the verses, "They had almost succeeded in inducing you. . ."[5] and "Every prophet We sent before you was such that, whenever he pressed for revelation. . ."[6] constitute evidence for the story of the goddesses, it is yet more incoherent than that of Sir Muir. It is sufficient to remember that the first group of verses include the statement, "Had We not confirmed you in your faith, you might have been tempted." This group shows that even if Satan had actually hastened to inspire Muhammad with something satisfying his wish and thus induced him to favor the unbelievers, God had confirmed the Prophet in his faith and prevented him from falling to the temptation. Had Muhammad really fallen, God would have inflicted upon him inescapable punishment. The point is, precisely, that he did not fall. Hence, these verses prove the opposite of what "these advocates assume them to prove. The story of the goddesses asserts that Muhammad did indeed incline toward the Quraysh, that the Quraysh had indeed induced him to add to the divine word, and that he indeed did attribute to God that which God had not said. The text, on the other hand, tells us the exact opposite, namely that God confirmed him in his faith and that he did not add to the divine word. Moreover, we should well bear in mind the fact that the books of exegesis and the books dealing with the causes and circumstances of revelation — regardless of whether or not they subscribe to the story in question — affirm that these verses had been revealed at a time other than that during which the story of the goddesses had presumably taken place. To resort to the story of the goddesses in order to disprove the infallibility of the prophets in their conveyance of divine messages not only runs counter to the whole history of Muhammad but constitutes a fallacy of incoherent reasoning and, hence, a futile and perverse argument.

As for "Every prophet We sent before you...," these verses are utterly devoid of relation to the story of the goddesses. Moreover, they clearly affirm that God will abrogate all that the devil may bring forth, that Satan's work is only a lure to those who are sick of mind and hard of heart, and that God, the all-wise and all-knowing, would keep His scripture absolutely pure and true.

Fallacious Reasoning of the Claim

Let us now turn to a critical and scientific analysis of the story. The first evidence which imputes suspicion to the story is the fact that it has been reported in many forms and versions. First there is the report that the fabricated verses consist of the following words: *"Tilka al gharaniq al 'ula; wa inna shafa'atahunna laturtaja."* Others reported them as consisting of, *"al gharaniqah al 'ula: inna shafa'atahum turtaja."* Still others reported that they consist of the following words, *"Inna shafa-'atahunna turtaja"* without mentioning the word *"al gharaniq"* or *"al gharaniqah"* at all. According to a fourth version, they were supposed to consist of the words: *"Innaha lahiya al gharaniq al 'ula."* A fifth version reads, *"Wa innahunna lahunna al gharaniq al 'ula wa inna shafa'atahunna lahiya allati turtaja."* The collections of Hadith have given us still more varied versions. The multiplicity of the versions proves that the report itself is fabricated, that it had been fabricated by the *zindiqs* — as ibn Ishaq had said earlier — and that the forgers had sought thereby to spread doubt into the message of Muhammad and to attack his candidness in conveying the message of his Lord.

The Story's Violence to the Contextual Flow of Surah "al Najm"

Another proof of the falsity of the story, stronger and more conclusive than the foregoing, is the fact that the contextual flow of *surah* "al Najm" does not allow at all the inclusion of such verses as the story claims. The *surah* reads:

لَقَدْ رَأَىٰ مِنْ آيَاتِ رَبِّهِ الْكُبْرَىٰ ۝ أَفَرَأَيْتُمُ اللَّاتَ وَالْعُزَّىٰ ۝ وَمَنَوٰةَ الثَّالِثَةَ الْأُخْرَىٰ ۝ أَلَكُمُ الذَّكَرُ
وَلَهُ الْأُنثَىٰ ۝ تِلْكَ إِذًا قِسْمَةٌ ضِيزَىٰ ۝ إِنْ هِيَ إِلَّا أَسْمَاءٌ سَمَّيْتُمُوهَا أَنتُمْ وَآبَاؤُكُم مَّا أَنزَلَ اللَّهُ بِهَا
مِن سُلْطَانٍ إِن يَتَّبِعُونَ إِلَّا الظَّنَّ وَمَا تَهْوَى الْأَنفُسُ وَلَقَدْ جَاءَهُم مِّن رَّبِّهِمُ الْهُدَىٰ ۝

"He has witnessed many of the great signs of his lord. Would you consider the case of al Lat, al 'Uzza, and of Manat, the third goddess? Would you then ascribe to God the females and to yourselves the males? Wouldn't that be a wretched ascription? All these are nothing but names, mere names which you and your ancestors had coined. Men are so prone to follow opinion! They credulously fall for the product of their own wishful thinking. But true guidance has indeed come from the Lord."

The logical and literary flow of these verses is crystal-clear. *Al Lat* and *al 'Uzza* are mere names devoid of substance given by the past and present unbelievers to works of their own creation. There is no deity such as the words name. The context does not allow any such addition as is here claimed. If, assuming such addition, the text were now to read: "Would you consider the case of al Lat, al 'Uzza, and of Manat, the third goddess? These are the goddesses on high. Their intercession is to be sought. Would you then ascribe to God the females and to yourselves the males? Wouldn't that be a wretched ascription?" its corruption and outright self-contradiction become obvious. The text would have praised al Lat, al 'Uzza, and Manat as well as condemned them within the space of four consecutive verses. Such a text cannot proceed from any rational being. The contextual background in which the addition is supposed to have been made furnishes unquestionable and final evidence that the story of the goddesses was a forgery. The forgers were probably the *zindiqs;* and the credulous whose minds are not naturally repulsed by the irrational and the incoherent, accepted the forgery and passed it as true.

The Linguistic Evidence

There is yet another argument advanced by the late Shaykh Muhammad 'Abduh. It consists of the fact that the Arabs have nowhere described their gods in such terms as "al gharaniq." Neither in their poetry nor in their speeches or traditions do we find their gods or goddesses described in such terms. Rather, the word *"al ghurnuq"* or *"al gharniq"* was the name of a black or white water bird, sometimes given figuratively to the handsome blond youth. The fact is indubitable that the Arabs never looked upon their gods in this manner.

The Story Contradicts the Fact of Muhammad's Candidness

There is yet one more final argument against the story of the goddesses that is based upon the nature of Muhammad's personal life. Ever since his childhood and throughout his adolescence, adulthood and maturity, he was never known to lie. So truthful was he that he had been nicknamed "al Amin" before he reached his twenty-fifth year of age. His truthfulness was unquestioned by anyone. He himself once addressed the Quraysh after his commission to prophethood: "Suppose I were to tell you that an enemy cavalry was advancing on the other side of this mountain, would you believe me?" His enemies themselves answered: "Yes, indeed! As far as we are concerned, you are innocent, for we have never found you to lie at all." How can we believe that such a man who had been known to be truthful in his relations with his fellow men from childhood to maturity, would be any less candid in his relation to God? How could such constant truthfulness allow him to lie and ascribe to his God that which He had not said? How could we believe that such a man did so in fear of the people and defiance of Almighty God? That is utterly impossible. Its impossibility is evident to all those who have studied these great; strong and distinguished souls of the prophets and religious leaders known for their dedication to the truth *pereat mundus.* How can we reconcile such an allegation with Muhammad's great declaration to his uncle that he will not adjure this cause even if his foes should put the sun in his right hand and the moon in his left? How can we accept such a claim when it imputes to the Prophet the heinous charge of attributing to God that which God had not said, of violating the very foundation of the religion he was commissioned to proclaim and teach to mankind?

Furthermore, we may ask, when, according to the story, did Muhammad turn to praise the gods of Quraysh? Ten years or so after his commission to prophethood is the reply. But, then that is also after ten years of patient sufferance of all kinds of injury and harm, all kinds of sacrifices, after God had reinforced Islam with the conversion of Hamzah and 'Umar, and, in short, after the Muslims had begun to feel themselves a significant power in Makkah and the news of their existence and exploits had begun to spread throughout Arabia, indeed to Abyssinia and other corners of the globe. Such a claim is not only uninformed, it is positively silly. The forgers of this story themselves must have realized its inadmissibility and sought to conceal its falsehood with the claim, "Muhammad hardly heard Quraysh's words of reconciliation once he granted to their gods the honor of interceding with God, when his compromise appeared to him objectionable and he felt compelled to repent and to review the text of revelation with the angel Gabriel when he visited him that same evening." This concealment, however, exposes the forgery rather than hides it. As long as the compromise appeared objectionable to Muhammad no later than he had "heard Quraysh's words of reconciliation," would he have not paused to reconsider it immediately and on the spot? How natural it would have been then for him instantly to recite the true version of the text! We may, therefore, conclude that this story of the goddesses is a fabrication and a forgery, authored by the enemies of Islam after the first century of the Hijrah.

Attack upon Tawhid

The forgers must have been extremely bold to have attempted their forgery in the most essential principal of Islam as a whole: namely, in the principle of *tawhid*, where Muhammad had been sent right from the very beginning to make proclamations to all mankind in which he has never accepted any compromise whatever; he was never swayed by anything the Quraysh had offered him whether by way of wealth or royal power. These offers had come, it must be remembered, at a time when Muhammad had very few followers within Makkah. Later persecution by the Quraysh of his companions did not succeed in swaying Muhammad away from the call of his God or away from his mission. The *zindiqs'* strategy to work their forgery around the first principle of the faith, where Muhammad was known to be the most adamant, only points to their own inconsequence. Acceptance of the forgery by the credulous only points to their naiveté in the most conspicuous of cases.

The story of the goddesses, therefore, is absolutely devoid of foundation. It is utterly unrelated to the return of the Muslims from Abyssinia. As we said earlier, the latter returned after the conversion of 'Umar, the strengthening of Islam with the same tribal solidarity with which he used to fight Islam hitherto, and the compulsion of Quraysh to enter into an armistice with the Muslims. Moreover, the Muslims' return from Abyssinia was partly due to the revolution which had broken out in that country and to their consequent fear of losing the Negus's protection. When the Quraysh learned of the Muslims' return, their fears reached a new level of intensity with the increase of Muhammad's followers within the city, and, therefore, they sought a new strategy. Their search for a new strategy was concluded with the signing of a pact in which they and their allied clans and tribes resolved to boycott the Banu Hashim in order to prevent any intermarriage with them, to stop all commercial relations and finally, to seek to kill Muhammad if they could only find the means.

7

The Malevolent Conduct
of Quraysh

The conversion of 'Umar to Islam reduced the power of Quraysh significantly in that 'Umar brought with him to the faith the tribal loyalties with which he had fought Islam earlier. He did not hide himself or conceal his Islam. On the contrary he proclaimed it to all the people and fought them for not joining him. He did not at all approve of the Muslims' hiding themselves or holding prayers in the outskirts of Makkah far beyond the Quraysh's reach. He continued to struggle against the Quraysh until he could pray near the Ka'bah where his fellow Muslims joined him. Henceforth, Quraysh became certain that no injury inflicted upon Muhammad or his companions would stop men from entering the religion of God since they could now rely upon the tribal protection of 'Umar, Hamzah, the Negus of Abyssinia, or others capable of protecting them. The Quraysh then sought a new strategy, and agreed among themselves to a written pact in which they resolved to boycott Banu Hashim and Banu 'Abd al Muttalib completely, prevent any intermarriage with them, and stop all commercial relations. The written pact itself was hung inside the Ka'bah, as was then the practice, for record and sanctification. They thought that this negative policy of boycott, isolation, and starvation would be more effective than the previous policy of harm and injury, though the latter was never stopped. The Quraysh blockaded the Muslims as well as the Banu Hashim and Banu 'Abd al Muttalib for two or three years during which time they hoped that these tribes would renounce Muhammad and thus cause him to fall under the hand of Quraysh. They

110

had hoped that such a measure would isolate Muhammad and remove all danger from his mission.

The new strategy of Quraysh served only to strengthen Muhammad's faith in God and his followers' determination to protect his person and God's religion against attack. It did not prevent the spreading of Islam, not only within the bounds of Makkah but outside of it as well. Muhammad's mission became widely known among the Arabs of the Peninsula, and the new religion became the subject of conversation everywhere. This growth, in turn, increased the fury and determination of Quraysh to oppose and fight the man who abandoned and blasphemed her gods and to prevent the spread of his cause among the Arab tribes. Loyalty of these tribes was indispensable for Makkan commerce and trade relations with other people.

The Arm of Propaganda

It is nearly impossible for us to imagine the intensity and extent of the efforts which Quraysh spent in its struggle against Muhammad, or its perseverance during many long years in that struggle. The Quraysh threatened Muhammad and his relatives, especially his uncles. It ridiculed him and his message, and it insulted him as well as his followers. It commissioned its poets to revile him with their sharpest wits and to direct their most caustic sting against his preaching. It inflicted injury and harm on his person and on the persons of his followers. It offered him bribes of money, of royalty and power, of all that which satisfies the most fastidious among men. It not only banished and dispersed his followers from their own country but injured them in their trade and commerce while impoverishing them. It warned him and his followers that war with all its tragedies would fall upon them. As a last resort, it began a boycott of them designed to starve them. All this notwithstanding, Muhammad continued to call men with kind and gentle argument unto the God of truth who sent him as a prophet and a warner. Would Quraysh lay down its arms and believe the man whom it had always known to be truthful and honest? Or would they, under the illusion that they could still win, resort to new means of hostility to save the divine status. of their idols and the hallowed position of Makkah as their museum?

No! The time had not yet come for the Quraysh to submit and to convert to the new faith. Rather, they were more apprehensive than ever when the religion began to spread outside of Makkah within the Arab tribes.

They had still another weapon which, though they had used it right from the very beginning, was yet capable of more power and damage. That was propaganda, or mental warfare, with all it implies by way of debate, counter-argument, spreading of false rumors, ridicule of the opponent's point of view, and positive apologetics in favor of their own view. The development of this weapon was not to be limited to Makkah but would apply to the whole countryside, to the whole desert, and to the tribes of the Peninsula. Threat, bribery, aggression, and gangsterism allayed the need for propaganda within Makkah. There was a great need for it, however, among the thousands who came into Makkah every year for trade or pilgrimage, and among the attendants of the markets of 'Ukaz, Majannah, and Dhu al Majaz, who later arrived at the Ka'bah for thanksgiving and worship near the Ka'bah idols. Therefore, it was expedient for the Quraysh, the moment the lines of battle against Muhammad were clearly drawn, to plan and organize its propaganda forces. It had all the more reason to do so since Muhammad himself had always taken the initiative of approaching the pilgrim and addressing him on the subject of restricting worship to God alone without associates. The idea of such initiative did not occur to Muhammad until years after his commission to prophethood. At the beginning, revelation had commanded him to warn his nearest relatives. It was only after he had warned Quraysh and those who wanted to convert had converted that his revelation commanded him now to address his warning to the Arabs as a whole. He was later to be commanded to address his call to all mankind.

The Charge of Magical Eloquence

As Muhammad began to approach the pilgrims coming from various corners of Arabia with his call to God, a number of Quraysh leaders met with al Walid ibn al Mughirah to consult for a possible strategy. What would they say regarding Muhammad to the Arabs coming for pilgrimage? Their answers to this question should be universally the same; otherwise they would constitute arguments in favor of Muhammad's claims. Some suggested that they should claim that Muhammad was a diviner. Al Walid rejected this suggestion on the grounds that what Muhammad recited was unlike the secret formulae of common diviners. Others suggested that they should claim that Muhammad was possessed or mad. Al Walid again rejected this view on the grounds that the symptoms of madness or possession were not apparent in Muhammad. Still others suggested that they should claim that Muhammad was a magician, but al Walid again rejected this view on the grounds that Muhammad did not practice the common tricks of magicians. After some discussion, al Walid suggested that they should tell the non-Makkan Arab pilgrim that Muhammad was a magician whose craft was eloquence — that by means of eloquent words he was capable of dividing the man against his father, his brother, his spouse and his own tribe. Al Walid advised that they could produce evidence for such nefarious eloquence by pointing to the division which befell Makkah after Muhammad began to practice his craft. Any consideration of the present division, internal struggle, and internecine fighting raging among the Makkans who were once the exemplars of tribal solidarity and social unity would convince the observer that Muhammad's influence had brought the worst. During the pilgrimage season the Quraysh made a special effort to warn every visitor to Makkah against ever lending his ear to Muhammad for fear that he would be mesmerized by his magic eloquence and then suffer in turn the same evils that had befallen Makkah and thus bring about a general war in Arabia detrimental to all.

Al Nadr ibn al Harith

A mental warfare of such order could not be expected to withstand or counteract Muhammad's so-called magic eloquence all alone. If genuine truth were to come on the wings of this so-called magic eloquence, what would prevent the people from accepting it? Is the acknowledgment of the distinction of the antagonist and the acknowledgment of the inferiority of the protagonist ever successful as a propaganda weapon? There must needs be other fronts on which to attack Muhammad in addition to this proposed mental warfare. Let the Quraysh seek this second front with al Nadr ibn al Harith. The said al Nadr was one of the sophisticated geniuses of Quraysh. He had studied at al Hirah the history, religion, wisdom, theories of good and evil, cosmology, and other literature of the Persians. Whenever Muhammad finished preaching his faith in an assembly calling men to God, and warning them of the consequences on the Day of Judgment — taking the bygone peoples and civilizations as examples of such divine punishment for failure to worship God — al Nadr would rise and tell his fellow Makkans about Persia and its religion. He would conclude by asking the assembly, "Why is Muhammad's speech better than mine? Does he not draw from the tales of antiquity just as I do?" The Quraysh used to memorize al Nadr's speeches and statements and circulate them around and outside Makkah as counter-measures to the claims of Muhammad and his message.

Jabr, the Christian

Muhammad used to tarry at the shop of a Christian youth called Jabr whenever he passed by the Marwah quarter of Makkah. The Quraysh took advantage of the fact and began to spread the rumor that this Christian Jabr had taught Muhammad all that he knew and that if anyone were expected to apostatize from the religion of his ancestors, the Christian should be the first one to do so. As this rumor spread, revelation itself answered the claim in the verse: "We know they claim that the Qur'an is taught to him by another man. But the man whom they suspect is Persian of tongue, whereas the tongue of this Qur'an is pure and clear Arabic."[1]

Al Tufayl ibn 'Amr al Dawsi

With this and like feats of propaganda the Quraysh sought to fight Muhammad in hope of achieving by these means more than they did by means of injury and harm to his person and followers. The clear and simple might of truth, however, shone brilliantly in Muhammad's preaching. While the struggle between the two forces continued, Islam spread more and more widely among the Arabs. When al Tufayl ibn 'Amr al Dawsi, a nobleman of great poetic talent, arrived in Makkah, he was immediately approached by the Quraysh and warned against Muhammad and his magical eloquence. They admonished him that Muhammad's craft might well divide him and his people and that his tribe might well suffer the same evil as had befallen Makkah. They asked him not to visit Muhammad or hear him if he wanted to avoid the evil. Al Tufayl, however, went one day to the Ka'bah and there heard a little of the preaching of Muhammad and liked it. He then thought, "Woe to me! Am I, the intelligent poet, the mature man, to fear that I may not distinguish between the genuinely beautiful and the really ugly in human discourse? Shouldn't I go to Muhammad, hear all that he has to say and apply my own judgment? If I should find it good, why shouldn't I accept it? And if I find it evil, surely I shall avoid it." He followed Muhammad one day to his house and there told him exactly what he thought and what he had decided. Muhammad welcomed him, presented to him the new religion, and recited for him the

Qur'an. Al Tufayl was immediately converted, recited the confession of truth, and returned to his people a missionary for Islam. He was responsible for the conversion of many, though not all, of his tribesmen. For many years, he continued his missionary activity and succeeded in converting the greater number of them. He and they joined themselves to the forces of Muhammad after the conquest of Makkah once the political structure of the Islamic community began to crystallize.

Al Tufayl ibn 'Amr al Dawsi is only one of many examples. The idol worshippers were not the only ones responding favorably to the message of Muhammad. While Muhammad was still in Makkah, twenty Christian men arrived, sent by their own people on a fact-finding mission concerning the new faith. They sat with Muhammad and asked him all kinds of questions and listened to him. They, too, were converted on the spot, believed in Muhammad and in the revelation. This conversion aroused great anger and resentment among the Quraysh. Indeed the latter addressed the new converts in these words: "Wretched fact-finding mission that you are! Your fellow religionists sent you here in order to investigate the man and bring them the factual news concerning him. But you have hardly sat down with him before you apostatized from your religion and believed him in everything he said." In vain did the Quraysh try to dissuade the Christian delegation from following Muhammad and converting to his faith. On the contrary, the Quraysh's attack against their sincerity had strengthened their faith in God and added to their monotheistic convictions since, before they heard Muhammad, they were already Christian and hence submissive to God.

Abu Sufyan, Abu Jahl, and al Akhnas

The struggle against Muhammad reached even greater proportions. The most antagonistic of the Quraysh began to ask themselves: "Is it true that this man is really calling unto the religion of truth? That what he promises us and threatens us with in the hereafter is true?" Abu Sufyan, Abu Jahl and al Akhnas ibn Shariq went out one night to hear Muhammad preach in his own house without anyone of them knowing what the other was about. Unobserved by his colleagues, each one of them took his place in some corner and spent the night listening to Muhammad preach, then pray and recite the Qur'an in the still of night, cantillating its holy verses with his beautiful voice. As dawn arrived and the three auditors repaired to their houses, they met one another on the road. Each one of them knew what the others were about and blamed the others for such behavior. Arguing that this would be a blow to the morale of the rank and file of the Quraysh if they ever knew of it, they mutually promised one another never to do it again. When the following night came, however, and the hours of yesterday struck, each one of them felt as if he were being carried to the house of Muhammad without being able to stop himself. An irresistible power was drawing them to spend another night of listening to Muhammad's prayer, preaching, and cantillation of the divine verses. Again they met one another at dawn on their way back and blamed one another anew. Even this repeated violation of their mutual threat and promise did not prevent them from going to the same place the third night. It was only after the third violation that they realized their weakness and the strong attraction they felt toward the voice of Muhammad, his faith, and Qur'anic recitation. They pledged solemnly never to return again, but what they had heard from Muhammad during the three previous nights left such a deep impression upon their souls that it disturbed their inner peace and reduced their spirit of resistance. Naturally, they were quite apprehensive that, being leaders of their people, their inner disturbance would some day be discovered by their followers and sap the morale of the whole community.

"He Frowned and Turned Away"

What prevented these men from following Muhammad? He had not asked of them either reward or power or kingship. Rather, Muhammad was a very modest man, full of love for his people, anxious to do good to them and to guide them in the true path. He was both strongly self-critical and fearful of bringing the least harm to the weak or the oppressed. In suffering the injuries inflicted upon him by others and forgiving their authors, he found peace and tranquility of conscience. Evidence of this personal characteristic of Muhammad may be found in the story of ibn Umm Maktum. Muhammad was once involved in serious conversation with al Walid ibn al Mughirah, one of the leading aristocrats of Quraysh, whom he hoped he would convert to Islam. Ibn Umm Maktum, the blind, stopped by and asked Muhammad to recite some Qur'anic verses for him. Preoccupied with his conversation, Muhammad did not answer. Ibn Umm Maktum insisted until he interrupted the conversation of the two men, to the severe annoyance of Muhammad. The conversation thus abruptly ended, Muhammad frowned, gave an angry look to the blind

man and moved on without satisfying his request. When Muhammad
carne to himself, he began to criticize himself for this maltreatment of the
blind man, and soon the following verses were revealed to him: "He
frowned and turned aside when the blind man approached him. Perhaps,
the blind man may have sought to purify himself, to remember the words
of God and to benefit therefrom. But to him who is disdainfully indiffer-
ent, you [Muhammad] pay great attention, though you are not responsible if he should never become purified. But he who came to you exerting
himself and striving in fear and reverence, him you neglected. No! No!
The whole matter is a reminder. So let him who so desires, be reminded
of it. The Qur'an is inscribed in honored sheets, exalted and purified, and
written by hands noble and virtuous."[2] If such was Muhammad's character, what did in fact prevent the Quraysh from following him and from
helping him in his cause, especially as their hearts had mellowed, as the
years had caused them to forget the obsolete traditions to which they had
lethargically attached themselves, and as they saw in Muhammad's message true majesty and perfection?

The Will to Perfection

But is it true that time makes men forget their obsolete past and
lethargic conservatism? Perhaps so, but only among those who are
endowed with superior intelligence and a will to perfection. Such people
spend their lives trying out and testing the truth which they have taken to
be such in order to keep it free of admixture, superstition, and error. The
minds and hearts of such people are cauldrons forever boiling, accepting
every new idea in order but to boil it down, purify it, and separate its good
from its evil as well as its beauty from its ugliness. Such souls seek the
truth in everything, everywhere, and from every source. In every nation
and age, such people are few; they are the chosen and the distinguished.
Such men always find themselves on the other side of any contest with the
rich, the established, and the powerful. The latter are forever apprehensive
of anything new lest it may adversely affect their wealth, prestige, or power
and, generally speaking, they do not know any other facts besides those of
concrete everyday living. Everything is true, in their opinion, if it leads to
an increase in the substance of this very life, and false if it implies the
slightest doubt regarding that substance. For the capitalist, virtue is good
if it increases the substance, evil if it dissipates it. Religion itself is indeed
true only if it serves his passions and desires, and false if it denies or fails
to satisfy them.

The man of political power and the man of social prestige stand here on a par with the capitalist. In their enmity to everything new and fearful, they mobilize the masses on whom their wealth, social prestige, or power depend against the innovator. This mobilization of the masses is carried out under an appeal to save the sanctity of the old order which may very well have become corrupt, obsolete, and spiritless. They present the old order they seek to save in great monuments of stone designed to delude the innocent rank and file. They pretend that the great spirit and value which moulded those monuments still lives therein with all its majesty and grandeur. The masses usually respond to their appeal with enthusiasm, for they are above all concerned with their daily bread; it is not easy for them to realize that any truth cannot remain for long imprisoned within the walls of any temple or monument, however beautiful or majestic it may be. It is hard for them to understand that it is of the nature of truth to be free, to invade the souls of men and to nourish them without discrimination between nobleman and slave; that no matter how hardily a system may defend itself against the truth and how closely it may be protected, the truth is always bound to win. How then could those Quraysh leaders who were seeking to listen to the Qur'an in secret, believe in its call when it proclaimed the wrath of God against the very practices which they were doing? How could they believe in a religion which did not differentiate between the blind pauper and the great capitalist except as regards the purity of their own souls? How could they believe in the call of Islam unto all men that "the greatest of you with God is the most pious and virtuous ?"[3] If, therefore, Abu Sufyan and his colleagues remained true to the religion of their ancestors, it was not due to their faith in its truth-value. Rather, it was due to their zeal to preserve the old order that not only protected them but also enabled them to achieve their position of wealth, social prestige, and power.

Jealousy and Competition

In addition to this anxiety and despair, jealousy and competition did their work to prevent the Quraysh from following the Prophet. Ummayyah ibn Abu al Salt was one of those who predicted the rise of a prophet among the Arabs; indeed, he hoped that he himself was such a prophet. He was full of resentment and jealousy when revelation came to Muhammad rather than to him; he could not, despite his own superiority over Muhammad as far as poetical composition is concerned, follow a person whom he believed was his competitor. When Muhammad heard the poetry of Ummayyah, he exclaimed: "What a man is Ummayyah! His poetry believes, but his heart does not." Likewise, al Walid ibn al Mughirah said: "It is incomprehensible to me that revelations would come to Muhammad and not to me while I am the greatest elder and master of Quraysh. Neither do I understand that revelation would not come to Abu Mas'ud 'Amr ibn 'Umayr al Thaqafi, the elder and master of Thaqif." It was in reference to such commonplace sentiments that the Qur'an says: "They said: would that this Qur'an be revealed to one of the great men in one of the two cities. Would they thus divide the mercy of your Lord? It is We who do so, as We do divide their livelihood among them in the world."[4] After Abu Sufyan, Abu Jahl, and al Akhnas had listened for three consecutive nights to Muhammad's recitation of the Qur'an, as we have reported earlier, al Akhnas visited Abu Jahl in his home and asked, "O Abu al Hakam, what do you think of what we heard from Muhammad?" Abu Jahl answered, "What did you hear? Our house and the house of Banu 'Abd Manaf have been competing for the honor: They have given the people to eat and so did we; they have carried the water to the pilgrims and so did we; they have assumed other burdens and so did we, they have given and so did we. Whenever we and they mount on our horses it always looks as if we are in a race. Now they are saying, among us is a prophet to whom revelation comes straight from heaven! When, if ever, will we achieve such a feat? Now, by God, we shall never believe in their prophet: we shall never accept what he says as true."

In these Bedouin souls of Muhammad's contemporaries, jealousy and competition were deeply rooted, and it would be a great mistake to overlook them. We should remember that such passions are not unique to the Arabs but are shared by all men. To neutralize their effects or get rid of them demands long and arduous self-discipline, a radical self-transformation that raises reason far above passion and ennobles one's spirit and heart to the degree of acknowledging the truth whithersoever it may come from, be he enemy or friend. It also demands believing that the possession of the truth is more precious than all the wealth of Midas, the glory of Alexander, or the power of Caesar. Such nobility and magnanimity of soul is hardly ever reached except by those whose hearts God Himself guides. Commonplace men are usually blinded by the wealth and pleasure of the world and by the present moment in which alone they spent their lives. Obviously, they are unable to rise to such spiritual height. In pursuit of quick satisfaction during the fleeting present, they struggle, fight, and kill one another. For its sake, nothing seems to prevent any of them from striking his teeth and claws into the very neck of truth, goodness and virtue, and from trampling to death the noblest and highest values. Seeing Muhammad's followers increasing in numbers and strength day by day, the Arabs of Quraysh were horrified by the idea that the truth which Muhammad proclaimed would one day achieve victory and power over them, over their allies and beyond, and over all the Arabs of the Peninsula. Heads shall roll rather than allow such a thing to happen, they thought. Counter-propaganda and mental warfare, boycott, blockade, injury and harm, persecution — all these and the vials of wrath shall be poured over Muhammad and his followers.

Fear of Resurrection and the Day of Judgment

A third reason prevented the Quraysh from following Muhammad, namely, the terror of the resurrection on the Day of Judgment with its punishment of hell. They were a people immersed in recreation and the pursuit of pleasure; trade and usury were their means to its attainment. Those of them who could afford to indulge in these pursuits did not see in them anything immoral and felt no imperative to avoid them. Through their idol worship they thought that their evil deeds and sins could all be atoned for and forgiven. It was sufficient for a man to strike a few arrows at the foot of the statue of Hubal for him to think that anything he was about to undertake was blessed if not commanded by the god. It was sufficient to sacrifice something to these idols for him to have his sins and guilt wiped out and forgotten. Therefore, to kill, to rob, to commit adultery, to indulge in unbecoming speech and indecency were all proper and permissible as long as one was capable of bribing those gods and placating them with sacrifices.

On the other hand, Muhammad was proclaiming that the Lord was standing in wait for them, that they will be resurrected on the day of judgment, and that their works will be their only credit. Moreover, he did so with verses of such tremendous, power that they shook men's hearts to the foundation and threw their consciousness into horror and panic. The Qur'an proclaimed: "But when the deafening cry is heard, when man would flee from his brother, from his father and mother, his wife and children, everyone will have enough to concern himself with his own destiny. On that day some faces will be bright, joyous and gay. Others will be dark and gloomy. The latter are the unbelievers, the wicked."[5] It proclaimed that the deafening cry would come — "the day when heaven will be like molten copper, when mountains will be like flakes of wool, when no friend will be able to concern himself for his friends. Beholding the fate which is to be theirs, the condemned will wish to ransom themselves with their own children, their wives and brothers, their tribes that gave them protection, even the whole of mankind if such could save them from the impending doom. No indeed! There shall be a flame of fire, burning and dismembering, grasping without relief him who turned his back to the call of God, who played deaf to the moral imperative, who hoarded wealth and withheld it from the needy. . . ."[6]

يَوْمَئِذٍ تُعْرَضُونَ لَا تَخْفَى مِنكُمْ خَافِيَةٌ ۞ فَأَمَّا مَنْ أُوتِيَ كِتَابَهُ بِيَمِينِهِ فَيَقُولُ هَاؤُمُ اقْرَءُوا كِتَابِيَهْ ۞ إِنِّي ظَنَنتُ أَنِّي مُلَاقٍ حِسَابِيَهْ ۞ فَهُوَ فِي عِيشَةٍ رَّاضِيَةٍ ۞ فِي جَنَّةٍ عَالِيَةٍ ۞ قُطُوفُهَا دَانِيَةٌ ۞ كُلُوا وَاشْرَبُوا هَنِيئًا بِمَا أَسْلَفْتُمْ فِي الْأَيَّامِ الْخَالِيَةِ ۞ وَأَمَّا مَنْ أُوتِيَ كِتَابَهُ بِشِمَالِهِ ۞ فَيَقُولُ يَا لَيْتَنِي لَمْ أُوتَ كِتَابِيَهْ ۞ وَلَمْ أَدْرِ مَا حِسَابِيَهْ ۞ يَا لَيْتَهَا كَانَتِ الْقَاضِيَةَ ۞ مَا أَغْنَى عَنِّي مَالِيَهْ ۞ هَلَكَ عَنِّي سُلْطَانِيَهْ ۞ خُذُوهُ فَغُلُّوهُ ۞ ثُمَّ الْجَحِيمَ صَلُّوهُ ۞ ثُمَّ فِي سِلْسِلَةٍ ذَرْعُهَا سَبْعُونَ ذِرَاعًا فَاسْلُكُوهُ ۞ إِنَّهُ كَانَ لَا يُؤْمِنُ بِاللَّهِ الْعَظِيمِ ۞ وَلَا يَحُضُّ عَلَى طَعَامِ الْمِسْكِينِ ۞ فَلَيْسَ لَهُ الْيَوْمَ هَاهُنَا حَمِيمٌ ۞ وَلَا طَعَامٌ إِلَّا مِنْ غِسْلِينٍ ۞ لَا يَأْكُلُهُ إِلَّا الْخَاطِئُونَ

"On that day you will be presented before God; none of your secrets will be hidden. Then, he who has received his record with his right hand will say: 'Come, read my record. I had rightly thought that I was to meet my reckoning.' Such a man will lead a blessed life in a lofty garden whose fruits are ripe and within reach. When he is brought therein he will be told: 'Eat and drink joyfully for in the days gone by, you have done the good deeds.' As for him who is given his record in his left hand he will say: 'Would I that I had never been given my record; that I never knew of my reckoning. Oh, would that death had made an end of me! My wealth is of no avail, and my power has come to naught.' To him God will say: 'Seize him and fetter him. Broil him in the fire. Then bind him in a chain seventy cubits long. For he did not believe in Almighty God, nor did he urge the feeding of the hungry. Today, he shall have no loyal friends and no food except what is foul, which none eat except his fellow sinners."[7]

After this I may ask the reader: Have you read this well? Did you ponder every word of it? Have you fully understood its meaning? Are you not

petrified and panic stricken? But that is only a portion of Muhammad's
warning to his people. You read these verses today and remember that you
have read them many times over before. Concurrently with your reading,
you will remember the Qur'an's description of hell. "On that day, We shall
ask hell, 'Are you full?' And hell will answer: 'Give me more!' . . .
Whenever their skins wear out, We shall give them new skins that they
may continue to suffer the punishment."[8] You can well imagine then the
horror which must have struck Quraysh, especially the rich among them
wallowing in the protection of their gods and idols whenever Muhammad
warned them of the imminent punishment. It would then become easy for
you to appreciate the degree of their enthusiasm in belying Muhammad,
opposing him, and urging the people to fight him. Previous to the
Prophet's preaching, the Arabs had no idea of the Day of Judgment or of
the resurrection, and they did not believe what they heard thereof from
non-Arabs. None of them thought that he would be reckoned with after
death for what he had done in this world. Whatever concern they had for
the future was limited to this world. They feared disease, loss of wealth
and children, of power and social prestige. This life, to them, was all there
is to life. Their energies were exhausted in the amassing of the means with
which to enjoy this life and to keep it safe from misfortune. The future was
utterly opaque. Whenever their consciences were disturbed by a premonition of evil following upon their misdeeds, they had recourse to divination
by arrows, pebbles, or bird-chasing in order to dissipate the fear or confirm it. If confirmed they would sacrifice to their idols and thereby avoid
the imminent misfortune.

   As for reckoning after death, resurrection, and the Day of Judgment
— paradise for the virtuous and hell for the unjust — all this completely
escaped them despite the fact that they had heard of it in connection with
the religion of the Jews and of the Christians. Nonetheless, they never
heard of it described with such emphatic, frightening, indeed horrifying,
terms and seriousness such as Muhammad's revelation had brought to
them. What they had heard of before Muhammad never succeeded in
pressing home to them the recognition that their continued life of pleasure, pursuit of wealth, exploitation of the weak, robbery of the orphan,
neglect of the poor, and excess in usury, would surely incur eternal punishment. They had no idea of impending suffering in the depth of hell, and
when they heard of it described in these terms, it was natural for them to
be seized with panic. How strongly they must have felt when they realized, though they did not openly admit it, that the other world with its

reward and punishment is truly there, waiting for them only one step beyond this life which was soon to end in death!

Quraysh and Paradise

As for God's promise to the virtuous of a paradise as large as heaven and earth, where there is neither evil word nor deed but only peace and blessedness, the Quraysh were quite suspicious. They doubted paradise all the more because of their attachment to this world and their anxiousness to enjoy its blessings right here and now. They were too impatient to wait for the Day of Judgment though they did not believe in any such day at all.

The Struggle of Good and Evil

One may indeed wonder how the Arabs locked their minds against any idea of the other world and its reckoning when the struggle of good and evil in this world has been raging eternally without let-up or peace. Thousands of years before Muhammad, the ancient Egyptians provided their dead with their needs for the other world. In the coffins, they enclosed *The Book of the Dead*, which was full of psalms, invocations, and other prayers, and in their graves they painted pictures of judgment and scenes of repentance and punishment. The Indians, too, conceived of the other world in terms of Nirvana and transmigration of souls. A soul, they held, may suffer for thousands and millions of years before it is guided to the truth, purified, and rehabilitated to the good life at the end of which is Nirvana. Likewise, the Zoroastrians of Persia recognized the struggle of good and evil, and their gods were gods of light and darkness. So, too, did the Mosaic and the Christian religions, both of which describe a life of eternity dependent upon God's pleasure or wrath. Did the Arabs not know any of all this, though they were a people of trade in continual contact through their voyages with all the adherents of these religions? How could the case be otherwise? Why did they not have similar notions of their own when, as people of the desert, they were closer to infinity and eternity, to a conception of the spiritual existence induced by the heat of noon and the darkness of night, to good and evil spirits, which they had already conceived of as residing within the statues which interceded for them with God? Undoubtedly, they must have had an idea of the existence of the other world, but since they were a people of trade, they were more realistic and hence appreciative of that which they could see and touch.

They were one and all *bon vivants* and, hence, all the more determined to deny punishment or reward in the hereafter. They thought that what man needs in this world is precisely the consequence of his deed whether good or evil. Further consequences of his deeds in the other world were therefore superfluous. That is why most of the revelations of Muhammad which warned, threatened, and made promises concerning the other world were revealed in Makkah at the beginning of Muhammad's commission. This revelation answered the need for saving those among whom Muhammad was sent. It was natural that Muhammad draw their attention as strongly as he could to their error and misguidance and that he call them to rise above idol worship to the worship of the One Almighty God.

For the Sake of Salvation

In the course of bringing spiritual salvation to his people and to all mankind, Muhammad and his followers suffered great harm. They were subjected to many travails of body and spirit, to emigration, to alienation from peers and relatives, and they bore these sacrifices with gallantry and patience. It was as if the more his people harmed Muhammad, the stronger became his love for them and the greater his desire and care to bring about their salvation. Resurrection and the day of judgment were the supreme ideas to which they were to give their attention if they were to be saved from their idolatry and evil deeds. Consequently, in the first years of Muhammad's prophethood, revelation constantly repeated divine threats and warnings that the Makkans might open their eyes and recognize the veracity of resurrection and the Day of Judgment. It was this constant assault by revelation which, in final analysis, had inflamed the terrible war between Muhammad and Makkah whose rage did not subside until God had given victory to Islam, His religion, over the religions of man.

8

From the Violation of the Boycott to al Isra'

Calling the Tribes to Islam during the Holy Months

The pact into which the clans of Quraysh had entered for boycotting Muhammad and blockading the Muslims continued to be observed for three consecutive years. During this time Muhammad and his family and companions fortified themselves against attack in one of the hills within Makkah. In their isolation, however, they suffered all kinds of privations; often they could not find enough food to satisfy their hunger. It was not possible either for Muhammad or the Muslims to mix with other people or to talk to them except during the holy months, when the Arabs would come to Makkah on pilgrimage and all hostilities would cease. In those months, no killing, persecution, aggression or vengeance was permitted. Muhammad used to approach the Arabs and call them unto the religion of God and warn them of His imminent punishment as well as announce to them the blessings of paradise. The pilgrims knew what Muhammad had suffered in the cause of his mission, and this stirred their sympathy and compassion for him as well as their sensitivity to his call. Indeed, this boycott imposed by Quraysh, and Muhammad's patient bearing of it for the sake of his cause, won for him and his cause many hearts. Not all men were as hard of feeling as Abu Jahl and Abu Lahab.

Blockade of the Muslims

The long duration of the blockade and, consequently, the great sufferings inflicted upon the Muslims by the Quraysh, caused a number of Makkans to realize the hardness and injustice to which their very brethren, in-laws, and cousins, had been subjected. Were it not for the few who compassionately furnished the Muslims food, the latter would have surely starved. Hisham ibn 'Amr was the most compassionate to the Muslims in their tragedy. He used to load his camel with food and other supplies, take it during the night and pass by the entrance to the quarter where the Muslims were isolated. He would detach the reins of the camel and let it go free, whipping it on the sides so that the camel would enter into the quarter and be seized by the Muslims. The more Muhammad and his companions suffered, the more disturbed a number of Qurayshis became. Unable to withhold his compassion, Hisham ibn 'Amr went to Zuhayr ibn Abu Umayyah, whose mother was 'Atikah, daughter of 'Abd al Muttalib. He said, "O Zuhayr, how could you eat and wear new clothes and marry and enjoy life when your uncles are locked up and isolated, unable to buy or purchase anything, to give or to take anyone in marriage? By God I swear that if the Muslims were the uncles of Abu al Hakam ibn Hisham and you had asked him to boycott them as he asked you to boycott the Muslims, he would have never fulfilled your request." Together the two men agreed to revoke the pact of the boycott and sought to convince others to do likewise, although secretly. Al Mut'am ibn 'Adiyy, Abu al Bakhtari ibn Hisham, and Zam'ah ibn al Aswad agreed to denounce the pact of boycott and to work together for its repudiation.

One day after circumambulating the Ka'bah seven times, Zuhayr ibn Abu Umayyah addressed the Makkans: "O People of Makkah, would you that we eat food and enjoy ourselves while the Banu Hashim are dying one after another unable to buy or acquire anything? By God, I shall not sit still until this unjust pact of the boycott is revoked." Upon hearing this, Abu Jahl immediately rose and said to Zuhayr, "You are a liar. The pact is sacred and inviolable." At this, Zam'ah, Abu al Bakhtari, al Mut'am, as well as Hisham ibn 'Amr, rose from their places to argue against Abu Jahl and to confirm Zuhayr in his request. At this show of strength, Abu Jahl realized that a previous agreement must have been reached between these men and that direct opposition to them might not prove advantageous. He therefore withdrew. Al Mut'am rose to tear up the pact hanging on the wall of the Ka'bah only to find that insects had already devoured most of it except the opening words "In the name of God." At this, Muhammad

and his companions were permitted to come out of their isolation and circulate in Makkah, to buy and to sell as usual, although the antagonism and
hostility remained as they were, and each party continued to look forward
to a day when it could overcome the other.

Infallibility of Muhammad in Conveying the Revelation

Some biographers claimed that the unbelievers who brought about
the revocation of the boycott pact went to Muhammad and asked him to
make some gesture of reconciliation toward the Quraysh in order to
strengthen them in their attempts and to put a stop to further harm. They
asked him to agree to give their gods a place, at least to grant them occa-
sional recognition with the fingers of his hand as the Makkans were accustomed to do. The same biographers claim that Muhammad inclined
toward doing some of this in gratitude for the good deeds just done to
him. They even allege that he said to himself: "What blame is there if I do
such a thing? God knows that I am innocent!" Other biographers report
that the same men who helped revoke the pact of boycott went one
evening to Muhammad, talked to him all night, and praised him so much
and endeared themselves to him, calling him "Our Master, Our Master,"
until he was moved to answer some of their demands. The first version
was reported by Sa'id ibn Jubayr; and the second by Qatadah. In both versions, it is reported that God protected Muhammad against their subversion and revealed to him the following verse: "They have almost succeeded in inducing you, under promise of their friendship, to attribute to Us,
against Our command, that which We did not reveal to you. Had We not
confirmed you in your faith, you might have been tempted and hence fall-
en under the inescapable punishment."[1]

It should be remembered that these verses were claimed to have been
revealed in connection with the forged story of the goddesses which we
have investigated earlier; the present reporters attribute it to the story of
the revocation of the boycott pact. The same verses have also been claimed
by ibn 'Abbas, as reported by 'Ata', to have been revealed in connection
with another story. That is the story of the delegation of Thaqif who came
to Muhammad to ask him to declare their valley holy just as Makkah had
declared her trees and birds and animals holy. It is claimed that the
Prophet — may God's peace be upon him — hesitated until these verses
were revealed. Whatever the historical circumstances which occasioned
the revelation of these verses, the verses themselves bespeak the greatness

of Muhammad as well as his candidness. The same aspects of Muhammad's personality are equally in evidence in the verses we have reported from *Surah* 80. Indeed, they are supported by the history of Muhammad's life as a whole. Muhammad had repeatedly told the people that he was only a man, that as a man God had revealed to him certain messages for their guidance, and that without God's special protection in this regard he was as fallible as anyone. Muhammad did in fact err when he frowned in the face of ibn Umm Maktum and sent him away. He almost erred as reported above in the verses from the *surah* "al Isra'" as well as in the foregoing verses which tell of his inclination away from that which had been revealed to him and of the people's invitation to Muhammad to invent a revelation. But revelation did, in fact, come to Muhammad and condemned what he did in connection with the blind beggar, his near succumbing to Quraysh's temptation. Muhammad, however, reported all these revelations to the Quraysh people with equal truthfulness and candidness. Neither self-esteem nor pride nor any other human feeling prevented him from conveying the revelation, whether it was for or against him. The truth and the truth alone was the essence of his message. He declared the truth even if it were against himself. We are accustomed to expect the great man to bear resolutely and patiently whatever harm he might be exposed to on account of his conviction, but we hardly ever expect the great man to acknowledge that he almost succumbed to his temptations. Such temptations are usually not talked about, and most great men are contented to reckon with themselves strongly only in secret. He was therefore greater than the great, for his soul enabled him to rise to the height where it would acknowledge the truth even regarding its own struggle and proclaim it to the public. Such greatness that is greater than the great belongs exclusively to the prophets. It demands of the prophet the very utmost in truthfulness and candidness in the conveyance of the message of truth that comes from God alone.

Death of Abu Talib and Khadijah

After the repudiation of the boycott pact, Muhammad and his companions emerged from their quarters. Muhammad immediately resumed his call to the Quraysh and to the tribes that used to come to Makkah during the holy months. Despite the spreading of his fame among the Arab tribes and the number of his followers, neither he nor they were quite yet safe from injury, and nothing he could do would have guaranteed such safety. A few months later two tragedies were to add to his troubles: First, the death of Abu Talib, his protector, and then that of Khadijah, his wife. Abu Talib died at about the age of eighty. When Quraysh knew of his approaching end, they feared that the conflict with the Muslims would reach a new height now that their leadership would pass into the less temperate hands of Hamzah and 'Umar, well known for their hardness and determined hostility. The leaders of Quraysh went up to Abu Talib and addressed him as he lay on his deathbed: "O Abu Talib, we hold for you great respect and we appreciate your counsel and wisdom. Now that you are about to leave us, and, knowing the conflict that has arisen between us and your nephew, do please call him and ask him to give us assurance as we are wont to give you for him, that he will leave us alone and we will leave him alone, that he will leave us to practice our religion and we shall leave him to practice his." Muhammad and his companions came to the meeting in his uncle's house. After he was told about their purpose he said: "Yes, indeed! All I want from you is this one word of assurance which, if given, will bring you mastery of all Arabia as well as Persia, namely..." "Speak out," interrupted Abu Jahl, "by your father we shall give it to you! Not one word but ten." Muhammad continued: "Namely, that you witness with me that there is no God but God and repudiate all that you worship besides Him." Some of them said to Muhammad: "Do you want to make all the gods one?" Turning to one another, the men of Quraysh said: "By God, this man is not going to give you any word of assurance such as you require." The leaders of Quraysh left Abu Talib's house without satisfaction, and Abu Talib died a few days later, the situation between him and the Quraysh being more hostile than ever before.

Later on, Khadijah, who supported Muhammad with her love and goodness, her purity, gentleness and strong faith, passed away. At her death, Muhammad lost an angel of mercy who reassured and reconciled him whenever he felt crushed under the burdens of his cause. Henceforth, Muhammad was forever to miss the believing eyes of Khadijah and her reassuring smile, just as he had lost in Abu Talib his protection and refuge from his enemies. How deeply these tragedies must have cut into Muhammad's heart! Surely they were strong enough to shake the most determined soul, to bring doubt and despair to the most resolute, and to leave behind the greatest degree of emptiness and despondence.

Increase of Quraysh's Hostility

Soon thereafter, the Quraysh were to increase their attacks against Muhammad. An example of the least of such injuries was the covering of Muhammad's head with soil thrown at him by one of the plebeians of Quraysh. Muhammad withdrew to his home where his daughter, Fatimah, moved to tears by the sight of her father, washed his head for him. It is certainly painful to us to hear our children cry, and more so to hear our daughters cry. Indeed, every tear dropped from a daughter's eye is a ball of fire fallen upon our hearts, causing us to cry in pain. The daughter's sob and painful murmur fall heavily upon the father's heart, and Fatimah's cries must have choked a compassionate father such as Muhammad. However, what was he to do to reassure a person who had just lost her mother and who is now appalled by the insults heaped upon her father? Nothing but to orient himself all the more to God, and to proclaim his conviction that God would give him final victory. He said to his daughter: "Do not cry, O Fatimah! Your father has God for protector." Often Muhammad would be heard saying: "By God. Quraysh never harmed me so much as after the death of Abu Talib."

Muhammad's Excursion to Ta'if (628 C.E.)

The Quraysh doubled and redoubled their injuries to Muhammad and his followers until Muhammad could bear it no longer. Alone, and without telling anyone, he undertook a trip to the city of Ta'if where he solicited the support of the tribe of Thaqif after calling them to Islam. When they refused, he asked them not to spread the news of their refusal to his enemies that they might not rejoice at his failure. The tribe of Thaqif, however, not only repudiated Muhammad's call but sent their servants to insult him and throw him out of their city. He ran away from them and took shelter near a wall which belonged to 'Utbah and Shaybah, sons of Rabi'ah. There, he sat under a vine pondering his defeat, within sight of the sons of Rabi'ah. He raised his hands to heaven and prayed with noticeable pain: "O God, please consider my weakness, my shortage of means, and the little esteem that people have of me. Oh, most Merciful God, You are the Lord of the oppressed, and You are my Lord. To whom would You leave my fate? To a stranger who insults me? Or to an enemy who dominates me? Would I that You have no wrath against me! Your pleasure alone is my objective. Under the light of Your faith which illuminates all darkness and on which this world and the other depend, I take my refuge. I pray that I may not become the object of Your wrath and anger. To You alone belongs the right to blame and to chastise until Your pleasure is met. There is neither power nor strength except in You."

'Addas, the Christian

For some time, the sons of Rabi'ah watched Muhammad until a feeling of compassion and sympathy for him began to stir within them. They sent their Christian servant, 'Addas by name, with a bunch of grapes. Before Muhammad partook of the grapes, he said: "In the name of God." 'Addas was surprised and said, "That is not what the natives of this country usually say." Muhammad then asked him about his religion and his country of origin, and when he learned that he was a Christian from Nineveh, he said, "Are you then from the City of the Righteous Jonah, son of Matthew?" Still more surprised, 'Addas asked, "What do you know about Jonah, son of Matthew?" Muhammad answered, "That was my brother; he was a true prophet and so am I." Moved with emotion, 'Addas covered Muhammad with kisses. The two sons of Rabi'ah were surprised at what they saw although they remained unmoved by Muhammad's religious claims. When their servant returned to them they counseled him: "O 'Addas, do not allow this man to convert you from your faith. Your faith is better for you than his."

Muhammad Offers Himself to the Tribes

The news of the injuries inflicted upon Muhammad lightened the hostility of the tribe of Thaqif, but it never succeeded in moving them to follow him. The Quraysh knew about this expedition and increased their injuries. Nothing, however, could dissuade Muhammad from continuing his call. At every season, whenever the tribes of Arabia came to Makkah, he offered himself and his cause to them, informed them that he was a commissioned prophet, and asked them to believe in him. His uncle 'Abd al 'Uzza, son of 'Abd al Muttalib, otherwise known as Abu Lahab, would not let him; he would follow Muhammad everywhere he went to dissuade the people from listening to him. Muhammad, for his part, did not only preach his religion to the tribes in the pilgrimage season in Makkah, but sought those tribes in their own quarters. He visited the tribe of Kindah and the tribe of Kalb, of Banu Hanifah, Banu 'Amir ibn Sa'sa'ah, each in its own province. None of them responded favorably to him, and they all repudiated his call — sometimes with insults, as did the tribe of Banu Hanifah. The tribe of Banu ʿAmir felt more ambitious and imagined that they could assume a position of leadership should the cause of Muhammad triumph. But when Muhammad told them, "The matter belongs wholly to God; He places leadership wheresoever He wishes," they turned away and repudiated his call like the rest.

Did all these tribes repudiate Muhammad's call for the same reasons for which Quraysh did before them? We have seen the disappointment of the tribe of Banu ʿAmir upon the frustration of their ambition of leadership and power. As for the tribe of Thaqif, they had a different opinion. In addition to the cool atmosphere and vineyards which made it a summer resort, the city of Taʾif was the center of worship of al Lat, for it was in its midst that the idol stood and on its account the city had become a place of pilgrimage. Should the tribe of Thaqif follow Muhammad, the goddess al Lat would lose her place of worship, the city its pilgrimage site, and ensuing hostility with Quraysh would soon cut off all summer visits by the Makkans. Every tribe had thus its own reason, economic or other, for which it refused to accept Islam besides the personal attachment to the religion of the fathers and the worship of old idols.

Muhammad's Engagement to ʿAʾishah

The rejection of Muhammad by the tribes increased his isolation, as the doubled and redoubled injuries of the Quraysh increased Muhammad's pain and grief. The period of mourning for Khadijah passed, and Muhammad thought of marrying again in the hope of finding consolation in a new companion. He also thought that marriage might even furnish a new occasion for strengthening the bond of brotherhood and commitment between himself and the earlier converts to Islam. He therefore asked Abu Bakr for the hand of his daughter, ʿAʾishah. Since she was still too young to marry, the engagement was announced, but the marriage was postponed for three more years until ʿAʾishah reached the age of eleven. In the meantime, Muhammad married Sawdah, the widow of one of the Muslim companions who emigrated to Abysinnia but died upon his return to Makkah. In both these instances, it is hoped that the reader will have a glimpse of the principle regulating Muhammad's later domestic life which we shall discuss in a forthcoming chapter.

Al Isra' (621 C.E.)

It was during this period that *al Isra'* and *al Mi'raj* had taken place.[2] On the night of *al Isra'*, Muhammad was staying in the house of his cousin, Hind, daughter of Abu Talib, who was also called Umm Hani'. Hind related that "The Prophet of God spent the night in my quarters. He recited his night prayers and went to sleep. Just before dawn, the Prophet of God awoke us and we all prayed the dawn prayer together. When the prayer was through, he said, "O Umm Hani', I prayed with you the night prayer in this place; then I went to Jerusalem and I prayed there, and as you see, I have just finished praying with you the dawn prayer.' I answered, 'O Prophet of God, do not tell this to the people for they will belie you and harm you.' He said, 'By God I shall tell them.'"

Was al Isra' in Body or in Soul?

Those who claim that *al Isra'* and *al Mi'raj* of Muhammad — may God's peace be upon him — had taken place in soul rather than in body refer to this report of Umm Hani'. They also refer to another report by 'A'ishah which says, "The body of the Prophet of God — may God's peace and blessing be upon him — was never missed from his bed. Rather, God caused him to travel in soul alone." Whenever Mu'awiyah ibn Abu Sufyan was asked about *al Isra'* of the Prophet, he used to answer, "It was a true vision from God." Those who share such a view confirm their claim with the Qur'anic verse, "The vision which We have shown you is but a trial to the people."[3] According to the other view, *al Isra'* from Makkah to Jerusalem took place in body. In confirmation of this, they mention that Muhammad had related what he saw in the desert on the way hither and add that his ascension to heaven was in soul. Others hold that both *al Isra'* and *al Mi'raj* were in body. As a result of this great controversy, thousands of books have been written on the subject. We have a view of this matter which we shall give shortly, a view that somebody else may have held before us. Before we proceed, however, we shall give the story of *al Isra'* and *al Mi'raj* as it was reported in the biography books.

Al Isra' as Given in Literature

The Orientalist Dermenghem has reported the following eloquent story culled from a number of biography books. We shall quote it as he related it:

"In the middle of a solemn, quiet night when even the night-birds and the rambling beasts were quiet, when the streams had stopped murmuring and no breezes played, Mahomet was awakened by a voice crying: 'Sleeper, awake!' And before him stood the Angel Gabriel with radiant forehead, countenance white as snow, blond hair floating, in garments sewn with pearls and embroidered in gold. Manifold wings of every colour stood out quivering from his body.

"He led a fantastical steed, Boraq ('Lightning'), with a human head and two eagles' wings; it approached Mahomet, allowed him to mount and was off like an arrow over the mountains of Mecca and the sands of the desert toward the North. . . The Angel accompanied them on this prodigious flight. On the summit of Mt. Sinai, where God had spoken to Moses, Gabriel stopped Mahomet for prayer, and again at Bethlehem where Jesus was born, before resuming their course in the air. Mysterious voices attempted to detain the Prophet, who was so wrapped up in his mission that he felt God alone had the right to stop his steed. When they reached Jerusalem Mahomet tethered Boraq and prayed on the ruins of the Temple of Solomon with Abraham, Moses, and Jesus. Seeing an endless ladder appear upon Jacob's rock, the Prophet was enabled to mount rapidly to the heavens.

"The first heaven was of pure silver and the stars suspended from its vault by chains of gold; in each one an angel lay awake to prevent the demons from climbing into the holy dwelling places and the spirits from listening indiscreetly to celestial secrets. There, Mahomet greeted Adam. And in the six other heavens the Prophet met Noah, Aaron, Moses, Abraham, David, Solomon, Idris (Enoch), Yahya (John the Baptist) and Jesus. He saw the Angel of Death, Azrail, so huge that his eyes were separated by 70,000 marching days. He commanded 100,000 battalions and passed his time in writing in an immense book the names of those dying or being born. He saw the Angel of Tears who wept for the sins of the world; the Angel of Vengeance with brazen face, covered with warts, who presides over the elements of fire and sits on a throne of flames; and another immense angel made up half of snow and half of fire surrounded by a heavenly choir continually crying: 'O God, Thou hast united snow and fire, united all Thy servants in obedience to Thy Laws.' In the seventh heaven where the souls of the just resided was an angel larger than the entire world, with 70,000 heads; each head had 70,000 mouths, each mouth had 70,000 tongues and each tongue spoke in 70,000 different idioms singing endlessly the praises of the Most High.

"While contemplating this extraordinary being, Mahomet was carried to the top of the Lote — Tree of Heaven flowering at the right of God's invisible throne and shading myriads of angelic spirits. Then after having crossed in a twinkling of an eye the widest seas, regions of dazzling light and deepest darkness, traversed millions of clouds of hyacinths, of gauze, of shadows, of fire, of air, of water, of void, each one separated by 500 marching years, he then passed more clouds — of beauty, of perfection, of supremacy, of immensity, of unity, behind which were 70,000 choirs of angels bowed down and motionless in complete silence. The earth began to heave and he felt himself carried into the light of his Lord, where he was transfixed, paralysed. From here heaven and earth together 'appeared as if imperceptible to him, as if melted into nothingness and reduced to the size of a grain of mustard-seed in the middle of a field. And this is how Mahomet admits having been before the Throne of the Lord of the World.

"He was in the presence of the Throne *'at a distance of two bows' length or yet nearer'* (Koran, liii), beholding God with his soul's eyes and seeing things which the tongue cannot express, surpassing all human understanding. The Almighty placed one hand on Mahomet's breast and the other on his shoulder — to the very marrow of his bones he felt an icy chill, followed by an inexpressible feeling of calm and ecstatic annihilation.

"After a conversation whose ineffability is not honored by too precise tradition, the Prophet received the command from God that all believers must say fifty prayers each day. Upon coming down from heaven Mahomet met Moses, who spoke with him on this subject:

"'How do you hope to make your followers say fifty prayers each day? I had experience with mankind before you. I tried everything with the children of Israel that it was possible to try. Take my word, return to our Lord and ask for a reduction.'

"Mahomet returned, and the number of prayers was reduced to forty. Moses thought that this was still too many and made his successor go back to God a number of times. In the end God exacted not more than five prayers.

"Gabriel then took the Prophet to paradise where the faithful rejoice after their resurrection — an immense garden with silver soil, gravel of pearls, mountains of amber, filled with golden palaces and precious stones.

"Finally, after returning by the luminous ladder to the earth, Mahomet untethered Boraq, mounted the saddle and rode into Jerusalem on the winged steed."[4]

Ibn Hisham's Report about al Isra'

Such is the report of the orientalist Dermenghem concerning the story of *al Isra'* and *al Mi'raj*. Every item he reported may be readily found, perhaps with greater or lesser detail, in many of the biographies. An example of the fertility of the reporters' imagination may be read in ibn Hisham's biography. Reporting on Muhammad's conversation with Adam in the first heaven, ibn Hisham wrote: "Then I saw men with lips like those of camels. In their hands were balls of fire which they thrusted into their mouths and collected from their extremities to thrust into their mouths again. I asked, 'Who are these, O Gabriel?' He said: 'These are men who robbed the orphans.' I then saw men with large bellies, the likes of which I have never seen before even on the road to the house of Pharaoh where the greatest punishment is meted out to the greatest sinners. These are trodden upon by men who when brought to the fire run like maddened camels. Those whom they tread upon remain immobile, unable to move from their place. I asked, 'Who are those, O Gabriel?' He answered, 'Those are the usurers.' I then saw men sitting at a table loaded with delicious and fat meat as well as spoilt and stinking meat. They were eating of the latter and leaving the former untouched. I asked, 'Who are these, O Gabriel ?' He answered, 'These are men who left their own women whom God had permitted them to enjoy and ran after other women illegitimately.' I then saw women hanging from their breasts and asked, 'Who are these, O Gabriel?' He answered, 'These are women who fathered on their husbands children not their own.' . . . He then took me into Paradise where I saw a beautiful damsel with luscious lips. As I was attracted by her I asked her, 'To whom do you belong?' She answered: 'To Zayd ibn Harithah.' The prophet of God — may God's peace and blessing be upon him — announced this glad tiding to Zayd ibn Harithah."

Whether in ibn Hisham's or in other biographies of the Prophet or in the books of Qur'anic exegesis, the reader will find many details besides the above-mentioned. It is certainly the historian's right to question how closely these reports have been scrutinized and investigated by their collectors, with the view to finding out how much of them may be truly ascribed to the Prophet and how much was the invention of the fancy of the Sufis and others. Although there is no room here to undertake such investigation, nor to decide the issue of whether or not *al Isra'* or *al Mi'raj* were both in body or in soul or the one in body and the other in soul, there is still no doubt that everyone of these views has reasons which their advocates claim to be legitimate. There is no *a priori* reason why one may not adhere to one of these views rather than another. Whoever wishes to hold the view that *al Isra'* and *al Mi'raj* were in soul and not in body, could turn to the evidence of the reports we have already cited as well as to the Qur'anic emphasis that

$$\text{قُلْ اِنَّمَا اَنَا بَشَرٌ مِثْلُكُمْ يُوْحَى اِلَيَّ اَنَّمَا اِلٰهُكُمْ اِلٰهٌ وَّاحِدٌ ۚ فَمَنْ كَانَ يَرْجُوا لِقَآءَ رَبِّهِ فَلْيَعْمَلْ عَمَلًا صَالِحًا وَّلَا يُشْرِكْ بِعِبَادَةِ رَبِّهٖ اَحَدًا}$$

"I am but a human like you unto whom a revelation is given that your God is one God;"[5] that the book of God is the sole "miracle" of Muhammad; and that "God does not forgive any association of aught with Him but He forgives to whomsoever He wishes anything else."[6]

Whoever holds a view of *al Isra* and *al Mi'raj* such as this is perhaps better entitled to inquire about the meaning of these ideas. And that is precisely the issue to which, perhaps for the first time ever, we want to address ourselves in the following sections.

Al Isra and the Unity of Being

As phenomena in the spiritual life of Muhammad, *al Isra'* and *al Mi'raj* carry great and noble meanings that are greater than the foregoing descriptions have suggested — much of which being the product of pure imagination. In the moment of *al Isra'* and *al Mi'raj*, Muhammad grasped the unity of being in all its totality and perfection. In that moment, neither space nor time could prevent his consciousness from encompassing all being; whereas our consciousness, determined by weaker perceptive and rational faculties, is incapable of transcending the limitations of space and time. In that moment, all frontiers fell before Muhammad's insight; and all being was, as it were, gathered in his soul. In that moment, he came to know totality from beginning to end and represented this totality as the self-realization of the forces of goodness, truth, and beauty in their struggle against and conquest of evil, untruth, and fraud. All this happened to Muhammad by God's grace.

No one is capable of such transcendent vision except by means of superhuman power. If any of the followers of Muhammad were unable to match him in his struggle to rise to or to achieve such vision and perception, there should be neither blame nor surprise. Men's degrees of endowment differ, and their vision of the truth is always determined by these limitations which our ordinary powers are unable to transcend. There is perhaps an analogy between Muhammad's understanding of the universe at that moment and that of any other person who has risen to the highest level of consciousness possible for man. It is that of the story of the blind men who, upon being brought into contact with the elephant, were asked to identify it. It will be remembered that the first thought it was a long rope because he had touched its tail; the second, a thick tree because he had touched its leg; the third, a spear because he had touched its ivory; and the fourth, a moving round tube because he had touched its trunk. These views are to the unimpaired view of the elephant as the understanding of most of us to that of Muhammad, implied in *al Isra'* and *al Mi'raj*, of the unity and totality of being. In Muhammad's vision, the finitude of space and time disappeared, and he beheld the universe all "gathered up" and present. Men capable of such great moments of consciousness see the details of space-time and problems of worldly living as mathematical atoms appended to the person without ever affecting him. None of them affect in the least the life of his body, the beat of his heart, the illumination of his soul, the enlightenment of his consciousness, nor his vibration with energy and life. For by existing, such a person enters into communion with all existence and all life, as it were, *ipso facto*.

A spiritual *Isra'* and *Mi'raj* cannot be different in its meanings of beauty, majesty, and transcendence than a bodily one.[7] In itself, the story is a very strong figurization of the spiritual unity of all being. Muhammad's detour for a stop on Mount Sinai where God spoke to Moses face to face, at Bethlehem where Jesus was born, and the spiritual meeting of Muhammad, Jesus, Moses and Abraham in the moment of prayer is another very strong figurization of the unity of religious experience and life, a unity constitutive of the world as it tends to value and perfection.

Al Isra' and Modern Science

In our modern age, science confirms the possibility of a spiritual *Isra'* and *Mi'raj*. Where there is a meeting of genuine forces, that which shines forth is genuine reality; just as a meeting of the same forces of nature configured by the genius of Marconi produced the real effect of lighting a light in distant Australia by means of an electric radiation directed at it on the waves of space from his ship in Venice. In this age of ours, science has confirmed the possibility of prestidigitation, of broadcast of sound through space by means of the radio, as well as of pictures and writing, all of which was considered too fanciful even for the imagination. The forces latent in nature are still being discovered by science, and every new day brings a new surprise. Strong and powerful spirits such as Muhammad's are perfectly capable of being carried in one night from Makkah to Jerusalem and of being shown God's signs. That is not opposed to reason, especially when the moral of it is the figurization of divine truths, of extraordinary meanings of beauty and transcendence, and of the unity of spirit and world so clearly achieved in the consciousness of Muhammad. Though extraordinary and unique to Muhammad, the experience is certainly possible for man upon removal of the illusions of this world, penetration of ultimate reality, and relation of oneself and the world thereto.

Doubt of Quraysh and Apostasy of Some Muslims

The Arabs of Makkah, however, were incapable of understanding such meanings. Therefore, as soon as Muhammad related his *Isra'*, they could not progress beyond the question of the possibility or otherwise of instantaneous bodily transportation to Jerusalem. Even those who followed Muhammad and believed in him were troubled by doubt. Some said, "This is clear and decisive. By God, camels run continually for a whole month to reach al Sham and another whole month to return. Would Muhammad achieve such a feat in one night?" Many of the Muslims apostatized. Those who were troubled by doubt went to Abu Bakr and related to him Muhammad's claim. Abu Bakr answered, "Surely you are telling me lies." They said, "There is Muhammad in the mosque telling the people of his trip." Abu Bakr answered, "By God, if Muhammad himself has said so, then it is true. He tells us that the word of God comes to him directly from heaven to earth in an hour of night or day and we believe him. Isn't this a greater miracle than what you are doubting today?" Abu Bakr came to the Prophet and listened to him describing Jerusalem and its mosque. When he finished, Abu Bakr said, "You said the truth, O Prophet of God." From that day on Muhammad called Abu Bakr "al Siddiq."[8]

Al Isra' in Body

Those who claim that *al Isra'* took place in body explain, in support of their view, that when the Prophet proclaimed the news, Muslims and non-Muslims asked him for proof. Muhammad described to them a caravan of camels he had encountered on the road to Jerusalem. He related how he led the leaders of that caravan to one of their beasts which had gone astray in the desert, how he drank from a water jar carried on the back of one of those camels, and how he lowered the lid of the jar after he drank from it. They related that the Quraysh had inquired about that caravan and that the reports of the caravan leaders confirmed Muhammad's claim and description. On the other hand, those who believe that *al Isra'* took place in spirit do not find such reports unbelievable now that science in our own days has confirmed the possibility of hypnotism and of the hypnotized one to report about events far removed from him. For a spirit holding in unity and presence the spiritual life of the universe *in toto*, for one so endowed with vision and power so as to penetrate the secret of all life from eternity to eternity, such a feat is not at all surprising.

Mosque of Ghazi Husrev Bay, Sarajevo, Yugoslavia

9

The Two Covenants
of al 'Aqabah

Muslim Weakness after al Isra'

Quraysh did not understand the meanings behind *al Isra'*. Neither did many of the Muslims who themselves apostatized in consequence, as we saw earlier. Encouraged by this relapse, Quraysh intensified its attacks against Muhammad and his followers until they could cope with it no more. Muhammad's hope of enlisting the tribes into his ranks was dissipated after his rejection by Thaqif at al Ta'if, as well as by the tribes of Kindah, Kalb, Banu 'Amir and Banu Hanifah at their annual pilgrimage in Makkah. After all these experiences, Muhammad nearly gave up hope of converting any more men from Quraysh. Realizing the isolation imposed upon Muhammad and the irreconcilable opposition of Quraysh to his cause, the other tribes of the Peninsula, especially those surrounding or having business relations with Makkah, became all the more reluctant to receive his calls. Despite his reliance upon Hamzah and 'Umar, and his confidence that Quraysh could not harm him any more than they had already done on account of the tribal loyalties and alliances involved, Muhammad realized that the spread of God's call, limited as it were to a small number of weak people, exposed to the danger of apostasy or extermination, had come to a halt unless some victory from God was forthcoming. Days passed while Muhammad's increasing isolation kept pace with Quraysh's ever-growing enmity.

Muhammad's Fastness

Did this isolation of Muhammad weaken his determination or impair his morale? No! Rather, it strengthened his faith in the truth which had come to him from his Lord. Such travails would have discouraged any person of ordinary spirit; but the noble, the truly gifted, they can only be stimulated to higher levels of conviction, of resolution, and self-exertion. Rather than being shaken, Muhammad and his companions continued to have the strongest faith that God would raise His religion above all religions and bring victory to them in the process. The storms of hatred raging around them did not shake the faith. Muhammad spent his year in Makkah unconcerned that his and Khadijah's wealth was being rapidly exhausted to the point that poverty and want were imminent. Only the victory which he was absolutely certain God soon would grant him occupied his thought. When the season of pilgrimage came again and men from all over the Arabian Peninsula gathered in Makkah, he renewed his call to the revealed truth, undaunted by any violent rejection with which these tribes might meet his call. The plebeians of Makkah renewed their attacks against his person whenever he preached in public, but their injuries did not reduce Muhammad's self assurance. He knew that it was Almighty God who sent him a messenger of the truth, that there could be no doubt but that God would confirm His truth and give it victory. He knew that God had asked him always to present his revelations to men with arguments yet more sound and gentle, counseling "and then, your enemy will become your very warm friend."[1] He knew too well that God has asked him to be gentle to men that they might remember and fear. It was in this certainty, therefore, that Muhammad received the attacks of the Quraysh and bore patiently their injuries and harm. All along, he knew that God is always with the patient.

The First Signs of Victory in Yathrib

Muhammad did not have to wait more than a few years before the first signs of victory began to loom on the horizon, in the direction of Yathrib. Muhammad was related to Yathrib in ways other than trade. He had relatives in Yathrib. Moreover, in Yathrib was his father's grave. In Yathrib lived Banu al Najjar, uncle of his ancestor 'Abd al Muttalib, and hence his relative. To that grave, Aminah, the loyal wife, as well as 'Abd al Muttalib, the father who lost his son at the very height of his youth and power, used to come for yearly visits. Muhammad himself accompanied his mother to Yathrib when he was six years old and visited his father's grave with her. On their way back to Makkah, his mother, Aminah, fell ill and died and was buried at al Abwa' midway between Yathrib and Makkah. It was no surprise to Muhammad that the first sign of victory came from a town to which he was so closely associated, a town which stood in the direction of al Aqsa Mosque in Jerusalem, toward which he prayed and where stood the shrines of his two predecessors, Moses and Jesus. No wonder that circumstances prepared the town of Yathrib for this great destiny that Muhammad might achieve victory therein and that it might become the capital from which Islam was to conquer and to spread over the world.

Al Aws, al Khazraj, and the Jews

For this illustrious career, the town of Yathrib was better fitted than any other. Both al Aws and al Khazraj were idolaters sharing their town with the Jews whom they hated and often fought, and were hated and fought by them. History relates that the Christians of al Sham who then belonged to the dominant church in the East Roman Empire hated the Jews very strongly, regarding them as the crucifiers and torturers of Jesus. These Christians had raided Yathrib in the past for the express purpose of killing its Jewish citizens. When they could not succeed, they sought the assistance of al Aws and al Khazraj in order to draw the Jews of Madinah into their trap. Such a plan was responsible for the death of many a Jew and deprived the Jewish community of its dominion and power within the city. It also raised al Aws and al Khazraj to a position of power greater than that which trade relations with the Byzantines had hitherto established for them. History further relates that once more the Madinese tried to destroy Jewish power in their city in order to extend their possessions and influence, and that they had succeeded. The surviving Jews hated al Aws and al Khazraj deeply. Enmity was hence deeply rooted in the hearts of both. However, the followers of Moses were quick to realize that they neither had the power nor the numbers needed to meet force with force, and that continuation of such adventures would in the end result in their own extermination should al Aws and al Khazraj ever find allies among their own co-religionists in Arabia. Hence they changed their tactics and, instead of victory in battle, they sought to divide and separate al Aws from al Kharzaj and cause the two tribes to hate and fight each other. In this they succeeded far better, for the two tribes were soon at each other's throats. Through the continuing hostility of the two Arab tribes, the Jews secured their position, increased their trade and wealth, and re-established the dominion, possession, and prestige which they had once enjoyed.

The Jews' Spiritual Influences

Besides this competition for power and dominion, there is a sphere in which the Jews exerted greater influence upon al Aws and al Khazraj than they had over any other tribe of Arabia. That is the realm of the spirit. As adherents of a monotheistic faith, the Jews had been castigating their idolatrous neighbors for worshipping at the feet of idols which they took to be intercessors for them with God. The Jews had been threatening them with the prediction that soon a prophet would arise among the Arabs who would destroy them and ally himself to the Jews. Nonetheless, they did not succeed in judaizing the Arabs for two reasons: the first was that perpetual enmity between Christianity and Judaism did not allow the Jews to entertain any hope of political dominion in Yathrib. To realize for themselves a measure of security and prosperity through trade was the highest desideratum to which they would aspire. The second was that the Jews had thought of themselves as God's chosen people and objected that any other people might share with them such favored position. They do not missionarize their faith, for they do not wish for it to include other than their own people, the children of Israel. This notwithstanding, neighborliness and trade between Arab and Jew enabled al Aws and al Khazraj to become more familiar with and more prepared for spiritual and religious discussion than other tribes. The evidence of this preparation is in the fact that nowhere had the Arabs responded to Muhammad's spiritual call with the same understanding and enthusiasm.

Suwayd ibn al Samit

Suwayd ibn al Samit was one of the noblest men of Yathrib. His people called him "the perfect" for his bravery, his eloquent poetry, his great honor, and his noble lineage. During this period Suwayd, who came to Makkah for pilgrimage, was approached by Muhammad, who called him unto God and Islam. Suwayd said, "Perhaps what you have, Muhammad, is like that which I have." Muhammad answered, "What is it that you have?" He answered, "The wisdom of Luqman." Muhammad asked him to explain this wisdom, and after hearing him, he said: "Your words are

good, but those which I have are even better. For they are a Qur'an
revealed by God to me as light and guidance." He read to him the Qur'an
and called him to Islam. Suwayd was pleased with what he heard, and
said: "That is indeed good." When he left Muhammad, he was in deep
thought; there are reports that when al Khazraj killed him he had already
become a Muslim.

Iyas ibn Mu'adh

Suwayd ibn al Samit was not the only example of the spiritual influence of the Jews upon the Arabs of Yathrib. The Jews had not only instigated the enmity of al Aws for al Khazraj and vice versa, but fanned its
flames as well. This enmity caused each of the two hostile tribes to seek
alliances with other tribes to consolidate its power. It was in search of an
alliance from the Quraysh against al Khazraj that Abu al Haysar Anas ibn
Rafi' came to Makkah with a number of men from Banu 'Abd al Ashhal,
including Iyas ibn Mu'adh. After Muhammad heard of their arrival, he
visited with them for a while, calling them unto Islam and reading to them
the Qur'an. When he finished, Iyas ibn Mu'adh, still young and of tender
age, rose and said: "O my people, this is by God far better than your religion." The delegation returned to Yathrib with one convert to Islam,
namely Iyas. Apparently, they were too busy to listen attentively to
Muhammad's preaching and too preoccupied with their war preparations.
Upon the return of Abu al Haysar and his delegation from Makkah, al
Aws engaged them in the war of Bu'ath where both parties suffered grave
losses. Nonetheless, the words of Muhammad — may God's peace be
upon him — left such a deep impression upon them that both al Aws and
al Khazraj came to see in Muhammad a prophet, a messenger of God, and
a worthy spiritual leader.

The Battle of Bu'ath

Al Aws fought the battle of Bu'ath against al Khazraj in which both
tribes gave full vent to their chronic enmity and hostility. So fierce did the
battle rage that each party was seriously considering exterminating the
enemy and finishing with the affair once and for all if it could only achieve
victory. Abu Usayd was the general not only of the legions of al Aws but
of their hate and resentment as well. In the first round of battle, al Aws
lost and they ran toward the desert for their lives. Al Khazraj, who accused

them of cowardice, began to sing in verse of their unmanliness and poltroonery. When Abu Usayd heard this, he plunged his own spear in his leg, fell from his horse and shouted, "Woe! Woe! By God I shall not move from this spot until they kill me. If you my people must forsake me, go ahead and run." Moved by this sacrifice of their own leader, al Aws returned to the battle with such enthusiasm and resoluteness — indeed despair — that they inflicted a terrible defeat upon al Khazraj. Pressing forth against their enemy, they burnt their houses as well as their orchards until stopped by Sa'd ibn Mu'adh al Ashhali. Indeed Abu Usayd had intended to wipe out the Khazraj tribe completely, house by house, tree by tree, and person by person, until not one of them remained alive. Abu Qays ibn al Aslat, however, stood in his way and begged him to save al Khazraj saying, "They are your co-religionists; it would still behoove you to keep them alive. They would be better neighbors for you than the foxes and beasts of prey of the desert."

Islamic Beginnings in Yathrib

After that day, the Jews recaptured their position of dominance in Yathrib. Both conqueror and vanquished realized the tragedy of what they had done, and they pondered their fate with gravity. Together they looked forward toward appointing a king to manage their affairs, a choice to fall upon 'Abdullah ibn Muhammad, of the vanquished al Khazraj, on account of his wisdom and sound opinions. The situation, evolved too rapidly, however, to allow a realization of this dream. A group of al Khazraj made a pilgrimage to Makkah where they were met by Muhammad and asked about their affairs. The Prophet knew they were clients of the Jews. In order to keep their clients in check, the Jews used to threaten them that a new prophet was about to appear whom they would follow and bring to any of their enemies that dared oppose them the total destruction which was meted out to the ancient tribes of 'Ad and Iram. When the Prophet talked to this group and called them unto God, they looked to one another and said, "By God, this is the Prophet by whom the Jews had threatened us. Let us acclaim him before they do." They responded favorably to Muhammad's call, were converted, and said, "We have left our people, al Aws and al Khazraj, who are alienated from one another and are full of hatred for one another. Would to God that they might meet you and unite under your leadership! Should this ever become the case, you will be the strongest man in Arabia." The group included in their numbers two men from Banu al Najjar, the uncles of 'Abd al Muttalib, and the grandfather of Muhammad who had protected him ever since his birth; the latter returned to Madinah and reported to their people their conversion to the new faith. The relatives received the news with joy and enthusiasm, for now they could boast of a religion that made them monotheists like the Jews — indeed more excellent than they. Soon, there was no house in al Aws or al Khazraj in which the name of Muhammad — God's peace by upon him — was not mentioned with reverence and awe.

The First Covenant of 'Aqabah

As the year passed and the holy months and the pilgrimage season returned, twelve men from Yathrib set out for Makkah. They met the Prophet at al 'Aqabah and entered with him into an alliance known as "the first covenant of al 'Aqabah." In this covenant they agreed to adhere to the absolute unity of God, neither to steal nor to commit adultery, neither to kill their children nor knowingly to commit any evil, and not to fail to obey God in His commandment of any good. They were satisfied that, in case they succeeded in living the life of virtue and obedience, their reward would be paradise; otherwise, their judgment belonged to God, His being the power to punish as well as to forgive. On their return to Yathrib, Muhammad sent with them Mus'ab ib 'Umayr to teach them the Qur'an and the precepts of Islam. After this covenant, Islam spread in Yathrib. Mus'ab resided with the Muslims of al Aws and al Khazraj and taught them the religion of God and the revelation of truth while their numbers increased with new converts every day. When the holy months returned, Mus'ab traveled to Makkah and reported to Muhammad the progress of the Muslims at Madinah in solidarity and power and informed the Prophet that a greater number of them, surpassing their predecessors in faith, would be arriving this season to perform the pilgrimage.

Muhammad Thinks of Emigration

Muhammad pondered the news which Mus'ab had brought for a long time. He thought of his followers in Yathrib who were increasing in number and power and who were progressing without let or hindrance from either Jews or others, unlike their colleagues in Makkah who suffered from Quraysh at every turn. He thought of Yathrib, the city of greater prosperity than Makkah on account of its large fields, its orchards and vineyards. It must have occurred to him to ask whether it might not be better that the Makkan Muslims emigrate to Yathrib, live with their co-religionists, and enjoy the security they missed so much at Makkah. In all likelihood, he pondered the observation which a member of the first group of converts from Yathrib once made, namely, that should al Aws and al Khazraj unite under him, he would be the strongest man in the country. Was it not better, now that God had united them under him, that he, too, should consider to emigrate to Yathrib? Muhammad did not want to return the injuries of Quraysh since he knew he was still weaker than they. As for his allies, Banu Hashim and Banu al Muttalib, it is one thing for them to come to his rescue as a sufferer of their injustice, but a totally different matter for them to support him in a war of aggression against the Quraysh. He also pondered the fact that Banu Hashim and Banu al Muttalib were not really capable of protecting all the Muslims in such an open war with Quraysh. It is true that religious conviction is man's strongest and most precious possession, for which he is prepared to sacrifice wealth, peace, freedom and life itself. It is equally true that the nature of religious conviction is such that physical injury inflames as well as strengthens it. Nonetheless, it is also true that persistence of injury, suffering, and sacrifice rob the believer of the possibility of the peaceful contemplation and precise vision necessary for the nourishment of faith and the deepening of man's awareness of ultimate reality. Previously, Muhammad had commanded his followers to emigrate to Christian Abyssinia because of its sound faith and just rule. There was all the more reason now to permit them to emigrate to Yathrib, to strengthen and be strengthened by their fellow Muslims in order to achieve a measure of peace and security against the evil designs of the enemy. There was all the more reason to ask them to do so in order to give them the chance to contemplate the religious truths, to cultivate their understanding, and to preach their faith to their fellow men. Islam had ruled out coercion and propagated itself through gentleness, persuasion, and conviction by argument alone.

The Second Covenant of 'Aqabah

The year 622 C.E. saw a great number of pilgrims, seventy-three men and two women, from Yathrib. When Muhammad learned of their arrival, he thought of concluding another pact with them which would not be limited to the preaching of Islam in the way followed during the last thirteen years. Beyond the preaching of gentleness and forbearance and sacrifice under attack, the times and their present dangers called for an alliance by which the Muslims would help one another to prevent as well as to repel injury and aggression. Secretly Muhammad contacted the leaders of the group and learned of their good preparation for a task such as this. They agreed to meet at al 'Aqabah during the night on the second day following the pilgrimage. The Muslims of Yathrib kept this appointment secret and did not inform the unbelievers among their own tribe. When the time came, they went to their rendezvous with the Prophet, stealing themselves away under the cover of night. When they reached al 'Aqabah, men and women ascended the mountain and there awaited the arrival of the Prophet.

Muhammad arrived with his uncle al 'Abbas ibn 'Abd al Muttalib. Al 'Abbas, who had not yet converted to Islam, knew from his nephew that this meeting was to conclude an alliance which might incite Quraysh to a war of aggression as much as it was designed to achieve peace and security. Muhammad had informed his uncle that together with some members of Banu al Muttalib and Banu Hashim he had agreed with the new group from Yathrib that they would protect him personally. Anxious to strengthen his nephew and people against a war whose losses might fall heavily upon Banu Hashim and Banu al Muttalib, al 'Abbas sought to make sure that among this group from Yathrib he would find real helpers and allies. Consequently, he was the first one to open the discussion. He said, "O men from Khazraj, Muhammad's eminence and prestige among us are known to you. We have protected him even against those of his own people who think as highly of him as we do. Among us, he stands strong and secure. But he insists on joining your party. If you find yourselves capable of fulfilling toward him what you have promised, then you may proceed. But if you would betray him and send him over to his enemies once he has joined your party, you had better now say so and leave him alone." After hearing this speech of al 'Abbas, the men from Yathrib said, "We have heard what you said, O 'Abbas," and turning to the Prophet, they continued, "O Prophet of God, speak out and choose for yourself and your Lord what you desire."

Muhammad, after reciting some verses from the Qur'an, preached his faith in God in moving terms. He then said to the men from Yathrib, "I covenant with you on the condition that you will protect me against all, just as you would protect your women and children." Al Bara' ibn Ma'rur, who was chief of his people and their elder, had entered into Islam after the first covenant of al 'Aqabah. Since then he had been fulfilling all that Islam required of him, except that he directed himself toward the Ka'bah whenever he prayed. Muhammad and all the Muslims were in the prac-

tice of turning their faces toward al Aqsa mosque in Jerusalem. His disagreement with his people on the subject of the *qiblah* was brought to the
attention of the Prophet upon their arrival to Makkah. The Prophet
enjoined al Bara' not to turn his face toward the Ka'bah during prayer.
Nonetheless, it was the same al Bara' who first stretched forth his hand to
covenant with the Prophet when the latter asked for the protection that
the people of Yathrib were wont to give their women and children.

Discussion before Conclusion of the Covenant

Al Bara' said, "We have covenanted with you, O Prophet of God. By
God, we are men of many wars; we are men of the sword, having inherited it from father unto son." Before al Bara' finished his words, Abu al
Haytham ibn al Tayyihan said, "O Prophet of God, there are pacts
between us and some Jews which we are going to denounce. Should your
cause succeed later on among your own tribe, would you return to them
and leave us alone?" Muhammad smiled and said, "No! Rather, your blood
is my blood and your destruction is my destruction. You are of me and I
am of you. I shall fight whomsoever you fight and make peace with
whomsoever you will make peace." The people were about to rise and give
covenant to Muhammad when al 'Abbas ibn 'Ubadah interrupted and
said, "O men of Khazraj! Are you fully aware of what you are about to
covenant with this man? You are about to covenant with him to make war
against all sorts of men without discrimination. If you have any fear that,
should you lose your wealth and should your leaders fall by the sword, you
might betray Muhammad, say so now and withdraw from this covenant.
For if you do not and then betray your oath, you will have lost this world
as well as the next. But if you feel certain that you can stand by him and
fulfill this oath, notwithstanding the loss of your property and the murder
of your dear ones, then go ahead and covenant with him. He is, by God,
the best gain in this world and in the next."

All the people present answered together, "We take him despite all
threats to property, wealth and life. Tell us, O Prophet of God, what will
be our reward if we remain true to this oath?" With his usual self-reliance
Muhammad answered, "Paradise." They stretched out their hands to him,
and he to them, and the covenant was concluded. Thereafter, the Prophet
said, "Elect among yourselves twelve representatives who will be responsible to me regarding your behavior and conduct." After they elected nine
from al Khazraj and three from al Aws, the Prophet addressed them in the

following words: "You are the guarantors of your people, just as the disciples were guarantors of theirs before Jesus, Son of Mary. I, for my part, am the guarantor of my people." Such was their second covenant which included the words, "We have covenanted to listen and to obey in health and in sickness, in fortune and misfortune, to tell the truth wherever we might be and, at all times, to fear none in the cause of God."

The Covenant

All this had taken place in the middle of the night atop one of the hills of al 'Aqabah in perfect isolation from the surrounding world. Only God, the covenantors felt certain, knew what they were about. No sooner had they terminated their meeting, however, than they heard a crier warning the Quraysh in the following words, "Muhammad and the apostates have covenanted to make war against you." The case of this, however, was unique. He had heard a little bit about the matter as he traveled to al 'Aqabah and, being a Qurayshi and idolator, he thought of spoiling the arrangement of Muhammad and of frightening the Muslims by pretending everything the Muslims did was known to their enemies. Al Khazraj and al Aws, however, stood firm by their covenant. Indeed, al 'Abbas ibn 'Ubadah told Muhammad immediately after he heard the crier, "By God, who has sent you with the truth, if you order us to pounce upon Mina tomorrow morning with our swords, we shall do so." Muhammad answered, "God has not commanded us to fight. Return to your quarters." The covenanters returned to their quarters and slept until the morning.

Quraysh and the Covenant of al 'Aqabah

The morrow had hardly come when the Quraysh, learning of the new pact, was disturbed by it. The Quraysh leaders went to al Khazraj in their own quarters and blamed them for what they had just done. The Quraysh reiterated that they sought no war against them and asked them why they had covenanted with Muhammad to fight them on his side. The unbelievers of al Khazraj denied that any of this had taken place. The Muslims, on the other hand, kept silent and were saved from embarrassment when the Quraysh believed the claim of their co-religionists. Thus the news was neither confirmed nor denied, and the Quraysh allowed the matter to stand until new evidence could be brought forth. The people of Yathrib returned to their city before the Quraysh had reached any certainty about what had happened. When later the Quraysh did learn the truth, they ran after the people of Yathrib who had exited the day before but could catch up with none except Sa'd ibn 'Ubadah. They took him to Makkah in chains and tortured him until Jubayr ibn Mut'am ibn 'Adiyy and al Harith ibn Umayyah ransomed him as their agent in Yathrib when they passed by there on their way to al Sham.

Tension between the Two Parties

Neither in its fear of them nor in its attempt to catch up with the people of Yathrib, who covenanted with Muhammad to fight against them, did the tribe of Quraysh overestimate the danger. For thirteen long years they had known and observed Muhammad. They had exerted enough effort in their war against Muhammad to exhaust their own as well as Muhammad's energies. The Quraysh knew Muhammad to be a very strong and tenacious man who held only to his God and the message He had entrusted to him. The Quraysh knew him as an unwavering man who feared neither harm nor death. For a moment it seemed to the Quraysh that after all the injuries they inflicted upon him, after blockading him within Makkah, and frightening the tribesmen enough to keep them from joining him, Muhammad's cause was about to fall. They predicted that Muhammad's activity would henceforth be restricted to his followers alone and that these would soon fall apart under the constant pressures of Quraysh to seek reconciliation. The new covenant brought a new determinant into the situation and gave Muhammad and his followers some hope of victory. It at least strengthened their freedom to conduct their missionary activity and renew their attack upon the idols of the Ka'bah and their worship. But who could predict what the situation would turn out to be throughout the Arabian Peninsula after Yathrib had come to the rescue of Muhammad and both its tribes of al Aws and al Khazraj were united under his leadership? The Quraysh were rightly apprehensive of the future since the covenant of al 'Aqabah rendered the Muslims safe against attack and gave them freedom to practice their new faith, to preach it to the others, and to welcome the new converts under their protection. Quraysh thought, therefore, that unless this movement was uprooted and destroyed completely, the future would continue to be threatening and the victory of Muhammad would be a most disturbing possibility.

The Quraysh thought very hard how it could counter-attack Muhammad and outmaneuver him in order to destroy this latent power. He, too, gave the same problem no less thought than did the Quraysh. He looked upon the covenant as a gate which God had unlocked before him in order to bring power and glory to His religion, to God's truthful words. The war between him and the Quraysh had then reached a new level of tension by becoming a matter of life and death for both parties. Muhammad trusted, however, that victory belonged to the truthful. He decided to rally his people to trust in God, in utter disregard to Quraysh and its plotting. He therefore must march forward, but with wisdom, precision, and sure step. The new situation called for the greatest possible statesmanship and the ablest generalship in time of battle.

The Muslims' Emigration to Yathrib

Subsequently, Muhammad commanded his companions to follow *al Ansar*[2] in Yathrib. He ordered them to exit from Makkah in very small groups so that they would not give cause to Quraysh to suspect or attack them. The Muslims began their exodus individually or in small groups. When the Quraysh realized what they were about, it began to return those whom it could catch to Makkah to suffer punishment and torture. This Makkan counter-measure was carried out with such zeal and determination that man and wife were separated whenever a pair wanted to exit from Makkah. Those who disobeyed were locked up in jail. But the Quraysh could not do more, fearful as they were of alienating the tribes by killing their Muslim members and thereby adding to their list of enemies. The Muslims, nonetheless, continued to exit from Makkah and to emigrate to Yathrib. Muhammad remained where he was, nobody knowing whether he, too, was planning to emigrate or not. None suspected him. Previously, he had permitted his companions to emigrate to Abyssinia without going there himself; he had stayed behind and continued to call the Makkans to Islam. Indeed, even Abu Bakr asked the Prophet for permission to emigrate to Yathrib. The Prophet advised, "Do not hurry; perhaps God may yet give you a companion for your trip." No more was said regarding this matter.

The Quraysh and the Prophet's Emigration

All this notwithstanding, the Quraysh were quite apprehensive lest the Prophet himself emigrate to Yathrib. The Muslims in that city had become so numerous that the dominion of the city was almost theirs. The *Muhajirun*,[3] who were arriving at Yathrib in numbers, consolidated and increased Muslim power. Should Muhammad himself go there, the Quraysh feared that under his wise and farsighted leadership and persistence, the people of Yathrib might even seek to attack Makkah or, at least, to cut off their trade route to al Sham. If this should ever become a real possibility, the Muslims would avenge the boycott and isolation of the Muslims in kind by cutting off the Makkan trade routes.

On the other hand, even if the Quraysh were to succeed in keeping Muhammad in Makkah and thus prevent him from joining his companions, the Quraysh were still exposed to the danger of the people of Yathrib's attacking them in defense of their Prophet. Hence, the Quraysh decided that there was really no alternative but to kill Muhammad and get rid of this persistent trouble once and for all. But in case they did succeed in killing him, Banu Hashim and Banu al Muttalib would surely seek to avenge his blood, and the civil war which they feared so much would break out within Makkah and bring a greater danger than that which they feared might come from the side of Yathrib. In al Nadwah, their community house, the Quraysh gathered in order to find a means and solution. One of them suggested, "Let us catch Muhammad and lock him up in jail. Then, wait to see happen to him that which has happened to other possessed people and poets like Zuhayr, al Nabighah, and others." This view found no supporters. Another suggested, "Let us carry him out of our country and banish him and then forget about him altogether." This, too, found no supporters because the Quraysh feared that Muhammad might then join his followers in Yathrib and lead them against Makkah — a frightful possibility, indeed. Finally, they concluded that the best solution is that each one of their clans delegate a strong youth and arm him with a sharp sword so that all these delegates can kill Muhammad together in one stroke; therefore, responsibility for his death would be equally divided among all, thus making vengeance on the part of Banu 'Abd Manaf virtually impossible. The clan of Muhammad would then be forced to accept his bloodwit, and the Quraysh would put an end to this instigator who had rent its unity and sapped its power. The Quraysh thought well of this counsel and carefully chose their executioners. They expected that the story of Muhammad was soon to come to a close, that his cause would soon be buried and forgotten, and that those who had migrated to Yathrib would soon return to their tribe, their former religion and gods, and that Quraysh would resume the unity and leadership which it had almost lost.

10

Al Hijrah or the Prophet's Emigration

The Command to Emigrate

Muhammad discovered that the Quraysh had plotted to kill him rather than to allow him to emigrate to Madinah where he might entrench the forces of Islam for a resolute stand against Makkah and from where he might cut off its trade with al Sham. No one doubted that Muhammad would henceforth seize any opportunity to carry out his plan for emigration. But no one knew of any plans he might have had; not even Abu Bakr, who had been commanded to keep two beasts alert and ready ever since he asked the Prophet for permission to emigrate and the Prophet advised him to wait. Muhammad remained in Makkah until he learned of the Quraysh's plot to assassinate him, and until none but the fewest Muslims were still left there with him. He waited for the command of his Lord for emigration. When, finally, that command did come, he went to the house of Abu Bakr and informed him of the permission God had granted. He asked Abu Bakr to accompany him on the trip.

'Ali in the Prophet's Bed

Here begins one of the greatest adventures history has known in the cause of truth and religious conviction. It is one of the noblest and most beautiful. Abu Bakr had chosen his two beasts and given them to 'Abdullah ibn Urayqit to graze until the time when they would be needed. When the two men planned to leave Makkah they were absolutely certain that Quraysh would follow them in their trail in order to seize them and bring them back. Hence, Muhammad decided to surprise his enemies by leaving under circumstances and at a time hardly conceivable to them. The young men whom the Quraysh had prepared for performing the assassination had blockaded his house during the night in fear that he might run away. On the night of the Hijrah, Muhammad confided his plan to 'Ali ibn Abu Talib and asked him to cover himself with the Prophet's green mantle from Hadramawt and to sleep in the Prophet's bed. He further asked him to tarry in Makkah until he had returned all things left with Muhammad to their rightful owners. The Quraysh men waiting to kill the Prophet felt reassured whenever, looking through a hole in the door, they saw somebody sleeping in the Prophet's bed. Just before dawn, Muhammad left without being noticed, picked up Abu Bakr at the latter's house and from there they proceeded through a back door southward toward the cave of Thawr. The southerly direction of their flight was inconceivable to everyone.

Nobody knew of their hiding place in the cave except 'Abdullah, son of Abu Bakr, his two sisters, 'A'ishah and Asma', and their servant 'Amir ibn Fuhayrah. 'Abdullah spent his day in Makkah listening to what the Quraysh said and plotted about Muhammad and then reported it to the pair at their hideout under cover of night. 'Amir grazed the sheep of Abu Bakr and passed by the cave in the evening in order to give them some milk and meat. Upon 'Abdullah's return from the cave, 'Amir would follow him with all his sheep and then conceal any trace of his steps. For three long days, the pair remained in the cave and the Quraysh persistently looked for them without avail. For the Quraysh it was absolutely necessary to find Muhammad and to prevent his emigration to Yathrib. Meanwhile, Muhammad spent most of his time praying to God and invoking his blessings, and Abu Bakr continually sought to find out whether they were being discovered and to look after their security.

The young men of Quraysh who were chosen to kill Muhammad continued their search and came close to the cave fully armed and ready for the kill. When they found a shepherd in the vicinity, they asked him about Muhammad and Abu Bakr. He answered, "Perhaps they are within the cave, although I have not seen anyone go in or out." When he heard the shepherd's answer, Abu Bakr trembled with fear and expected the Quraysh to break into the cave any moment. He withdrew into a corner and, trusting in God, remained motionless. Some members of the

Quraysh party climbed up to the cave, and the foremost among them turned round as soon as he saw the cave entrance. His companions asked him, "Why have you not gone into the cave?" He answered, "Its entrance is covered with cobwebs, and there is a pair of wild pigeons on the threshold. Obviously, no one could have gone in without disturbing the pigeons and destroying the cobwebs." At that moment, Muhammad prayed while Abu Bakr continued to shake with fear. To Abu Bakr, who pressed ever closer to Muhammad, the latter whispered, "Do not grieve; God is with us." According to some Hadith books, it is reported that when the Quraysh party arrived at the cave entrance, Abu Bakr exclaimed: "If anyone of them looks at his feet he will find us," and that the Prophet had answered, "O Abu Bakr, how can you fear for two men whose constant companion is God Himself?" The Quraysh men were further convinced that the cave was empty when they saw the entrance to the cave covered — indeed blocked — with branches growing from a tree nearby. They then agreed to leave and called one another for their return to Makkah. Only then did the two refugees within the cave feel reassured. Abu Bakr's faith in God and His Prophet became stronger, and Muhammad prayed: "Praise be to God! God is greater than all!"

The Miracle of the Cave

The cobwebs, the two wild pigeons, and the tree and its branches — these are the miracles which the biography books relate concerning the hiding in the cave of Thawr. The miracle is that none of these things were there when the Prophet and his companion entered the cave, and that thereafter, the spider hurried to weave its cobwebs, the two pigeons to build their nest and to lay their eggs, and the tree to grow its branches around the door. In this connection the orientalist Dermenghem wrote, "These three things are the only miracles recorded in authentic Mussulman history: the web of a spider, the love of a dove, the sprouting of a flower — three miracles accomplished daily on God's earth."[1]

Some Biographers Omit the Story

This miracle received no mention in Ibn Hisham's biography. His version of the story of the cave ran as follows: "They [Muhammad and Abu Bakr] went to the cave of Thawr, on the south side of Makkah. Abu Bakr ordered his son 'Abdullah to stay in Makkah during the day, listen to the news of the Quraysh and bring them knowledge thereof in the evening. He ordered his servant, 'Amir ibn Fuhayrah, to continue to graze his sheep and to come by the cave at night. Asma', daughter of Abu Bakr, brought them provisions of food in the evening, also. The Prophet of God — may God's peace and blessing be upon him — stayed in the cave three days. The Quraysh had announced a prize of one hundred camels to whosoever would bring back Muhammad to Makkah. 'Abdullah, son of Abu Bakr, used to spend his day in Makkah listening well to the plotting and gossip of the Quraysh, and when visiting the pair in the evening, related the news to them. 'Amir ibn Fuhayrah, servant of Abu Bakr, used to graze the flock of sheep around Makkah and, in the evening, passed by the cave and gave milk and meat to the pair. When 'Abdullah, son of Abu Bakr, returned home to Makkah, he was followed by 'Amir ibn Fuhayrah and his sheep in order to cover over his footprints. Three days later, when the interest of the Quraysh in this search had subsided, the man whom Abu Bakr had appointed to graze the two camels for the trip came with the three camels, two for Muhammad and Abu Bakr, and a third for himself. . . ." That is all that Ibn Hisham says concerning the story of the cave.

In the same connection, the following verses of the Qur'an were revealed:

وَ اِذْ يَمْكُرُ بِكَ الَّذِيْنَ كَفَرُوْا لِيُثْبِتُوْكَ اَوْيَقْتُلُوْكَ اَوْ يُخْرِجُوْكَ ۚ وَيَمْكُرُوْنَ وَيَمْكُرُ اللّٰهُ ۚ وَاللّٰهُ خَيْرُ الْمَاكِرِيْنَ ۞ . . . اِلَّا تَنْصُرُوْهُ فَقَدْ نَصَرَهُ اللّٰهُ اِذْ اَخْرَجَهُ الَّذِيْنَ كَفَرُوْا ثَانِيَ اثْنَيْنِ اِذْ هُمَا فِى الْغَارِ اِذْ يَقُوْلُ لِصَاحِبِهٖ لَا تَحْزَنْ اِنَّ اللّٰهَ مَعَنَا ۚ فَاَنْزَلَ اللّٰهُ سَكِيْنَتَهٗ عَلَيْهِ وَاَيَّدَهٗ بِجُنُوْدٍ لَمْ تَرَوْهَا وَجَعَلَ كَلِمَةَ الَّذِيْنَ كَفَرُوا السُّفْلٰى ۚ وَكَلِمَةُ اللّٰهِ هِيَ الْعُلْيَا ۚ وَاللّٰهُ عَزِيْزٌ حَكِيْمٌ ۞

"When the unbelievers plotted to imprison you, to kill you or to banish you, God planned on your behalf, and He is the best of planners. . . If you [the people] do not help Muhammad, then know that God Will. For God helped him when the unbelievers drove him out, and he and his companion hid in the cave. At that time, the Prophet said to his companion, 'Grieve not for God is with us.' It was then that God sent down his peace upon him and assisted him with hosts invisible that the word of God might be supreme and that of the unbelievers might be repudiated. God is almighty and all-wise."[2]

The Trip to Yathrib

On the third day, when they felt certain that the Quraysh had called off the hunt for them in the vicinity, Muhammad and Abu Bakr commanded their servant to bring them their camels for escape. The servant managed to bring a third camel for himself. Asma', daughter of Abu Bakr, brought them provisions. As they mounted, they could not find ropes with which to tie their provisions of food and water. Asma' cut her robe in two and used one half of it for the purpose while covering herself with the other half. For this reason she was called "the woman with the two half-robes." Their provisions taken care of, the three men went forth. Abu Bakr carried five thousand Dirhims,[3] which was all that was left of his wealth. Lest the Quraysh should find them, they cautiously took an untrodden path toward their destination. Their servant and guide, 'Abdullah ibn Urayqit, from the tribe of Banu al Du'il, headed south of Makkah and then to the mountain range of Tihamat close by the shore of the Red Sea. From there he took an unknown path northward parallel to the shore but far removed from it. His purpose was always to remain off the beaten track. All night and most of the day the riders pressed forth unaffected by fatigue or hardship, for every hardship was preferable — indeed easy by comparison — to what the Quraysh was prepared to do to destroy them and their cause! Muhammad never doubted that God would come to his help, but God had also commanded man not to expose himself to open risks. God had counselled that He would assist man only as long as man helped himself and his brother. The two men were successful in their hiding in the cave. However, the Quraysh's announcement of a hundred camel prize to whoever would bring them back or furnish information which would lead to their capture was sufficient to mobilize the wealth-seeking Makkans for the search, even if it was a criminal one. Still, the Arabs of Quraysh had additional motivation to conduct such a search, for they regarded Muhammad as their enemy *par excellence,* and they were so revengeful and passionate in their hate that no consideration could stop them from exploiting the weak and injuring the harmless. Therefore, they redoubled their attentiveness and renewed their vigor for the search.

The Story of Suraqah

Their intuition did not fail them. A man soon arrived at Makkah to report that on his way he met three riders whom he thought were Muhammad and his companions. Upon hearing this report, Suraqah ibn

Malik ibn Ju'shum immediately said, "Those are the sons of so and so." His purpose was to lead his companions into disregarding the report so that he might capture Muhammad single-handed and win the prize of the hundred camels. A moment later, he returned home, loaded himself with arms, and ordered his servant to take his horse to the outskirts of the city so that no one would see him go. There, he arrayed himself for battle, mounted his horse, and galloped toward the spot where Muhammad was reported to have been seen. Muhammad and his two companions had at that time repaired to a tree to rest a little under its shade, to eat a meal and to replenish their energies.

The time was close to evening. Muhammad and Abu Bakr began to ready their beasts to resume their ride. Suraqah was still as far from them as the eye could see. Exhausted with fatigue from all its galloping, Suraqah's horse fell twice on the way. When the travelers came into his sight, and he realized he could now capture or kill them, Suraqah forgot that his horse had fallen twice already. He spurred it once more and hurried it toward them. The horse fell to the ground with its rider. At this turn, Suraqah felt very apprehensive that the gods were against the execution of his scheme and that he might be exposing himself to grave danger should he spur his horse forward for the fourth time. After stopping, he called to the travelers: "I am Suraqah ibn Ju'shum. Wait for me so that I may talk to you. By God, I shall do you neither harm or injury." When he arrived, he asked Muhammad to write him a note with which to prove his present encounter. At the Prophet's command, Abu Bakr wrote a note to this effect which Suraqah took and returned home. Made contrite by his unfortunate venture, he spread the news that the riders were not Muhammad and his party at all!

The Hardships of the Road

Muhammad and his two companions set forth toward Yathrib across mountains, hills, and deserts whose sands were glowing with heat. Since they were off the beaten track, they found hardly anything with which to alleviate the hardships of sun and thirst. Furthermore, they were ever apprehensive that the Quraysh or some other people might surprise and overtake them. Their only consolation was their patient trust in God and the truth revealed to His Prophet. For seven consecutive days they travelled, lying low during the heat of day and moving with great haste under cover of night. In the stillness of night and the brilliance of its stars lay their only security and assurance. When they reached the quarters of the tribe of Banu Sahm, where elder chieftain Buraydah came over to greet them, their fears lessened, and for the first time, their hearts palpitated with the hope and assurance of victory. They had almost reached their destination.

Awaiting the Prophet in Yathrib

During Muhammad's long and exhaustive trip, the news reached his companions in Yathrib that he had emigrated from Makkah in order to join them. Aware of the enmity of the Quraysh and of their attempts to follow and to seize the Prophet, the Muslims waited anxiously for his arrival and looked very much forward to hearing the details of his escape. Many of them had never seen the Prophet before although they had heard a great deal about his eloquence and resolution. Naturally, they were quite anxious to meet him. We can imagine the enthusiasm of these men when we know that a number of notables from Yathrib had followed Muhammad even though they had never seen him before. Their knowledge of him depended on his companions who had spoken to them of their love for him and who had been staunchly carrying his message about.

The Spread of Islam in Yathrib

Sa'd ibn Zurarah and Mus'ab ibn 'Umayr once sat in one of the courtyards of Banu Zafar listening to the speech of those who entered into Islam. Their news had reached Sa'd ibn Mu'adh and Usayd ibn Hudayr, chieftains of their tribes. Sa'd said to Usayd, as one chieftain to another, "Go out to these two men who came here to subvert the weaklings among us. Chastise them and forbid them to come here again. You can do this better than I because Sa'd ibn Zurarah is a cousin of mine and I cannot be harsh enough to him." Usayd went out to seek the two men. Mus'ab said, "Will you not sit down and listen to us? If you hear something worthwhile, accept it. If, on the other hand, you hear something unworthy, you may put a quick end to it." Usayd replied, "You are fair." He stuck his spear into the ground and sat down listening to Mus'ab's preaching of Islam. No sooner had Mus'ab finished than Usayd was converted to Islam. When he returned, his fellow chieftain, Sa'd, was annoyed at this and sought out the two men in person. They offered him the same choice, and he, too, was converted. Following upon this, Sa'd went to his people and said, "Oh, Banu 'Abd al Ashhal, what do you think of me?" They answered, "You are our chieftain, our dearest relative, our wise leader and righteous representative." He said, "Then I shall forbid myself to speak to any of your men and women until you believe in God and in His prophet." Banu 'Abd al Ashhal then entered into the faith *en bloc*.

Islam had spread so widely in Yathrib and the Muslims had gathered so much strength before the emigration of the Prophet that some Muslim youths were encouraged to attack the idols of the unbelievers. Apparently Islam had enjoyed a strength that the Muslims of Makkah had never dreamt of before. 'Amr ibn al Jamuh had a wooden idol which he called Manat and which he kept in his house according to the custom of the nobility, for he was one of the noblemen of Banu Salamah. When the youths of his tribe joined Islam, they raided his house at night and, without his knowledge, would steal away the idol and place it in the refuse dump outside the city. In the morning, 'Amr would miss his statue and look for it. When he found it, he would cleanse, purify, and return it to its place. All along, he would curse and threaten the offenders in the strongest terms. The youth of Banu Salamah continued their attacks upon this idol until one day 'Amr hung his sword on the shoulder of the statue and said to it, "If there is any power in you, there's my sword, defend yourself." The following morning, however, he found the idol robbed of its sword and tied to a dead dog inside an empty pit. At that moment, his people talked to him and showed him how unworthy of man is idolatry. He was convinced and entered Islam.

With all these successes which Islam had been scoring in Yathrib, the people of Yathrib looked forward quite eagerly to the arrival of Muhammad when they heard of his emigration. For many days before his arrival, they went out to the outskirts of their city at dawn to spend the morning seeking signs of the Prophet's arrival.

The month was July and the days were hot. Muhammad reached Quba', two leagues from Madinah,[4] and stayed there four days with Abu Bakr being constantly with him. During this interval, he founded a mosque and before he left for Madinah, 'Ali ibn Abu Talib had joined his party. 'Ali had returned the trusts left with Muhammad which Muhammad had asked him to return to their rightful owners, and he came to Yathrib on foot, walking during the night and hiding during the day. He had been on the road for two whole weeks in order to join the Prophet and his fellow Muslims in Madinah.

Muhammad's Entry into Madinah

One day, as the Muslims waited the arrival of Muhammad, a Jew of Yathrib announced to them, "O People of Qaylah, your man has finally arrived." It was a Friday, and Muhammad performed his prayer in Madinah at the mosque situated in the valley of Ranuqna. The Muslims of Yathrib arrived there from all quarters in order to see the man whom they had not seen, but whom they loved with all their minds and hearts, in whose message they had believed, and whose name they had mentioned many times in their daily prayers. A number of notables invited the Prophet to stay in their houses and to enjoy the comforts, security, and protection of their quarters. As Muhammad apologized, he rode his camel, which he allowed to go free, toward the city. As it ran forth surrounded by the Muslims who opened the way for it, the people of Yathrib, whether Jews or unbelievers, looked with surprise on the new agitation and vitality that had suddenly seized their city. They looked at this great visitor who was equally acclaimed by al Aws and al Khazraj, who had until recently been death enemies of each other. No one among them apparently grasped the new direction which history was taking at that auspicious moment, nor the great destiny at work to make their city immortal. The Prophet's camel continued to run until it stopped at a yard belonging to two orphans of Banu al Najjar. There, the camel lay down and the Prophet dismounted. Upon inquiring who the owner of the yard was, he learned from Mu'adh ibn 'Afra' that it belonged to Sahl and Suhayl, sons of 'Amr, of whom he was the guardian. He asked the Prophet to build a mosque there and made a promise to satisfy the two orphans. Muhammad accepted the request by building his mosque as well as his living quarters there.

A map of Al Madinah al Munawwarah and vicinity
appears on the following two pages.

al Jurf

al Ghābah

Mt. Tha

Zughābah

Mt. Uhu

Orchards
ʿAyn al
al Darīh
al

Rūmah Well
Mt. Ḥabashah
ruins
Palace of
Saʿīd ibn al ʿĀs

Jabal ʿAynayn
al Saʿ

Mosque of Nuḥs
al

Yathrib
Mosque

Wādī al ʿArṣah al Kubra
Wādī al ʿAqīq
al ʿArṣah al Ṣughrā

Road to Shām
Road to

11

Harrah al Wabrah

al Khandaq

Jammāʾ ʿĀqil

Palaces of al ʿAqīq

Road to
Yanbuʿ

Well of
Suqyā

al Ḥāwla

old grave

Jammāʾ Umm Khālid

Road to Qubāʾ

Jammāʾ Tudāru

Wādī

Wādī Ranūnā

al Jamʿah
Mosque

Well of ʿUrwah

Well of Arīs

Mosque

Aṭum al Daḥyānī
ʿAyn al Azraq

Qa

Hou
House

Dhū al Ḥulayfah

Dams

al

Mt. ʿAsīr

AL MADĪNAH
AL MUNAWWARAH

AND VICINITY

North

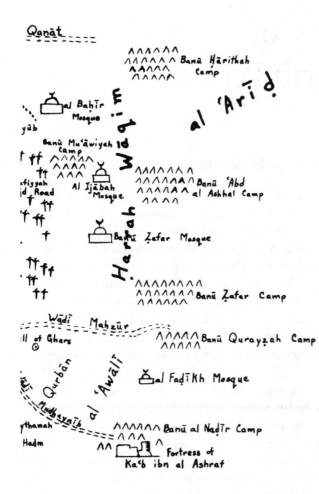

Qanāt

Banū Hārithah Camp

al Bahīr Mosque

al 'Arīd

yūb

Banū Mu'āwiyah Camp

Harrah Waqim

Al Ijābah Mosque

Banū 'Abd al Ashhal Camp

afiyyah id Road

Banū Zafar Mosque

Banū Zafar Camp

Wādi Mahzūr

ll of Ghars

Banū Qurayzah Camp

al 'Awālī

Qurbān

al Fadīkh Mosque

Mudhaynib

ythamah

Banū al Nadīr Camp

Hadm

Fortress of Ka'b ibn al Ashraf

KEY

mountain	
valley	
forest	
orchards	↑↑↑↑
date palms	↑↑
ditch	
dam	
campsite	∧∧∧
house	▣
spring ('ayn)	•
well	◎
grave	
mosque	

1 Thaniyyah al Wadā'
2 Mt. al Mustandir
3 Saqīfah Banū Sā'idah
4 Thaniyyah 'Ath'ath
5 Dar al Diyāfah
6 Al Sāhah Quarter
7 Al 'Aynī Road
8 Sūq al Hadrah
9 Al Suqyā Mosque
10 Al Ghumāmah Mosque
11 Gate of al Shām
12 Gate of al Jum'ah
13 Gate of al 'Awālī
14 Gate of al Qubā'
15 Gate of al 'Anbariyyah
16 Well of Dharwān

11

Beginning of the Yathrib Period

Explanation of the City's Welcome

Having heard the news of his emigration, of Quraysh's plot to kill him, and of his travel in mid-summer on an untrodden path ridden with hardships — across rocky mountains and valleys aglow with fire under the torrid sun — individuals and groups of men and women went out to welcome Muhammad to their city. Excited by their own curiosity after the spread of the news of Muhammad's mission throughout the Arabian Peninsula, the people of Yathrib went out to see and meet the author of this call to renounce the holy faith and sacred beliefs of their ancestors. More importantly, they went out to meet Muhammad and to welcome him because his intention was henceforth to live with them in their own city. Every clan and tribe of Yathrib well knew what political, social, and other advantages it stood to gain should it succeed in convincing the new guest to reside in its midst. Indeed, they went out to take a look at this man that they might confirm their intuition concerning him. Hence, neither the unbelievers of Yathrib nor its Jews were any less enthusiastic than the Muslims, whether Muhajirun or Ansar. That is why they came from all sides to walk in his procession although each was naturally moved by different feelings. As Muhammad allowed his camel to run loose, they followed him in a disorderly manner; it was as if he had intended it that way in order to give each one of them a chance to come closer to him to take a nearer glimpse of his face. It was as if everyone had come out in order to gather in one moment of consciousness all that he had heard about and all that he could see of the person to whom he had given the grand oath of allegiance at al 'Aqabah where he pledged to lay down his life when necessary in fighting any man whatever that stood in the way of the faith. It was, furthermore, as if everyone wanted to see the man who taught the unity of God based upon a scientific investigation of the cosmos and an objective search for the truth: a doctrine for the sake of which he had abandoned his native town, its people, and borne their enmity and harm for some thirteen consecutive years.

Building of the Prophet's Mosque

We have seen that the Prophet's camel stopped in the courtyard of Sahl and Suhayl. The Prophet bought the land in order to build his mosque there. While the mosque was being erected, he stayed in the house of Abu Ayyub Khalid ibn Zayd al Ansari. In the construction of the mosque, Muhammad worked with his own hands as did the Muslims, whether Muhajirun or Ansar. When the mosque was completed, they built on one side of it living quarters for the Prophet. These operations did not overtax anyone, for the two structures were utterly simple and economical. The mosque consisted of a vast courtyard whose four walls were built out of bricks and mud. A part of it was covered with a ceiling made from date trunks and leaves. Another part was devoted to shelter the poor who had no home at all. The mosque was not lit during the night except for an hour at the time of the night prayer. At that time some straw was burned for light. Thus it continued to be for nine years, after which lamps were attached to the tree trunks on which stood the ceiling. The living quarters of the Prophet were no more luxurious than the mosque although they had to be more closed in order to give a measure of privacy.

Upon completion of the building, Muhammad left the house of Abu Ayyub and moved into the new quarters. He began to think of this new life which he had just initiated and the wide gate it opened for his mission. The various tribes and clans of this city were already competing with one another; and they differed among themselves in ways and for reasons unknown to any Makkan. Yet it was equally obvious that they all longed for peace and freedom from the differences and hostilities which had torn them apart in the past. Moreover, they were ambitious for and willing to build a peaceful future capable of greater prestige and prosperity than Makkah had ever enjoyed. That is not to say that these matters concerned

Muhammad in the least. Rather, his concern, whether immediate or ultimate, was the conveyance of the message God had entrusted to him. The
people of Makkah had resisted that message with every weapon they
knew, and their hostility prevented its light from shining in the hearts of
most men. The injury and harm the Quraysh were wont to inflict upon
anyone who ventured into the new faith was sufficient to prevent conversion of those who were not yet convinced of its truth and value. Hence it
was a cardinal need that Muslims as well as others feel certain that whoever followed the new guidance and entered into the religion of God was
absolutely secure against attack. This precaution was necessary in order to
confirm the believers in their faith and to enable the weak, the fearful, and
the hesitant to enter into the faith with confidence. This consideration
preoccupied Muhammad as he moved to the security of his new home in
Yathrib. In the years to follow, it constituted the cornerstone of his policy.
All biographies have emphasized this orientation of Muhammad's poli-
cies. At the time, he thought of neither property, nor wealth, nor trade, but
only of realizing the security of his followers and their right to worship as
they pleased on an equal footing with men of other faiths. It was absolutely necessary that the Muslim, the Jew, and the Christian have an equal
opportunity in their exercise of religious freedom as well as in their freedom to hold different opinions and to preach their own faiths. Only such
freedom can guarantee victory for the truth and progress of the world
toward perfection in the higher unity of mankind. Every war against this
freedom furthers the cause of falsehood. Every limitation of it gives power
to the forces of darkness to cut off the light shining within the soul calling man to unity with mankind and the world to an eternal bond of harmony and love instead of alienation, war, and extinction.

Muhammad's Aversion to War

Ever since the Hijrah, revelation persistently confirmed this orientation of Muhammad and caused him strongly to incline toward peace,
away from fighting, hostility or war. It made him regard fighting as the
last resort in defense of this freedom and this faith. When, at the cry of
the Qurayshi spy, the people of Yathrib who pledged to him their allegiance at the second al 'Aqabah meeting proclaimed, "By God who sent
you as a messenger of the truth, if you wish us to pounce on the quarter
of Mina tomorrow morning with swords drawn, not one of us will stay
behind," did Muhammad not respond: "God has not commanded us to

fight"? Did not the first verse granting such authority say: "Permission to fight is granted to those who are being fought, for they suffer injustice, and God is certainly capable of coming to their assistance"?[1] Was not this verse immediately followed by the revelation,

$$ وَقَاتِلُوهُمْ حَتَّى لَا تَكُونَ فِتْنَةٌ وَ يَكُونَ الدِّينُ كُلُّهُ لِلَّٰهِ $$

"And fight them until all persecution has stopped and religion has become all God's"?[2]

Muhammad's thought was then guided by one final objective, namely, the guarantee of freedom of religion and thought. It was for the sake of this freedom alone that fighting was permitted. It was in its defense that repulsion of the aggressor was allowed, that no one might be persecuted on account of his faith and that no injustice might befall anyone because of his faith or opinion.

The Thinking of Yathrib

While Muhammad was occupied by this line of thought and pondered over the measures necessary for guaranteeing this freedom, the people of Yathrib entertained different ideas. Each clan and party followed a line of thought peculiar to itself. The Muslims were either Muhajirun or Ansar; the unbelievers belonged to either al Aws or al Khazraj and were committed to a long history of mutual hostility, as we have shown earlier. There were also the Jews, of whom the Banu Qaynuqa' lived within the city, the Banu Qurayzah in the suburb of Fadak, the Banu al Nadir, nearby, and those of Khaybar toward the north. As for the Muslims, Muhammad feared that, despite the strongest ties with which the new religion had bound them together, the old hatred and prejudice might some day break out anew between them. The unbelievers, from al Aws or al Khazraj, were exhausted by the previous wars; they found themselves situated, in the new configuration of society, between the Jews and the Muslims. The unbelievers' strategy concentrated on dividing Jew and Muslim and pulling them farther apart. The Jews, for their part, gave Muhammad a good welcome in the hope of winning him over to their side. Their strategy demanded that they make use of the new unity of the Peninsula which he could help forge to bolster their opposition to

Christendom. For to avenge their banishment from Palestine, the land of promise, and their national home, was the guiding concern of the Jews who saw themselves as God's chosen people. Each group followed its own train of thought and began to seek the means to realize its objective.

Muslim Brotherhood

At this time a new stage, unlike any other prophet before him, began in the career of Muhammad. Here began the political stage in which Muhammad showed such great wisdom, insight, and statesmanship as would arrest attention first in surprise and then in awe and reverence. Muhammad's great concern was to bring to his new home town a political and organizational unity hitherto unknown to Hijaz, though not to ancient Yaman. He consulted with Abu Bakr and 'Umar, his two viziers, as he used to call them. Naturally, the first idea to occur to him was that of reorganizing Muslim ranks so as to consolidate their unity and to wipe out every possibility of a resurgence of division and hostility. In the realization of this objective, he asked the Muslims to fraternize with one another for the sake of God and to bind themselves together in pairs. He explained how he and 'Ali ibn Abu Talib were brothers, how his uncle Hamzah and his client, Zayd, were also brothers, as were likewise Abu Bakr and Kharijah ibn Zayd, and 'Umar ibn al Khattab and 'Itban ibn Malik al Khazraji. Despite the Muhajirun's rapid increase in number, following the emigration of the Prophet, everyone of them was now bound to a member of al Ansar group in a bond of mutual assistance. The Prophet's proclamation in this regard transformed that bond into one of blood and real fraternity. A new, genuine brotherhood arose which forged the Muslim ranks into an indivisible unity.

The Traders

Al Ansar showed their Muhajirun brethren great hospitality which the latter had first accepted with joy. For when they emigrated from Makkah, they had left behind all their property, wealth, and goods and entered Madinah devoid of the means with which to find their food. Only 'Uthman ibn 'Affan was able to carry with him enough of his wealth to be prosperous in his new residence. The others had hardly been able to carry much or little that was of use to them. Even Hamzah, the Prophet's uncle, had one day to ask the Prophet to give him some food to eat. 'Abd al

Rahman ibn 'Awf and Sa'd ibn al Rabi' were bonded together in brother-hood. The former had nothing. The latter offered to split his wealth with him. 'Abd al Rahman refused and asked that he be shown the market place. There he began to sell cheese and butter and in short time achieved a measure of affluence fair enough to enable him to ask the hand of a Madinese woman as well as to send caravans in trade. Many other Muhajirun followed the example of 'Abd al Rahman; for the Makkans, it should be remembered, were quite adept in trade. Indeed, they were so expert at it that it was said of them that they could by trade change the sand of the desert into gold.

The Harvest

Those who could not engage in trade such as Abu Bakr, 'Umar, 'Ali ibn Abu Talib and others, took to farming on the land owned by al Ansar under the system of sharecropping. Another group of truly helpless peo-ple, with a past full of suffering and hardship, put their hand to menial jobs, preferring hard labor to living as parasites on the earnings of others. Despite their meager earnings, they found consolation in the new peace and security of their own persons and of their faith. There was yet anoth-er group of emigrants so poor and helpless that they could not find even a place to sleep. To these, Muhammad permitted the use of the covered part of the mosque during the night. That is why they were called "Ahl al Suffah," "*suffah,*" meaning the covered area of the mosque. To these, Muhammad assigned a ration from the wealth of the more affluent Muslims, whether Ansar or Muhajirun.

Muhammad's Friendliness to the Jews

By this new brotherhood, Muhammad achieved an operational Muslim unity. Politically, it was a very wise move destined to show Muhammad's sound judgment and foresight. We shall better appreciate its wisdom when we learn of the attempts to divide al Aws against al Khazraj, and al Ansar against al Muhajirun. The politically greater achievement of Muhammad was his realization of a unity for the city of Yathrib as a whole, his construction of a political structure in which the Jews entered freely into an alliance of mutual cooperation with the Muslims. We have already seen how the Jews gave Muhammad a good welcome in the hope of winning him as an ally. He, too, returned their greeting with like gestures and sought to consolidate his relations with them. He visited their chiefs and cultivated the friendship of their nobles. He bound himself to them in a bond of friendship on the grounds that they were scripturists and monotheists. So much had Muhammad defended the Jews that the fact that he fasted with them on the days they fasted and prayed toward Jerusalem as they did increased his personal and religious esteem among them. Everything seemed as if the future could only strengthen this Muslim-Jewish friendship and produce further co-operation and closeness between them. Similarly, Muhammad's own conduct, his great humility, compassion, and faithfulness, and his outgoing charity and goodness to the poor, oppressed and deprived, as well as the prestige and influence which these qualities had won for him among all the people of Yathrib — all these enabled him to conclude the pact of friendship, alliance, and cooperation in the safeguarding of religious freedom throughout the city. In our opinion, this covenant is one of the greatest political documents which history has known. Such an accomplishment by Muhammad at this stage of his career had never been reached by any prophet. Jesus, Moses, and all the prophets that preceded them never went beyond the preaching of their religious messages through words and miracles. All of them had left their legacy to men of power and political authority who came after them; it was the latter who put their powers at the service of those messages and fought, with arms where necessary, for the freedom of the people to believe. Christianity spread at the hands of the disciples of Jesus and after his time, but only in extremely limited measure. The disciples as well as their followers were persecuted until one of the kings of the world favored this religion, adopted it, and put his royal power behind its missionary effort.[3] All other religions in the East and the West have had nearly the same history, but not the religion of Muhammad. God willed that Islam be spread by Muhammad, and that the truth be vindicated by his hand. He willed Muhammad to be prophet, statesman, fighter, and conqueror, all for the sake of God and the truth with which he was commissioned as prophet. In all these aspects of his career Muhammad was great, the exemplar of human perfection, the *typos* of every realized value.

The covenant of Madinah concluded between Muhajirun and Ansar on one side and Jews on the other, was dictated by Muhammad. It was the instrument of their alliance which confirmed the Jews in both their religion and position in society, and determined their rights as well as their duties. Following is the text of this important document:

"In the name of God, the compassionate, the merciful. This is a covenant given by Muhammad to the believers and Muslims of Quraysh, Yathrib, and those who followed them, joined them, and fought with them. They constitute one Ummah to the exclusion of all other men. As was their custom, the Muhajirun from Quraysh are bound together and shall ransom their prisoners in kindness and justice as believers do. Following their own custom, Banu 'Awf are bound together as they have been before. Every clan of them shall ransom its prisoners with the kindness and justice common among believers. [The text here repeats the same prescription concerning every clan of the Ansar and every house including Banu al Harith, Banu Sa'idah, Banu Jusham, Banu al Najjar, Banu 'Amr ibn 'Awf and Banu al Nabit.] The believers shall leave none of their members in destitution without giving him in kindness what he needs by way of ransom or bloodwit. No believer shall take as an ally a freedman of another Muslim without the permission of his previous master. All pious believers shall rise as one man against whosoever rebels or seeks to commit injustice, aggression, sin, or spread mutual enmity between the believers, even though he may be one of their sons. No believer shall slay a believer in retaliation for an unbeliever; neither shall he assist an unbeliever against a believer. Just as God's bond is one and indivisible, all believers shall stand behind the commitment of the least of them. All believers are bonded one to another to the exclusion of other men. Any Jew who follows us is entitled to our assistance and the same rights as anyone of us, without injustice or partisanship. This *Pax Islamica* is one and indivisible. No believer shall enter into a separate peace without all other believers whenever there is fighting in the cause of God, but will do so only on the basis of equality and justice to all others. In every military expedition we undertake our members shall be accompanied by others committed to the same objective. All believers shall avenge the blood of one another whenever anyone of them falls fighting in the cause of God. The pious believers follow the best and most upright guidance. No unbeliever shall be allowed to place under his protection against the interest of a believer, any wealth or person belonging to Quraysh. Whoever is convicted of killing a believer deliberately but without righteous cause, shall be liable to the relatives of the killed. Until the latter are satisfied, the killer shall be subject to retaliation by each and every believer. The killer shall have no rights whatever until this right of the believers is satisfied. Whoever has entered into this covenant and believed in God and in the last day shall never protect or give shelter to a convict or a criminal; whoever does so shall be cursed by God and upon him shall the divine wrath fall on the day of judgment. Neither repentance nor ransom shall be acceptable from him. No object of contention among you may not be referred to God and to Muhammad — may God's peace and blessing be upon him — for judgment. As the Jews fight on the side of the believers, they shall spend of their wealth on equal par with the believers. The Jews of Banu Aws are an *ummah* alongside the believers. The Jews have their religion and the Muslims theirs. Both enjoy the security of their own populace and clients except the unjust and the criminal among them. The unjust or the criminal destroys only himself and his family. The Jews of Banu al Najjar, Banu al Harith, Banu Sa'idah, Banu Jusham, Banu al Aws, Banu Tha'labah, Jafnah, and Banu al Shutaybah — to all the same rights and privileges apply as to the Jews of Banu Aws. The clients of the tribe of Tha'labah enjoy the same rights and duties as the members of the tribe themselves. Likewise, the clients of the Jews, as the Jews themselves. None of the foregoing shall go out to war except with the permission of Muhammad — may God's peace and blessing be upon him — though none may be prevented from taking revenge for a wound inflicted upon him. Whoever murders anyone will have murdered himself and the members of his family, unless it be the case of a man suffering a wrong, for God will accept his action. The Jews shall bear their public expenses and so will the Muslims. Each shall assist the other against any violator of this covenant. Their relationship shall be one of mutual advice and consultation, and mutual assistance and charity rather than harm and aggression. However, no man is liable to a crime committed by his ally. Assistance is due to the party suffering an injustice, not to one perpetrating it. Since the Jews fight on the side of the believers they shall spend their wealth on a par with them. The town of Yathrib shall constitute a sanctuary for the parties of this covenant. Their neighbors shall be treated as themselves as long as they perpetrate no crime and commit no harm. No woman may be taken under protection without the consent of her family. Whatever difference or dispute between the parties to this covenant remains unsolved shall be referred to God and to Muhammad, the Prophet of God — may God's peace and blessing be upon him. God is the guarantor of the piety and goodness that is embodied in this covenant. Neither the Quraysh nor their allies shall be given any protection. The people of this covenant shall come to the assistance of one another against whoever attacks Yathrib. If they are called to cease hostilities and to enter into a peace, they shall be bound to do so in the interest of peace. If, on the other hand, they call upon the Muslims to cease hostilities and to enter into a peace, the Muslims shall be bound to do so and maintain the peace except when the war is against their religion. To every smaller group belongs the share which is their due as members of the larger group which is party to this covenant. The Jews of al Aws, as well as their clients, are entitled to the same rights as this covenant has granted to its parties together with the goodness and charity of the latter. Charity and goodness are clearly distinguishable from crime and injury, and there is no responsibility except for one's own deeds. God is the guarantor of the truth and good will of this covenant. This covenant shall constitute no protection for the unjust or the criminal. Whoever goes out to fight as well as whoever stays at home shall be safe and secure in this city unless he has perpetrated an injustice or committed a crime. God grants His protection to whosoever acts in piety, charity and goodness."

New Horizons in Political Life

The foregoing political document, which Muhammad wrote down fourteen centuries ago, establishes the freedom of faith and opinion, the inviolability of the city, human life, and property, and the forbiddance of crime. It certainly constitutes a breakthrough in the political and civil life of the world of that time. For that age was one in which exploitation, tyranny, and corruption were well established. Though the Jews of Banu Qurayzah, Banu al Nadir, and Banu Qaynuqa' did not sign this covenant at its conclusion, they did enter later on into like pacts with the Prophet. Thus Madinah and all the territories surrounding it became inviolate to their peoples who were now bound to rise to their defense and protection together. These peoples were now bound to guarantee one another in the implementation of the covenant, in the establishment of the rights arising therefrom, and in the provision of freedom it has called for.

The Prophet's Marriage to 'A'ishah

Muhammad was satisfied with the result of his negotiations. The Muslims felt secure in their religion and began to practice its duties and precepts as individuals and groups in public, without fear of attack or harm from any source. At this time Muhammad married 'A'ishah, daughter of Abu Bakr, who was then ten or eleven years old. She was a beautiful, delicate, and amiable young girl, emerging out of childhood and blossoming into full womanhood. Although she was fully grown, she was still quite attracted by amusement and play. She had a room of her own near that of Sawdah alongside the mosque. In Muhammad, she found not only a sympathetic and loving husband but also a compassionate father who was not at all offended by her inclination to play games and amuse herself with trifles. On the contrary, she was for him a source of relaxation from the continuous tension imposed upon him by his great burden to which the government of Yathrib had just been added.

Adhan or the Call to Prayer

It was during this interval in which the Muslims felt secure in their religion that the duties of *zakat*, fasting, and legal sanctions of Islam were imposed and its dominion was firmly established in Yathrib. Ever since Muhammad arrived in Madinah, whenever the time of prayer came, the people assembled around the Prophet without call. It occurred to him to have the Muslims called for prayer by means of a horn, following the style of the Jews, but he found the idea unbecoming. He had also thought of using the clapper, in the manner of the Christians. After consulting 'Umar and a number of Muslims, according to one report, and by the command of God, according to another, he changed his idea to the *adhan* and commanded 'Abdullah ibn Zayd ibn Tha'labah: "Get up with Bilal and dictate the call to prayer to him, but let him deliver it forth for he has a more beautiful voice than yours." A woman of Banu al Najjar owned a house next door to the mosque which was higher than the latter. Bilal used to ascend to the roof of that house and deliver the call to prayer from there. Thus the people of Yathrib all began to hear the call to prayer many times a day beginning at dawn. The Islamic call to prayer was equally a call to

Islam sung beautifully by a beautiful voice and carried on the waves of the
air unto all corners of the horizon. It was a call which penetrated the ear
of life itself. It said, "God is greater. God is greater. I witness that there is
no God but God. I witness that Muhammad is the Prophet of God. Rise
to prayer. Rise to felicity. God is greater. God is greater. There is no God
but God." Henceforth, the Muslims' fears were dissipated and they felt
secure. Yathrib became Madinah al Nabiy or "the City of the Prophet."
While the non-Muslim inhabitants began to fear Muslim power —
knowing well that it stemmed from the depth of hearts which had tasted
sacrifice and persecution for the sake of faith, the Muslims collected the
fruits of their patience and enjoyed their religious freedom. There peace
and freedom were now made constitutional by the Islamic principles that
no man has any authority over any other, that religion belongs to God
alone, that service is to Him alone, that before Him all men are absolutely equal, and that nothing differentiates them except their works and
intentions. In Madinah, the atmosphere was finally cleared of all impediments, and Muhammad openly proclaimed his teachings. The theater was
ready and the stage was set for Muhammad to constitute by his conduct
the ideal exemplification and embodiment of these teachings and principles, and for his laying down the foundation stone of Islamic civilization.

Brotherhood: Foundation of Islamic Civilization

The rock bottom foundation of Islamic civilization is human brotherhood, a brotherhood under which man does not become truly human until
he has loved for his brother what he loves for himself and implemented
this love by deeds of goodness and mercy without weakness or servility. A
man once asked Muhammad, "Which Islam is better?" Muhammad
answered, "That you give food to the needy and that you greet those
whom you know as well as those whom you don't." He opened the first
sermon he delivered in Madinah with the statement, "Whoever can protect his face from the fire even with a basket of dates, let him do so; and
whoever does not find even that much, then let him do so with a good
word, for the good word brings a reward ten times greater than itself." In
his second sermon he said, "Worship God and do not associate any being
with Him. Fear and revere Him as He ought to be feared and revered. Be
true unto Him by saying always the best than can be said. Love one
another in the spirit of God. God is displeased whenever His covenant is
violated." By this and like exhortations, Muhammad used to counsel his

companions and preach to the people in his mosque, leaning against one of the date trunks supporting the ceiling. Later on, he ordered a pulpit of three steps to be made for him, the first to stand upon when delivering a sermon and the second to sit down upon.

Muslim Brotherhood

The brotherhood which Muhammad made the cornerstone of Islamic civilization did not rest on his preachings alone. It was embodied in its highest perfection in his deeds and concrete example. True, he was the Prophet of God, but he consistently refused to adopt any of the appearances of power, authority, kingship, or temporal sovereignty. He emphatically repeated to his companions, "Do not praise me as the Christians have praised the son of Mary, for I am but the servant of God. Rather, call me the servant of God and His Prophet." Once, he arrived at a gathering of his companions leaning on a stick and they all rose up in respect for him. He said, "Do not stand up for me as the Persians do in aggrandizement of one another." Whenever he joined his companions, he always sat at the edge of the space they occupied. He used to joke and mix with them, to talk to them about their own affairs, to pamper and coddle their children, and to answer the call of freeman, slave, maid servant and destitute alike. He used to visit the sick in the farthest district of Madinah, to take the initiative in greeting whomever he met, and to stretch his hand in welcome to his visitors. No man came to visit Muhammad and found him in prayer but he shortened his prayer, attended to his visitor and returned to his prayer after the visitor had left. He was the most charitable of people, always smiling in the face of everyone except when revelation came to him or when he delivered a speech or a sermon. In his home, he felt no superiority over the members of his family. He washed his own robe and mended it by his own hand. He milked his own goat, repaired his own sandals, attended to himself and to his camel, ate with his servant, and fulfilled the request of the weak, the oppressed and the destitute. Whenever he found somebody in need, however lowly or plebeian, he preferred to attend to him first rather than to himself or to his family. That is why he never saved anything for the morrow, and when he died his shield was in possession of a Jewish pawnbroker as lien for a loan made to Muhammad to spend on his family. He was exceedingly modest and extremely loyal. When a deputation from the Negus of Abyssinia arrived to see him, he rose to serve them. His companions sought to stop him, but he said to them: "The Abyssinians were kind to our companions when they went to their country; I would like to treat them likewise and reward them." He was so loyal to Khadijah that whenever she was mentioned he gave her the best of praises so that 'A'ishah used to say, "I have never been jealous of a woman as I have been of Khadijah for all that I have heard the Prophet praise her." Once when a woman came to him, he rose to greet her, spoke to her gently, and attended to her pleas; people asked him who she was. He answered, "She used to befriend us in the days of Khadijah; loyalty to one's friends is of the faith." Indeed, he was so compassionate and gentle that he did not mind his grandsons playing with him during his prayer. Once, he even prayed while Umamah, his granddaughter through Zaynab, sat on his shoulders and had to be put down when he prostrated himself.

Muhammad's Kindness to Animals

His kindness and mercy, on which he founded the new Islamic civilization, were not limited to man alone but extended to animals. Muhammad used to rise and open the door for a cat seeking to enter. He attended with his own hands to a sick rooster and rubbed down his own horse with his own sleeve. When 'A'ishah rode on an obstinate camel and began to pull him hardly, he said to her, "Softly and gently please." Thus his kindness and mercy embraced all that ever came in touch with him — every creature that sought to stand near his person.

The Brotherhood of Justice and Mercy

Muhammad's mercy did not proceed from weakness or servility, nor was it ever vitiated by pride, haughtiness, or the expectation of gratitude. It was done purely for the sake of God. Hence, nothing was excluded from it. This kindness differentiates the foundation of the civilization of Islam from all other civilizations. Islam puts justice side by side with kindness and judges that kindness is not kindness without justice.

فَمَنِ اعْتَدَىٰ عَلَيْكُمْ فَاعْتَدُوا عَلَيْهِ بِمِثْلِ مَا اعْتَدَىٰ عَلَيْكُمْ

"Whoever commits an aggression against you, return to him his aggression in like manner."[4]

وَلَكُمْ فِي الْقِصَاصِ حَيَوةٌ يَأُولِي الْأَلْبَابِ

"In punishment a whole life lies implicit, O you who have minds to reason with!"[5]

Kindness is felicitous and the good deeds that issue from it are praise-worthy only when the motivation is internal, the will is free, and the pur-pose is the seeking of God's sake alone. Kindness should proceed from a strong soul that has known no submission to anything but God, has not succumbed to weakness, does not go to extremes in the name of piety, and knows no fear or contrition except on account for a misdeed it has done or a crime it has committed. As long as the soul is under alien dominion, it can never be strong; it can never be strong, either, if it stands under the dominion of its own passions and desires. Muhammad and his compan-ions emigrated from Makkah precisely in rebellion against the dominion of Quraysh who attempted to weaken their souls by means of dominion and the injuries it perpetrates. On the other hand, the soul is said to be under the dominion of passions and desires whenever the body's demands take precedence over those of the spirit, when passion vanquishes reason, when external life exerts any power over internal life — in short, when the soul does not know that it has no need of either passion or desire and is really their final master.

Muhammad's Power to Surmount Life

Muhammad provided the highest example of the power to overcome life. He achieved such a degree of mastery over life that he did not hesi-tate to give all that he had whenever he wanted to give. A contemporary of Muhammad once said of him, "Muhammad gives as if he has no fear of want at all." In order not to allow anything to exercise any power over him but rather to enable himself to determine it, Muhammad led a very ascetic life. Despite his strong desire to know the secrets of life and under-stand its structure, he was quite contemptuous of its joys and attractions. He slept in a bed of palm fibers; he never ate his fill; he never ate barley bread on two consecutive days, gruel being his main daily meal together with dates. Neither he nor his family had ever had enough *tharid*.[6] He felt the pangs of hunger more than once, and learned to press a stone against his stomach as a means to silence those pangs. This remarkable restraint, however, did not prevent his enjoying the delicacies of God's bounty if such were available, and he was known to love to eat leg of lamb, squash, honey, and other sweets.

In his dress he was as ascetic as he was in his food. His wife once gave him a new robe because he was in need of one. One of his companions asked him for something with which to shroud a dead relative, and Muhammad gave him the new robe he had just received. His wardrobe consisted of shirts and robes made out of wool, cotton, or linen. But on special occasions he had no objection to wearing a luxurious robe from Yaman should it be called for. He used to wear a simple sandal, and he did not wear slippers until the Negus of Abyssinia sent him some together with other clothes.

Muhammad's denial of the world and its luxuries was not pursued for its own sake. Nor was it a duty imposed by religion. The Qur'an said: "Eat of the delicacies of God's providing," and "Do seek the other world in what God has given you of this, but do not give up your share of this world. Do good, as God has done good to you."[7] In the traditions of the early Muslims it is said, "Work for this world as if your life in it is eternal; work for the other world as if you were to die tomorrow." Certainly Muhammad sought to give mankind the highest possible example of a mastery of life absolutely free of weakness, in which no goods, wealth, or power dedicated to another being beside God could have any effect. When brotherhood is based upon such a power over life and its attractions issue into such exemplary deeds as Muhammad had done, it is pure, candid, and has no other object whatever besides the lofty fraternalism of man and man. In it, justice dovetails with mercy, and the subject is not determined except by his own free and deliberate judgment. Islam places both mercy and forgiveness side by side with justice. It insists that if they are to be themselves at all, mercy and forgiveness must issue from power. Only then will their purpose be the genuine good of the neighbor and his reconstruction.

The Sunnah of Muhammad

The foundation for a new civilization which Muhammad laid down was expressed very succinctly in a report by 'Ali ibn Abu Talib. He asked the Prophet of God concerning his Sunnah, and the latter replied: "Wisdom is my capital, reason the force of my religion, love my foundation, longing my vehicle, the remembrance of God my constant pleasure, trust my treasure, mourning my companion, knowledge my arm, patience my robe, contentment my booty, poverty my pride, asceticism my profession, conviction my strength, truthfulness my intercessor, obedience my argument, holy war my ethics, prayer my supreme pleasure."

Beginning of Jewish Fears

Muhammad's teachings, example, and leadership had the deepest effect upon the people. Large numbers of men joined the ranks of Islam and their conversion consolidated and increased Muslim power in Madinah. It was at this stage that the Jews began to rethink their position *vis-a-vis* Muhammad and his companions. They had concluded a pact with him and were still ambitiously hoping to win him over to their side in order to increase their power against the Christians. Muhammad, however, was becoming more powerful than both Christians and Jews, and his command was growing in effect and application. Muhammad had even begun thinking of Quraysh, of their banishment of him and the Muhajirun from Makkah, and of their forced conversion of some Muslims to the old idolatry. It was at this time that the Jews asked themselves whether they should let his call, spiritual power, and authority continue to spread while remaining satisfied with the security they enjoyed under his protection and the increased trade and wealth which his peace had brought to their city. Perhaps they might have done so had they felt certain that his religion was not going to spread in their midst and their own men would not abjure the exclusivism of Jewish prophethood and the people of Israel to convert to Islam. A great number of their priesthood and a learned rabbi, 'Abdullah ibn Salam, approached the Prophet and announced to him his conversion as well as that of his own household. 'Abdullah himself feared the calumny of the Jews and their defamation of him should they learn of his conversion. He therefore asked the Prophet to inquire of them about him, before any of the Jews had learned of his conversion. The Jews answered Muhammad, "'Abdullah ibn Salam is our master, son of our master, our priest, and learned rabbi." When, however, 'Abdullah went back to them as a Muslim and called them to Islam, they attacked him and spread in the Jewish quarters of Madinah all sorts of calumnies against him. This was the event which triggered their suspicions of Muhammad and their denial of Muhammad's prophethood. Those members of al Aws and al Khazraj tribes who never entered Islam or who did so in hypocrisy or for an ulterior purpose were quick to rally

around the Jews once their opposition to Muhammad and to Islam began
to crystallize.

The War of Words between Muhammad and the Jews

A war of words between Muhammad and the Jews, which proved to
be greater and more sinister than that which raged between Muhammad
and Quraysh, followed ibn Salam's conversion. Unlike the hostility with
Quraysh, the new war in Yathrib witnessed the connivance of treason,
deception, and scriptural knowledge for the attack against Muhammad,
his message, and his companions, whether Muhajirun or Ansar. The Jews
sent some of their rabbis to feign conversion to Islam in order to enter
Muslim ranks and councils. While showing all piety, these rabbis were
commissioned to disseminate doubt and suspicion of Muhammad among
his own people. They asked Muhammad questions which they thought
might shake the Muslims' conviction and arouse doubt in the message
Muhammad was teaching. A number of hypocrites from al Aws and al
Khazraj tribes joined Islam for the same purpose. Both Jews and unbelievers, however, reached such levels of deception that they denied either
Torah or God in order to ask Muhammad, "If God created creation, who
then created God?" Muhammad used to answer them with the divine
verses: "Say, 'God is One, the Eternal. He was not born, nor did He give
birth to anyone. None is like unto Him.'"[8] The Muslims soon detected
their purpose and uncovered their attempts. When some of them plotting
in secrecy in one of the mosque's corners were discovered one day by the
Muslims, Muhammad had to command that they be expelled from the
mosque. However, their efforts to split Muslim ranks continued. A Jewish
leader called Shas ibn Qays passed one day by a group of al Aws and al
Khazraj tribesmen enjoying one another's company in good harmony. He
remembered how they were once divided and warring against each other,
and thought that should the Banu Qaylah[9] remain united in this territory the Jews would not be able to live in peace for long. He therefore
instructed a young Jew who frequented their sessions to seek an opportunity to arouse memories of the Day of Bu'ath when al Aws vanquished al
Khazraj. The youth did speak and recalled the memory of that war and
succeeded in arousing the old pride and hatred of the two tribes, convincing some that a return to that *dies nefastus* was possible as well as desirable.
When Muhammad learned of this, he hurried with his companions and
reminded the divisive elements how Islam had sweetened their hearts and

made of them mutually loving brethren. Muhammad continued to talk to them, emphasizing their Islamic unity and brotherhood until their tears ran down in emotion and they embraced one another.

The war of words between Muhammad and the Jews increased in intensity. The evidence therefor is what the Qur'an has to say about it. The first eighty-one verses of *Surah* "al Nisa'," mention the people of the book, their denial of their own scripture, and condemns their unbelief and denial in strong terms:

وَلَقَدْ اتَيْنَا مُوسَى الْكِتَبَ وَقَفَّيْنَا مِنْ بَعْدِهِ بِالرُّسُلِ وَ اتَيْنَا عِيسَى ابْنَ مَرْيَمَ الْبَيِّنتِ وَاَيَّدْنهُ بِرُوْحِ
الْقُدُسِ ۚ اَفَكُلَّمَا جَآءَكُمْ رَسُوْلٌ بِمَا لَا تَهْوَى اَنْفُسُكُمُ اسْتَكْبَرْتُمْ ۚ فَفَرِيْقًا كَذَّبْتُمْ وَفَرِيْقًا تَقْتُلُوْنَ ۝
وَقَالُوْا قُلُوْبُنَا غُلْفٌ ۚ بَلْ لَّعَنَهُمُ اللّٰهُ بِكُفْرِهِمْ فَقَلِيْلًا مَّا يُؤْمِنُوْنَ ۝ وَلَمَّا جَآءَهُمْ كِتبٌ مِّنْ عِنْدِ اللّٰهِ
مُصَدِّقٌ لِّمَا مَعَهُمْ ۙ وَكَانُوْا مِنْ قَبْلُ يَسْتَفْتِحُوْنَ عَلَى الَّذِيْنَ كَفَرُوْا ۚ فَلَمَّا جَآءَهُمْ مَّا عَرَفُوْا كَفَرُوْا بِهٖ فَلَعْنَةُ
اللّٰهِ عَلَى الْكٰفِرِيْنَ

"Verily, We revealed to Moses the scripture and called after him messengers to follow in his footsteps. To Jesus, Son of Mary, We gave manifest signs and We strengthened him with the spirit of holiness. 'Will you then, O Jews, every time a prophet comes to you with what you yourselves do not like take to false pride and arrogantly belie some and kill others?' They rationalize and seek to excuse themselves by admitting to dimness of vision. God, however, curses them for their disbelief. Little are they convinced of the truth! And when the book which came from God and which confirmed their own scripture was brought to them and invoked for their benefit they denied it. Hitherto they were boasting of such revelation and deriding the unbelievers for never receiving any. Now that the same truth which they had known beforehand has come to the believers from God they reject it. God's wrath will surely fall upon the unbelievers."[10]

The Story of Finhas

Sometimes, controversy and argument between Jews and Muslims reached such a level of intensity that the participants attacked each other. In order to appreciate how provocative the Jews were in their war of words against the Muslims, suffice it to remember the story of Finhas. The gentleness, patience, and *largeur de coeur* of Abu Bakr are proverbial. And yet he too could and did lose his temper. He once talked to Finhas calling the latter unto Islam. Finhas answered, "By God, O Abu Bakr, we do not need God. Rather, it is He who needs us. It is not I who pray to Him, it is He who prays to us. We are self-sufficient and He is not. If God were self-sufficient, He would not borrow our wealth as your Prophet claims. If He were truly not in need of us, He would not have prohibited usury to you and allowed it to us." Finhas was actually referring to the Qur'anic verse which said: "Will you then lend God a good loan which He will repay to you many times over?"[11] At this point in the conversation, Abu Bakr lost his patience and struck Finhas on the face saying, "By God, were it not for the covenant between your people and mine, I would have struck your head off, O enemy of God." The said Finhas took his complaint to the Prophet and denied his blasphemy. It was then that this verse was revealed: "God has heard those who said, 'He is poor and we are rich.' On the day of judgment, God will remember this as well as their murder of the prophets. Then will he say: "Taste the punishments of hell."[12]

Not satisfied with their attempt to divide the Muhajirun and Ansar, al Aws and al Khazraj, in order to dissuade the Muslims from their religion and return them to idolatry — without ever seeking to convert them to Judaism — the Jews even tried to trap Muhammad himself. A number of their rabbis, elders, and noblemen went to him one day and said: "You know who we are and you know well our prestige with our people. You know that if we should follow you, the Jews would do likewise. Would you then not help us against our people by giving a verdict in our favor when we bring to you our litigation with them to arbitrate? If you do, we shall then follow you and believe in you. At this the following divine words were revealed: "Judge between them by that which God has revealed, and do not follow their desires. Take care lest they sway you away from some of the revelations made to you. If they turn away from you, know that God is punishing them for some of their misdeeds. Most of them are immoral. What? Do they seek judgment on the basis of the idolatrous principles of pre-Islam? Is not God's judgment preferable? But they are people devoid of certain knowledge."[13]

Orientation to the Ka'bah in Prayer

By this time, the Jews had lost their patience and began to plot against Muhammad. They sought to get him to leave Madinah as the Quraysh had succeeded in causing him and his companions to leave Makkah. Their method, however, was different. They said to Muhammad that each and every prophet hitherto had gone to Jerusalem and there established his residence. They challenged him by asserting that if he were a true prophet, he would only do as his predecessors had done in considering Madinah only as an intermediate station between Makkah and the city where al Aqsa Mosque stood. Muhammad, however, did not have to think hard to realize that they were plotting against him. It was then, seventeen months after his emigration from Makkah, that God commanded him to orient himself in prayer toward the holy mosque, the house of Ibrahim and Isma'il. It was then that the verse was revealed: "We see your yearning for a direction to take in prayer. Let us then guide you to a direction that you will accept. Orient yourself in prayer toward the holy mosque of Makkah, and wherever you may be, turn your face toward it."[14] The Jews condemned Muhammad for this and sought to trap him once more. They went to him pleading that they would all enter into his faith if he would but return to Jerusalem, his old direction in prayer. In this connection, God revealed the following verses:

سَيَقُولُ السُّفَهَآءُ مِنَ النَّاسِ مَا وَلَّهُمْ عَن قِبْلَتِهِمُ الَّتِي كَانُوا عَلَيْهَا ۚ قُل لِّلَّهِ الْمَشْرِقُ وَ الْمَغْرِبُ ۚ يَهْدِى مَن يَشَآءُ إِلَىٰ صِرَاطٍ مُّسْتَقِيمٍ ۝ وَكَذَٰلِكَ جَعَلْنَاكُمْ أُمَّةً وَسَطًا لِّتَكُونُوا شُهَدَآءَ عَلَى النَّاسِ وَيَكُونَ الرَّسُولُ عَلَيْكُمْ شَهِيدًا ۗ وَمَا جَعَلْنَا الْقِبْلَةَ الَّتِي كُنتَ عَلَيْهَا إِلَّا لِنَعْلَمَ مَن يَتَّبِعُ الرَّسُولَ مِمَّن يَنقَلِبُ عَلَىٰ عَقِبَيْهِ ۚ وَإِن كَانَتْ لَكَبِيرَةً إِلَّا عَلَى الَّذِينَ هَدَى اللَّهُ ۗ

"Some foolish people will ask, 'What caused them to change their old orientation?' Say: 'To God belongs the East as well as the West. He guides unto His straight path whomsoever he wills." Thus We have caused you to be a nation following the course of the golden mean, witnessing unto mankind and witnessed to by the Prophet. The whole question of the orientation in prayer was intended by us to sift the true believers from the apostates and deceptors. To change orientation is a big travail only to those who have missed the divine guidance."[15]

The Christian Delegation from Najran

While the war of words was raging between Muhammad and the Jews in full intensity, a delegation from the Christians of Najran consisting of sixty riders arrived in Madinah. Among them were some of the nobles, learned men, and religious leaders of the tribe whom the emperors of Byzantium had been protecting, encouraging, financing, and assisting in the building of churches. Perhaps this delegation arrived in Madinah after they learned of the conflict between Muhammad and the Jews with the hope of adding fuel to the fire so that neighboring Christendom, whether in al Sham or in Yaman, might relax and feel safe from Jewish plots and Arab aggression. The three scriptural religions thus confronted one another in Madinah. The delegation entered with the Prophet into public debate and these were soon joined by the Jews, thus resulting in a tripartite dialogue between Judaism, Christianity and Islam. The Jews were obstinately denying the prophethood of Jesus as well as of Muhammad, as we have seen earlier, and pretending that Ezra was the son of God. The Christians were defending trinitarianism and the divinity of Jesus. Muhammad was calling men to recognize the unity of God and the spiritual unity of mankind. Most Jews and Christians asked Muhammad which prophets he believed in. He answered: "We believe in God, in what has been revealed to us, to Ibrahim, Isma'il, Ishaq, Ya'qub, and his children. We believe in what has been revealed to Moses, to Jesus, as well as in all the revelations which the prophets have received from their Lord. We do not differentiate between them. And we have submitted ourselves to God."[16] Muhammad criticized both Jews and Christians in very strong terms for their compromise of the monotheistic faith that God is one, for tampering with the words of God in their scriptures, and for interpreting them in ways violating the understanding of the prophets whose prophethood they themselves acknowledged.

He criticized them for asserting that the revelation of Jesus, Moses, and their predecessors in prophethood differed in many essential matters from his own revelation. In support of this, Muhammad argued that what those prophets had received from God was the same eternal truth as that revealed to him. Being the truth, its light shines forth clear and distinct, and its content is majestic and simple to any researcher submitting to none but God and to anyone capable of seeing the world as a connected and integrated unity rather than as ephemeral intimations of desire, passion, and ulterior motives. Being the truth, it must be readily recognized by the man liberated from blind submission to old wives' tales or to the sanctified legends of the fathers and ancestors. By nature, such truth must be open and possible for everyone to perceive.

Congress on the Three Religions

This was a truly great congress which the city of Yathrib had witnessed. In it, the three religions which today dominate the world and determine its destiny had met, and they did so for the greatest idea and the noblest purpose. It had neither political nor economic aims, but stood beyond the materialistic objectives which our present world is anxiously, yet so vainly trying to realize. The objective of the congress was purely spiritual. Whereas in the case of Christianity and Judaism the spiritual objective was backed or motivated by political, capitalistic, and worldly ambitions, Muhammad's spiritual purpose was pure and advocated for the sake of humanity as a whole. It was God that gave this purpose of Muhammad's its form, and this same form was proclaimed not only to the Jews but to the Christians and all mankind. Muhammad was commanded to address the delegates of both faiths,

قُلْ يَا أَهْلَ الْكِتَبِ تَعَالَوْا إِلَى كَلِمَةٍ سَوَاءٍ بَيْنَنَا وَبَيْنَكُمْ أَلَّا نَعْبُدَ إِلَّا اللَّهَ وَلَا نُشْرِكَ بِهِ شَيْئًا وَلَا يَتَّخِذَ بَعْضُنَا بَعْضًا أَرْبَابًا مِنْ دُونِ اللَّهِ فَإِنْ تَوَلَّوْا فَقُولُوا اشْهَدُوا بِأَنَّا مُسْلِمُونَ ⑰

"Say, 'O People of the Book, come now to a fair principle common to both of us, that we do not worship aught but God, that we do not associate aught with Him and that we do not take one another as lords besides God.' But if they turn away, then say, 'Bear witness that we are Muslims.'"[17]

Withdrawal of the Christian Delegation

What can Jews, Christians, or any other people say of this call to worship none but God, to associate none with Him and never to take one another as lords besides God? The spirit which is sincere and truthful, which is endowed with reason and candid emotion cannot but believe in this call and in it alone. But human life is not entirely dominated by such noble dispositions. There is yet the materialistic consideration. Man is indeed weak; and it is this inclination to material gain which causes him to subject himself to the dominion of another man for material advantage. Man suffers terribly from false pride, his considerateness, self-respect and reason are destroyed thereby. It was this materialistic ambition for wealth, worldly prestige and social eminence that caused Abu Harithah, the most

learned of the people of Najran, to tell a friend of his that he was perfectly convinced of the truth of which Muhammad was teaching. When that
friend asked him why he did not then convert to Islam, he answered: "I
cannot do so on account of what my people have done to me. They have
honored, financed, and respected me; and they insist on differing from
him. Should I follow him, they would take away from me all this that I
now have."

It was to this message that Muhammad summoned Jews and
Christians alike. Muslim relationships with the former were already under
the governance of the Covenant of Madinah. Those of the latter depended upon the Christians' response to Muhammad's invitation. Though they
did not join Islam at this time, the Christians resolved neither to oppose
Muhammad nor the missionary activity of his followers. Appreciating the
perfect justice of Muhammad's new order, they asked him to appoint for
them a Muslim to act as judge in their own disputes at home. Muhammad
sent with them Abu 'Ubaydah ibn al Jarrah, who was vested with the
proper judicial authority.

Rethinking the Problem of Quraysh and Makkah

Muhammad continued to consolidate the civilization for which his
teaching and example provided the foundation. Together with his
Muhajirun companions, he thought over the problem of Quraysh, which
had vexed them ever since their emigration. The Muslims were moved by
many considerations. In Makkah stood the Ka'bah, the house of Ibrahim,
pilgrimage center to them as well as to all the Arabs. Until their exile, they
had performed this sacred duty in season, every year. In Makkah too many
of their friends, relatives, and loved ones had stayed behind and were still
practicing the old idolatry. In Makkah, their wealth, worldly goods, trade,
and properties were still under the jurisdiction of the Quraysh. Madinah
itself was struck with epidemic diseases which attacked the Muslims and
inflicted upon them great suffering; indeed, the very trip to Madinah on
foot and without provisions had so worn them out that they entered the
city on their first arrival already diseased and exhausted. This hard journey
had naturally increased their longing for their hometown. Moreover, they
did not leave Makkah of their own accord but under compulsion and full
of resentment for their overlords who threatened them with all kinds of
punishments and sanctions. It was not in their nature to suffer such injustices or to submit to such tyranny for long without thinking of avenging

themselves. Besides these determinants, there was the natural motivation of longing to return to one's homeland, to one's home where one was born and grew up. There was the natural longing for the land, the plain, and the mountains, the water and the vegetation, all of which had constituted their earliest associations, friendships, and love. The land in which he grows and to which he returns at the end of his life has a special appeal for man. It determines his heart and his emotion and moves him to defend it with all his power and wealth as well as to exert all possible effort — indeed his life — for its guardianship and well being. It is to the land from which we came out, as it were, that we want to return and be buried in at death. This natural feeling added a degree of intensity to the other emotions. Indeed, the Muhajirun could never forget Makkah nor stop thinking about the problem of their relation with the Quraysh. From the very nature of the case, and after thirteen long years of persecution and conflict in which they held their ground firmly, the Muslims could not possibly entertain any ideas of withdrawal or giving up. The religion itself to which they had converted and for the sake of which they had emigrated did not approve of weakness, despair, servile submission, or the patient bearing of injustice. Although it was strongly opposed to aggression and condemned it in no uncertain terms, and although it called for and promoted fraternity and brotherhood, it demanded that man rise up to the defense of his person, of his dignity, of the freedom of religion, and the freedom of homeland. It was for this defense and purpose that Muhammad concluded with the Muslims of Yathrib the great covenant of al 'Aqabah. Now the question posed itself: how may the Muhajirun fulfill this duty imposed upon them for the sake of God, His holy house, and their beloved homeland, Makkah? Toward the realization of this objective will the policy of Muhammad and of the Muslims now turn. This objective was to preoccupy them all until the conquest of Makkah had been achieved, and the religion of God, and the truth which it proclaimed, had become supreme.

The Mosque of the Prophet in Madinah, Saudi Arabia.

12

The First Raids
and Skirmishes

Muslim Policy in Madinah

The Muslims were all well settled in Madinah only months after the Hijrah. Their longing for Makkah increased with every new day, as they thought of their loved ones whom they had left behind, of their property and wealth which they had forsaken, and of the injuries which the Quraysh had inflicted upon them in the past. What they would now do was for them a constant question. The majority of historians think that the Muslims, led by Muhammad, thought of avenging themselves on the Quraysh and of declaring war against them. Some even claim that the Muslims had thought of declaring this war ever since they arrived in Madinah, and that if they had not opened hostilities at that time it was because they were preoccupied with the business of settling down and organizing their own lives. They reasoned that Muhammad had concluded the great covenant of al 'Aqabah precisely in order to wage war against all opponents and that it was natural for his and his companions' attention first to fall upon the Quraysh — a fact proven by Quraysh's own mobilization upon hearing of the conclusion of the said pact.

The First Raids

This general hypothesis of the historians is supposedly proved by events which took place eight months after the Hijrah of Muhammad.

194

The Prophet then sent his uncle Hamzah ibn 'Abd al Muttalib with forty riders from the Muhajirun, rather than the Ansar, to the seacoast near al 'Is where Abu Jahl ibn Hisham was camping with three hundred Makkan riders. Hamzah was just about to enter into battle with the Quraysh force when Majdiy ibn 'Amr al Juhani, who was in peaceful relation with both parties, interfered to separate them before the battle had begun. At the same time, Muhammad sent 'Ubaydah ibn al Harith with sixty riders from the Muhajirun to go to a well in the valley of Rabigh in Hijaz where they met more than two hundred riders led by Abu Sufyan. The Muslim forces withdrew without engaging the enemy, except for the report that Sa'd ibn Abu Waqqas shot one single arrow, later to be called, 'the first arrow shot in the cause of Islam.' It is also reported that Muhammad had sent Sa'd ibn Abu Waqqas to lead a number of Muhajirun riders (eight according to one version and twenty according to another) into the Hijaz, but he returned without engaging the enemy.

Raids Led by the Prophet

As further evidence to all the foregoing it is said that the Prophet himself had undertaken the leadership of the raids on al Abwa' twelve months after the Hijrah and appointed Sa'd ibn 'Ubadah as his vice-regent in Madinah during his absence. In their search for the Quraysh as well as the Banu Damrah, the Muslims reached Waddan. They did not meet any man from Quraysh on that expedition, but they did succeed in winning Banu Damrah as allies. A month later, Muhammad led a force of two hundred riders from both the Muhajirun and Ansar camps with Buwat as their objective, where a caravan of 1,500 camels accompanied by one hundred riders under the leadership of Umayyah ibn Khalaf was reported to be passing. No engagement took place because the caravan had taken an untrodden, unknown route. Two or three months after Muhammad's return from Buwat by way of Radwa, he appointed Abu Salamah ibn 'Abd al Asad to take his place in Madinah while he and more than two hundred Muslim riders went on an expedition to 'Ushayrah in the district of Yanbu'. There he spent the whole month of First Jumada and a few days of Second Jumada of the second year A.H. (October 623 C.E.) waiting for a Quraysh caravan headed by Abu Sufyan to pass, without success, for it had already gone earlier. During his stay in the area, he concluded a pact of friendship with the tribe of Banu Mudlaj and their allies from Banu Damrah. He had hardly spent ten days in Madinah after his return when

Kurz ibn Jabir al Fihri, an ally of Quraysh, raided the camels and cattle of Madinah. The Prophet immediately led a force after him, appointing Zayd ibn Harithah as his representative during his absence. The force marched until it reached a valley called Safawan in the district of Badr and again missed their objective, the said Kurz ibn Jabir al Fihri. It is to this raid that biographers refer as the first raid of Badr.

The Historians' View of the First Raid

Does not all this constitute evidence that the Muhajirun as well as Muhammad sought first of all to avenge themselves on the Quraysh and to open hostilities against them? There is full evidence, according to these historians, that for these expeditions and raids the Muslims had two objectives: first to seize the caravans of the Quraysh, on their way to or from al Sham during the summer, in order to take possession of the goods which they carried; second to cut off the Quraysh caravan routes to al Sham. This latter goal was to be achieved by concluding covenants and pacts with the various tribes settled along these routes. Thus, it would be all the easier and safer for the Muhajirun to attack these caravans without fear of detection or attack from the local inhabitants, and the caravans themselves would then be at the total mercy of the Muslims. The raids which the Prophet sent out under the leadership of Hamzah, 'Ubaydah ibn al Harith, and Sa'd ibn Abu Waqqas, as well as the pacts of friendship and peace which he concluded with Banu Damrah, Banu Mudlaj, and others, confirmed this second objective and proved that the Muslims had definitely aimed at cutting the road to al Sham for the Quraysh and Makkah.

Our View of These Raids

That by means of these raids, begun six months after their settlement in Madinah and undertaken by the Muhajirun alone, the Muslims sought to wage war against Quraysh and to attack its caravans is an opinion which cannot be accepted without hesitation and scrutiny. The expedition of Hamzah did not consist of more than thirty men, that of 'Ubaydah, sixty, that of Sa'd eight, according to one version, and twenty according to another. The number of fighters assigned by the Quraysh to the protection of their caravan was in each case many times the number of riders the Muslims had sent out. Moreover, ever since Muhammad emigrated to

Madinah and began to forge a chain of alliances around the city, the
Quraysh multiplied the number of escorts for their caravans and improved
their weapons. Whatever the personal courage of Hamzah, 'Ubaydah, and
Sa'd among the leaders of those expeditionary forces of the Muhajirun,
their military equipment was not such as would encourage them to make
war. They were satisfied with threatening the Quraysh rather than engaging them in battle. The only exception to this was the single arrow shot by
Sa'd, as reported above.

Exposure of Quraysh's Trade to Danger

The caravans of Quraysh were protected by escorts of the people of
Makkah who were related to many Muhajirun as members of the same
tribe, the same house and clan, and often the same family. It was not easy,
therefore, for them to decide to enter into an engagement in which members of the same tribe, clan, and family would kill one another and then
expose to retaliation all their fellow tribesmen on each side, in fact to
expose the whole of Makkah and Madinah at once to the *lex talionis* of the
desert. Hardly any change affected the inability and unwillingness of
Muslims and others to launch a civil war which both parties had ably
struggled to avert for thirteen long years, from the commission of
Muhammad to prophethood to the day of his emigration to Madinah.
The Muslims knew too well that the covenant of al 'Aqabah was a defensive one which both al Aws and al Khazraj had undertaken to protect
Muhammad. These tribes of Madinah have never agreed either with
Muhammad nor with anyone else to commit aggression on anyone. It is
not possible, therefore, to accept the view of the earliest historians, who
did not begin to write the history of the Prophet until two centuries or so
after his death, that the first raids and expeditions had actually been
intended for fighting. Hence, we must understand these events in a more
reasonable way to harmonize with what we know to have been the policy
of the Muslims in this early period of Madinah, and to be consistent with
the Prophet's policy of common understanding, mutual friendship, and
co-operation to obtain religious freedom for all.

It is more likely, therefore, that these early expeditions had only psychic objectives, and were meant to press home to the Quraysh the realization that their own interest demanded that they come into some kind of
understanding with the Muslims. The Muslims were, after all, their own
people, compelled to migrate from their own city to escape the persecu-

tion so far inflicted. Rather than to bring war and hostility, these expeditions were intended to put an end to the old hostility, to guarantee to the Muslims the freedom they sought for calling men to their religion, and to ensure for Makkah the security it needed for its caravans to al Sham. This trade, in which both Makkah and Ta'if were involved and which Makkah used to carryon with the south as well as with the north, had built up large interests and businesses. Some caravans consisted of two thousand camels or more, and carried a load whose value amounted to fifty thousand Dinars.[1] According to the estimates of the Orientalist, Sprenger, the annual exports of Makkah amounted to 250,000 Dinars or 160,000 gold pounds. If the Quraysh could be made to realize that this precious trade and wealth were exposed to danger by their own sons who had migrated to Madinah, perhaps they might be inclined to reach an understanding with the Muslims in order to grant them the freedom to preach their faith, visit Makkah, and perform the pilgrimage, which was all they really sought. Such an understanding was not possible, however, unless the Quraysh were brought to realize that their emigrant sons were capable of impeding that trade and inflicting some material harm. To my mind, this explains the return of Hamzah and his riders without battle after their encounter with Abu Jahl ibn Hisham on the seacoast when Majdiy ibn 'Amr al Juhani intervened between him and the Quraysh. It also explains the fact of the small numbers of riders which the Muslims sent on these expeditions in the direction of the trade routes of Makkah. Otherwise, it would be unreasonable that the Muslims go out to war in such small numbers. This also explains Muhammad's alliances of peace which he concluded with the tribes settled along the routes of these caravans while Quraysh persisted in its hostility toward the Muhajirun. Apparently, Muhammad had hoped that the news of these alliances would reach the Quraysh and cause them to reconsider their position and, perhaps, open the road to some understanding.

Al Ansar and Offensive Attack

The foregoing hypothesis is corroborated by a very reliable tradition to the effect that when the Prophet — may God's blessing be upon him — went with his men to Buwat and to al 'Ushayrah, a great number of Ansar from Madinah accompanied him. These Ansar had covenanted with him for his protection, not in order to launch any offensive attack against anyone. This point will become clear when we study the great battle of Badr. There, Muhammad hesitated whether or not to permit the fighting to take place until the people of Madinah had clearly agreed to join that specific sortie. Although the Ansar saw no violation of their covenant with Muhammad if the latter entered into other covenants of peace and friendship, they were not thereby committed to join him in a war against Makkah which no Arab morality or custom would approve. The effect of the alliances which Muhammad concluded with the tribes settled along the trade route was surely that of endangering Makkan trade. But how far removed is such an attempt from declaring and entering into a full scale war! We may conclude, therefore, that the views that Hamzah, 'Ubaydah ibn al Harith, and Sa'd ibn Abu Waqqas were sent to fight the Quraysh, and that their expeditions should be called military raids, are unsound and unacceptable. Likewise, the view that Muhammad had gone to al Abwa, Buwat, and al 'Ushayrah for purposes of war is refuted by the considerations we have just given. The fact that such a view is held by the historians of Muhammad does not constitute a sound argument because the said historians did not write until toward the end of the second century A.H. Furthermore, the said historians were looking at these events as they occurred after the great battle of Badr. Hence, they looked upon them as preliminary skirmishes preceding that great battle and leading toward it. It was a natural mistake for them to add these sorties to the list of battles the Muslims fought during the Prophet's lifetime.

Nature of the Madinese

A large number of Orientalists have perceived these facts and realized their opposition to the said claim, although they did not expressly say so in their works. We are moved to accredit them with this realization despite their following the Muslim historians in their general attribution to Muhammad and the Muhajirun of the intention to make war against Makkah from the first days of residence in Madinah. They point out that these early expeditions were, rather, intended as raids on the caravans to rob their goods, and they argue that this kind of robbery was embedded in the nature of the people of the desert and that the Madinese were attracted by prospective booty to cooperate in violation of their pledge at al 'Aqabah. This is spurious reasoning, of course, and to be rejected outright. The people of Madinah were not people of the desert living on robbery and raids. Rather, like the people of Makkah, they had other sources of income and were motivated the same way as all settled people who live on agriculture and trade. Such people do not make war except for an extraordinary and stirring purpose. On the other hand, the Muhajirun were entitled to seize Quraysh goods in retaliation for the goods which the Quraysh had seized from them. But they did not have recourse to such action before the battle of Badr. This was not, therefore, the reason for those expeditions. Besides, fighting had not yet been permitted in Islam. Neither Muhammad nor his companions could have indulged in it for the nomadic purpose erroneously explained by the Orientalists. Fighting was permitted in Islam, and carried out by Muhammad and his companions, in order to stop their being persecuted for their faith and to have all the freedom they needed to call men to it. Later, when we see the details and the proofs of this, it will become clear that in all these alliances Muhammad's purpose was the consolidation of the defense of Madinah. The objective was to remove Madinah beyond any design the Quraysh might have against its Muslim inhabitants. Muhammad could not have forgotten that the Makkans once sought to extradite the Muslims from Abyssinia. At that time, Muhammad did not see any objection at all to entering into a treaty of peace with Quraysh. Such a treaty would have stopped persecution, given him the freedom to call unto the new faith, and to witness for God unto all men.

Threat to the Jews

Perhaps, too, by these expeditions and armed sorties, Muhammad sought to warn the Jews of Madinah and the neighboring area. We have already seen how, upon Muhammad's arrival at Madinah, the Jews hoped to bring him into alliance with them and how, after befriending him and pledging to honor his freedom to practice and preach the new religion, they had begun to oppose and plot against him. In fact, no sooner had Muhammad settled down and the prospects of Islam had begun to improve, than the Jews, for their part, began their undeclared war against him. Their opposition and hostility were never open. Above all, they feared lest any harm might befall their trade; and, although they had fanned and fueled the fires of civil war in the past, they adeptly avoided every possible involvement. Henceforth, their covenant with Muhammad at least prevented them from any such open involvement; and they recoursed to every hidden way to instigate enmity and hostility between the Muhajirun and Ansar so as to revive the old hatreds between al Aws and al Khazraj by reminding them of the day of Bu'ath in reciting the war poetry which had been composed on that occasion.

Jewish Plots

The Muslims realized what the Jews were about, for the latter were neither gentle nor discrete. Their instigation was always overdone. The Muslims accused those who entered into the Covenant of Madinah of hypocrisy, and classified them with the *munafiqun*.[2] Some Jews were once violently expelled from the mosque, and were later isolated and boycotted. After failing to convince them of the truth of Islam, the Prophet — may God's blessing be upon him — let them alone. But to let them alone religiously did not mean that they should be allowed to instigate the Muslims to a civil internecine war. Politically speaking, it was not enough to warn them and to warn the Muslims of their instigation. It was necessary to impress them with the fact that the Muslims were sufficiently strong to stamp out any such war as the Jews were instigating as well as to uproot its causes. A good way for pressing this realization upon them was the sending out of Muslim forces on military expeditions in all directions on condition that such sorties entail no actual fighting and no military setback. This account seems to be factual, for men like Hamzah, whom we know to have been quick to fly into a rage, turned around in front of the enemy without engagement. The appearance of an honored friend asking for peace is not enough to separate two parties either of which is bent upon fighting. Rather, non-engagement was a deliberate and carefully laid out plan. Its specific purpose was on one side to threaten and warn the Jews, and, on the other, to seek an understanding with the Quraysh to let the religious call take its course freely, without impediment or recourse to war or fighting.

Islam and Fighting

This peaceful show of strength by Islam does not at all mean that Islam, at that time, forbade fighting in defense of personal life and of religion, or to put a stop to persecution. Indeed, Islam did not. Rather, it imposed such defense as a sacred duty. What it did really mean at that time, as it does today or will ever do, was to condemn any war of aggression. "Do not commit any aggression," God commands. He counsels, "God does not love the aggressors."[3] If, at that time, the Muhajirun felt justified in seizing the property of the Quraysh in retaliation for the latter's confiscation of their property when they emigrated, they certainly realized that to protect the Muslims against apostasy from their faith was a greater duty in the eyes of God and His Prophet. The latter was the main purpose for the sake of which God had permitted the Muslims to fight at all.

'Abdullah ibn Jahsh's Expedition

The proof of the foregoing contention may be found in the expedition of 'Abdullah ibn Jahsh al Asadi, who was sent by the Prophet of God at the head of a number of Muhajirun in the month of Rajab of the second year A.H. The Prophet gave him a document and asked him not to look at it until two days after the start of his journey. He was then supposed to follow its instructions without forcing any of his companions to comply with them. Two days after he started off, 'Abdullah, having unsealed the document, read the following instructions: "As soon as you have read this document, proceed to Nakhlah between Makkah and Ta'if, and there seek to learn for us the news of the Quraysh and their movements." When his companions learned that they were under no compulsion to go along with him, they all decided to do so except for Sa'd ibn Abu Waqqas al Zuhri and 'Utbah ibn Ghazwan, who preferred to look, on their own, for some of their camels which the Quraysh had seized. 'Abdullah and his companions proceeded as instructed. At Nakhlah, they saw a donkey caravan carrying trade goods for the Quraysh which were guarded by 'Amr ibn al Hadrami. The date was the end of the month of Rajab. Remembering the old persecutions of the Quraysh and the latter's seizure of their wealth and property, 'Abdullah ibn Jahsh, after consulting with his Muhajirun companions, said: "Surely, if you allow the caravan to pass through tonight unmolested, they will reach the holy territory tomorrow and will thereby become forbidden to you. And yet, if you kill them today, you will have killed them in the holy month when killing is forbidden." The hesitant Muslims were afraid to attack the caravan; but, encouraging one another, they agreed to kill whomever they could and to seize the goods in his possession. One of them shot an arrow at 'Amr ibn al Hadrami and killed him. The Muslims captured two men from the Quraysh.

Sedition Greater Than Murder

'Abdullah ibn Jahsh arrived in Madinah together with the two Quraysh captives and the donkey caravan loaded completely with goods. He had already earmarked one-fifth of the booty to the Prophet. But when the Prophet saw them, he said: "I have not instructed you to fight during the holy months." He stopped the caravan in its place as well as the two captives and refused to take any part of the booty. He castigated 'Abdullah ibn Jahsh and his companions and, later on, they were further scolded and punished by their fellow Muslims for what they had done. The Quraysh seized the opportunity to spread the propaganda everywhere that Muhammad and his companions had violated the sanctity of the holy month by having killed, robbed and captured. The Muslims of Makkah answered that the event had taken place not in the holy months but during the following month of Sha'ban. The Jews immediately joined the chorus of Quraysh propaganda with the hope of engaging the Muslims in a war with the Quraysh over a case in which the Muslims were apparently in the wrong according to Arabian custom. It was then that God revealed the judgment:

يَسْأَلُونَكَ عَنِ الشَّهْرِ الْحَرَامِ قِتَالٍ فِيهِ قُلْ قِتَالٌ فِيهِ كَبِيرٌ وَصَدٌّ عَن سَبِيلِ اللّهِ وَكُفْرٌ
بِهِ وَالْمَسْجِدِ الْحَرَامِ وَإِخْرَاجُ أَهْلِهِ مِنْهُ أَكْبَرُ عِندَ اللّهِ وَالْفِتْنَةُ أَكْبَرُ مِنَ الْقَتْلِ وَلَا
يَزَالُونَ يُقَاتِلُونَكُمْ حَتَّى يَرُدُّوكُمْ عَن دِينِكُمْ إِنِ اسْتَطَاعُوا

"They ask you concerning the holy month whether or not fighting is permitted therein. Answer: to fight therein is a grave misdeed. But to impede men from following the cause of God, to deny God, to violate the sanctity of the holy mosque, to expel its people from its precincts is with God a greater wrong than fighting in the holy month. Moreover, to divide the community of Muslims against itself is greater yet. Your enemies continue to fight you by all these means in order to compel you to abjure your religion."[4]

This revelation brought the Muslims relief, and the Prophet accepted his share of the booty. When the Quraysh sought to ransom the two captives, the Prophet answered: "We shall not accept your ransom for the two captives unless you return our two men whom you have captured, namely

Sa'd ibn Abu Waqqas and 'Utbah ibn Ghazwan. If you kill them we shall likewise kill your two men." Sa'd and 'Utbah were returned and the two Quraysh captives were released. One of them, al Hakam ibn Kaysan, was immediately converted to Islam and spent the rest of his life in Madinah. The other returned to Makkah where he remained to the end.

It is well worth our while to pause here for further consideration of the evidence which this expedition of 'Abdullah ibn Jahsh and the Qur'anic verse, which was revealed in that connection, furnish for our generalization concerning the political theory of Islam. The event occurs as it were at the very crossroads of the development of Islamic policy. In kind, it is new. It points to a spirit strong in its nobility, human in its strength, a spirit which orders the material, moral, and spiritual aspects of life very strictly while enhancing man's quest of perfection. The Qur'an answered the question of the idolaters concerning whether or not fighting is permissible in the holy months and approved their view that it is a grave misdeed. But it also warned against something yet greater in its evil and immorality: that is to impede men from following the path of God and to deny Him, to stop men from entering the holy mosque, to expel the worshipers therefrom, or to sway and lure man away from his religion by promise, threat, bribery, and persecution. All these are greater misdeeds than fighting during the holy months or any months. The Quraysh and the idolaters who blamed the Muslims for killing during the holy months were themselves still fighting the Muslims by these means in order to compel them to renounce their religion. If the Quraysh and the idolators perpetrated all these misdeeds together, the victims of their misdeeds cannot be blamed for fighting during the holy months. Rather, the real misdeed is that of perpetrating these evils during the holy month against the innocent and the peaceful.

The Qur'an and Fighting

Fitnah, or sedition, is a greater crime than murder. It is a right, nay a duty, of whosoever witnesses it, whether perpetrated against an individual or a whole community, to take up arms and fight for the sake of God and thus put an immediate end to it. It is here that the Orientalists and the missionaries raise their eyebrows and voices, shouting: "Do you see? Here is Muhammad agreeing that his religion actually calls to war, to *jihad* in the cause of God, that is, to compel man by the sword to enter into Islam. Isn't this precisely what is meant by fanaticism? Now contrast this with

Christianity, which denies fighting and condemns war, which calls for peace and advocates tolerance, which binds men in bonds of brotherhood in God and in Christ. . . ." In arguing this point I do not wish to mention the statement of the New Testament, "I have not come to send peace but a sword. . . ."; nor do I want to analyze the meanings implicit in such statements. The Muslims understand the religion of Jesus only as interpreted by the Qur'an. Rather, I want to begin by refuting the claim that Muhammad's religion calls for fighting and coercion of men into Islam. That is a false accusation denied by the Qur'anic judgment:

$$ لَآ اِكْرَاهَ فِى الدِّيْنِ ۛ قَدْ تَّبَيَّنَ الرُّشْدُ مِنَ الْغَيِّ ۛ $$

"There is no compulsion in religion — the truth is now distinct from error," as well as by the command, "Fight in the cause of God those who fight you, but do not commit any aggression. God does not love the aggressor."[6]

The same directives are contained in a number of other verses.

War in the Cause of God

Jihad, or war for the sake of God, is clearly defined in the verses which we have mentioned and which were revealed in connection with the expedition of 'Abdullah ibn Jahsh. Its definite meaning is to fight those who sway the Muslim away from his religion and prevent him from walking in the path of God. This fight is waged solely for the freedom to call men unto God and unto His religion. To use a modern expression consonant with the usage of the present age, we may say that war in Islam is permitted — nay, it is rather a duty — when undertaken in defense of freedom of thought and opinion. All weapons used by the aggressors may be used against them. If somebody seeks to sway a man from conviction or opinion, and he effectively uses propaganda and logic without physical coercion, persecution, discrimination, or use of illicit means such as bribery, no man may stop him except by answering his argument and analyzing and exposing his logic. However, if he resorts to armed force to prevent a man from holding a certain opinion, then it becomes necessary to answer his armed power with equal armed power wherever practical. Man has no dignity if his convictions have none. Convictions are far more precious than wealth, position, power or life itself. To those who appreciate the meaning of humanity, convictions are far more precious than the material life which man shares with the animals. If man's humanity consists of no more than eating and drinking, growing and struggling for survival, he is one with the animals. Man's spiritual and moral convictions constitute the moral bond which unites him to his fellow-men, the spiritual link between him and God. The life of conviction is man's great distinction from the animal kingdom. By it, man wills for his brother that which he wills for himself; by it, he inclines to share his wealth with the poor, the destitute, and the miserable, though such sharing may imply some deprivation to his near relatives; by it, man enters into communion with the universe to perform that which enables the universe to realize the perfection which God has prescribed and established for it.

Should conviction take possession of a man and should another man attempt to make him renounce it under conditions in which self-protection or defense are impossible, such a man would do what the Muslims did before their emigration from Madinah, namely, to bear patiently all injury, persecution, and injustice. Neither hunger nor deprivation of any kind would cause him to succumb to ignoble desires; patient forbearance was precisely what the Muslims practiced in Makkah as well as what the early Christians had practiced. But those who suffer in patience for the sake of their convictions are not the majority of mankind nor the plebians among them. They are, however, the select and chosen few whom God has endowed with such moral strength that they are capable of standing up against any injury or injustice, however great. It was precisely this kind of conviction which the New Testament has associated with the judgment that whoever is endowed therewith "shall say unto this mountain, remove hence to yonder place, and it shall remove."[7] But if it is possible for man to defend himself against aggression with the same arms as the aggressor, to fight the man who blocks the path of God by use of his own means, then it is his duty to do so. Otherwise, one would be weak of faith and doubtful in conviction. That is what Muhammad and his companions did after they had achieved a measure of security for themselves in Madinah. That is equally what the Christians did after they had achieved power in Rome and Byzantium, after the conversion of the Roman emperors.

Christianity and Fighting

The missionaries say, "But the spirit of Christianity condemns fighting altogether." I do not wish to pause here for investigating the truth, or lack of it, of such a claim. The history of Christianity, however, is a legitimate witness in this matter and so is the history of Islam. From the dawn of Christianity until today every country of the world has been soaked with blood in the name of Jesus Christ. The Romans and the Byzantines of old as well as the European peoples of modern times are guilty of shedding blood in religious causes. The Crusades were launched and their fires fanned by Christians, not by Muslims. For hundreds of years, one army after another rolled out of Europe in the direction of the Muslim Orient to fight, to destroy, and to shed blood. In every case, the popes who claimed to be the vicars of Jesus Christ, blessed and encouraged these armies and hurried them to Jerusalem and other destinations. Were all these popes heretics? Was their Christianity spurious? Or was everyone of them a pretender, an ignoramus, unaware that Christianity absolutely condemns fighting? The missionaries rejoin, "Those were the Middle Ages, ages of darkness, unfit as evidence against Christianity." If this is an argument on which they pin some hope, let us then turn to the twentieth century in which we now live and which they call "the century of the highest human civilization." This century has indeed seen the same darkness as did the Middle Ages. Lord Allenby, representing the allied forces of England, France, Italy, Rumania, and America, stopped in Jerusalem in 1918 after his conquest of that city toward the end of the first World War and said: "Today the Crusades have come to an end."

The Saints in Islam and Christianity

If in every age and period, there have been Christian saints who have condemned fighting and who rose to the pinnacles of human brotherhood — indeed, of brotherhood among all elements of the universe — so there were among the Muslims saints who have reached these very pinnacles and related themselves to all existence and being in a bond of brotherhood, love, and illumination and who realized within their souls the very unity of being. These saints, however, whether Muslim or Christian, do not represent human life in its constant development and struggle toward perfection. Rather they represent the highest example of the realization of that perfection. The general run of men, however, seek to understand and realize such perfection, but neither their reason nor their imagination succeeds in doing so with any amount of precision or completeness. Their attempts to realize it are understandable as preliminaries and trials. One thousand three hundred and fifty-seven years have so far passed since the emigration of the Arab Prophet from Makkah to Madinah. Throughout these years men have increased their capacities to fight, improved their devilish art of war, and made its weapons more destructive than ever. However, disarmament and the cessation of war are still words of mere propaganda spread before the eyes of the credulous in war after war, each more devastating than the preceding. These noble ideals have hardly been more than propaganda claims made by people thus far incapable — and who knows, perhaps never capable — of realizing any such desiderata, of bringing true peace into the world, a peace of brotherhood and justice instead of an armed peace which is only a preliminary to another war.

Islam, the Natural Religion

The religion of Islam is not one of illusion and fantasy. Neither is it a religion which addresses only the individual as such and urges him to rise to perfection. Rather, Islam is the natural religion, the religion which naturally belongs to all men, individuals as well as groups. It is the religion of truth, of freedom, and of order. As long as it is also the nature of man to fight and to make war, to discipline that nature and to limit this inclination within the narrowest frontier is all that is possible for men to bear and abide by; it is all that humanity can hope to achieve in its struggle toward goodness and perfection. By far the best disciplining of this inclination to war is to limit it to pure defense of one's person, one's faith, one's freedom of opinion, and one's freedom to preach. The greatest wisdom is to regulate the making of war so that all the rights and dignities of man may be respected and observed to the utmost. And this is precisely what Islam has sought to do, as we have seen and as we shall have occasion to see later. That is precisely what the Qur'an has commanded, as we have seen, and shall have occasion to see in the sequel.

13

The Great Battle of Badr

The expedition of 'Abdullah ibn Jahsh constituted the crossroads of Islamic policy. It was the occasion when Waqid ibn 'Abdullah al Tamimi shot an arrow at 'Amr ibn al Hadrami and killed him, thus shedding blood by a Muslim hand for the first time. It was in regard to this sortie that the Qur'anic verses constituting the Islamic position on war and fighting were revealed. And it was in consequence of this revelation that fighting was permitted, but only against those who seek to compel the Muslims to renounce their religion and who stand in the way of calling men unto God. The same expedition constituted also the crossroads of Muslim policy toward Quraysh, for it now opened the door for the two parties to compete in military power and strength as they had done formerly in word and idea. It was after that expedition that the Muslims began to think seriously of extracting their goods from Quraysh by force and conquest. The Quraysh saw in this an opportunity to stir up the whole peninsula against Muhammad and his companions, and therefore accused them of the most heinous crime in the eyes of all Arabs, namely the desecration of the holy months. In the resultant situation, Muhammad became convinced that there was no more hope of reaching any kind of agreement with them. Toward the beginning of autumn of the second year A.H., Abu Sufyan led a great caravan toward al Sham. It was this trade which the Muslims had previously threatened when the Prophet — may God's peace and blessing be upon him — joined the expedition to al 'Ushayrah in person. When the Muslims reached that locality, the caravan of Abu

209

Sufyan had passed two days earlier. The Muslims decided to withdraw and wait for the caravan's return. When that time came and the caravan was supposedly in the vicinity of Madinah, Muhammad sent Talhah ibn 'Ubaydullah and Sa'id ibn Zayd to reconnoiter its whereabouts. The two men ran in the direction of the usual trade route and arrived at the campsite of Kashd al Juhaniy in al Hawra'. There, they hid until the caravan passed. They returned quickly to Madinah in order to give Muhammad the information he asked for.

The Muslims Mobilize for Badr

Muhammad did not await the return of his two messengers from al Hawra'. He had already heard that the caravan in question was a very large one and that practically all the Makkans were involved in the trade it carried since all Makkan capitalists had already bought a share in it. The goods the caravan carried were estimated at 50,000 dinars. Muhammad feared that if he were to await the news of his two messengers, the caravan would pass him by on its return to Makkah as it had passed him by on its northward trip to Syria earlier. Consequently, he called the Muslims together and addressed them in the following words: "Yonder is the caravan of Quraysh. Mobilize your forces and seek to capture it. Perhaps God may give it to you as booty." Some Muslims responded and others did not. Some non-Muslims were anxious to join, but Muhammad prevented them from doing so until they had believed in God and his Prophet.

Abu Sufyan's Messenger to Quraysh

On the other side, Abu Sufyan had also heard of Muhammad's sortie to intercept his caravan on its way north to al Sham, and he was equally apprehensive that the Muslims would again attempt to do so on his return. He therefore sought to learn of their movements as assiduously as the Muslims sought to learn of his. He was especially apprehensive of the return trip because his trade, so far, had been particularly successful. The same al Juhaniy who played host to Muhammad's messengers at al Hawra' was asked by Abu Sufyan concerning the Muslims. Al Juhaniy did not tell the truth to Abu Sufyan; but this did not matter inasmuch as Abu Sufyan already knew as much about the Muslims as the Muslims knew about him. He feared a catastrophe because his caravan had but thirty or forty men to guard it. Anticipating danger, he decided to send Damdam ibn

'Amr al Ghifari in haste to Quraysh with the message that Muhammad and his companions had set out to intercept the caravan and to appeal to them to send men for escort. As instructed by Abu Sufyan, just before he entered Makkah, Damdam cut off the ears of his camel, broke its nose, turned its saddle sideways, tore his own robe in front and in back, and entered the city standing on the back of his camel shouting: "O People of Quraysh, your wealth and trade are being lost. Abu Sufyan and the caravan are being intercepted by Muhammad and his companions. Perhaps you may still catch them. Help! Help!" As soon as he heard the news, Abu Jahl called upon all Makkans to join in the rescue operation. He, a man of acid temper, eloquent speech, and strong insight, could inflame any audience. The Quraysh, however, were not in need of eloquent speeches to rise against Muhammad. Everyone of them had a share in the trade this caravan carried.

Old Enmity of Quraysh and Kinanah

At the time, a group of Makkans felt that Quraysh had been too unjust toward its Muslim members for having compelled them to emigrate first to Abyssinia and then to Madinah. This group, hesitant to answer the call of Abu Jahl, simply hoped that the caravan would not be destroyed. This same group remembered that the Quraysh and Kinanah tribes were quite alienated from each other and were only waiting for an opportunity to avenge themselves against each other. They feared that should the Quraysh all go out to meet Muhammad and protect their caravan, the Banu Bakr of Kinanah might seize the opportunity to attack them from behind. This cautious judgment would nearly have carried the day against the appeal of Abu Jahl were it not for the arrival upon the scene of Malik ibn Ju'shum al Mudliji, a nobleman and leader of Banu Kinanah. He said, addressing the Makkans: "I deliver myself to you as a surety that Kinanah will not pounce upon you in your hour of need." With this, the group supporting Abu Jahl and 'Amr ibn al Hadrami for general mobilization and war against Muhammad and his companions, succeeded in convincing the Makkans in favor of war. No reason remained for any Makkan capable of fighting to stay behind, or for the incapable to equip and send somebody in his stead. None of the noblemen of the Quraysh stayed behind except Abu Lahab, who sent in his stead al 'As ibn Hisham ibn al Mughirah in compensation for some four thousand dirhams the latter owed him which he was not able to pay back. 'Umayyah ibn Khalaf, a very old and obese man, decided to stay behind. He was visited in the mosque by 'Uqbah ibn Abu Mu'ayt and Abu Jahl. The first carried an incense burner; the second, instruments of beautification for women. 'Uqbah placed the incense burner in Umayyah's hands and said, "O Abu 'Ali, fill your atmosphere with incense for you are a woman." Abu Jahl handed over the instruments of beautification and said, "O Abu 'Ali, beautify yourself for you are only a woman." At this, Umayyah rose and said, "Buy for me the best and strongest camel in Makkah." He rode it and joined the force. Because of this and like tactics, no man capable of bearing arms remained behind.

The Path of the Muslim Army

The Prophet — may God's blessing be upon him — had started off from Madinah with his companions on the eighth day of Ramadan in the second year A.H. He had appointed 'Amr ibn Maktum to lead the prayer in Madinah, and Abu Lubabah, whom he called back from al Rawha', to govern Madinah in his place during his absence. The Muslim force was preceded by two black flags, and their camels counted seventy. Since three or four men were assigned to one camel, each one rode for only a brief while. Muhammad's share in riding was like that of his companions. He, 'Ali ibn Abu Talib, and Marthad ibn Marthad al Ghanawi had one camel assigned to them. Abu Bakr, 'Umar, and 'Abd al Rahman ibn 'Awf shared another. The total number of men on this expedition amounted to three hundred and five. Eighty-three of them were Muhajirun, sixty-one belonged to al Aws, and the rest to al Khazraj. Their pace was swift because they feared Abu Sufyan would pass them by if they tarried. They arrived to a place called 'Irq al Zubiah where they found a Bedouin whom they asked concerning the caravan but could not learn anything from him. They continued on their march until they arrived at a valley called Dhafiran where they encamped. It was at this moment that the news reached them that the Quraysh had come out in force to meet them and protect the caravan. This news radically changed the situation. It was no more a question of intercepting Abu Sufyan, his caravan, and the thirty or forty escorts who were no match for Muhammad and his companions. The whole of Makkah, led by its nobles and elders, was out to protect its trade. If the Muslims were to catch up with Abu Sufyan, overcome his men and take away his camels and all they carried, would the Quraysh not follow and catch up with them, stirred up by this new attack of the

Muslims and encouraged by their great numbers and armaments? Would they not catch up with the Muslims and fight them to the finish? On the other hand, if Muhammad were to return without victory, would not both the Quraysh and the Jews of Madinah realize his weakness and seek to take advantage of it? Would he then not have to compromise and, perhaps, suffer a Jewish tyranny in Madinah such as the Quraysh tyranny he had suffered in Makkah? In such eventuality, how could the revelation of truth and the religion of God ever become successful or achieve victory?

Muhammad consulted the members of his expedition concerning the news just received. After Abu Bakr and 'Umar presented their views, al Miqdad ibn 'Amr stood up and said: "O Prophet of God, press forward toward that which God has shown you. We are with you. By God, we shall never say to you, as the Jews had said to Moses, 'Go alone with your Lord and fight with Him for us, while we remain here and await your return.' Rather, we say, 'Go forth, you and your Lord to fight, for we are fighting with you.'" Al Miqdad's speech was followed by silence. The Prophet said: "Speak out, O men, and give me your counsel." He was especially anxious to hear al Ansar's view who, on the day of al 'Aqabah, pledged to protect him as they would their children and women but not to permit any aggression with him outside their own area. When al Ansar realized that he was waiting for them to speak, Sa'd ibn Mu'adh, their leader, rose and addressed Muhammad: "Does it seem, O Prophet of God, that you are seeking to hear our view?" The Prophet answered, "Indeed." Sa'd said, "We have believed in you, and we have witnessed that what you have brought to us is the truth. We have covenanted with you to hear and to obey. Go ahead with whatever you decide, for we are with you. By Him who sent you as a prophet, if you lead us toward the sea, we shall enter into it with you and not one of us will stay behind. We do not fear that you cause us to face our enemy tomorrow. We shall hold fast to our ground and stand firm or press forward toward the enemy in solid ranks. We hope that God will show you such of our deeds as you may not be disappointed therein but may be proud of. Lead us forth with God's blessing." Sa'd had hardly finished his words when Muhammad's face radiated with joy and his eyes shone with energy. He said: "Go forward and be optimistic; for God had promised me one of the two — either the caravan or the Makkan army. By God, it is as though I see the enemy lying prostrate in the field." When the force arrived at Dhafiran, Muhammad advanced on his camel alone and, reaching an old Bedouin settler in the area who did not know him, asked about Quraysh, as well as about Muhammad and his companions, and learned that the caravan of Quraysh was indeed close by.

Reconnaissance and Espionage

When Muhammad returned to his party, he sent 'Ali ibn Abu Talib, al Zubayr ibn al 'Awwam, and Sa'd ibn Abu Waqqas with a number of other companions to the well of Badr to seek out fresh news. The little group returned with two boys who, upon interrogation by Muhammad, revealed that the Quraysh army stood behind the hill on the further side. When they could not answer his questions regarding the strength of the Quraysh army, Muhammad asked how many animals they killed for food every day. The boys answered, "Nine on one day and ten on the other." The Prophet concluded from this that their number must be between nine hundred and one thousand. He also learned from the two boys that the leaders of Quraysh were all present. Turning to his own companions he said, "There is Makkah confronting you with all its sons in one body." It was therefore absolutely necessary, he thought, that Muslims mobilize all efforts, harden their hearts and wills, and prepare themselves for a battle so fierce that none would emerge victorious from it except those whose hearts were completely possessed by faith in God alone.

Escape of the Caravan and Abu Sufyan

As 'Ali and his companions came back from Badr with the two youths and some information about Quraysh, two other Muslims went in a slightly different direction to seek news of the caravan. They came to a sandhill not too far from the springs of Badr. There they took a jug and went down to the spring to get some water. While they were there they overheard two maid servants involved in an argument in which the one was asking the other to pay back her debt to her; the latter answered that either on the next day or the day after the caravan would come for whom she would work, and she would earn enough to pay her back. The two men returned to Muhammad and reported what they heard. As the caravan approached the area, Abu Sufyan marched ahead reconnoitering the territory, apparently fearful that Muhammad might have preceded him to the place. When he arrived at the spring, he met Majdi ibn 'Amr, whom he asked whether anyone had been seen in the vicinity. Majdi answered that he had not seen anyone except two idlers who stopped at the nearby sand dune, and pointed to the spot where the two Muslims stopped in order to get the water. Abu Sufyan came to the spot and found some refuse of their two camels. As he examined it, he found it contained grains which he recognized as coming from crops known to be grown and used in Madinah. He returned quickly to his caravan and altered its course. By leading it toward the sea coast with great speed, he managed to escape.

The morrow arrived while the Muslims were still awaiting the arrival of the caravan. The news now reached them that the caravan had passed them by on a different route and that the Quraysh army were still in the vicinity close by. With this news, whatever hope for booty some of them may have entertained collapsed. The Prophet discussed with his companions whether or not they should now return to Madinah and not force a showdown with the Quraysh army. In this connection, the following verses of the Qur'an were revealed: "Now that God has promised that one of 'the two' shall fall to you, you wish that it would be the one devoid of strength or resistance. But, rather than easy booty, God wishes that the truth become supreme, that justice be done, and that the unbelievers be scattered."[1]

Prospects of Battle

For their part, the Quraysh asked themselves the same question. What need do they have to fight now that their caravan had escaped? Was it not better for them to return to their homes and to let the Muslims return to theirs empty handed? These were the thoughts of Abu Sufyan, who sent word to the Quraysh to this effect. He told them, "You have prepared for war and come out in strength in order to protect your caravan, your men, and your goods. God has saved all these. Return, then, home." Some men agreed. Abu Jahl thought otherwise. To Abu Sufyan's message, he responded, "By God, we shall not return home until we have come to Badr, spent three nights in eating good food, drinking wine, and reveling, that all Arabs may hear of our sortie, our strength, and continue to fear us." The locality of Badr was the center of a seasonal gathering in that part of Arabia. For the Quraysh to withdraw soon after the escape of their caravan might be interpreted as fear of Muhammad and his companions. This event would increase Muhammad's power and encourage the spread of his cause. Such would especially be the case as the expedition of 'Abdullah ibn Jahsh, the killing of ibn al Hadrami, the capture of two Qurayshis, and Quraysh's loss of the caravan were all common knowledge throughout the desert.

The Muslims Camp at Badr

There was some hesitation in the camp of Quraysh, whether to follow Abu Jahl or return home. Banu Zuhrah, under the leadership of al Akhnas ibn Shariq, listened to Abu Sufyan's counsel and returned home; but they were alone. All the rest followed Abu Jahl in deciding to encamp as if in preparation for war and to consult with one another later on. They set up camp on the farthest side behind a sand dune which they took as center. The Muslims, on the other hand, having now missed the booty, decided together to stand firm should the enemy engage them. They hurried to the springs of Badr while a rain which fell upon them from heaven helped their quick advance to that place. When they reached the first water well, Muhammad dismounted with the intention of camping there. Cognizant of the area, al Hubab ibn al Mundhir ibn al Jamuh approached the Prophet and said: "O Prophet of God, is this spot where you have dismounted a place to which God has guided you and, therefore, may we neither step beyond it nor stay far behind it? Or is this simply a question of ordinary war strategy, of measures and moves and counter measures and moves?" Muhammad answered, "It is indeed the latter, just as you said." Al Hubab then said, "O Prophet of God, this is not a good place to be. We should move forward until we reach the well closest to the enemy. There we would bring a trough to it to fill with water and then fill the well with sand. We would fight the enemy; and when we withdraw we would be able to drink, whereas they would not." Muhammad, immediately agreeing, rose to go forward with his force. He sent a reminder to all his companions that he is but a man like them, that all decisions have to be taken by all of them in consultation with one another, that he will not decide anything without them finally, and that he stands in great need of their good counsel.

Building a Booth for the Prophet

When they completed the building of the trough, Sa'd ibn Mu'adh addressed the Prophet thus: "O Prophet of God, let us build a booth for you to stay in, and let us prepare for you some mounts before we engage our enemy. If God gives us the strength and we are victorious, that would be fine and well. If otherwise, you would then ride these mounts, join the rear ranks of our forces and return home. Many Muslims have stayed in Madinah who do not love you any less than we do. No one had expected that our expedition would turn out to be one of war. Had they realized this, they would not have let you go out without them. On your return to Madinah, they would be there to protect you, counsel you and fight with you." Muhammad thanked Sa'd and prayed for him. The booth was readied for the Prophet and preparations were made for his return in case of defeat so that he would not fall into the hands of his enemies as a captive.

The True Faith of the Muslims

We must pause here to appreciate with wonder the faithfulness of the Muslims, their great love for Muhammad, and their absolute conviction of the truth of his prophethood. They knew too well that Quraysh far exceeded them in number; in fact, their enemy had three times as many fighters as they. Nonetheless, they decided to stand firm in the cause and to fight. After they saw their booty escape, whatever motivation they had for material gain must now be discounted. All this notwithstanding, by siding with the Prophet they confirmed his prophethood and strengthened his ranks. They were not sure of victory, though they wished for it; and they were afraid of defeat. Nonetheless, they thought of protecting the Prophet and arranged lest he should fall a captive in the hands of his enemies. They planned for him to return to Madinah and join the Muslims behind. What stand is more wonderful than this! What faith guarantees victory as this faith of theirs!

Hamzah Kills Ibn 'Abd al Asad

The Quraysh arranged and readied themselves for battle. Their spies had informed them that the Muslims were three hundred strong or a little more, that they had neither provisions nor a hiding place, and that their only protection was their swords, determined as they were to kill before falling. As the cream of Quraysh forces had joined this expedition, the wise among them feared that should a number of these fall by Muslim hands, Makkah would soon lose its position of leadership. However, they could not speak out for fear that Abu Jahl would accuse them of cowardice. Nonetheless, 'Utbah ibn Rabi'ah did. "O men of Quraysh," he advised his peers, "we will surely not achieve anything by meeting Muhammad and his companions in battle. If we should defeat them, everyone of us would recognize in their dead a cousin, an uncle, or a relative from his own clan and tribe. Return to your homes and leave

Muhammad alone among the tribes. Should they kill him and defeat him, your purpose would have been met. Should it turn out to be otherwise, you will not have to suffer the consequences." But when Abu Jahl heard these words of 'Utbah, he raged in anger, sent after 'Amr ibn al Hadrami, and said to him: "Your ally is shamelessly courting men to return to Makkah now that you have beheld your enemy with your own eye. There is your enemy, on whom you ought to avenge yourself. Rise and avenge the slaying of your brother." 'Amir stood up and yelled, "Woe! 'Amr shall be avenged! To battle! To battle!" With this, the last chance of peace was shattered. Al Aswad ibn 'Abd al Asad al Makhzumi, springing out of the ranks of the Quraysh toward the Muslims, sought to destroy the trough which they had just built. Hamzah ibn 'Abd al Muttalib struck him with his sword. The blow cut off his leg, and the victim fell on his back with his leg bleeding profusely. Immediately Hamzah struck him again and killed him. Nothing draws the swords out of mens' sheaths faster than the sight of blood. Nothing stirs the will to kill more than the sight of a friend slain by an enemy hand in front of his own people.

Engagement of the Two Armies

As soon as al Aswad fell, 'Utbah ibn Rabi'ah, flanked by his brother Shaybah on one side and his son al Walid ibn 'Utbah on the other, sprang forth and challenged the Muslims to duel. A number of youths from Madinah went out to meet them. When Shaybah recognized them, he said: "We have not come to fight you. Rather we want to fight our own tribesmen." The Quraysh crier called forth: "O Muhammad, send out our own peers of our own tribe to fight us." At this, Hamzah ibn 'Abd al Muttalib, 'Ali ibn Abu Talib, and 'Ubaydah ibn al Harith advanced forth. A duel was fought in which Hamzah killed Shaybah, and 'Ali killed al Walid. Then both of them came to assist 'Ubaydah who had not yet finished off 'Utbah. When the Quraysh army saw this, they advanced in force and the two armies collided. It was the morning of Friday, seventeenth of Ramadan, 2 A.H.

Muhammad's Prayer and Invocation

Muhammad led the Muslims and organized their ranks. As he looked over the Quraysh army and compared them with his thin ranks and poor equipment, he felt quite apprehensive. He returned to his booth with Abu

Bakr, strongly moved by fear and pity for the career of Islam should the Muslims lose on this day. Turning his face to Makkah and his whole soul to God, he began to pray, calling on God to give him victory. He prayed to God for a very long while, and was heard repeating the following words: "O God, here is Quraysh with all her tribe seeking to belie your Prophet. O God, give us the assistance which You promised. O God, if this little army perishes, when will You be worshiped again?" Muhammad prayed with hands raised to heaven. His mantle fell off and Abu Bakr had to pick it up and put it back on his shoulders. Abu Bakr said to him: "O Prophet of God, enough calling on God; He will surely give you what He promised." Muhammad continued to pray, pouring out his whole soul in pious invocation to God to help him in this hour of precipitous danger. After near collapse, he came back to himself and told of a vision he saw of God's victory. With radiant face, he went out to meet his men and incited them to put their faith in God and enter the battle without fear. He assured them one by one: "By Him who controls Muhammad's soul, not one of you today fights and falls but God will enter him into His paradise."

Muslim Morale

Out of Muhammad's strong soul a stronger power than God might have imparted on any other occasion spread among the Muslim ranks, fortifying their will and determination and making each and everyone of them the equivalent of two — nay ten — men in strength. We can easily imagine the effect of this sudden reinforcement of Muslim morale upon their personalities when the cause is as morally justified as theirs has been. The feeling of patriotism with which modernity is familiar is certainly one such supporting moral justification in modern wars. The soldier who exposes himself to all kinds of danger in the belief that he is defending his fatherland walks into battle with superior morale; the greater his love for and faith in his fatherland, the more frightful the risks he stands prepared to take. Consequently, nations inculcate upon their young at a very tender age the love of the fatherland and the will to sacrifice for its sake. Conviction of the fatherland's right to justice, freedom, and the higher human values reinforce the soul; and this, in turn, doubles the material power issuing from the person. Those who remember the allied propaganda against the Germans during World War II will recall that the allies saturated the atmosphere with their claim that they were fighting a war for the sake of freedom and justice, and were laying down their lives in a last war against the militaristic state of Germany precisely in order to usher in an age of peace and security and light. This allied propaganda not only doubled the strength of their soldiers but provided them as well with a warm welcome freely given by most peoples of the world. But what patriotism and what cause of peace and security dare compare with what Muhammad was calling for! For Muhammad, it was a matter of one's communion with ultimate reality, of union with all being in a bond giving man determining power in the universe, and of blazing for him the path of goodness, blessedness and perfection. Yes, indeed: What kind of patriotism or cause of peace dares to stand beside the communion with God which puts to an end the persecution of the believers for their faith in Him and removes the hindrances of idolatry and associationism from the path of God? If patriotism increases the power of the soul by as much power as corresponds with the value of fatherland, and if the love of peace for mankind increases the power of the soul by as much power as corresponds with the value of the whole of mankind, how great must have been the power of the soul when it was reinforced by faith in total being as well as in the Creator of total being? Surely it makes that soul capable of moving mountains, of determining the heavenly bodies, of exerting its power and influence supremely over all men endowed with less faith? Moral power doubles and redoubles material power. When, before the battle, this strength was not at its highest because of division within Muslim ranks, Muslim material power suffered in consequence. But the situation changed, and their power increased tremendously under the inspiration of Muhammad. And it was this new resurgence of power by this means that compensated the Muslims for their small number and poor equipment. It was in connection with this spiritual phenomenon that the two Qur'anic verses were revealed:

يَٰٓأَيُّهَا ٱلنَّبِىُّ حَرِّضِ ٱلْمُؤْمِنِينَ عَلَى ٱلْقِتَالِ إِن يَكُن مِّنكُمْ عِشْرُونَ صَٰبِرُونَ يَغْلِبُوا۟ مِا۟ئَتَيْنِ وَإِن يَكُن مِّنكُم مِّا۟ئَةٌ يَغْلِبُوٓا۟ أَلْفًا مِّنَ ٱلَّذِينَ كَفَرُوا۟ بِأَنَّهُمْ قَوْمٌ لَّا يَفْقَهُونَ ۞ ٱلْـَٰٔنَ خَفَّفَ ٱللَّهُ عَنكُمْ وَعَلِمَ أَنَّ فِيكُمْ ضَعْفًا فَإِن يَكُن مِّنكُم مِّا۟ئَةٌ صَابِرَةٌ يَغْلِبُوا۟ مِا۟ئَتَيْنِ وَإِن يَكُن مِّنكُمْ أَلْفٌ يَغْلِبُوٓا۟ أَلْفَيْنِ بِإِذْنِ ٱللَّهِ وَٱللَّهُ مَعَ ٱلصَّٰبِرِينَ ۞

"'O Prophet, urge the believers to fight.' If there be twenty steadfast men they will overcome two hundred. And if there be a hundred, they will overcome a thousand unbelievers. These are a people devoid of knowledge, faith, or conviction. For the present, God has lightened your burden. He knows that there is weakness in you. So if there be a hundred steadfast men among you, they will overcome two hundred; and if there be a thousand, they will overcome two thousand by God's permission. God is surely with those who are steadfast."[2]

Bilal Kills Umayyah ibn Khalaf

At Muhammad's urging and inspiration, his standing in their midst and inciting them against the enemy, and his announcement that paradise belongs to the men of valor who plunge fearlessly into the ranks of the enemy, the Muslims doubled and redoubled their strength. Before entering battle, they resolved to direct their attention to the leaders and nobles of the Quraysh. They planned to seek them and to kill them first, remembering the persecution and travails they suffered at their hands in Makkah, especially the blocking of the road to God and to the holy mosque. Bilal saw Umayyah ibn Khalaf and his son on the field surrounded by a number of Muslims who had recognized him and sought to take him as captive. This Umayyah was Bilal's previous master who used to torture him by forcing him down to the ground where he placed a large rock on his chest, letting him burn under the torrid sun in order to force him to abjure Islam. Bilal survived all these travails in certainty of his faith while repeating continuously, "God is one! God is one!" When his eyes fell upon Umayyah in the field, he shouted, "Umayyah, the head of idolatry! Death to me if he escapes!" and charged furiously toward him. The Muslims surrounding Umayyah sought to prevent Bilal from reaching him. Bilal called to them at high voice: "O Helpers of God! The head of idolatry is Umayyah ibn Khalaf. Death to me if he escapes!" He charged again toward Umayyah and killed him. Mu'adh ibn 'Amr ibn al Jamuh killed Abu Jahl ibn Hisham. Hamzah, 'Ali and other Muslim heroes penetrated deeply into enemy lines, forgetting themselves, their small numbers, and their being surrounded by their enemies. Muslims hurled themselves into the melee. The dust rose, the battle raged at its hottest and wildest, and the heads of the Quraysh flew off their bodies. Possessed by their faith and chanting, "God is one! God is one!" the Muslims exerted tremendous power and pressed ever forward. It was as if space and time had lost their meaning, and God's angels were hovering above to encourage and draw them ever forward. They were so great that even their arms brandishing their swords in the air and striking the necks of their enemies seemed as if they moved not by ordinary human power but by the supernatural power of God Himself. Muhammad was in the midst of the battlefield fighting as well as observing his companions. At one moment he took dirt in his hand and threw it in the face of an advancing party of Quraysh, commanding his companions to stand firm. The Muslims stood their ground and forced the superior enemy to withdraw. It did not matter to the Muslim that he was surrounded by his enemies. His soul was filled with the breath of God; this divine spirit made him ever-firm and gave him the very power with which he wielded his arms. It was of this battle that God said: "Your lord revealed to the angels that He is with you and commanded them to give firmness to those that believe. He announced that He will cast terror into the hearts of those who disbelieve. God commands: 'Smite your enemies; strike off their heads and forearms. . . You killed them not when you did, but it was God who killed them; and you threw not when you did throw your arrows but it was God who threw them."[3] When the Prophet saw that God had fulfilled His promise and given the Muslims victory, he returned to his booth. The Quraysh were not only withdrawing but running away, and the Muslims were pressing after them to capture those of them whom they did not kill on the battlefield.

The Muslims Spare the Just

This was the great battle of Badr that established Muslim power throughout the Arabian Peninsula and began the movement of Arab unity under the leadership of Islam. It was the beginning of a large Islamic empire which gave the world a civilization which has so far played and will ever play a very important role in the history of the universe. It may surprise some readers to learn that as he urged his companions to fight the enemy and scatter their forces, Muhammad asked them not to kill Banu Hashim and some other leaders of the Quraysh despite the fact that they were all arrayed in battle on the other side. In so doing, he was not seeking any advantage for his tribe or relatives. Muhammad was too noble to be moved by such considerations. Rather he wanted to reward Banu Hashim for their protection of him and of his cause during thirteen long years between his commission to prophethood and emigration. It should be remembered that his uncle, al 'Abbas, was the one who concluded the covenant of al 'Aqabah. He also remembered other members of the Quraysh besides the Banu Hashim, who once sought to revoke the boycott pact which imprisoned the Muslims in one of the districts of Makkah with little or no food supplies. Muhammad considered a good deed as worthy of regard — of a gesture equal to it in charity and good will — despite the idolatry of its author. Thus, he interceded with the Muslims at the hour of battle on behalf of those Makkans who did the good deeds. Some of them, however, refused Muhammad's good will move and kind gesture. Such was the case of Abu al Bakhtari, who was responsible for the rescinding of the boycott pact but who fought and was killed in battle.

People of the Grave

The people of Makkah ran away from the field despondent, dejected, and mourning their dead. They would hardly catch sight of their companions when their eyes would fall down in shame for what had happened. The Muslims remained at Badr until the end of the day. They collected the dead of the Quraysh and buried them on the spot. Muhammad and his companions spent that night on the battlefield burying the dead, collecting the booty and keeping their eyes on the captives. As the night drew on, Muhammad sat down to think both of this victory, which God had just given the Muslims despite their small number, and the terrible defeat He had inflicted upon an enemy devoid of a sound faith capable of fusing their large numbers into one strong will. He pondered the matter over many long hours of the night. He was even heard addressing the dead in their new graves: "O people of the grave!" he murmured, "O 'Utbah ibn Rabi'ah! O Shaybah ibn Rabi'ah! O Umayyah ibn Khalaf! O Abu Jahl ibn Hisham!" After calling by name the fallen one by one, he addressed them in these words: "Have you really found that which your Lord had promised you? I have found what my Lord had promised me. But have you? The Muslims who overheard him asked, "Are you calling the dead?" and the Prophet answered, "They hear me no less than you do, except that they are unable to answer me." The Prophet of God looked Abu Hudhayfah ibn 'Utbah straight in the face and realized that he was pale. He asked him, "O Abu Hudhayfah, are you despondent over the sad fate your father met today?" Abu Hudhayfah answered, "No, by God, O Prophet of God! I have not censured my father or bemoaned his fate. I have known him to be a wise and good man, and I had hoped that his wisdom and virtue would one day lead him to Islam. When I saw what befell him, I remembered his idolatry despite all the hope I had entertained for him. Thus I am only sorry for him." The Prophet of God spoke to him gently and prayed for him.

Muslim Differences Concerning Booty

When the morning came and it was time for the Muslims to return to Madinah, they began to consider the disposition of the booty. Those who collected it claimed it as their own. Those who ran after the enemy and captured the captives said: "By God, we deserve it more than they; for without us it would not have been realized." Those who were guarding Muhammad and protecting him against a resurgence of the enemy forces, said: "Neither one of you deserve the booty. We surely could have killed the enemy and taken possession of his goods, but we preferred to protect the Prophet of God and, therefore, we stayed behind near him while you went out capturing and collecting it." At this Muhammad commanded every Muslim to return every piece of the booty he had taken and to keep all the booty together until he had reached judgment regarding it, or God had revealed the way it should be disposed of.

Equal Division of the Booty

Muhammad sent to Madinah 'Abdullah ibn Rawahah and Zayd ibn Harithah to bring news of the victory to the people of Madinah. He and his companions returned to Madinah accompanied by the captives and carrying the booty of war. He had appointed 'Abdullah ibn Ka'b as the guardian of it. After reaching the valley of al Safra', Muhammad camped on a hill and there began to divide the booty among the Muslims in equal parts. Some historians claim that Muhammad had divided the booty after he had appropriated one-fifth of it in accordance with the Qur'anic command: "And know that whatever you take as spoils in war, a fifth thereof shall go to God, His Prophet, the kindred, the orphans, the needy, and the wayfarer. If you believe in God and in what We send down to Our servant and the day of decision [the day of Badr] when the two armies met, you will accept this division. God has power over all things."[4] Most biographers, especially the earlier among them, believed that this verse was revealed after the battle of Badr as well as after Muhammad's division of its booty. They hold that Muhammad had divided the booty in equal parts, giving to the fighter with a horse twice the amount he gave to the fighter on foot, and allowing the share of the Muslims who were killed at Badr to go to their heirs. They also hold that Muhammad had assigned a share to the Muslims who were left behind in Madinah on assignment to work for the Muslim cause there during the absence of the army in Badr, or who had remained in Madinah for good reason. Muhammad divided the booty justly. Not only did he include in his division the soldier but also everyone who worked for the cause and helped achieve this victory, whether on the battlefield or far from it.

Execution of Two Captives

While the Muslims were on their way back to Madinah, two of the captives were executed, al Nadr ibn al Hirith and 'Uqbah ibn Abu Mu'ayt. Neither Muhammad nor his companions had until that moment any law regarding the captives regulating their execution, ransom, or enslavement. Al Nadr and 'Uqbah were terribly hard on the Muslims in Makkah and had inflicted upon them all the harm and injury they could. Al Nadr was executed when the captives were arrayed in front of the Prophet near the locality called al Uthayl. As the Prophet looked at al Nadr, the latter trembled and called to his neighbor: "Muhammad is surely going to kill me. He had looked at me with eyes in which I saw the judgment of death." His neighbor rejoined: "You are a coward." Al Nadr approached Mus'ab ibn 'Umayr, the closest of the captives to Muhammad and asked him: "Please approach your relative concerning me. Let him allow me to be one of his companions. If you do not, I am certain he is going to kill me today." Mus'ab replied, "You used to speak all kinds of calumnies against the Book of God and His Prophet; you also used to persecute and harm his companions." Al Nadr said, "Had Quraysh taken you captive, I would have never allowed them to kill you as long as I was alive"; to which Mus'ab replied, "By God I do not believe you; I am not like you; Islam has severed my relations with you." Al Nadir was the captive of al Miqdad who expected to receive a great ransom from the captive's family. When al Miqdad heard the conversation regarding the execution of al Nadr, he said: "Al Nadr is my captive. Hands off!" At this the Prophet — may God's blessing be upon him — said: "Strike his neck. O God, give al Miqdad plenty of Your bounty instead." 'Ali ibn Abu Talib executed the Prophet's order with the sword. As the party arrived at 'Irq al Zubyah, the Prophet ordered the execution of 'Uqbah ibn Abu Mu'ayt. When 'Uqbah pleaded, "Who will take care of my children, O Muhammad?" Muhammad answered, "The fire." According to one version, it was 'Ali ibn Abu Talib who executed him; according to another, it was 'Asim ibn Thabit.

News of the Victory in Madinah

Before the Prophet and the Muslims reached Madinah, the two messengers, Zayd ibn Harithah and 'Abdullah ibn Ka'b, had arrived and entered the city from different directions. 'Abdullah galloped through the city on his horse and Zayd ibn Harithah followed him riding on al Qaswa', Muhammad's she-camel. Both were calling al Ansar and announcing to them the victory, mentioning the names of the fallen idolators. The Muslims, pleased to hear the news, went out of their houses and gathered in the streets acclaiming this great victory. As for the Jews and the idolators of Madinah, they were saddened by this turn of events. Indeed, they even tried to convince themselves as well as the Muslims in Madinah that it was not true. They proclaimed at the top of their voices: "Muhammad was killed, and his companions were defeated. There is his she-camel which we all know. Had he achieved victory, his she-camel would have stayed there. Zayd said otherwise because he lost his mind out of terror in the course of fighting." The Muslims, however, quickly confirmed the news and went on with their celebration. Only the death of Ruqayyah, daughter of the Prophet, which had occurred on that day, marred their joy. As his daughter was sick on the day Muhammad left for Badr, he ordered her husband, 'Uthman ibn 'Affan, to stay behind and take care of her. When the idolators and *munafiqun* realized that the news of victory was true, they felt that their position was degenerating into one of weakness and isolation. A Jewish leader said, "Death for us is better on this day than life. What kind of life can we have now that the noblest of men, their lords and kings — the Makkan guardians of security and peace — are dead or vanquished?"

The Captives of Badr

The Muslims entered Madinah without the captives who were to follow the next day. When they did, Sawdah, daughter of Zam'ah and wife of the Prophet, was returning from a morning visit to the relatives of the two sons of 'Afra'. She saw Abu Yazid Suhayl ibn 'Amr, one of the captives, whose hand was bound to his neck. Unable to control her indignation at the sight, she approached him and said, "O Abu Yazid! Did you give yourself up, and surrender voluntarily? Woe! The pity that you had not fallen nobly and met a heroic death on the battlefield!" Muhammad called her away and said to her, "O Sawdah, are you inciting the man against God and against His Prophet?" She answered, "O Prophet of God, by Him who sent you a Prophet of the truth, I could not control myself when I saw Abu Yazid with his hand tied to his neck and felt impelled to say what I said." Muhammad distributed the captives among his companions and said to them, "Treat them well." The question of what to do with them, to kill them or to accept ransom for them, continued to trouble him. Many of them are strong warriors; their hearts are now filled with hatred following their defeat and shameful captivity. If he were to accept ransom for them, surely they would wage another war against him. And yet, if he were to kill them would he not incite their people in Quraysh to further acts of violence? To a new height of enmity which might be avoided if he were to accept their ransom?

Abu Bakr and 'Umar's Views Regarding the Captives

Muhammad submitted the matter to the Muslims and sought their advice. He wanted them to share freely in the decision. The Muslims, for their part, discovered that the captives desired to live and, therefore, that a great amount of wealth could be reaped from them as ransom. The captives sent word to Abu Bakr knowing that he was the nearest to the Quraysh and the most merciful and compassionate of the Muslims as well as the closest adviser and friend of Muhammad. They said to Abu Bakr: "O Abu Bakr, among us are fathers, brothers, uncles, and cousins of the Muslims. The most distant of us is still a relative. Approach your friend on our behalf and ask him to forgive us or to allow us to be ransomed. Abu Bakr promised them to do his best. At the same time, they feared that ibn al Khattab would counsel against Abu Bakr's pleas; therefore, they sent after him to ask as they did Abu Bakr. 'Umar ibn Khattab looked at them in anger and did not answer. The two approached Muhammad and each presented his point of view. Abu Bakr appealed to Muhammad's gentleness and stirred his compassion. He pleaded, "O Prophet of God, you are dearer than my father and my mother. Your captives consist of men who are parents, sons, cousins, uncles and brothers of your own people. The most removed of them is still a member of your clan and a blood relative. Be good to them and forgive them. God will forgive you and be good to you. Otherwise allow them to be ransomed and take from them that which would increase the Muslims in power. Perhaps, by such action, God will soften their hearts toward Islam." Muhammad listened without answering. 'Umar, coming after Abu Bakr, sat in his place and pleaded: "O

Prophet of God, these are the enemies of God. They have belied you, fought you, and banished you. Strike their necks. They are the leaders of idolatry and misguidance. By this course God will consolidate Islam and bring low the idolators." Again Muhammad did not answer. Later, Abu Bakr returned to Muhammad and sought once more to stir his compassion by reminding him of the captives' relation and hoping for their conversion to Islam in case they were allowed to live. 'Umar, too, the exemplar of stern justice, returned to Muhammad to plead once more still unmoved as ever by any feelings of leniency or mercy. When both Abu Bakr and 'Umar said all they had to say, Muhammad withdrew to his room to ponder the matter alone. When he came out, he found the Muslims divided between Abu Bakr's view and 'Umar's. He consulted them again, characterizing both Abu Bakr and 'Umar for their benefit. Abu Bakr, Muhammad said, was like Michael, a carrier of God's pleasure and forgiveness. Compared with the prophets he is like Ibrahim who was sweeter to his people than honey itself. Ibrahim's people had condemned him to the fire and threw him into it, but all he could say to them was, "Fie on you and on that which you worship instead of God! Would you not use your reason? . . . Whoever follows me is surely of me, but whoever disobeys me, God is merciful and forgiving."[5] Abu Bakr is like Jesus when the latter said: "If You punish them they are only Your servants; and if You forgive them, You are the All-wise and Almighty."[6] 'Umar, on the other hand, is like Gabriel among the angels. He is the carrier of God's wrath and condemnation of His enemies. Among the prophets he is like Noah when the latter said: "O God, spare not one of the unbelievers;" or like Moses when he said: "O God, destroy their wealth and confirm them in their error that they may not believe until they receive the painful punishment."[7] Then turning to the Muslims, the Prophet said: "You have families to support. Do not therefore let any of these captives escape before you receive a ransom from him. Otherwise, strike off his neck." As the Muslims consulted with one another, one of the captives, a poet by profession, and Abu 'Izzat 'Amr ibn 'Abdullah ibn 'Umayr al Jumahi by name, stepped forward toward the Prophet and said: "I have five daughters whom I must support. Do give me to them as your charity, O Muhammad. For my part I pledge to you that I shall never fight you nor will I ever criticize you." The Prophet forgave him and sent him back to his family without ransom. He was the only captive thus liberated. But he violated his pledge and fought again against the Muslims in the battle of Uhud, a year later. There he was taken captive, and, this time, executed.

After a while, the Muslims reached a consensus to accept ransom for the captives. The following verse of the Qur'an was revealed on this occasion:

$$\text{مَا كَانَ لِنَبِيّ أَنْ يَكُونَ لَهُ أَسْرَى حَتَّى يُثْخِنَ فِى الْأَرْضِ تُرِيدُونَ عَرَضَ الدُّنْيَا وَ}$$

$$\text{اللهُ يُرِيدُ الْأَخِرَةَ وَ اللهُ عَزِيزٌ حَكِيمٌ}$$

"It does not behoove a prophet to hold captives; nor to tyrannize in the world. You seek the advantages of this world whereas God wishes you to seek the advantages of the other. God is almighty and all-wise."[8]

Orientalists' Controversy

A number of Orientalists pause at this affair of the captives of Badr and especially at the execution of al Nadr and 'Uqbah. They argue: Doesn't this prove the thirst of this new religion for blood? Without such thirst, the two captives would not have been executed. It would have been more charitable and nobler for the Muslims after they won the battle to return the captives and to be satisfied with the booty they acquired. The Orientalists' argument is designed to stir mercy and compassion simply in order to provide means for condemning Islam and its Prophet. But such emotions were utterly out of place on the day of Badr, and much more so a thousand or more years after that battle. The incoherence of the argument is evident upon comparison of the execution of al Nadr and 'Uqbah with what happens today and will always happen as long as western civilization rules the world under the banner of Christianity. Is their execution comparable in any possible manner to what the Christian imperialists do when they put down the uprisings of their colonies against their rule? Is it equivalent to any part, however, infinitesimal, of the slaughter that took place in the first or second World War? Is it at all comparable to the events of the French Revolution, or the many other revolutions which have taken place among the Christian nations of Europe?

Revolution against Idolatry

There is no doubt that the whole matter between Muhammad and his companions was one of a strong revolution led by Muhammad against idolatry and its adherents. It was a revolution that started in Makkah where Muhammad and his companions were subjected to all kinds of suffering for thirteen long years. Thereafter, the Muslims emigrated to Madinah and there organized themselves and built up their strength under revolutionary principles dominating the scene in both their camp and the Quraysh's. The Muslims' emigration to Madinah, the peace they had concluded with the Jews, all the skirmishes preceding the battle of Badr as well as the battle of Badr itself — all these were steps in the general plan of revolution, but not its guiding principles. They constitute the policy line decided by the leader of this revolution and his companions as instruments in the realization of principles which the Prophet had received from God. The policy of a revolution should not be confused with its principles. The plan followed cannot be identified with the purpose for which it was drawn. Since Islam made human brotherhood the foundation of its civilization, it had to seek that civilization by following whatever means are necessary, including violence.

The Slaughter of St. Bartholomew's Day

What the Muslims did with the captives of Badr was an instance of sublime mercy and charity when compared with what happened in the revolutions praised by the western peoples as embodiments of justice and mercy. What happened to the captives of Badr was really nothing compared to the many slaughters carried out in the name of Christianity such as that which occurred on St. Bartholomew's Day in France. This slaughter is really a curse in the history of Christianity unmatched by anything in the whole history of Islam. It was a slaughter planned deliberately during the night. The Catholics rose the next morning to slaughter systematically the Protestants of Paris and France with deception, wantonness, and the lowliest and worst kind of cruelty. If the Muslims had killed two of the fifty captives for the cruel suffering they had previously inflicted upon the Muslims during thirteen years in Makkah, it was an act of further mercy and benefit which occasioned the revelation of the already quoted verse: 'It does not behoove a Prophet to hold captives; nor to tyrannize in the world. You seek the advantages of this world, while God wishes you to seek the advantages of the other. God is almighty and all-wise."[9]

Warning to Makkah

While the Muslims were celebrating the victory God had granted to them, al Haysuman ibn 'Abdullah al Khuza'i was making his way toward

Makkah. He was the first one to reach the city to announce to its people the defeat of the Quraysh and the fall of its leaders and nobles. Makkah was so shaken by the news that it hardly believed what it heard. Al Haysuman, however, was not angry but insisted on the veracity of his news and shared their grief. When the Makkans finally realized what had happened, they were so shocked that they fell to the ground. Indeed, Abu Lahab was immediately seized by a fever and died seven days later. The Quraysh, consulting together on the course of action to follow, agreed not to mourn their dead lest Muhammad and his companions he pleased at their suffering. They also decided not to seek to ransom their captives lest Muhammad and his companions increase their demands. A number of days passed while the Quraysh bore their tragedy silently. But an occasion soon presented itself. Mikraz ibn Hafs arrived seeking to ransom Suhayl ibn 'Amr. 'Umar ibn al Khattab hated to see Suhayl return home unharmed. He therefore asked Muhammad: "O Prophet of God, let me pull out Suhayl's front teeth so that he would never be able to exercise his oratory against you." Without hesitation, Muhammad gave this supremely noble answer: "I shall not mutilate anyone under any circumstance. God would mutilate me though I am His Prophet."

Ransom and Conversion of Abu al 'Asi ibn al Rabi'

Zaynab, daughter of the Prophet, sent out to ransom her husband Abu al 'Asi ibn al Rabi'. Included in the wealth she sent for the ransom was a necklace that once belonged to Khadijah, the Prophet's wife, which the latter had given to her daughter on the day of her wedding to Abu al 'Asi. When the Prophet saw the necklace, he remembered his former wife and was deeply moved. He said to his companions: "If you find fit to send her captive back to her and to return to her what she paid, do so." The Prophet had also agreed with the captive, Abu al 'Asi, that he would divorce his wife Zaynab now that Islam had separated the two spouses. Muhammad sent Zayd ibn Harithah and another companion to escort Zaynab to Madinah. Soon, however, Abu al 'Asi left Makkah on a trade trip to al Sham. When he passed by the vicinity of Madinah, a Muslim patrol discovered and confiscated his caravan. While in Madinah he managed to reach his wife Zaynab under the shadow of night and begged her to intervene on his behalf. She did and his goods were returned to him. He ran back to Makkah with his goods and there returned to each his due. He asked all his creditors to speak out in case they had any claim against him. When none spoke out and everyone thanked him for his loyalty, he announced to his fellow Makkans: "I witness that there is no God but God, and that Muhammad is His servant and prophet. By God, I have not refrained from joining Islam earlier except out of fear of suspicion that I have run away with your goods. Now that everyone has received his due and my reputation is safe, I declare my conversion." He returned to Madinah, and the Prophet permitted his wife Zaynab to return to him. The Quraysh continued to ransom their captives with varying amounts running from 1000 to 4000 dirhims per person. As for those prisoners who were too poor to afford a ransom, Muhammad granted them their liberty as a gift.

Quraysh Mourns Her Dead

Having ransomed her captives, Quraysh still felt the wounds of her tragedy. Makkah could find no reason to make peace with Muhammad, and the memory of defeat at his hand remained alive for a long time to come. For one whole month, the women of Quraysh mourned their dead. They shaved off their hair, whipped themselves, and cried when a dead man's camel or mare was paraded in the streets. Only Hind, daughter of 'Utbah and wife of Abu Sufyan, did not cry in public at all. She was once asked by other Quraysh women about this mastery of nerve: "Would you not publicly mourn your father, your brother, your uncle, and your other fallen relatives?" She answered: "Were I to mourn them publicly, the news will reach Muhammad and his companions and the women of Banu al Khazraj who will all be pleased at my misfortune. No, by God, I shall not mourn them publicly until I have avenged them. Fat and perfume shall be forbidden to me until we have defeated the enemy. By God, if crying would take away sadness from my heart I would have cried. But I know that sadness will not leave me until I have seen with my own eye vengeance taken on the murderers of my dear ones." True to her vow, Hind never touched fat or perfume, nor came close to her husband's bed until the battle of Uhud; and she spared no moment or occasion to incite her fellow Makkans to war. As for her husband, Abu Sufyan, he vowed never to wash himself until he had defeated Muhammad.

One of the Gates of Al Haram al Sharif, Makkah al Mukarramah, Saudi Arabia.

14

Between Badr and Uhud

The Effect of Badr in Madinah (January, 624 C.E.)

We have just taken note of the deep effect that the Battle of Badr had upon Makkah. Above all, this effect included the will of the Quraysh to seek revenge against Muhammad and the Muslims at the first opportunity. The effect of this battle in Madinah was, however, much more obvious and more closely connected with the survival of Muhammad and his fellows. The Jews, associationists, and hypocrites felt Muslim power increase after Badr. They realized that this alien who came to them less than two years ago as an escaping emigrant from Makkah had increased his power and influence almost to the point of dominating not only the Muslims but their city as a whole. As we have had occasion to see, the Jews had begun to complain even before Badr that they had had many skirmishes with the Muslims and that were it not for the Covenant of Madinah, the explosion would have come sooner. Consequently, soon after the Muslims' victorious return, the non-Muslims of Madinah began to meet clandestinely and to encourage the composition and recitation of divisive poetry. It was as if the battlefield had moved from Makkah to Madinah and the dispute from religion to politics. It was not Muhammad's call to God that was being fought; rather, it was his political power, his worldly influence, and his success which incited these parties not only to plot against him but even to think of assassinating him. None of this, of course, was beyond Muhammad's ken. All the happenings within his city, including the rumors, reached him in constant flow. Simmering in hatred and anger against each other, Muslims and Jews lay in wait for one another.

Muslims Kill Abu 'Afk and 'Asma'

Before the victory of Badr the Muslims used to fear the Madinese non-Muslims, for they were still too weak to return any aggression inflicted upon them. But when they returned victorious from Badr, Salim ibn 'Umayr took upon himself the job of getting rid of Abu 'Afk, a tribesman of Banu 'Amr ibn 'Awf. The latter was a poet who composed verses disparaging Muhammad and the Muslims and inciting his own tribe to rise against them. Even after Badr, Abu 'Afk still composed and disseminated abusive verse. Salim attacked Abu 'Afk in his sleep in his own yard and killed him. Likewise, 'Asma', daughter of Marwan, of the tribe of Banu Umayyah ibn Zayd, used to insult Islam and the Prophet by encouraging bad feeling against the Muslims. The Battle of Badr did not make her reconsider. One day, 'Umayr ibn 'Awf attacked her during the night while she was surrounded by her children, one of whom she was nursing. 'Umayr was weak of sight and had to grope for her. After removing the child from his victim, he killed her; he then proceeded to the Prophet and informed him of what he had done.

When her relatives returned from the funeral, they asked him whether he had killed her. "Indeed so," said 'Umayr, "You may fight me if you wish. By Him Who dominates my soul, if you should deny that she composed her abusive poetry, I would fight you until either you or I fall." It was this courage of 'Umayr that caused the Banu Khutmah, the tribe of 'Asma's husband, to turn to Islam. Having converted to Islam but fearing persecution at the hand of their fellow tribesmen, some of them had hidden their conversion. Henceforth, they no longer did so.

Murder of Ka'b ibn al Ashraf

It is sufficient to add to these two examples the murder of Ka'b ibn al Ashraf. When learning of the fall of the noblemen of Makkah, he exclaimed, "Those were the nobles of Arabia, the kings of mankind. By God, if Muhammad has vanquished these people, the interior of the earth is a better dwelling than the top of it." Having assured himself of the news of defeat, he traveled to Makkah to incite its people against Muhammad, to recite war poetry, and to mourn the victims. Furthermore, it was he who falsely accused the Muslim women upon return to Madinah. The reader is perhaps aware of Arab custom and ethic in this regard, and can appreciate the Muslims' anxiety over such false accusations directed against their women's honor. Indeed, they were so incensed and irritated by him that, after unanimously agreeing to kill him, they authorized Abu Na'ilah to seek his company and win his confidence. Abu Na'ilah said to Ka'b, "The advent of Muhammad was a misfortune to all of us. The tribes have become our enemies and fought against us; our roads are cut off, our families separated and dispersed, and our lives exhausted." With this and similar remarks, Abu Na'ilah won Ka'b's confidence and asked him to lend some money to himself and his friends, pledging to pawn his and their armor. Ka'b agreed and asked the Muslims to return. They came to his house in the outskirts of Madinah after dark. Abu Na'ilah called out to him. Despite his wife's warning, Ka'b went out to meet his new friend. The two men walked in the night and were later joined by the companions of Abu Na'ilah, whom Ka'b never suspected. Together they walked for a whole hour and covered a long distance, conversing and complaining about the hardships Muhammad had brought upon their community, thus reassuring Ka'b of their sincerity. From time to time Abu Na'ilah would touch the hair of Ka'b and exclaim, "I have never smelled such perfume in my life!" Then, after gaining Ka'b's complete trust, Abu Na'ilah seized him by the hair, pulled him down to the ground, and said to his companions, "Kill the enemy of God!" They struck him with their swords.

Jewish Fears and Aggression

The murder of Ka'b increased the fears of the Jews to the point that not one of them felt secure. Nonetheless, they continued to attack Muhammad and the Muslims and incite the people to war. A desert woman came one day to the Jews' market in the quarter of Banu Qaynuqa' seeking to remodel some jewelry at one of their shops. They persistently asked her to remove her veil, but the woman refused. Passing behind her without her knowledge, one of them tacked her robe with a pin to the wall. When the woman got up to leave, the robe was pulled down and her nakedness exposed. The Jews laughed and the woman cried. Seeing what happened, a Muslim passerby jumped upon the shopkeeper and killed him on the spot. The Jews gathered around the Muslim and likewise killed him. The Muslims' relatives called for help against the Jews and a general fight between them and the Banu Qaynuqa' erupted. Muhammad first

asked the Jews to stop their attacks and keep the covenant of mutual peace
and security or suffer the kind of treatment meted out to the Quraysh.
They ridiculed his request saying: "O Muhammad! Fall not under the illusion that you are invincible. The people with whom you have fought were
inexperienced. By God, if you were to turn your arm against us, you will
find us adept in the arts of war." After this, little option was left to the
Muslims but to fight the Jews. Otherwise, Islam would suffer political
deterioration, and the Muslims would become the ridicule of Quraysh
when they had just succeeded in making the Quraysh the ridicule of
Arabia.

Blockade of Banu Qaynuqa'

For fifteen consecutive days, the Muslims blockaded Banu Qaynuqa'
within their quarters, preventing any exit or entry. The Jews had no alternative but to surrender and yield themselves to Muhammad's judgment.
After consulting the Muslim leaders, Muhammad decided to kill his captives. 'Abdullah ibn Ubayy ibn Salul, allied to both Jews and Muslims,
asked Muhammad to be merciful toward his allies. When the Prophet
declined, 'Abdullah repeated his request, and the Prophet declined again.
'Abdullah then seized the Prophet by his shield and would not let him go.
At this, the Prophet seemed rather angry and said with a loud voice,
"Leave me; hands off!" Ibn Ubayy replied, "No, by God, I shall not let you
go until you give mercy to my *protégés*. Three hundred armed and four
hundred unarmed men have so far protected me against every sort of people. Would you kill them all at once? By God, I will never agree to such a
judgment, for I fear the turns of fortune." 'Abdulla was still a man of great
power, having command of the associationists of the Aws and Khazraj
tribes, although this power had largely waned with the growth of Muslim
power. His insistence caused the Prophet to regain his good temper and
patience, especially since 'Ubadah ibn al Samit had joined ibn Ubayy in
making the same plea. He therefore decided to stretch his hand to
'Abdullah, to all his *protégés*, whether associationists or Jews, and to grant
them all his mercy and benevolence. He decreed only that the Banu
Qaynuqa' should evacuate Madinah in punishment for their misdeeds.
Once more, ibn Ubayy tried to plead with Muhammad on behalf of his
protégés that they be allowed to remain in Madinah. One of the Muslims,
however, prevented ibn Ubayy from reaching the Prophet and forced him
to remove himself. The tribesmen of Banu Qaynuqa' then announced that

"By God, we shall not remain in a city where ibn Ubayy is pushed by force and we are unable to protect him." 'Ubadah subsequently led them in the surrender of their arms and jewel-making machinery and in the exodus from Madinah. They went to Wadi al Qura where they tarried a while and then proceeded northward until they reached Adhri'at near the frontier of al Sham, where they settled. Perhaps they went there because they wanted to be nearer the Land of Promise that attracted the Jews then as it still does today.

Political Unity in Madinah

Jewish power in Madinah was considerably reduced after the expulsion of Banu Qaynuqa', for most of the Jews who called themselves Madinese lived far from Madinah, in Khaybar and Umm al Qura. It was this political objective at which Muhammad had aimed, and it reveals most clearly his political wisdom and foresight. It was the first of a number of political consequences of Muhammad's strategy. Nothing could be more harmful to the unity of a state than internal division. And if internal strife is inevitable, it is equally inevitable that one faction will finally establish its authority and dominion over all the others. Some historians have criticized the conduct of the Muslims toward the Jews. They claim that the incident of the Muslim woman at the jeweler's shop was relatively easy to settle as long as each party had already paid with the loss of one of its members. In answer to this claim, we may say that the victimization of the Jew and the Muslim did not efface the insult which the Muslims suffered at the hands of the Jews in the person of that woman. We may also argue that among the Arabs, more than among any other people, such an insult produces far greater commotion and, according to custom, would have easily caused continual war between two tribes for many long years. Examples of such incidents and the wars which followed them are legion in Arab history. Besides this consideration, however, there is yet a stronger one. The incident at the jeweler's shop was to the blockade of Banu Qaynuqa' and their expulsion from Madinah as the murder of the Austrian heir-apparent in Sarajevo in 1914 was to World War I, which enveloped the whole of Europe. The incident was only the spark which inflamed Muslims and Jews and caused them to explode. The fact was that the presence of Muslims, Jews, associationists and *munafiqun* in one city with all their disparate ideals and customs made that city a political volcano replete with explosive power. The blockade of Banu Qaynuqa' and their expulsion were a prologue to the coming explosion.

The Campaign of Al Sawiq

After the expulsion of Banu Qaynuqa', the non-Muslims of Madinah naturally withdrew from public life and the city appeared peaceful and quiet. The peace lasted one whole month and would have lasted longer were it not for Abu Sufyan who, unable to bear the memory of Makkan defeat at Badr, resolved to venture again outside of Makkah. He sought to reimpress the Arabs of the Peninsula with the notion that Quraysh was still strong, dominant and capable of attack and war. He mobilized two hundred Makkans (forty according to other versions) and led them out in secret in the direction of Madinah. Upon arrival in the vicinity of Madinah, they attacked at night a locality called al 'Urayd. Only one Madinese and his client were in the locality at the time. They were killed and their house and orchard destroyed. Abu Sufyan thought his vow to attack Muhammad had now been fulfilled, and he and his associates therefore left the scene quickly, fearing pursuit by the Prophet or his men. The Muslims did in fact pursue Abu Sufyan as far as Qarqarat al Kudr. In order to hasten their flight, Abu Sufyan and his party every now and then threw away some of their provisions of wheat and barley flour. While the Muslims followed their trail, they picked up these provisions; they soon realized, however, that the Makkans had escaped, and they decided to return home. By this raid Abu Sufyan had sought to console Quraysh after its defeat at Badr and to recapture its lost pride. In fact, his scheme turned against him and his flight in face of his pursuers brought further shame to Quraysh. Because of *al sawiq (i.e.,* the flour), which the men of Quraysh dropped on their path, this expedition was given the name "Al Sawiq Campaign."

Threat to the Shore Route of al Sham

The news of this event spread throughout the Arabian Peninsula. The distant tribes remained safe in their distance and concerned themselves but little with the affairs of those Muslims who, until the recent Battle of Badr, were nothing more than a weakly group of refugees in Madinah. Even though the Muslims had resisted Quraysh successfully, expelled Banu Qaynuqa' from Madinah, humbled 'Abdullah ibn Ubayy, frightened Abu Sufyan away, and broke the traditional pattern of power distribution in the desert, it was only the tribes close to Madinah which realized what threat this whole movement of Muhammad posed. Only they were aware of the serious consequences of the contest for power between the Quraysh of Makkah and the Muslims of Madinah. The shore route to al Sham was Makkah's well trodden path of trade that brought significant economic advantages to these tribes. Muhammad had entered into threatening alliances with a number of tribes flanking the shore route and thereby exposed Makkah's commerce to serious danger. The tribes which lived on this commerce feared that Quraysh might now choose another route. Before the Hijrah of Muhammad and his companions to Yathrib, indeed before Muslim victory at Badr, these tribes had felt relatively safe and secure. Now they pondered the future and the threat to their prosperity. If Makkan trade were to take another route, how would they sustain themselves in their arid and barren lands?

The Tribes' Fear of the Muslims

The Battle of Badr struck fear into the hearts of these tribes. Their leaders considered whether or not to strike against Madinah now, before the situation got utterly out of hand. Soon enough, it came to the ear of Muhammad that an army of Ghatafan and Sulaym tribesmen were marching in the direction of Madinah; in turn, he led an expedition of Muslim fighters to Qarqarat al Kudr to meet them. When the Muslim force arrived, they found camel traces but no men. Muhammad sent a number of his companions to reconnoiter the upper levels of the valley. While waiting for them to return, he met a young boy by the name of Yasar and asked him about the whereabouts of the enemy. The boy answered that they had gone to the spring at the higher extremity of the valley. The Muslims seized the camels they found in the area without battle and divided the booty as the Qur'an demanded, one-fifth going to Muhammad. It was reported that their booty amounted to five hundred camels of which the Prophet took one-fifth and distributed the rest equally among his companions, each one getting two camels. Later on, it reached the ear of Muhammad that Tha'labah and Muharib tribesmen had gathered at Dhu Amarr with aggressive designs. The Prophet immediately led an expedition of four hundred and fifty fighters to search out the enemy in their own grounds but without meeting them. He did, however, come across a man from Tha'labah whom he questioned regarding the whereabouts of the enemy. This man warned the Prophet that, should they hear of his advance, they would run away to the mountain heights; and he offered his services as a guide. The enemy soon heard of Muhammad's approach and retreated to the mountains. Later learning that a great force of Banu Sulaym tribesmen from Bahran were advancing on Madinah, the Prophet went out in haste with a Muslim force of three hundred to meet them. A day's distance from Bahran, the Muslims came across a man from Banu Sulaym who reported, upon questioning by the Prophet, that the tribesmen had dispersed and returned home. All these tribesmen were stricken with panic and fear for their future. They plotted against the Muslims and oft went out in force to fight them. But no sooner did they hear of Muhammad's sortie with his companions to meet them, than they would lose heart and run away.

The Jews' Fear of Muhammad

It was during these times that Ka'b ibn al Ashraf was killed. This event instilled in the Jews such fear that none of them dared leave his house. Muhammad's blockade and expulsion of Banu Qaynuqa' intensified these fears. They then came to Muhammad pleading their cause and accusing the Muslims of having killed Ka'b deliberately, in spite of his personal innocence. Muhammad answered, "The man whom you claim to be innocent has indeed harmed us deeply and composed libelous poetry against us. Had he remained quiet like his co-religionists, nothing would have befallen him." After long discussion of the matter, Muhammad invited the Jews to enter with him into a new covenant agreeable to both and which both would henceforth respect. But this covenant did not allay fears. Their plotting against Muhammad continued as later events were to make evident.

The 'Iraq Route to al Sham

How was Quraysh to conduct her trade now that Muhammad had cut off its route? Makkah, it must be remembered, lived on trade. Without trade, its whole economy was bound to founder. By cutting her trade route as he did, Muhammad had practically imposed a blockade on her which would soon destroy her place and influence in Arabia. It is reported that Safwan ibn Umayyah advised the Quraysh at this stage that "Muhammad and his companions have spoiled our trade. What shall we do with him and his companions if they do not remove themselves from the coastal area? The Muslims befriended the tribes who inhabited the coastal regions and most of these have even joined their party. What shall we do with ourselves? To live in Makkah devoid of trade is tantamount to eating

up our capital funds and then starving. Our whole life in the city, therefore, depends upon our summer trade with al Sham and our winter trade
with Abyssinia." To this al Aswad ibn 'Abd al Muttalib replied that the
Makkans ought to abandon the coastal route to al Sham and henceforth
take the eastern route passing through al 'Iraq. To help satisfy this requirement, al Aswad suggested to Safwan that he should appoint Furat ibn
Hayyan, a tribesman of Banu Bakr ibn Wa'il, to show him the new route
he should take. Furat explained to them that the eastern route was safe
because none of Muhammad's companions ever approached it, but that it
was an empty, waterless desert. The desert did not frighten Safwan
because the season was winter and the need for water relatively small. He
gathered merchandise amounting to one hundred thousand Dirhams and
prepared to start off toward al Sham. Nu'aym ibn Mas'ud al Ashja'i, who
was in Makkah at the time, learned of the preparation of this caravan.
Upon returning to Madinah he reported this news to Muhammad. The
Prophet sent Zayd ibn Harithah with a hundred riders to intercept the
caravan at the oasis of al Qardah in the center of Najd. The Makkans ran
away at the encounter, leaving behind the caravan which the Muslims
took away as booty. Upon Zayd's return to Madinah, Muhammad took
one-fifth of the booty and divided the rest among his men. Furat ibn
Hayyan, the guide of the caravan, accepted Islam and thereby saved himself.

Muhammad's Marriage to Hafsah

Did all these successes convince Muhammad that his position was
really secure? Did his present victories delude him about the dangers of
the future? Did the fear of Makkah and the various booty he had seized
from Quraysh persuade him that the word of God and His Prophet was
really safe and secure? Did his faith in God's timely help and providence
cause him to let things take care of themselves on the grounds that divine
government is supreme? Certainly not. Although time and space belong
to God, yet the world runs according to unalterable laws innate to human
nature and everywhere the same. Quraysh, for instance, enjoyed mastery
over Arabia. It was not possible to expect her to give it up without a fight.
Therefore, the fate of the caravan of Safwan ibn Umayyah succeeded only
in increasing their eagerness to avenge themselves and to double their
preparation for the day of vindication. Neither could this escape
Muhammad's vision, foresight, or wise planning. It was necessary there-

fore, in anticipation of hostilities, for him to seek to strengthen his relationship with his fellow Muslims. However closely Islam had knitted the wills of its adherents and however strong the resultant social fabric, Muhammad must have deemed further consolidation and unity desirable. For him to link himself to them in familial bonds was regarded by Muhammad as well as by his companions as meeting this noble objective. Thus he married Hafsah, daughter of 'Umar ibn al Khattab, just as formerly he had married 'A'ishah, daughter of Abu Bakr. The former was the widow of Khunays, an early convert to Islam, who died seven months previously. The Prophet's marriage to Hafsah increased ibn al Khattab's attachment to him. In the same spirit, Muhammad gave his daughter Fatimah in marriage to 'Ali, his cousin, though the latter had loved Muhammad perhaps more than anyone else and had remained loyal to him ever since he was a child. When the Prophet's daughter, Ruqayyah, passed away, Muhammad gave 'Uthman ibn 'Affan, her bereaved husband, his other daughter, Umm Kulthum. Thus he united in a bond of family and blood Abu Bakr, 'Umar, 'Uthman, and 'Ali, the four strongest personalities of his community. By this and similar action, Muhammad guaranteed the solidarity of Muslim ranks. He assured them that the booty they seized in their conquests would be theirs. He encouraged them to go to war by combining in a single objective service to God and fighting for His sake with the desire to make up their lost possessions in Makkah with captured Makkan booty. Muhammad, by following the news of Quraysh very closely throughout this period, always kept himself abreast of her preparations for war. It was common knowledge that Quraysh was preparing for her day of revenge and for the reopening of the coastal trade route to al Sham. She was preparing for a war to preserve her commercial and religious position without which it was impossible for her to exist.

15

The Campaign of Uhud

Quraysh's Preparations for Revenge

Ever since the Battle of Badr, Quraysh had not been at ease. The debacle of its al Sawiq campaign and the recent loss of its caravan on the route of al 'Iraq to the Muslims under the command of Zayd ibn Harithah had intensified its resentment and bent its mind upon the avenging of Badr. The tribesmen of Quraysh, lords, notables, and noblemen of Makkah, could not forget their fallen brethren. How could they do so while Makkah women were still mourning their sons, brothers, fathers, husbands, and other relatives? Ever since Abu Sufyan ibn Harb reached Makkah with the caravan that had caused the confrontation at Badr, he, together with those who participated in the battle and other notables of Quraysh, such as Jubayr ibn Mut'im, Safwan ibn Umayyah, 'Ikrimah ibn Abu Jahl, al Harith ibn Hisham, Huwaytib ibn 'Abd al 'Uzza and others, agreed to deposit the whole caravan in the community house of Makkah (Dar al Nadwah) for public auction so that the proceeds might be used in preparing an army to fight Muhammad. Their plans called for equipping a great strong army and inciting the tribes to join in this war of revenge. They had already incited Abu 'Azzah, the poet, a captive of Badr who was forgiven by the Prophet, to defect to their side. Likewise, they invited their Abyssinian clients to join ranks with them. The women of Quraysh, for their part, insisted on accompanying the army in order to witness and to enjoy the revenge. In deliberating whether or not to permit them to do

244

so, some argued that for the women to march alongside the men and sing the songs of war would remind the soldiers of their fallen relatives and further arouse them to fight. Those who argued in this vein were truly desperate, for they were unwilling to return to their homes without either avenging themselves or perishing in the process. Others thought otherwise. Some said, "O Men of Quraysh, it is not wise to expose your women to your enemies. Since it is not absolutely impossible that you may have to run away for your lives, shame would then befall your women." As the people deliberated, Hind, daughter of 'Utbah and wife of Abu Sufyan said: "Indeed! We shall accompany the army and watch the fighting. None may stand in our way or force us back to our homes as happened at al Juhfah[1] on that *dies nefastus* when our beloved ones fell in battle. And on the Day of Badr, had the women been there to witness the soldiers run away from the battle front, this would never have happened." Hind thus attributed the defeat at Badr to the absence of women to arouse their men to sufficient self-exertion in battle. Her little speech sealed the argument, and the Quraysh began its march against Muhammad together with the women who were now led by the most resentful woman of all, Hind, who suffered at Badr the loss of two dearest relatives, her father and brother. The Makkan army started off in solemn procession from Dar al Nadwah in three divisions. Only a hundred men were from Thaqif whereas all the others were Makkans and Arab or Abyssinian clients of Makkah equipped with great amounts of armour, two hundred horses, and three thousand camels. They also counted seven hundred men clad in heavy armour.

The Makkans' March against Madinah

While all these preparations were taking place with the consent and enthusiasm of everyone, al 'Abbas ibn 'Abd al Muttalib, the Prophet's uncle, watched from a distance and pondered. Despite his loyalty to the faith of his fathers and the religion of his people, he was moved in his feeling toward Muhammad by a sense of admiration complemented by a feeling of tribal solidarity within him. He recalled how well Muhammad had treated him on the Day of Badr. It was the same sort of admiration and tribal solidarity which had previously moved him to conclude the Great Covenant of al 'Aqabah with al Aws and al Khazraj tribes of Madinah, for the purpose of guaranteeing the same safeguard and protection to Muhammad, his nephew, as those which belonged to Madinese women and children. At the time, he warned those tribes that were they ever to falter in providing such protection to his nephew, they should withdraw and give up Muhammad's protection to his own people. The same kind of feeling stirred within him when he saw Quraysh's ubiquitous enthusiasm against Muhammad and when he witnessed this great army marching forward toward Madinah. He wrote a letter describing the whole preparation, military equipment, and number of Makkan soldiers and gave it to a man from Ghifar whom he trusted to deliver to the Prophet in time. Soon, the Quraysh army reached al Abwa' where Aminah, daughter of Wahb and mother of Muhammad, was buried. Some Makkans thought of digging up her grave. However, their leaders stopped them, fearful lest they set a precedent among the Arabs, and recalling that the Muslims too could retaliate with the Makkans' own dead buried in their vicinities. Upon arrival at the locality of al 'Aqiq, the Makkan army camped at the foot of Mount Uhud, five miles from Madinah.

Al 'Abbas's Message to the Prophet

The man from Ghifar, carrying the letter of al 'Abbas ibn 'Abd al Muttalib, arrived at Madinah and found that Muhammad was at Quba'. There he proceeded; and, upon meeting Muhammad at the door of the mosque when he was just about to leave, handed over the letter to him. The message was read for Muhammad by Ubayy ibn Ka'b who was then asked to keep its contents secret. Muhammad proceeded to Madinah and called upon Sa'd ibn al Rabi' at his home, told him the content of the message, and asked him to keep it secret. Sa'd's wife, however, who was at home at the time overheard the conversation and the matter could no longer remain secret. Muhammad then sent Anas and Mu'nis, the two sons of Fadalah, to reconnoiter the movements of Quraysh. They found out that the army had approached Madinah and let its horses and camels loose to graze in the plantations surrounding the city. Muhammad then sent another scout, al Hubab ibn al Mundhir ibn al Jamuh. When enough information had reached him to confirm the news his uncle had sent, Muhammad became gravely concerned and perplexed. Salamah ibn Salamah reported thereafter that the Quraysh cavalry was coming closer and closer to Madinah and that they were about to enter the city. He rushed to his people and warned them of the imminent danger. All the inhabitants of Madinah were apprehensive due to the descriptions of the might and equipment of the enemy. Their Muslim leaders even saw fit to guard the person of the Prophet with their own swords throughout the night. Sentries were posted at all corners of the city. When morning came, the Prophet called upon all Muslims, whether sincere or insincere,[2] for a public consultation on the fate of the city and the means by which they should meet the enemy.

Varying Opinions on Madinah's Defense

The Prophet — May God's blessing be upon him! — suggested that the Muslims should hold fast to Madinah, reinforce themselves therein, and keep out the Quraysh. Should the enemy decide to attack, the Muslims would fight from within and, knowing their own ground, should be better able to repulse the enemy. 'Abdullah ibn Ubayy ibn Salul agreed with the Prophet and added: "Prophet of God, in the past we always fought our enemies in Madinah by placing our women and children safely in the upper stories of the houses and building walls connecting one house with another on the perimeter of the city, thus making the town a single fortress. When the enemy advanced on us, the women and children would hit them with stones with which they had been amply provided while we would meet them with our swords in the streets. Our city, O Prophet of God, has never been violated by an enemy because none has ever entered it without meeting defeat. On the other hand, we have never met an enemy outside our city without loss to ourselves. Please listen to me in this matter and follow this wise plan which I inherited from the greatest leaders and wise men of Madinah who have gone before."

The Prophet, as well as the prominent among the Prophet's companions, whether Muhajirun or Ansar, agreed with this view. However, the young Muslims who had not participated in Badr, as well as others who had witnessed Badr but became thereafter convinced that Muslim power was invincible, desired to go out of Madinah and meet the enemy wherever he might be. They were disturbed by the idea that unless they spoke to this effect, they might be suspected of cowardice. They argued that since the enemy was not too far from Madinah, the Muslims would be stronger than at Badr when they fought many miles away from their people and land. An advocate of this view said: "I hate to see the Quraysh return to Makkah saying that they have locked up Muhammad in the houses and buildings of Yathrib and have prevented him and his companions from going out. Such talk would undoubtedly incite the Quraysh to further acts of aggression. Now that they have entered our very orchards and plantations, shown off their numbers and strength, and incited the

Arab tribes and Abyssinian clients to follow them, how could we allow them to blockade us in our own homes and let them return without injury? Should we do that, they would surely return to raid our frontiers, to blockade us again, and to cut off our roads to the outside world." A number of other speakers spoke in favor of going out to meet the enemy, arguing that in case God gave them victory they would have met their objective. This would be a substantiation of the promise which God made to His Prophet. On the other hand, should they be defeated and die, they would have fallen as martyrs and would have won Paradise.

Call to Bravery and Martyrdom

This bold talk about bravery and martyrdom moved every Muslim heart and incited the community as a whole to spring to its feet in enthusiasm over a prospect of fighting in God's cause. With their eyes on Muhammad, their hearts filled with faith in God, in His Prophet, Book, and Judgment, the image of their victory over this aggressive force standing out to attack them dissipated every other idea. They began to imagine themselves marching deep within enemy ranks, cutting them down with their swords and seizing their booty. The picture of paradise hovering before their eyes as martyrs in God's cause was just as the Qur'an had described it. It was a garden replete with everything desirable and beautiful where they would be reunited with the martyrs of Badr who preceded them, therein to dwell eternally, and "where there is neither gossip nor accusation and where every conversation is a talk of peace."[3] At this juncture, Khaythamah Abu Sa'd ibn Khaythamah said: "Perhaps, God will give us victory over them, or our turn will be one of martyrdom. Despite my great desire to be at Badr, it was not my fortune to go, but my son's. God was pleased to grant him his martyrdom. Last night, I saw him in a dream calling to me, 'Hurry up, Father, and join us in Paradise, for here I have truly found everything that God had promised me.' By God, Prophet, of God, I now long to join my son in Paradise. I am advanced in years and my hair has turned gray. Surely do I yearn to meet my Lord." Overwhelmed by this and similar speeches, the Muslims present inclined toward going out to meet the enemy. Muhammad nonetheless advised against it, as if apprehensive of what it was to bring. But everybody insisted, and he had to agree with them. Community consensus and decision had always been his system of worldly government, and he departed from it only in case of a direct revelation to the contrary.

Discipline and Mutual Consultation

The day was a Friday. Muhammad led the prayer and informed the congregation that their victory depended on their patience and careful preparation for war. After the mid-afternoon prayers, he returned home with Abu Bakr and 'Umar, who helped him put on his armour and handed to him his sword. In the meantime, the people were waiting outside and arguing with one another. Usayd ibn Hudayr and Sa'd ibn Mu'adh, who had argued in favor of remaining in Madinah, addressed the people in these words: "You must have noticed that the Prophet was of the opinion that we should remain in Madinah and meet our enemy here. In saying what you did, you dissuaded him from this position against his will. Had you not better delegate the matter to him entirely, follow his verdict, and obey him?" The protagonists of the opposite view were suddenly struck by the idea that they might have opposed the Prophet in a matter in which God might have guided him. When he came out of his house wearing his armour and carrying his sword, they came to him pleading that they did not mean to disagree with him. They declared themselves prepared to abide by his and God's judgment whatever that may be. Muhammad answered: "I have previously called you to follow such a course but you resisted. The Prophet is not one to put away his armour and sword once he puts them on until God's judgment is rendered between him and his enemies. Obey me henceforth. Victory will be yours provided you bear yourselves in patience." Thus, besides the principle of consensus, Muhammad placed order at the foundation of government. Once the community has made up its mind after due deliberation, it should not alter it in haste, but endeavor resolutely to see through. It is then the responsibility of its executive to see to it that the course followed does indeed accomplish the objective sought.

The Muslims' March

Muhammad set out at the head of his force in the direction of Uhud. His first stop was at a locality called al Shaykhan where he met a group of people unknown to him and who, upon inquiry, turned out to be the Jewish allies of ibn Ubayy. The Prophet ruled that unbelievers may not be taken as allies against unbelievers unless they become Muslims. The Jewish column therefore was commanded to return to Madinah. The friends of ibn Ubayy began to whisper in his ear that Muhammad had

slighted him by disregarding the ancestral wisdom which he had put at the
disposal of Muhammad but which the latter had rejected in favor of the
childish views of the Muslims. Soon ibn Ubayy became convinced that the
Muslims were following the wrong course and returned with his own men
to Madinah. The sincere believers who remained with the Prophet numbered seven hundred as against the three thousand Makkan fighters of the
Quraysh tribe.

Ordering the Ranks for Battle

The Muslim force reached Uhud toward the morning. They crossed
the valleys and ascended over dunes. Muhammad ordered his companions
in rows and placed fifty archers on the side of the mountain. Fearing that
the enemy might surprise the Muslims from the rear, he ordered the
archers to protect that side under all circumstances. Specifically, he commanded them never to leave their place regardless of whether the Muslims
plunged into the enemy camp and won, or fell in their places at the hand
of the enemy. Should the enemy cavalry charge, it was the duty of the
archers to repel that charge with arrows. He commanded everyone not to
begin the fight except on his command, but he ordered the archers to
attack the enemy on sight and before he reached Muslim ranks.

Quraysh Women

Quraysh, too, ordered its forces in rows, placing Khalid ibn al Walid
on the right and 'Ikrimah ibn Abu Jahl on the left. They gave the command to 'Abd al Uzza Talhah ibn Abu Talhah. The women were running
back and forth between the lines of the fighters striking their drums and
tambourines and, led by Hind, daughter of 'Utbah and wife of Abu
Sufyan, sang:

"Ho Ho, Sons of 'Abd al Dar!
Ho Ho, Guardians of the land!
Strike down your enemies!
Advance forward and we shall embrace you!
Advance forward and we shall spread the carpets for you!
Turn your backs and we shall avoid you!
Turn your backs and we shall never come to you!"

Abu Dujanah and His Death-Scarf

Thus the two parties were poised for battle and the leaders aroused their own men to fight, the Quraysh by summoning the memory of Badr and its victims, the Muslims by remembering God and the promise of His victory. Muhammad raised his sword in front of his companions and invited them to come forward to get it provided they could fulfill one condition. A number of them rushed to him but were sent back. Abu Dujanah Simak ibn Kharashah, brother of Banu Sa'idah, rose and asked, "What is the provision, O Prophet of God?" The Prophet answered, "That you continue to strike the enemy with it until it breaks." Abu Dujanah was a very brave man who had a red scarf which, as everybody knew, signaled that he was bent on fighting until victory or death. As he drew this scarf and wrapped it around his head, the Prophet gave him the sword. He took it and started to dance in joy between two rows of fighters, as he was wont to do before entering into battle. When Muhammad saw him perform this dance, he said that "Such would be hateful to God except under the circumstances."

Abu 'Amir, slave of 'Amr ibn Sayfi al Awsi, was the first to start the hostilities. Previously, he had moved from Madinah to Makkah in order to arouse the Quraysh to fight Muhammad. He had not witnessed the Battle of Badr. Anxious not to miss this time, he came to Uhud with a retinue of soldiers consisting of fifteen al Aws tribesmen and a number of slaves from Makkah. Once he claimed that he could persuade his fellow tribesmen who converted to Islam to fight with Quraysh against Muhammad. Putting this large claim to the test, he called to them and announced his identity. But his tribesmen replied with curses and damnations. Infuriated at the result, he approached Muslim ranks and started to fight. To the left, 'Ikrimah ibn Abu Jahl with a company of slaves attempted to penetrate Muslim lines at the flank. The Muslims met them with stones and caused them to withdraw. At this moment, Hamzah ibn 'Abd al Muttalib gave the war cry, "Die! Die!" and sprang forward into the thick of the Quraysh lines. Talhah ibn Abu Talhah, carrier of the Makkan flag, sprang forward asking the Muslims to duel with him. 'Ali ibn Abu Talib advanced forth to fight with him. The encounter was soon over as 'Ali struck his enemy a single fatal stroke. Exalted, the Prophet and the Muslims yelled, "God is Great," and advanced for the general charge. Abu Dujanah, with the Prophet's sword in hand and its head wrapped in the "scarf of death," as he called it, killed everyone with whom he fought. He saw one Makkan fighting a Muslim with his fingernails. As he prepared to deal with him, he discovered that it was a woman and that it was Hind, daughter of 'Utbah. He immediately withdrew and saved the Prophet's sword from ever touching a woman's blood.

The Martyrdom of Hamzah

The Quraysh forces advanced ferociously, and the general *melée* between the disproportionately balanced forces began. The larger army was motivated by resentment and a consuming will to vengeance; the smaller by its faith in God and His religion and the will to defend its homeland as well as its interests. Those who sought revenge surpassed them in number and equipment. They were heartened and cheered by the women, each of whom promised one soldier or another her most precious possessions if he could only avenge for her previous loss of her father or brother, husband, or relative. Hamzah ibn 'Abd al Muttalib was one of the greatest and most courageous of Arab heroes. At Badr, it was he who killed 'Utbah, father of Hind, as well as her brother and a number of other close relatives of hers. True to his reputation, Hamzah distinguished himself in battle on the Day of Uhud. He killed Artat ibn 'Abd Shurahbil, Siba' ibn 'Abd al 'Uzza al Ghubshani, and a number of others. His sword seemed invincible. Hind had promised Wahshi, the Abyssinian client of Jubayr, a great amount of wealth should he succeed in killing Hamzah. To encourage him further, Jubayr ibn Mut'am, his master whose uncle was also killed at Badr, promised Wahshi his freedom if he succeeded. The story following was later told by Wahshi: "I set out among others, planning to fight with my javelin as all Abyssinians do, for I hardly ever miss my objective with it. When the great encounter took place, I looked around for Hamzah and caught him with my eyes. I saw him right in the middle of the *melée*, standing out as clearly as a black camel in the herd and felling everybody around him with his sword. I swung my javelin and, making sure it was well balanced, I threw it at him and it fell right on him hitting him in the abdomen and piercing him through. I left my javelin and its victim pinned down under it until he died. Later on I came to him and pulled my javelin away and returned then to the camp and fought no longer. I had killed him in order to win my liberty, and that I had now achieved. When I returned to Makkah, my manumission was officially recognized."

Those in the Muslim camp fell into two categories: The sincere Muslims and the *munafiqun*. The prototype of the latter was Quzman, who joined Islam but never really believed in it. When the Muslim army left Madinah, Quzman refused to march. The next morning the women of Banu Zafar began to shame him for his cowardice. "O Quzman," they said to him, "have you lost your sense of shame or have you become a woman to stay behind while all the men are out fighting?" Incensed, Quzman went to his home, put on his armour, bow, arrows and sword, and set out to join the Prophet's army. He was known to be a brave soul. When he arrived on the scene, he found the Prophet ordering the ranks of the Muslim soldiers. He went straight through to the first row and was the first to throw himself into the battle. He shot his arrows and pierced many an enemy's chest. Toward the end of the day, he was still determined to fall fighting, and he continued to fight until he did. He killed seven of the enemy in one short hour in addition to all the others whom he had killed with his arrows. Passing by him and finding him about to die, Abu al Ghaydaq congratulated him on his achievement of martyrdom. Quzman answered, "O Abu 'Amir, I have not really fought for the faith. I have fought only in order to prevent Quraysh from invading our territory and violating our homes and properties. By God, I fought only in order to protect my people and my land. Without those I would never have done it."

The other group were the true believers. They were not over seven hundred strong and they faced three thousand of the enemy. What has so far been said concerning the deeds of Hamzah and Abu Dujanah reveals an idea of the power of Muslim morale. This was a power before which the soldiers of Quraysh reeled like worms, despite all the courage and heroism for which they were famous throughout Arabia. Their flag was carried so proudly that none would allow it to lay fallen; and as soon as it fell, another soldier would raise it anew. When 'Ali ibn Abu Talib killed its carrier, Talhah ibn Abu Talhah, it was immediately raised again by 'Uthman ibn Abu Talhah. And when 'Uthman fell at the hands of Hamzah, it was raised again by Abu Sa'd ibn Abu Talhah. At the moment he raised the Makkan flag he shouted at the Muslims, "Do you pretend that your martyrs are in paradise and ours in hell? By God, you lie! If anyone of you truly believes such a story, let him come forward and fight with me." His challenge attracted 'Ali[4] who killed him on the spot. The Banu 'Abd al Dar kept on carrying the Makkan flag until they lost nine men. The last of them was Su'ab, the Abyssinian slave of Banu 'Abd al Dar, whose right hand carrying the flag was struck by the aforementioned Quzman. Su'ab seized the flag and raised it high with the left arm. Quzman struck it with his sword again. Having lost both arms, Su'ab now seized the flag and pressed it to his chest with whatever was left of his arms and even bent his back to support it while saying "O Banu 'Abd al Dar, have I not done my duty?" Either Quzman or Sa'd ibn Abu Waqqas killed him. When all the party in charge of the Makkan flag were decimated, the Makkan associationists realized their defeat and began to run for their lives. Even their women were now exposed, and the statue which they had brought with them on camel back to bless them had now fallen to the ground and was broken.

Muslim Victory on the Morning of Uhud

Actually, the victory the Muslims achieved on that morning was a genuine war miracle. Some may attribute it to the sound judgment of Muhammad in placing the archers on the mountain side so that they could hit the enemy cavalry before they could reach the Muslim lines while at the same time protecting the rear of all Muslim forces. Muhammad's good judgment is undoubtedly true. But it is equally true that when six hundred Muslims threw themselves against an enemy force five times greater than theirs, they could not possibly have done so and achieved such bravery unless their deeds sprang from their candid faith in the righteousness of their own cause. Whoever believes in the cause of truth is not bothered by the material preponderance of any power, however great, and his will would not be shaken even if all the forces of evil rallied against him. Sincere faith in God Almighty is the greatest power, the greatest idea. It is invincible. As long as its subject remains sincere and loyal to it, there is no doubt that sincere faith must obtain all it wills. Therefore, Quraysh was shattered and defeated with all its three thousand fighters by the six hundred Muslims. That is why the women of Quraysh were about to be taken captive. When the Muslims followed up their enemies far from the battlefield, those who remained fell upon the large booty left behind. Indeed, many Muslims were thus drawn away from pursuing the defeated enemy.

The Muslims' Preoccupation with Booty

The archers whom Muhammad had commanded not to leave the mountainside even to rescue the Prophet and his companions from what might seem to them to be certain death watched the battle from their height, and saw the defeated enemy running away and the pursuing

Muslims seizing the booty. This whetted their appetites. For a moment, they argued with one another in seeking to convince themselves that no purpose would be served by keeping their position now that God had defeated their enemy. As they watched their fellow Muslims gather the booty, they strongly felt like joining them. When a wiser voice reminded them that the Prophet had commanded them not to leave their position even for rescuing the Muslims from certain death, they rationalized that he had not intended for them to remain in their positions that long, certainly not after the defeat of the enemy. 'Abdullah ibn Jubayr advised them not to violate the Prophet's commandment whatever the circumstances. The majority did not heed his advice, however, but descended to the plain. Ten men only kept their ground. This provided Khalid ibn al Walid, Commander of the Makkan cavalry, the golden opportunity to attack and seize the mountainside where the archers were. He eliminated the remainder of the Muslim archers and occupied the mountainside. The other Muslims were not aware of what was happening, preoccupied as they were in gathering everything of value on the field. After he occupied the mountainside, ibn al Walid signaled to the Quraysh to attack again and he advanced upon the Muslims from the rear. The defeated Makkans rallied to his call, turned about and resumed the fighting. The Muslims dropped the booty they carried, drew their swords and defended themselves. But their victory was lost. Their ranks were disorderly and their unity was in shreds. Quraysh took a heavy toll of Muslim lives. Earlier, the Muslims were fighting by the command of God and out of their faith in Him and in victory; now they fought in order to save their own lives from certain death and humiliation. Earlier, the Muslims were fighting in a united and orderly manner, under a strong and resolute leadership; now they fought without order or leadership. So great was the disorder that some may have struck their own fellows. Finally, when somebody raised the cry that Muhammad was killed, chaos reined supreme, Muslim morale plunged to the bottom and Muslim soldiers fought sporadically and purposelessly. This chaos was responsible for their killing of Husayl ibn Jabir Abu Hudhayfah by mistake, as everyone sought to save his own skin by taking flight except such men as 'Ali ibn Abu Talib whom God had guided and protected.

The Prophet's Injury

When the Quraysh heard of the fall of Muhammad, their forces fell upon Muslim ranks with renewed vigor. Everyone of them was seeking to hit Muhammad, even if dead, that he might have the honor and pride of having participated in his downfall. The Muslims who stood close to the Prophet protected him and drew a close circle around him. Their faith had come back to them and they now stood their ground anxious to lay down their lives in order to save their Prophet. The fact is that one of the stones thrown by the Quraysh had hit the Prophet and caused him to fall to the ground, with a cut lip, a wounded face, and a broken tooth. The stone that hit the Prophet was thrown by 'Utbah ibn Abu Waqqas. It landed with such force that it pushed two links of Muhammad's helmet chain into his wound. Muhammad attempted to stand up behind a shield of his companions, but he fell again, this time in a hole which Abu 'Amir had dug as a trap for the Muslims. 'Ali ibn Abu Talib ran to Muhammad and gave him his hand and, together with Talhah ibn 'Ubaydullah, lifted him again to his feet. He and his companions then began to retreat toward the mountain of Uhud while fighting their pursuing enemies.

Desperate Defense of the Prophet's Person

In a moment, however, a number of other Muslims joined the circle of the Prophet, and these were so determined and desperate in their defense that they formed an impregnable barrier between the Prophet and the enemy. Umm 'Amarah al Ansariyyah, the Madinese, had been on the battlefield since the morning to give water to the Muslim fighters to drink. When the Muslims suffered defeat, she threw down her water jug, drew her sword, and joined the other fighters around the Prophet for his protection. She shot a number of arrows until she herself was wounded. Abu Dujanah placed himself as a shield before the Prophet and even exposed his back to the falling arrows lest they should hit the Prophet. Sa'd ibn Abu Waqqas shot arrows which Muhammad passed to him while lending him encouragement. A little earlier, Muhammad himself was using his bow and shot at the enemy until the string of his bow broke. Those who thought that Muhammad had perished, including Abu Bakr and 'Umar, went toward the mountain and sat down. When Anas ibn al Nadr inquired why they were giving up so soon, and was told that the Prophet of God had been killed, he retorted: "And what would you do with yourselves and your lives after Muhammad died? Rise, and die like he did." He turned, charged against the enemy, and fought gallantly. He kept on fighting despite his wounds and did not give up until he was hit seventy times. His body was so torn up with wounds that only his sister could identify it by means of his fingers alone.

The Prophet's Escape

Quraysh took the news of Muhammad's death with exhilaration and joy, and Abu Sufyan began a search for his body on the battlefield. The Muslims around Muhammad did not deny the news of his death in obedience to Muhammad's own commandment designed to prevent any new onslaught by the Quraysh against him. Ka'b ibn Malik, however, came close to the circle and, bending himself over Abu Dujanah, noticed that the Prophet was there and still alive. He proclaimed at the top of his voice: "O Believers, be glad, for the Prophet of God is here and still alive." The Prophet, however, asked him to keep quiet. The Muslims then reinforced the protective circle around the Prophet and moved with him farther up toward the mountain; they were led by Abu Bakr, 'Umar, 'Ali ibn Abu Talib, al Zubayr ibn al 'Awwam and others. The cry of Ka'b brought about a different effect upon the Quraysh. Most of the latter did not believe it but regarded it as an enemy trick designed to rally the Muslims to fight again. A few Makkans ran toward the Muslims shouting, "Where is Muhammad? Death to me if he lives!" The Prophet hurled the javelin of al Harith ibn al Simmah at the oncoming party. It hit the leader, threw him off his horse, and killed him. When the Muslims reached the entrance to the valley on the other side, 'Ali filled his shield with water, washed Muhammad's face and poured some water on his head. Abu 'Ubaydah ibn al Jarrah pulled out the two links of chain from Muhammad's wound, and his two front teeth fell off in the process. While this was taking place, Khalid ibn al Walid pursued the Muslims on the hillside with a small force of Makkan cavalry. But they were repelled by 'Umar ibn al Khattab and a number of the Prophet's companions. The Muslims continued their retreat. So great was their exhaustion that when it was noon, the Prophet led the prayer seated, suffering as he was from his wounds, and the Muslims prayed behind him seated also.

Mutilation of the Muslim Dead

Quraysh was intoxicated with her victory and deemed her vengeance for Badr fully taken. The occasion gave Abu Sufyan such cause for pride that he said, "A great day was won against the day of Badr. Next year will see the same." His wife Hind, daughter of 'Utbah, was not satisfied with this victory. Nor was she satisfied with the death of Hamzah ibn 'Abd al Muttalib. With her women companions she ran toward the battlefield and began the mutilation of the Muslim dead. She cut off a number of noses and ears in order to make a string and a necklace of them. She then cut the body of Hamzah open and pulled out his liver which she began to chew. These ugly deeds of hers and of her women companions were so unbecoming that even Abu Sufyan, her husband, denounced her. He said to one of the Muslims: "Your dead were indeed mutilated; but I swear by God that I have never approved of such deeds. How can I be accused of commanding them?"

Muhammad's Mourning of Hamzah

The Quraysh returned to Makkah after burying their dead. The Muslims returned to the battlefield to bury theirs, and Muhammad sought out the body of his uncle, Hamzah. When he saw that his body was mutilated, Muhammad felt profoundly sad and vowed that he would never allow such a hateful thing to happen again and that he would some-day avenge these evil deeds. It was on this occasion that the revelation was made:

وَإِنْ عَاقَبْتُمْ فَعَاقِبُوا بِمِثْلِ مَا عُوقِبْتُمْ بِهِ وَلَئِنْ صَبَرْتُمْ لَهُوَ خَيْرٌ لِّلصَّابِرِينَ۞ وَاصْبِرْ وَمَا صَبْرُكَ إِلَّا بِاللَّهِ وَلَا تَحْزَنْ عَلَيْهِمْ وَلَا تَكُ فِي ضَيْقٍ مِّمَّا يَمْكُرُونَ۞

"And if you punish, inflict the same punishment as has been meted out to you. But if you bear patiently, it is certainly better for you. Do bear then patiently; for the reward of your patience is with God. Do not feel sad nor give way to anger because of their plotting."[5]

The Prophet of God then pardoned, bore patiently, and laid down an absolute prohibition against mutilation. Hamzah was given burial on the spot where he lay, Muhammad conducting the funerary prayer and Hamzah's sister, Safiyyah, daughter of 'Abd al Muttalib, participating. All prayed for God to show them His mercy. The Prophet then commanded burial for all the dead, which numbered seventy; and, when this was completed, he led his party back to Madinah. The Muslims were quite sad and solemn for having encountered such defeat after their victory, and such humiliation after their splendid accomplishment. They fully realized that it was the archers' disobedience of Muhammad as well as the Muslims' preoccupation with booty that had exposed them to this sad turn of events.

Need for Recapturing the Lost Prestige

The Prophet went home and thought deeply. The Jews, the *munafiqun*, and the associationists of Madinah were elated at the news of the setback. Muslim power in Madinah had been such that none could effectively oppose it. Now it stood ready to be shaken. 'Abdullah ibn Ubayy ibn Salul did not participate in the Battle of Uhud because Muhammad as well as the Muslims did not wish to listen to his advice. Moreover, Muhammad declared himself angry against 'Abdullah's clients, the Jews. Were this setback at Uhud the last judgment on the Muslims *vis-a-vis* the Quraysh, the fate of Muhammad and his companions would have been easily disposed of by the tribesmen of the Peninsula, and their political power in Yathrib would have crumbled. The Muslims would have become objects of universal derision. In such circumstances, the associationists and pagans would surely have been emboldened to attack the religion of God, and that would have been the greatest tragedy. It was necessary, therefore, to direct some strike against the enemy in order to offset the defeat of Uhud and to recapture Muslim morale as well as to instill fear in the hearts of the Jews and the *munafiqun*. Such a measure was necessary if the political power of Muhammad and his companions in Yathrib was to regain its strength.

Resumption of Fighting on the Morrow

On the morrow, which fell on Sunday the 16th of Shawwal, the *mu'adhdhin* of the Prophet called upon the Muslims to regroup and pursue the enemy. Only those who had participated in the previous day's battle were, however, allowed to proceed. When the Muslims set out toward the Makkan force, Abu Sufyan immediately learned that his enemies had returned from Madinah with new reinforcements. Muhammad reached Hamra' al Asad while Abu Sufyan and his companions were still at al Rawha'. Since he passed by both camps, Ma'bad al Khuza'i, who was still an associationist, was asked by Abu Sufyan about Muhammad and his forces. He replied that "Muhammad and his companions are coming after you with such a large army that I have never seen the like of it. Those who were not present yesterday are all with him today shouting with anger and seeking revenge." Abu Sufyan, on the other hand, though he wanted to run away from any more confrontations with Muhammad, pondered the consequences of such a flight. Would not the Arabs say of Quraysh in

such an eventuality what he himself would have liked to say of
Muhammad and his companions? But then, were he to return to
Muhammad and the Muslims defeat them this time, would not the
Quraysh be destroyed once and for all? He therefore made recourse to a
trick. With some riders of 'Abd al Qays proceeding to Madinah, he sent a
message to Muhammad that the Quraysh had decided to pursue the
Muslims in order to finish them off. When this message reached
Muhammad at Hamra' al Asad, his will and determination remained constant and his decision unchanged. The whole Muslim force, which
remained in place for three days and three nights, made large bonfires during the night in order to show the world that they were there to stay.
Finally, disagreeing with Abu Sufyan, the Quraysh preferred to save the
memory of their victory of Uhud and to return to Makkah. Thereafter,
Muhammad returned to Madinah with more confidence in Muslim
power, though the insincere believers began to raise their heads in derision
of the Muslims and asked: "If the battle of Badr was a sign from God
proving the veracity of Muhammad's prophethood, what was the sign of
the battle of Uhud ?"[6]

16

The Effects of Uhud

Muhammad's Policy after Uhud

After Uhud, Abu Sufyan returned to Makkah preceded by the news of his victory. He arrived home exalted and overjoyed for having removed from Quraysh the stain of defeat at Badr. As soon as he entered the city and before setting foot in his residence, he went to the Ka'bah where he offered thanksgiving and prayers to its high god Hubal. He then shaved his sideburns and returned to his residence feeling that the vow he had made not to touch his wife until he had defeated Muhammad had now been fulfilled. The Muslims, on the other hand, despite the fact that they spent three whole days in the open, challenging their enemy to return and engage them without avail, were derided by the Madinese. Nobody mentioned the Muslim victory in the first round of battle. Evidently, Madinah was simply not favorable to the Muslims, Muhammad's great political power notwithstanding. The Prophet — May God's peace and blessing be upon him — felt this hostility strongly, not only from Madinah but also from all the surrounding Arab tribes who only a few days earlier feared and respected Muslim power. The Battle of Uhud had enabled the non-Muslim elements of Madinah and its surroundings to dare to stand in the face of Muhammad and even to oppose him. Hence Muhammad took especial care to keep himself abreast of developments within and without the city, and he prepared himself for recapturing and reestablishing Muslim power and reputation.

261

The Campaign of Abu Salamah ibn 'Abd al Asad

The first news of enemy movement that came to Muhammad's ear told that Tulayhah and Salamah, sons of Khuwaylid and leaders of Banu Asad, were inciting their tribesmen and clients to attack Madinah and to seek Muhammad in his own house. They were also inciting them to raid the city outskirts to seize the cattle of the Muslims. Apparently, they were emboldened by the consideration that Muhammad and his companions were still shaken by defeat and that their power was on the decline. As soon as the Prophet heard of this, however, he sent forth Abu Salamah ibn 'Abd al Asad at the head of an expeditionary force of one hundred and fifty fighters including Abu 'Ubaydah ibn al Jarrah, Sa'd ibn Abu Waqqas, and Usayd ibn Hudayr. He ordered the force to march by night along untrodden paths, to lie still by day, and to surprise the enemy wherever possible. Abu Salamah followed the instructions of the Prophet and found his enemy unprepared. Shortly before dawn, he talked to his men, inspiring them to holy war, and they attacked. The enemy ran away in defeat. The Muslims pursued them and returned after having stripped them of all their possessions. They divided the booty among themselves after saving one fifth of it for God, His Prophet, the poor, and the wayfarer; then they returned to Madinah victorious. Their accomplishment restored some of the Muslim prestige which had been lost at Uhud. Abu Salamah, however, did not live long after this raid, for his wound at Uhud had not been completely cured. His participation in this raid, during which he reopened the wound, finally brought about his death.

The Campaign of 'Abdullah ibn Unays

Later Muhammad learned that Khalid ibn Sufyan ibn Nubayh al Hudhali was either at Nakhlah or 'Uranah arousing the people and inciting them to raid Madinah. He commanded 'Abdullah ibn Unays to travel to Madinah in order to reconnoiter for him. After going forth, 'Abdullah found Khalid in the company of women. When asked by Khalid about his identity, 'Abdullah answered, "I am an Arab tribesman who has heard of you and of the army you are raising to fight Muhammad and I have come to you to join your ranks." Khalid did not hide the fact that he was actually raising an army in order to attack Madinah. In a moment of separation from his men, and in the company of his women, 'Abdullah asked Khalid to walk with him a little while in order to discuss certain

affairs. When they were at a safe distance, he fell on him with his sword
and killed him. Khalid's women were the only witnesses and they began
to cry and mourn for him. 'Abdullah returned home and informed the
Prophet of his exploits. This singlehanded campaign had the effect of
silencing the Banu Lihyan branch of the Hudhayl tribe for some time. But
the Banu Lihyan began to think of ways and means to avenge the murder
of their leader.

The Battle of al Raji' (625 C.E.)

About this time, a group of tribesmen living in the district of
Muhammad came to him saying, "There are some Muslims among us.
Please send with us some of your companions to teach us the law of Islam
and to recite the Qur'an." Muhammad was in the habit of sending his
companions upon request to such areas and tribes in order to perform such
religious functions and to call men to the true faith and guidance as well
as to find new political allies. It will be recalled that Muhammad sent such
companions to Madinah after the great covenant of 'Aqabah. In fulfillment of this new request, Muhammad sent six of his notable companions.
When they were all camping at a well belonging to the tribe of Hudhayl
in the Hijaz at a place called al Raji', their host betrayed them to the
Hudhayl tribe. The six Muslims arose to find that they were surrounded
by enemies with drawn swords. They drew their swords too and prepared
for battle. But the Hudhayl tribesmen said, "It is not our intention to kill
you but to sell you as captives to the people of Makkah. Lay down your
swords and we solemnly promise that we shall not kill you." The Muslims
looked to one another and decided that a humiliating captivity in Makkah
was far worse than loss of life. Rejecting the promise of Hudhayl, they
began to fight knowing that they were outnumbered. Hudhayl killed three
of them and overpowered the other three. They tied their hands and drove
them toward Makkah. 'Abdullah ibn Talib managed to pull his hands free
and seized his sword to fight his captors. But they overwhelmed and killed
him. The other two captives were brought to Makkah and sold by the
Hudhayl. Zayd ibn al Dathinah was purchased by Safwan ibn Umayyah
in order to be killed in revenge for his father, Umayyah ibn Khalaf. The
captive was given over to Safwan's servant Nastas for execution. Abu
Sufyan questioned the captive: "Tell me, O Zayd, would you not prefer
that Muhammad were here in your place to receive this last punishment
while you were at home with your people?" Zayd answered, "No! By God,

I certainly prefer that Muhammad be where he is, safe from all harm. That is more preferable to me than reunion with my people." Stupefied, Abu Sufyan rejoined, "Never have I seen anyone more beloved by his companions than Muhammad." Nastas executed the order of his master and killed Zayd, the man who remained true to his religion and Prophet. As for Khubayb, he was kept in jail until such time as they would crucify him. In his last hour, he asked to be allowed to pray, and they let him. After completion of his prayer, he exclaimed: "By God, were I not afraid that you might think I was not ready to die, I would have prolonged my prayer." They lifted him to the cross and tied him to it. With great passion, he prayed to God: "O God, reduce their numbers, rout, and disperse them, do not let anyone of them escape." There was such a ring in his voice that his executioners were seized with panic and fell to the ground as if his curse had really struck them. Like Zayd before him, Khubayb died a martyr, true to his Creator, and loyal to His religion and Prophet. It would have been possible for these two pure souls to save themselves from death if they had apostatized. But their conviction of God, of His Spirit, of the Day of Judgment — the Day on which every soul will receive its due, and no vicarious substitutes will be allowed — caused them to see death as a fitting finale for the life of faith. Undoubtedly, they must have believed that their innocent lives now being laid down on Makkan soil would one day arouse their Muslim brethren to conquer that city, destroy its idols, and purify it from paganism and associationism. They were certain that someday the Ka'bah should rightly be sanctified as the House of God ought to be and that someday its walls would reverberate with none but the name of God alone.

The western Orientalists do not note this event as they do the execution of the two captives of Badr by the Muslims. None of them has even condemned this treacherous execution of two innocent Muslims who participated in no war but who were dragged stealthily into the enemy camp while they were teaching the very men who were planning their murder or sale to their enemies. None of them had thought to condemn the Quraysh despite the fact that its behavior in this case was nothing short of cowardice and cold-blooded murder. The rules of the most primitive justice would have required of those western Orientalists who condemned the Muslims' execution of the two Badr captives that they condemn, *a fortiori*, this treason of Quraysh and of the men who sold her the two captives after killing their four colleagues. Neither did Quraysh capture them in an honest fight. It bought them from people who tricked them into their camp by inviting them to be the teachers of truth, to instruct, and to enlighten them in matters of the faith.

Muhammad and the Muslim community were saddened by the news of the martyrdom of their six colleagues as a result of the treachery of Hudhayl. Hassan ibn Thabit, the Muslim poet, composed a poem in their memory in which Khubayb and Zayd were objects of the warmest compassion and mourning. The event gave Muhammad reason to ponder and to fear deterioration of Muslim prestige in case such events were to recur. Nothing, of course, is more harmful to one's prestige than to be slighted by the larger community. As he was engaged in these thoughts, he was approached by Abu Bara' 'Amir ibn Malik, to whom Muhammad offered the faith of Islam. Abu Bara' turned down the offer of Muhammad, but he did not show any enmity to the new faith. On the contrary, he asked Muhammad to send some of his companions to the people of Najd in order to preach Islam to them. "Perhaps," he said, "they may respond favorably and enter the faith." Muhammad feared that any such companions whom he might send to Najd might be subject to treacherous attack as had befallen Khubayb and his companions on the part of the Hudhayl tribe. Unmoved, he therefore rejected Abu Bara's request. Abu Bara' said, "I shall be their guardian and protector. Send them over, therefore, and let them preach the faith." Abu Bara' was a notable with large influence among his people. No one had reason to fear when Abu Bara' had extended his personal protection to him. With this consideration, Muhammad sent al Mundhir ibn 'Ami', brother of Banu Sa'idah, together with other men chosen from the foremost Muslim ranks.

The Battle of Bi'r Ma'unah

Delegates and escorts proceeded together until they reached the well of Ma'unah, at the frontier between Banu 'Amir and Banu Sulaym. From there, they sent Haram ibn Milhan to 'Amir ibn al Tufayl with Muhammad's message. 'Amir, not even bothering to read Muhammad's letter, killed its carrier forthwith. He then called on the tribesmen of Banu 'Amir to kill all the Muslims. When his tribesmen refused to violate the protection already extended by Abu Bara', 'Amir summoned other tribes to do the job. A number of these responded to his call, gave fight to the Muslims, surrounded them completely, and killed them. Not one Muslim survived this battle except Ka'b ibn Zayd and 'Amr ibn Umayyah. The former was left wounded in the field on the assumption that he was dead, and the latter was set free by 'Amir ibn al Tufayl as atonement for a vow involving a man's life which his mother owed. On his way home, 'Amir met two men on the road whom he mistook as part of the enemy hosts which killed his companions. He waited until they had gone to sleep and then sprang upon them and killed them. When he reached Madinah, he gave the Prophet a full report of what he did and what had happened. It then turned out that the two men whom he killed were clients of 'Amir and *protégés* of Abu Bara', with whom the Prophet had entered into a covenant of good neighborliness. The Prophet therefore commanded him to pay their bloodwits.

The fall of the Muslim martyrs at the well of Ma'unah deeply grieved Muhammad. He blamed Abu Bara' for this loss since he was the author of the request which Muhammad had satisfied, but only with apprehension and after much hesitation. Abu Bara' for his part, was extremely wrathful against 'Amir ibn al Tufayl for violating his protective covenant with the Muslims; and sent his own son, al Raji', to kill 'Amir in vengeance for the violated honor. Mourning his colleagues for one whole month, Muhammad asked God fervently at every morning prayer to enable him to avenge their death. All the Muslims were deeply affected by this tragedy that had befallen their brethren in religion, though they believed that the martyrs were all in Paradise.

The Jews and Munafiqun of Madinah

The Jews and the *munafiqun* of Madinah found in the tragedies of Al Raji' and Bi'r Ma'unah occasion to remember the victory of Quraysh at Uhud and to forget the Muslim victory over Banu Asad. In consequence, the prestige of the Prophet and his companions declined, and grave concern was directed to the Muslims' political fortune. With proper foresight, Muhammad realized that this deterioration of Muslim prestige in Madinah had exposed the whole cause to the greatest danger. Nothing would so inspire the tribes to dig their claws into Madinah as the suspicion that an attack upon the Muslims would immediately bring about civil war within their city. Muhammad also observed that both the Jews and the *munafiqun* were plotting against him. He therefore decided to force them into betraying their intentions. As the Jews of Banu al Nadir were the allies of Banu 'Amir, Muhammad went to them near Quba', together with ten of his prominent companions — including Abu Bakr, 'Umar, and 'Ali — and asked them to cooperate in furnishing the bloodwit money for the two victims whom 'Amr ibn Umayyah had killed by mistake, not knowing of their covenant with the Muslims.

Jewish Plots against Muhammad

When Muhammad submitted his request to them, they pretended acquiescence to his demand. But it was also noticeable that while some of them were showing signs of reconciliation, others were plotting at a safe distance. They whispered to one another in presence of the Muslims, and the Prophet overheard them mentioning the murder by the Muslims of Ka'b ibn al Ashraf. When one of them, 'Amr ibn Jahsh ibn Ka'b, entered the house on whose wall Muhammad was leaning, in a suspicious and stealthy manner, Muhammad could no more contain his doubts which their talk and hush-hush conversation made gradually more certain. He rose and withdrew from their midst, leaving behind his companions and giving the impression that he was soon to return. The Jews knew that he was leaving for good and addressed his companions incoherently and hesitantly. They realized that if they were to kill his men, Muhammad would surely take a bitter revenge. But if they let them go, the Jewish plot against Muhammad would not be betrayed, and at any rate they could count on the Muslims to continue to honor their part of the covenant. They therefore tried to convince their Muslim guests of their good intentions and to counteract any suspicions that their guests may have entertained. Soon, the companions began to complain that the Prophet had not returned and that they had better leave and look for him. They met a man on the way who assured them that Muhammad had safely returned to the mosque. When they joined him, the Prophet told them of his suspicions and of the Jewish plot to kill him. They then realized the meaning of Jewish behavior and understood their moves at the recent interview. They became convinced of the Prophet's penetrating insight, which seemed all the more convincing when joined to the evidence of their own observations.

Warning to Banu al Nadir

Commanding Muhammad ibn Maslamah, the Prophet said: "Go to the Jews of Banu al Nadir and tell them that I have sent you to them with the command that they should leave this country. Tell them that by plotting to kill me, they have violated the covenant which I gave them. Tell them also that I give them ten days to evacuate after which any Jew seen in this area will be killed." When they heard of this command, Banu al Nadir lost hope. In vain they looked for means to change the verdict. Seeking to sway the Prophet's messenger to their own side, they said: "O Muhammad ibn Maslamah, we did not expect that such command be conveyed by an old ally of ours like you, a man from al Aws tribe which is our ally against the Khazraj." Ibn Maslamah replied, "The times have changed and so have the affiliations."

Instigation to Defy the Prophet

The Jews spent a number of days preparing for war. In the meantime, 'Abdullah ibn Ubayy sent to them two messengers with the message that they should not depart from their land and property, that they should remain in their fortresses, and that soon he himself would be coming to their assistance with two thousand Jewish and Arab fighters prepared to defend them to the death. Banu al Nadir pondered over the message of Ibn Ubayy and wondered how he could have felt so certain of victory. They recalled that the same man had previously promised help to Banu Qaynuqa', just as he was doing today, but betrayed them when his help was needed by running for his life. They considered that since Banu Qurayzah had contracted a peace with Muhammad, they would not be prepared to come to their rescue. Hence, they inclined toward removing themselves to Khaybar or a nearer place, considering that they could still come to Yathrib to harvest their crops and return to their fortresses at Khaybar with no appreciable loss. Huyayy ibn Akhtab, their leader, finally resolved against this view. "No," he said, "I shall send to Muhammad telling him that we shall not leave our homes and properties and that we refuse to comply with his orders. As for us, all we have to do is to consolidate our fortresses, to fill up our granaries, to barricade our streets, to supply ourselves with stones, and to get ready. We have enough food reserves to keep us for a full year and our water supply never runs dry. At any rate, Muhammad will not blockade us for as long a time as a year." The ten days therefore passed and no Jew left Madinah.

Blockade of Banu al Nadir

The Muslims took up arms and began to fight the Jews. For twenty days and nights the battle raged. Whenever a Jew showed up on the public street or outside of his quarters, the Muslims would engage him in battle. But the Jews would withdraw quickly and often would even destroy their own property or houses before withdrawal to deeper lines. Subsequently, Muhammad ordered his companions to cut down the date trees and to burn them in order to reduce the Jews' will to stay in Madinah to protect and enjoy their properties. The Jews were angry and argued, "O Muhammad, how could you, who always forbade corruption and injustice and castigated their perpetrators, command the destruction of our date orchards?" On this occasion the following verse was revealed: "Whatever tree you have cut down or left standing, you have done so with God's permission that the unjust may be overwhelmed."[1] The Jews waited in vain for military assistance to come from the side of ibn Ubayy or from that of some other Arab tribes, and they dreaded the fate which awaited them in case they prolonged the hostilities. In despair and with hearts trembling with fear, they asked Muhammad to guarantee their lives and properties and to give them safe passage. Muhammad agreed, permitting each one to take with him three camel loads of whatever property of goods they wanted to take away. Huyayy ibn Akhtab, their leader, led this exodus; the emigrants settled either at Khaybar or at Adhri'at in al Sham. They left behind them large amounts of booty consisting of food, fifty pieces of armour, three hundred and forty swords, and large areas of land. This prize was greater than anything the Muslims had so far seized. These properties were not divided among the Muslims as war booty. They were all considered as a trust which the Prophet of God divided among the early emigrants, after putting away some for the purposes of the poor and deprived. Thus the necessary economic support of the Muhajirun by al Ansar was alleviated for the first time, the Muhajirun having now acquired as much wealth as their hosts. None of the Ansar received any of this new wealth except Abu Dujanah and Sahl ibn Hunayf. When they pleaded to Muhammad that they were really in need, Muhammad gave them as liberally as the Muhajirun. All the Jews of Banu al Nadir left Madinah except two who converted to Islam and kept their property.

It is by no means easy to appreciate the true significance of the Muslim victory and of the forced evacuation of Banu al Nadir from Madinah. The Prophet's apprehension of what their presence in Madinah might lead to by way of civil strife, of emboldening the *munafiqun* to plot against the Muslims whenever the latter suffered a set-back, and of the actual threat of civil war in case of outside attack — all these weighed heavily in the Prophet's consideration. On the occasion of the evacuation of Banu al Nadir, the whole *Surah* of "al Hashr" was revealed. In it God said: "Would you not see the *munafiqun*, how they falsely promise their brethren — the faithless among the People of the Book — to join them in evacuation if that were imposed, to refuse obedience to anyone against them, and to come to their rescue in case of war? God knows that they lie. The People of the Book are forced to evacuate; yet, the *munafiqun* would not leave with them, and should the former be fought, they would not come to their assistance but would run away without giving rescue. Indeed, they fear you more than they fear God, little that they think or know."[2]

The *Surah* continues with a discussion of faith and its power over the human soul and asserts that only recognition of God gives the human soul value and dignity such as no other recognition of any power can give. The Qur'an said:

> هُوَ اللهُ الَّذِى لَا إِلٰهَ إِلَّا هُوَ عَلِمُ الْغَيْبِ وَالشَّهَادَةِ هُوَ الرَّحْمٰنُ الرَّحِيْمُ ۞ هُوَ اللهُ الَّذِى لَا إِلٰهَ إِلَّا هُوَ اَلْمَلِكُ الْقُدُّوسُ السَّلٰمُ الْمُؤْمِنُ الْمُهَيْمِنُ الْعَزِيْزُ الْجَبَّارُ الْمُتَكَبِّرُ سُبْحٰنَ اللهِ عَمَّا يُشْرِكُوْنَ ۞ هُوَ اللهُ الْخَالِقُ الْبَارِئُ الْمُصَوِّرُ لَهُ الْاَسْمَآءُ الْحُسْنٰى يُسَبِّحُ لَهُ مَا فِى السَّمٰوٰتِ وَالْاَرْضِ وَهُوَ الْعَزِيْزُ الْحَكِيْمُ ۞

"God is the Being besides Whom there is no other God. He knows that which no man knows and He is the Merciful, the Compassionate. God is the Being besides Whom there is no other God. He is the King, the Holy, the Peace-giver, the Securer, the Dominant, the Mighty, the Great, the Unchallengeable. Praised be He above everything they associate with Him. God is the Creator, the Fashioner, the Form-giver. To Him belong the noble names. To Him everything on earth and in heaven gives praise. He is the Omnipotent, the Wise."[3]

The Prophet's Secretary

Until the exit of Banu al Nadir from Madinah, the Prophet's secretary was a Jew. He had chosen him for his capacity to write letters in Hebrew and Syriac, as well as Arabic. After the evacuation of the Jews from Madinah, the Prophet no longer trusted a non-Muslim to write his letters. He therefore commanded Zayd ibn Thabit, a Madinese youth, to learn the two languages and appointed him his secretary for all affairs. The same Zayd ibn Thabit collected the Qur'an during the caliphate of Abu Bakr, supervised the collection of the Qur'an when the readings of it varied during the caliphate of 'Uthman, and finally established the text known as "the recension of 'Uthman," after which all other texts were destroyed.

The city of Madinah recovered its peace after the evacuation of Banu al Nadir. The Muslims no more feared the *munafiqun*, and the Muhajirun were quite satisfied with the new lands they had acquired. On the other hand, al Ansar were equally happy that there was no further need to support the Muhajirun. The period was generally one of peace and tranquility as well as prosperity for both Muhajirun and Ansar. This continued until the following year when, on the occasion of the memory of Uhud, Muhammad remembered the promise of Abu Sufyan to fight the Muslims again a year thence to the day. Muhammad also recalled that Abu Sufyan had challenged to meet him once more at Badr, on the Day of Badr, a year later. The year was one of drought and Abu Sufyan wished to postpone the encounter for another year. Nonetheless, he sent Nu'aym to Madinah to inform the Muslims that Quraysh had rallied a tremendous army such as the Arabs had never seen before, that Makkah was planning to fight them and destroy them once and for all and inflict upon them unheard of misery and destruction. The Muslims first reacted with apprehension and fear and were more eager to remain in Madinah than go out to meet their enemy at Badr. Muhammad was indignant. He castigated their cowardice and warned them that be was going to Badr even if he had to do so alone.

The Would-be Encounter at Badr

After this show of anger on the part of the Prophet, it was not surprising that all hesitation and all fear on the part of the Muslims dissolved and that they picked up their arms in order to run to Badr. The Prophet appointed 'Abdullah ibn 'Abdullah ibn Ubayy ibn Salul to govern Madinah in his absence. The Muslims arrived at Badr and waited there for the Quraysh army to come forth. Quraysh, on the other hand, sent two thousand fighters under the leadership of Abu Sufyan. Abu Sufyan, however, was not enthusiastic about the whole affair, and he decided to return to Makkah two days after he left. He advised his people that since they could not do well in war outside of Makkah except in a fertile and prosperous year, and since that year was one of drought and poverty, it was bet-

ter for them to return home and not to fight Muhammad. He returned to
Makkah and the army returned with him while Muhammad awaited
them eight long days in their encampment at Badr. While waiting for
their enemy to appear, the Muslims began a little trade and they made
large gains for which they thanked God. It was on the occasion of this
would-be encounter that the following Qur'anic verses were revealed:

الَّذِينَ قَالُوا لِإِخْوَانِهِمْ وَقَعَدُوا لَوْ أَطَاعُونَا مَا قُتِلُوا قُلْ فَادْرَءُوا عَنْ أَنفُسِكُمُ الْمَوْتَ إِن
كُنتُمْ صَادِقِينَ ۞ وَلَا تَحْسَبَنَّ الَّذِينَ قُتِلُوا فِى سَبِيلِ اللَّهِ أَمْوَاتًا بَلْ أَحْيَاءٌ عِندَ رَبِّهِمْ
يُرْزَقُونَ ۞ فَرِحِينَ بِمَا آتَاهُمُ اللَّهُ مِن فَضْلِهِ وَيَسْتَبْشِرُونَ بِالَّذِينَ لَمْ يَلْحَقُوا بِهِم مِّنْ
خَلْفِهِمْ أَلَّا خَوْفٌ عَلَيْهِمْ وَلَا هُمْ يَحْزَنُونَ ۞ يَسْتَبْشِرُونَ بِنِعْمَةٍ مِّنَ اللَّهِ وَفَضْلٍ وَ
أَنَّ اللَّهَ لَا يُضِيعُ أَجْرَ الْمُؤْمِنِينَ ۞ الَّذِينَ اسْتَجَابُوا لِلَّهِ وَالرَّسُولِ مِن بَعْدِ مَا أَصَابَهُمُ
الْقَرْحُ لِلَّذِينَ أَحْسَنُوا مِنْهُمْ وَاتَّقَوْا أَجْرٌ عَظِيمٌ ۞ الَّذِينَ قَالَ لَهُمُ النَّاسُ إِنَّ النَّاسَ قَدْ
جَمَعُوا لَكُمْ فَاخْشَوْهُمْ فَزَادَهُمْ إِيمَانًا وَقَالُوا حَسْبُنَا اللَّهُ وَنِعْمَ الْوَكِيلُ ۞ فَانقَلَبُوا بِنِعْمَةٍ مِّنَ اللَّهِ وَ
فَضْلٍ لَّمْ يَمْسَسْهُمْ سُوءٌ وَاتَّبَعُوا رِضْوَانَ اللَّهِ وَاللَّهُ ذُو فَضْلٍ عَظِيمٍ ۞ إِنَّمَا ذَٰلِكُمُ
الشَّيْطَانُ يُخَوِّفُ أَوْلِيَاءَهُ فَلَا تَخَافُوهُمْ وَخَافُونِ إِن كُنتُم مُّؤْمِنِينَ ۞

"To those who did not go to war but remained behind complaining,
'Had they only listened to us and not gone out to war they would not have
been killed,' [Allah says,] 'If you are truthful in your allegation, will you
not seek to avoid death altogether and become immortal? Think not that
those who have laid down their lives for the sake of God are dead. Rather,
they are alive, in presence of their Lord, and they receive His gifts. They
are happy with what God had given them of His bounty and they are
awaiting with joy the arrival of those who were not as fortunate but who
have neither reason to grieve nor to sorrow. They are jubilant with God's
bounty and grace, for God never suffers the reward of the believers to be
lost. On the other hand, those who responded to God's call and the
Prophet's even after they had been wounded in previous battles, and to
those of them who have done well and have been pious, will fall the great
reward. As to those whom the enemy wished to frighten by reports of the
rallying of great armies, but whose faith grew stronger at the challenge
and who said, "Sufficient for us is God, for He is the most excellent

Guardian," to them God will show His favor and grant His bounty. No evil has befallen them, only God's blessing and benediction. God is the Lord of great bounty. It is Satan, rather, that instills fear in his friends and associates. Do not fear your enemies, therefore, but fear Me if you are true believers.'"⁴

This would-be encounter at Badr erased completely every trace of Uhud. Quraysh had no alternative but to wait another whole year, enduring in the meantime an opprobrium no less great than that of her first defeat at Badr.

Campaign of Dhat al Riqa'

Fully satisfied with the implicit victory God had sent to him, Muhammad returned to Madinah. He was content that the Muslims recaptured their prestige, but he kept constant vigilance lest the enemy should cheat him once more. In the meantime, the news reached him that a group from Ghatafan in Najd were rallying an army to fight him. He planned to surprise them before they could complete their preparations. Gathering a force of four hundred, he led his men to Dhat al Riqa' where the Banu Muharib and Banu Tha'labah of Ghatafan had rallied. The Muslims took the initiative of surprise attack, and the enemy ran away leaving behind their women, equipment, and property. Of these the Muslims carried what they could and returned to Madinah. Taking care lest the enemy launch a surprise attack against them in turn, the Muslims established night and day sentries, and Muhammad would only allow short prayers to be held. While some of them prayed, the others would face the enemy fully prepared for defense. The enemy, however, never showed his face; and the Prophet returned to Madinah fifteen days after they had left it, jubilant and victorious.

Campaign of Dawmat al Jandal

A little later, the Prophet led another campaign to Dawmat al Jandal. This is an oasis on the frontier between al Hijaz and al Sham, midway between the Red Sea and the Persian Gulf. There again, Muhammad could not find the tribes whom he had come to punish for their attack upon the caravans. For as soon as any heard that he was on his way, they would run, unmindful of what the Muslims might carry away of their property as booty. The geographic location of Dawmat al Jandal shows the ample extent of Muhammad and his companions' political influence and military sway. In fact, the Arabian Peninsula shook under their feet. The foregoing accounts give equally clear evidence of Muslim endurance, of their disregard for excessive heat, for the desolateness of the countryside and shortage of water. These reports testify to the Muslims' readiness to lay down their lives for the cause of God and to the determination of their faith in Him as One.

After all these exploits and campaigns, it was time for Muhammad to settle down in Madinah for a few months before Quraysh would trouble him again in fulfillment of Abu Sufyan's resolution to make annual battle with the Muslims. In the meantime, the Prophet had plenty to do to complete the organization of the nascent Islamic society and to order and structure its various elements on the basis of revelation, *i.e.,* of what may be safely deduced from revealed truths. Muhammad elaborated a complete system of rules for the guidance of man, state and society, which his companions canonized after his death and which still stands viable for all ages.

17

The Prophet's Wives

The Zaynab Affair and the Orientalists

In the interval in which the events of the last two chapters took place, Muhammad married Zaynab, daughter of Khuzaymah, Umm Salamah daughter of Umayyah ibn al Mughirah, and Zaynab, daughter of Jahsh, after she had been divorced by Zayd ibn Harithah. The last named is the same Zayd who was adopted by Muhammad and set free after he was bought by Yasar for Khadijah. It is here that the Orientalists offer their highest condemnation, in chorus with the Christian missionaries. Glowing with vindictiveness, they say,

"Muhammad who in Makkah called men to asceticism and contentment, to monotheism and abstinence from the pleasures of this life, has now become a man of lust whose appetite every woman could whet. He is not satisfied with three women whom he has so far taken into marriage but has now taken the three additional wives just mentioned. Indeed, he was to marry three more yet in addition to Rayhanah. Nor was he to be satisfied by marrying the widow. He fell in love with Zaynab, daughter of Jahsh, while she was the wife of Zayd ibn Harithah, his own client. Once, when he passed by the house of Zayd in the latter's absence, he was met by Zaynab wearing clothes which exposed her beauty. Muhammad's heart was inflamed. It is reported that

275

when his eyes fell upon her, he exclaimed, 'Praise be to God who changes the hearts of men!' and that he repeated this expression at the time of his departure from her home. Zaynab heard him say this and noticed desire in his eye. Proudly, she reported what happened to her husband. Zayd immediately went to see the Prophet and offered to divorce his wife. Muhammad answered, 'Hold to your wife and fear God.' Thereafter, Zaynab was no longer a docile wife and Zayd had to divorce her. Muhammad did not marry her immediately despite his love for her. He waited until an express revelation came which permitted him to do so. Addressing Muhammad, God said: 'You said to Zayd, to whom God gave of His bounty and you gave of yours, "Hold fast to your wife and fear God." Would you hide, O Muhammad, that which God was going to bring to light? Would you fear the gossip of the people? Isn't God more worthy of being feared? After a term of married life with her husband, We permitted you to marry her so that it may hence be legitimate and morally blameless for a believer to marry the wife of his adopted son provided that wife had already been divorced. That is God's commandment which must be fulfilled.'[1] Thereupon, Muhammad married this woman and satisfied his desire and lust. Now, what kind of Prophet is this? How could he permit himself that which he forbade to others? How can he violate the law which he himself had said had come to him from heaven? How would he amass this harem which calls to mind the behavior of the old lustful and pleasure seeking kings rather than the righteous reforming prophets? How could such a prophet fall prey to lust and desire in the case of Zaynab that he would force his adopted son to divorce her only so that he might marry her thereafter? That was definitely taboo in pre-Islamic Arabia, and the Prophet of Islam lifted this taboo in order to satisfy his own lust and fulfill his own desire."

Thus appears the Western Orientalists' claim.

The Orientalists' Portrait of Zaynab

Western Orientalists and missionaries pause in order to give full vent to their resentment and imagination. In this chapter of Muhammad's biography, some of them take inordinate pain to paint a sensual portrait of

Zaynab. They relate that when Muhammad saw her, she was half-naked, that her fine black hair was covering half her body, and that every curve of her body was full of desire and passion. Others relate that when Muhammad opened the door of the house of Zayd the breeze played with the curtains of the room of Zaynab, thus permitting Muhammad to catch a glimpse of her stretched out on her mattress in a nightgown. They then tell their readers that this view of her stormed the heart of Muhammad who was extremely passionate in his love and desire for women. They relate that Muhammad had hidden his secret desire, though he could hardly bear to conceal it for long! This and many like pictures have been painted arduously by Orientalists and missionaries and may be read in the works of Muir, Dermenghem, Washington Irving, Lammens, and others. It cannot be denied that these stories are based upon reports in fanciful Muslim biographies and Hadith books. But these books are questionable. And it is extremely regrettable that our authors have used them without scrutiny. It is inexcusable that these scholars had built "Castles in Spain" regarding Muhammad's relations with women, castles which they thought were sufficiently justified by the fact that Muhammad married a plurality of wives, probably nine, or even more according to some versions.

Great Men and the Law

It is possible to refute all these claims with one argument. If supposed to be true, they constitute no flaw in the prophethood of Muhammad, in his own greatness or that of his message. The rules which are law to the people at large do not apply to the great. *A fortiori*, they have no application on prophets, the messengers of God. Did not Moses — May God's peace be upon him — kill the gentile whom he noticed was fighting with one of his compatriots? That was murder, forbidden by God, and there was no war or hostility to justify it. It was a clear violation of the law. Nonetheless, this did not impair Moses' prophethood, his greatness, or his status with God. The case of Jesus violates the law even more flagrantly than either Moses or Muhammad or for that matter any other prophet. For his case is not one of a unique exemplification of power or desire but a persistent violation of natural law from birth to death. First, the spirit of God appeared to Mary, his mother, in the likeness of a handsome man to give her a fair son. Second, she herself was surprised and said, "How can I have a son when no man ever touched me and I have never lost my chastity?" The messenger replied that God wished her son to be a sign to mankind.

Thirdly, when she gave birth to her son she said: "I wish I was dead, given to oblivion, and lost before this." Her son, however, called unto her, "Do not grieve, for God has made rivers to issue under your feet." Fourthly, when she brought her son to her people, and they accused her of adultery, Jesus answered them from the cradle: "I am the servant of God. . . etc." However the Jews may have denied the facts of this story, and however they may have attributed Jesus' paternity to Joseph, the carpenter — a claim believed today to be true by such rationalists as Renan — the greatness and prophethood of Jesus constitute a miracle, and a miracle is precisely a breech of natural law, the cosmic pattern, and the rules of creation. It is surprising that Christians and missionaries call men to believe such breaches of the cosmic pattern in the case of Jesus and yet blame Muhammad for much less. Muhammad's violation was not one of a cosmic law but one of a social law, which is permissible to every great man. Such status above the social laws of the community is usually accorded to all kings and heads of states. Constitutional law usually grants to such persons immunity which shields them from the pursuing hand of the law.

Incoherence of the Orientalists' Account

It is possible for us to give such an answer and to thereby refute all these Orientalists' claims, the arguments of the missionaries and of those who follow in their tracks. But if we did so we would be doing a great injustice to history itself as well as to the true greatness of Muhammad and the magnanimity of his message. For the fact is that Muhammad was not a man given to passion and desire as the Orientalists and missionaries have pictured him. He did not marry his wives for lust, desire, or love. If some Muslim writers in certain periods of history have allowed themselves to attribute such things to the Prophet and thereby to present with good intent an argument to the enemies of Islam, that is because their conservatism caused them to adopt a materialistic view of things. In such a manner they pictured Muhammad as superlative in everything including the lusts of this world. But the picture they drew was clearly false. The history of Muhammad denies it outright, and the logic of Muhammad's life is utterly inconsistent with it.

As Husband of Khadijah

Muhammad married Khadijah when he was twenty-three years old, i.e. at the height of his youth, the fullness of manhood, and the apex of power and handsomeness. He remained true and loyal to Khadijah for twenty-eight years until he was over fifty years old. This had been the case at a time when polygamy was normal among the Arabs. Moreover, since no male offspring of Khadijah survived, Muhammad had all necessary justification to marry another woman considering that newborn daughters were customarily buried alive and male offspring alone were regarded as rightful heirs. Before Muhammad became a prophet he had lived seventeen years of married life, and thereafter eleven more years without ever thinking of marriage with any other woman. Throughout his married life with Khadijah as well as during his celibate years, Muhammad was never known to be one susceptible to womanly attractions at a time when women wore no veils and showed their beauty and ornaments publicly — the evidence of which is implicit in Islam's prohibition of the same later on. It is unnatural, therefore, now that Muhammad had passed the fifty year mark, for him to suffer such a transformation as would make him fall suddenly in love with Zaynab, daughter of Jahsh, while he was already married to five other women, among whom was 'A'ishah whom he loved dearly and constantly. It is therefore unnatural that such a man would have given Zaynab, daughter of Jahsh, any thought at all, and certainly unlikely that she had occupied his thought night and day, as the Orientalists claim. It is certainly unnatural that Muhammad, now past fifty years old, would collect in the short span of five years more than seven wives, and two years later to increase the number to nine simply on account of sexual desire. Such a claim, first made by Muslim authors and then uncritically imitated by the Western Orientalists, is absurd. It is inconsistent with the natural predilection of the commonplace, not to speak of the great, whose work has transformed the world, altered the course of history, and still plays a role in retransforming the world and reorienting historical development toward radically new goals. This claim is irrational and does not correspond with the facts. It is contrary to nature to assume that the same man who caused Khadijah to bear all her children before he reached fifty, and caused Mariyah to conceive Ibrahim while he was sixty, could cause none of his numerous wives to bear any children when they were all still young enough and capable of doing so. Nor were they barren, since each of them had borne children before her marriage to Muhammad. This fact, true of each of the nine women, would defy explanation if the

Orientalist and missionary claim is true. We must add to this consideration the fact that Muhammad, a man like other men, was certainly anxious to obtain a male offspring. His prophetic status had made him father
to all Muslims at once from a purely spiritual point of view. But that does
not deny the human urge to fatherhood.

Muhammad's Marriage to Sawdah

History and the logic of its events furnish an unquestionable refutation of the Orientalist and missionary claim regarding the Prophet's wives.
As we have seen earlier, Muhammad did not share his bed with any other
woman besides Khadijah for twenty-eight years. When she finally passed
away, he married Sawdah, daughter of Zam'ah, widow of Sakran ibn 'Amr
ibn 'Abd Shams. No one ever described Sawdah as a beautiful woman, and
no one has ever reported that she possessed any wealth or social position
which might have given a material reason for anyone to marry her. Rather,
Sawdah was a wife of one of the early converts of Islam who suffered
much harm for the sake of the faith and who migrated to Abyssinia following the instructions of the Prophet in order to find a measure of safety. Sawdah had embraced Islam with her husband and migrated with him.
She suffered as he did and bore Makkan oppression as patiently as her
husband did. If Muhammad married her thereafter in order to provide for
her and to raise her position to that of a "Mother of Believers,"[2] he certainly did a most worthy and appreciable deed.

'A'ishah and Hafsah were daughters of his two viziers, Abu Bakr and
'Umar, respectively. It was this relation of their fathers to Muhammad
which caused the latter to cement his relationship with them by blood.
That is why he married their two daughters; that is why he gave in marriage his two daughters to 'Uthman and 'Ali. If it is true that Muhammad
did in fact love 'A'ishah, it must have been a love which arose after marriage, surely neither before nor at the time of marriage. He had asked her
hand from her father while she was only nine years old, and did not marry
her until two years later. It is contrary to logic to claim that he could have
fallen in love with her while she was at this tender age. Further evidence
on this point is the report of 'Umar that Muhammad's marriage to his
daughter was not based on love. His report ran as follows: "In pre-Islamic
times, we did not attach any importance to women; but we changed radically after God revealed what He did and assigned to them the rights He
did. Once, my wife tried to change my mind about something and sug-

gested that I do otherwise. When I asked her to let my business alone, she answered, 'How strange of you, O Son of al Khattab ! You forbid me to criticize you while your daughter is permitted to criticize the Prophet of God himself — May God's peace and blessing be upon him — and to do so so well that he would spend the whole day angry.' When I heard this I immediately went to my daughter Hafsah and inquired whether this was true. Hafsah confirmed her mother's report. I was stupefied. I warned her that God's punishment as well as the wrath of the Prophet would fall upon her if she persisted. I told her that she should not count either on her beauty or on the Prophet's love for her, for I knew too well that the Prophet of God did not love her and that were it not for my sake, he would have even divorced her." There is then ample evidence that Muhammad did not marry either 'A'ishah or Hafsah out of any love or desire but in order to consolidate the ties of mutual brotherhood within the new Islamic community, and especially between himself and his two viziers. There is equally clear evidence that the Prophet married Sawdah in order to teach the Muslim fighters that should they fall martyrs in the cause of God, they would not leave their women and children without support but that the community would take care of them.

Another conclusive proof of this sense of social concern is the case of Muhammad's marriages to Zaynab, daughter of Khuzaymah, and Umm Salamah. The former was the wife of 'Ubaydah ibn al Harith ibn al Muttalib who fell at the Battle of Badr. Surely she was not beautiful, but she was so kind and gentle that she acquired the nickname of "mother of the destitute." She was past her prime in age and lived only one or two years after her marriage to Muhammad. Besides Khadijah she was the only wife of the Prophet who died before him. As for Umm Salamah, she was the wife of Abu Salamah for whom she bore many children. It has already been mentioned that Abu Salamah was wounded at Uhud, that he seemed to be recovering from his wound when the Prophet assigned to him the duty of fighting Banu Asad whom he defeated and whose wealth he seized. It was during the second campaign of Abu Salamah that his wound reopened, and it caused his death a few days later. The Prophet visited him in his last days and remained constantly by his bedside praying for him until he died. Four months after his death, when the Prophet asked the hand of Umm Salamah, she apologized by using the large number of her children and her old age as an excuse. But the Prophet insisted until she accepted and he assumed the duty of caring for and bringing up her offspring. Would then the missionaries and the Western Orientalists

claim that Umm Salamah was a woman of rare beauty and that this is why
Muhammad had married her? If Muhammad was indeed looking for
beauty, there were scores of virgin daughters of both Muhajirun and Ansar
far surpassing his women in beauty, in youth, in position and wealth, in
vitality, for him to choose from and to take in marriage. He did not have
to choose those women who would bring to him large liabilities of mouths
to feed and old people to take care of. The fact is that Muhammad married Umm Salamah because of this noble motivation of his, the same reason for which he married Zaynab, daughter of Khuzaymah. It was this
same reason which caused the Muslims to love their Prophet all the more
and honor him as the Prophet of God and to see in him a father to the
destitute and the deprived and the weak and the poor as well as to everyone who had lost his father as a martyr in the cause of God.

Historical Analysis and Its Results

What does true historical analysis conclude from all this? It concludes
that Muhammad stood for monogamy and counseled its observance. This
is the substance of the example of his married life with Khadijah, as well
as that of the Qur'anic commandments,

$$\text{فَانكِحُوا مَا طَابَ لَكُم مِّنَ النِّسَاءِ مَثْنَى وَثُلَاثَ وَرُبَاعَ فَإِنْ خِفْتُمْ أَلَّا تَعْدِلُوا فَوَاحِدَةً أَوْ مَا مَلَكَتْ أَيْمَانُكُمْ}$$

"Marry such women as seem becoming to you, two, three, or four. But
if you fear that you may not be just, then marry only one, or your slaves"[3];
and,

$$\text{وَلَن تَسْتَطِيعُوا أَن تَعْدِلُوا بَيْنَ النِّسَاءِ وَلَوْ حَرَصْتُمْ فَلَا تَمِيلُوا كُلَّ الْمَيْلِ فَتَذَرُوهَا كَالْمُعَلَّقَةِ}$$

"You will not be able to do justice to more than one wife however
much you may try. And if you must marry another wife, do not incline
excessively to one and leave the other like a thing suspended."[4]

These verses were revealed toward the end of the eighth year of the Hijrah after the Prophet had married all his wives. The purpose of these verses is to limit the number of wives to four whereas, until their revelation, there was no limit to the number of wives a Muslim could marry. This historical fact repudiates the claim that Muhammad has allowed himself that which he had forbidden to the people. Furthermore, these verses were revealed in order to stress the superiority of monogamy over polygamy. The Qur'an commanded the limiting of one's self to one wife out of fear of the possibility of injustice and conviction that justice to more than one wife is not within the limits of men's capability. The revelation, however, realized that in the exceptional circumstances of a people, it is quite possible that there might be a need for more than one wife; but it has limited polygamy to four and conditioned its practice to capacity for fairness and justice on the part of the husband. Muhammad called the Muslims to realize these values by exemplifying them in his own life in a period in which Muslims made battle and fell as martyrs on every occasion. But could anyone in truth decide once and for all that monogamy is the absolute commandment in all conditions and circumstances? What would be the effect of such a law when wars and epidemics and revolution cut down thousands and millions of men in a brief while? Would then monogamy still be better than polygamy when restricted to the exceptional circumstances? Can the people of Europe in this age following World War I assert categorically that monogamy is the law of life of their own citizens, even if they may say it is the law in the books? Are not the social and economic disturbances which the world witnessed in Europe following the War the direct result of this imbalance between the two sexes, of their inability to bring about harmony and prosperity in their marital relations, and hence of their insistence to seek that harmony outside the marriage bond? It is not my intention to decide the issue here. But I leave the matter to the reader to ponder. I do wish to repeat, however, that the happiness of the family and that of the community can best be served by the limitation which monogamy imposes. That is so, however, if and only if the life of the community itself is normal.

The Story of Zaynab, Daughter of Jahsh

As for the story of Zaynab, daughter of Jahsh, the chroniclers, Orientalists, and missionaries have mixed it with such products of vivid imagination that they have made of it a story of love and passion. Critical history, on the other hand, concludes that it is one of the truly great facets of Muhammad's personality. It proves beyond question that Muhammad was the perfect example of faith and conviction, for it is an instantiation of the principle that the faith of man is complete only when he truly loves for his brother that which he loves for himself. Muhammad had made himself always the exemplar of his own legislation, especially of such laws as were intended to replace the tradition and customs of pre-Islamic Arabia. He was the exemplar of the new system which God revealed through him as a mercy and guidance to mankind. For a repudiation of the whole story of Zaynab as reported by these chroniclers or Orientalists and missionaries, it is sufficient to realize that the said woman was the daughter of Umaymah and grand-daughter of 'Abd al Muttalib the uncle of the Prophet of God — May God's peace and blessing be upon him. It is sufficient to remember that this woman was brought up in sight of Muhammad and under his care, and on this account was regarded by him as a daughter or a young sister; that he knew too well whether she was beautiful or not before she ever married Zayd; that he saw her and followed her growth from childhood to maturity and youth; and that it was he who asked her hand for Zayd, his adopted son. Once the reader knows these historical data, then all the fictitious elements and tales spun about him, namely, that he passed by her house in the absence of her husband and was struck by her beauty; that he opened the door of her house and, as the breezes played with the curtains of her room, he saw her stretched in her nightgown like a real "Madame Recamier," that his heart was so struck by her beauty that he instantly forgot Sawdah, 'A'ishah, Hafsah, Zaynab, daughter of Khuzaymah and Umm Salamah, his wives — not to mention the memory of Khadijah of whom 'A'ishah used to say that she had never felt jealous of any woman except Khadijah on account of the memory he kept of her — all these tales must dissolve. If any grain of them was true, Muhammad would have taken her in marriage himself at first, rather than give her in marriage to Zayd. This historical relationship between Zaynab and Muhammad rules out as utterly fictitious and groundless all the stories which have been attributed to Zaynab's attractiveness.

History, however, has more yet to tell. It proves that Muhammad asked for the hand of his own cousin Zaynab for his adopted son Zayd. Her brother, 'Abdullah ibn Jahsh, refused to let his sister, the Hashimi and Qurayshi noble girl that she was, and the first cousin of the Prophet in addition, become the wife of a slave whom Khadijah had bought and whom Muhammad had set free. Such a union was regarded by him as well as by the Arabs in general as a thing of great shame. For the daughters of the aristocracy to marry their slaves, even though their slaves had become free, was plainly unthinkable. But Muhammad sought to wipe out these racial and class distinctions between men. He sought to educate the whole world to the truth that no Arab is superior to any non-Arab unless it be in virtue and piety. For it was God who said,

$$\text{اِنَّ اَكْرَمَكُمْ عِنْدَاللهِ اَتْقَكُمْ}$$

"Highest in God's view is the most virtuous."[5]

Muhammad did not choose to force this noble principle upon a woman outside his own tribe and clan. Let it then be Zaynab, he thought, his very cousin, that will carry the first burden of this flagrant violation of Arabian custom. Let her be the destroyer of these pagan traditions. Let her cause herself, and therewith the whole tribe and religion of Muhammad, to endure all the criticisms that such an act would engender. And let Zayd, his own adopted son, be the person of lesser lineage to marry the noble Makkan aristocrat. On the other hand, Arab custom and tradition demanded that the adopted son inherit from his adopted father, like the latter's legitimate children. And since this custom too was the object of Muhammad's attack, his choice of Zayd as the spearpoint of the first reform, would actually make of him — if he were prepared to give up the inheritance to which Arabian custom gave him title — the spearhead of another Islamic legislation prohibiting inheritance to any but the blood heirs and relatives of the deceased. Thus, Muhammad insisted that Zaynab agree to marry Zayd and that her brother 'Abdullah ibn Jahsh accept Zayd as a brother-in-law. Indeed, this furnished the occasion for the revelation that "No believer, whether man or woman, has freedom to choose otherwise than as God and His Prophet have resolved in any given case. To do so is to disobey God and His Prophet, to err and fall into manifest misguidance."[6]

Once the foregoing verse was revealed, neither 'Abdullah nor his sister Zaynab had any alternative but to acquiesce in the Prophet's order. The Prophet helped Zayd furnish a dowry for his bride-to-be and the marriage took place. After the wedding, the husband found in his wife a woman very hard to manage and to live with. Her pride continued to know no bounds. Indeed, she continued to deride Zayd, to boast of her lineage in his presence and to look down on him because of his having once been a slave. Zayd complained about her to the Prophet more than once and even consulted with him in the matter of divorcing her. All along, the Prophet would counsel him in these terms: "Hold fast to your wife and fear God." Zayd's home life, however, did not improve and, unable to bear her false pride any longer, Zayd divorced her.

Adoption in Islam

The All-Wise Legislator willed to undo the Arab practice of adopting children and passing onto them the adopter's genealogy and name, his investment of them with all the rights of the legitimate son including that of inheritance and the prohibition of marriage on grounds of consanguinity. The divine Legislator willed to give the adopted son only the right of a client and co-religionist. In this sense, the verse was revealed that: "God did not make your adopted son as your own sons. To declare them so is your empty claim. God's word is righteous and constitutes the true guidance."[7] It follows from this revelation that the adopter may marry the ex-wife of his adopted son and vice-versa. But how is such provision to be implemented? Who, among the Arabs, could implement this legislation and thereby openly repudiate the ancient traditions? Even Muhammad himself, despite his tremendous willpower and profound understanding of the wisdom implicit in the divine command, found himself disinclined to implement this judgment by marrying Zaynab after Zayd had divorced her. Indeed, the criticisms of the commonplace and the vituperations with which he was indicted in the public eye for breaking down such well established custom did, for a time, influence Muhammad's judgment and affected his decision. It was at this stage that the following divine criticism was addressed to Muhammad: "Would you hide, O Muhammad, within yourself that which God was going to bring to light anyway? Would you fear the gossip of the people? Isn't God more worthy of being feared ?"[8] The truth is, however, that Muhammad was the exemplar of obedience to God; his life was the implementation of that which he was entrusted to convey to mankind. The outcome, therefore, was that Muhammad would not give any weight at all to the gossip of the people if he were to marry the ex-wife of his adopted son, since the fear of social condemnation is nothing comparable to that of

condemnation by God, of disobedience to divine commandment. Thus, Muhammad married Zaynab in order to provide a good example of what the All-Wise Legislator was seeking to establish by way of rights and privileges for adoption. In this regard, God said: "After a term of married life with her husband, We permitted you to marry her so that it may hence be legitimate and morally blameless for a believer to marry the wife of his adopted son provided that wife has already been divorced. That is God's commandment which must be fulfilled."[9]

Return to the Orientalists' Views

Such is the evidence critical history furnishes in the case of Zaynab, daughter of Jahsh, and of her marriage to Muhammad. She was his first cousin whom he knew well long before Zayd ever married her. It was he who asked for her hand on Zayd's behalf. Muhammad often saw Zaynab even after her marriage to Zayd, for the veil was not then known. It was also the custom, on account of Zaynab's blood relation to Muhammad and Zayd's relation as adopted son, that the couple would refer to the Prophet any complaint each may have against the other. As Zayd was not happy in his marriage with her, it was natural that both of them would seek advice and judgment in their domestic disputes. All these provisions of the divine law have been revealed, and they have been instanced in the case of Zayd and Zaynab's marriage and divorce, and of Zaynab's later marriage to Muhammad. These provisions had one purpose, namely the raising of the manumitted slave to the full status of freedom, and the repudiation of all the rights of masters, protectors, and adoptive parents in clear and unequivocal terms. There is hence no ground for these fictitious stories woven by Orientalists and missionaries and repeated by Muir, Irving, Sprenger, Weil, Dermenghem, Lammens and other biographers of Muhammad. Their so-called scholarship is a scandalous piece of missionarizing. It is a masquerade of science. Their traditional antagonism to Islam, going back to the Crusades, has simply taken possession of their conscience, dictating and determining all that they write on the subject. It is this fundamental prejudice which vitiates their writing. Their "history" is a crime against history itself, for they choose to see, to note, and to report only the most scurrilous and fictitious reports to satisfy this end. Even if, though impossible, their claims were true, we would still refute them with the simple argument that the great stand above the law; that Moses, Jesus, Jonah, and others before Muhammad have likewise risen above the laws of nature as well as of society, some in their birth, others in their lives. None of this has affected their greatness. Muhammad, moreover, legislated for man and society by means of his Lord's revelation. He executed those laws equally by his Lord's command. His life constitutes the highest ideal, the perfect example, and the concrete instance of his Lord's command. Would those missionaries have Muhammad divorce his wives in order not to exceed the limit of four prescribed by Islamic law after Muhammad? Wouldn't they then subject him to more severe criticism? But Muhammad's treatment of his wives was just and noble. We have seen in the above-mentioned tradition of 'Umar ibn al Khattab some evidence thereto, and we shall see more yet in the sequel. Evidently, Muhammad not only honored woman more than did any other man, but he raised her to the status which truly belongs to her — an accomplishment of which Muhammad alone has so far been capable.

18

The Campaigns of al Khandaq and Banu Qurayzah

Muhammad's Caution and Arab Instinct

After the forced evacuation of Banu al Nadir from Madinah, and the events of the "second Badr," the campaigns of Ghatafan and Dawmat al Jandal, it was high time the Muslims felt a measure of security within their city. Hence, they applied themselves to the task of organizing their own internal affairs. Their constant preoccupation with security and war had largely prevented their engagement in agriculture or commerce. Nonetheless, their state of privation and need was largely ameliorated by the booty they acquired through these campaigns. Though Muhammad felt relatively secure, he was always cautious lest the enemy strike without notice. He therefore had to maintain eyes, ears, and channels of communication throughout the Arabian Peninsula in order to learn of all the news of the tribes so that the Muslims might have time to prepare for defense in case of emergency. It is easy for us to appreciate the need for all these precautions after hearing of the treacherous attacks of Quraysh and other tribes against the Muslims. The Arabian Peninsula of those days was covered with autonomous little republics, each of which extended over the territory inhabited or used by its various clans, and depended for its security on an intricate system of inter-tribal customs, pacts, and traditions, which we do not usually expect to find in the organizations of states in modern times. Since Muhammad himself was an Arab and understood the will to retaliate innate in Arab character, he took extreme care to guard the Muslim community from all sides. Quraysh, the Jews of Banu Qaynuqa' and Banu al Nadir, the tribes of Ghatafan and Hudhayl as well as those living in the vicinity of al Sham, were all lying in wait for Muhammad and his companions. Each one of these groups awaited the opportunity to avenge itself on this man who had divided the Arabs in their religion, and, though emigrating from Makkah devoid of power or ally, had acquired, within the last five years by virtue of his great faith, such prestige and power as to make him a real threat to the strongest cities and tribes of Arabia.

Jewish Enmity

The Jews were perhaps the most cognizant of Muhammad's teachings and the most apprehensive of the success of his message. They knew too well what consequences to them would be implied in the victory of Islam. In Arabia, having distinguished themselves through their monotheistic teachings, they competed with the Christians and were hoping soon to wrest all power from them throughout Arabia. They were right in their expectation inasmuch as the Semitic soul was by nature more inclined toward monotheism than to Christian trinitarianism. As if to spoil that promise and dash those hopes, Muhammad, the pure Arab and pure Semite, was calling men to the monotheistic truth with strong and emphatic words which penetrate to the nethermost depths of consciousness. His revelation overwhelmed and intoxicated the soul. It caused man to transcend himself. Furthermore, Muhammad achieved such political and worldly power that he had forced the evacuation of Banu Qaynuqa' from Madinah, and the Banu al Nadir from their lands. Would they then leave him alone and return to their previous abodes in al Sham and in the promised land of Jerusalem, or would they confront him here in Arabia by rallying the Arab tribes to seek revenge from him?

Jewish Preference of Paganism to Islam

It was the latter idea that finally gripped Banu al Nadir. In pursuit of it, their leaders Huyayy ibn Akhtab, Sallam ibn Abu al Huqayq, Kinanah ibn al Huqayq, together with Hawdhah ibn Qays and Abu 'Ammar, both of the tribe of Banu Wa'il, went to Makkah for consultation with the Quraysh leaders. When Huyayy was asked about his tribe, he told the Quraysh that he had left them between Khaybar and Madinah awaiting the arrival of the Makkans that they might join them in battle against Muhammad and his companions. When the Makkans inquired about Banu Qurayzah, he answered that they had remained within Madinah in order to plot against Muhammad and to spring against his men from behind once the Makkans launched their attack. The Quraysh hesitated. They knew only too well that in the last analysis, there was no difference between them and Muhammad except in this matter of his new faith; and even in it, they were not quite certain that Muhammad was entirely wrong since his worldly power had been on the increase every day. The Quraysh therefore asked the Jews to tell them, since they were the first People of the Book and held the keys of knowledge in the matters in which the Quraysh disagreed with Muhammad, whether or not Muhammad's religion was better than Makkan religion. The Jews answered by giving preference to Makkan religion over Islam and to Makkan rights over Muhammad's. It was to this that the Qur'an referred when it said, "Would you consider those who were given part of the scripture, that they believe in evil and injustice and commend to the unbelievers their own unbelief as guidance superior to the true faith of those who believed? Such men are accursed of God. And whosoever God curses, will never prevail. Nor will anyone ever come to his rescue."[1] This attitude of the Jews toward Quraysh and their favoring of the latter's paganism over the monotheism of Muhammad was the subject of a severe rebuke by Dr. Israel Wolfenson, who wrote in his *The Jews in Arabia:* "It was the duty of the Jews not to allow themselves to get involved in such a scandalous mistake. They should have never declared to the leaders of Quraysh that the worship of idols was better than Islamic monotheism even if this were to imply frustration of their requests. The Jews, who have for centuries raised the banner of monotheism in the world among the pagan nations, who have remained true to the monotheistic traditions of the fathers, and who have suffered throughout history the greatest misfortunes, murders, and persecutions for the sake of their faith in the One God should, in loyalty to this tradition, have sacrificed every interest — nay their very lives — to bring about the downfall of paganism. Furthermore, by allying themselves with the pagans they were in fact fighting themselves and contradicting the teachings of the Torah which commands them to avoid, repudiate — indeed to fight — the pagans."

The Jews' Rallying of the Arab Tribes

This brazen self-contradiction, this favoring of paganism over monotheism and the encouragement of pagan forces to rise against the monotheistic forces — all this was not enough for Huyayy ibn Akhtab and the Jewish leaders who accompanied him on his trip to Makkah. After securing a definite date from the Makkans for the attack against Muhammad, the same leaders went to the Ghatafan clan of Qays Ghaylan, to the tribes of Banu Murrah, Banu Fazarah, Ashja', Sulaym, Banu Sa'd, Asad, and all those who had fought with the Muslims to instigate a general mobilization on the side of Quraysh for a revengeful war on Muhammad. In order to placate these tribes, the Jews commended and praised their pagan practices and prophesied that victory would certainly belong to paganism. All these parties which the Jews had rallied against Muhammad marched against Madinah. The Quraysh sent an expeditionary force of four thousand infantrymen, a cavalry of three hundred, and a camel corps of one thousand five hundred. This huge army was led by Abu Sufyan in person. The flag of Makkah and, hence, the leadership of battle was assigned to 'Uthman ibn Talhah, whose father had been killed carrying that same flag in the Battle of Uhud. The Banu Fazarah tribe sent a large number of infantrymen and a camel corps of one thousand under the leadership of 'Uyaynah ibn Hisn ibn Hudhayfah. The tribes of Ashja' and Murrah supplied four hundred soldiers each, under the leadership of al Harith ibn 'Awf and Mis'ar ibn Rukhaylah respectively. Sulaym, the tribe which engaged the Muslims at the battle of the well of Ma'unah, sent seven hundred soldiers. To this tremendous number, the tribes of Banu Sa'd and Banu Asad added more soldiers and more cavalry until the total number reached ten thousand or more. This whole army moved in the direction of Madinah under the general leadership of Abu Sufyan. After they had reached the outskirts of Madinah and encamped, the leadership of the army as a whole really revolved among the leaders of the various tribes.

The Muslims' Panic

When news of this tremendous mobilization reached Muhammad and the Muslims in Madinah, it struck them all with panic. The mobilization of the whole of Arabia against them instilled fear in their hearts as they faced the prospect of being not only defeated but wiped out. The gravity of the situation was evident in the fact that the army the Arab tribes had now raised surpassed in number and equipment anything the Peninsula had ever seen before. If the Quraysh had won a victory over the Muslims at Uhud singlehanded, what was likely to be the outcome of a battle in which the enemy's force was many times greater in number and equipment? What would they do against such an overwhelming preponderance of men, horses, camels, arms, and ammunitions? Obviously, there was no defense open to them except self-fortification within the walls of Yathrib, the invincible city, as 'Abdullah ibn Ubayy had previously described it. But would such fortification stand in face of such overwhelming power? Salman al Farisi, who knew far more of the techniques of warfare than was common in the Peninsula, advised the digging of a dry moat around Madinah and the fortification of its buildings within. The Muslims hurried to implement this counsel. The moat was dug and the Prophet — May God's peace and blessing be upon him — worked with his hands alongside his companions lifting the dirt, encouraging the Muslim workers, and exhorting everyone to multiply his effort. All the Muslims picked up their digging utensils, their picks and shovels, and borrowed more tools from the Qurayzah Jews who remained true to their covenant with Muhammad. With tremendous effort and exertion, the whole moat was dug in six days. At the same time, the walls of the buildings on the perimeter of the city facing the enemy were also reinforced, their inhabitants were evacuated and the buildings were reserved for military use. The women and children were removed to the interior and placed within fortified walls. Rocks were gathered and placed on the inner side of the moat for use as possible projectiles against the enemy if the need arose.

Quraysh in Front of the Dry Moat

The Quraysh and their allies arrived at Uhud hoping to meet the Muslim forces there. Disappointed in this, they proceeded to Madinah where, to their surprise, they found an impassable ditch surrounding the whole city. They never expected this kind of defense, and their anger and resentment became so strong that they accused the Muslims of cowardice for taking refuge behind such an unusual trick of war. Their army encamped in the plain called Rumah, and the forces of Ghatafan and its allies encamped in the plain called Dhanab Naqama. Muhammad amassed three thousand Muslims on the side of Sal' mountain in

Madinah. Only the ditch separated him from the enemy. There the Muslim army built a number of tents to prepare itself for the long siege, and Muhammad had his own red tent erected for his use. The Quraysh and the Arab tribes realized the impossibility of crossing the moat and were, therefore, forced to restrict their military activity to the exchange of javelins for a number of days.

Soon, Abu Sufyan and his colleagues became convinced that they were going to have to lay siege to Yathrib for a very long time before they could storm it. The season was winter, the cold unbearable, and wind and storm continually threatened heavy rain. It was possible for the people of Makkah and Ghatafan to protect themselves from the storm only if they were in the shelter of their own cities. But here, the tents which they had put up before Yathrib provided little or no protection. They had joined the expedition in search of easy victory, expecting the whole affair to last a day or two, as did the Battle of Uhud. They expected to return quickly home, there to celebrate with songs of victory while dividing all kinds of wealth and booty. How could the army of Ghatafan return empty handed when the sole reason for its participating in this war was the Jewish promise that in case of victory a whole year's crop of the orchards of Khaybar would be theirs as a free gift? Now, they realized that victory was not going to be easy, for it was going to cost at least the trouble of spending the whole wintry season, and this alone counterbalanced all the fruits and crops of the orchards. As for Quraysh, they were eager to avenge themselves for the previous defeats. But it was becoming amply clear that victory was impossible as long as Muhammad controlled the other side of the ditch while the Banu Qurayzah supplied Madinah with enough food provisions to enable them to hold to their fortress for months and even years. No wonder, then, that some of the allies of Makkah began to think of return-ing home. Their leaders realized, however, that the remobilization of such an overwhelming force would not be easy to accomplish once they were demobilized and allowed to disperse. Led by Huyayy ibn Akhtab, the Jews had been capable of mobilizing these tribes as they sought to avenge themselves on Muhammad for all the injuries he had inflicted upon them as well as upon the Banu Qaynuqa'. If this opportunity were to escape, would it ever return again? If Muhammad were to gain an easy victory by the withdrawal of the Makkans and their allies, would he then not turn against the Jews?

Jewish Fear of Makkan Withdrawal

Huyayy ibn Akhtab weighed all these considerations. He realized that there was no escape from using the very last trump card he had. He told his allies that he would convince the Banu Qurayzah to violate their covenant with the Muslims in order to join his camp, and that Muslim supplies would then be cut off and a road to the interior of Yathrib would lie open. Quraysh and Ghatafan were quite pleased with the news. Pursuing this scheme, Huyayy went to the quarter of Banu Qurayzah and asked to see Ka'b ibn Asad, their leader, whose door was slammed shut in his face. Apparently, Banu Qurayzah knew too well that treason might bring some advantages in case of Muslim defeat but that it would provide cause for extermination in case of Muslim victory. Huyayy, however, insistently kept knocking at the door until the gate was opened and he was let in. He asked Ka'b to listen to his warning that he had come with the greatest army ever assembled in Arabia, the armies of Quraysh, Ghatafan, and all their leaders and noblemen. He pleaded that all these allies and leaders had pledged not to leave the place until Muhammad and his companions were utterly destroyed. Ka'b hesitated, remembering Muhammad's loyalty to his covenant. He feared the evil consequences a sad turn of events might bring. Huyayy determinedly continued to reiterate the sufferings which the Jews had borne at the hand of Muhammad and which they would have to bear in case the war did not succeed. At last Ka'b weakened and began to lend his ear. Huyayy described the forces of the Makkan allies, their equipment and number, and reasoned that only the ditch prevented the forces from assaulting the Muslims and finishing them off in a brief hour. To Ka'b's question as to what would be the fate of the Banu Qurayzah in case the Makkans and their allies were to withdraw, Huyayy answered that he and his party of Jews would then join the Banu Qurayzah in their own quarter and share with them whatever fate might bring. At this, Ka'b's Jewish feeling stirred, moving him to yield to Huyayy, to accept his demands, to repudiate his covenant with Muhammad and the Muslims, and to join the ranks of their enemies.

The Prophet's Warning to Banu Qurayzah

The news of this betrayal by the Banu Qurayzah reached Muhammad and his companions and shook them greatly. Sa'd ibn Mu'adh, leader of al Aws, and Sa'd ibn 'Ubadah, leader of al Khazraj, together with 'Abdullah ibn Rawahah and Khawwat ibn Jubayr, were ordered by Muhammad to ascertain the news and report back to him. They were instructed not to announce their findings in case the news was true, for fear it might adversely affect the army's morale. The delegates came to the Jewish quarter and found the situation worse than it had been reported. They sought by argument to bring the Jews back to honoring their covenant with Muhammad. But Ka'b impertinently required that the Muslims return the Jews of Banu al Nadir back to their quarters in Madinah. Sa'd ibn Mu'adh, with whose tribe the Banu Qurayzah were closely allied, sought to convince Ka'b that the fate of Banu al Nadir or something worse might befall them in case they persisted in this treason. Giving full vent to their resentment, the Jews began to insult the Prophet — May God's peace be upon him. Ka'b said: "And who is this so-called Prophet of God? There is neither covenant nor peace between us and him." The conversation was quickly ended, and the Muslims left the scene hastily to prevent the possible outbreak of open fighting.

Morale of the Makkans and Their Allies

Muhammad's delegates returned and reported to him what they had seen and heard. Muslim leaders were gravely apprehensive. They feared that the side of Qurayzah would now open for the Makkans and their allies, that the latter would enter the city and rout them. Their fear was not imaginary but quite real. As was expected of them, Banu Qurayzah immediately cut off all supplies to the Muslims. On the Makkan side, there was rejoicing when Huyayy ibn Akhtab reported the treason of Banu Qurayzah, and their rallying to Quraysh and Ghatafan. The morale of the Makkan forces took a sharp rise as they began to prepare for the day of battle. The Banu Qurayzah had actually requested the Makkans, first, to wait ten days before invading Madinah so that they might prepare themselves; and second, to keep constant pressure upon the Muslims and thus prevent any Muslim attack upon them before their military preparations were complete. That was exactly what happened. The enemy divided itself into three main brigades. The first, led by Ibn al A'war al Sulami, was to assault the Muslims from across the valley. The second, led by 'Uyaynah ibn Hisn, was to attack from the flank. Finally, the third under the command of Abu Sufyan was to launch its attack across the ditch. It was with reference to this deployment of enemy forces that the Qur'an said

إِذْ جَآءُوكُم مِّن فَوْقِكُمْ وَمِنْ أَسْفَلَ مِنكُمْ وَإِذْ زَاغَتِ الْأَبْصَارُ وَبَلَغَتِ الْقُلُوبُ الْحَنَاجِرَ وَ
تَظُنُّونَ بِاللَّهِ الظُّنُونَا۠ ﴿١۰﴾ هُنَالِكَ ابْتُلِيَ الْمُؤْمِنُونَ وَزُلْزِلُوا زِلْزَالًا شَدِيدًا ﴿١١﴾ وَإِذْ يَقُولُ الْمُنَافِقُونَ
وَالَّذِينَ فِي قُلُوبِهِم مَّرَضٌ مَّا وَعَدَنَا اللَّهُ وَرَسُولُهُ إِلَّا غُرُورًا ﴿١٢﴾ وَإِذْ قَالَت طَّآئِفَةٌ مِّنْهُمْ
يَا أَهْلَ يَثْرِبَ لَا مُقَامَ لَكُمْ فَارْجِعُوا ۚ وَيَسْتَأْذِنُ فَرِيقٌ مِّنْهُمُ النَّبِيَّ يَقُولُونَ إِنَّ بُيُوتَنَا عَوْرَةٌ
وَمَا هِيَ بِعَوْرَةٍ ۖ إِن يُرِيدُونَ إِلَّا فِرَارًا ﴿١٣﴾

"When they attacked you from above and from below, when your eyes knew no more where to turn and your hearts were ready to give up and you entertained all sorts of thoughts about God, then the believers were truly shaken and faced disaster. Then did the false pretenders and the disheartened doubt that what God had promised them and His Prophet was all in vain. Then did a group of them counsel the people of Madinah against war and suggested withdrawal while another group sought the Prophet's permission to withdraw on the ground that their houses were exposed whereas their houses were neither exposed nor in danger, but the suppliants only sought to flee."2

It was only too human for the people of Yathrib to grumble with fear and panic. They were disappointed at this turn of events. Whereas Muhammad had promised them the wealth and treasures of Chosroes and Caesar, they now felt as afraid to venture outside the confines of their own city as did those who were disheartened at the prospects of the war. Did they not see death advancing upon them, shining in the brilliance of the swords which were being brandished by the Quraysh and Ghatafan tribesmen? Did they not have reason to be disheartened when their immediate neighbors, the Banu Qurayzah, threatened to attack them treacherously from within and to enable their enemies to infiltrate behind their lines? Would it not have been better for them, they pondered, to have utterly destroyed the Banu al Nadir rather than allow them to emigrate and take their possessions with them? Had the Muslims finished them then, Huyayy and his companions would not have now instigated this general Arab war. Certainly, this was a moment of great apprehension and danger. Surely this was a terrible and fateful day. Its disposal was in the hand of the Almighty alone.

Engagement of the Forces

The Makkans and their allies were encouraged and their morale was uplifted by the news of the new alliance. Some Quraysh horsemen, including 'Amr ibn 'Abd Wudd, 'Ikrimah ibn Abu Jahl, and Dirar ibn al Khattab sought to advance across the ditch. After finding a point where the ditch was narrow, they succeeded in entering it and took position on its inner side near Sal'. 'Ali ibn Abu Talib and other Muslims proceeded to meet them and to seal the breach through which they advanced. 'Amr ibn 'Abd Wudd challenged the Muslims to a duel. When 'Ali ibn Abu Talib answered his call, 'Amr replied: "Why, O Cousin! By God, I do not wish to kill you." 'Ali answered, "But I do." The duel started, and no sooner had it got under way than 'Ali killed 'Amr and the companions of the latter ran for their lives. They jumped over the ditch thinking only of the death which was following them. Nawfal ibn 'Abdullah ibn al Mughirah sought to jump over the ditch shortly after sunset on that same day. But the ditch was too wide and both horse and rider fell into it to their death. Abu Sufyan then demanded one hundred camels as bloodwit. The Prophet rejected the demand, however, and condemned Nawfal as an aggressor whose death was unworthy of bloodwit.

The Makkans and their allies now launched a tactical war of nerves against the Muslims in order to destroy their spirit. In order to frighten the Muslims, tribesmen of Banu Qurayzah began to descend from their fortifications and occupy the houses closer to the Muslim quarters. Safiyyah, daughter of 'Abd al Muttalib, was at Fari', the fortress of Hassan ibn Thabit, which was also full of women and children. A Jew approached their house and started to circumscribe it, inspecting its sides and fortifications. Safiyyah asked old Hassan to go out and kill the Jew because he was obviously reconnoitering the fort preliminary to storming it. At the time the Prophet and his companions were busy with other matters, and Safiyyah felt that the danger should be eliminated at once by herself, if not by Hassan. When Hassan declined to do as she requested, she seized a solid bar, went to the Jew, and beat him with it until she killed him. When she returned, she asked Hassan to go down and to dispossess the Jew of what he had. She apologized, saying that she would have finished the job herself had the victim not been a man. Nonetheless, Hassan refused to budge.

Dividing the Enemies against Themselves

While the people of Madinah suffered from fear and threat, Muhammad concentrated his thoughts on finding means of saving the community. Certainly no purpose would be fulfilled by forcing a confrontation with the enemy. The only alternative left for him was to attempt a ruse. He therefore sent a messenger to Ghatafan with the promise of one third of the total crop of Madinah if they withdrew and went home. Actually, Ghatafan was beginning to show signs of exhaustion and disapproval of this long siege for which they were not prepared. They had joined in this venture simply in order to appease Huyyay ibn Akhtab and his other Jewish companions. On the other hand, the Prophet sent Nu'aym ibn Mas'ud to the Banu Qurayzah, their old friend from pre-Islamic days whose conversion to Islam was not yet known to them, with the message that they should not join the ranks of the Makkans and fight with them unless and until the latter would give them a concrete guarantee that they would not be left alone to the mercy of Muhammad should the tide of battle turn against them. Nu'aym had been a very good friend of the Banu Qurayzah for a long time before his conversion, and they therefore had no reason to doubt him. He reminded them of this friendship and warned them that their rallying to the side of Quraysh and Ghatafan against Muhammad was liable to bring disaster, especially since neither Quraysh nor Ghatafan were likely to continue the siege for long. In that eventuality, nothing would prevent Muhammad from inflicting upon them great harm. This made such good sense that the Banu Qurayzah were dissuaded from their treacherous course. Nu'aym then proceeded to the Quraysh camp and there intimated to their leaders that the Banu Qurayzah had repented their violation of the covenant with Muhammad and that they were seeking to appease and befriend him anew by plotting to give up the noblemen of Quraysh that Muhammad might execute them. Furthermore, he counseled them not to send their men to the Banu Qurayzah for fear that the latter might seize them and give them up to Muhammad. Nu'aym then proceeded to Ghatafan and there repeated the same offer and warning. His ruse worked, and the leaders of Quraysh and Ghatafan began to probe each other on the matter. When Abu Sufyan sent to Ka'b, leader of Banu Qurayzah, asking him to advance against the Muslims on the morrow and promising to follow up their advance with an advance of their own by Makkan forces, his messenger was turned back with the message that since the next day was a Saturday the Jews would neither fight nor work. Angry at their disobedience, Abu Sufyan believed the words of Nu'aym. He sent word to them that they had better hold their Sabbath on another day as fighting Muhammad had become extremely necessary and the need for engaging him immediate. Abu Sufyan also warned that unless they joined the Makkans in battle on Saturday he would declare his pact with them null and void and, indeed, subject them to the brunt of Makkan attack. When the Banu Qurayzah heard this message of Abu Sufyan, they reiterated their resolution not to violate the Sabbath, reminding the messenger of divine wrath against its desecration. Moreover, they demanded guarantees for their future security. Their response dissipated any lingering doubts in Abu Sufyan's mind regarding Nu'aym's report. Discussing the problem with the leaders of Ghatafan, he discovered, much to his great dismay, that they deliberately hesitated to start the fight because of the Prophet's promise to them of one-third of the crops of Madinah. Evidently, the Muslims' maneuver worked, much as it was objected to at the time by Sa'd ibn Mu'adh, the leaders of al Aws and al Khazraj tribes, and other elderly consultants of the Prophet.

The Anger of Nature

On that same night a very strong wind blew and an extremely heavy rain fell. Thunder deafened the ears and the lightning was blinding. The storm was so wild that it swept the tents of the enemy off the ground and brought havoc to their camp. It struck fear into their hearts, and they believed that the Muslims were seizing this opportunity to launch their attack. Tulayhah ibn Khuwaylid was the first to rise and openly to suggest to the Makkans and their allies to flee for their lives. He claimed that these evil omens signaled the start of Muhammad's attack. Abu Sufyan followed him with the same counsel. "O people of Quraysh," he said, "Surely this is no place for you. The date trees around are uprooted and our work camels have perished. The Banu Qurayzah have abandoned us and cooperated with our enemies; the storm has taken its toll. All these things have brought terrible disadvantage to us. Let us move away from here. I shall be the first to give up." The armies prepared to withdraw, and each man carried as little as his camel, horse, or shoulders could bear and began to move while the storm continued to rage. The withdrawal was led by Quraysh, followed by Ghatafan and their allies. When the morning came, there was not one of them to be seen in the area. The Muslims returned to their homes in Madinah with the Prophet and gave praise and thanks to God for their escape from the travails of war.

The Campaign against Banu Qurayzah

Muhammad pondered the general situation of the cause of Islam. God had seen fit to remove the outside enemy, but the Banu Qurayzah remain in the midst of Madinah. Surely they were capable of repeating their treason in another season. Were it not for the internal division and sudden withdrawal of the Makkans and their allies, the Banu Qurayzah would have attacked Madinah and helped in the routing of the Muslims. Did not the common saying counsel, "Do not cut off the tail of the viper and allow it to go free?" The Banu Qurayzah, therefore, must be completely destroyed. The Prophet — May God's peace and blessing be upon him — ordered a *mu'adhdhin* to proclaim: "No pious Muslim will hold the mid-afternoon prayer except in the quarter of Banu Qurayzah," and a general invasion began. He appointed 'Ali commander of the operation. Despite their exhaustion after the long siege, the Muslims advanced fully confident of the result. It is true that the Banu. Qurayzah had fortified houses like those of Banu al Nadir. But if these were sufficient for defending them from Makkan attack, they were futile against the Muslims who were already in possession of the lands surrounding the Banu Qurayzah. Upon arrival at the Banu Qurayzah quarters, the Muslims found Huyayy ibn Akhtab al Nadiri bitterly reviling Muhammad, refuting his message and attacking the honor of his women. It was as though the Banu Qurayzah had a notion of what was coming to them now that the Makkans and their allies had withdrawn. When the Prophet arrived at the scene, he was met by 'Ali, who asked him not to approach the Jewish camp. Upon enquiry, Muhammad heard the Jews reviling him, and he said: "Miserable wretches that you are, didn't God Himself put you to shame and send His curse upon you?" In the meantime, the Muslims continued to pour into the area, and soon thereafter Muhammad ordered the siege to begin.

The siege lasted twenty-five days and nights during which only a few javelins, arrows, and stones were shot between the two combatants. The Banu Qurayzah did not dare leave their quarters a single time. When, exhausted, they realized that their fortifications were not going to avail them, and that they must sooner or later fall into Muslim hands, they sent word to the Prophet asking for Abu Lubabah, an al Aws tribesman and former ally, to negotiate with them. As he arrived, he was met by women and children in tears whose sight touched his heart. The Jews asked whether he counseled acquiescence to Muhammad's judgment. He answered, "By all means!" And, passing his hand over his throat, he said:

"Otherwise, it will be a general carnage." Some biographers report that Abu Lubabah later regretted having given them this counsel. After he left, Ka'b ibn Asad, their leader, suggested that they follow Muhammad and convert to his faith, thereby securing themselves, their children, properties, and wealth from any harm. But the majority refused, promising not to abandon the Torah or exchange it for anything else. Ka'b then suggested that they kill their own women and children and go out to meet the Muslims with drawn swords free of any apprehension for their loved ones, and to fight Muhammad to the bitter end. His idea was that should they lose, there would be neither family nor children for which to worry, but if they should win, Muslim women and children would all become theirs. Once more, the Banu Qurayzah said "No." They argued that life without their families was not worth the effort. Finally, Ka'b said that there remained no alternative for them but to acquiesce in Muhammad's disposal of their case. After consulting one another, they decided that their fate would not be worse than that of Banu al Nadir, that their friends and former allies from al Aws tribe would give them some protection and that if they were to remove themselves to Adhri'at in al Sham, Muhammad would have no objection to letting them go.

Arbitration of Sa'd ibn Mu'adh

Banu Qurayzah sent word to Muhammad proposing to evacuate their territory and remove themselves to Adhri'at, but Muhammad rejected their proposal and insisted on their abiding by his judgment. They sent to al Aws pleading that they should help them as al Khazraj had helped their client Jews before them. A group of al Aws tribesmen sought Muhammad and pleaded with him to accept from their allies a similar arrangement to that which he accepted from the allies of al Khazraj. Muhammad asked, "O men of al Aws, would you be happy if we allowed one of your men to arbitrate the case?" When they agreed, he asked them to nominate whomsoever they wished. This was communicated to the Jews, and the latter, unmindful of the fate that was lying in store for them, nominated Sa'd ibn Mu'adh. Sa'd was a reputable man of al Aws tribe, respected for his sound judgment. Previously, Sa'd was the first one to approach the Jews, to warn them adequately, even to predict to them that they might have to face Muhammad one day. He had witnessed the Jews cursing Muhammad and the Muslims. After his nomination and acceptance as arbitrator, Sa'd sought guarantees from the two parties that they would abide by his judgment. After these guarantees were secured, he commanded that Banu Qurayzah come out of their fortress and surrender their armour. Sa'd then pronounced his verdict that the fighting men be put to the sword, that their wealth be confiscated as war booty, and that the women and the children be taken as captives. When Muhammad heard the verdict, he said: "By Him Who dominates my soul, God is pleased with your judgment, o Sa'd; and so are the believers. You have surely done your duty." He then proceeded to Madinah where he commanded a large grave to be dug for the Jewish fighters brought in to be killed and buried. The Banu Qurayzah did not expect such a harsh judgment from Sa'd ibn Mu'adh, their former ally. They thought that he would plead on their behalf as 'Abdullah ibn Ubayy had done in the case of Banu Qaynuqa'. It must have occurred to Sa'd that if the Makkans and their allies had achieved victory through the treachery of Banu Qurayzah, the Muslims would surely have been subjected to the same fate of being killed and mutilated. He therefore imposed upon them the fate to which they sought to subject the Muslims. That the Jews showed great patience in the midst of tragedy is recorded for us in the story of Huyayy ibn Akhtab when he was brought for execution. The Prophet said to him, "Had not God put you to shame, O Huyayy?" Huyayy answered, "Every man is going to taste of death. I have an appointed hour which has now come. I do not blame myself for arousing your enmity." He then turned toward the people present and said, "O Men, it is all right to suffer God's decree. This tragic fate has been decreed by God for Banu Isra'il." Al Zubayr ibn Bata al Quraziyy, another Jew, had done a favor to Thabit ibn Qays on the day of Bu'ath when he let him free after capturing him. Thabit wanted to reciprocate the good deed on this occasion and asked the Prophet to grant him the favor of al Zubayr's life. The Prophet approved Thabit's request. When this came to the knowledge of al Zubayr, he pleaded that being an old man condemned to live in separation from his family and children, he had no use for life. Thabit then begged the Prophet of God to grant him also the life of Zubayr's wife and children, and the sparing of his property that al Zubayr might live in happiness. The Prophet again granted his request. After al Zubayr heard of his family's salvation, he inquired about Ka'b ibn Asad, Huyayy ibn Akhtab, 'Azzal ibn Samaw'al, and other leaders of the Banu Qurayzah. When he was told that they had all been killed, he asked to be dispatched with them, pleading: "I ask you, O Thabit, to dispatch me with my people, for life without them is not worth living, and I shall have no patience until I have rejoined my loved ones." Thus, he was killed at his own demand. The Muslims were always opposed to killing any women or children. On that day, however, a Jewish woman was executed because she had killed a Muslim by dropping a millstone on his head. It was of this woman that 'A'ishah used to say: "By God, I shall never cease to wonder how serenely that woman met her death." On that day, four Jews converted to Islam and were saved from death.

Quyayy's Responsibility for the Tragedy

We have seen how the lives of Banu Qurayzah were dependent upon Huyayy ibn al Akhtab, though the lives of both were terminated at the same time. It was he who violated the covenant that he, himself, had entered into with Muhammad when the latter forced Banu al Nadir's evacuation from Madinah without killing a single person. Also, it was he who so incited the Quraysh, Ghatafan, and the other Arab tribes to fight Muhammad that he became the very embodiment of Jewish-Muslim enmity. It was he who indoctrinated the Jews with the idea that they should have no peace unless Muhammad and the Muslims were utterly destroyed. Likewise, it was he who inspired Banu Qurayzah to violate their covenant with Muhammad and to repudiate their neutrality in the struggle needlessly and at such terrible cost. Finally, it was he who came to the Banu Qurayzah after the withdrawal of the Makkans and aroused them to engage the Muslims in a hopeless fight that was doomed before it started. Had the Banu Qurayzah acquiesced in the judgment of Muhammad from the first day, and acknowledged their mistake in violating their previous covenant, their lives would have been saved. Unfortunately, Huyayy's soul was possessed by a consuming Jewish enmity to the Muslims. He imparted such a measure of this enmity to the Banu Qurayzah that their own ally, Sa'd ibn Mu'adh, believed that even if they were forgiven, they would soon rally the tribes again to fight the Muslims anew. Such was their obsession with hatred of Muhammad and the Muslims that the Jews believed no life was worth living as long as the Muslim power was not broken and the Muslims were not subjugated or killed. However harsh the verdict which the arbitrator had reached in this regard, it was dictated by self-defense, as the arbitrator had become convinced that the presence or destruction of the Jews was a question of life and death for the Muslims as well.

The Spoils of War

The Prophet divided the properties, women, and children of Banu Qurayzah among the Muslims after he had separated one-fifth for public purposes. Each man of the cavalry received two shares, one for himself and one for his horse. On that day, the Muslim force included thirty-six cavalrymen. Sa'd ibn Zayd al Ansari sent a number of Banu Qurayzah captives to Najd where he exchanged them for horses and armour in order to increase Muslim military power.

Rayhanah, a captive woman of Banu Qurayzah, fell to the share of Muhammad, who offered her Islam. But she refused obstinately. Muhammad even offered to marry her, but she preferred to remain his captive. It was her strong attachment to her religion and people which must have prevented her from joining Islam as well as from marrying the Prophet. Her hatred for the Muslims and for their Prophet must have continued. No one had spoken of her beauty as they spoke of Zaynab, daughter of Jahsh, though a slight mention of this could be found in the chronicles. There was some disagreement as to whether she, upon entering the quarters of the Prophet, was asked to wear a veil as the protocol of the Prophet's house demanded, or whether she remained like most other women of the Peninsula without a veil. One thing, however, is certain: namely, she remained in the quarters of Muhammad until her death.

This expedition of the Makkans and their allies with its resultant destruction of the Banu Qurayzah enabled the Muslims to establish themselves as Madinah's absolute masters. The power of the *munafiqun* was finally broken, and all Arab tribes admired Muslim power, dominion, and the new prestige of Muhammad as sovereign of Madinah. The Islamic message, however, was not meant for Madinah alone but for the whole of mankind. The Prophet and his companions still faced the task of preparing for the greater task ahead, namely bringing the word of God to the wide world, calling all men to the true faith and making that faith secure against all enemies. That is precisely what awaited them, and what we shall study in the sequel.

19

From the Two Campaigns to the Treaty of Hudaybiyah

Organization of the Arab Community

After the Battle of the Ditch and the destruction of Banu Qurayzah, the situation in Madinah stabilized in favor of Muhammad and the Muslims. The Arab tribes so feared the Muslims that many Qurayshis began to think that it might have been better for their tribe to have made peace with Muhammad, especially since he himself was a Quraysh tribesman and the Muhajirun were all among its leaders and noblemen. The Muslims felt quite secure after they had destroyed Jewish power within and outside Madinah once and for all. For six months, they remained in Madinah during which their commerce prospered and they enjoyed a spell of peace and comfort. At the same time, the message of Muhammad crystallized in the minds of his followers, and they learned better to appreciate his teachings and observe his precepts. The Muslims followed their Prophet in reorganizing and remodeling the Arab community. Departing from tradition and reshaping society according to model principles were necessary steps in the making of that new society that Islam sought to establish in the world. In pre-Islamic days, the only social system known to the Arabs was that which their own customs had sanctified. In the matters of family and its organization, of marriage and its laws and divorce, and of the mutual relations of parents and children — in all these human relations — pre-Islamic Arabia had not gone beyond the elementary dictates of its hard topography; namely, extreme *laissez-faire* on the one hand and extreme conservatism reaching to slavery and oppression on the other. Islam was therefore called upon to organize a nascent society which as yet had developed no traditions and looked with disdain on its heritage of social customs. Muslim society had great ambitions, however, for it looked forward to becoming within a short time the nucleus of a great civilization ready for a destiny of absorption of the Persian, Roman, and Egyptian civilizations. Islam was to give this nascent civilization its character and gradually to impress it with its own ethos and brand until, some day, God might find it proper to say of it:

$$\text{ٱلْيَوْمَ ٱلْمَلْتُ لَكُمْ دِينَكُمْ وَأَتْمَمْتُ عَلَيْكُمْ نِعْمَتِي وَرَضِيتُ لَكُمُ ٱلْإِسْلَامَ دِينًا}$$

"Today I have completed for you your religion; my bounty and grace have been conferred upon you conclusively; and I am pleased that your religion shall henceforth be Islam."[1]

Relations between Men and Women

Whatever the nomadic nature of Arabian civilization had been before Islam, and regardless of whether or not such cities as Makkah and Madinah had enjoyed a level of civilization unknown to the desert, relations between men and women had never extended much beyond the sexual. According to the witness of the Qur'an, as well as of the traditions of that age, such relations were determined only by considerations of class or tribe, and were quite primitive in every other respect. The women used to show themselves off not only to their husbands but to any other men they pleased. They used to go out into the open country singly or in groups and meet with men and youths without hindrance or sense of shame. They exchanged with men glances of passion and expressions of love and desire. This was done with such blasé frankness and lack of shame that Hind, wife of Abu Sufyan, had no scruples whatever about singing on such a public and grave occasion as the Day of Uhud:

"Advance forward and we shall embrace you!
Advance forward and we shall spread the carpets for you!
Turn your backs and we shall avoid you!
Turn your backs and we shall never come to you."

Arab Eroticism

Among a number of tribes, adultery was not at all regarded as a serious crime. Flirting and courting were common practices. Despite the prominent position of Abu Sufyan and his society, the chroniclers tell, concerning his wife, a great many tales of love and passion with other men without implying any stain on her reputation. Whenever a woman gave birth to an illegitimate child, she felt no restraint about proclaiming the identities of all the men with whom she had had love affairs so that her child might be attributed to the man whom he most resembled. Likewise, there was no limit to the number of wives a man could take or to the number of his women slaves and concubines. Men were completely free to do as they pleased, and women were perfectly free to give birth as they pleased. The whole domain of man-woman relations had no seriousness or gravity except where a scandal was uncovered which brought about disputes, fighting, or libel between one clan and another within the larger tribe. Only on such occasions did the flirtations, courtings, and adulterous rendezvous become reasons for shame, vituperation, or war. When hostility broke out between one house and another, men and women alike felt free to claim and accuse as they wished. The Arab's imagination is by nature strong. Living as he does under the vault of heaven and moving constantly in search of pasture or trade, and being constantly forced into the excesses, exaggerations, and even lies which the life of trade usually entails, the Arab is given to the exercise of his imagination and cultivates it at all times whether for good or for ill, for peace or for war. Should a man, for instance, pour out his imagination in the most sentimental and affected forms when addressing his sweetheart in private, one would think that was normal. But when the same man readily and publicly pours out that same imagination, in the event of war against his sweetheart's tribe or in personal disaffection for her, by describing her neck, breast, waist, hips, and all other aspects of her feminine form, we must conclude that that imagination knows little more of the woman than her sex, feminine form, and adeptness at making love. Despite the decisive blow which Islam had directed at this excessive cultivation of the imagination, much of it was embedded in the Arab psychic character described in the poetry of 'Umar ibn Abu Rabi'ah. Indeed, Arabic love poetry has hardly ever been free of this trait; a measure of it can still be found in the modern poetry of our own day.

Woman in Other Civilizations

The foregoing account may have struck the reader who is full of admiration for the Arabs and their civilization, including the Arabs of pre-Islam, as somewhat exaggerated. Such a reader is certainly excused for so thinking, for he must be comparing the picture we have given with the actualities of the present age, intermingled as they certainly are with the ideal relations between man and woman, parents and children. Such comparisons, however, are false and lead the investigator astray. If the comparison is to be fruitful, one should undertake to contrast Arab society as we have described it in the seventh century C.E. with other societies of the same period. I do not think it is an exaggeration to say that Arab society, despite all its aberrations, was far superior to the societies of Asia and Europe. We do not have enough information to speak with authority on Chinese or Indian society of that age. But we do know that Europe was wallowing in such darkness that its family structure stood little higher than the most primitive levels of human organization. The *Imperium Romanum,* possessor of the law, master of the world, and the sole competitor of the Persian Empire, regarded woman as far more inferior to man than she was in the Arabian desert. In Roman law, woman was regarded as a piece of movable property, owned by a man and disposable by him in any way he wished. The Roman male citizen exercised the right of life and death over his women, and did so by law. The law enabled the Roman citizen to treat his women as he would his slaves, making no distinction between them. It regarded a woman as the property of her father, then of her husband, and finally of her son. The right of property exercised over her person was complete, just as complete as the right of property over animals, things, and slaves. Moreover, woman was looked upon as a source of desire. Like an animal, she was not expected to have any control over her sex life. Because morality did not apply to her, it was necessary to fabricate the western artificial framework of absolute chastity in order to instill a sense of ethics in man-woman relations. This necessary though artificial framework furnished the womanly ideal of that society for several centuries afterwards. It will be recalled that Jesus — May God's peace be upon him — was quite compassionate toward women, and that when his disciples expressed surprise at his fair treatment of Mary Magdalene, he proclaimed: "He that is without sin among you, let him first cast a stone at her."[2] Despite this charitable attitude toward women on the part of Christianity, Christian Europe continued to deride woman and to hold her in the greatest contempt very much as pagan Europe had done before.

Europe did not only regard the relation of man to woman merely as a relation of male and female. It coalesced with this relationship that of owner to owned, master to slave, and the honorable to the dishonorable and contemptible. These attitudes have so determined the mind of Europe so long that for centuries the Europeans have asked whether woman has a soul; whether she is a morally responsible being; whether she is to render account on the Day of Judgment; or whether, like an animal, she is devoid of soul, subject to neither judgment nor responsibility, and entitled to no place at all in the kingdom of God.

Muhammad and Social Reconstruction

Led by divine revelation, Muhammad recognized that there can be no social reconstruction of society without the cooperation of all its men and women members in mutually helping, loving, and sympathizing with one another. He realized that no society is viable where women do not enjoy rights as well as duties, where these rights and duties are not exercised in cooperation, reciprocal love and respect, and where men are nonetheless the leaders. To realize these conditions in Arab society quickly and by force of authority was not an easy affair. However strong the faith of Muhammad's Arab followers, to take them slowly forward without exposing them to undue hardships was surer to succeed than otherwise. Slow progress intensifies the faith of the adherents and wins more converts, whereas forced progress creates dissension and weakens the faith of many. The same was true of every social reconstruction God prescribed for the Muslims. Indeed, the same progressive reconstruction characterized the religious duties of Islam, namely prayer, fasting, *zakat*, abstaining from gambling, eating pork, and the like. Muhammad began to teach social reconstruction and to define the rights and duties of men and women to one another by talking about exemplary instances occurring between himself and his wives which all Muslims could witness. The veil was not imposed upon the wives of the Prophet until shortly before the Campaign of al Khandaq, and the limitation of polygamy to four was not imposed until after that Campaign, indeed a whole year thereafter. It would be interesting to see how the Prophet anchored the relationships of man and woman to sound foundations and how he prepared his followers for the equality of men and women under Islam. Islam wanted its women to have the same rights even as they have duties. But it wanted these rights and duties to be exercised in an atmosphere of mutual love, fairness, and compassion, and its men to enjoy the position of leadership.

Islam Forbids Fornication

As we saw earlier, the relationship between man and woman among the Muslims of the period, as among all Arabs, was limited to that of male to female. Fornication, exposure of the woman's flesh and ornaments in a way inviting molestation by men and arousing in them sexual desire, dominated the relationship. There was little or no room for any relationships expressing human spirituality, or for any communion between man and woman in their service to God. The presence of Jews and *munafiqun* in Madinah and their hostility to the new faith caused many of their men to molest the Muslim women and led, as in the case of Banu Qaynuqa', to serious harm and injury to Muslim women. A great many unnecessary problems resulted from this situation. Had the Muslim women not exposed themselves outside their homes, thus inviting fornication, their identities would not have been known to the public and they would not have been harmed. Had this been the case, the Muslims would have avoided all these problems and could have made a fair start toward realizing the equality which Islam sought to realize between the sexes. This ideal might have been realized even without hardship to Muslim men and women. It was in this spirit that the Qur'an announced:

> "Those who harm the believers unjustly, whether men or women, do great wrong. O Prophet, command your women, your daughters, and the women of the believers to lengthen their garbs that they may not be harmed. God is merciful and compassionate. If the *munafiqun,* those who are ill of heart or cause agitation in the city do not stop their evil work, We shall give you mastery over them and the power to terminate forthwith their residence in your midst. They shall be accursed wherever they go, seized, and put to the sword. That is the pattern of God, already realized in earlier history and immutable for ever and ever."[3]

With this simple introduction, the Muslims were taught the necessity of outgrowing the customs of their predecessors. The Islamic legislation aimed at reorganizing society on a foundation of pure family life, free of intrusion from the outside. To reach this purpose, Islam declared adultery a grave sin. In consequence, the Muslims learned to appreciate the evil inherent in a woman's fornication and entanglement outside her family. The Qur'an said,

قُلْ لِلْمُؤْمِنِينَ يَغُضُّوا مِنْ أَبْصَارِهِمْ وَيَحْفَظُوا فُرُوجَهُمْ   ذَلِكَ أَزْكَى لَهُمْ   إِنَّ اللّهَ خَبِيرٌ بِمَا
يَصْنَعُونَ*   وَقُلْ لِلْمُؤْمِنَاتِ يَغْضُضْنَ مِنْ أَبْصَارِهِنَّ وَيَحْفَظْنَ فُرُوجَهُنَّ وَلَا يُبْدِينَ زِينَتَهُنَّ
إِلَّا مَا ظَهَرَ مِنْهَا وَلْيَضْرِبْنَ بِخُمُرِهِنَّ عَلَى جُيُوبِهِنَّ وَلَا يُبْدِينَ زِينَتَهُنَّ إِلَّا لِبُعُولَتِهِنَّ أَوْ
آبَائِهِنَّ أَوْ آبَاءِ بُعُولَتِهِنَّ أَوْ أَبْنَائِهِنَّ أَوْ أَبْنَاءِ بُعُولَتِهِنَّ أَوْ إِخْوَانِهِنَّ أَوْ بَنِي إِخْوَانِهِنَّ أَوْ بَنِي
أَخَوَاتِهِنَّ أَوْ نِسَائِهِنَّ أَوْ مَا مَلَكَتْ أَيْمَانُهُنَّ أَوِ التَّابِعِينَ غَيْرِ أُولِي الْإِرْبَةِ مِنَ الرِّجَالِ أَوِ الطِّفْلِ
الَّذِينَ لَمْ يَظْهَرُوا عَلَى عَوْرَاتِ النِّسَاءِ   وَلَا يَضْرِبْنَ بِأَرْجُلِهِنَّ لِيُعْلَمَ مَا يُخْفِينَ مِنْ زِينَتِهِنَّ
وَتُوبُوا إِلَى اللّهِ جَمِيعًا أَيُّهَ الْمُؤْمِنُونَ لَعَلَّكُمْ تُفْلِحُونَ*

"Command the believers to lower their eyes and to live a life of chastity. That is better for them, for God knows what they do. Command the women believers also to lower their eyes, to live the life of chastity, not to show off their beauty and ornaments except what must be shown in the course of daily life. Command them to cover themselves up, not to show their beauty and ornamentation except to their husbands, their fathers, the fathers of their husbands, their sons or the sons of their husbands, their brothers or the sons of their brothers, the sons of their sisters, their women-slaves or eunuchs, or immature children. Command them not to stamp their feet in order to show off their hidden ornaments. O Believers, repent to God that you may achieve felicity."[4]

Thus Islam worked toward the transformation of man-woman relations into one in which sex is possible only when legitimate, and illegitimate sexual relationships are condemned as evil. In all other matters of human life, the relationships of men to women and vice versa are based on a foundation of absolute equality. Everybody is a servant of God, and everybody is mutually responsible for promoting virtue and the fear of God. If anyone stirred the sexual passion in other people, he would be guilty and obliged to repent and atone to God.

All this, however, was not sufficient to transform Arab character and wean it away from its original customs. Unlike the repudiation of associationism, the transformation of character could not be brought about with speed. This was only natural, for once a material has been given a certain form, it is not easy to transform that material except slowly and progressively. Even so, the desired change cannot be too radical. Human life is such that inherited custom and local traditions knead and mold it into a definite pattern. If this pattern is to bring change, it must be done slowly by degrees. Moreover, no such gradual change may be undertaken unless man transforms his inner self. It is possible for man to change one aspect of himself by removing the hindrances abetting such change in that aspect. That is precisely what Islam did with the Muslims when it converted them to the unitization of God, to faith in Him, in His Prophet, and in the Day of Judgment. But many other aspects of Arab character, especially the material or social aspects, were not so radically transformed but remained nearer to what they had been before Islam. Arab laziness and love of conversation with women, traits kneaded into their character by life in the desert, were chronically resistant to change.

The Prophet's Home and His Wives

In spite of the aforementioned rectification by the new religion of the relationships between the sexes, the Muslims did not depart radically from their previous customs. Often, one of them would enter the Prophet's house and stay there for a long time enjoying conversation with the Prophet or with his wives. But the Prophet had no time to spend on listening to each of his visitors, nor could he tolerate them to converse with his wives and broadcast their gossip. Seeking to free the Prophet from these minor cares, God revealed the following verses:

> "O Men who believe, do not enter the house of the Prophet without permission. Do not wait there until meal time, but eat if food is served. Enter therein if you are invited; but once fed, disperse and do not tarry. Such gossiping in his presence harms the Prophet, who is shy to ask you to leave. But God is not shy of saying the truth. And if you ask the wives of the Prophet for something, then talk to them from behind a curtain. That is purer and more seemly for you and for them. It behooves you not to hurt the Prophet of God nor to marry his wives after him. If you do, your deed will be a great crime in God's eye."[5]

While this verse was addressed to the believers, the following was addressed to the Prophet's wives:

"O Wives of the Prophet, you are distinguished only as long as you are righteous. Do not, therefore, be soft or tempting in speech lest the ill-hearted fall to temptation. Be always gentle and good. Maintain your homes with dignity and do not show off yourselves as pre-Islamic women were wont to do. Observe prayer, pay the *zakat*, and obey God and His Prophet. God only wishes to keep you pure and to remove from you all uncleanliness and temptation."[6]

Social Foundations of Muslim Brotherhood

On this foundation Islam sought to construct the social order of the human community. Its core was the new relationship between man and woman. By its means Islam sought to remove the unchallenged dominion sex had hitherto exercised over this relationship. Its aim was to direct the community to a higher life where man might enjoy the pleasures of this world without corrosion of his moral fabric, and to lead man to a spiritual relationship with all creatures transcending agriculture, industry, trade, and the other preoccupations of life — the relationship implicit in the life of faith which makes man the partner of angels. Other means which Islam employed for that same purpose were fasting, prayer, and zakat — by virtue of what each commands against adultery, injustice and evil doing and by virtue of what each enjoins by way of self-purification, submission to God alone, fraternity between the believers, and communion between man and all that is.

The Campaign of Banu Lihyan

The slow reorganization of society in preparation for the great transformation for which Islam was preparing humanity did not prevent Quraysh and the tribes from lying in wait for Muhammad. Nor did it prevent Muhammad from taking the requisite precaution and being always on the alert, ready to strike terror in the hearts of his enemies should the need arise. A case in point was the campaign of Banu Lihyan. Six months after the destruction of Banu Qurayzah, it came to Muhammad's notice that the Banu Lihyan were marching from a locality near Makkah. Immediately, he remembered the case of Khubayb ibn 'Adiy and his companions, who were murdered by Banu Lihyan at the well of al Raji' two years ago, and sought to avenge them. However, he did not announce his purpose for fear that the enemy might be alerted and take refuge. He therefore announced that he wanted to go to al Sham and, after mobilizing his forces, he led them toward the north. When he felt secure that neither the Quraysh nor their neighbors were aware of his intentions, he turned to Makkah and proceeded in its direction full haste until he reached the camping grounds of the tribe of Banu Lihyan at 'Uran. Some people, however, had noticed his change of direction, and eventually the Banu Lihyan were informed of his plan. They took refuge in the heights of the surrounding mountains, gathering with them their cattle and property. The Prophet, therefore, could not reach them. He sent Abu Bakr and a hundred cavalrymen in hot pursuit until they reached a place not far from Makkah called 'Usfan. He himself returned to Madinah on a day that was remembered for the hardship to the traveler which its extreme heat presented, as the following tradition clearly states: "We returned and, by God's leave, we repent to God and praise Him. We take shelter and refuge in God from the travail of travel, the sadness of tragedy, and the realization of loss in relatives and property."

The Campaign of Dhu Qarad

A few days after Muhammad returned to Madinah, a group led by 'Uyaynah ibn Hisn raided the outskirts of the city, seized the camels grazing in the area, killed their shepherd, and carried off his wife. Apparently, he thought that the Muslims would not realize what had happened in time to catch up with him. Salamah ibn 'Amr ibn al Akwa' al Aslami, however, who happened to be going that way to the forest with bow and arrows, beheld the raiders running away with their booty as they passed through the place called Thaniyyah al Wada' near al Sal'. He followed them, shot arrows at them and called for help throughout the pursuit. His call was soon heard by the Prophet who alerted the people of Madinah, and Muslim cavalrymen came out from every direction. Muhammad ordered them to pursue the raiders immediately, and he followed a little later with another force until he arrived at the mountain of Dhu Qarad. 'Uyaynah and his companions pressed ever faster toward Ghatafan where they could find protection from its tribesmen and escape from the Muslims. The Madinese cavalry overtook the enemy's rear, seized the stolen camels, and liberated the captive woman. Some companions were prepared to press the pursuit further and avenge the Muslims against 'Uyaynah. The Prophet advised against this course, knowing that 'Uyaynah and his companions had already reached the tribe of Ghatafan and had fallen under their protection. The Muslims therefore returned to Madinah bringing with them the liberated woman and the camels. While in captivity and driving her own camel, the Muslim woman vowed that should that camel ever bring her back home, she would sacrifice it to God. When she informed the Prophet of her vow in Madinah, the Prophet answered: "What a terrible reward you propose to the camel which served you and carried you to freedom! That is clearly an evil act, and no vow to perform an evil is valid."

The Campaign of Banu al Mustaliq

Muhammad remained in Madinah for about two months, until the campaign of Banu al Mustaliq at al Muraysi', which has arrested the attention of every biographer of the Arab Prophet and every historian. The importance of this campaign lies not in its military significance, but rather, in the internal division which it almost caused within the Muslim community, and which the Prophet settled resolutely. Another important aspect of this campaign is its connection with the Prophet's marriage to Juwayriyyah, daughter of al Harith. A third aspect is its connection with the malignant slander of 'A'ishah who, though hardly seventeen years of age, was able to repulse these falsehoods by her strong faith and sublime character.

The news reached Muhammad that the Banu al Mustaliq, a clan of Khuza'ah tribe, were mobilizing for war in the vicinity of Makkah and inciting the Arab tribes around them to assassinate Muhammad. Their leader was al Harith ibn Abu Dirar. Acting quickly in seizing the initiative, Muhammad hastened to strike and take them by surprise as was his custom. The two divisions of al Muhajirun and al Ansar which rallied to his immediate call were led by Abu Bakr and Sa'd ibn 'Ubadah, respectively. The Muslims encamped near a well called al Muraysi', not far from the encampment of their enemies. The allies of Banu al Mustaliq ran away upon hearing the news of the advancing Muslim army, with the result that the Banu al Mustaliq themselves were quickly encircled. In the short engagement which followed, the Muslims lost one man, Hisham ibn al Khattab by name, who was killed accidentally by a fellow Muslim. After losing ten men, the Banu al Mustaliq realized that they had better surrender to the Muslim forces. They were all made captives and their cattle confiscated.

The Plot of 'Abdullah ibn Ubayy

'Umar ibn al Khattab had a servant charged with taking care of his horse. After the Campaign of Banu al Mustaliq was over, this servant crowded out one of the al Khazraj tribesmen from the proximity of the well. As they quarreled together the man from Khazraj called on al Ansar for help; the other called for help from al Muhajirun. 'Abdullah ibn Ubayy, who had accompanied the Muslim forces on this expedition in order to secure some booty, arose when he heard the call and, venting his old hatred of al Muhajirun as well as of Muhammad, said to al Ansar :

> "Indeed, al Muhajirun have not only crowded us here but even in our own homes. The case of our hospitality to them has been nothing short of the common saying, 'Feed your beast and one day it will devour you.' Surely when we return to Madinah, the stronger party shall force the evacuation of the weaker. Such is the fate that you have incurred with your own hands. You have allowed the Muslims to occupy your lands; you have willingly shared your wealth and crops with them. By God, if you could only deny them these privileges, they would have to leave you alone and seek somebody else's help."

The news of this speech of 'Abdullah ibn Ubayy was soon reported to the Prophet of God. Muhammad, satisfied that operations against the enemy had all been completed, was visiting with 'Umar ibn al Khattab at the time. When the latter heard the report, 'Umar suggested that Bilal be sent out to kill him instantly. With his usual foresight, patience, experience, and sense of leadership, the Prophet declined 'Umar's suggestion, saying: "O 'Umar, what would the people think if they heard that Muhammad had begun to kill his own companions?"

Nonetheless, the Prophet calculated that unless he took some resolute action, the situation might worsen. He therefore commanded his people to start off on their return to Madinah despite the inappropriateness of the hour. Ibn Ubayy in turn heard what had been reported to the Prophet, and he ran to him to deny the report and to explain that he had never entertained such ideas. This action did not affect Muhammad's resolution to command the return. He traveled with his people continuously throughout the whole day and night and most of the second morning until they could bear the desert sun no longer. As soon as the people dismounted or sat down, they were so exhausted that they fell asleep. Their exhaustion caused them to forget the affair of Ibn Ubayy; and after they had rested, they hurried to Madinah carrying the captives and booty from Banu al Mustaliq. One of those captives was Juwayriyyah, daughter of al Harith ibn Abu Dirar, the leader of the vanquished tribe.

Ibn Ubayy's Resentment of the Prophet

After his return to Madinah with the victorious Muslims, Ibn Ubayy could not reconcile himself to their success, and his resentment of Muhammad and the Muslims stirred with unabated vigor. His hatred continued despite his apparent adherence to the faith and his emphatic claim that what was reported to the Prophet at al Muraysi' was false. It was on this occasion that the *Surah* "al Munafiqun" was revealed in which we read the following verses:

هُمُ الَّذِينَ يَقُولُونَ لَا تُنْفِقُوا عَلَى مَنْ عِنْدَ رَسُولِ اللهِ حَتَّى يَنْفَضُّوا ۗ وَلِلهِ خَزَآئِنُ
السَّمَاوَاتِ وَالْأَرْضِ وَلَٰكِنَّ الْمُنَافِقِينَ لَا يَفْقَهُونَ ۚ يَقُولُونَ لَئِنْ رَجَعْنَا إِلَى الْمَدِينَةِ
لَيُخْرِجَنَّ الْأَعَزُّ مِنْهَا الْأَذَلَّ ۗ وَلِلهِ الْعِزَّةُ وَلِرَسُولِهِ وَلِلْمُؤْمِنِينَ وَلَٰكِنَّ الْمُنَافِقِينَ
لَا يَعْلَمُونَ ۚ

"It is the *munafiqun* who counsel against spending anything for the benefit of the Muhajirun so that the latter may get out of Madinah. But it is to God that all the treasures of heaven and earth belong. The *munafiqun* are simply ignorant. They threaten that when the Muslims return to Madinah, the stronger will force the evacuation of the weaker. But they do not know that might belongs to God, to his Prophet, and to the believers."[7]

Some people believed that the revelation of these verses was a verdict of death passed on Ibn Ubayy and that Muhammad would soon command his execution. Upon learning of this revelation, 'Abdullah, son of 'Abdullah ibn Ubayy, who was a true and loyal Muslim, ran to the Prophet and said: "O Prophet of God, I have heard that you are seeking to kill 'Abdullah ibn Ubayy because of reports which have reached you about him. If this is true, I ask that you command me to do the execution, and I promise to bring to you his head forthwith. By God, it is known that nobody supported al Khazraj tribe as my father did. Should anyone else besides me kill him, I will have to suffer myself to see the murderer of my father go about without avenging him. But I cannot bear such a torture, and the results may be that I will kill the murderer of my father, thereby killing a believer and incurring eternal punishment for myself in hell." Such were the words of 'Abdullah ibn Ubayy's son to Muhammad. It is hardly possible to appreciate the struggle within' Abdullah's soul of filial loyalty, genuine faith, tribal chivalry, concern for the preservation of peace, and the prevention of blood feuds among the Muslims. Though he realized that his father was going to be killed, he did not plead to save the condemned life. He believed that the Prophet does what he is commanded by his Lord, and was absolutely certain of his father's treason. But his filial loyalty, personal dignity, and Arab chivalry demanded that he avenge the death of his father. Hence, he was prepared to undertake the killing of his own father, however such a deed might rend his heart and expose his conscience to ruinous self-reproach. He found consolation for his tragedy in his own faith in the Prophet and in Islam. This faith convinced him that if he were to follow the voice of Arab chivalry and filial piety and kill the executioner of his father, he would incur eternal punishment. His was a sublime struggle between faith, emotion, and moral character; and his tragedy was beyond comparison. After hearing his plea, the Prophet answered: "We shall not kill your father. We shall be kind to him, and we shall appreciate his friendship as long as he wishes to extend it to us."

The sublimity and greatness of forgiveness! Muhammad was touched and he stretched forth a kindly hand toward the one who had incited the people of Madinah to rise against the Prophet and his companions. His gentleness and pardon were to have far greater effect than punishment. After this episode, whenever an occasion arose for the Muslims to criticize 'Abdullah ibn Ubayy, they used to remind him that his very life was a gift Muhammad had made to him. One day, when the Prophet was conversing with 'Umar on the affairs of the Muslim community, the criticism ibn Ubayy was meeting from his peers was mentioned. Muhammad asked 'Umar: "Had I commanded him to be killed the day you advised me to do so, many men would have never entered Islam. These same men, were I to command them today to kill him they would do so without hesitation." 'Umar apologized and acknowledged the Prophet's superior judgment.

'A'ishah at the Campaign of Banu al Mustaliq

All the foregoing took place after the Muslims had returned to Madinah with their fruits of victory. Something else had happened on that expedition which was far removed from military affairs and concerning which there was little talk at first. The Prophet was in the habit of drawing lots among his wives whenever he went on an expedition, and would take in his company that wife whose lot happened to be drawn. On the occasion of the campaign of Banu al Mustaliq, it was the lot of 'A'ishah that was drawn. 'A'ishah was petite, slim and light; her presence inside the palanquin in which she rode was hardly noticeable by the men who would lift it for placement on camelback. As the Prophet and his expeditionary force were returning to Madinah after their long and exhaustive journey, they camped not far from Madinah in order to spend the night and recover their energies. At dawn or before, Muhammad gave the sign to resume the travel. 'A'ishah had stepped out of the Prophet's tent while her palanquin was placed at the entrance of it that she might ride therein and travel be resumed. On her way back she realized that she had lost her necklace. She quickly retraced her own footsteps, looking for the lost necklace. It took her a long time to find it. She had had very little sleep the previous day, and it is possible that she might have fallen asleep in her search for the necklace. At any rate, by the time she returned to her tent, she discovered that her servants had disappeared with the palanquin and that the whole company had vanished into the desert. Apparently thinking that 'A'ishah was inside for there was hardly any difference in its overall weight, the servants attached it to the camel's back and proceeded unaware that the "Mother of the Believers" was left behind. 'A'ishah looked around herself, and though not finding anyone, she did not panic; for she believed that her people would soon discover her absence and would return to seek her. She judged that it would be better for her to stay where she was rather than to strike out in the desert on her own and risk getting lost. Unafraid, she wrapped herself in her mantle and laid down waiting for her people to discover her.

While she waited, Safwan ibn al Mu'attal al Salami, who had been out of camp on an errand in the desert, returned to camp to find that he had missed his companions who were already on their way to Madinah. When he came close to 'A'ishah and discovered that she was indeed the wife of the Prophet, he stood back surprised and angry that she had been left behind. He asked her why she had been left behind and, receiving no reply, he brought her his camel and invited her to ride on it. 'A'ishah rode on the camel and Safwan rushed toward Madinah as fast as he could, hoping to join the Muslims before their entry into the city. The Muslims, however, were traveling at a very fast pace, purposely commanded by the Prophet of God in order to keep them exhausted and unable, as it were, to bring to a head the old hatreds between the various Muslim factions which 'Abdullah ibn Ubayy had been fomenting. Safwan arrived at Madinah in full daylight; 'A'ishah was riding on his camel. When he reached the Prophet's house, 'A'ishah dismounted and entered her home. No one present ever entertained any suspicion of unusual behavior on anybody's part, and the Prophet himself never suspected either the daughter of Abu Bakr, or Safwam, the loyal Muslim and pious believer, of the slightest misdemeanor.

Considering that 'A'ishah entered Madinah during the day and in front of everybody, and that her return was soon after the return of the Muslim forces, nobody could entertain any suspicion as to her behavior. She entered Madinah bearing her usual pride and unperturbed by any feeling of guilt. The whole city went about its business as usual, and the Muslims occupied themselves with dividing the captives and booty which they had seized from the Banu al Mustaliq. Their life in Madinah was actually becoming more prosperous as their faith gave them more power over their enemies. Their faith had reinforced their wills and had encouraged them to think lightly of death, whether in the cause of God and of His religion, or in defense of religious freedom which they had earned after such a long and hard struggle against their own fellow tribesmen.

Muhammad's Marriage to Juwayriyyah

Juwayriyyah, daughter of al Harith, was one of the captives of the Banu al Mustaliq. She was a noble and attractive woman and her lot fell to a man of al Ansar. She sought to ransom herself but her captor, knowing that she was the daughter of the leader of the Banu al Mustaliq, demanded a very high price which he thought her people were capable of paying. Afraid of him and his ambition, Juwayriyyah sought the Prophet in the house of 'A'ishah and, announcing her identity as the daughter of al Harith ibn Abu Dirar, chief of the Banu al Mustaliq, she asked for the Prophet's assistance in ransoming herself from captivity. After listening to her story, the Prophet thought of a better fate for her. He suggested that he ransom and marry her as well. Juwayriyyah accepted his proposal. When the news reached the people, everyone who held a captive of the Banu al Mustaliq granted that particular captive his or her freedom in deference to the new status the new captives had acquired as the in-laws of the Prophet. 'A'ishah had said of her: "I know of no woman who brought as much good to her people as Juwayriyyah."

Such is the story according to one version. Another version tells that al Harith ibn Abu Dirar came to the Prophet to ransom his daughter, and that after talking to the Prophet, he believed in him and declared his conversion. The same version tells that Juwayriyyah followed her father and was converted to Islam, whereupon the Prophet asked for her hand and offered her a dowry of four hundred dirhams. A third version tells that her father was not agreeable to her marriage to the Prophet and that a relative of hers intervened and gave her to the Prophet against the will of her father. Muhammad did in fact marry Juwayriyyah and built for her a room adjoining his other quarters by the mosque. By this, Juwayriyyah became one of the "Mothers of the Believers." While still busy in the aftermath of the wedding, some people began to whisper about 'A'ishah's delayed return to the camp mounted on the camel of Safwan. Safwan was a young and handsome man. Zaynab, daughter of Jahsh, had a sister called Hamnah who knew too well that 'A'ishah was preferred by Muhammad to her own sister. It was this Hamnah who began to broadcast gossip about 'A'ishah. In Hassim ibn Thabit she found a helper and in 'Ali ibn Abu Talib, an audience. 'Abdullah ibn Ubayy found her gossip of inestimable value in dividing the community and satisfying his hatred. He therefore spread the news in the market places. Al Aws tribesmen defended 'A'ishah, however, for they knew she was an example of nobility, chastity and purity. This story and the gossip to which it gave rise almost led to civil war.

'A'ishah's Illness

When the gossip finally reached the ear of Muhammad, he felt deeply hurt. He could not believe 'A'ishah would violate her marriage vows. Such indictment was impossible. 'A'ishah was pride and purity personified. She enjoyed such fervent love and strong affection from her husband that the mere thought of accusing her was the greatest crime. Yes indeed! But then, woe to women! Who can ever understand them or reach with certainty to their inner core? 'A'ishah was still a child. For, how could she lose her necklace and then retrace her steps looking for it in the middle of the night? And why didn't she say anything about her loss when she came to the camp? These and other questions bothered the Prophet; he did not know what to believe and what not to believe.

As for 'A'ishah, nobody dared inform her of the people's gossip. She noticed that her husband was unusually laconic and unfriendly to her, a departure from his usual tenderness and preoccupation with her. She fell

severely ill and was attended by her mother. But when Muhammad visited her, he hardly said any more than, "How are you?" Indeed, noticing this
coolness on the part of the Prophet, 'A'ishah asked whether or not
Juwayriyyah had now taken her place in his heart. These strained relations
being too much for her patience, she one day asked her husband's permission to move to her parent's quarters where her mother could take care of
her. After permission was granted, she moved to her parent's house all the
more alarmed at this new expression of unconcern. She remained bedrid-
den for over twenty days, and no knowledge of the gossip spreading
around her was ever brought to her notice. The people continued to gossip and annoyed the Prophet so much that he found himself obliged to
mention the matter in one of his speeches. "O Men," he said, "why are
some of you staining the reputation of my family by accusing them falsely? By God, the members of my family have always been good. Why are
you staining the reputation of one of my companions whom I know to be
good and who has never entered my house except in my company?" Usayd
ibn Hudayr rose and said, "O Prophet of God, if the false accusers are our
own fellows of al Aws tribe, we promise that we shall put a quick stop to
them. But if they are of the tribe of al Khazraj, then command us and we
shall obey. By God, to whichever tribe they belong, they are worthy of
having their heads struck off." Sa'd ibn 'Ubadah commented on Usayd's
proposition that the latter had made it because he knew too well that the
false accusers belonged to al Khazraj tribe. A spirit of civil dispute and
strife hovered over the whole community that took the Prophet's wisdom
and sound judgment to dissipate.

The Gossip and 'A'ishah

The gossip finally reached 'A'ishah through a woman of al Muhajirun.
When she learned of it she almost collapsed in alarm. She cried so hard
that she felt as if she were falling apart. Despondent and dejected, she
went to her mother and blamed her with broken voice. "May God forgive
you, O Mother," she said. "People talk as they do and you do not inform
me of it?" Realizing her anguished state, her mother sought to alleviate her
pains and said, "O, my daughter, relax and take things lightly. Surely, hardly ever has a beautiful woman such as you, more loved by her husband
than his other wives, not been slandered and gossiped about by those
wives." 'A'ishah, however, was not consoled by this. It began to dawn upon
her that the Prophet's coolness and disaffection which had recently

replaced his gentleness and affection must have been the result of this gossip and of the suspicion which it has caused. But what could she do now? Would she openly discuss the matter with him? Would he believe her if she swore to him that she was innocent? Or would she acquiesce in the false accusations and seek to offset them by her faith and pleading? Would she show him the same cold shoulder which he had shown her? But he is the Prophet of God, and he has loved her more than any of his other wives. It is surely not his fault that the people have gossiped about her delay in returning to the camp and her return to Madinah with Safwan. Would to God that she could discover some way of convincing Muhammad of the truth so that the real facts might be made clear once and for all and that Muhammad would return to his old love and gentle treatment of her!

The Revolt of 'A'ishah

Muhammad was not in a better position. The gossip of the marketplace had hurt him so much that he was forced to consult on the matter with his personal friends. He proceeded to the house of Abu Bakr and there called 'Ali and Usamah ibn Zayd to join him. Usamah denied all that had been attributed to 'A'ishah as falsehood and lies. He claimed that the people had no more knowledge of any inclination to disloyalty on the part of 'A'ishah than he had. On the contrary, they knew as much about her loyalty and innocence. As for 'Ali, he answered, "O Prophet, women are many. Perhaps you might get some information out of the servant of 'A'ishah, loyal as we all know her to be to you." The servant was called in and 'Ali immediately seized her and struck her painfully and repeatedly as he commanded her to tell the truth to the Prophet of God. The servant, however, continued to deny all the gossip and assert that she knew nothing but good as far as 'A'ishah was concerned. Finally, Muhammad had no alternative but to put that question directly to his wife, asking that she confess and tell him the truth. He went into her room and, in the presence of her parents and another woman of al Ansar, he found her and that woman crying together. As he entered the room, 'A'ishah could see the suspicious look on his face and this cut most deeply into her heart. The man whom she loved and adored, the man in whom she believed and for whom she was prepared to lay down her life, loved her no more. On the contrary, he suspected her. As she composed herself, she listened to him say: "O 'A'ishah, you have heard what the people are saying about you. Fear

God. If you have done an evil such as they say you did, repent to God for God accepts the repentance of His servants." No sooner had he finished than 'A'ishah sprang to her feet, her tears completely vanished, her blood rushing to her face. She glanced at her father and mother hoping that they would speak out for her. But when they remained silent, her rebellious spirit could hold her tongue no longer. She shouted to the top of her voice addressing her parents: "Don't you answer? Won't you speak out?" Despondently, her parents replied that they had nothing to say. At that moment 'A'ishah broke out in tears, and this seemed to temper the fire of the storm raging within her. Her tears drying again, she turned suddenly to the Prophet and said: "By God, I will not repent to God because I do not have anything to repent for. If I were to agree with what the people are saying, God knows that I am innocent and that I would be admitting that which is not true. And yet if I persist in my denial, you do not seem to believe me." After a pause, she said: "Rather, I shall say to myself as did the father of Joseph of his lying sons: 'Patience and more patience. God is my refuge against what you describe.'"

Revelation of 'A'ishah's Innocence

Silence reigned for a while; nobody could describe it as long or short. Muhammad had not moved from his spot when revelation came to him accompanied by the usual convulsion. He was stretched out in his clothes and a pillow was placed under his head. 'A'ishah later reported, "Thinking that something ominous was about to happen, everyone in the room was frightened except me, for I did not fear a thing, knowing that I was inno-cent and that God would not be unjust to me. As for my parents, when the Prophet recovered from his convulsion, they looked pale enough to die before the gossip was proven true." After Muhammad recovered, he sat up and began to wipe his forehead where beads of perspiration had gathered. He said, "Glad tidings! O 'A'ishah, God has sent down proof of your inno-cence."

'A'ishah exclaimed, "May God be praised." Immediately Muhammad went to the mosque and there read to the Muslims the verses which had just been revealed to him.

"Those who brought forth this lie and spread it are some of you. However, do not regard this, O Muhammad, as an evil. You may yet draw good therefrom. Everyone of those who spread the

lie shall have his share of due punishment. As for him who has
taken the chief part in that gossip, his will be the greatest punishment. . . . When you heard the great lie, you thought that it was
unbecoming of you to listen or to respond to it, and you condemned it saying, 'Holy God, that is a great calamity!' God
admonishes you never to do such a thing if you are believers. He,
the Omnipotent, the All-Wise, shows forth His signs to you.
Those who like to see immorality spread among the believers will
receive a painful punishment in this world as well as in the next.
God knows and you do not."[8]

It was on this occasion that the punishment for false accusation of
adultery was promulgated through the revelation of the following verse:
"Those who falsely accuse chaste women of adultery and do not bring
forth four witnesses to this effect shall be flogged with eighty stripes and

وَالَّذِينَ يَرْمُونَ الْمُحْصَنَتِ ثُمَّ لَمْ يَأْتُوا بِأَرْبَعَةِ شُهَدَآءَ فَاجْلِدُوهُمْ ثَمَانِينَ جَلْدَةً وَّ
لَا تَقْبَلُوا لَهُمْ شَهَادَةً أَبَدًا ۚ وَأُولَٰئِكَ هُمُ الْفَاسِقُونَ

their witness shall never be admitted as evidence in any matter. Those are
the decadent, the immoral."[9]

In pursuit of this Qur'anic injunction, Mistah ibn Athathah, Hassan
ibn ThAbit, and Hamnah, daughter of Jahsh, who had spread the false
accusation of 'A'ishah in the marketplace were flogged eighty stripes each,
and 'A'ishah returned to her rightful place in the house as well as in the
heart of Muhammad.

Commenting on this event in the life of the Prophet, Sir William
Muir concluded: "The whole career and life of 'A'ishah before that event
as well as after it furnishes unquestionable evidence that she was sincere
and innocent. There should therefore be no hesitancy in rejecting every
report of malconduct imputed to her." Despite his grave misdemeanor,
Hassan ibn Thabit repented, made amends with Muhammad and was
able to win back the latter's friendship. On the other hand, Muhammad
himself asked Abu Bakr not to deny Mistah ibn Athathah the kindness
which he used to extend to him. Henceforth, the whole event was forgot-

ten in Madinah. 'A'ishah's health improved rapidly, and, after returning to her quarters in the Prophet's residence, she recaptured her favorite position with him and with all the Muslims. Thus, the Prophet was able to devote all his energies to his message, to the administration of policy, and to preparing himself for the events leading to the Treaty of Hudaybiyah that would bring to the Muslims new and certain victories.

20

The Treaty of Hudaybiyah

Six years had passed since the emigration of the Prophet and his companions from Makkah to Madinah. During that time, they were constantly occupied with war and conflict, now with the Quraysh, now with the Jews. All along, Islam was gaining converts as well as power. From the first year of the Hijrah, Muhammad changed his orientation in prayer from al Aqsa Mosque to the Mosque of Makkah. The Muslims turned toward the house of God which Ibrahim had built in Makkah and which was renewed and reconstructed during Muhammad's youth. The reader will remember that it was Muhammad who lifted and placed the Black Stone in its position in the wall of that house, long before he could have ever thought that he was to become the recipient of a revelation from God on High.

Proscription of the Sanctuary to Muslim Entry

For hundreds of years, this Mosque had been the center toward which the Arabs turned in their worship and to which they went in pilgrimage during the holy month of every year. Everybody entering the area of the Mosque was to be safe and secure. The most hostile enemies met on its grounds without anyone ever drawing his sword or shedding the blood of his enemy. Ever since Muhammad had emigrated with the Muslims to Madinah, the Quraysh resolved to prevent them from entering the

Mosque. This prohibition applied only to the Muslims among all the Arabs of the Peninsula. To this effect, God said in the Qur'anic verses revealed during the first year of the Hijrah:

يَسْأَلُونَكَ عَنِ الشَّهْرِ الْحَرَامِ قِتَالٍ فِيهِ قُلْ قِتَالٌ فِيهِ كَبِيرٌ وَصَدٌّ عَنْ سَبِيلِ اللهِ وَكُفْرٌ بِهِ وَ الْمَسْجِدِ الْحَرَامِ وَ إِخْرَاجُ أَهْلِهِ مِنْهُ أَكْبَرُ عِنْدَ اللهِ

"They challenge you regarding the sacred month, that there should be no fighting whatsoever during its whole course. Answer, that fighting in the holy month is a great transgression. But to hinder men in their pursuit of God's path, to be blasphemous to Him and to the Holy Mosque, to force the worshippers out of the Mosque — all these are greater transgressions in the eye of God."[1]

Likewise, the following verse was revealed after the Battle of Badr: "And why should they not be punished by God when they prevent men from entering the Holy Mosque for worship? Surely, they are not its guardians. The guardians of the Holy Mosque are only the pious and righteous. But most of them are utterly ignorant. As for their worship in the House of God, it is nothing but whistling and clapping and garbling. They should then be punished for their ungodliness. The unbelievers spend of their wealth for the purpose of hindering men from the path of God. Their expenditure is wasted and will bring about their own ruin. For it is to Hell that they shall finally be assigned."[2] During these six years many other verses were revealed centering on the Mosque of Makkah which God had declared to be a place of repentance and of security for mankind. But the Quraysh never saw in Muhammad and his companions who turned their backs on the idols of that house — namely, Hubal, Isaf, Na'ilah and the others — anything but men who ought to be fought and combatted and denied the privilege of pilgrimage to the Ka'bah until they repented and returned to the gods of their ancestors.

Muslim Yearning for Makkah

During the whole time the Muslims were kept from fulfilling their religious duty, they suffered deeply. The Muhajirun especially felt this privation more strongly as it was combined with banishment from their own hometown and people. All the Muslims, however, were convinced that God would soon give victory to His Prophet and to them and would raise Islam high above all other religions. They firmly believed that the day would soon come when God would unlock for them the gates of Makkah that they might perform their pilgrimage to the ancient house and thus fulfill the duty which God had imposed upon all men. If so far the years had passed one after another with frequent campaigns and battles, beginning with Badr, Uhud, the Ditch and others, so too the day of victory which they believed to be necessary must soon come. How strong was their longing for this day! And how intensely did Muhammad himself share their very faith in the proximity of that day of victory!

The Arabs and the Ka'bah

The truth is that the Quraysh had done a great injustice to Muhammad and his companions by forbidding them to visit the Ka'bah and to perform the duties of pilgrimage and 'umrah.[3] The ancient sanctuary of Makkah was not a property of the Quraysh but of all the Arabs together. The Quraysh enjoyed only the services attached to the Ka'bah such as the sidanah, siqayah, and other functions pertinent to the sanctuary or to the care for its visitors. The fact that one tribe worshiped one idol rather than another never permitted the Quraysh to forbid any tribe from visiting the Ka'bah, from circumambulating it, or from filling any religious duties or acts of worship demanded by the tribe's loyalty to that god. If Muhammad came to call men to repudiate idol worship, to purify themselves from paganism and associationism, to raise themselves to the worship of God alone, devoid of associates, to conduct themselves for the sake of God in a manner free of all moral flaws, to elevate their spirit to consciousness of the unity of being and the unity of God, and if the new faith imposed on its adherents the duty of pilgrimage and 'umrah to the sanctuary of Makkah, it would be sheer aggression and injustice to prevent the followers of that faith from fulfilling their religious duty. The Quraysh, however, feared that were Muhammad and his Makkan companions to visit Makkah, they might persuade the majority to follow them, especially since they were related to the Makkans with bonds of blood and family and had been separated from them long enough to arouse in them the strongest longing. Such a development would start a civil war in Makkah which the Quraysh wanted to avoid. Moreover, Makkan leaders and noblemen had not forgotten that Muhammad and his companions had destroyed their faith, cut off their trade route to al Sham, and antagonized them so deeply that no common loyalty to the sanctuary and no common feeling that it belonged to God and to all the Arabs could compose their differences. The Quraysh could not be convinced that their relationship to the house was merely one of taking care of it and of its visitors.

The Muslims and the Ka'bah

Six whole years had passed since the Hijrah, during which the Muslims longed to visit the Ka'bah and perform the pilgrimage and 'umrah. One day, while they congregated in the mosque in the morning, the Prophet informed them of a vision he had seen that they should enter the holy sanctuary of Makkah secure, shaven, and unarmed, and without fear for their safety. As soon as the Muslims heard of the news, they praised God for His grace and spread the tidings all over Madinah. No one, however, could imagine how this was going to be accomplished. Would they fight and enter Makkah after battle? Would they force the evacuation of Quraysh and pull down its guardianship of the Ka'bah? Or would Quraysh open the road to them in humiliation and acquiescence?

Muhammad's Proclamation Concerning Pilgrimage

No! There was to be neither war nor fighting. Muhammad proclaimed to the people that pilgrimage to Makkah would take place in the holy month of Dhu al Qi'dah. He had sent his messengers to the tribes, whether Muslim or otherwise, inviting them to participate with the Muslims in a visit to the sanctuary of God in security and peace. Apparently, he sought to make the group performing the pilgrimage the largest possible. His objective was to let the whole Peninsula know that this expedition of his during the holy month was intended purely for pilgrimage and not for conquest, as well as to proclaim the fact that Islam had imposed pilgrimage to Makkah just as pre-Islamic Arab religion had done and, finally, that he had actually invited even the Arabs who were not Muslims to join in the performance of this sacred duty. If, despite all this, the Quraysh insisted on fighting him during the holy month and preventing him from the performance of a duty commonly held by all Arabs regardless of their personal faith, the Quraysh would surely find themselves isolated and condemned by all. In that eventuality, the Quraysh would find the Arabs unwilling to help them in fighting the Muslims. In the eyes of all the tribes, the Quraysh would have indicted themselves. They would have to appear as stopping men from visiting the sanctuary, as combating the religion of Isma'il and of his father, Ibrahim. By this means, the Muslims would guarantee that the Arab tribes would not rally against them under Makkan leadership as they did hitherto in the campaign of the Ditch, and their religion would itself gain some credit among the tribes who had not yet been converted to it. What would the Quraysh say to a people who came to their doors armless except for their undrawn swords, and in a state of ritualistic purity, accompanied by the cattle which they planned to sacrifice near the Ka'bah and whose every care was simply to circumambulate the House, the duty common to all the tribes of the Peninsula?

Muhammad publicly proclaimed that the pilgrimage had started and asked the tribes, including the non-Muslim, to accompany him on that holy mission. Some of the tribes rejected his invitation and others accepted. His procession set forth on the first of Dhu al Qi'dah, one of the holy months; and it included al Muhajirun, al Ansar, and a number of other tribes. He led the procession riding on his she-camel, al Qaswa'. Their total number was about one thousand four hundred men. They took with them seventy camels and donned the garb demanded by the ritual of 'umrah that the people might know that this was no military campaign but a pilgrimage to the holy sanctuary and a fulfillment of religious duty. When he reached Dhu al Hulayfah, the pilgrims shaved their heads, purified themselves as the ritual demanded, and isolated their sacrificial cattle by placing them to their left. The sacrificial cattle included the camels of Abu Jahl which were seized in the Battle of Badr. No man in the whole group carried any arms except the undrawn sword usually worn by all travelers. Umm Salamah, the wife of the Prophet, accompanied him on this trip.

Quraysh and Muslim Pilgrimage

When the Quraysh learned that Muhammad and his companions were approaching Makkah for purposes of pilgrimage, they were filled with fear and pondered whether or not Muhammad was now playing a war game against them in order to enter Makkah after they and their allies had failed to enter Madinah. Their fear was not dissipated when they learned that the pilgrims had actually donned the ritual garb demanded by 'umrah, nor by Muslim proclamation across the Peninsula that they were coming solely to fulfill a religious duty approved and accepted by all the Arabs. None of this prevented them from resolving to stop Muhammad from entering Makkah at whatever cost. Quickly, they mobilized an army, including a cavalry force of two hundred. They gave the command to Khalid ibn al Walid and 'Ikrimah ibn Abu Jahl This army advanced to Dhu Tuwa and took up position to prevent the Muslims' religious march to Makkah.

Encounter

Muhammad and the Muslims continued their march. At 'Usfan, they met a tribesman of Banu Ka'b whom the Prophet questioned regarding the Quraysh. The man answered: "They heard about your march; so they marched too. But they wore their tiger skins, their traditional war apparel, pledging that they will never let you enter Makkah. Their general, Khalid ibn al Walid, set up camp for his cavalry at Kara' al Ghamim." Upon learning this, Muhammad said: "Woe to Quraysh! Their hostility is undoing them. Why should they object to letting me settle this affair with all the tribes without intervention? If the Arab tribes destroy me, that will be the realization of their objective. If, on the other hand, God gives me victory, then they can enter into Islam with dignity; and if they resist, they can then fight with good cause. What does the Quraysh think? By God, I shall continue to serve that for which God has commissioned me until the divine message has become supreme or I lose my neck in the process." Pondering over the issue, he thought that, whereas he did not come thither as a conqueror but as a Muslim pilgrim seeking the sanctuary as a religious duty, he might be compelled to fight and perhaps lose unless he should take the precaution of arming his people. Should he lose in such an engagement, the Quraysh would parade their victory throughout the Peninsula and thus deal a tragic blow to the Muslim position. Indeed, it is perhaps for that reason that the Quraysh delegated the command of their army to Khalid ibn al Walid and 'Ikrimah, their most illustrious generals, that they might attain this very objective, knowing that Muhammad was not prepared to fight on this occasion.

Muhammad's Caution to Safeguard the Peace

While Muhammad pondered these issues, Makkan cavalry was looming on the horizon. The presence of the enemy prepared for war showed the Muslims that it was impossible for them to reach their objective without going through these lines and engaging in a battle in which the Quraysh had come prepared to repulse the threat to their dignity, honor, and homeland. Such would have been a battle undesired and uncalled for by Muhammad and forced upon him. The Muslims were not afraid of battle. With the high morale they enjoyed, their swords alone would be sufficient to stop this new aggression of the Makkans. But if they did fight the Makkans, the peaceful purpose of the whole affair would not be realized. On the contrary, the Quraysh would use such fighting as proof of Muhammad's guilt before the tribes. Muhammad was too farsighted to allow such a course to be followed. He therefore asked his party to find someone who could show them a road to Makkah other than the main one which was blocked by the Quraysh. Apparently, he was still of the same mind as before he started out from Madinah. A man was found to lead the procession by a different route which was yet more desolate and full of hardships. That road led them to a valley at the end of which a turn by al Murar brought them to the locality of al Hudaybiyah, south of Makkah. When the Quraysh discovered the movement of Muhammad and his companions, they returned quickly to Makkah in order to defend it against what they thought to be a Muslim invasion from the south. Upon arrival at the plain of al Hudaybiyah, al Qaswa', she-camel of the Prophet, stopped. The Muslims thought the she-camel was exhausted; but the Prophet explained that it was stopped by the same power which stopped the elephant from entering Makkah. He continued, "If only the Quraysh would ask us for guarantees of Muslim intentions based upon our blood relationship to them, we should be happy to give them the same." He then called upon the Muslims to encamp. When they complained that the place was waterless, he sent a man with a stick to one of the wells of the area and asked him to verify the existence of water. When the man plunged his stick into the bottom of the well, water sprang up; the people felt reassured, and they put up camp.

Quraysh's Delegates to the Muslims

The Muslims encamped and the Quraysh observed their moves. The Makkans had resolved to prevent the Muslims by force from entering their city. To them, this was a clear and final commitment. The Muslims, on the other hand, did not know whether or not they were heading for an all-out war with the Quraysh which would decide the matter between them once and for all. Undoubtedly, some people on both sides preferred a settlement by the sword. The 'Muslims who approved of this course thought their victory would bring about a final destruction of the Quraysh. The Quraysh's reputation throughout the Peninsula as well as their *sidanah* and *siqayah* functions in pilgrimage — indeed, their pride and religious distinction — would be eliminated. The two camps were poised seeking an answer. Muhammad did not change his original plan to perform the *'umrah* in peace and to avoid war unless attacked. In case of attack, there would be no escape from recourse to the sword. As for the Quraysh, while hesitant, they decided to send some delegates to the Muslim camp, partly to reconnoiter Muslim strength and partly to dissuade Muhammad from executing his plan. For this purpose, Budayl ibn Warqa' arrived at the Muslim camp, together with some tribesmen from Khuza'ah. Inquiry into Muhammad's objectives convinced them that he did not come to fight but to honor the sanctuary and pay to it the homage due. The delegation returned to the Quraysh and counseled that the Muslims be permitted to fulfill their religious wish. The Quraysh, however, remained unconvinced. Indeed, they accused their own delegates of conniving with Muhammad. They argued that even though Muhammad might not have come to make war, he should not be allowed to enter Makkah against their will and with such preponderant numbers. Otherwise, the Quraysh would become the mockery of Arabia. In order to make sure that their first delegates told them the truth, the Quraysh sent another delegation which returned with exactly the same reports, which the Quraysh now believed. The Quraysh were depending for their war against Muhammad upon their Ahabish allies.[4] They thought of sending the Ahabish leader to talk to Muhammad with the hope that the two leaders would misunderstand each other and the Quraysh ally would become increasingly committed to fight on Makkah's side against Muhammad. Al Hulays, as the leader of the Ahabish was called, went to the Muslim camp to see for himself. When the Prophet saw him arriving, he ordered the sacrificial cattle paraded in front of him as material proof of Muslim intention to perform the pilgrimage and to honor the sanctuary. Al Hulays saw the seventy sacrificial camels shaved and readied for sacrifice and was moved by the view of this display of Arab religiosity. He soon became convinced that the Quraysh were doing an injustice to those people who had come neither for war nor for hostility. Without bothering to meet Muhammad and converse with him, he returned to Makkah and told the Quraysh of his opinion. Full of resentment, the Quraysh slighted al Hulays as a Bedouin and neglected his advice as that of one uninstructed. Al Hulays was naturally angered, and he threatened them that he had not allied himself with them in order to stop pilgrims from performing their religious duties. He even threatened that unless they allowed Muhammad and his party into the sanctuary, he would remove himself and his tribe from Makkah. The Quraysh feared the consequences of such a move and begged him to give them time to reconsider.

The Delegation of 'Urwah ibn Mas'ud al Thaqafi

The Quraysh then thought of sending somebody whom they could trust and whose judgment stood beyond suspicion. They approached 'Urwah ibn Mas'ud al Thaqafi and apologized to him for having slighted the delegate whom they had sent before him to negotiate with Muhammad. When they assured him of their respect and pledged their compliance with his advice, he agreed to meet with Muhammad. He proposed to the latter that since Makkah was his own hometown whose honor it was his duty to safeguard, it would be opprobrious for him to prefer the commonplace people he brought with him to the noblemen of Quraysh who were none other than his own people. 'Urwah stressed the point that such opprobrium would attach to Muhammad as well as to the Quraysh even though the two had been at war with each other. On hearing this, Abu Bakr objected loudly to 'Urwah's request that the Prophet of God separate himself from the people. While talking to Muhammad, 'Urwah touched Muhammad's beard in supplication, and al Mughirah ibn Shu'bah, standing on the side of the Prophet, struck the hand of 'Urwah every time it was stretched toward Muhammad's beard despite the fact that 'Urwah had ransomed al Mughirah by paying the bloodwit of the thirteen men whom all Mughirah had killed prior to his conversion to Islam. Accordingly, 'Urwah returned to Makkah after convincing himself that Muhammad had not come to wage war but to honor the holy sanctuary in fulfillment of a divine imperative. Upon return to the Quraysh, he said to them: "O Men of Quraysh, I have visited Chosroes, Caesar, and the Negus in their respective courts. By God, I have never seen a king attaching himself to his people as Muhammad does. His companions love him and honor him and revere him so much that they carefully lift every hair that falls off his body, and they save the water with which he performs his ablutions. They will never allow any hand to fall on him. Judge then accordingly."

Muhammad's Delegation to Quraysh

In this way, negotiations between Muhammad and the Quraysh lasted a long time. Muhammad wondered whether or not the delegates of
Quraysh had enough courage and initiative to convince the Quraysh with
the facts which they had noted. He therefore sent a delegate from his own
camp to inform the Quraysh of the Muslim view. The Makkans slew the
camel of Muhammad's delegate and were about to kill him when the
Ahabish intervened and let him go free. This conduct of the Makkans
only confirmed their hostile spirit and, consequently, the Muslims began
to lose patience and think of fighting their way through. While still considering what to do, some plebeians from Makkah went out under the
cover of night to throw stones at the tents of the Muslims. The latter sent
out forty or fifty men who encircled the attackers, captured them and
brought them to the Prophet for judgment. To the surprise of everyone,
Muhammad forgave the attackers and allowed them to go free in accordance with his general plan for peace and in deference to the holy month
in which no blood was to be shed in al Hudaybiyah, an area falling within the holy ground of Makkah. The Quraysh for their part were stupefied
by this conduct of Muhammad and lost every argument they had that
Muhammad wanted war. It had become absolutely certain that any attack
on the part of the Quraysh against Muhammad would be regarded by all
Arabs as a sneaking, treacherous act of aggression which Muhammad
would be perfectly entitled to repel with all power at his disposal.

The Prophet of God — May God's blessing be upon him — tested
the patience of the Quraysh once more by sending a delegate from his
camp to negotiate with them. He called 'Umar ibn al Khattab for the job
of conveying his message to the noblemen of Quraysh. 'Umar, however,
pleaded with the Prophet of God that since none of his people, the Banu
'Adiyy ibn Ka'b, were left in Quraysh, he would be unprotected prey for
them to pounce upon in revenge for his many offenses against them. He
counseled the Prophet to send another man, 'Uthman ibn 'Affan, who was
far more protected among the Quraysh than he. The Prophet called
'Uthman ibn 'Affan, his son-in-law, and sent him to Abu Sufyan and the
noblemen of Quraysh. 'Uthman proceeded to Makkah, and on its outskirts was met by Aban ibn Sa'id who extended to him his protection for
the duration of time that it would take him to convey his message.
'Uthman approached the noblemen of Quraysh and handed over the
Prophet's message. They suggested to him that he might circumambulate
the sanctuary if he wished. But he declined, saying, "I shall never do so

until the Prophet of God had done so himself." He continued to insist that the Muslims had come to Makkah simply in order to visit the holy shrine and to glorify it and to perform the religious duty of pilgrimage. He pointed out that the Muslims had brought with them their sacrificial animals and pleaded that if they were allowed to sacrifice them, they would return in peace. The Quraysh pleaded that they had already sworn defiantly that Muhammad would not be allowed to enter Makkah this year. The negotiations lasted a long time during which 'Uthman was forced to stay in Makkah. Soon the Muslims began to suspect that he had been treacherously put to death. Perhaps during this time the noblemen of Quraysh were busy conversing with 'Uthman in an attempt to find a common form in which their pledge not to allow Muhammad to enter Makkah this year, and the Muslim's desire to visit the Holy House and to fulfill their religious duty, could be composed. Perhaps, too, they appreciated 'Uthman's frankness and sincerity and were seriously engaged in discussing with him how best to reorganize the relations with Muhammad in the future.

The Covenant of al Ridwan

Whatever the reason, 'Uthman's failure to return quickly caused the Muslims at Hudaybiyah no little anxiety. They began to give vent to their imagination by picturing the Quraysh treacherously attacking them in the holy month despite the sanctity of the occasion and of the purpose for which they came. They feared that the Quraysh would violate the religious conscience of all Arabia with impudence, even within the holy sanctuary or on the holy grounds of Makkah. With tension rising in the Muslim camp, and everybody reaching for his sword, Muhammad assured them that he would not allow them to return without challenging their enemies. He called his companions to him under a large tree in the middle of that valley, and there they covenanted with him to fight to the last man. Their faith was certain, their conviction was strong, and their will was determined to avenge the blood of 'Uthman whom they thought the Quraysh had murdered in Makkah. This covenant was called the Covenant of al Ridwan; and in its regard, the following verse was revealed: "God is pleased with the believers who have covenanted with you under the tree. God knows what is in their hearts and, therefore, He has granted them His peace and will soon give them great victory."[5] When the Muslims concluded their covenant, Muhammad — May God's peace and blessing be upon him —

pledged the same covenant on behalf of 'Uthman, and the latter was regarded as if he were present. Thereupon, swords shook in their scabbards and the Muslims realized that war was now inevitable. Everybody looked forward to the day of victory or martyrdom with a mind convinced and satisfied, and a heart reassured and at peace. While in this state, the news reached them that 'Uthman had not been murdered, and soon the man himself returned safe and sound. The Covenant of al Ridwan, however, like the great Covenant of al 'Aqabah, remained a great landmark in Muslim history. Muhammad was particularly pleased with this covenant for the evidence it furnished of the strength of the bonds which tied him and his companions together, and for the readiness of the Muslims to face the greatest dangers without fear. For whoever is willing to face death will find that death itself shies away from him, life itself surrenders to him, and victory is always his own to reach.

The Quraysh's Response

Upon return, 'Uthman conveyed to Muhammad the message of the Quraysh. They entertained no more doubt that the Muslims had come to Makkah for anything but the religious purpose of pilgrimage to the Holy House, and they realized that they had no right to prevent any Arab from performing his pilgrimage or 'umrah during the holy month. Nonetheless, they had mobilized their army under the leadership of Khalid ibn al Walid to prevent Muhammad and his companions from entering Makkah, and some skirmishes had taken place between the two parties. After all this had happened, to let Muhammad enter Makkah would allow the tribes to conclude that the Quraysh had been defeated and, as a result, their position in the Peninsula would suffer greatly. Therefore, the Quraysh argued, they must insist on maintaining this decision of theirs in order to preserve their reputation and prestige. They invited Muhammad to think out with them both his and their position that together they might find an outlet from this difficulty. By themselves they saw no escape from a war which they would have to wage whether they wanted to or not. Rather, they wished they might not have to fight during the holy months because of their religious sanctity and out of fear that should those months be violated, then the tribes would never feel secure that they would not be violated again in the future. The result of a present conflict would be that the security of passage to Makkah and to its market, of the religious rites and of the prosperity of the Makkans and Arabs alike would all go aground.

Negotiations

Another round of negotiations between the two parties followed. The Quraysh sent Suhayl ibn 'Amr to reconcile Muhammad and to ask him to return for the same purpose the following year. They argued that in such an arrangement the tribes would not claim that Muhammad had entered Makkah in defiance of the Quraysh. Suhayl began his negotiations with the Prophet, and these lasted a long time during which they were interrupted and resumed again by both parties, anxious as they were for the negotiations to succeed. In the Muslim camp the Muslims listened in on these negotiations and often lost patience at their involvement and length, the obstinacy with which Suhayl refused to make any concessions, and the leniency with which the Prophet made his. Were it not for the absolute confidence the Muslims had in their Prophet, they would have never accepted the terms reached by those negotiations. They would have fought with the Makkans and either entered Makkah victorious or perished in the process. Even such a great man as 'Umar ibn al Khattab lost patience and said to Abu Bakr, "O Abu Bakr, isn't Muhammad the Prophet of God and aren't we Muslims?" Abu Bakr answered in the affirmative. 'Umar then said, "Why then should we give in to the unbelievers in a matter vital to our faith?" Abu Bakr replied, "O 'Umar, do not trespass one inch where you ought not to go. Remember that I witness that our leader is the Prophet of God." Angrily, 'Umar acquiesced by replying: "I, too, witness that our leader is the Prophet of God."

Conclusion of the Treaty (March, 628 C.E.)

'Umar turned to Muhammad and complained to him with the same anger and resentment, but could not alter the Prophet's determination and patience. Their talk was concluded with the Prophet's statement that he was the servant of God and His Prophet and that he would not deviate from the divine commandment nor entertain any doubt of divine support. So patient was Muhammad in these negotiations that many Muslims remembered anecdotes which speak most eloquently to this effect. It is reported, for instance, that Muhammad called 'Ali ibn Abu Talib and said to him: "Write, 'In the name of God, the Merciful, the Compassionate.'" Suhayl, the non-Muslim delegate of Quraysh interrupted. "Stop," he said, "I do not know either 'the Merciful' or 'the Compassionate.' Write, 'In your name, O God.'" The Prophet of God instructed 'Ali to write accordingly and continued: "Write, 'Following is the text of a pact reached by Muhammad, the Prophet of God and Suhayl ibn 'Amr.'" Suhayl again interrupted. "Stop it. If I accepted you as a Prophet of God I would not have been hostile to you. You should write only your name and the name of your father." The Prophet of God instructed 'Ali to write accordingly, referring to himself as Muhammad ibn 'Abdullah. The text of the treaty was redacted and agreed upon. In the opinion of most biographers, the treaty specified that the peace was to last for ten years. According to al Waqidi, the peace was stipulated for only two years. The pact also specified that any person from Quraysh emigrating to Muhammad's camp without permission from his guardian would have to be returned to Makkah, whereas any Muslim emigrating from Muhammad's camp to Makkah would not have to be returned. It also specified that any tribe was free to ally itself to Muhammad without incurring any guilt or censure from Quraysh, and likewise, any tribe seeking an alliance with Quraysh could do so without let or hindrance from the Muslims. The pact stipulated that Muhammad and his companions would leave the area of Makkah that year without fulfilling their religious function but that they might return the next year, enter the city and stay therein three days for this purpose while carrying no more than swords in their scabbards.

Promulgation of the Treaty

As soon as this pact was solemnly concluded by the parties concerned, the tribe of Khuza'ah entered into an alliance with Muhammad and that of Banu Bakr with Quraysh. Soon after, Abu Jandal ibn Suhayl ibn 'Amr left Makkah forever and came to the Muslim camp seeking to join the Muslims. When Suhayl, the delegate of Quraysh to the Muslim camp, saw his son change loyalties in his presence, he struck him in the face and pulled him by the hair to return to the Quraysh. Abu Jandal was calling upon the Muslims to save him from the fate of being returned to the unbelievers who would persecute him for his faith. This greatly increased the Muslims' resentment and their dissatisfaction with the pact the Prophet had just concluded with Suhayl. But Muhammad spoke to Abu Jandal. "O Abu Jandal," he said, "have patience and be disciplined; for God will soon provide for you and your other persecuted colleagues a way out of your suffering. We have entered with the Quraysh into a treaty of peace and we have exchanged with them a solemn pledge that none will cheat the other." Abu Jandal returned to Quraysh in compliance with the demand of this treaty and Suhayl returned to Makkah. Muhammad, too, was disconcerted with the resentment and dissatisfaction of the Muslims around him. After reciting his prayers he felt reassured, sought his sacrificial animal, and slaughtered it. Then, he sat down and shaved his head, thus declaring the 'umrah, or lesser pilgrimage, complete. His soul was satisfied and his heart full of contentment, as if the peace of God had come upon him. When the people saw what he did and observed the peace of soul shining through his face, they began to slaughter their animals and to shave off their hair. Some of them shaved off their hair completely and others only in part. Muhammad said, "God Bless those who shaved their heads." The people asked him about those who only cut their hair short, and Muhammad repeated his blessing for the benefit of those who *shaved* their heads. After the people asked him three times and he repeated the same blessing three times, he was asked: "Why, O Prophet of God, do you exclude those who cut off their hair short from your blessing?" He answered, "Because the shavers did not doubt, whereas the others did."[6]

The Treaty of Hudaybiyah: A Genuine Victory

Nothing remained for the Muslims to do except to return to Madinah and there await the arrival of the coming season for another trip to Makkah. Most of them accepted this idea grudgingly, and consoled themselves purely on the grounds that the unwelcome compliance therewith was only the command of the Prophet himself. They were not accustomed to acquiesce in a defeat or to surrender without a fight. Moreover, in their faith in God and in the timely assistance that God would grant to His Prophet, his religion and themselves, they could entertain no shadow of a doubt of their ability to storm Makkah if only Muhammad had commanded it. They stayed in al Hudaybiyah a few days questioning one another regarding the wisdom of this pact which the Prophet had concluded. Some of them were inclined to doubt its wisdom. But they bore in patience and then returned home. On their way home between Makkah and Madinah, the *surah* "al Fath" was revealed to the Prophet, and he recited it to his companions.

اِنَّا فَتَحْنَا لَكَ فَتْحًا مُبِينًا لِيَغْفِرَ لَكَ اللهُ مَا تَقَدَّمَ مِنْ ذَنْبِكَ وَمَا تَأَخَّرَ وَيُتِمَّ نِعْمَتَهُ عَلَيْكَ وَ يَهْدِيَكَ صِرَاطًا مُسْتَقِيمًا

"We have granted to you a clear victory that God may forgive you your past and future shortcomings, grant you His blessings, and guide you to the straight path."[7]

There was hence no reason to doubt that the Hudaybiyah Treaty was a victory for the Muslims. History has shown that this pact was the product of profound political wisdom and farsightedness and that it brought about consequences of great advantage to Islam and indeed to Arabia as a whole. It was the first time that Quraysh acknowledged that Muhammad was an equal rather than a mere rebel and runaway tribesman. It was the first time that Makkah acknowledged the Islamic state that was rising in Arabia. Makkan acquiescence in the right of the Muslims to visit the sanctuary and to perform the pilgrimage was equally a recognition on her part that Islam was an established and approved religion in the Peninsula. Furthermore, the peace of the following two or ten years gave the Muslims the peace and security they needed on their southern flank without fear of an invasion from Quraysh. The peace also contributed to the spread of Islam. Even Quraysh, the most determined enemy of Islam and its greatest antagonist, had by this pact come to recognize Islam and its community, and to acquiesce in that in which it had never acquiesced before. Indeed, Islam spread after this treaty more widely and quickly than it had ever spread before. While those who accompanied Muhammad to Hudaybiyah counted one thousand and four hundred, those who accompanied him on his conquest of Makkah two years later counted well over ten thousand. The greatest objection to those who doubted the wisdom of the Hudaybiyah pact was directed to the provision that any Quraysh member joining the Muslims without the permission of his guardian would have to be returned to Quraysh, and that any apostate from Islam would not have to be returned to Madinah. Muhammad's opinion in this matter centered on the consideration that the apostate from Islam who seeks the shelter of Quraysh is not really worthy of readmission to the Muslim community; that for the convert who wished to join that community but who was not allowed to at present, God would soon find an outlet. Events have confirmed this judgment of Muhammad far more quickly than his companions anticipated, and given evidence that Islam had actually drawn great advantages. Indeed, the treaty even made it possible two months later for Muhammad to begin to address himself to the kings and chiefs of foreign states and invite them to join Islam.

The Story of Abu Basir

Events succeeded one another very rapidly, all of which confirmed Muhammad's judgment and wisdom. Abu Basir became a Muslim and escaped from Makkah to Madinah. Obviously, the provisions of the Hudaybiyah Treaty applied to him and demanded his return to the Quraysh, for he had not obtained the permission of his master. Azhar ibn 'Awf and al Akhnas ibn Shariq wrote to the Prophet to this effect and sent their letter with a tribesman of Banu 'Amir and a slave of theirs. When the demand was made, the Prophet called Abu Basir and said to him: "We have covenanted with the Quraysh to honor the Treaty of Hudaybiyah which you well know. In our religion, we are not permitted to cheat. You should therefore return to your people. God will grant to you and to the other persecuted Muslims a means of emancipation in His good time." Abu Basir objected to the Prophet that the unbelievers would force him to apostatize. The Prophet, however, repeated the same judgment to him. Abu Basir had, therefore, to give himself up to the two messengers and accompany them back to Makkah. Once they arrived at Dhu al Hulayfah, Abu Basir asked the Banu 'Amir tribesman to show him his sword, and as soon as he laid his hand upon it, he struck the tribesman with it and killed him. The Makkan slave ran toward Madinah and into the Prophet's presence with obvious signs of fear and panic on his face. When interrogated, the slave told the Prophet that Abu Basir had killed his master. Soon, Abu Basir himself arrived brandishing his sword and addressing Muhammad: "O Prophet of God, you have fulfilled your duty under the Treaty and God has relieved you of your obligation, for you have in fact surrendered me to my people as the treaty prescribed. But I was not willing to allow myself to be persecuted, enticed away, or forced to abjure my religion." The Prophet did not hide his admiration for him and wished that he had many companions. Later on, Abu Basir went to al 'Is on the sea coast, on the road which the Quraysh followed to al Sham and which the Treaty of Hudaybiyah prescribed to keep open for Makkan trade. When his story and that of Muhammad's admiration of him reached Makkah, the Muslims still residing there were elated, and about seventy of them ran away to al 'Is to follow him as their chief. Abu Basir and his companions began to cut off the trade route on their own initiative, killing any unbeliever they caught and seizing any camels belonging to Quraysh. Only then did it dawn on the Quraysh what a loss they had incurred by insisting as they did on keeping their Muslim members or slaves in forced residence in Makkah. They realized that the man who is truly committed to

Islam was a greater handicap to them than the loss of him altogether to the Muslim camp. Such a man would escape at the first opportunity without entering into the camp of Muhammad and, hence, without becoming an outlaw under the prescriptions of the Hudaybiyah Treaty. He would then wage a terrible war against the Makkans in which the Makkans had everything to lose and nothing to gain. Remembering too well that Muhammad had cut off the caravan road after his emigration to Madinah, the Quraysh feared that Abu Basir would do likewise. They therefore wrote to the Prophet asking him, in violation of the Hudaybiyah Treaty, to accept their fugitives into his camp in order to keep the caravan route open. In the consequent negotiation, the Quraysh relinquished the privilege emphasized by Suhayl ibn 'Amr so strongly, namely, that the Muslims of Quraysh who escape therefrom without approval of their masters or guardians be returned to Quraysh. Thus, the concession criticized by 'Umar ibn al Khattab and for the sake of which he revolted against Abu Bakr was dropped by request of the Quraysh. Muhammad then invited all the Muslims to enter Madinah, and the caravan route to al Sham became once more secure.

Muslim Women Emigrants

As for the Muslim women of Quraysh who escaped to Madinah, Muhammad had a different opinion. Umm Kulthum, daughter of 'Uqbah ibn abu Mu'ayt, escaped from Makkah to Madinah after the Hudaybiyah Treaty, and her two brothers 'Umarah and al Walid came to the Prophet demanding her return under terms of the Treaty. The Prophet refused, judging that the treaty did not apply to women and that if women called for assistance and shelter, their request could not be turned down. Furthermore, when a woman becomes a Muslim, she is no more legally tied to her husband who is an unbeliever. Dissolution of the bond of marriage is then automatic. On this point, the revelation is clear: "O Men who believe, if the women believers come to you for shelter, examine them, remembering that God knows the nature of their faith better than anyone. If you find them to be true believers, do not return them to the polytheists to whom they are no longer legitimate. Return to them that which they have spent and marry them if you wish; for there is no blame upon you if you do so, provided you give them their dowries. Do not hold to your matrimonial ties with women unbelievers, but ask them to return what you have spent and return to them what they have spent and separate yourselves from each other. That is the judgment of God and He wishes to see it observed among you. God is All-Knowing and All-Wise."[8] Thus events confirmed Muhammad's wisdom, foresight, and deep political insight. History has indeed proved that the Treaty of al Hudaybiyah actually laid down a very important foundation for Islam's political career as well as for its spread throughout the world. That is the meaning of the clear victory God had promised.

Relations between Quraysh and Muhammad became quite peaceful and settled after the Treaty of al Hudaybiyah. Both parties felt secure. The Quraysh embarked on enlarging trade, hoping to recapture the losses which had resulted from the war with the Muslims in which the road to al Sham was cut. As for Muhammad, he embarked on a wider policy of mission, seeking to bring his message to all men in all corners of the earth and to lay down the foundations for the happiness and success of the Muslims throughout the Peninsula now that their security was guaranteed. Both these considerations enabled him to send his messengers to the kings in the surrounding empires and, especially after the Battle of Khaybar, to expel the Jews from the Arabian Peninsula altogether.

The Campaign of Khaybar and Missions to Kings

Muhammad and the Muslims returned from al Hudaybiyah to Madinah three weeks after the signing of the treaty with Quraysh and the agreement that they would not enter Makkah that year but the following year. Many of them returned with wounded pride. They continued to feel dejected and despondent until *surah* "al Fath,"[1] revealed on the road to Madinah, alleviated their despondency. While in Hudaybiyah as well as after the return to Madinah, Muhammad thought about what he should do to strengthen the faith of his companions and to spread the message of Islam. He thought of sending messengers to Heraclius, Chosroes, the Archbishop of Alexandria, the Negus of Abyssinia, King al Harith of Ghassan, and the satrap of Chosroes in Yaman. He also pondered the necessity of eliminating Jewish influence in the Arabian Peninsula once and for all.

Crystallization of the Islamic Call

In fact, the Islamic message had by this time reached a high level of crystallization and comprehensiveness. The time was ripe for its dissemination among mankind. Besides the doctrine of the unity of God and its implications for worship and ethics, the Islamic message developed so widely as to include within its purview all aspects of social activity and human relations. These it sought to regulate and infuse with its ethos and spirit. It attached such importance to man's social relations that it put its precepts for social behavior on a level with the doctrine of the unity of God. The system of principles Islam elaborated came nearer than any other to enable man to attain perfection and to realize the absolute, or the highest ideals in space-time. Hence, a large number of specific proscriptions were revealed during this period to regulate man's social relationships.

The Proscription of Alcohol

Biographers of the Prophet have disagreed regarding the time of the prohibition of alcohol. Some assert that it took place in the fourth year A.H. Most of them; however, agree that it took place in the same year as the Hudaybiyah pact. The purpose of the prohibition of alcohol was purely a social one, unrelated to the unity of God as a purely theological doctrine. The evidence for this is the fact that the Qur'an remained silent on this problem for a period of approximately twenty years after Muhammad's commission to prophethood. Throughout this period, the Muslims continued to use alcohol. Further evidence to this effect comes from the fact that the prohibition itself was not categorically laid down all at once, but was revealed progressively and at intervals. There was a series of prohibitions, each prescribing a limitative measure of use. Total abstinence was not demanded until near the end of the Madinese period of the revelation. It is told that 'Umar ibn al Khattab inquired about the drinking of wine and prayed for God to show the Muslims His will in this regard, and that it was in this connection that the verse was revealed saying, "When they ask you about drinking wine and gambling, answer that they constitute great evil as well as advantage to the people but that their evil is greater than their good."[2] Despite the indication this verse gave, the Muslims who were in the habit of drinking did not stop. Some of them in a state of drunkenness would pray without knowing what they were reciting. Again 'Umar prayed God to show more of His will in this matter. The common Arabic saying, "Alcohol causes the loss of both mind and money," is attributed by tradition to him. Later, another step toward prohibition was taken with the following revelation: "O Men who believe, do not hold the prayers while you are in a state of drunkenness. Recover yourselves first until you become fully conscious of what you are about to recite."[3] From that day on, the town crier of the Prophet proclaimed at the times of prayer: "Let no drunken man come to prayer." Despite this new limitation upon alcohol, 'Umar continued to pray to God to send down yet clearer revelation concerning it. Personally, 'Umar was quite opposed to alcohol because the Arabs often drank to the point of losing decorum, pulling one another's beards and hitting one another. It so happened that at a banquet which included Muhajirun and Ansar, a member of the former group boasted of his peoples' superiority over the latter group. A member of al Ansar, equally intoxicated, wounded the former in the nose by hitting him with a skull bone. Under the influence of liquor, the two groups quarreled, fought, and generated all kinds of hatred toward one another until they almost destroyed their previous harmony and mutual esteem. On this occasion, God said in a special revelation:

يَٰٓأَيُّهَا ٱلَّذِينَ ءَامَنُوٓاْ إِنَّمَا ٱلْخَمْرُ وَٱلْمَيْسِرُ وَٱلْأَنصَابُ وَٱلْأَزْلَٰمُ رِجْسٌ مِّنْ عَمَلِ ٱلشَّيْطَٰنِ فَٱجْتَنِبُوهُ لَعَلَّكُمْ تُفْلِحُونَ إِنَّمَا يُرِيدُ ٱلشَّيْطَٰنُ أَن يُوقِعَ بَيْنَكُمُ ٱلْعَدَٰوَةَ وَٱلْبَغْضَآءَ فِى ٱلْخَمْرِ وَٱلْمَيْسِرِ وَيَصُدَّكُمْ عَن ذِكْرِ ٱللَّهِ وَعَنِ ٱلصَّلَوٰةِ فَهَلْ أَنتُم مُّنتَهُونَ

"O men who believe, alcohol, gambling, idols, and divination arrows are an abomination of Satan's handiwork. Avoid them, therefore, that you may be felicitous. Satan wishes to infuse enmity and hatred among you through alcohol and gambling. He wishes to keep you intoxicated that you may not remember God, and hence fail to hold prayer. Will you not listen and stop being his tools?"[4]

On the day this revelation was made and the prohibition of alcohol was instituted, Anas, the wine seller and server, spilled all the alcohol in his possession. Other men who were not pleased by the new legislation asked: "Could alcohol be a real abomination even though it was consumed by some of the martyrs of Uhud and Badr?" In response to them, the following verse was revealed: "Those who believed and did the good may not be blamed for what they consumed, inasmuch as they feared God, believed, and did good works. For God loves the virtuous."[5]

By commanding mercy and compassion, the doing of good works, disciplining the soul and character by means of worship, and eliminating false pride by means of kneeling and prostration in prayer, Islam became the natural perfection of all previous religions, the religion to which all men are called.

The Persian and Byzantine Empires

Heraclius and Chosroes were at the time the chiefs of the Roman and Persian empires, the greatest states of the age and the makers and arbiters of world policy and world destiny. Between them war was continual, as we have had occasion to see. The Persians were at first victorious and conquered Palestine and Egypt. They governed Jerusalem from where they moved away the cross of Christ. Later, the arm of destiny moved, and it was the Roman flag that flew over Egypt, Syria, and Palestine. Heraclius recovered the cross and put it back in its original place after a pilgrimage to Jerusalem on foot in fulfillment of a vow he had taken before victory. One can easily appreciate the position of the two empires if one remembers the tremendous fear which their very names inspired in any person who fell within their reach. Men were so awed by the two empires that no state or community could think of opposing them, and every man kept on good terms with their authorities and representatives as essential to survival. Since the world of the time was one divided between the spheres of influence of these two giants, it was natural for the Arabian Peninsula to fall within the one or the other. 'Iraq was under Persia while Egypt and al Sham were under the influence of Rome. Hijaz and the entire remainder of the Arabian Peninsula were divided between the two. Whatever prosperity the Arabs enjoyed depended wholly upon trade between Yaman and al Sham. It was absolutely essential, therefore, that the Arabs enjoy the friendship of Khosrau as well as of Heraclius if their trade was to be successful. The Arab population consisted of tribes, sometimes mutually hostile, sometimes peaceful, but never related to one another by a bond constituting a political structure capable of counteracting the influence of either of the two great powers. It was hence amazing that Muhammad would think of sending his messengers to the two great kings, as well as to Ghassan and Yaman, to Egypt and Abyssinia, and to call them all to his religion without fear of the consequences of such deeds for the Arabian Peninsula as a whole, or without fear that Roman and Persian influence in Arabia might actually be transformed into a solid yoke of subjugation.

The Prophet's Delegates

Muhammad, however, did not hesitate to call all these men to the religion of truth. One day, addressing his companions, Muhammad said: "O men, God has sent me to be a Prophet of mercy to all mankind. Do not, therefore, disagree and divide as the disciples of Jesus, son of Mary, did after him." When his companions asked him to explain, he replied: "Jesus had called his disciples to the same truth to which I have called you. Those of them whom he sent to places close by accepted and observed the truth that Jesus had conveyed; those whom he sent to faraway places did not like that truth and could not accept it." Muhammad mentioned to them that he was planning to send messengers to Heraclius, the Archbishop of Alexandria; to al Harith of Ghassan, King of al Hirah; to al Harith of Himyar, King of Yaman; and to the Negus of Abyssinia, calling them all to Islam. The companions approved and made for him a seal out of silver which read "Muhammad, the Prophet of God." Muhammad sent letters to these chiefs, an example of which is the message sent to Heraclius. It read as follows: "In the name of God, the Merciful, the Compassionate. From Muhammad ibn 'Abdullah to Heraclius, Emperor of Byzantium. Peace be upon the rightly guided. I call you to the religion of Islam. If you convert, you will be saved and God will double your reward. If you do not convert, responsibility for the salvation of your subjects rests with you.[6] O People of the Book, come now to a fair principle, common to both of us, namely, that we worship only God, that we do not associate aught with Him and that we do not take one another as lords besides God. But if they refuse, then say, 'Take note that we are Muslims.'"

The Prophet gave this message to Dihyah ibn Khalifah al Kalbi and asked him to convey it to Heraclius. He dictated a similar letter to Chosroes and asked 'Abdullah ibn Hudhafah al Sahmi to convey it to him. Another letter addressed to the Negus was handed to 'Umar ibn Umayyah al Damri. A letter to the Archbishop of Alexandria was handed to Hatib ibn abu Balta'ah; to the King of Yamanah, to Salit ibn 'Amr; to the King of Bahrayn, to al 'Ala' ibn al Hadrami; to al Harith of Ghassan, King of the Approaches of al Sham, to Shuja' ibn Wahb al Asadi; to al Harith of Himyar, King of Yaman, to Ibn Umayyah al Makhzumi. All these men went out each to the destination assigned to him by the Prophet. Most historians affirm that they started their journeys in various directions at the same time. Some, however, assert that they were sent at different intervals.

Persia and Byzantium

That Muhammad sent such missions to the kings of the world is truly surprising. More surprising still is the fact that within barely thirty years

of the time he sent those missions, the kingdoms of these kings were conquered by the Muslims and most of their inhabitants converted to Islam.
The surprise, however, is dissipated when one remembers that the two
great empires disputing the leadership of the world and dividing it
between their two civilizations were really disputing only the material
possessions of the world. In both of them, spiritual power had long been
decaying. Persia, for its part, was divided between paganism and
Zoroastrianism. The Christianity of Byzantium, on the other hand, was
rife with dispute and controversy between various sects. There was no single conviction, neither faith nor world view, to inspire the hearts and satisfy the minds of the people. Rather, religion had become a series of rites
and superstitions by which the Church was exercising its control and
exploitation of the masses of mankind. As for the new call of Muhammad,
it was purely spiritual, raising man to the highest levels of his humanity.
Wherever matter contends with spirit, wherever care for the present contends with the hope for eternity, matter and concern for the present are
sure to lose.

Furthermore, despite their greatness, both Persia and Byzantium had
lost the power of initiative, creativity, and culture-building. In thought,
feeling and action, the two empires had declined to the level of ancestor-
imitation where every novelty was looked upon as misguidance and abomination. But human society, like individual men and all living organisms,
must renew itself every day. Either it remains youthful renewing itself,
recreating, reconstructing, and always adding to its life, or it reaches old
age and, being incapable of recreation and reconstruction, spends its own
life-capital. Its ensuing history is a continuing reduction and downfall
toward a tragic end. Any human society which has thus fallen is susceptible to renewal and recreation by another society youthful enough to instill
new life into anything it touches. Such a new element, full of life power
and youth and growing in close proximity to Persia and Byzantium was
Muhammad. His mission was so new and vigorous that it breathed new
life into the masses of mankind whose spirit had been destroyed internal-
ly by the vacuitous rites and superstitions of the decaying societies in the
great empires. The fire of the new faith which illumined the soul of the
Prophet and the indomitable power of his soul explain the fact of his calling the kings of the earth to Islam, the religion of truth and perfection, the
religion of God — May He be revered! The great kings were called to the
religion which liberated the mind to reason and the heart to see for itself.
Islam was the religion which gave man, whether in the life of worship or

in the ordering of society, general principles which harmonized the powers of spirit and matter and made possible the highest levels of life on
earth. Where such harmony prevails, there is neither weakness nor false
pride. After going through all the stages of necessary development, human
society can reach the highest possible level of existence designed for it.

Elimination of Jewish Influence in Arabia

But would Muhammad send his missions to the foreign kings while
his own domain was threatened by the treacherous Jews who were still living to the north of Madinah? It is true that the Treaty of Hudaybiyah had
secured his southern flank, especially from Quraysh. But what about the
north, where both Heraclius and Chosroes might attack Madinah in
cooperation with the Jews of Khaybar who were anxious for an opportunity to take revenge upon Muhammad? It would be relatively easy for
either emperor to remind the Jews of the fate of their co-religionists, the
Banu Qurayzah, Banu al Nadir, and Banu Qaynuqa', who had previously
been expelled from their dwellings after blockade, fighting, and war, and
to incite them to new ventures against Muhammad. For their enmity and
bitterness surpassed that of Quraysh. They were more attached to their
religion, more intelligent, and more learned. On the other hand, it was not
possible to reconcile them with a peace treaty like that of Hudaybiyah
since the covenant of Madinah had been violated by them ,much to their
own detriment. Were help to come to them from the side of Byzantium,
their natural inclination to rise again against Muhammad could not be
contained. Hence, it was thought necessary to put a final end to their
influence in the Arabian Peninsula, and to do so quickly without giving
them the time to forge any new alliances with Ghatafan or any of other
tribe hostile to Muhammad.

And such Muhammad did. He had hardly spent fifteen days after his
return from al Hudaybiyah — a month according to another version —
when he commanded the people to prepare for the campaign of Khaybar,
restricting the call to arms to those who had accompanied him to al
Hudaybiyah. His purpose was to leave behind all those interested in booty,
and to go out with the truly loyal followers who sought service for the sake
of God. The Muslims marched forth one thousand and six hundred
strong, including a cavalry of one hundred. They were confident of God's
assistance and victory, and recalled *surah* "al Fath" which was revealed
shortly after the signing of the Hudaybiyah treaty; "When you go forth

and booty lies ahead of you, those who remained behind and did not participate in the previous campaign will ask to accompany you that they
might share in the spoils. Thus they seek to change the decrees of God.
Say to them, 'It is not given to you to accompany us, for that is the decree
of God which has been given.' They will accuse you of jealousy and envy,
but their understanding is meager and their intelligence is dim."[7]

The March against Khaybar

Muhammad and his men crossed the distance between Khaybar and
Madinah in three days. Khaybar did not learn of their move until the
Muslims' forces stood in front of their fortifications. In the morning,
when the Khaybar workmen went out of their homes to go to their plantations, they saw the Muslim army for the first time and ran away shouting to one another, "There is Muhammad and his army." When
Muhammad heard them, he said: "Khaybar is doomed; whenever we enter
the enemy's land, the fate of that enemy is sealed."

Jewish Reaction

Nonetheless, the Jews of Khaybar did in fact anticipate Muhammad's
move and thought of ways and means of escape. Some leaders advised
Khaybar to form a block with the Jews of Wadi al Qura and Tayma' and
to take the initiative in attacking Madinah first. This group saw no point
in depending upon Arab tribes. Other leaders advised that it was more
salutary for them to enter into a new pact with the Prophet in order to
mitigate Muslim hatred and hostility, especially among al Ansar. This suggestion was particularly appealing after the experience in Madinah, when
Huyayy ibn Akhtab and his party had instigated the Arab tribes to attack
Madinah and sack its fortification in the Campaign of al Khandaq. The
truth is, however, that neither Jews nor Muslims were ready for any conciliation, especially since the Muslims had killed Sallam ibn Abu al
Huqayq and al Yasir ibn Razzam, two Khaybar chieftains, before venturing out on their present expedition against Khaybar. As a consequence, the
Jews were constantly in touch with the tribe of Ghatafan and sent to them
for help as soon as they discovered Muhammad's army in their domain.
Historians differ regarding Ghatafan's answer to Khaybar's call, whether
they actually did come to Khaybar's rescue or whether the Muslim army
prevented any such assistance from reaching Khaybar.

The Two Armies

Regardless of whether Ghatafan had actually helped the Jews or not, it soon renounced its attachment to them and became neutral as early as Muhammad promised it a share in the spoils of war. The campaign of Khaybar was one of the greatest. The masses of Jews living in Khaybar were the strongest, the richest, and the best equipped for war of all the peoples of Arabia. The Muslims, for their part, were certain that as long as the Jews held any power in the Peninsula, the two religions would have to compete with each other endlessly. That is why they advanced so resolutely and fought so valiantly. The Quraysh as well as the whole Arabian Peninsula watched the campaign and awaited its results. Some Quraysh tribesmen wagered with one another concerning its outcome; many believed that the tables would now be turned against the Muslims, knowing how fortified were the dwellings, how impregnable the city stood perched over rocks and mountains, and how experienced its people were in the arts of war.

The Muslims' Blockade

The Muslims, on the other hand, brought to Khaybar all the equipment and preparation they could muster. After consulting one another and listening to Sallam ibn Miskham, their chief, the Jews decided to assemble their wealth and children in the fortified quarters of al Watih and al Sulalim, to place their ammunition at Na'im, and to deploy their fighting men at Natat where Sallam ibn Mishkam would lead them in battle to the bitter end. The two armies met at Natat and fought each other strongly. The encounter, however, was not decisive. There were fifty wounded among the Muslims on the first day and probably many more than this among the Jews. When Sallam ibn Mishkam was killed, al Harith ibn Abu Zaynab took over the leadership of the Jewish forces. Charging from the fortress of Na'im, the new leader attacked the Muslim army at the flank, but he was soon repulsed by Banu al Khazraj', who were deployed in that area. As a result of this engagement, the Muslims tightened their encirclement of Khaybar. Realizing that this was their last stand in Arabia, the Jews fought desperately. As the days went by, the Prophet sent Abu Bakr with a contingent and a flag to the fortress of Na'im; but he was not able to conquer it despite heavy fighting. The Prophet then sent 'Umar ibn al Khattab on the following day, but he fared no better than Abu Bakr. On the third day, the Prophet called 'Ali ibn Abu Talib and, blessing him, commanded him to storm the fortress. 'Ali led his force and fought valiantly. In the engagement, he lost his armor and, shielding himself with a portal he had seized, he continued to fight until the fortress was stormed by his troops. The same portal was used by 'Ali as a little bridge to enable the Muslim soldiers to enter the houses within the fortress. The fortress of Na'im fell after the Jewish leader, al Harith ibn Abu Zaynab, was killed in battle. Evidently, both Jews and Muslims were determined to fight it out to the end.

Having stormed the fortress of Na'im, the Muslims then directed their attention to the fortress of al Qamus which they stormed after equally strenuous fighting. Provisions were becoming rather scarce within the Muslim army, and many began to approach Muhammad personally to ask him for something with which to stave off their hunger. Unable to find provisions, Muhammad permitted them to eat horse meat. Later on, a Muslim soldier noticed a herd of goats entering one of the fortifications of the Jews, launched an immediate attack, and seized two animals which were immediately killed and consumed. Not until after they had conquered the fortress of al Sa'b ibn Mu'adh was their shortage relieved. For within that fortress, they found large stores of food that enabled them to continue the blockade of other fortresses. Throughout this campaign, the Jews would not give up a single inch of territory without putting up a heroic struggle for it. Whenever they retreated, it was only before preponderant Muslim forces. At one stage in the campaign, Marhab came out of one of the fortresses fully covered with his military attire and singing the following verses: "Khaybar knows that I am Marhab, that I am an experienced hero fully prepared for war. I deal blows to my enemies and I strike them. Even the lions I face with drawn sword. The ground I hold is unassailable. Even the most experienced in war dares not approach it." Muhammad asked his companions, "Who will rise to meet him?" Muhammad ibn Maslamah rose and said, "Send me, O Prophet of God. For I am the angry bereaved who lost his brother yesterday." The Prophet permitted him and he sprang to meet Marhab. The pair fought valiantly and, at one stage, Marhab almost killed the Muslim. Ibn Maslamah, however, intercepted the falling sword with his shield which bent under its weight and was cut so that the sword could not be pulled out and disengaged. Muhammad ibn Maslamah seized the opportunity and gave Marhab a fatal blow. This war between Muslim and Jew was a hard and savage struggle, and the fortifications of the Jews made it even more so.

Jewish Despair and Collapse

The Muslims then directed their attention to the fortress of al Zubayr and surrounded it for a long time, waging a number of harsh attacks without being able to storm it. At one stage, they seized the water supply of the fortress and stopped its flow. The Jews were forced to come out and engage the Muslims in battle but, faced with preponderant Muslim forces, they fled. Their fortresses fell one after another into Muslim hands, the last of them being those of al Watih and al Sulalim in the al Katibah area. Only then did the Jews become truly desperate, and they begged for peace. The Prophet had already seized most of their possessions at the fortresses of al Shaqq, Natat, and al Katibah. In the circumstances, they had only their own skins to seek to save. Muhammad accepted their plea and permitted them to stay on their land whose title now passed to him by right of conquest. The terms of their surrender provided that they would be given half their crops in compensation for their labor.

The Jews of Khaybar were thus treated differently from those of Banu Qaynuqa' and Banu al Nadir who were forced to evacuate their lands altogether. With the fall of Khaybar, Jewish power no more threatened Islam or the Muslims. Moreover, Khaybar had large areas of orchards and groves of date trees whose maintenance needed an experienced labor force. Although al Ansar, the Muslims of Madinah, were agriculturalists, they were needed back home to tend their own gardens and orchards. The Prophet also needed his men for the purpose of war and could not afford to demobilize his army for the sake of agriculture. The Jews of Khaybar were hence allowed to continue to work their own groves after their political dominion had been destroyed. Despite Muhammad's sharecropping arrangement, the agricultural economy of Khaybar retrogressed after the destruction of Jewish political power. 'Abdullah ibn Rawahah, Muhammad's deputy for the division of the Khaybar crops, dealt justly with the Jews, following in this regard the instructions of the Prophet himself. So honorable was his conduct that he returned to them copies of the Torah seized by the Muslims in the course of the hostilities. This is in direct contrast to the manner in which the Romans treated the Jews when they conquered Jerusalem and burned all the sacred writings they found in the temple and trampled them under foot. It is also far from the Christian persecution of the Jews in Spain where every Torah seized was put to the torch.

As the Jews of Khaybar pleaded for peace while the Muslims blockaded al Watih and al Sulalim at Khaybar, the Prophet sent a message to the Jews of Fadak asking them to surrender their properties and wealth or accept his terms. The people of Fadak were so panic-stricken at the news of Khaybar that they agreed to give up half their wealth without fighting. The wealth of Khaybar was to be distributed among the members of the Muslim armed forces according to rule because they had fought to secure it. The wealth of Fadak, on the other hand, fell to Muhammad,[8] as no Muslims and no fighting were involved in its acquisition.

The Prophet prepared to return to Madinah by way of Wadi al Qura where the Jews of that area prepared to fight the Muslims. Some fighting did indeed take place, but the Jews realized the futility of their resistance and pleaded for peace as Khaybar and Fadak had done before. As for the Jews of Tayma', they accepted to pay the *jizyah* without fighting. Thus, all the Jews of the Peninsula submitted to the authority of the Prophet and their political influence was brought to an end. The northern flank of Muslim power, namely the whole area north of Madinah, was now as secure as the south had become through the Treaty of al Hudaybiyah. With the collapse of Jewish political power, Muslim hatred of the Jews mellowed, and this was especially true of the Ansar of Madinah who even closed their eyes when a number of Jews returned to Madinah to resume their normal trades and professions. Indeed, the Prophet himself sympathized with such Jewish returnees and joined with them in mourning 'Abdullah ibn Ubayy by presenting condolences to his son. Moreover, the Prophet took especial care to instruct Mu'adh ibn Jabal not to sway the Jews from their religion but to allow them to practice it as they had done before. He did not impose any *jizyah* on the Jews of al Bahrayn despite the conservatism of the latter and their attachment to the faith of their forefathers. The Prophet also reconciled the Jews of Banu Ghaziyah and Banu 'Arid and offered them his covenant and protection provided they agree to pay *jizyah*. On the whole, the Jews of the Peninsula lost their political power and fell under that of the Muslims. So much had their prestige deteriorated, however, that they soon found themselves having to emigrate from a land which once felt their influence. According to some versions, this Jewish emigration took place during the lifetime of the Prophet; according to others, shortly after his death.

Jewish acquiescence in their fate under the dominion of Islam did not take place at one and the same time or immediately after their military defeat, for they were exceedingly resentful and full of hatred for their Muslim fellows. Zaynab, daughter of al Harith, and wife of Sallam ibn Mishkam, cooked a goat and presented it to Muhammad after the peace treaty with Khaybar and Jewish-Muslim relations returned to normal. Muhammad sat down at the table with his companions to eat of this Jewish prepared food. Taking the first mouthful, he realized that the taste was strange. Bishr ibn al Bara' likewise had the same realization and could hardly swallow the first mouthful. As he threw his away, the Prophet said: "I have a premonition that this dish is poisoned." He then called Zaynab and questioned her, and she confessed. In defense of herself, she said to the Prophet: "You know what has befallen my people at your hand, and you can appreciate my resentment and hatred. In pondering the whole event, I arrived at the conclusion that if you, the source of all the evil, were a king like other kings, then to put an end to your life would bring peace to me and my people. If, on the other hand, you are a true prophet, then surely you would find out that the food was poisoned and you would not eat." The one mouthful which Bishr ate was fatal to him. The chroniclers disagree regarding the fate of Zaynab. Most of them agree that the Prophet appreciated her defense, forgave her, and sympathized with her loss of father and husband. Others relate that she was killed in revenge for the life of Bishr.

Muhammad's Marriage to Safiyyah

This treacherous deed of Zaynab adversely affected the attitudes of the Muslims. It destroyed whatever confidence they still had in the Jews. Indeed, it confirmed their presentiment that there could be no peace with the Jews as long as they were not finally destroyed. Safiyyah, daughter of Huyayy ibn Akhtab of Banu al Nadir, was one of the captives the Muslims had seized inside the fortresses of Khaybar. Her husband, Kinanah ibn al Rabi', was known by the Muslims to have been the guardian of all the wealth of Banu al Nadir. When the Prophet had asked Kinanah about his treasure, the latter solemnly declared that he did not know where it was hidden. Muhammad threatened him that in case the treasure was found hidden in his place he would be put to death. Kinanah agreed. One day when Kinanah was seen moving about an uninhabited house in the out-skirts, his movement was reported to the Prophet. After the Prophet ordered the inside of the house be dug out, part of the treasure was revealed. Kinanah was killed as a result. When a companion learned of Safiyyah's captivity, he approached the Prophet with the suggestion that, since she was the lady of Banu Qurayzah and Banu al Nadir, she was fit to become the wife of the Prophet alone. The Prophet granted her her

freedom and then married her, following the example of the great conquerors who married the daughters and wives of the kings whom they had
conquered, partly in order to alleviate their tragedy and partly to preserve
their dignity. Abu Ayyub Khalid al Ansari, however, feared that Safiyyah's
tragic loss of father, husband, and people might incite her to avenge herself against the Prophet. He therefore spent the night near Muhammad's
tent where the wedding had taken place, with sword drawn. When the
morning came and the Prophet saw him in that state, he asked him for an
explanation. Abu Ayyub answered that he feared for the Prophet that this
woman, who until very recently had been a non-Muslim, might attack
him. The truth, however, was otherwise. Safiyyah remained loyal to
Muhammad throughout his life. In his last illness, when the Prophet was
surrounded by his wives, Safiyyah came forward and said: "O Prophet of
God, I surely wish that that from which you suffer might be in me rather
than in you." Muhammad's wives winked at one another and the Prophet,
observing their reaction, said: "Go on and wink at one another! By God,
I know that Safiyyah is truthful and loyal." Safiyyah, who survived
Muhammad, lived until the time of the caliphate of Mu'awiyah. She was
buried at al Baqi'.

Delegation to Heraclius

Whatever happened to the messengers whom Muhammad sent to
Heraclius, Chosroes, the Negus, and other kings and men of power surrounding Arabia? Did they go forth before the Campaign of Khaybar, or
did they participate in that Campaign until Muslim victory had been
achieved and traveled thereafter? Historians differ so widely in this respect
that it is very difficult to reach a conclusion. We are inclined to think that
they did not all go forth at the same time, that some of them began their
travel before the campaign of Khaybar and others thereafter. More than
one chronicler has asserted that Dihyah ibn Khalifah al Kalbi participated in the operations at Khaybar. Yet it was he who was commissioned by
the Prophet to go to Heraclius. The Prophet's messenger met Heraclius at
the time of the latter's victorious return from the war with Persia and his
recapture of the cross which had been taken by the Persians when they
occupied Jerusalem. The vow which Heraclius had made, namely, to perform a pilgrimage to Jerusalem on foot and return the cross to its original
place, could now be fulfilled. It was on this pilgrimage of Heraclius,
specifically when the imperial procession had reached the city of Hims[9]

that the message of Muhammad was received. Whether Muhammad's letter was handed to the Emperor by one of the latter's employees after Dihyah surrendered it to the Byzantine governor of Bosra, or whether the group of Muslims headed by Dihyah was granted a court audience at which Dihyah submitted the Prophet's letter in person, is not known for certain. At any rate, it is known that the Prophet's letter did reach Heraclius, and that the Emperor was not irritated by it. Instead of sending an army to conquer Arabia, Heraclius did in fact send a gentle letter in reply to Muhammad's message. It was this gentle response to Muhammad's message that a number of historians mistook as meaning that Heraclius had joined the ranks of Islam.

At the same time, al Harith of Ghassan sent to Heraclius a message to the effect that he had just received a letter from Muhammad, a message which Heraclius thought was similar to what he himself had received from the same source calling him to Islam. Al Harith applied for permission to send an expeditionary force against this new "pretender." Heraclius saw otherwise and instructed al Harith to come to Jerusalem and attend with him the ceremonies at which the cross would be reinstated. Heraclius was apparently more interested in the pomp and circumstance of those ceremonies than in the call of a new religion. He could not imagine that only a few years would pass before Jerusalem, as well as the whole of al Sham, would fall under Islamic dominion; that the Islamic capital would move to Damascus; that the struggle between the Islamic state and the Byzantine Empire would not subside until the Muslims had conquered Constantinople in 1453 and converted its great church[10] into a mosque in which the name of that Prophet would be inscribed in honor; and that that same church would remain a mosque for many centuries until the Muslim Turks would change it into a museum of Byzantine art in modern times. Such was to be the influence of this Prophet whose message Heraclius did not think sufficiently worthy to deserve attention.

Delegation to Chosroes

As soon as the message of Muhammad was read out to Chosroes, the Emperor of Persia, he went into a rage, destroyed the letter, and dictated an order to his satrap in Yaman commanding him to send forth to the capital the head of his Prophet-pretender in al Hijaz. Perhaps he was moved to such a decision out of a need for self-assertion following his defeat by Heraclius. When the Prophet heard of Chosroes's response, he cursed him as well as his empire. Bazan, the satrap of Yaman, sent his messengers in search of Muhammad, in compliance with the command of his emperor. In the meanwhile, however, Chosroes passed away, and his son, Cyrus, ascended the throne. Knowing the news of the accession, the Prophet informed the messengers of Bazan and asked them to carry his call to Islam to Bazan rather than carry out Bazan's instructions. The people of Yaman had learned of the defeat of Persia and realized that Persian dominion was on the decline and would soon pass away. They had heard, also, of the victories Muhammad had scored over Quraysh and of his total destruction of Jewish power and dominion. When Bazan's messengers returned and told their master of Muhammad's response, he immediately converted to Islam and accepted Muhammad's appointment as governor of Yaman. But what would Muhammad require of Bazan, as long as enemy Makkah separated the two? Since he did not have much to fear, but rather everything to gain because Persian dominion was on the wane, and because the new power rising on the horizon of the Peninsula could, in fact, demand of him no price in return, Bazan preferred to enter into friendly relations with Muhammad. Possibly, Bazan did not quite appreciate the fact that his joining the ranks of Islam gave the latter a very viable *point d'appui* in the south corner of the Peninsula, as events were to show two years later.

Delegation to the Archbishop of Egypt

The Coptic Archbishop of Egypt answered in a radically different way from his superior Heraclius, or from Chosroes. He informed Muhammad of his belief that a Prophet was indeed to appear in the world, but in al Sham. He accorded to Muhammad's messenger a good reception and sent with him a gift to the Prophet consisting of two slave girls, a white mule, a donkey, some money, and a variety of Egyptian products. The two slave girls were Mariyyah, whom Muhammad took in marriage and who gave birth to Ibrahim, and Sirin, who was given in marriage to Hassan ibn Thabit. The mule was given by the Prophet the name of Duldul, for its unique whiteness of skin which the Arabian Peninsula had never seen before. The donkey was called 'Ufayr or Ya'fur. The Archbishop explained that he did not convert to Islam because of his fear of discharge by his superior, and that were he not a man of authority and power, he would have been rightly guided to the true faith.

Delegation to Abyssinia

It was natural that the answer of the Negus of Abyssinia was favorable, for his country had always been on good terms with the Muslims. Indeed, some historians assert that the Negus was converted to Islam — a claim which the Orientalists suspect very strongly. The Prophet sent to the Negus a second letter asking him to send back the Muslims who had been living in Abyssinia under his protection. The Negus provided these Muslims with two ships that carried them to the shore of Arabia. They were led by Ja'far ibn Abu Talib, and the group included Umm Habibah, Ramlah, daughter of Abu Sufyan and wife of 'Abdullah ibn Jahsh who went to Abyssinia as a Muslim, converted to Christianity and died there a Christian. Following her return from Abyssinia, the same Umm Habibah became one of the wives of the Prophet, a "Mother of the Believers." Some historians asserted that the Prophet married her in order to forge a blood relation with the house of Abu Sufyan and to confirm thereby the Treaty of al Hudaybiyah. Other historians saw in the marriage of Umm Habibah to Muhammad an attempt on the part of the latter to punish and annoy Abu Sufyan who was still a pagan.

Explanation to the Kings' Replies

Finally, as for the princes of Arab tribes and regions, it should be recorded that the Amir of Yaman and 'Uman sent the Prophet a very antagonistic answer. The Amir of al Bahrayn sent a favorable reply and became a Muslim. The Amir of al Yamamah declared his preparation to enter into Islam if his chair and office could be secured. The Prophet cursed him for laying down conditions to his conversion, and the historians assert that the man lived but one year after the event.

The reader might well pause to consider the preponderant friendliness and appreciation which most of the kings and princes showed in response to Muhammad's call. None of Muhammad's messengers was killed or imprisoned. Everyone of them returned to Madinah with the response with which he had been entrusted. Some of these messages were coarse and harsh, but most of them were gentle and sweet. Two questions naturally arise: Why did all these kings receive the new religion without seeking to destroy the man who called them to it, and why did they not unite to destroy him? The answer to these questions lies in the fact that the world of those days was, like the world of today, one in which matter had come to dominate everything, affluence and luxury had become the *summum bonum*, and nations fought and destroyed one another for the sake of power and in satisfaction of the ambitions of its king and ruling circles, or in order to increase their affluence and luxury. In such a world, faith deteriorates to mere ritual, and men perform these rituals without believing any of the truths which the rituals were meant to express. In such kingdoms, the masses seldom care but to belong to such regimes as will provide them with *panem et circencis*, with wealth and luxury. Under such circumstances, a religion is adhered to only in proportion to the material advantage its practice promises. When such advantage is not in sight, the masses of people quickly lose their attachment, and their power of resistance to another religion evaporates. That is why as soon as these masses heard the voice of the new religion with its strength and simplicity, its call to equality before the one God, the only Being worthy of worship and prayer, and the only One capable of giving true good to man, they began to thirst after the new faith and the spiritual satisfactions it provides. Verily, a ray of God's blessing dissipates the fury of all the kings of the earth combined! The fear of His wrath shakes the human soul to its very depths even though the kings of the earth might have smothered that soul in blessings and favors. The hope of God's forgiveness moves every man deprived of grace to repent, to believe and to do good works. When the people heard that the author of this new call was capable of vanquishing the enemies who persecuted him and who inflicted upon him and his followers all sorts of injustice and suffering, it was not surprising that they stretched out their necks and lent their ears to see him and hear him. For them to witness Muhammad's victory over all the material forces assembled against him and to see his power grow despite his original weakness, poverty, and deprivation, for them to see this Prophet achieve that which no one else had ever dreamt of achieving — be it in his own town or throughout the Arabian Peninsula — all this was enough to incite them to examine this faith and to want to belong to it. Were it not for their fear of the immediate consequences, most of them would not have kept themselves separated from the truth. Hence, the majority of the sovereigns answered with a consideration and sympathy which reinforced the Muslims' faith and conviction.

Muslim Return from Abyssinia

Muhammad returned from Khaybar, and Ja'far and the Muslims returned from Abyssinia. The messengers of Muhammad returned from those lands whither Muhammad had sent them. All of them met again and were reunited in Madinah. Inspiring each of them was the longing to go to Makkah in the following year and to do so in security, with shaven heads or short hair, and to perform their pilgrimage without fear. Muhammad was so pleased to be reunited with Ja'far that he said he could not tell which was the greater: victory over Khaybar or reunion with Ja'far. It was in this period that, according to a certain report, a Jew called Labid charmed Muhammad and put him under a spell. The report is self-contradictory and highly questionable. The claim that Muhammad did anything at any time without consciousness or under a spell is a sheer fabrication and hence devoid of truth.

The Muslims were safe in Madinah where they led a prosperous and affluent life. During this period they thought neither of war nor of fighting despite the fact that they had to send some expeditionary forces to punish those who aggressed upon their lands or seized any of their property. As the year[11] came to a close, in the month of Dhu al Qi'dah, the Prophet set out with two thousand men to perform the lesser pilgrimage, in accordance with the provisions of the Hudaybiyah Treaty, and to satisfy the Muslim longing to visit the holy sanctuary and to perform the holy ritual.

22

The 'Umrah
or Lesser Pilgrimage

The Muslims' March to Makkah

A full year had passed since the Treaty of al Hudaybiyah. Muhammad and his companions were accordingly free to enter Makkah and to visit the Ka'bah under the terms of that treaty. The Prophet, therefore, proclaimed to the people that they might now prepare themselves to go to Makkah for performance of the lesser pilgrimage. It is easy to appreciate the enthusiasm of the Muslims in response to Muhammad's call. Many among them, the Muhajirun, were emigrants from Makkah who had left their hometown seven years ago. Others, the Ansar, conducted wide trade with Makkah and felt great love and loyalty to the holy sanctuary which they longed to visit. Those who responded to Muhammad's call exceeded two thousand in number. Hence, there were six hundred or more than in the previous year. In compliance with the terms of the Hudaybiyah Treaty, none of them carried any arms except his sword which he kept in its scabbard. Muhammad feared treachery. He therefore equipped a hundred cavalrymen and assigned them to Muhammad ibn Maslamah. He instructed them to reconnoiter the fields ahead of the procession of Muslims but not to tread on the holy ground surrounding Makkah. His order was that they should turn to a nearby valley as soon as they reached the canyon of al Zahran. The Muslims herded before them the sacrificial animals; the entire procession was led by Muhammad riding his she-camel, al Qaswa'. They set out from Madinah in the direction of Makkah moved by the strongest emotion to circumambulate the House of God and to see the places where they were born. Each longed to visit the house and quarter where he had grown up and played as a child. They were quite anxious to visit their old friends whom they had had no opportunity to see during those long years, and, in short, to breathe the air of their dear homeland. The non-Makkan Muslims were equally anxious to see and touch this blessed holy city which had brought out the Prophet of God and in which the revelation of God was first heard. One can imagine this great procession of Muslims numbering over two thousand, pushing forward toward Makkah with their hearts practically leaping out of their breasts in exaltation and reverence. At every opportunity, a pilgrim would tell his companion what he knew of Makkah and would recall nostalgically the days of his childhood or youth in that city. He would tell about his friends that were still there and the wealth and property which he had abandoned for the sake of God when he left it. One can imagine this unique procession animated by faith, indeed bursting with religious enthusiasm, pulling forward toward the universally revered sanctuary. The reader may well imagine the jubilation of this procession of men who for the last seven years had been prevented from performing this sacred duty but who were now certain they could enter Makkah in peace, with shaven head or cut hair, for an opportunity to re-express their loyalty to God.

The Quraysh Evacuate the City

The Quraysh learned of the arrival of Muhammad and his companions, and they evacuated the whole town as the treaty demanded. They removed themselves with their families to the hills surrounding Makkah where they erected tents for this purpose. Those who could not afford tents spent the time in the shade of trees. From the mountains of Abu Qubays and Hira' as well as from every mound or hill surrounding Makkah, the Makkans looked down upon their city which appeared to be invaded by this "refugee" and his companions. The Muslims entered the city without resistance, indeed without meeting any Makkans at all, and they poured into the sanctuary. They entered from the north led by Muhammad on the back of al Qaswa' whose reins were held by 'Abdullah ibn Rawahah. The Prophet was surrounded by his elder companions, and behind him followed the rank and file of Muslims, whether mounted or on foot. When the Holy house came into view, every Muslim tongue was loosened with a single call: "At Your command, O Lord! At Your command, O Lord!" Their hearts and souls were totally turned to God, the Lord of Majesty.

Circumambulation of the Sacred House

In surrounding the Prophet the multitudes expressed their hope and reverence to the man whom God had sent to convey His guidance and true religion and whom He promised to vindicate against the adherents of all other religions. In truth, it must have been a unique and truly great spectacle, defying history itself. Upon witnessing it, even those most obstinate in their paganism or hostility to Islam were softened and even attracted to the new faith. Such a spectacle simply mesmerized the Makkans. The voice of the Muslims calling, "At your command, O Lord!" rocked the horizon as well as their ears and hearts. When the Prophet reached the Ka'bah he wrapped his mantle under his right arm, baring his shoulder and praying, "O God, have mercy on anyone performing this rite today and showing the enemy a side of his spiritual strength!" He then stopped near the black stone to begin circumambulation of the House. Followed by his companions and going at a trotting pace, Muhammad circumambulated the holy shrine three times, pausing whenever he reached the black stone at each turn. The Muslims, all two thousand of them, followed Muhammad in every move while the Quraysh were looking upon them from the height of Abu Qubays. Undoubtedly, the Quraysh were stupefied by what they saw. Every notion they previously entertained of the Muslims' weakness, exhaustion, and moral bankruptcy was shattered. In the enthusiasm of the moment, 'Abdullah ibn Rawahah wanted to challenge the Quraysh by shouting a war cry at them. But he was stopped by 'Umar. The Prophet then advised him to recite the following prayer instead: "There is no God but God alone. He is always true to His word. He it is Who gave victory to His servant, Who reinforced His army, Who defeated all the allies assembled against His people." Ibn Rawahah recited this prayer at the top of his voice, and the Muslims, in repeating these words after him rocked the horizons thereby and inspired terror in the hearts of all the spectators of this ritual.

The Muslims' Sojourn in Makkah

When the Muslims completed their circumambulation of the Ka'bah, Muhammad led them toward al Safa and al Marwah.[1] There, he covered the distance between the two hills seven times mounted on his camel, just as the Arabs used to do, and then proceeded to slaughter the sacrificial animals at al Marwah. He then shaved his head and thereby completed the duty of the *'umrah* or lesser pilgrimage. On the morrow, Muhammad entered into the Ka'bah and there remained until noon. Despite the fact that the Ka'bah was still full of idols, Bilal ascended to its top, gave the call to the noon prayer and, led by the Prophet, the two thousand Muslims held the noon prayer around the Holy House. It should be remembered that for seven years the Muslims had been prevented from performing their religious functions in the sanctuary. The Muslims remained in Makkah three whole days as the Treaty of Hudaybiyah prescribed, and during these days, not a Makkan remained in town or came to it. The Muslims roamed throughout the city without suffering any harm or being obstructed by anyone. The Muhajirun among them visited their old houses, showing them to their Madinese companions, the Ansar, and generally behaving as if they were the real hosts to them. Everyone, by complying with every function Islam prescribed for the day, deepened his Islamic awareness and effaced every trace of pre-Islamic vanity. The Muslims were charitable to one another, the strong among them helping the weak, the rich giving to the poor, and the Prophet moving among them as a loving and beloved father, meeting the smile of the one, reconciling the other, and teaching the truth to all. The Quraysh and all other Makkans, looking down from their tents on the mountains, pondered the behavior of the Muslims. They observed that the Muslims were extremely good to one another, that they displayed exemplary nobility and morality, never touching intoxicating drink, neither doing evil nor allowing food, drink, or treasure ever to tempt them. They could not be seen disobeying God's commandments even once. What effect did such a spectacle have on the Makkans? What could they think of this new religion which raised man to the greatest heights of spirituality and virtue possible? It is easy for the reader to appreciate the awe and admiration for Islam all this inspired. Only a few months later, Muhammad returned at the head of an army of ten thousand Muslims; but Makkah opened its gates without a struggle.

Muhammad's Marriage to Maymunah

Umm al Fadl, the wife of al 'Abbas ibn 'Abd al Muttalib, the uncle of the Prophet, had been asked by her sister Maymunah to be her agent in seeking a husband. Maymunah was twenty-six years old, and she was the aunt of Khalid ibn al Walid. Umm al Fadl delegated her function to her husband al 'Abbas. When Maymunah saw the Muslims performing the 'umrah, she was attracted to Islam and permitted al 'Abbas to talk to Muhammad, his nephew, on the subject of marrying her. Muhammad agreed and offered her four hundred Dirhams in dowry. In the meantime, the three days prescribed by the pact of al Hudaybiyah had passed. Muhammad sought to make of his marriage to Maymunah an occasion to consolidate the mutual understanding between him and the Quraysh which the Hudaybiyah Treaty had brought about. When Suhayl ibn 'Amr and Huwaytib ibn 'Abd al 'Uzza, delegates of the Quraysh, came to Muhammad and asked him to leave the city because the time allowed by the treaty had expired, Muhammad asked them that his marriage be performed in Makkah, and invited Quraysh to attend both the ceremony and the banquet which the Muslims would prepare for the occasion. Muhammad issued this invitation to them knowing very well the powerful reconciliatory effect his performance of the pilgrimage ritual had had on the hearts of the Quraysh. The Prophet sought to further this feeling by having them participate in a joyous occasion, one which would undoubtedly furnish the Makkans with further evidence of Muhammad's sincerity and love of peace. He had hoped that if he could talk to them leisurely and in an atmosphere such as a wedding ceremony and banquet would provide, he could further allay their fears and, perhaps, Makkah would then open its gate and heart freely to its Muslim children. That was precisely what Suhayl and Huwaytib feared in Muhammad's invitation. Hence, they answered: "No, we do not need your food. Please evacuate our city forthwith." Muhammad did not hesitate to comply with their request because it complied with the terms of the Treaty, and he called his men to prepare for withdrawal to Madinah. He led the exodus of the Muslims out of Makkah, leaving behind him his client Abu Rafi' to take care of Maymunah and to accompany her on her trip northwards. Maymunah joined the Muslim group at Sarif outside of Makkah, where Muhammad married her. Maymunah hence became a "Mother of the Believers," and the last wife of the Prophet. She survived him by fifty years, and before she died she asked to be buried at the site of her wedding. Muhammad took under his care the two sisters of Maymunah, namely Salma, widow of his uncle Hamzah, and 'Imarah al Bikr, who never married.

Conversion of Khalid ibn al Walid and Others

The Muslims returned to their residence in Madinah. Muhammad did not doubt that the pilgrimage which he and his companions had just performed had made the greatest possible favorable effect upon the Quraysh and all the Makkans. The subsequent days proved Muhammad's expectations. Indeed, as soon as the Muslims had left Makkah, Khalid ibn al Walid, the greatest soldier of the Quraysh and the hero of the Battle of Uhud, said to his fellow Makkans: "It has become absolutely clear to any person with the least intelligence that Muhammad is neither a poet possessed nor a magician inspired. His words are truly the words of God, of the Lord of the Universe. It follows then that every man with common sense ought to follow him." 'Ikrimah ibn Abu Jahl was alarmed when he heard Khalid say this and said to him in reply: "O Khalid, you have been brainwashed." Khalid answered, "Neither brainwashed nor intoxicated, but simply Islamized." 'Ikrimah said: "By God, if any man in Quraysh ought not to say what you have just said, it is you." Khalid asked, "Why?" and 'Ikrimah answered: "Because Muhammad stained your father's honor when he wounded him and when he killed your uncle and his son in the Battle of Badr. By God, I will never allow myself to be Islamized, nor will I ever allow myself to say such words as you did. Don't you see that the Quraysh are all ready to fight Muhammad?" To this Khalid replied: "All you say is ignorant, tribalistic, and shows only the prejudices of pre-Islam. But now I am a Muslim and the whole truth lies clear before my eyes." Khalid sent to the Prophet his own mares together with a message that he had accepted Islam and acknowledged Muhammad as the Prophet of God. When Abu Sufyan learned of the conversion of Khalid, he sent for him enquiring whether or not it was true. When Khalid answered in the affirmative, Abu Sufyan flew into a rage and said: "By al Lat and al 'Uzza, if I were certain I heard you right, I would kill you before I kill Muhammad." To which Khalid replied, "By God it is the truth, and you have heard right. Let the consequences be what they may!" Abu Sufyan rushed toward him but was stopped by 'Ikrimah who witnessed the conversation. The latter said to Abu Sufyan: "Slowly! By God I, too, would have said exactly what Khalid has just said, and would have joined his faith, had I not feared the crumbling of the Quraysh. Now, you seek to kill Khalid because of a view he has just adopted while the whole of Quraysh has invested him with leadership. I fear that hardly a season will pass before the whole of Makkah will follow their leader in his new faith."

Khalid left Makkah and came to Madinah where he joined the ranks of the Muslims.

After Khalid, 'Amr ibn al 'As and 'Uthman ibn Talhah, the guardian of the Ka'bah, converted to Islam. Many Makkans followed them after hearing of their conversion to the religion of truth. With their entry, the power of Islam grew considerably and the conquest of Makkah by Muhammad became a future certainty.

23

The Campaign of Mu'tah

Skirmishes before the Campaign

Knowing that time was on his side, Muhammad was in no hurry to conquer Makkah. The Treaty of Hudaybiyah was hardly more than a year old, and nothing had happened to warrant its abrogation. Being a man of his word who never failed to honor a promise, Muhammad was satisfied to return to Madinah and wait for his time in peace. During the few months that followed his return, a few skirmishes took place. He sent five men to Banu Sulaym for the sole purpose of teaching them Islam, and he endured their cold-blooded murder by their hosts. Only their leader managed to escape, and he did so purely accidentally. He also sent fifteen men to Dhat al Talh on the outskirts of al Sham in order to call its people to Islam. There, too, the messengers of Muhammad and missionaries of the faith were put to death in cold blood. The Prophet also sent some of his men to the Banu al Layth which they successfully raided, bringing back both captives and booty. He also sent a force to punish the Banu Murrah for their previous treachery. Al Sham and the whole northern district were of particular concern to the Prophet, especially since he had already secured the south through the Treaty of Hudaybiyah and the conversion of the governor of Yaman. The Prophet looked upon the north as the gateway to the spread of Islam beyond the frontiers of the Arabian Peninsula. Al Sham and the adjoining territories were the first object of his mission beyond Arabia. Consequently, only a few months after his return to

Madinah he readied an army of three thousand fighters, some of whom
had previously fought at Mu'tah, for possible deployment in the north.
According to other versions, the number of the men involved was one or
two hundred thousand.

Causes of the Campaign

Historians differ in explaining the expedition against Mu'tah. Some
give the murder of Muhammad's companions at Dhat al Talh as the cause.
Others relate that the Prophet had sent a messenger to the Byzantine governor of Busra, that this messenger was killed by a tribesman of Ghassan
in the name of Heraclius, and that Muhammad sent this force as a puni-
tive expedition against that governor and the empire he represented.

Just as the Treaty of Hudaybiyah was the forerunner of the pilgrimage, and this in turn of the conquest of Makkah, so was the campaign
against Mu'tah an introduction to Tabuk, and this, in turn, to the conquest
of al Sham which took place shortly after the Prophet's death. It is imma-
terial whether or not the cause which led to the conquest of Mu'tah was
the murder of the Prophet's messenger to the governor of Busra or that of
the fifteen missionaries he had sent to Dhat al Talh. The fact is that the
Prophet — May God's peace and blessing be upon him — called up in
the month of Jumada I of the year 8 A. H. (629 C.E.), three thousand of
his best men and appointed Zayd ibn Harithah as their leader. In the
event of Zayd's fall, Ja'far ibn Abu Talib was to assume command of the
army. In the event of Ja'far's death, 'Abdullah ibn Rawahah was to take his
place. Khalid ibn al Walid, the recent convert from Makkah, volunteered
to join this expedition in order to prove his loyalty to the new faith. The
people of Madinah bid the army farewell, and Muhammad saw them off
at the outskirts of the city. He commanded them not to kill any women,
children, or invalids, and not to destroy either houses or trees. Together
with his companions, he prayed for them: "May God be with you! May
He shield you with His protection, and may He bring you back to us safe,
sound, and victorious." Most of the leaders of this army thought to surprise their enemy, as the Prophet had done on previous occasions, and thus
to achieve a quick victory and return home with the spoils of war. They
advanced till they reached Ma'an in the territory of al Sham without
knowing what lay ahead of them.

Byzantine Mobilization

However, the news of their march preceded them. Shurahbil, Heraclius's commissioner in al Sham, mobilized all the tribes around him and sent word to Heraclius asking for more Greek and Arab armies. Some historians assert that Heraclius himself came over with his armies and camped in Ma'ab [Moab], in al Balqa', with one hundred thousand Byzantine soldiers. They also relate that another hundred thousand men joined his main force from Lakhm, Judham, al Qayn, Bahra', and Baliyy. It is also related that Theodorus, Heraclius's brother, rather than Heraclius himself, was the leader of this army. While the Muslims were at Ma'an, they heard of this mobilization, and for two days and nights they did not know what to do. One of them advised that a message be sent to the Prophet — May God's peace and blessing be upon him — informing him of the force of the enemy and asking him for more men or for other orders. This counsel was about to receive unanimous approval when 'Abdullah ibn Rawahah, who was as proud and chivalrous as he was eloquent in poetry, rose and said: "O people! By God, that which you fear might happen to you is precisely why you came here — namely, martyrdom. We Muslims do not fight either with numbers, physical strength, or material equipment. Our only power lies in this religion which God has been gracious enough to give to us. Rise to battle and march forward! One of the two greatest blessings must befall you: either victory or martyrdom." The bravery of this eloquent poet was contagious, and soon the whole army reverberated with the same war cry. Everybody approved of ibn Rawahah's counsel. They marched forward toward al Balqa' and a village called Masharif, where the Byzantine armies were encamped. When the enemy attacked, the Muslims withdrew to the village of Mu'tah which presented to them strategic advantages, and they fortified their position. It was there that the battle was fought by three thousand Muslims against some one or two hundred thousand of the enemy.

Fall of the Martyrs

The majesty of religious conviction! The sublimity of the strength of faith! Zayd ibn Harithah raised the banner of the Prophet and marched forward toward the enemy. He plunged deep into their ranks fully certain of the death that awaited him. But to die under such conditions is precisely to fall a martyr in the cause of God. Martyrdom is not one whit lesser a blessed fate than victory. Zayd fought desperately until he was torn apart by enemy arrows. Ja'far ibn Abu Talib, then a brave man of thirty-three, picked up the Prophet's banner and fought valiantly until his horse was completely surrounded by enemy soldiers. When his horse fell under him, he pressed ever forward on foot to cut the enemy ranks down with the sword. He was carrying the banner in his right hand. When it was cut off, he picked up the banner with his left; and when he lost his left hand, he kept the banner high by pressing it between his legs until he died. It is related that a Byzantine soldier struck him with his sword and cut him in two. At the death of Ja'far, Ibn Rawahah seized the Prophet's banner, mounted on his mare but hesitated to advance toward the enemy's lines. His mind being braver than his will, he composed the following verses to encourage himself: "O Soul, I have sworn that you will fight in battle deliberately, or that I shall force you to fight. When people assemble and shout the war cry, why do you not advance with them? Or do you hate to enter Paradise?" Aroused by his own eloquence, he drew his sword, plunged into the thick of battle and fought valiantly until he died.

The three commanders, Zayd, Ja'far, and ibn Rawahah, all fell as martyrs in the cause of God in the first engagement. When the Prophet learned of their death, he was extremely sad. He said of them that they were lifted to Paradise on thrones of pure gold, just as men see in their dreams. He pointed out that in his vision of the three martyrs, he noticed the throne of 'Abdullah ibn Rawahah hovering in the heights and not rising as rapidly as the other two; upon enquiry he was told that the other two advanced straight forward whereas 'Abdullah hesitated. What sound advice and good counsel the Prophet meant to give! Surely, he meant to impress upon the Muslims that the believer should not hesitate or fear to die in the cause of God, but rather he should carry his life on his palm ever ready to lay it down when he marches forward in the cause of God and homeland. He should firmly realize that his fate is either to succeed and realize that cause or to fall martyr and give the supreme example to posterity. In martyrdom lies a final and lasting memory that one has deemed the value of life to be wholly in that for which the sacrifice had taken place; that tenacity to life in humiliation and subjection is indeed a betrayal and destruction of life. To hold the contrary is, in fact, to lose the right to be counted among the living. Likewise, the man who exposes himself to the danger of death but does so for a mean cause; or saves his life from the danger of death when God, the Lord of Majesty, calls upon him to lay down that life in the cause of truth, has already met his death — but in ignominy. If the slight hesitation of ibn Rawahah merited for him a place inferior to that of Zayd and Ja'far despite the fact that he still fought and laid down his life as a martyr; if, in short, he was unworthy of the reward of those who plunge into the thick of battle and fly to martyrdom with joy, what would be the fate of one who retraced his steps and withdrew altogether in order to save his life or to attain the advantage of wealth or glory? His is surely the fate of a miserable insect, no matter how great his glory among the multitudes, or how abundant his wealth. Is the human soul capable of any joy greater than that which sacrifice for the sake of conviction brings? Is man capable of any nobler fate than that of martyrdom in the cause of truth?

Ibn al Walid's Strategy

Upon the death of ibn Rawahah, Thabit ibn Arqam, a tribesman of Banu 'Ajlan, picked up the Prophet's banner and asked the Muslims to appoint a leader. Many nominated him, but he declined. The people then asked Khalid ibn al Walid to assume command. Khalid accepted despite the disintegration of Muslim power and the disorganization of their ranks. Making full use of his great military experience and unique wisdom and foresight in battle, he first commanded the Muslims to reorganize their ranks and recoup their forces. He allowed only skirmishes with the enemy in order to gain time. Soon night came and the two armies disengaged until the following morning. During the night, Khalid carefully laid out his plan. He sent a number of men toward the rear deploying them in such a way as to give the impression the next morning that massive reinforcements from Madinah were arriving to join the battle. The ruse worked. Recalling their losses and the Muslims' fierce acts of war on the previous day, the Byzantines decided to abandon the battlefield. The Muslims, pleased by the withdrawal of the enemy, withdrew toward Madinah. It was a battle in which the Muslims were not victorious. Neither did they lose.

Muslim Disappointment and Muhammad's Assurance

As soon as Khalid and the army reached Madinah, Muhammad and the Muslims went out to meet them, Muhammad carrying on his arm 'Abdullah, the son of Ja'far, the second commander of the Muslim force. Upon learning of the news, the people flung dust in the face of the

Muslim soldiers and accused them of fleeing in the face of the enemy and abandoning the cause of God. The Prophet of God argued with his people that the soldiers did not flee but simply withdrew in order, with God's will, to advance again. Despite this justification on the part of Muhammad of the Muslim army, the people were not willing to forgive them their withdrawal and return. Salamah ibn Hisham, a member of this expedition, would neither go to the mosque for prayer nor show himself in public in order to avoid being chastised for fleeing from the cause of God. Were it not for the fact that these same men, especially Khalid ibn al Walid, later distinguished themselves in battle against the same enemy, their reputations would have remained forever stained.

Muhammad was deeply saddened by the death of Zayd and Ja'far. After hearing the sad news, he went to the latter's house where his wife, Asma', daughter of 'Umays, had baked her bread, washed and dressed up her children, and awaited the return of her husband. The Prophet embraced Ja'far's children and cried. Asma' immediately grasped what the Prophet was about to say to her and said: "O Prophet of God, woe to me if you should cry! Have you heard any news about Ja'far and his companions?" The Prophet answered: "Yes indeed, and they have fallen this very day." The Prophet cried and sobbed and Asma' began to cry and shout in mourning. Before leaving the house, Muhammad commanded the people who assembled to take care of Ja'far's family and to provide food for them. Upon meeting the daughter of his client, Zayd, he picked her up and cried on her shoulder. When those who saw them expressed astonishment, he explained to them that it was all too natural. The martyrs were not only his people, but his own personal friends.

According to one version, the remains of Ja'far were carried to Madinah where he was buried three days after the return of Khalid and the army. On that day, the Prophet commanded the Muslims to stop mourning their lost ones. To reassure the bereaved relatives, he announced that God had given Ja'far, instead of the two arms he lost on the battlefield, two wings with which to fly to Paradise.

The Campaign of Dhat al Salasil

A few weeks after the return of Khalid, Muhammad sought to make up the losses in Muslim prestige in the northern parts of the Peninsula which the previous engagement with the Byzantines had caused. He therefore commissioned 'Amr ibn al 'As to rouse the Arabs to march against al Sham. He chose 'Amr for this task because the latter's mother belonged to one of the northern tribes, and he hoped that' Amr could use this connection to facilitate his mission. As he arrived at a well called al Salasil, in the land of Judham, fearing the enemy might overtake him, he sent word to the Prophet asking for more forces. The Prophet sent Abu 'Ubaydah ibn al Jurrah at the head of a corps of Muhajirun which included Abu Bakr and 'Umar. The Prophet feared that 'Amr, new as he was in his conversion to Islam, might disagree with Abu 'Ubaydah, one of the earliest and oldest among the Muhajirun. He therefore advised Abu 'Ubayah when he assigned to him the leadership of the expedition not to disagree with 'Amr. When Abu 'Ubaydah and his men joined forces with 'Amr, the latter reminded Abu 'Ubaydah that he had come not as a commander but only as a relief force to operate under 'Amr's command. Abu 'Ubaydah was a very affable, ascetic, and humble man, and he instantly assured 'Amr that he stood under the Prophet's commandment to obey 'Amr at all costs and under all circumstances. 'Amr led the army in prayer as well as in battle. With his reinforcements, he not only engaged the enemy but dispersed and routed them, thereby recovering the Muslim prestige lost in the campaign of Mu'tah.

At the same time, Muhammad was thinking of Makkah and of its affairs. In this regard, he was bound by the Treaty of Hudaybiyah for two years, and he meant to abide by its terms. Therefore, the only engagements he allowed his forces in the south were small skirmishes designed merely to calm down the tribes inclined toward rebellion. This was not difficult to do, and many delegations were already arriving in Madinah from all corners of Arabia to declare their conversion. It was during this interval that the Quraysh violated the Treaty of Hudaybiyah, thereby triggering the chain of events which led to the conquest of Makkah and the establishment of Islam therein. Unlike any other conquest, the Muslim conquest of Makkah conferred upon it the greatest sanctity ever enjoyed by any city.

24

The Conquest of Makkah

Effects of the Previous Campaign

After the Campaign of Mu'tah, the Muslim army led by Khalid ibn al Walid returned to Madinah neither victorious nor vanquished, but happy to be able to return at all. Their return affected the Byzantines, the Muslims of Madinah, and the Quraysh in the most diverse ways. The Byzantines were glad that the Muslim army, despite its small size compared to their one or two hundred thousand, had withdrawn; and they gave thanks that the war did not last long. Regardless of whether the satisfaction of the Byzantines was due to the cessation of a war so fierce that nine swords had fallen apart in Khalid ibn al Walid's hand, or to that of a war fought with such strategy that untold forces were thought to reinforce the Muslim army, the tribes living in the outskirts of al Sham were left stupefied in admiration of the Muslim exploit. Farwah ibn 'Amr al Judhami, commander of a Byzantine army division, was at the same time chieftain of one of those tribes. Soon after Mu'tah, he proclaimed his conversion to Islam. He was arrested by order of Heraclius and accused of high treason; however, he was told that Heraclius would let him go free if he were to repent and return to Christianity. Indeed, he was promised the return to his position as army commander. Farwah refused and insisted on following the faith of Islam and was hence put to death. As a result of his execution, Islam spread widely among the tribes adjoining al 'Iraq and al Sham under Byzantine suzerainty.

Spread of Islam in the North

The chaos and insecurity attending the Byzantine Empire further encouraged the people to convert to the new faith of Islam. Its situation was truly chaotic. Entrusted by the emperor with paying the members of the armed forces their wages, one of Heraclius' governors discharged the soldiers with the announcement that the emperor had no money. Adding insult to injury, he said: "My Emperor has neither money nor food to distribute among his dogs." It was natural that such men would become disillusioned regarding Heraclius and his state and that the new order of Islam would shine with more brilliant light in their eye. It is no wonder that such men felt more inclined to it and thus followed the new guidance to divine truth. The foregoing explains, though necessarily only in part, the conversion to Islam of thousands from the tribe of Sulaym, under the leadership of al 'Abbas ibn Mirdas; of the tribes of Ashja' and Ghatafan, the old allies of the vanquished Jews of Khaybar; and of those of 'Abs, Dhubyan and Fazarah. Thus, it may be said that the campaign of Mu'tah caused the consolidation of the Muslim front north of Madinah all the way to the frontiers of al Sham.

The effect of that Campaign upon the morale of the Muslims in Madinah, however, was different. We may recall that as soon as Khalid and the army returned to Madinah without the proofs of victory, they were called deserters. Many soldiers and commanders felt so humiliated that they stayed at home in order not to be seen and insulted in public. The campaign of Mu'tah gave the Quraysh the impression that the Muslims and their power had now been destroyed and that both their dignity and the fear they previously inspired in others had all but disappeared. This made the Quraysh incline strongly to the conditions prevalent before the Treaty of Hudaybiyah. They thought that they could now launch a war against which the Muslims were incapable of defending themselves, not to speak of counterattacking or making retaliation.

Quraysh's Violation of Her Treaty

The Treaty of Hudaybiyah prescribed that any non-Makkans wishing to join the camp of Muhammad or that of the Quraysh may do so without obstruction. On the basis of this provision, the tribe of Khuza'ah joined the ranks of Muhammad, and that of Banu Bakr joined the Quraysh. Between Khuza'ah and Banu Bakr a number of old unsettled blood feuds had to be suspended on account of the new arrangement. With the Quraysh now believing that Muslim power had crumbled, Banu al Dil, a clan of Banu Bakr, thought that the occasion had come to avenge themselves against Khuza'ah. In this, they were encouraged by Quraysh, especially by 'Ikrimah ibn Abu Jahl and others who furnished them with arms and equipment. While Khuza'ah tribesmen were camping one day near a well of theirs called al Watir, Banu Bakr launched a surprise attack against them. The Khuza'ah party fled to Makkah and took refuge in the house of Budayl ibn Warqa', complaining that the Quraysh and their Banu Bakr allies violated their treaty with the Prophet. After running in full haste toward Madinah, 'Amr ibn Salim al Khuza'i related to Muhammad and the Muslims in the mosque what had happened and asked for assistance. The Prophet of God answered: "Certainly, O 'Amr ibn Salim, we shall come to your rescue." Another group of Khuza'ah tribesmen followed him to Madinah together with their Makkan host, Budayl ibn Warqa', and confirmed their predecessor's report. Realizing that this flagrant violation by the Quraysh of their treaty was forcing his hand to conquer Makkah, the Prophet sent word to the Muslims all over the Peninsula to mobilize at once. The objective, however, he kept as a secret.

Quraysh's Fears

The wise elders of Quraysh realized the danger to which 'Ikrimah and his youthful companions had exposed Makkah for their action was a clear violation of the Hudaybiyah Treaty. Should Muhammad decide to avenge his Khuza'ah allies against the Makkans, the holy city would be exposed to the strongest danger. What should they do? It occurred to them to send Abu Sufyan to Madinah to reaffirm the peace treaty and seek a prolongation of its two year term to ten. Abu Sufyan, chief statesman and leader of Makkah, proceeded to Madinah to conduct negotiations. On his way there, he met Budayl ibn Warqa' and his companions near 'Usfan, and feared that Muhammad might have preceded him to this place with an army bent on revenge, thus making his mission all the more difficult. Budayl denied that he had seen Muhammad before, but the shrewd Abu Sufyan could tell from the refuse of Budayl's horse that he had recently been in Madinah. He therefore decided that upon arrival to Madinah, he had better see his daughter, Umm Habibah, the Prophet's wife, rather than Muhammad himself.

The Failure of Abu Sufyan's Efforts

Umm Habibah knew well the Prophet's emotions regarding the Quraysh, though she did not know of his plans for Makkah. Such was the case with all Muslims in Madinah. Entering into his daughter's quarters, Abu Sufyan was about to sit upon the mattress of the Prophet when Umm Habibah moved it away. When he asked her whether she had done so in order to save her father from the mattress or the mattress from her father, she replied: "This is the mattress of the Prophet of God — May God's peace and blessing be upon him. You are an associationist and hence impure. You may not therefore be allowed to sit on the Prophet's mattress." Abu Sufyan was enraged by this reply and left the house, saying to his daughter, "By God, after you left my house, you must have become utterly mad." His strategy exposed, he proceeded to see Muhammad. The Prophet, however, refused to give him an audience. Abu Sufyan decided to go to Abu Bakr and ask him to intervene with the Prophet. Again, his request was turned down. He then approached 'Umar ibn al Khattab, who rejected him with the harsh rebuke: "Do you expect me to intervene with the Prophet of God for you? By God, if nothing is left for me but the sand of the desert, I will still fight you." Abu Sufyan went to 'Ali ibn Abu Talib and talked to him in the presence of his wife Fatimah. 'Ali spoke to him gently and apologized that nobody could change the mind of Muhammad once it was made up. Finally, the mighty delegate of Quraysh begged Fatimah to allow him to use her son, al Hasan, in his search for support among the people of Madinah as a means of convincing Muhammad to prolong the peace. Fatimah answered that nobody could dissuade the Prophet of God by this method. As the gates closed in the face of Abu Sufyan one after another, he returned to 'Ali and sought his advice. 'Ali replied that he knew of no measure which would alleviate the situation. He told him, however, that since he was the chief of Banu Kinanah, he could invoke his own tribal connections for a while and quickly return home. 'Ali informed Abu Sufyan that he did not think even that measure would work but that Abu Sufyan could turn to it *faute de mieux*. Abu Sufyan went to the Mosque and there proclaimed on behalf of his tribe his willingness to make peace with the people. He then mounted his horse and returned to Makkah. His heart was full of sorrow and his pride badly wounded, partly by his own daughter and partly by the rejection of those who, prior to their emigration from Makkah, had longed for the least bit of consideration or compassion from the great and mighty leader.

Abu Sufyan returned to Makkah and reported to his people the frustration of his efforts. He informed them of his proclamation in the Mosque of Madinah and of Muhammad's refusal to come to any terms of peace. The Makkans chastised him for allowing himself to be so contemptuously treated and continued their deliberations on the fate of their city.

Muslim Preparations for War

It was Muhammad's plan not to give the Quraysh the time to prepare for war. Armed by his confidence in Muslim power and in God's assistance, he sought to surprise the enemy before they could build up their defenses. His aim was to conquer without bloodshed. He therefore first commanded the people to get ready and informed them of his plans for Makkah later. He asked the Muslims to hurry and prayed that Quraysh would not find out his plan before it was too late.

While the Muslim army prepared to leave Madinah, Hatib ibn Abu Balta'ah wrote a letter informing the Quraysh about the Muslim move and gave it to a woman called Sarah, a client of some members of the house of Banu 'Abd al Muttalib. He commanded her to take it to Makkah and to hand it over to the Quraysh leaders. Hatib was one of the foremost Muslims. How then could he now turn informant for the enemy? Apparently, there are sides of the human soul which remain weak despite the great strength achieved by other sides, and man remains forever at the mercy of his weaknesses despite his conscious effort to overcome them. At any rate, Muhammad, soon learned of Hatib's attempt and sent 'Ali ibn Abu Talib and al Zubayr ibn al 'Awwam to intercept the messenger. The latter was arrested and her horse and saddle searched, but no letter was found. 'Ali threatened her that unless she produced the letter voluntarily, he would be forced to search her own person and to unveil her body in the process. When the woman realized how serious 'Ali was, she unloosened her pigtails, brought out the letter and handed it over to 'Ali. The woman was returned to Madinah, and Hatib was called to account. In his own defense, Hatib said: "O Prophet of God, by God I swear that I am still a believer in God and in His Prophet. My faith has not changed by one jot or tittle. But I am a man here in the Muslim camp devoid of relatives, family or clan, whereas in Makkah, I have children, family, and relatives whom I want no evil to befall." Upon hearing his reply, 'Umar ibn al Khattab asked the Prophet's permission to strike his neck on the grounds that he had apostatized. The Prophet answered: "O 'Umar, perhaps God has looked favorably on the men who fought at Badr and has permitted them to do whatever they wish; for their merit with God is truly great." Hatib was one of those who fought at Badr. In this connection, the following verse was revealed: "O Men who believe, do not take My and your enemies as friends. Show such people no amity."[1]

The Muslims' March on Makkah

The Muslim army proceeded from Madinah to Makkah bent upon conquering that city and seizing the sanctuary which God had declared a place of peace, security, and religious sanctification to all mankind. This army had more men than Madinah had ever seen before, since the tribes of Sulaym, Muzaynah, Ghatafan, and others had joined the Muhajirun and the Ansar in such numbers and with such armaments that the wide expanses of the desert were filled with them. As the force moved forward it covered the desert from horizon to horizon and no end of it could be seen. They moved fast, and at every station many more tribes joined their ranks and added to their armaments and equipment. Every soul was filled with the faith of Islam and entertained no doubt that God's help will bring them victory. Muhammad led this army at the forefront. His greatest concern was to seize the holy house without shedding any unnecessary blood. By the time the army arrived at al Zahran, four miles from Makkah, its number had reached ten thousand. Until then, the Quraysh knew nothing about it, and its leaders continued to consult with one another, to agree and to disagree regarding the measures to be taken by them to meet Muslim anger. Al 'Abbas ibn 'Abd al Muttalib, uncle of the Prophet, withdrew from the conversation of the Quraysh leaders, took all members of his family, and went out in the direction of Madinah. At al Juhfah he met Muhammad and converted to Islam.[2] It is rather likely that a group of the Banu Hashim heard a rumor regarding the Prophet's new expedition and sought to join him before the battle began. Two other Makkans came to join the ranks of the Muslims at Niq al 'Uqab, both cousins of the Prophet: Abu Sufyan ibn al Harith ibn 'Abd al Muttalib and 'Abdullah ibn Abu Umayyah ibn al Mughirah. The Prophet, however, refused to grant them their request, replying to Umm Salamah, who approached him on their behalf, that he had no need for either cousin. The first had previously injured the Prophet, and the second, the Prophet's brother-in-law, had broadcast all sorts of libels and calumnies about him. When a report of the Prophet's decision reached the ears of

Abu Sufyan, he swore that either Muhammad would grant him this permission or he would take his son and strike out aimlessly into the desert and perish of thirst and hunger. Muhammad felt compassion toward him and his son, and permitted them to be received within the Muslim ranks. They entered his audience and were converted to Islam.

Al 'Abbas ibn 'Abd al Muttalib saw that the armies of his nephew were disturbingly preponderant in power and numbers. Although a Muslim, he felt quite apprehensive for what might befall his own native city should this hitherto unrivalled army advance on it with hostile intention. After all, the city he had just left behind was full of his own people, friends and relatives, and he did not consider those relationships terminated by his entry into Islam. Perhaps he intimated some of these fears to the Prophet when he asked, "What would the Prophet do in case Quraysh asked for a guarantee of its own security?" And perhaps Muhammad was pleased that al 'Abbas had broached the subject with him. It might even be conjectured that the Prophet thought of using al 'Abbas as a delegate to the Quraysh that his apprehensiveness might be transmitted to the Makkans. Such measure would prevent the shedding of blood and enable the Muslims to enter Makkah without war. The sanctity of the city would thus be Raved and its picture in the Arab mind as a place of security, refuge, and peace would be preserved. In fact, al 'Abbas was soon sent back to Makkah, riding on the Prophet's own white mule. When he approached the locality of al Arak, al 'Abbas looked for anyone from Makkah, be it a lumberman or herdsmen, with whom he might send a message informing the Makkan leadership of the Muslim's preponderant armies and advising them to come out to meet the Prophet and reconcile themselves to him before he should take Makkah by storm.

Abu Sufyan's Audience with the Prophet

The Quraysh, for their part, felt gravely apprehensive ever since the Muslims arrived at al Zahran. They sent Abu Sufyan, Budayl ibn Warqa', and Hakim ibn Hazzam, the relative of Khadijah, to reconnoiter the field and assess the danger. While riding in the area on the Prophet's white mule, al 'Abbas overheard a conversation between Abu Sufyan and Budayl ibn Warqa'. To Abu Sufyan's exclamation that he had never seen any lights or encampments as wide and great as those which he had just beheld that night, Budayl answered that the said lights and encampments must belong to Khuza'ah tribe, now aroused to do battle. Abu Sufyan rejected this view of Budayl, affirming that Khuza'ah was known to be much fewer in number and much poorer than to afford all such lights and camps. Overhearing the voice of Abu Sufyan and recognizing it for what it was, al 'Abbas called out to him using his title "Abu Hanzalah". Abu Sufyan, who recognized the voice, answered by using the title of al 'Abbas, "Abu al Fadl". Al 'Abbas said: "Watch out, O Abu Sufyan! What you see is the Prophet of God leading his people. Woe to the Quraysh tomorrow morning, when his armies storm their city." Abu Sufyan answered: "Oh the misery of it! What shall we do?" Al 'Abbas invited him to mount on his mule, sent his companions back to Makkah and returned with him to the Muslim camp. As the Muslims recognized the mule of the Prophet, they let it pass unhurt with Abu Sufyan on its back. It ran between rows of thousands of Muslims who had built enormous bonfires. As the mule passed by the fire of 'Umar ibn al Khattab, 'Umar recognized Abu Sufyan and surmised that al 'Abbas was about to take Abu Sufyan under his protection. He hurried to the tent of the Prophet and asked the latter to permit him to strike the neck of Abu Sufyan. Al 'Abbas entered the tent of the Prophet saying: "O Prophet of God, I have extended my protection to this man on account of the urgent need of this hour of the night." After what must have been a hot discussion between 'Umar and al 'Abbas, Muhammad said: "O 'Abbas, take your guest to your tent and bring him over in the morning."

On the next day, Abu Sufyan was brought to the Prophet and, in front of a court composed of the elders of the Muhajirun and al Ansar, the following conversation took place. Addressing himself to Abu Sufyan, the Prophet said: "Is it not time for you to know that there is no God but God, O Abu Sufyan?" Abu Sufyan answered: "How great, noble, and generous you are, O Prophet of God! By God I swear that if God had an associate, such had ample time to prove himself. But he didn't." The Prophet said : "Woe to you, O Abu Sufyan, is it not time for you to learn that I am the Prophet of God?" Abu Sufyan answered: "How great, noble and generous you are, O Prophet of God! While I entertain no more doubt that God has any associate, I am still not so sure about this claim." At this point, al 'Abbas intervened and asked Abu Sufyan to convert to Islam and to witness, before he was put to death, that there is no God but God and that Muhammad is the Prophet of God. Faced with the threat, Abu Sufyan converted and recited the confession of faith. Al 'Abbas then turned to the Prophet — God's peace be upon him — and said: "O Prophet of God, Abu Sufyan is a proud man. Would you not grant him some privilege?"

The Prophet answered: "Yes, indeed! Whoever enters the house of Abu Sufyan shall be secure; whoever remains in his own house shall also be secure; and whoever enters the Mosque shall be secure."

The Historians' Estimate of These Reports

The veracity of the foregoing event is agreed upon by all historians and biographers. Some of them question whether these events took place accidentally or by previous arrangement. They point to the fact that when al 'Abbas sought the Prophet, he meant to travel to Madinah, but we find him confronting the Muslim army at al Juhfah. They also point to the fact that Budayl ibn Warqa' and Abu Sufyan ibn Harb left Makkah in order to reconnoiter, whereas we do know that the same Budayl had gone to Madinah and related to the Prophet how he encountered Khuza'ah on the road and learned from the Prophet that the Banu Khuza'ah had become the Prophet's allies. How, then, is this consistent with the view that Abu Sufyan had left Makkah without prior knowledge that Muhammad and his army were already on the road to Makkah? Some historians therefore suggest that some prearrangement, whether little or much, must have taken place before these events unfolded, and that it was under some such prearrangement that al 'Abbas went out to meet Muhammad. They point out that such an arrangement between Makkans and Muslims is implicit in the meeting of al 'Abbas and Abu Sufyan in the night. Abu Sufyan stood in need of no argument to convince al 'Abbas that Quraysh had no more means to stop Muhammad, especially since he had been in Madinah seeking to extend the term of the Hudaybiyah Treaty without success. These historians and biographers suggest that Abu Sufyan must have thought that if he could cooperate with the Prophet and prepare for the Muslim conquest of Makkah, his position of leadership in Makkan society would be safeguarded. That such a prearranged agreement did not go beyond Muhammad and the few persons concerned, the evidence of 'Umar's request to kill Abu Sufyan eloquently proves. At any rate, it is conjecture for us to judge. But we certainly may decide, and do so with utmost conviction, that regardless of whether these events took place incidentally or by previous arrangement, they prove beyond doubt Muhammad's skill, sure insight, and precision in winning the greatest victory of Islamic history without war or bloodshed.

The March on Makkah Continued

The conversion of Abu Sufyan did not dissuade Muhammad from taking all necessary precautions before entering Makkah. Although understood that victory is a gift of God granted to whomsoever He pleases, it is still true that God does not grant His gift except to those who prepare for it perfectly and who avail themselves of every possible precaution to achieve it. Only in this way can it be explained why the Prophet ordered that Abu Sufyan be held at the gate of the valley in the outskirts of Makkah. He deemed it desirable that Abu Sufyan watch the Muslim armies at close range and describe them to his people accurately. But he was careful not to give the enemy any time to mobilize an army or to prepare any kind of opposition before the Muslims had entered the city. As the tribes passed by Abu Sufyan, he was in no way so much impressed as by the "green company" in which Muhammad stood surrounded by the Muhajirun and al Ansar. So close were their ranks and so well equipped that all one could see was a solid mass of iron. After they passed, Abu Sufyan said to al 'Abbas: "O Abu al Fadl, no force can stand in the face of this. By God, the dominion of your nephew has become truly great." He then rushed toward Makkah calling to his people at the top of his voice: "O men of Quraysh, here comes Muhammad with an army such as you have never seen before. Put up no resistance. Whoever enters into my house shall be secure; whoever remains in his own house shall be secure; and whoever enters the Mosque shall be secure."

Muhammad advanced with the army until he reached Dhu Tuwa. From there he realized that Makkah lay in front of him devoid of any army to give him battle. He stopped his forces, stood over this mount, and bent himself in prayers and thanksgiving. He was grateful to God that he had enabled him to conquer the first theatre of revelation. The sanctuary of the holy House was now to be opened to all the Muslims in peace and security. At the same time, Abu Quhafah who had not yet been converted to Islam like his son, asked a granddaughter of his to take him over to the mount of Abu Qubays. Being blind, he asked his granddaughter what she saw once they got to the top. She answered, "A black mass is all I see." He said, "That must be the cavalry." She said, "By God the black mass is spreading out." He said, "The cavalry must have been given orders to march over Makkah. Take me quickly to my home." Before they reached Makkah, however, the Muslim cavalry had entered the city and intercepted him on the road.

Deployment of the Muslim Forces

Muhammad praised God and thanked him for the conquest of Makkah. Nonetheless, he continued to take every precaution. He had divided the army into four groups and commanded them all not to engage in any fighting or shed any blood except in cases of extreme emergency. He gave the command of the left wing to al Zubayr ibn al 'Awwam and ordered him to enter Makkah from the north. He gave the command of the right to Khalid ibn al Walid and ordered him to enter Makkah from the south. He gave the command of the Madinese to Sa'd ibn 'Ubadah and ordered him to enter Makkah from the west. As for Abu 'Ubaydah ibn al Jarrah, he gave him the command of the Muhajirun and ordered him to enter Makkah from the north near Hind Mountain and joined his own company to the Muhajirun. While about to march, Sa'd ibn 'Ubadah was heard saying: "Today is the day of battle, the day of the great war, the day when all taboos will be lifted." Had he been permitted to proceed, this general would have violated the Prophet's commandment that no blood should be shed in Makkah. Hence, as soon as the Prophet learned of his attitude, he relieved him of the command of the forces and appointed his son, Qays, to replace him. The son was less active than the father on account of his voluminous size, but he was of a far more gentle disposition.

The armies entered and occupied Makkah without opposition. Only the front assigned to Khalid ibn al Walid put up any resistance. That area, the south of Makkah, was populated by the most hostile and antagonistic members of Quraysh. Many of them were among the attackers of Khuza'ah who, together with their Banu Bakr allies, had violated the Treaty of Hudaybiyah. Not moved by the call of Abu Sufyan, they prepared for battle. Those of them ready to fight were led by Safwan, Suhayl, and 'Ikrimah ibn Abu Jahl. When Khalid's army entered their quarter, they showered it with arrows. Khalid, however, quickly dispersed them, losing two of his men and killing thirteen of the enemy, according to one version, and twenty-eight according to another. It is even said that the two soldiers missing from Khalid's army were not lost in battle but had strayed into the wilderness and lost their way. Safwan, Suhayl, and 'Ikrimah took to flight as soon as they realized the futility of their stand, leaving their own men whom they had incited to resistance at the mercy of Muslim arms. Standing with a group of Muhajirun on a Makkan height and surveying the various quarters of the city he had just conquered without violence, Muhammad noticed toward the south the shining of swords in battle with the local inhabitants. The Prophet became angry and repeated his command that there should be no fighting. He was soon told the facts of the case and accepted God's judgment in the matter.

The Muslims Enter Makkah

The Prophet camped on a height opposite the mountain of Hind and in the proximity of the graves of Abu Talib and Khadijah. He was asked whether he wanted to rest in his old house in Makkah and answered, "No! They have leveled it." The Prophet then retired to his tent grateful to God for this glorious and victorious return, and for bringing to its knees the cruel city which had tortured and banished him. For a moment, he turned his gaze toward the valley of Makkah as well as to the surrounding hills. He recalled that in those hills he often found refuge from the persecution of Quraysh; that one of them, Hira', was the scene of his periodical retreats. Vividly, he represented to himself the moment when, in the cave of that same mountain, the first verses of the Qur'an were revealed; he could hear the holy words resound in his ears:

اِقْرَأْ بِاسْمِ رَبِّكَ الَّذِى خَلَقَ خَلَقَ الْإِنْسَانَ مِنْ عَلَقٍ اِقْرَأْ وَرَبُّكَ الْأَكْرَمُ الَّذِى عَلَّمَ بِالْقَلَمِ عَلَّمَ الْإِنْسَانَ مَا لَمْ يَعْلَمْ

"Read! Read in the Name of your Lord, Who created man from a clot! Read! For your Lord is the Most gracious. He has taught man to read and to write! He has taught man that which he does not know!"[3]

The Prophet was naturally attracted by the view of Makkah spread out in expanding circles before him between these hills, at the center of which stood the sanctuary and its holy House. Muhammad, moved by the sight of Makkah and by the remembrance of God's revelation, let tears fall from his eye as he thanked God, praised Him, and witnessed that there is no truth and no power except in Him. He felt that his task as leader was coming to a natural conclusion. So agitating were all these feelings that he was unable to settle down to rest or, indeed, even to restrain himself within the tent. Mounting his she-camel, al Qaswa', he rode toward the Ka'bah where he circumambulated the House without dismounting. He then dismounted and called upon 'Uthman ibn Talhah to open the Ka'bah for him. Muhammad stood at the door surrounded by the many worshippers who had found their way to the holy House. He delivered a speech to the people present in which he said, quoting the Qur'an:

$$\text{يَٰأَيُّهَا ٱلنَّاسُ إِنَّا خَلَقْنَٰكُم مِّن ذَكَرٍ وَأُنثَىٰ وَجَعَلْنَٰكُمْ شُعُوبًا وَقَبَآئِلَ لِتَعَارَفُوٓا۟ إِنَّ أَكْرَمَكُمْ عِندَ ٱللَّهِ أَتْقَىٰكُمْ إِنَّ ٱللَّهَ عَلِيمٌ خَبِيرٌ}$$

"O men, We have created you from male and female and constituted you into peoples and tribes that you might know and cooperate with one another. In the eye of God, highest among you is the most virtuous. God is omniscient and all-wise."[4]

He continued: "O Men of Quraysh, what do you think I am about to do with you?" "Everything good," they answered, "for you are a noble brother and a noble nephew of ours." Muhammad went on: "Rise, then, and go. For you are free."

With this word, Muhammad gave a general amnesty to all Quraysh and all the Makkans.

The Prophet's General Amnesty

Oh, the beauty of pardon and forgiveness on the part of the mighty and powerful! How great is the soul of Muhammad which rose above hatred and above revenge, which denied every human feeling and ascended to heights of nobility man had never reached before! There were the Quraysh among whom were people whom Muhammad well knew had plotted to kill him, had persecuted him, and inflicted upon him and his companions all kinds of injury and harm, who fought him at Badr and at Uhud, who blockaded him in the Campaign of al Khandaq, who incited the Arab tribes to rise against him, and who would even then tear him apart if only they had the power. There, the whole of Quraysh stood totally under Muhammad's hand, indeed under his feet, totally subject to his command. Indeed, their very life depended upon the first word emerging from his lips. All these thousands of men, of Muslims in battle array, stood on the ready waiting for that one word to wipe out the whole of Makkah and its people within minutes. Muhammad, however, was no less than Muhammad! He was no less than the Prophet of God! No alienation, antagonism, or hostility could find any permanent abode in his heart. His heart was absolutely free of injustice, of malice, of tyranny or false pride. In the most decisive moment, God gave him power over his enemy. But Muhammad chose to forgive, thereby giving to all mankind and all the generations the most perfect example of goodness, of truthfulness, of nobility and magnanimity.

Cleansing the Ka'bah of Its Images

When Muhammad entered the Ka'bah, he saw that its walls were painted with pictures of angels and prophets. His eyes fell upon a picture of Ibrahim holding the divination arrows and a pigeon made out of twigs. He seized the pigeon, broke it into pieces and threw it to the ground and, looking at the picture of Ibrahim, he said: "Accursed be the Makkans! They have made our ancestor an idolater and a diviner. What does Ibrahim have to do with divination arrows? He was neither a Jew nor a Christian nor yet an associationist, but a *hanif,* and a Muslim." On the walls of the Ka'bah, the angels were pictured as beautiful women. Turning to them, Muhammad denied that angels had any such bodily forms, that they were either male or female. He commanded the obliteration of all pictures and images. Attached with lead to the walls of the Ka'bah were the idols which the Quraysh worshipped as the associates of God; the idol Hubal stood in the center of the Ka'bah. Muhammad designated every one of these idols with his stick and recited the verse of the Qur'an:

$$\text{وَقُلْ جَآءَ الْحَقُّ وَزَهَقَ الْبَاطِلُ ۚ إِنَّ الْبَاطِلَ كَانَ زَهُوقًا}$$

"Say, the truth is now manifest. Falsehood is truly confuted. And it is right that it should be."[5]

The idols were then torn down and broken, and the holy House was purified. That which Muhammad had called for during the last twenty years was now accomplished before the first day of the conquest of Makkah was over. That which Makkah had opposed most strongly was now a fact of history. The destruction of the idols and the wiping out of paganism in the holy sanctuary was now completed before the very eyes of Quraysh. The Makkan idols, the objects of reverence and worship inherited from the ancestors, crumbled to bits under the hammering blows of Muhammad.

Al Ansar's Fears and the Prophet's Reassurance

As the Ansar of Madinah witnessed all this, and as they saw Muhammad on top of al Safa mountain invite the Makkans to embrace Islam, they feared he might now abandon Madinah and reestablish himself in his native city. Some of them inquired of one another, seeking to reassure themselves whether or not this was the case. Their apprehension was not out of place. Victor in his own home town where stood the sanctuary, the holy House of God and center of worship, it was quite likely that the Prophet would now make Makkah his capital. Muhammad had hardly finished his prayer and preaching when he inquired concerning their fears. When, after long hesitancy, they intimated to him their concern, the Prophet said: "Never, by God! I have covenanted to join you in life and death. I shall remain true to my covenant." Evidently, neither relatives, nor native city, nor even the holy sanctuary itself could dissuade Muhammad from honoring a pledge he once gave to those who stood by him at his hour of need. His word given at the conclusion of the Covenant of 'Aqabah was to be honored in exemplary faithfulness and loyalty, and the occasion proved to be just what the moral teacher needed. When the Ka'bah was purified of its idols, the Prophet ordered Bilal to mount to its top and from there to recite the *adhan*, to give the call to worship. The Muslims gathered and, led by Muhammad, performed the prayer. From that time until today, for fourteen long centuries without interruption, Bilal as well as his countless successors have recited the *adhan* calling men to prayer five times a day from that same spot on top of the Ka'bah. For fourteen long centuries since that day, Muslims all over the globe have worshipped God and invoked His blessing upon His Prophet, their face turned toward this holy House which Muhammad cleansed on that day of its images and idols and reconsecrated to the One Almighty God.

Quraysh, resigned to its fate, felt reassured by Muhammad's general pardon. They watched the Muslims go about their city with great surprise, not without a measure of fear and caution. Seventeen Makkans were excepted from Muhammad's general amnesty and were ordered executed even if found clutching to the coverings of the Ka'bah. Some of them went into hiding and others ran away from the city altogether. They all stood convicted of atrocious crimes they had committed. One of these men was 'Abdullah ibn Abu al Sarh who once converted to Islam and wrote down the revelation for Muhammad, but who then apostatized, returned to Quraysh, and there spread tales about his falsification of the revelation. Another convict was 'Abdullah ibn Khatal who converted to Islam, killed one of his clients, apostatized, and commanded his two slave women, one of whom was called Fartana, to castigate Muhammad in song. Both slave women were indicted and ordered executed with their master. Another was 'Ikrimah ibn Abu Jahl, the most persistent enemy, who could not accept the Muslim conquest of Makkah and put up strong resistance in the face of Khalid ibn al Walid on the southern front.

Pardon Extended to The Convicts

As soon as he entered Makkah, Muhammad ordered that no blood should be shed and that only the seventeen people would receive their just punishment. While some of the seventeen condemned hid, others ran away from Makkah with their families. As the situation settled down and the news of the Prophet's clemency and all-embracing forgiveness became fully known and appreciated by all, some companions dared to think that even the condemned could also be forgiven. 'Uthman ibn 'Affan, brother-in-nursing of Ibn Abu al Sarh, approached the Prophet in this regard and sought an order for the safe passage of his *protégé*. Muhammad was silent for a long time sunk in thought, but he then consented to grant forgiveness. Umm Hakim, daughter of al Harith ibn Hisham and the wife of 'Ikrimah ibn Abu Jahl who ran away to Yaman, converted to Islam and sought pardon for her husband directly from Muhammad. She was granted it. She then went to Yaman and returned with her husband. Muhammad also forgave Safwan ibn Umayyah who accompanied 'Ikrimah on his escape toward the sea and thence to Yaman. Both had been caught just before their ship was to sail. Muhammad also forgave Hind, wife of Abu Sufyan, who chewed the liver of Hamzah, uncle of the Prophet, after his martyrdom at the Battle of Uhud. Indeed, most of the men condemned to death had been forgiven. Only four were executed: al Huwayrith who tempted Zaynab, the Prophet's daughter, when she returned from Makkah to Madinah; two Muslims guilty of murder in Madinah who escaped to Makkah and apostatized; and one of the slave women of Ibn Khatal who used to castigate the Prophet in song. The other slave-woman ran away, but was brought back and later forgiven.

Reconsecration of Makkah: The City as Inviolate

Following the conquest of Makkah, the Khuza'ah tribe discovered a Hudhayl tribesman in their midst who was still a pagan and killed him. Upon hearing the news, the Prophet was so angry that he delivered a speech in which he said: "O men, God made Makkah a holy place on the day heaven and earth were created. Makkah is therefore holy, holy, holy to the end of time. No man believing in God and the Day of Judgment may therefore shed any blood or destroy any tree in its precincts. Makkah has never been desecrated by anyone before me and it shall never be desecrated by anyone after me. Only for the brief hour of conquest and because of God's wrath upon its people, it was permitted to me to enter it with arms. But now Makkah fully enjoys her previous holiness. Let the present inform the absent. Whoever argues with you that the Prophet of God fought in Makkah, answer him that God had desanctified the city for His Prophet but not for anyone else, and surely not for you, O Tribesmen of Khuza'ah! All killing must stop, for it is evil crime and brings no advantage when indulged in. You have killed a man, and I shall have to pay his bloodwit to his people. Henceforth, the heirs of a victim shall have the choice between executing the murderer or receiving bloodwit." Muhammad immediately paid the bloodwit of the Khuza'ah tribesman to his people. By his disposal of the case in this manner and his general proclamation concerning murder and retaliation, Muhammad struck a further example of clemency and justice. The force of Islam's appeal to the Makkans became irresistible, and they began to convert. The town crier proclaimed: "Whoever believes in God and the Day of Judgment will destroy on this day every idol and vestige of paganism in his home." The Prophet commissioned some Khuza'ah men to repair the walls of the holy city, thereby giving further proof of his respect for it. Under the circumstances, the love and esteem for Muhammad could only increase. Muhammad told the Makkans that he loved them the most, that they were the highest in his regard, and that he would have never left them had they themselves not rejected and banished him. With this praise, the Makkans' esteem for Muhammad broke all bounds.

Abu Bakr brought his own father, Abu Quhafah, the old blind man who went up to the mount of Abu Qubays guided by his daughter to find out what was happening before the Muslims entered the city, and placed him in the presence of the Prophet. When seeing him, Muhammad reproached Abu Bakr for bringing the old man over and said that it was he, Muhammad, that should have come to Abu Quhafah. Paying no attention to Abu Bakr's rejoinder that it was his father's duty to come to the Prophet and not vice versa, he asked the man to sit by him, wiped his face for him and invited him to enter into Islam. Abu Quhafah converted and became an ardent Muslim. Through this noble behavior of the Prophet, this magnanimous conduct, Muhammad succeeded in winning over a people who had nursed for him the strongest hatred. Thereafter, the

Makkans revered the person of Muhammad, embraced Islam, and whole-heartedly subjected themselves to his rule.

Ibn al Walid and the Tribe of Jadhimah

Muhammad resided in Makkah fifteen days during which he organized its affairs and instructed its people in Islam. During this period, he sent forth delegations to call men peaceably to Islam to destroy the idols without shedding any blood. Khalid ibn al Walid was sent to Nakhlah to destroy al 'Uzza, goddess of Banu Shayban. His task accomplished, ibn al Walid proceeded to Jadhimah. There, however, the people took up arms at his approach. Khalid asked them to lay down their arms on the grounds that all people had accepted Islam. One of the Jadhimah tribesman said to his people: "Woe to you, Banu Jadhimah! Don't you know that this is Khalid? By God, nothing awaits you once you have laid down your arms except captivity, and once you have become captives you can expect nothing but death." Some of his people answered: "Do you seek to have us all murdered? Don't you know that most men have converted to Islam, that the war is over, and that security is reestablished?" Those who held this opinion continued to talk to their tribesmen until the latter surrendered their arms. Thereupon, ibn al Walid ordered them to be bound, and he killed some of them. When he heard of the news, the Prophet lifted his arms to heaven and prayed: "O God, I condemn what Khalid ibn al Walid has done." The Prophet gave funds to 'Ali ibn Abu Talib and sent him to look into the affairs of this tribe, cautioning him to disregard all the customs of pre-Islam. Upon arrival, 'Ali paid the bloodwit of all the victims and compensated the property owners for their damages. Before leaving, he surrendered the rest of the money which the Prophet had given him to the tribe just in case there were any other losses which may have escaped notice at the time.

During the two weeks which Muhammad spent in Makkah, he wiped out all the traces of paganism in the city. All the offices attached to the holy House were abolished except two: the *sidanah* which the Prophet assigned to 'Uthman ibn Talhah, his children, and progeny after him till the end of days, and the *siqayah*, which he assigned to his uncle al 'Abbas. Thus Umm al Qura[6] embraced Islam and raised high the torch of genuine monotheism, illuminating the whole world for generations and centuries to come.

25

Campaigns of Hunayn and al Ta'if

After its conquest, the Muslims remained in Makkah for two weeks during which they showed their joy over the victory which God had granted to them. They gave thanks that such a great victory had been achieved with such little bloodshed. They hurried to the sanctuary every time Bilal delivered the *adhan* calling them to prayer. They strove to be near the Prophet wherever he went. The Muhajirun visited their old houses and their relatives and friends whom God had guided to the truth after the conquest. Everybody was satisfied that Islam was now firmly established and that the greater part of the holy war had been victorious. Fifteen days of their stay in Makkah had hardly passed when news broke out which shook the Muslims out of their joy and feeling of security. They learned that Hawazin, the tribe living a few miles to the southeast of Makkah, had mobilized its forces and was marching against the Muslims in Makkah. This tribe had learned of the conquest of Makkah by the Muslims and of the subsequent destruction of the idols of the Ka'bah. Apparently, their men feared that the time would soon come for the Muslims to fight them on their own ground. Anxious to prevent such a tragedy, they thought this hour of Muslim intoxication with victory the right time to mobilize their forces for an attack. Their purpose, however, was the larger one of wrecking the Muslims' general plan of uniting all the tribes of the Peninsula under the banner of Islam.

Malik ibn 'Awf's March against the Muslims

It was toward this end that Malik ibn 'Awf al Nadri succeeded in uniting the Hawazin and Thaqif tribes and rallying the tribes of Nasr and
Jusham in one front opposing the Islamic movement as a whole. Only the
Ka'b and Kilab clans of Hawazin refused to join the new alliance. Durayd
ibn al Simmah, of the Jusham tribe, was a very old man, too old to fight,
but he was extremely wise and had the advantage of an extensive military
experience and career. The anti-Islamic alliance had mobilized all its
members, men, women, and children, and carried to battle all the treasures it possessed. It completed its mobilization in the valley of Awtas.
When Durayd, who was blind, heard the braying of donkeys and lowing
of cattle mixed in with the crying of children and the bellowing of goats,
he asked Malik ibn 'Awf why he had brought women, children, and treasures to the front. Malik answered that he meant thereby to encourage the
fighting men and to incite them to greater self-exertion in war. Durayd
answered: "But what do we do in case of defeat? Does the vanquished ever
keep anything he brings to the battlefield? If we are to be victorious, surely such victory will be brought about not by the women or children but by
the fighting men and their swords, arrows, and javelins. But if we should
lose the war, then we would be shamed and scandalized by the capture of
our families and treasures." Malik disagreed with Durayd, and the people
followed the former. Malik was a youth of thirty years, a man of strong
will and firm resolution. Durayd, anxious to safeguard the newly forged
unity, decided, against his better judgment, to go along with the majority.
Malik commanded his people to stand by on the tops of the Sulaym hills
at the entrance to the valley and, at the proper signal, to fall upon the
Muslims like one man and break their ranks as they passed in file through
the canyon. Such a plot would reduce the Muslim ranks to a rabble, and
the Muslims would not be able to distinguish their own soldiers from the
enemy. They would be vanquished; and with their defeat, their victory
over Makkah would be cancelled and to the tribes of Hawazin and
Hunayn would belong the honor of destroying a power which came close
to engulfing the whole Peninsula. The tribes obeyed the orders of Malik
and dug themselves in on the sides of the canyon.

The Muslims March to Hunayn

As for the Muslims, they went forth under the leadership of
Muhammad with such power and such numbers that they themselves had

never seen before. There were twelve thousand of them, ten thousand of which were those who conquered Makkah and two thousand who were newcomers from Quraysh including Abu Sufyan. Their war equipment was excellent and their armies were preceded by their cavalry and camel corps carrying their provisions and ammunition. Theirs was an army the like of which the Arabian Peninsula had never seen before. It consisted of many tribes, and each tribe had its own banner which it carried high above its ranks. It was a sight convincing any spectator of Muslim invincibility. Indeed, many Muslims told one another: "To say the least, our numerical strength has today made us invincible." They arrived at Hunayn in the evening and camped at the entrance of the valley until dawn. At dawn the following day the army began to move, and Muhammad, riding his white mule, was in the rear while Khalid ibn al Walid, commanding a group of soldiers from Banu Sulaym, was in the vanguard.

Muslim Defeat

As the Muslims passed through the canyon of Hunayn, Malik ibn 'Awf ordered his army to attack in the darkness before dawn, first with arrows and then with a general charge. The Muslims' ranks broke up and were stricken with panic. Some of them ran out of the canyon as fast as they could in search of safety. Witnessing what had befallen the Muslims, Abu Sufyan felt no little pleasure at the defeat of his previous enemies who until now had been celebrating their victory over Makkah. He said, "The Muslims will not be defeated until they are thrown into the sea." Shaybah ibn 'Uthman ibn Abu Talhah, whose father was killed at Uhud, said, "Today is my day of vengeance from Muhammad." Likewise, Kaladah ibn Hanbal said, "Today, the fate of the Muslims is cast," only to be answered by his brother Safwan: "Silence! Cursed be your tongue. By God, to be lorded over by a man from Quraysh is better than by a man of Hawazin." These remarks were exchanged while Muslim ranks were falling apart, and soldiers, fleeing in face of the enemy, were bypassing the Prophet in the rear unaware of his presence.

Muhammad's Resoluteness and Bravery

What would Muhammad do? Would he allow the sacrifices of twenty years to be lost in this moment of pre-dawn darkness? Could he think that God had abandoned him in this hour? Such could never be! Better death and annihilation. Better that Muhammad die in the thick of battle! At any rate, when one's hour has struck, to what purpose is delaying or advancing it a little? Muhammad therefore held his ground and was surrounded by a number of Muhajirun, Ansar, and immediate relatives. As his men passed by, he called out to them and sought to rally them back to the ranks. But they neither heard nor wanted to hear. The sudden onslaught of Hawazin and Thaqif robbed them of their senses. This terrible picture the Muslims had of the enemy was not exaggerated. From the sides of the canyon the tribesmen of Hawazin poured down in overwhelming numbers. Their leader rode a red camel and held a black banner attached to a long spear which he plunged into the chest of every Muslim that came anywhere near him. Hawazin and Thaqif tribesmen, as well as their allies, fought in the same way. It was a sea of drawn spears. At one moment, Muhammad almost plunged with his mule into enemy lines to stop their torrent of blows. Abu Sufyan ibn al Harith ibn 'Abd al Muttalib hold back the reins of the mule and prevented it from carrying the Prophet forward.

Al 'Abbas's Call for Regrouping

Al 'Abbas ibn 'Abd al Muttalib was a man of large stature who had a very resonant voice. He called loudly enough to reach all the Muslims: "O Ansar Company! O Men who opened their homes and helped Muhammad! O Muharijrun Company! O Men who pledged their allegiance under the tree! Muhammad is still alive. Charge forward with him." Al 'Abbas repeated his call until the whole valley reverberated with its echo. Then, the miracle happened. The covenanters of al 'Aqabah and the Muhajirun heard. They remembered Muhammad and their oaths of allegiance to him as well as their sacrifices in the cause of Islam. The other Muslims also heard and realized that Muhammad was still there, alive, holding his ground, and fighting the enemy just as he had held his ground and fought the enemy at the Battle of Uhud. Suddenly, they were gripped by a consciousness of shame at their conduct and of apprehension at what might befall their Prophet and God's religion in case the associationists carried the day. Al 'Abbas's call continued to reverberate through the valley; the Muslims' hearts were immediately touched and their wills kindled. There and then, from every corner and quarter came the resounding cry, "At Your command, O God, at Your command!" The Muslims returned to battle and fought with utmost resolution and gallantry.

Muslim Counterattack and Victory

Muhammad was reassured as he saw them return to the battlefront. In the meantime, the whole Hawazin camp had come out of their trenches in the hills and confronted the Muslims face to face in the valley. At that time, too, the darkness was dissipated by sunrise. Around the Prophet a few hundred soldiers stood and repelled the attacks of the Hawazin. Their ranks began to swell as the fleeing Muslims returned. The Ansar began to call to one another, "Rally forth to battle." They quickly reorganized themselves according to tribes and clans while Muhammad watched the progress of the battle. As the Muslim soldiers refilled their ranks and began to march shoulder to shoulder together, the Prophet proclaimed: "Now the battle has begun. God will not fail the Prophet and will fulfill the promise He gave him." Then, turning to al 'Abbas and asking for a handful of pebbles, the Prophet threw the pebbles in the face of the enemy with the war cry, "Woe to the enemies of God!" With this, the Muslims charged, throwing themselves upon their enemies. They were convinced that theirs would be the victory and the fate of the martyr would even be greater than that of the surviving victor. The battle raged and men fell on all sides. Soon Hawazin, Thaqif, and their allies realized that their efforts were vain and that they faced annihilation. They turned around and started to flee, leaving behind them their women, children, and all their properties: 22,000 camels, 40,000 goats, and 4, 000 ounces of silver. The captives which numbered 6, 000, were transported under Muslim protection to the valley of al Ji'ranah where they were held until the Muslims returned from their pursuit of the enemy and from their blockade of Thaqif tribe in the city of al Ta'if.

The Muslims' Pursuit of Their Enemies

The Muslims gave their enemy close pursuit, and they were further encouraged by the Prophet's proclamation that whoever killed an associationist would receive his victim's booty. Ibn al Dughunnah overtook a camel carrying an open palanquin which he thought might be carrying a woman whom he could take captive. He brought the camel to its knees, looked into the palanquin and discovered an old man unknown to him. The old man asked his pursuer what he wanted. Ibn al Dughunnah answered, "I wish to kill you," and hit him with his sword. The blow was so light that the old man was not even cut. A ware of the shame that had befallen him and his people, the old man had no desire to live; he addressed his attacker in these words of disdain and pride: "Woe to your mother who taught you how to bear arms! Take my sword from my saddle and strike with it. Hit neither the chest nor the head but apply all your strength to one blow against the neck. In this way I used to kill my own enemies in days gone by. And if your miserable mother should ask you whom you killed in this fashion, tell her that you have killed Durayd ibn al Simmah. By God, it was a wretched day on which I extended my protection to your women and saved them by my arm." When Rabi'ah ibn al Dughannah returned and told the story to his mother, she cried in agonies of conscience and said to her son: "To fire with both your arms! What crime have they perpetrated! Durayd sought to remind posterity of our obligation to him. By God, it was he who granted freedom to three of your own mothers in one day; myself, my mother, and the mother of your father." The Muslims followed Hawazin all the way to the plain of Awtas where they inflicted upon them the most terrible defeat, capturing all their women and property. Only then did they return to Muhammad. Malik ibn 'Awf al Nadri gave the Muslims some resistance but then ran away with his people and some Hawazin tribesmen to Nakhlah. From there he escaped to al Ta'if where he took refuge.

Thus, Muslim victory was complete. The unbelievers were vanquished after they had almost defeated the Muslim army. The advantage they had secured by their surprise attack in pre-dawn darkness was shattered when the Prophet called his men back to their ground. The steadfastness of Muhammad and of the small number of believers that surrounded him turned the tide and proved the Muslims invincible. In this regard, the following verses were revealed:

لَقَدْ نَصَرَكُمُ اللّٰهُ فِى مَوَاطِنَ كَثِيرَةٍ ۙ وَيَوْمَ حُنَيْنٍ ۙ إِذْ أَعْجَبَتْكُمْ كَثْرَتُكُمْ فَلَمْ تُغْنِ عَنْكُمْ شَيْئًا وَضَاقَتْ عَلَيْكُمُ الْأَرْضُ بِمَا رَحُبَتْ ثُمَّ وَلَّيْتُمْ مُدْبِرِينَ ۙ ثُمَّ أَنْزَلَ اللّٰهُ سَكِينَتَهُ عَلٰى رَسُولِهِ وَعَلَى الْمُؤْمِنِينَ وَأَنْزَلَ جُنُودًا لَمْ تَرَوْهَا وَعَذَّبَ الَّذِينَ كَفَرُوا ۙ وَذٰلِكَ جَزَاءُ الْكَافِرِينَ ۙ ثُمَّ يَتُوبُ اللّٰهُ مِنْ بَعْدِ ذٰلِكَ عَلٰى مَنْ يَشَاءُ ۗ وَاللّٰهُ غَفُورٌ رَحِيمٌ ۙ يَا أَيُّهَا الَّذِينَ آمَنُوا إِنَّمَا الْمُشْرِكُونَ نَجَسٌ فَلَا يَقْرَبُوا الْمَسْجِدَ الْحَرَامَ بَعْدَ عَامِهِمْ هٰذَا ۚ وَإِنْ خِفْتُمْ عَيْلَةً فَسَوْفَ يُغْنِيكُمُ اللّٰهُ مِنْ فَضْلِهِ إِنْ شَاءَ ۚ إِنَّ اللّٰهَ عَلِيمٌ حَكِيمٌ ۙ

"God has given you victory on many occasions as well as on the Day of Hunayn. The numerical superiority of which you were so proud did not avail you. The tide overwhelmed you and you ran away in face of the enemy. But God brought down His peace upon the Prophet and believers. He sent forth soldiers whom you could not see to fight on the Prophet's side, and inflicted upon the unbelievers the great punishment they deserved. However, God accepts the repentance of whomsoever He pleases. He is merciful and forgiving. O Men who believe, the unbelievers are impure. They shall hence not enter the holy Mosque. In case you fear a reduction of your incomes as a result of this proscription, remember that God gives you of His bounty. For God is all-wise and all-knowing."[1]

The Price of Victory

Victory was not cheaply achieved. The Muslims paid a very high price. True, they could have done it at much lesser loss had they not fallen back at the beginning and occasioned Abu Sufyan's derisive remark that they would be thrown into the sea. Although the source books of biography have not listed all the casualties of the battle, they did mention that two tribes of Muslims were almost totally annihilated, and that the Prophet held a funerary prayer for them in which he asked God to let them enter Paradise. Partially offsetting this tremendous cost in human lives was the unquestioned supremacy the victory brought to the Muslims. Moreover, victory brought more captives and booty than the Muslims had ever seen before. As long as the war itself is an honorable one, victory, its final objective, must be achieved regardless of prices. That is why the Muslims did not mind the initial loss, celebrated the victory, and awaited the distribution of the booty.

Muhammad, however, had other plans. Seeking to make the victory still more spectacular, he commanded the Muslims to march immediately. Malik ibn 'Awf, leader of the enemy alliance, had taken refuge in the city of al Ta'if with the tribe of Thaqif, his allies against Muhammad. Full justification was therefore provided for the next Muslim move. Observing the same strategy employed at Khaybar following the Battle of Uhud, and at Qurayzah following the campaign of al Khandaq, the Prophet ordered the army to march against al Ta'if. Perhaps Muhammad remembered on that day how, many years before the Hijrah, he came to al Ta'if calling its people to Islam; how he was met with derision, driven away and pelted with stones; and how he sought shelter from its street children inside the closed vineyard. Perhaps he remembered how at that time he was alone, weak, and devoid of all support except God's; and how he had nothing but the great mountain-moving faith which filled his soul. Today, Muhammad found himself going again to the same city but at the head of a Muslim army the like of which Arabia had never seen before.

The Siege of al Ta'if

The city of al Ta'if, capital of the Thaqif tribe and refuge of Malik ibn 'Awf, loomed before Muhammad and his companions as the next objective. It was a fortified city and, like most Arab towns in that period, had gates which shut out the undesirable intruder. Its people had wide military experience, especially in the art of siege. Their great wealth had enabled them to make their fortifications the strongest in the world. As the Muslims approached al Ta'if, they passed by Liyyah where stood a fortress of Malik ibn 'Awf. The fortress as well as a nearby building belonging to a tribesman from Thaqif were destroyed. The army was commanded to put up camp in the vicinity, and the Prophet called his companions together to map out a strategy. Ta'if, on the other hand, learning of their approach, observed Muslim movements from the top of its fortresses and towers, and showered the Muslims with volleys of deadly arrows. It was not possible for the Muslims to storm these strong fortresses with their old weapons. New means of waging war, destructive and innovative weapons were needed. It was suggested that perhaps they could starve Ta'if into surrender by simply maintaining the siege. Those who favored a frontal attack could not find the necessary means with which to launch it. One immediate decision had to be taken at once, namely, to move the Muslims' camp and forces beyond the reach of al Ta'if's arrows. Once this danger was removed, the Muslims thought they could afford the leisure requisite for a sound decision as to strategy. At the Prophet's command, the Muslims erected their tents at a distance from the fortresses. There they built a mosque which was handed over to the city after its surrender and conversion to Islam. This preliminary measure was unavoidable considering that the arrows of Ta'if had accounted for the deaths of 18 Muslims and the wounding of a great number, including one of the sons of Abu Bakr. In the same locality two red tents were erected for the Prophet's wives, Umm Salmah and Zaynab, who had accompanied him throughout this expedition. It was near his tents that Muhammad used to call men to prayer, and, perhaps, it was precisely in that spot that the mosque of Ta'if was subsequently built.

Bombardment of al Ta'if by Catapult

The Muslims encamped and waited for new orders. Some tribesmen spoke to the Prophet in favor of a prolonged siege, claiming that nothing the Muslims had would help them scale Ta'if's fortifications. Time alone, they argued, would eventually force Ta'if's people out of their safe fox-holes. Muhammad, however, found it difficult to return without having achieved a victory over Ta'if. Banu Daws, one of the tribes living to the south of Makkah, were fully acquainted with the use of the catapult and had experience in tank-led assaults upon high fortifications. Al Tufayl, one of its leaders, who had accompanied Muhammad ever since the conquest of Khaybar, stood at the Prophet's side always on the ready to fulfill his wishes. At Muhammad's command, al Tufayl speeded to his tribe with a request for their assistance, and they responded by bringing with them their tools of war. Reaching al Ta'if four days after the Muslim siege began, they put their catapult to immediate use. They also brought their tanks into the battlefield, and sent a number of their men under their cover to the fortified walls. The soldiers of Ta'if, however, were clever enough to force the men of Banu Daws to flee. Having heated pieces of iron to red hot temperatures, they threw these missiles onto the tanks and put them to flame. The Muslim soldiers which the tanks were covering had to flee or be burnt alive. As they emerged from under their tanks, they were shot at with arrows and a number of them were killed. Having failed at this new effort, the Muslims became convinced that there was no way to storm the fortresses of Ta'if.

Destruction of al Ta'if's Orchards

What was left for them to do? Muhammad pondered this question for a long while. Suddenly, the thought occurred to him that he had achieved victory over Banu al Nadir and forced their evacuation simply by destroying their orchards. The vineyards of Ta'if were far more important than the orchards of Banu al Nadir and were known throughout Arabia for their produce. It was due to them that the city of al Ta'if acquired the reputation of being a little paradise in the desert. Without further ado, Muhammad gave the order, and the Muslims began systematically to cut down and burn the orchards. Upon discovering this destruction and realizing that Muhammad really meant to spare none of their vineyards, the Ta'if tribesmen sent to him pleading that they would rather give away their vineyards to Muhammad, or to those citizens of al Ta'if — and there were large numbers of them — who were bound to Muhammad in blood relationships. Muhammad stopped his men temporarily and called out to the besieged city that he would set free any man who surrendered to him. Twenty people responded to his appeal. From them he learned that enough ammunition and provisions were available that the city could withstand the siege for a very long time. Considering that his own men were anxious to return home and enjoy the fruits of their victory over Hawazin — indeed, that their patience would be at an end if the siege were prolonged — Muhammad ordered the Muslims to withdraw. With the arrival of the new moon (the month of Dhu al Qi'dah) the siege had become one month old, and the holy season during which no war was permitted had begun. Muhammad returned to Makkah with his army, visiting the holy places and performing the lesser pilgrimage or 'umrah. He announced that he would resume the war against al Ta'if at the expiration of the holy months.

Hawazin Captives Liberated and Returned to Their Tribe

In their withdrawal to Makkah, the Muslims turned in the direction of al Ji'ranah where they had left their booty and captives. There, they stopped long enough to divide their spoils. The Prophet separated one-fifth for himself and distributed the rest among his companions. Before they finished, a delegation from the Hawazin tribe who had already accepted Islam appealed to Muhammad to return to them the women, children, and property that the Muslim army had seized. They complained that they were anxious to see their families and that they had suffered enough from this war. Muhammad met this delegation in person and listened attentively as one of them said: "O Prophet of God; the captives in the wards of your army are themselves your relatives. Among them are your aunts on your father or mother's side and your nurse-mothers who held you in their arms as a baby. Had our women played similar roles to al Harith ibn Abu Shimr, or to al Nu'man ibn al Mundhir, and had any of these kings inflicted upon us what you have inflicted, he would have granted every request of ours if we but asked for his mercy and compassion and reminded him of his obligation. You, on the other hand, are the

most merciful and compassionate and the least needful of being reminded of your obligations." The Hawazin delegation did not err in reminding
Muhammad of his blood relationship to them. Among the captives, an
older looking woman whom the soldiers had treated roughly shouted in
their faces: "Woe to you! Learn that I am the sister of your leader by virtue
of having had the same wet nurse as he." The soldiers did not believe her
and brought her to Muhammad to verify her story. The Prophet immediately recognized her. She was al Shayma', daughter of al Harith ibn 'Abd
al 'Uzza. Muhammad went out to meet her and spread out his mantle for
her to sit on. After reassuring her of his devotion and respect, Muhammad
asked the old lady whether she chose to stay in his camp or to return to
her people. When she chose to return, Muhammad gave her some gifts
and returned her to her people unharmed. It was natural for Muhammad,
considering his relationship to the Hawazin Muslims who came pleading
for mercy, that he granted their request. Such loyalty, remembrance, and
considerateness to anyone who had shown him any respect or consideration, were second nature with Muhammad. Gratitude was with him a
matter of course, and compassion for the wounded-at-heart was innate.
After hearing their plea, Muhammad asked: "Which are more precious to
you, your women and children or your property? They answered, "O
Prophet of God, if you are giving us a choice between our relatives and our
property, we take the former." Muhammad said: "All that I have set aside
for me and for Banu 'Abd al Muttalib is yours. After the noon prayer, rise
in the midst of the worshippers and plead: 'We appeal to all the Muslims
in the name of the Prophet of God, and to the Prophet of God in the
name of all the Muslims for the return of our women and children.' I shall
then publicly declare that I relinquish my share as well as my tribe's share."
The delegation followed the advice of the Prophet and pleaded as he
taught them. No sooner than they did, the Prophet declared his plan as he
had promised them. Thereupon, the Muhajirun rose and said: "Anything
that is ours belongs automatically to the Prophet of God and is hereby
relinquished." Al Ansar and all the Muslims did likewise except al Aqra'
ibn Habis, speaking for Tamim; 'Uyaynah ibn Hisn, speaking for himself;
and al 'Abbas ibn Mirdas, speaking for Banu Sulaym. The last named was
immediately contradicted by his people. The Prophet said: "Anyone
among you who has declined to give up his right in this instance has my
word that if he does, I will make it up to him sixfold on the next campaign." Thus, all the captives of Hawazin were returned and the tribe converted to Islam *en masse*.

The People's Fear of Losing Their Booty

Muhammad inquired from the Hawazin delegation concerning Malik ibn 'Awf al Nadri and learned that he was still in al Ta'if. The Prophet asked the delegation to inform Malik that should he surrender and convert to Islam, Muhammad would return to him his family and property as well as make a gift to him of 100 camels. Upon hearing of this promise and invitation of the Prophet, Malik did not hesitate to steal out of al Ta'if on his mare under cover of night. Upon arrival at the Prophet's camp, he proclaimed his conversion to Islam, picked up his family, his property, and the prize of 100 camels and then went home. Indeed, the people even feared that should Muhammad continue such giveaways to the defectors from the other camp, soon there would be little left of the booty. They therefore insisted that each Muslim should receive his share, and they whispered one to another to this effect. As this whispering reached the ears of Muhammad, he pulled out a hair of the camel nearest him, lifted it up for his people to see and said: "O Men! By God, no part of your booty shall come to me that exceeds my legitimate share by as much as this hair, and this very share of mine I hereby return to you." The Prophet then asked everyone to return what he had taken that Muhammad might redistribute it to each according to his due. The Prophet proclaimed that anyone unjustly taking anything however little, would be guilty of eternal shame and hellfire.

Muhammad made this proclamation while enraged against those of his followers who had picked up his mantle thinking that it was part of the spoils of war. However, they returned it to him after he called out to them: "Return my mantle to me, O Men. By God, even if your cattle were as numerous as the trees of Tihamah, I would still divide it all among you in absolute fairness and justice, without avarice, fear, or deception. That which I have given away belongs to the fifth which is my due." It was out of the fifth which was due him that Muhammad distributed some spoils to those who were previously Islam's strongest and most hostile enemies. He gave, for instance, 100 camels each to Abu Sufyan, to his son Mu'awiyah, to al Harith ibn al Harith ibn Kaladah, to al Harith ibn Hisham, to Suhayl ibn 'Amr, and to Huwaytib ibn 'Abd al 'Uzza as well as to each of the nobles and chieftains of the tribes which he had won over after the conquest of Makkah. He gave 50 camels each to the lesser notables of the same tribes. Those who were so rewarded counted a few score, but the effect of this giving was far reaching. The Prophet of God was praised as the exemplar of hospitality and mercy by the very people who until recently — indeed, until the day before — had been fighting him with all their power. Now, they joined in an eloquent chorus of praise and gratitude. There was no request which Muhammad did not manage to fulfill for them. When 'Abbas ibn Mirdas complained that Muhammad had given more favorable treatment to 'Uyaynah, to al Aqra', and others than to him, the Prophet sent his companions to give him more until he was perfectly satisfied.

Al Ansar and the Reconciliatory Gratuities

The reconciliation of the enemies of yesterday which the Prophet had just effected caused al Ansar to murmur that the Prophet had done what he did because the people involved were his own tribesmen and people. Sa'd ibn 'Ubadah reported this murmur to the Prophet but sided with them and justified their complaint. The Prophet commanded him to bring his people together. When they were assembled, the Prophet said: "O Ansar! It has been reported to me that you were personally angry, that you do not approve of my distribution of the booty. Do tell me, when I came to you, did I not find you languishing in misguidance and error and did not God guide you to the truth through me? Did I not find you in a state of need and did not God make you affluent? Did I not find you enemies of one another and did not God reconcile your hearts?" Confused, al Ansar answered: "Indeed! God and his Prophet have been very generous and very loving;" and they fell into silence. Muhammad continued: "Will you not then say more than this, O Ansar? By God, had you replied, 'Rather, it was you Muhammad, who were under our obligation. Did you not come to us belied by your fellow men and did we not believe in you? Did you not come to us vanquished and defeated and did we not come to your rescue? Did you not come to us banished and repulsed and did we not give you shelter? Did you not come to us in want and need and did we not give you of our bounty?' Had you replied to me in this vein you would have said nothing but the truth and I would have had to agree. O Ansar, are you angry because I have given away some goods to those whom I sought to win to Islam? Because I deemed their faith confirmable by material goods whereas I deemed yours to be based on solid conviction, to be candid beyond all dissuasion? Are you not satisfied, O Ansar, that all the people return from this conquest loaded with goods and camels whereas you return with the Prophet of God? By Him who dominates Muhammad's soul, except for the fact of my birth, there is no people to whom I love to belong beside al Ansar. If all mankind went one way, and al Ansar went another, I would certainly choose the way of al Ansar. O God, bless al Ansar, their children, and their grandchildren. Show Your mercy to them and keep them under Your protection."

The Prophet said these words out of great affection for all the men of al Ansar who had pledged their loyalty and allegiance to him, who had helped him, who had reinforced his ranks and found their strength in him. Indeed, he was so moved by his feelings for them that he cried. The Ansar cried with him and declared their contentment.

Thus the Prophet showed that he was above the temptation of wealth. Although the booty of the Hunayn War surpassed anything he had ever seen, he showed that he had no wish for it. Rather he made of it a means for reconciling the hearts of those who had been associationists. He hoped that they might find in the new faith some happiness in this world besides the happiness of the hereafter. If in distributing this wealth Muhammad encountered such difficulties that the Muslims almost accused him of injustice, and if by giving liberally to those whose hearts he sought to soften he had infuriated al Ansar, he also proved his justice, farsightedness and such deep wisdom in administering the affairs of his people that he was able to cause the thousands to return home happy, contented and prepared to lay down their lives in the cause of God. The Prophet left al Ji'ranah to visit the holy places in Makkah. After performing the 'umrah, or lesser pilgrimage, he appointed 'Attab ibn Usayd governor of Makkah, and Mu'adh ibn Jabal to teach the religion and the Qur'an. Together with al Ansar and al Muhajirun, Muhammad returned to Madinah to await the birth of his son Ibrahim and to enjoy a moment of peace and security before undertaking the next expedition to Tabuk on the frontiers of al Sham.

26

Ibrahim and the
Wives of the Prophet

Effect of the Conquest of Makkah upon the Peninsula

Muhammad returned to Madinah after his conquest of Makkah, his victory at Hunayn, and his siege of al Ta'if. He had convinced all that no power could match his power within the Arabian Peninsula and that no tongue might henceforth vituperate him or spread any false information regarding himself or his cause. Both al Ansar and al Muhajirun returned heartened with joy that God had crowned His prophet's endeavor with such success; that He enabled Muhammad to conquer the city of the holy Mosque, that He guided its people to Islam; and that He inspired all Arab tribes to pledge their allegiance, loyalty and obedience to him. They all returned to Madinah in order to settle down in peace. Muhammad had taken care to appoint 'Attab ibn Usayd as governor of Umm al Qura, or Makkah, and Mu'adh ibn Jabal as teacher of the people in matters of religion and in the Qur'an. This victory, the like of which the whole history of Arabia and all its traditions have never known, left a profound impression upon the Arabs. Whether lords and masters of land and cities, men to whom it had never occurred that a day might come when they would be subject to Muhammad or accept his faith as their religion, or poets who labored as mouthpieces of those masters in exchange for their patronage and protection, or, finally, simple tribesmen for whom personal freedom was till death the most priceless possession, the Arabs were all strongly affected by the conquest of Makkah, Hunayn and the siege of al Ta'if. To one and all, it now seemed that the poetry of the poets, the mastery of the chieftains, and the personal freedom of the tribesmen were all to no avail before the tremendous power of Muhammad and his followers.

Conversion of Ka'b ibn Zuhayr

Muhammad's success among the Arabs of the Peninsula influenced them so profoundly that Bujayr ibn Zuhayr wrote a letter to his brother, Ka'b, after the Prophet's withdrawal from al Ta'if, informing him that Muhammad had killed a number of men in Makkah who had slandered his reputation by spreading false rumors concerning him. Bujayr, after informing his brother that a number of these men had run away in all directions, advised him to hurry to Madinah to give himself up and repent. He assured him that the Prophet would not kill anyone who came to him repentant and warned him that unless he was prepared to do so, he should escape to the most distant place on earth to remain alive. Bujayr had indeed told the truth. Muhammad commanded the execution of only four persons, one of whom was a poet who had vituperated the Prophet severely, and two of whom had hurt his daughter, Zaynab, when with her husband's permission, she sought to emigrate to Makkah to join her father. Ka'b recognized the veracity and timeliness of his brother's advice; and, anxious not to spend the rest of his life as an outlaw, he hurried to Madinah, spent the night at a friend's house, and came to the Prophet in the morning at the mosque to declare his conversion and pledge his allegiance. In the Prophet's presence, Ka'b recited his famous poem which opened with the verse: "Great distance now separates me from Su'ad. My heart is orphaned and bereaved. It awaits the sacrifice which will ransom my beloved." The Prophet forgave him and he became a good Muslim.

Conversion of Zayd al Khayl and Others

Another consequence of the same influence was that the tribes began to come to the Prophet to pledge their allegiance. Such was the case of a delegation headed by Zayd al Khayl who came to Madinah to pledge allegiance of the tribe of Tay'. Muhammad gave the delegation a fair welcome, conversed with their leader, and was so well pleased with him that he said: "No Arab has ever been praised before me but that when I finally met him I discovered that his eulogy surpassed his reality, except Zayd al Khayl concerning whom I had heard less than I have found." The

Prophet then changed the name of his guest from Zayd al Khayl (meaning literally, "increase of horses") to Zayd al Khayr ("increase of goodness"), and the whole tribe of Tay' entered into Islam under Zayd's leadership.

'Adiyy ibn Hatim al Ta'iy was a Christian who felt the strongest hatred for Muhammad. As he witnessed the rise of the Prophet and the Muslims and the spread of their dominion over the Peninsula, he loaded his goods, family, and children on his camel and joined his fellow Christians in al Sham. Indeed, 'Adiyy escaped at the very time that 'Ali ibn Abu Talib destroyed, at the Prophet's command, the idol of Tay' and seized a number of captives, including the daughter of Hatim and sister of 'Adiyy and a large amount of booty. 'Adiyy's sister was brought to Madinah and was held in the captives' quarters by the Mosque's gate. As the Prophet passed through the gate one day, she said to him from behind the bars: "O Prophet of God! My father has perished and my supporter has deserted. Be merciful to me, that God may be merciful to you." When the Prophet learned that her supporter was 'Adiyy ibn Hatim al Ta'iy, the escapee, he refused to talk to her. She tried once more, and this time she succeeded. In conversation, the Prophet mentioned to her her father's old prestige and noble reputation in pre-Islamic days. He praised him for the good name his hospitality had given to all Arabs. The Prophet then granted her her freedom, gave her respectable clothes and pocket money to satisfy her other needs, and sent her to her people with the first al Sham-bound caravan. Upon joining her brother, she mentioned to him the noble treatment Muhammad had accorded her. 'Adiyy was so impressed by the Prophet's chivalry that he returned with her to Madinah and joined the ranks of Islam immediately.

Likewise, following the conquest of Makkah, the victory of al Sham, and the siege of al Ta'if, the great and the poor, the tribes and the individuals, all came to Muhammad to acknowledge his mission and to convert to Islam. In the meantime, Muhammad remained in Madinah and, feeling reassured that God has given him victory, he enjoyed a measure of peaceful existence.

Muhammad's Bereavement

The measure of peaceful existence which Muhammad enjoyed was not to last. His daughter, Zaynab, was seriously ill. After al Huwayrith and Habbar hurt her when she attempted to emigrate from Makkah, Zaynab suffered from a miscarriage from which she never recovered. With her loss, Muhammad's only surviving child was Fatimah, for Umm Kulthum and Ruqayyah had passed away earlier. Muhammad was saddened by the loss of Zaynab. He surely appreciated her compassionate disposition and loyalty to her husband, Abu al 'Asi ibn al Rabi', whom she had ransomed after his fall as captive at the Battle of Badr with jewelry her father had given her on her wedding. It did not matter that she, a Muslim, sought to ransom her husband, an unbeliever; nor that this unbeliever husband had fought against her father in a battle in which, had the Quraysh been victorious, Muhammad would have surely lost his life. The Prophet praised Zaynab's good disposition and strong loyalty to her husband, and bemoaned her suffering from sickness during the whole time since her emigration from Makkah. It is no wonder that he felt bereaved at her loss. He felt the same deep concern for the well-being and happiness of others. It was his nature to sympathize with every sufferer, every bereaved, and to take the trouble to go everywhere within and outside of Madinah to visit the sick, console the destitute, and reassure the wounded. The hand of fate had here touched his own daughter. His tragedy was not the first of its kind, but the fifth, as he had previously lost two of his daughters and two sons. If he had found in God's favorable disposition toward him a measure of consolation, he surely well deserved it.

The Birth of Ibrahim, Muhammad's Son

Soon, Muhammad's loss was to be compensated. Mariyah, his Coptic wife, gave birth to a son whom Muhammad called Ibrahim after the ancestor-father of the Arabs as well as of hanifism and Islam. Until that day, and since the Archbishop of Alexandria had presented her to the Prophet, Mariyah had the status of a slave. She did not enjoy the benefits of a living quarter by the mosque as did the other wives of the Prophet, "the Mothers of Believers." Muhammad had provided Mariyah with a second-story residence in one of the outskirts of Madinah, called today Mashrabat Umm Ibrahim. Her house, which was surrounded with vineyards, was where Muhammad used to visit her every now and then. He had chosen her for himself and gave her sister Sirin to Hassan ibn Thabit. Muhammad did not expect to have any more children as none of his wives except the late Khadijah had ever conceived, though some of them were quite young and capable of bearing children. When Mariyah gave birth to Ibrahim, the event brought to Muhammad, a man past sixty years of age, great joy and filled his heart with reassurance and jubilation. By giving birth to a child, the status of Mariyah was raised in the Prophet's esteem; he now looked upon her as a free wife, indeed, as one enjoying a most favored position.

Jealousy of the Prophet's Wives

It was natural that this change would incite no little jealousy among his other wives who continued to be barren. It was also natural that the Prophet's esteem and affection for the newborn child and his mother increased that jealousy. Moreover, Muhammad had liberally rewarded Salma, the wife of Abu Rafi', for her role as midwife. He celebrated the birth by giving away a measure of grain to all the destitute of Madinah. He assigned the newborn to the care of Umm Sayf, a wet nurse, who owned seven goats whose milk she was to put at the disposal of the newborn. Every day Muhammad would visit the house of Mariyah in order to take another look at his son's radiant face and to reassure himself of the newborn's continued health and growth. All this incited the strongest jealousy among the barren wives. The question was, how far would these wives be able to bear the constant challenge?

One day, with the pride characteristic of new parents, the Prophet carried his son on his arm and walked into 'A'ishah's quarters in order to show him to her. He pointed out to her his great resemblance to his offspring. 'A'ishah looked at the baby and said that she saw no resemblance at all. When the Prophet observed how much the child was growing, 'A'ishah responded waspishly that any child given the amount of milk which Ibrahim was getting would grow just as big and strong as he. Indeed, the birth of Ibrahim brought such disaffection to the wives of the Prophet as would go beyond these and similar unfriendly answers. It reached such proportions that revelation itself voiced a special condemnation. Undoubtedly, the whole affair had left its imprint on the life of Muhammad as well as on the history of Islam.

Such far-reaching effects were natural in the circumstances. For Muhammad had granted to his wives a position hitherto unknown in Arabia. 'Umar ibn al Khattab said, "By God, in pre-Islamic days, we never gave consideration to our women. It was only after God had revealed in their regard what He did that we started to do so. My wife came once seeking to dissuade me from doing what I had planned to do. When I answered her that this was none of her business, she said: 'How strange of you, 'Umar ibn al Khattab! You refuse to be told anything whereas your daughter may criticize her husband, the Prophet of God — May God's peace and blessing be upon him — and do so so strongly that he remains worried the whole day long.' Upon hearing this, I took my mantle and went straight to my daughter, Hafsah, and said to her: 'O my daughter, is it true that you criticize the Prophet of God and do so so strongly that he remains worried the whole day long?' Hafsah answered: 'Indeed, I and his other wives do criticize him.' I said: 'You had better be warned that this will bring both the punishment of God and the wrath of His Prophet upon you. O Daughter, do not be deceived by that woman who became too proud of herself because of her beauty or Muhammad's love for her.' I left my daughter and went to visit Umm Salamah, another wife of the Prophet and a close relative of mine. Upon asking her the same question, Umm Salamah replied: 'How strange of you, O Ibn al Khattab! Are you going to interfere in everything, even in the Prophet's own domestic affairs?'" 'Umar continued: "With this I was utterly rebuffed and I abandoned every thought I had entertained." Muslim has related in his *Sahih* that Abu Bakr once sought the permission of the Prophet to visit him, and so did 'Umar. Upon entrance into the Prophet's living quarters, they found him sitting still and silent, surrounded by his wives. After announcing that he was about to break the silence with a story which he hoped the Prophet would find entertaining, he said: "O Prophet of God, if the daughter of Kharijah,[1] *i.e.*, my wife, were ever seen or heard asking me for money, I would surely pull her hair." The Prophet laughed, saying, "Here are my wives surrounding me and asking me for money." Immediately, Abu Bakr rose to his daughter 'A'ishah and pulled her hair and so did 'Umar to his daughter, Hafsah. Both Abu Bakr and 'Umar said to their daughters: "Do you dare ask the Prophet of God what he cannot afford to give?" They answered: "No, by God, we do not ask him any such thing." Actually, Abu Bakr and 'Umar had sought to see the Prophet because the latter was conspicuously absent at the previous prayer in the mosque, and the Muslims had asked one another the cause of his absence. It was in connection with this conversation between Abu Bakr and 'Umar and their daughters that the following verse was revealed:

يَٰٓأَيُّهَا ٱلنَّبِىُّ قُل لِّأَزْوَٰجِكَ إِن كُنتُنَّ تُرِدْنَ ٱلْحَيَوٰةَ ٱلدُّنْيَا وَزِينَتَهَا فَتَعَالَيْنَ أُمَتِّعْكُنَّ وَأُسَرِّحْكُنَّ سَرَاحًا جَمِيلًا ۞ وَإِن كُنتُنَّ تُرِدْنَ ٱللَّهَ وَرَسُولَهُ وَٱلدَّارَ ٱلْءَاخِرَةَ فَإِنَّ ٱللَّهَ أَعَدَّ لِلْمُحْسِنَٰتِ مِنكُنَّ أَجْرًا عَظِيمًا ۞

"O Prophet, tell your wives that in case they want the pleasures of this world and its ornaments, you will give them their freedom and send them on their way in fairness that they may elsewhere seek what they desire. But if they want God, His Prophet, and the other world, then remind them that God has prepared for the virtuous among them a great reward."[2]

The Wives' Plotting

As a matter of fact, the wives of the Prophet went as far as to plot against their husband. Muhammad was in the habit of visiting them immediately after the midafternoon prayer. According to one report, he once visited Hafsah (or Zaynab, daughter of Jahsh according to another version) and paid her an unusually long visit. This made all the other wives jealous. 'A'ishah reported: "Hafsah and I plotted together that any wife whom the Prophet — May God's peace and blessing be upon him — will visit will complain to him that she finds his breath undesirable, and will ask him whether he has eaten any *maghafir* (i.e., sweets with bad smells, and the Prophet could not stand bad smells). As he entered upon one of his wives, she asked him that question to which he answered: "No, but I have taken some honey at the quarters of Zaynab, which I will never do again." Having agreed to the plot of 'A'ishah and Hafsah, Sawdah related that when the Prophet approached her, she asked him whether he ate any *maghafir* to which he answered, "No." She asked him: "Where then does this bad odor come from?" Muhammad replied: "Hafsah gave me a little honey, so then it must be that the bees that made that honey had picked it up from the blooms of the awful tree which produces the *maghafir*." When he entered upon 'A'ishah, the latter repeated to him the question of Sawdah, which he heard again from Safiyyah, whereupon he vowed never to touch that honey again. Upon hearing the other wives' reports, Sawdah said: "May God be praised! We have deprived him of something he truly likes." 'A'ishah, however, looked askance at Sawdah and asked her to keep quiet.

Since the Prophet granted to his wives such an unusual position at a time when Arab women amounted to nothing at all in society, it was natural for his wives to abuse the liberty which none of their peers had known before, a liberty which went so far as to enable any of them to criticize the Prophet so severely as to spoil his disposition the rest of the day. He often ignored some of his wives, and avoided others on many occasions, precisely in order to discourage their abuse of his compassion. Even so, one of them was so moved by jealousy as to exceed all limits of decency. But when Mariyah gave birth to Ibrahim, they were incensed. They lost all the composure and self-mastery which Muhammad had for years been trying to instill into them. It was for this reason that 'A'ishah had gone to the extreme of denying all resemblance between him and his son, a denial which amounted to an accusation of adultery on the part of the innocent Mariyah.

Their Rebellion

One day Hafsah went to her father's house complaining about this situation. While the Prophet was in her room, Mariyah came to him and stayed with him some time. Upon Hafsah's return she found the Prophet and Mariyah in her quarters and, as she waited for them to come out, her jealousy broke all bounds. When, finally, Mariyah left the quarters and Hafsah entered, she said to the Prophet: "I have seen who was here. By God, that was an insult to me. You would not have dared do that if I amounted to anything at all in your eyes." At the moment Muhammad realized that such deep-lying jealousy might even move Hafsah to broadcast what she had seen among the other wives. In an attempt to please her, Muhammad promised that he would not go unto Mariyah if she would only refrain from broadcasting what she had seen. Hafsah promised to comply. However, she could not keep her promise as jealousy continued to affect her disposition. Hence, she intimated the secret to 'A'ishah, who in turn reported it to the Prophet. He took it as evidence of Hafsah's failure to keep her promise. Perhaps the affair did not stop with Hafsah and 'A'ishah but spread to the other wives. Perhaps, too, all of them had noticed the high esteem in which Mariyah was held and sympathized with 'A'ishah and Hafsah's opposition to the Prophet. There is nothing unusual in the whole story, such gossip and petty jealousies being commonplace between man and his many wives. A man's affection belongs where he puts it within his household, and the controversy which the daughters of Abu Bakr and 'Umar had woven around the Prophet's affection for Mariyah was utterly groundless. Previously we had seen that some disaffection had risen between the Prophet and his wives on various occasions because of the pocket money he allocated to them, or because of the honey Zaynab used to serve. Therefore, they had all the more reason to feel slighted and no little alienated when they discovered their husband's inclination toward 'A'ishah or his esteem for Mariyah.

An explosion was soon to come. One day, while the Prophet was staying with 'A'ishah, his other wives delegated Zaynab, daughter of Jahsh, to
go in and, in their name, to accuse him of injustice and unfairness to them,
and to plead that his love for 'A'ishah was a violation of the code which he
himself had set down of a day and night for each of his wives. On the
other hand, realizing that the Prophet did not care very much for her
charms, and being no longer anxious to please him, Sawdah had given up
her day and night to 'A'ishah. But Zaynab was not satisfied with expressing the other wives' indignation at this apparent injustice. She attacked
'A'ishah personally. The latter was anxious to defend herself, but kept still
in response to the Prophet's reconciliating pleas. Seeing that 'A'ishah was
defenseless, Zaynab went to excess in her accusations, and the Prophet
finally had to permit his favorite wife to take her defense into her own
hands. 'A'ishah spoke out with great eloquence in refuting Zaynab's claims.
The Prophet listened with obvious satisfaction and admired the perspicacity of Abu Bakr's daughter.

Indeed, favoritism for some of his wives had created such controversy
and antagonism among the "Mothers of the Believers" that Muhammad
once thought of divorcing some of them, but they soon agreed to let him
distribute his favors as he pleased. When Mariyah gave birth to Ibrahim,
their jealousy was at its strongest, especially in the case of 'A'ishah.
Certainly, Muhammad's leniency and gentleness encouraged rebellion,
and the new status which he had conferred upon women in society fanned
their vanity. Muhammad, however, was not free to spend his time dealing
with household problems. The need soon came to be felt for a decisive lesson to reestablish discipline and to liberate him for teaching the message
and fulfilling the mission of his prophethood. Hence, he decided to ignore
his wives and, indeed, to threaten them with divorce. A lesson had to be
taught to them, and the time had apparently come for a decision. Either
these women were to return to reason or they would be given their freedom in a mutually convenient divorce.

The Prophet's Separation from His Wives

Muhammad isolated himself from all his women for a full month and
refused to talk about them to anyone. Nor did anyone dare talk to him
concerning them. During this month, his mind was absorbed by his mission and the requirement of carrying the message of Islam beyond the
Arabian Peninsula. Abu Bakr, 'Umar, and his other in-laws as well, were

deeply concerned over the sad fate that awaited the "Mothers of the Believers" now that they had exposed themselves to the anger of the Prophet and the consequent punishment of God. It was even said that Muhammad had divorced Hafsah, 'Umar's daughter, after she had divulged the secret she had promised to keep. The marketplace of Madinah hummed with rumors about the impending divorce of the Prophet's wives. The wives, for their part, were repentant and apprehensive. They regretted that their jealousy of one another had carried them away, that they had abused and harmed their gentle husband who was to each one of them at all times an elder brother, a compassionate father, a nearest kin, and the best of everything that might be hoped for in this life and the next. Muhammad spent most of his time in a storeroom he owned, placing his servant Rabah at its doorstep as long as he was inside. Therein he used to sleep on a very hard bed of coarse date branches.

'Umar's Reconciliation of the Prophet and His Wives

At the end of the month during which Muhammad vowed to separate himself from his wives, the Muslims were despondent over the prospect of Muhammad's domestic affairs. Many signs of dejection and sorrow were apparent on their faces as they gathered in the mosque. 'Umar ibn al Khattab sought out the Prophet in his isolation. He went to the storeroom and called out to his servant, Rabah, asking for permission to enter. Rabah went in to speak to the Prophet but came out silent, a sign that Muhammad did not wish to see anyone. 'Umar asked once more. Once more Rabah went in and came out silent. At this, 'Umar raised his voice that the Prophet might hear and, repeating his request for an audience, said: "O Rabah, seek permission for me to see the Prophet of God. I fear that he thinks that I have come to intercede for my daughter, Hafsah. By God, if he were to ask me to strike off her head, I would do so without hesitation." The Prophet then permitted him to enter. He came in, sat down as his eyes roved around the room, and began to cry. Muhammad asked him why he was crying. Actually 'Umar cried out of severe shock at seeing the Prophet lying on the only piece of furniture in the room, the miserable straw mat, whose pattern of weaving had imprinted itself on the Prophet's side. He cried out of compassion for the Prophet's isolation in a room absolutely empty except for a little barley, a skin, and a small container of water. After hearing 'Umar's explanation, Muhammad taught him a lesson on the necessity of renouncing the pleasures of the world in order to achieve inner peace. 'Umar then said: "O

Prophet of God, what difficulties do your wives present? If you have truly lost them through divorce, you still have God, His angels Jibril and Mikha'il, Abu Bakr and me, and all the Muslims on your side." He kept on talking to the Prophet in this vein until the latter felt pleased and even smiled. As the Prophet's mood changed for the better, 'Umar told him about the despondency of the Muslims gathered in the mosque and their bemoaning of his separation from his wives. The Prophet explained that he had not divorced his wives but that he meant only to teach them a les-son. 'Umar immediately asked for and was granted permission to inform the Muslims waiting in the mosque. He hurried thither to announce the good news that the Prophet of God — May God's peace and blessing be upon him — had not divorced his wives. It was in connection with this incident that the following verses of the Qur'an were revealed: "O Prophet, why do you forbid yourself that which God has made legitimate for you, namely, to seek to please your wives? God is certainly compassion-ate and merciful. God has made it legitimate for you to release yourself from your vows. He is your Lord, and He is the All-Wise and All-Knowing. The Prophet had intimated information to one of his wives, but she did not keep the secret. When God brought knowledge to the Prophet of her insincerity, and the Prophet blamed her for it, her asking who had told him the news thus divulged her secret. The Prophet answered that God, the All-Knowing and Omniscient, had informed him of the deed. If the insincere wife and her insincere confidante were to repent to God and purify their thoughts, then they would be forgiven. But if they persist in striving against him, then God will compensate him with His friendship, with that of Jibril, Salih, the believers and angels, who will assist him in his plight. In case he should divorce his wives, God might even replace them with better ones, with women who are Muslims, believing, pious, repentant, and virtuous, whether widowed or virgins."[3] With this revela-tion, the whole affair was brought to a close. The wives of the Prophet, having regained their wisdom and common sense, returned to their hus-band repentant, pious, and confirmed in their faith. Once reconciled by their repentance, Muhammad returned to his wives and his domestic life resumed its peace — the necessary prerequisite for any man with a mis-sion to perform.

The Judgment of Critical Historiography

In my opinion, the foregoing is the true account of the story of Muhammad's self-imposed isolation from his wives, of the choice he gave them, of the incidents which led to his isolation as well as of its causes and consequences. This account is confirmed by all the evidence of the books of Qur'anic exegesis and of Hadith, as well as by the accounts of various biographies. The fact remains, however, that not one of these biographies has presented all these data in the proper sequence, beginning with the causes and ending with the consequences in the manner we have done here. Most of the biographers have passed by this matter too quickly and too simplistically. They give the impression that they found the material too rough to handle. Some accounts have pondered the story of the honey and *maghafir* at length but have omitted to point to the affair of Hafsah and Mariyah. As for the Orientalists, they regard the story of Hafsah and Mariyah and the former's divulgence to 'A'ishah of the secret she promised to keep as the cause of all that had happened. Their purpose is precisely to add to their already alienated readers further occasion to condemn the Arab Prophet by presenting him as a shameless runner after women. It is also my considered opinion that the Muslim historians are not justified in ignoring these incidents, or in omitting to examine all the data available with a view to giving them an objective interpretation. That is what we have sought to do here, though only in part. While the mistake of the Muslim historians was to underestimate the importance of these events, that of the western Orientalists is to exaggerate their importance, to violate historiographic precision, and to vent their Christian prejudice. Genuine historical criticism will not attribute to any man as great as Muhammad such a petty conduct as would be implied by referring his self-imposed exile solely to Hafsah's divulgence of a domestic secret to 'A'ishah. In fact, Muhammad had nothing to hide since the women in question were all his own legitimate wives. Indeed, whatever the nature of that domestic secret, it is too insignificant to cause Muhammad to threaten to divorce all his wives. Genuine historical criticism would also refuse to explain these events as due to the "honey" affair. A man as great, forbearing, and compassionate as Muhammad, as all historians and biographers acknowledge, would not regard such incidents as justifying a whole month's isolation, let alone divorce. The critical attitude is satisfied only when all these incidents are arranged in such historical sequence as would not violate the causal interrelationships between them. Only such history-writing satisfies the requirements of objectivity and presents its data as elements in factual interrelationships acceptable to reason. The arrangement we have given these events seems to us to have achieved precisely this, and to accord perfectly with what is known of Muhammad's wisdom, greatness, determination and farsightedness.

Refutation of the Orientalists' Claim

Referring to some of the verses at the beginning of *surah* "Al Tahrim" quoted above, some orientalists argue that none of the holy books of the Orient make any mention of domestic problems such as those of Muhammad. I do not think we need to quote here the similar stories and accounts of other scriptures. Suffice it to mention here the People of Lot and their argument with the two angelic visitors of Lot, the story of Lot's wife and her vagrancies. Indeed, the Torah does tell the story of Lot's two daughters, of their deliberately intoxicating their father with wine that he might commit incest and save their seed, and how they then suffered the punishment they deserved. We may say that in fact, contrary to the Orientalists claim, all the holy books have told stories about the prophets and have given accounts of what happened to them so that they might serve as examples for the education of mankind. Likewise, the Qur'an tells many stories for the same purpose, stories which God related to His prophets for the best of purposes. The Qur'an was not revealed for Muhammad's benefit alone but for that of all men. Muhammad is a prophet and a messenger preceded by many prophets and messengers, some of whose tales the Qur'an took upon itself to tell. That the Qur'an should find it fitting to tell some of the stories of Muhammad's life and to give some account of his biography to provide examples for the education of Muslims, and that it should find it fitting to give aspects of Muhammad's wise, pious, and virtuous conduct so that the Muslims might find in him an example to emulate, is no different from the contents and purpose of any other holy book. Moreover, what the Qur'an reported about Muhammad is not different in content or purpose from what it reported of the lives of the former prophets. If, therefore, it is now asserted that Muhammad isolated himself from his wives, not for any single reason deducible from that fact, nor for Hafsah's divulgence to 'A'ishah of Muhammad's legitimate love for Mariyah — a right which belongs to any man toward his free and slave wives — this would not be far from the truth. But it does expose the Orientalists whose claim stands on the shallowest grounds and whose historiography flies in the face of the biographical data common to all holy scriptures.

Minaret of the National Mosque, Masjid Negara, Kuala Lumpur, Malaysia.

27

Campaign of Tabuk and the Death of Ibrahim

Institution of Zakat and Kharaj

All the foregoing conflicts between the Prophet and his wives did not in the least affect the conduct of public affairs. After the conquest of Makkah and the conversion of its people, the cause of Islam confronted less danger than hitherto. The whole Peninsula had begun to feel the passing of inter-Arab war. The holy sanctuary held as sacred by the Arabs, to which they had performed pilgrimages for generations, had become an integral institution of the new religion. Its attendant functions of *sidanah, rifadah,* and *siqayah*[1] had been equally integrated into the order of Islam as Makkah passed under the control of Muhammad. The conquest of Makkah therefore led to a strengthening of public Muslim life and civil order, and the Muslims felt more confident as their power increased everywhere throughout the Peninsula. With the widening of Muslim society, public functions naturally demanded an increase in public expense. It was therefore inevitable that the Muslims be asked to pay *zakat* of *al 'ushr*,[2] and that the Arabs who decided to maintain their pre-Islamic faith to pay whatever *kharaj*[3] was imposed upon them. Taxes are always uncomfortable, and taxpayers might always complain or even rebel against them. Nonetheless, the new order imposed by the new religion on the Peninsula necessitated a large public expense, impossible to meet without the additional incomes from *zakat al 'ushr* and *kharaj*. For this purpose, soon after his return from Makkah, Muhammad sent his collectors to levy and col-

427

lect a tenth of the income of the tribes now converted to Islam. He commanded the collectors explicitly to restrict themselves to the incomes, never to touch the people's capitals. These collectors went in different directions to fulfill their duty.

The tribes welcomed the collectors and remitted to them the amounts due wholeheartedly with the exceptions of a branch of the tribe of Banu Tamim and another of Banu al Mustaliq which refused to pay. While the collector, 'Uyaynah ibn Hisn, was in the neighborhood making collections, a branch of Banu Tamim, called Banu al 'Anbar, jumped upon him with their arrows and swords and threw him out of their territory even before he had asked them to remit their due. When 'Uyaynah ibn Hisn told the news to Muhammad, he was sent right back at the head of fifty riders to reestablish order. 'Uyaynah launched a surprise attack against the Banu al 'Anbar, captured over fifty men, women, and children and seized some of their wealth. The Prophet received the captives and the seized properties and kept them in Madinah. Some of the Banu Tamim had been converted to Islam a long time before and had fought alongside the Prophet in the battles of Makkah and Hunayn while others were still unconverted. When these Muslims knew what their relatives, the Banu al 'Anbar, had done and what had happened to them, they sent a delegation of notables to seek the Prophet. They asked for an audience in the Mosque of Madinah calling out to the Prophet to come out to meet them. This impropriety disturbed the Prophet so much that he decided not to see them. Soon, however, the time of prayer arrived and 'Utarid ibn Hajib called the Prophet to lead the worship in the mosque as was his custom. After prayer, the delegation approached the Prophet and related to him what 'Uyaynah had done with their people. They took especial pains to remind him of his comradeship in arms with those of them who had joined Islam as well as of their high esteem among the Arabs. They then said to him, "We have come here in order to compete with your followers in poetic eloquence and rhetoric. Would you please permit our poet to recite some of his poems for you?" 'Utarid ibn Hajib, their orator, rose and delivered his speech. When he finished, the Prophet of God called Thabit ibn Qays to respond; when he finished, al Zabriqan ibn Badr, their other poet, rose and recited his eulogy in verse, whereupon Hassan ibn Thabit responded in verse also. When this contest was ended, al Aqra' ibn Habis said, "I swear that this man (i.e., Muhammad) is surely going to win, for his orator is more eloquent and his poet more poetic than ours. Indeed, the voices of the Muslims are higher than our voices." With this confession, the tribesmen converted to Islam, and the Prophet set the captives free and enabled them to return home.

When the Banu al Mustaliq saw the tax collectors run away, they feared the consequences and immediately sent word to the Prophet explaining to him that the *zakat* collector has nothing to fear from their quarter and that the whole affair with Banu al 'Anbar was a regrettable misunderstanding.

Indeed, not one of the provinces of the Arabian Peninsula failed to feel the power of Muhammad, Every tribe or clan that attempted to resist faced the Prophet's overwhelming power and was compelled either to convert to Islam and pay the *zakat* or submit to Muslim political power and pay the *kharaj*.

The Threat of Byzantine Invasion and Muslim Reaction

While still engaged in bringing security and order to the distant regions of the Peninsula, the news reached Muhammad that Byzantium was mobilizing an army to invade the northern approaches of Arabia to avenge the last engagement at Mu'tah. It was also rumored that this imperial army would seek to stamp out the nascent power of the Muslims who now stood at the frontier of both the Byzantine and Persian empires. At once and without hesitation, the Prophet decided that the imperial army must be met and destroyed so completely that the Byzantines would not think again of attacking Arabia or interfering in its affairs. It was autumn, but the desert heat, being greater in the beginning of autumn than in summer, was all the more deadly. Moreover, a long distance separated Madinah from al Sham. Any venture to cross it required great amounts of water and provisions. Inevitably, therefore, Muhammad had to tell the people of his plan if they were to prepare themselves adequately, Equally, it was necessary this time to alter his old diversionary strategy of ordering the army to march in the opposite direction, for no such expedition as he was preparing for could be kept a secret. Indeed, Muhammad sent messengers to all the tribes asking them to mobilize the greatest army ever, and to the Muslims of large means everywhere to give liberally for the equipment of the army. The Muslim force, the Prophet decided, should be so large and preponderous as to overwhelm an enemy long known for their numbers and military equipment.

The Muslims' Response to Muhammad's Call to Arms

How were the Muslims to receive this new call to leave their families and properties in the height of summer heat, to venture in desolate and waterless deserts, and to confront an enemy powerful enough to defeat Persia and even too mighty to be defeated by the Muslims? Would their Islamic conviction, love for the Prophet, and loyalty to God's religion inspire them to give up wealth, armour, and life, and to do so in such proportion as to instill terror in the heart of such an enemy? Or, would the discomforts of desert and summer heat, of thirst and hunger, force them to sit back and refuse to move? In those days, Muslim ranks included two kinds of people: those who entered Islam with hearts full of guidance and light and minds certain of their convictions, and those who did so in search of material gain or out of fear of Muslim arms. Those who belonged to the former group volunteered their own persons and offered all the equipment they could muster. They put themselves and their wealth entirely at the Prophet's disposal. Among them were the poor who walked on foot and the wealthy who provided for themselves and others. All hoped for martyrdom and closeness to God. The other group complained and looked for excuses to justify their recalcitrance. Secretly, they derided Muhammad's call to arms and ridiculed its timing and strategy. These were the *munafiqun* about whom *Surah* "Al Tawbah" had spoken. How great was its call to *jihad!* And how terrible the punishment it promised to he who failed to answer the Prophet's call!

Al Munafiqun

Some of the *munafiqun* counseled one another not to venture out in the desert at that time. In response to them, God said:

وَقَالُوا لَا تَنفِرُوا فِي الْحَرِّ قُلْ نَارُ جَهَنَّمَ أَشَدُّ حَرًّا لَّوْ كَانُوا يَفْقَهُونَ ٠ فَلْيَضْحَكُوا قَلِيلًا وَلْيَبْكُوا كَثِيرًا جَزَاءً بِمَا كَانُوا يَكْسِبُونَ ٠

"They counseled against venturing out in the desert heat. Answer: 'The fire of hell is hotter, if only they knew.' They laugh now, but their pleasure is short lived. They shall weep far more, and they will have deserved every bit of it."[4]

The Prophet asked an older tribesman of Banu Salamah: "Uncle, will you fight the Byzantines?" The man answered: "O Prophet of God, permit me to stay behind and do not tempt me. For I am known to be a ladies' man and I am especially weak in front of Byzantine women." Commenting upon him, the Qur'an said: "Among the *munafiqun* some impertinently begged to be permitted to stay behind so as not to be exposed to temptation. In temptation shall be their undoing. Then will they be cast into hell."[5] Those who in secret hated Muhammad and resented his leadership seized the opportunity to strengthen the *munafiqun's* suspicion and disobedience. Fearing that they might get bolder unless they were shown some firmness, and learning that they were meeting in the house of a Jew called Suwaylim, the Prophet angrily sent Talhah ibn 'Ubaydullah to deal with them. Talhah and his companions put Suwaylim's house on fire while the *munafiqun* were meeting inside. As the flames' engulfed the house, one of them jumped from the roof and broke his leg. The others escaped without injury, but they never dared to meet again in Madinah.

Recruitment of Jaysh al 'Usrah

This firmness in dealing with the *munafiqun* was not devoid of effects on all fronts. Even the wealthy Muslims came out to spend more liberally of their wealth in equipping the army. 'Uthman ibn 'Affan alone spent one thousand Dinars. Many others spent of their wealth each according to his means. Those who were capable of equipping themselves did so on their own. But there were many others who offered all they had: their energies and their lives. The Prophet took as many of them as he could equip and apologized to the rest. These wept in sorrow at their poverty and were for this reason called *al bakka'un,* or "the weepers." The army was finally assembled and counted thirty thousand men. Because of the difficulties encountered in its mobilization, this army was given the name *Jaysh al 'Usrah,* or the "hardship army."

The Muslims' March

While Muhammad was busy settling the affairs of Madinah — handing over the reins of government to Muhammad ibn Maslamah, appointing 'Ali ibn Abu Talib as guardian of his household and giving to each the necessary instructions — he left the army under the command of Abu

Bakr. The latter led the assembled men in prayer, and when the Prophet
returned, he handed the command back to him. Responding to
Muhammad's call, 'Abdullah ibn Ubayy came out at the head of a little
band of soldiers and asked for permission to march alongside the Muslim
army. The Prophet, however, preferred that 'Abdullah stay in Madinah, for
he was not quite sure of his good faith. At Muhammad's command, the
army began its march, raising great dust and making a tremendous roar.
The people of Madinah hurried to the rooftops to see this great mass of
men, animals, and equipment move toward al Sham. They were anxious
to catch a glimpse of this large mass of humanity venturing out against
heat, thirst, and all kinds of hardship in order to fulfill their duty to God
and to win His pleasure, the pleasure which they had deemed worthier
than all the good things they had left behind. Indeed, the sight of this
army on the march pioneered by ten thousand cavalrymen and the stupefied people of Madinah watching it, moved to action those whom the very
command of the Prophet failed to stir. Such was the case of Abu
Khaythamah who, after seeing the Muslim army, went straight to his
house where each of his two wives had cooked for him a delicious meal,
drew some fresh water to drink, and sprinkled the tent and surroundings
to cool off the place. Abu Khaythamah could not advance into his own
house a single step before exclaiming, "The Prophet of God is battling the
heat, sand, and thirst of the desert and I, Abu Khaythamah, languish in
the cool, eat delicious food, and enjoy the company of beautiful women?
No, by God, that cannot be! Prepare for me quickly some provisions that
I may join him." He shot off like an arrow. There were probably many
more who did likewise after realizing the shame that would befall them if
they remained in the city.

Encampment at Al Hijr

The army arrived at al Hijr where the rock-hewn remains of Thamud
stood, and the Prophet commanded the army to dismount for a watering
and a brief rest. When it was time to leave, he ordered against drinking
the water or using it for ablutions. "If you have used any of it to knead
bread," he said, "give your dough to the camels and do not eat it. Let no
one go out into the open desert alone." Muhammad knew that the place
was desolate and often struck by blinding sandstorms. Two men disobeyed
and went out of camp. One was carried away by the wind and the other
buried in the sand. When morning came and the people saw that the

sandstorm had filled the well with sand, they panicked. Soon rain fell upon them from a passing cloud. They drank, filled their skins, and felt reassured. Some of them thought this was a miracle. Others thought it was only a passing cloud.

Byzantine Withdrawal, Covenants of Peace with the North

The army then marched in the direction of Tabuk. News of its approach had already reached the Byzantines who immediately withdrew to the safety of their hinterland. When Muhammad learned of their fear and withdrawal, he saw no reason to pursue them within their territory. Instead, he roamed over the border inviting all either to fight or befriend him. His purpose was to secure the frontiers of Arabia. Yuhanna ibn Ru'bah, Governor of Aylah, received such an invitation. He came in person carrying a golden cross, presented gifts, declared his submission, and handed over the keys of his island to the Prophet. So did the people of al Jarba' and Adhruh, and they all paid the *jizyah*. The Prophet gave each of them a covenant which read as the following document given to Yuhanna. "In the name of God, the Merciful, the Compassionate. This is a covenant of security granted under God by Muhammad, the Prophet of God, to Yuhanna ibn Ru'bah and the people of Aylah. Their ships, vehicles, and routes on land and on sea are secure under God's guaranty and Muhammad's. So are all those who accompany them whether of the peoples of al Sham, Yaman, or beyond the seas. Whoever among them perpetrates a crime shall be liable for it in his own person, and it shall be legitimate for Muhammad to confiscate his wealth. It shall not be legitimate to prevent anyone of them from using a well or a road on land or sea which they have been in the habit of using." When the Prophet applied his seal to the document, he presented Yuhanna with a mantle woven in Yaman and showed him every courtesy, respect, and friendship. It was further agreed that Aylah would remit a yearly *jizyah* of three hundred Dinars.

Ibn al Walid's Campaign against Dumah

With the withdrawal of the Byzantines and the binding of the frontier provinces with treaties and covenants of peace, Muhammad had no reason to march any further. The only one he feared was Ukaydir ibn 'Abd al Malik al Kindi, the Christian prince of Dumah. This prince was suspected of preparing to launch a treacherous attack as soon as the

Byzantine forces could return. Taking no chances, Muhammad sent Khalid ibn al Walid with five hundred cavalrymen to deal with this threat and commanded the army to return to Madinah. Khalid hurried to Dumah and, discovering that its king was out on a hunting trip with his brother Hassan, attacked it without finding any appreciable resistance outside the city; its gates, however, remained tightly closed. Khalid seized Ukaydir and his brother Hassan as they returned home. He killed Hassan and threatened to kill Ukaydir unless the gates of the city were opened. Ukaydir and his city yielded. After seizing two thousand camels, eight hundred goats, four hundred loads of grain, and four hundred coats of arms, Khalid carried them, together with his captive, Prince Ukaydir, to Madinah. Muhammad offered Islam to Ukaydir, and the latter converted. He was then reinstated on his throne and became the Prophet's ally.

The Muslims' Return

Leading all these thousands of troops back to Madinah across the wide wastes which separate it from al Sham required no little feat of leadership on the part of Muhammad. Not many of them understood the Prophet's purpose or saw the value of the treaties he concluded with Aylah and other northern states. Evidently they could not appreciate the fact that Muhammad has thereby guaranteed the frontiers of Arabia and created buffer zones between it and Byzantium. All they saw was the plain fact that they had crossed long desert wastes full of hardships, lingered in the vicinity of Tabuk some twenty days, and returned without a fight, without capturing anyone, or seizing anything. Was this reason enough to justify their leaving Madinah at harvest time? Some of them began to whisper to one another derisive remarks about the whole expedition. Others, more faithful, reported the rumors to the Prophet. Muhammad dealt with the guilty, sometimes harshly and sometimes with leniency, his purpose being to maintain discipline in the body of the army. When the army was just about to enter Madinah, Khalid ibn al Walid caught up with and joined them, together with his captive Ukaydir and the booty he seized from Dumah. Ukaydir wore a golden, brocaded garment which caught the attention of everyone in Madinah.

The Recalcitrants

Upon the Muslims' return, those who failed to answer the call to mobilize and remained behind came to give account of their failure. They were given such harsh judgment that all those of questionable faith, including those soldiers who derided the outcome of the campaign just concluded, trembled in fear or changed their minds. The recalcitrants presented their reasons which were anything but spurious. The Prophet listened and, for the most part, let them go free pending God's final judgment. Three others told the truth frankly but repentantly. They were Ka'b ibn Malik, Murarah ibn al Rabi', and Hilal ibn Umayyah. Muhammad ordered them to be boycotted by the Muslims for fifty days, after which they were forgiven and rehabilitated within the community. In this regard the following verses of the Qur'an were revealed: "God has forgiven the Prophet, and the Muhajirun and Ansar who followed him on the 'hardship expedition.' Some of them had almost swerved away from faith. But they repented and God has forgiven them. He is the Merciful, the Compassionate. The three men who remained behind were accused, indicted, and castigated by their own consciences; they came forth repentant, however, as they realized that there is no escape from Him except by His judgment and mercy. God has accepted their repentance and forgiven them, that they may lead a new life. God is the Forgiver, the Merciful."[6]

Severe Treatment of the Munafiqun

From then on, Muhammad dealt more and more severely with the *munafiqun*, whose presence and influence among the Muslims became increasingly grave and demanded decisive solution. Muhammad did not doubt God's promise to give His religion victory and His word power, or that the Muslims would soon increase in very large numbers. Previously, when Islam was limited to the confines of Madinah and its vicinity, it was possible for him personally to supervise all Muslim affairs. Now that Islam had spread to the farthest reaches of Arabia and stood ready to cross its frontiers, any leniency toward the *munafiqun* might lead to grave consequences. Hence, there was all the more reason for the Prophet to eradicate this source of potential disruption. A group of *munafiqun* built a mosque at Dhu Awan, an hour's ride from Madinah, wherein to meet to concoct and plan their divisive strategy and misinterpret and misrepresent the words of God to the people. Before he left for the campaign of Tabuk, the Prophet was even asked by them to dedicate their mosque. The time, however, was pressing and the Prophet asked to be excused. After his return, the Prophet learned more about this group and their purposes, and hence ordered their mosque assigned to the flames. The *munafiqun* shook with fear and went into hiding. Henceforth, there remained only their elder, 'Abdullah ibn Ubayy, to lead and protect them.

'Abdullah, however, did not live long after Tabuk. He fell ill two months later and died. To the knowledge of everyone, 'Abdullah nursed the strongest hatred and resentment for the Prophet ever since the Hijrah. This notwithstanding, Muhammad was careful enough to let no Muslim inflict any harm upon him. Indeed, more. When he learned of 'Abdullah's death, Muhammad was quick to conduct a funeral service for him, to pray for him, and to see to it that he was given proper burial. With 'Abdullah's passing, however, the *munafiqun* lost their strongest pillar, and most of them hurried thereafter to repentance and genuine faith.

The Prophet's Last Campaign

With the campaign of Tabuk, the word of God became supreme throughout the whole Peninsula. Arab frontiers became secure and the peoples of Arabia began to enter Islam *en masse* and to merge into greater unity under Muhammad. The campaign of Tabuk was the last one the Prophet conducted. Henceforth, he remained in Madinah contented with what God had done for him. His son, Ibrahim, who was then sixteen or eighteen months old, was to him a source of constant joy. Whenever he finished with the day's official engagements and receptions, and satisfied himself that his duties to God, family, and friends were fulfilled, he would sit with his son, fondling and playing with him. He watched his son grow, become daily more resembling his father and, like any other father, Muhammad became more and more attached to him. Throughout these months the child was in the care of his nurse Umm Sayf, to whom Muhammad gave some goats to complement her milk supply.

Illness and Death of Ibrahim

Muhammad's attachment to his son had nothing to do with either his faith or with his mission. Repeatedly, he used to say: "We, the prophets, have nothing to pass on as inheritance to anyone. Any wealth we may leave behind must go for charity." Muhammad's case was purely one of a common human emotion, though in him, it has reached its highest and noblest expression. In the Arab, this human emotion expressed itself in causing him to see in his male progeny a form of eternity. It explains fully Muhammad's love for his son, however strong it may have been. Indeed,

Muhammad had more reason for such strong attachment since he had lost his two sons, al Qasim and al Tahir, at a tender age, and his daughters — even after they grew to maturity, married, and bore children — so that only Fatimah remained of all his progeny. Naturally, these sons and daughters who passed away one after the other and were buried by Muhammad's own hand left their father with a severe sense of bereavement. It was natural that a father so bereaved would feel excessive joy and the strongest personal pride and hope at the birth and growing of a son.

The promise and hope which Ibrahim represented were not to last long. Soon, the child fell seriously ill. He was moved to a date orchard near Mashrabat Umm Ibrahim, where his mother and Sirin, her sister, looked after him. When his state worsened and it became apparent that he will not live long, Muhammad was called. He was so shocked at the news that he felt his knees could no more carry him, and asked 'Abd al Rahman ibn 'Awf to give him his hand to lean upon. He proceeded immediately to the orchard and arrived in time to bid farewell to an infant dying in his mother's lap. Muhammad took the child and laid him in his own lap with shaking hand. His heart was torn apart by the new tragedy, and his face mirrored his inner pain. Choking with sorrow, he said to his son, "O Ibrahim, against the judgment of God, we cannot avail you a thing," and then fell silent. Tears flowed from his eyes. The child lapsed gradually, and his mother and aunt watched and cried loudly and incessantly, but the Prophet never ordered them to stop. As Ibrahim surrendered to death, Muhammad's hope which had consoled him for a brief while completely crumbled. With tears in his eyes he talked once more to the dead child: "O Ibrahim, were the truth not certain that the last of us will join the first, we would have mourned you even more than we do now." A moment later he said: "The eyes send their tears and the heart is saddened, but we do not say anything except that which pleases our Lord. Indeed, O Ibrahim, we are bereaved by your departure from us."

Aware of Muhammad's sorrow, the wise among the Muslim sought to remind the Prophet that he himself had commanded against indulgence in self-pity after a bereavement. Muhammad, however, answered: "I have not commanded against sadness, but against raising one's voice in lamentation. What you see in me is the effect of the love and compassion in my heart for my lost one. Remember that whoever feels no compassion toward others will not receive any compassion." These may not have been his exact words, but the meaning remains the same. Muhammad tried to sublimate his sadness and lighten his sorrow, and, looking toward Mariyah and Sirin, he said to them in appeasement that Ibrahim would have his own nurse in Paradise. Umm Burdah, or according to another version, al Fadl ibn 'Abbas, washed the body of the child in preparation for burial. He was carried on a little bed by the Prophet, his uncle al 'Abbas, and a number of Muslims to the cemetery of Abu Bakr where, after a funeral prayer recited by the Prophet, he was laid down to rest. As Muhammad ordered the grave closed, he filled it with sand, sprinkled some water, and placed a landmark on it. He then said: "Tombstones do neither good nor ill, but they help appease the living. Anything that man does, God wishes him to do well."

The death of Ibrahim coincided with the eclipse of the sun, a phenomenon the Muslims saw as a miracle. They went about saying that the sun was eclipsed in sadness over the death of Ibrahim. The Prophet heard them. Would his exceeding love for Ibrahim and deep sorrow over his loss not enable him to find in such rumors a measure of consolation? Would he not at least keep his silence and thus allow the people to believe what they had taken to be a miracle? Certainly not. Such an attitude surely belongs to those who exploit the ignorance and credulity of the people; for those whom suffering and sorrow push beyond reason and common sense. It does not belong to the man of genuine wisdom, nor *a fortiori*, to the great Prophet. Hence, looking to those who claimed the sun was in eclipse because of the death of Ibrahim, Muhammad said, "The sun and the moon are signs of God. They are eclipsed neither for the death nor birth of any man. On beholding an eclipse, therefore, remember God and turn to Him in prayer." What greatness! Even in his moment of greatest personal disaster this Prophet preserved his cool presence of mind. He remained fully conscious of his message and most serious in his commitment to it. And even the Orientalists could not hide their admiration and wonder when they came across this fact in the life of Muhammad. Even they could not fail to acknowledge the genuineness of the man who insisted on truth even in face of the greatest personal adversity.

One wonders what the attitude of the wives of the Prophet was toward the loss of Ibrahim and Muhammad's strong sense of bereavement. Muhammad himself found consolation in God, in the divine assistance he received in the fulfillment of His message, and in the successful spread of Islam that was shown by all the delegations that appeared in Madinah from every direction with the rise of each new day. So wide was the spread of the religion of God and so many peoples entered its ranks that this year, the 10th of the Hijrah, was called "the Year of Deputations." It is also the year in which Abu Bakr made the pilgrimage to Makkah.

28

The Year of Deputations and Abu Bakr's Leadership of the Pilgrimage

The Effects of the Campaign of Tabuk

With the campaign of Tabuk the word of God was fulfilled throughout the Arabian Peninsula. Muhammad had firmly secured it against all attacks. In fact, as soon as he returned to Madinah from Tabuk, the associationists of Arabia began to ponder their fate. The Muslims who accompanied Muhammad on his march toward al Sham suffered many hardships, bore the heat and thirst of the desert, and returned somewhat disappointed, nay resentful, that they were not given a chance to fight and to enjoy the fruits of victory. The Byzantines had withdrawn to the interior where they stood better fortified. Nonetheless, their withdrawal before a marching Arab army left the tribes severely shaken, anxious over the fate of their pagan religion and of their society. The tribes of southern Arabia, of Yaman, Hadramawt, and 'Uman were specially affected in this manner. The Byzantines, they thought, were those who vanquished the Persians, recaptured the cross and reinstated it in Jerusalem with imperial pomp and grandeur. This happened at a time when Persia held dominion over Yaman and the surrounding countryside, territories which Persia had ruled for many decades. Since the Muslims were now close to Yaman — indeed close to every quarter of the Peninsula — why should these territories not join the greater unity under the banner of Muhammad, the aegis of Islam? Such a step would at least save them from the imperialism of both Byzantium and Persia. So they thought regarding their relations

439

with the outside world. On the internal front the princes of the territories and the tribal chieftains knew very well that Muhammad would confirm any leader or sovereign in his leadership or sovereignty if he but converted to Islam. Why then, they thought, should they not join this greater unity, which would bring them clear advantage without prejudice to their particular structure of power? And so it was. The tenth year of the Hijrah was indeed the "Year of Deputations," in which men entered into the religion of God *en masse*. The Campaign of Tabuk and the withdrawal of the Byzantines before the Muslims brought forth results as great as the conquest of Makkah, the Muslim victory at Hunayn, or the blockade of al Ta'if.

Conversion of 'Urwah ibn Mas'ud and His Murder

Fortunately, it was al Ta'if, the city which resisted the Prophet despite the long blockade and which the Muslims had had to bypass without conquering, that came first to declare its allegiance to Muhammad after Tabuk. 'Urwah ibn Mas'ud, one of the chieftains of the tribe of Thaqif, was absent in Yam an during the Prophet's blockade of his city following the Battle of Hunayn. Upon his return to al Ta'if and his realization of the Prophet's victory in Tabuk, he hastened to Madinah to declare his conversion as well as his commitment to call his fellow tribesmen unto the religion of God. 'Urwah was not ignorant either of Muhammad or of the power which the latter had so far achieved, for he was one of the notables of Arabia who entered the negotiations regarding the peace of Hudaybiyah on behalf of Quraysh. 'Urwah's conversion reassured the Prophet that the voice of Islam would reach the tribesmen of Thaqif inside al Ta'if. A ware of Thaqif's attachment to their goddess al Lat, and of their determination to die in defense of their idol, Muhammad warned 'Urwah that his tribesmen would fight him. 'Urwah, however, felt too sure of his position and influence with his people. He answered: "O Prophet of God, my people love me more than they do their own eyes." 'Urwah proceeded to Thaqif and preached Islam to his people. They consulted among themselves and gave him no reply. In the morning, 'Urwah ascended to the top of his high house and from there gave the Islamic call to prayer. It was then that the Prophet's prediction came to be realized. Deeming 'Urwah's behavior utterly dishonorable, his people attacked him with arrows on all sides and killed him. As his relatives panicked around him, 'Urwah told them just before he breathed his last that: "This is indeed an

honor granted to me by God, the honor to die as a martyr in His cause.
For my case is identical to that of all the other martyrs who gave up their
lives at the gates of this city while the Prophet of God — May God's
peace and blessing be upon him — was laying siege to it." He then asked
to be buried together with those martyrs who were buried in that area.

Thaqif's Delegation to the Prophet

'Urwah had not laid down his life in vain. The tribes which lived in
the neighborhood of al Ta'if on all sides had already been converted to
Islam. Thaqif's quick disposal of one of its chieftains was regarded by the
surrounding tribes as a hideous and contemptible crime. Naturally, this led
to the decline of security in the area, for no Thaqif's tribesmen crossed the
territories of these tribes without exposing himself to the gravest dangers.
Soon Thaqif realized that unless it reached peace with the Muslims, its
fate would be doomed. The tribesmen consulted with one another and
approached an elder of theirs called 'Abd Ya Layl to go to the Prophet and
negotiate with him. 'Abd Ya Layl feared to meet a fate not unlike that of
his predecessor 'Urwah ibn Mas'ud. He therefore declined to go to
Muhammad unless Thaqif would delegate him five more chieftains
belonging to different clans and capable of committing those clans to
whatever decision the five would reach with Muhammad. Thaqif agreed
and their delegation was formed. As they approached Madinah, al
Mughirah ibn Shu'bah met them first at the outskirts of the city. When
he discovered their purpose, he hastened to the Prophet to inform him.
Abu Bakr met him on the road and, finding out the cause of his hurry,
pleaded with al Mughirah to give him the pleasure of announcing the
great news to the Prophet. It was therefore Abu Bakr who made the
announcement to the Prophet.

The delegation consisted of proud chieftains who had the greatest
esteem for their city and people. They remembered too well — and of
course resented — the Prophet's blockade of their city. Despite al
Mughirah's instruction of them in Islamic protocol, they refused to greet
the Prophet except in the pre-Islamic manner. Furthermore, they requested that a special tent be put up for their use within the mosque of
Madinah, for they trusted no one to be their host. It was Khalid ibn Sa'id
ibn al 'As who played the role of middleman between them and the
Prophet of God; and it was he who had to taste of every food which the
Prophet furnished to them in order to convince them that it had not been

poisoned. Finally, on their behalf, Khalid informed Muhammad of their preparation to convert to Islam on condition that the Prophet exempt them from prayer and promise not to destroy their idol, al Lat, for three years. Muhammad strongly rejected their proposal. They changed their proposal to two years, and then to one year, and indeed to one month after their return home. But Muhammad rejected all their terms. This was naturally to be expected of a prophet calling man to the religion of God, the One, the Mighty, of a prophet committed to stamp out all idolatry. How could he spare any idol, no matter how cherished it might be by its own devotees? On this matter, there can be no middle ground. Either man believes or he is victim to doubt and suspicion. Doubt and conviction do not unite, just as faith and unbelief are ever disparate. The sparing of al Lat would definitely imply that Thaqif would mingle its worship of God with that of the idol. That is plain associationism, condemned by God in clear and unequivocal terms. That is unfaith. Thaqif also pleaded for exemption from prayer. This, too, Muhammad rejected, saying: "There is no good in a religion in which prayer is ruled out." Finally, Thaqif accepted Islam on Muhammad's terms. They agreed to both the destruction of al Lat and the institution of regular prayers. They demanded, however, that they be exempted from having to destroy their own idol with their own hands. Since they were new converts and since they still had the task of convincing their fellows to accept the terms they were bringing back from Muhammad, their request was natural and could well be understood. It was too much to ask them to destroy with their own hands idols which they themselves had been worshipping the day before, idols which their people honored as the object of their ancestors' worship, and to do so at a time when their people's confidence in them was absolutely necessary if their call to Islam was to succeed. Hence, Muhammad was not adamant on this point. For him, it was all one whether al Lat was destroyed by Thaqif tribesmen or by others. What was important to him was that the idol was soon to be destroyed and that Thaqif was henceforth to turn to the worship of God alone. Addressing himself to the delegation, the Prophet — May God's blessing be upon Him — said: "As for the destruction of your idols with your own hands, we exempt you from it." Muhammad appointed 'Uthman ibn Abu al 'As, the youngest among them, as leader despite his youth; for he sensed in him the strongest desire to learn the Qur'an and the most brilliant mind for studying the law. Abu Bakr and other early Muslims attested to 'Uthman's competence. The delegation remained in Madinah as guests of the Prophet during the rest of

Ramadan, fasting with the Prophet and eating of the food which he presented to them at sunset and before dawn. When it was time for them to leave and return home, Muhammad counseled their leader, 'Uthman ibn Abu al 'As, saying, "Be brief when leading the prayers, and measure the people by the weakest among them. Remember that among them are the old men, the youth, the weak, and the deprived."

Destruction of the Idol al Lat

The delegation returned home accompanied by Abu Sufyan ibn Harb and al Mughirah ibn Shu'bah, who knew the tribe of Thaqif and felt toward its people great friendship and compassion. They were assigned by the Prophet the job of destroying al Lat. Abu Sufyan and al Mughirah approached the sanctuary, and the latter began the job of destruction while the women of Thaqif stood around moaning and crying. Not one tribesman, however, dared to stop al Mughirah in the fulfillment of his duty, for everyone had ratified beforehand the agreement the delegation had concluded with the Prophet. Al Mughirah further seized the wealth of al Lat and its jewelry and, at the direction of the Prophet and in agreement with Abu Sufyan, settled the debts of 'Urwah and al Aswad. With the destruction of al Lat and the conversion of al Ta'if, the conversion of the Hijaz was complete. Muhammad's power expanded from the frontiers of Byzantium in the north to al Yaman and Hadramawt in the south. The territories of South Arabia were all preparing to join the new religion and integrate themselves into a system of defense. That is why delegations from all corners proceeded to Madinah to declare allegiance to the new order and to convert to the new faith.

Abu Bakr Leads the Pilgrimage

As these delegations followed one another to Madinah, the months went by until it was time again for pilgrimage. Until that time, the Prophet — May God's blessing be upon him — had not performed the pilgrimage in exactly the same way as it is performed today. It will be remembered that the previous pilgrimages had all been performed under extraordinary circumstances. Would the Prophet go out to perform the pilgrimage this year in gratitude for the victory God had granted him over the Byzantines, or for the conversion of al Ta'if and the numerous peoples who sent all these delegations to Madinah? Many persons in the Arabian

Peninsula did not believe either in God or His Prophet. Unbelievers, Jews, and Christians were still in their places. The unbelievers continued to observe their ancient custom of going on pilgrimage to the Ka'bah during the holy months. But the unbelievers were anathema. Would the Prophet therefore not remain in Madinah until God's word was more completely fulfilled, until express permission from above were granted him for the purpose? Thus the Prophet reasoned, and he instructed Abu Bakr to lead the pilgrimage in his place.

Abu Bakr proceeded to Makkah together with three hundred Muslims. There was apprehension that the years would follow one another while the unbelievers continued to perform pilgrimage to the holy sanctuary and mingle with the Muslims in religious worship. After all, there was a general pact between Muhammad and the Arabs that none should be prevented from reaching the Holy House if he so desired, that none should be attacked during the holy months. Likewise, the relations with various Arab tribes were governed by pacts whose terms had not yet expired. As long as these pacts had not expired, the associationists had the same right to perform the pilgrimage to the Holy House as the Muslims. For sometime yet, the Muslims would have to continue to see pre-Islamic worship performed side by side with theirs around the Ka'bah.

True, most of the idols worshipped by the Arabs had by then been destroyed, as were the idols and images of the Ka'bah. The pilgrimage institution was, however, still confused. In the sacred months the sanctuary of Makkah was the scene of idolators worshipping their gods as well as of Muslims in revolt against idolatry. A religious institution with a texture such as this is in contradiction with itself. It may be possible to understand the pilgrimage of Jews and Christians to Palestine because it is the land of promise for the former and the birthplace of Jesus Christ for the latter. But it is incomprehensible that two systems of worship meet in the same sanctuary, the one destroying the idols of that sanctuary and the other worshipping the idols destroyed. Hence, it was necessary to stop the associationists from entering a sanctuary just cleansed of associationism and ridden of its idols and images. Thus, the *Surah* of "Bara'ah" was revealed at the right time but too late for implementation in this pilgrimage. The Hajj season had begun and already thousands of associationists had converged upon Makkah as they were accustomed to do for generations. Though this was obviously not the time to implement the revelation, it was time to proclaim it and to let the associationists know that, henceforth, no covenant between Muslims and associationists would be valid unless it specified a given term. In this case, the covenant would be honored for the duration of its term.

For this purpose, the Prophet sent 'Ali ibn Abu Talib to Makkah to join Abu Bakr and to address the congregation of pilgrims assembled at 'Arafat. He was entrusted with the duty to proclaim the commandments of God and His Prophet. When the two met, Abu Bakr asked: "Do you come to us as commander or messenger?" 'Ali answered, "Indeed as messenger," and informed Abu Bakr of his mission. When the pilgrims congregated at Mina, 'Ali rose and delivered the following address, quoting the Qur'an :

"This is a complete absolution from God and His Prophet regarding all obligation arising from pacts made with the associationists. The unbelievers may travel throughout the land for four months in freedom and security. Certainly, they cannot frustrate the plans of God, nor will they escape His final humiliation of them. This proclamation from God and His Prophet is for the benefit of all people on the day of the greater pilgrimage. God and His Messenger are clear of all obligation toward the associationists. It is better for them that they repent; but if they do not and turn away, they should know that they will not frustrate God's plan. Rather, to them belong the tidings of a severe and painful punishment. [These verses constitute a general and a particular absolution of obligations incumbent upon the Muslims toward the associationists. —Tr.] The "particular" absolution will not apply in those cases where those who covenanted with the Muslims have not subsequently violated their covenant nor aided anyone against the Muslims. Such covenanters shall enjoy the benefit of their pact until it expires. God loves the righteous. As for the others, when the holy months have passed, then you are free to kill the associationists wherever they may be, to take them prisoners, to beleaguer and blockade them, and to lie in wait for them at every place of ambush. However, if they repent, observe prayer, and pay the zakat, let them go free, for God is forgiving and merciful. And at any rate, if any of them ask for your protection, grant it to him so that he may hear the words of God. Extend your protection to him until he reaches his home in safety, remembering that he is ignorant and needs your mission. As for the others, how can there be any covenant between them and

God and His Prophet? Certainly, those with whom a pact of
peace has been concluded near the holy sanctuary are protected
thereby, and the Muslims are obliged to remain true to their
covenant as long as the associationists are true to theirs. God loves
the righteous; but the others can have no peace. Should they prevail against you, they will honor neither blood tie nor covenant of
peace. They will delude you with sweet words while their hearts
are full of perfidy and resentment. It was they who bartered God's
word for a mean price; it was they who put obstacles in the way
of men seeking the pleasure of their Lord. Evil indeed is everything they have done. They honor neither relation nor covenant.
It is they who are the transgressors. Nonetheless, if they repent,
hold prayer, and pay the *zakat*, then treat them as your brethren
in the faith. Thus do We explain Our word to men with knowledge. But if they break their oath after their covenant and attack
your religion, then fight these leaders of unfaith, these scions of
ungodliness, for they are unworthy of their covenants. Fight them
that they may desist from their path of error. As for you, the
Muslims, will you hesitate to fight a people who have broken their
oath, who have expelled the Prophet, and who were the first to
open hostilities against you? Will you fear them? Is not God worthier of your fear, you who call yourselves true believers? Fight
them then so that God may inflict upon them His punishment
through you. that He may humiliate them and give you victory,
and that He may avenge the believers for the wrongs they have
suffered and dissipate the wrath of their hearts. God will then forgive whomsoever He pleases, for He is All-Knowing and All-
Wise. Or, would you think that you would be abandoned and forsaken, assuming that God did not know which of you truly strive
for His sake or which of you faithfully refuse to regard as their
friend anyone but God, His Prophet, and the believers? Would
you think that God is not well aware of everything you do? The
associationists have no right to visit the mosques of God to bear
witness against themselves of their own unbelief. It is they whose
works shall be in vain and who will dwell eternally in the fire. The
mosques of God are for those who believe in Him, in the Day of
Judgment, and who hold the prayers, pay the *zakat*, and fear only
God. Only they may be counted among the righteous. True, the
unbelievers have been responsible for providing food and drink to

the pilgrims and for maintenance of the sanctuary. But would you confuse the moral worth of these services with the believers' faith in God and the Day of Judgment, with their fighting in the cause of God? Surely, they are unequal. The unjust are not guided by God. The worth of those who believed, who emigrated and fought for the sake of God, and who spent of their wealth and laid down their lives, is far greater with God. Theirs will be the true triumph. To them God will grant His mercy, His pleasure, and His gardens full of lasting bliss. God's reward is surely the greatest. O Men who believe, do not take your parents and brothers as friends as long as they prefer unfaith to faith. Whoever among you befriends them will do wrong. Remember, if parents, sons, wives and relatives, clans and tribes, wealth and property, prosperity and affluence which you fear might be adversely affected, a trade recession, and dwellings and material things you wish to preserve — if these are dearer to you than God or His Prophet and self-exertion in His cause, then God's judgment will soon fall upon you. Such immoral people are not guided by God. God has given you victory on many occasions. but when you became too proud of your numbers, that is on the day of Hunayn, your numbers availed you nothing. The earth with all its vastness became too small for you and you had to run away, vanquished and in retreat. Then did God send His peace upon His Prophet and the believers. He sent down His hosts to fight on their side, hosts which you did not see. Then did the unbelievers meet their due punishment. Then, too, did God forgive whomsoever He wills. For He is most forgiving and merciful. O Men who believe! The associationists are anathema. After this year they shall not approach the holy Mosque. Do not fear the economic consequences of this proclamation. God will give you of His bounty as He pleases. Surely God is All-Knowing and All-Wise. Fight, therefore, those 'People of the Book' who do not believe either in God or in the Day of Judgment, who do not forbid that which God and His Prophet have forbidden, nor follow the religion of truth, until they pay the *jizyah* and acknowledge their subjection. The Jews claim Ezra to be the son of God, and so do the Christians claim Jesus to be the son of God. That is what they actually claim in their own words. By claiming this they surpass even the unbelievers of old in unbelief. God's curse be upon them wherever they turn. They have taken their rabbis, priests, and monks as lords beside God, and so have they regarded the Messiah, son of Mary. But they were never commanded to worship any but God alone, the One, besides whom there is no other. Praised be God above their associations! Evidently they seek to extinguish the divine light by what they claim. But God will not be frustrated and His light will illumine the world in spite of them. It is He who sent His Prophet with genuine guidance and the religion of truth; and it is He who will make this religion prevail over all other religions, however much the unbelievers may resent it. O Men who believe, many of the rabbis, priests, and monks devour the wealth of the people by false means and turn men away from the true path of God. Many of them hoard gold and silver and do not spend it in the cause of God. To such of them as do this will belong painful and strict punishment. Their punishment shall be a scorching fire, a fire branding their foreheads, sides, and backs, and they will be told that such punishment is reward for what they have hoarded, a taste of what they themselves have treasured. Remember also that God reckoned the months to be twelve, ever since He created heaven and earth, and that four of them are sacred. That is the right religion. Do not therefore wrong yourselves during these months by committing any act of aggression. When the sacred months are over, then fight the associationists in all-out war just as they fight you. Know that God is always on the side of the pious and the virtuous."[1]

'Ali delivered all these verses from *Surah,* "Al Taubah,"[2] which we have quoted in full for a reason which will soon become apparent. After he finished his recitation of the Qur'an, he continued in his own words: "O Men, no unbeliever will enter Paradise; no associationist will perform pilgrimage after this year; and no naked man will be allowed to circumambulate the Holy House. Whoever has entered into a covenant with the Prophet of God — May God's peace and blessing be upon him — will have his covenant fulfilled as long as its term lasts." 'Ali proclaimed these four instructions to the people and then gave everybody four months of general peace and amnesty during which anyone could return safely home. From that time on no associationist performed the pilgrimage and no naked man circumambulated the Holy House. From that day on, the Islamic state was established.

The Moral Foundations of the Islamic State

It was precisely for the purpose of clarifying the foundation of the Islamic state that we have quoted the verses of *Surah* "Al Tawbah" at length. This was equally the purpose of 'Ali's recitation, namely, to enable all the Arabs to understand this foundation. That is why the Prophet had asked him, according to a number of sources, to recommend that these verses be recited to the people each in his own house and quarter. If one were to give close and conscientious examination to the opening pages of this *Surah,* he would be convinced that it contains all that constitutes the moral base of any nascent state. The revelation of this *Surah* of the Qur'an at a time following the last of the Prophet's campaigns, after conversion of the people of al Ta'if, of Hijaz, Tihamah and Najd, after all these territories and many of the tribes of the south had made common cause with Muhammad and Islam, was meant to clarify the moral foundation on which the new state was to be erected. It was then necessary, as it is now, for the state to have a general moral ideology in which its people believe and for the sake of which they would be prepared to fight with all their power and energy. The *Surah* in question seems to be saying to the Muslims in particular and to mankind in general that there is no ideology greater than faith in God alone, in God devoid of associates.

No idea, no faith and no conviction of any kind can exercise greater power over the soul of man than that soul's entry into communion with reality as a whole, with reality at the point of its greatest and most sublime manifestation — in short, with God. Here, man is without master except God; his conscience is without judge except God. The *Surah* seems to be laying down the principle that those who flout this general conviction which ought to be the foundation of the state are the rebels, the immoral, and the nucleus of subversion and hateful destruction. Such ones should be entitled to no covenant and the state ought to fight them. If their rebellion against the general faith of the state is overt, then they should be fought and brought to subjection. If it is not overt, as was the case with the people of Tabuk, then they should pay the *jizyah* in acknowledgment of their subjection.

A close but unbiased consideration of the problem from the historical and social points of view will enable us to appreciate the moral which the foregoing verses of the *Surah* were supposed to teach. Those who hastily have jumped to conclusions condemning Islam and its Prophet do not consider this aspect of the matter and regard these very strong verses of the *Surah* as a call to fanaticism and intolerance inconsistent with genuine civilization. They take the verses calling for fighting the associationists and killing them wherever they may be found without compassion or mercy as a call to raise the political state on a foundation of power and tyranny. Such false claims one often reads in the books of western Orientalists. They are the claims of those who have no talent for social and historical criticism even though, sometimes, they themselves be Muslims. They are claims which fly in the face of historical truth and run counter to every fact of social life. The prejudice with which such claims are advocated compel their authors to interpret the pertinent verses of this and other *Surahs* of the Qur'an in violence to the whole biography of the Prophet. Their interpretation contradicts the logic of the life of the great Prophet and the sequence of events from the day God commissioned him to prophethood to his death.

The Principle of Freedom in Western Civilization

In order to establish the foregoing point, it behooves us to inquire what is the moral foundation of the dominant civilization of modern times and then to compare it with the foundation on which Muhammad sought to base the civilization of Islam. The moral foundation of contemporary civilization is the limitless freedom of opinion, a freedom which cannot be limited except by due process of law. On this account, freedom of opinion is a first principle which men are prepared to defend, whatever the sacrifice, and to realize in their societies, whatever the cost, including war. The advocates of this freedom regard this principle as one of their greatest glories. They boast of it and call themselves greater than all previous generations and periods on its account. It is because of their commitment to this principle that the above mentioned Orientalists call Islam's condemnation of those who believe neither in God nor in the Day of Judgment a will to fanaticism incompatible with freedom. But the fallacious nature of this point of view becomes flagrantly obvious when one realizes that the value of an opinion lies in the ability to express, to propagate, and to implement it. Islam did not call for fighting the Arab associationists who acknowledged the dominion of Muhammad and did not propagate their unbelief or display their pagan rituals. Likewise, the dominant civilization of today wages a war to the knife against any ideology which runs counter to its own, and does so more resolutely and fiercely than the Muslims fought the Arab associationists. Indeed, it imposes upon its own "People of the Book" *(i.e.,* those who reside in its midst but disagree with its basic premises) that which is a thousand times worse than the *jizyah* of Islam.

The West's War against Communism

To illustrate this point, we may refer to the fight against slavery. In its war against those of its members who adhered to the institution of slavery, modern western civilization gave no heed to the fact that those adherents believed in their institution, that they did not regard slavery as taboo. By this we do not mean that Islam approves of slavery, though it must be remembered that Islam did not require us to fight anything but that which God had clearly and unequivocally condemned. The two cases are not dissimilar. Therefore, rather than invoking this case, let us look at Europe, the contemporary carrier of dominant western civilization together with America and all those countries of South and East Asia which run in her orbit. Europe has fought Bolshevism and continues to do so with the strongest determination. We, too, in Egypt are also prepared to cooperate with the western countries in fighting Bolshevism. But Bolshevism is only an economic view, an ideological opinion which runs counter to that of the dominant western countries. Can one therefore say that the call of Islam to fight the unbeliever who violates his own covenant after it has been given is a call to fanaticism, an "empty liberalism," and at the same time say that the call to fight Bolshevism, the destroyer of the West's economic system, is one which upholds the principle of freedom of faith and opinion and which respects and honors that freedom?

The West's War against Nudism

Furthermore, in more than one European country it has been thought that moral discipline cannot be separated from bodily discipline, that hiding some parts or organs of the human body under clothing is more sexually arousing, and hence, more corrupting than the exposure of the whole human body in total nakedness. The advocates of this view began to implement it and founded resorts in a number of cities where those who want to discipline themselves to total nakedness can pursue their desire without hindrance. However, as soon as this view began to spread, the rulers of most of the countries concerned decided that the practice constituted a grave threat to the morality of the majority. They thus declared these "health centers" out of bounds and fought the advocates of nudism.

They propagated laws forbidding the organization or construction of any nudist centers. And were nudism to envelop a whole nation, there is no doubt but that nation would become the object of a new war waged against it by all other nations on the grounds that it constituted a denial of the morality of man. Many a nation was threatened with war by other nations on account of its toleration of slavery, prostitution, or commerce in narcotics. How could such wars be justified? Surely, they could be justified solely on the grounds that freedom, despite its absoluteness, is a value only as long as it is limited to those bounds protecting the community from harm. Wherever the exercise of freedom exceeds those limits, it is deemed a threat to the social, economic, and moral health of the community, an evil worthy of being combated on all fronts. In such an instance, all public exercise of freedom is stopped, and the opinion itself whose freedom is in question is fought. The degree of brutality to which such a war may have to resort is determined by the nature of the threat which the ideological principle in question poses for the particular community.

Legislation May Restrict Freedom

Such is the social truth acknowledged by the dominant civilization of today. Were we to cite every expression and effect of this truth among the various nations, these pages would hardly suffice. Generally speaking, it may be safely asserted that every piece of legislation designed to combat a social, economic, or political movement is a denial of the freedom of opinion and an act of war against that movement. Such denial of freedom to that to which freedom gives birth can be tolerated only on the grounds that the free implementation of those principles entails harm to society. If, therefore, we are to appreciate Islam's war against associationism and its adherents, and its resolution to pursue the fighting till surrender, it is necessary to consider the social implications of associationism. Without such consideration, it is not fair to pass judgment on the legitimacy of the war. Now, if it can be established that associationism brought great harm to human society in all stages and periods, then Islam's call to war against it is not only legitimate but obligatory.

Social Aspect of Associationism

The associationism which was prevalent when Muhammad — May God's peace and blessing be upon him — began to call men to the religion of God was not only a matter of idol worship. Even if it were so, fighting it would still be obligatory. For it is an insult to the human mind, to the dignity of man, that any member of society should worship a stone. But that is not all. Associationism represented a system of traditional customs, beliefs, and practices; indeed, a total social structure which was far worse than slavery, Bolshevism, or any other social evil in the Twentieth Century. Associationism implied the burial of daughters alive and limitless polygamy whereby a man could marry thirty, forty, one or three hundred women. It implied the most cruel forms of usury and the most degrading license and immorality. The society of Arab pagans of Muhammad's time was truly one of the worst that has existed on earth. We ask every man of reason the following question: If a certain nation today were to adopt for itself the same system of beliefs and customs as the pagan Arabs, including the burial of daughters alive, limitless polygamy, slavery with or without cause, economic exploitation and usury, would an internal movement that seeks to destroy that order and alter its system be accused of fanaticism and violation of freedom? Suppose a social group neighboring the degraded community, realizing its own exposure to the contagion of such social evils as dominated their neighbors, were to challenge them to a war. Would such a war be justified or not? Would it not be even better justified than World War I in which millions of men were slaughtered for no other reason except the gluttony and recklessness of the colonialist states? If this argument is valid, what is the value of the Orientalists' criticism of the Qur'anic verses from *Surah* "Al Tawbah" which we have just brought to the attention of the reader? What would be the point of their critique of Islam's call to combat associationism and its adherents who seek to establish the evil order which we have just described?

Legitimacy of the War against Associationism

If such was the historical truth of that pattern of life which was prevalent in the Arabian Peninsula under the banner of associationism and paganism, it is not without implications for the historical truth of the life of the Prophet. It must be recalled that, ever since his commission to prophethood thirteen years before, Muhammad had been calling men to the religion of God with argument and the kindest of words. All the campaigns which he undertook against his enemies were purely defensive. In none of them had he been guilty of aggression. On the contrary, he undertook those campaigns in defense of his Muslim converts, of their freedom to preach the religion in which they believed and which they cherished more than their lives. The stringent call to fight the associationists because they were anathema and had violated the covenant and amnesty freely concluded between them and the believers was in fact revealed to the Prophet after the last of his campaigns, *viz.* the campaign of Tabuk. Islam arose in a land saturated with associationism and unbelief, a land in which associationism had established its destructive economy and immoral social system. If, therefore, the Prophet commanded the Muslims to ask Arabia to exchange its order for one allowing that which God legitimitized and forbidding that which He proscribed, no fair observer could but agree to rise against the associationists and to pursue the fight against them to victory. Such victory is the victory of truth and goodness, of the religion which is all God's.

'Amir ibn al Tufayl

'Ali's recitation of the Qur'anic *Surah* "Al Tawbah," and his calling Muslim attention to the divine order that henceforth no unbeliever would enter Paradise or would perform pilgrimage, and no naked man would circumambulate the Holy House, brought forth the best of fruits. Above all, it removed all hesitancy in the minds of those tribes which had not yet resolved to enter into Islam. Moreover, the territories of Yaman, Mahrah, Bahrayn, and Yamamah immediately joined the ranks of Islam. No one was left to oppose Muhammad nor to contend with him except a few deluded individuals. One of them was 'Amir ibn al Tufayl, who refused to convert. His people had enlisted him to serve as a member of their delegation to the Prophet proclaiming their conversion. When the delegation obtained audience with the Prophet, 'Amir refused to go forward. He even proclaimed himself the Prophet's equal. Muhammad invited him to a talk and tried to convince him of the truth of Islam — to no avail. 'Amir walked out threatening with war: "By God", he swore, "I shall fill your spaces with men and cavalry." Muhammad prayed God to restrict 'Amir. On his way home, the persistent unbeliever was struck with cancer in his neck and died in an inn belonging to a woman from the tribe of Banu Salul. It is reported that he expired while lamenting, "O Banu 'Amir, do you leave me to be stifled to death by a lump in my neck as big as a camel's lump here in the house of a woman of Banu Salul?"

Another persistent associationist was Arbad ibn Qays. He, too, refused to convert and returned to Banu 'Amir where he perished by lightning shortly after his arrival at the marketplace. However, neither 'Amir nor Arbad, whether dead or alive, could stop their people from joining Islam. Worse yet was the case of Musaylimah ibn Habib who accompanied the delegation of his tribe, the Banu Hanifah of Yamamah, to the Prophet. His companions assigned him the job of watching their horses while they entered the court of the Prophet to present their submission and receive his blessing. They did not forget him, but they mentioned his case to Muhammad, and the latter ordered that he be given exactly what his companions received. Indeed, Muhammad praised him for agreeing to stay behind and watch his people's property. But when Musaylimah heard of this, false pride took possession of him and he claimed to be himself a prophet. He not only started to argue that God had associated him with Muhammad in prophethood but as well to compose rhymes and verses in imitation of the Qur'an. He recited such verses as "God blessed the pregnant woman. He brought forth from her the breath of life, embedded within a well-padded womb." Musaylimah proclaimed wine and adultery legitimate, and he absolved men from the obligation of prayer. He preached widely but was met with ridicule. Except for these individual cases, Arab groups from all corners of the Peninsula, led by some of the greatest men of the period such as 'Adiyy ibn Hatim and 'Umar ibn Ma'di Karib, entered the religion of God. The kings of Himyar sent a messenger to the Prophet declaring their conversion to Islam, and the Prophet accepted their conversion and wrote to them explaining their rights and obligations under God. It was then that Muhammad sent some of the early converts to teach the new Muslims in the south the institutions of their faith and to deepen their understanding of it.

The Other Deputations

Unlike some early biographers, we shall not spend time relating the details of the delegations of tribes who came to declare their entrance into the faith. In his *al Tabaqat al Kubra*, the historian Ibn Sa'd devoted fifty long pages to those details. Suffice it here to mention only their names. These were: Muzaynah, Asad, Tamim, 'Abs, Fazarah, Murrah, Tha'labah, Muharib, Sa'd ibn Bakr, Kilab, Ru'as ibn Kilab, 'Uqayl ibn Ka'b, Ja'dah, Qushayr ibn Ka'b, Banu al Bakka', Kinanah, Ashja', Bahilah, Sulaym, Hilal ibn 'Amir, 'Amir ibn Sa'sa'ah, Thaqif; the Rabi'ah group of 'Abd al Qays, Bakr ibn Wa'il, Taghlib, Hanifah, Shayban; the Yamani tribes of Tay', Tujib, Khawlan, Ju'fiyy, Suda', Murad, Zubayd, Kindah, al Sadif,

Khushayn, Sa'd Hudaym, Baliyy, Bahra', 'Udhrah, Salaman, Juhaynah, Kalb, Jarm, al Azd, Ghassan, al Harith ibn Ka'b, Hamdan, Sa'd al 'Ashirah, 'Ans, al Dariyyin, al Rahawiyyin branch of Madhhtaj, Ghamid, al Nakha', Bajilah, Khath'am, al Ash'arayn, Hadramawt, Azd 'Uman, Ghafiq, Bariq, Daws, Thumalah, al Huddan, Aslam, Judham, Mahrah, Himyar, Najran, and Jayshan. There remained not one of the tribes of the Peninsula, or of its clans, but had entered into Islam.

Such was the fate of the associationists who lived in the Arabian Peninsula. They hastened to enter into Islam and to abandon the worship of idols until the countryside was cleansed of idols and idol-worship. All this was accomplished after the campaign of Tabuk and willingly and in freedom without a single soul being coerced or a single drop of blood being spilled. But what did the Jews and Christians do with Muhammad, and what did the latter do to them?

Jami' Mosque, Nairobi, Kenya.

29

The Farewell Pilgrimage

Ever since 'Ali ibn Abu Talib recited the opening verses of the *Surah* "Al Tawbah" to the Muslims and associationists who came to perform the pilgrimage under the leadership of Abu Bakr, and ever since the announcement that henceforth no associationist would enter paradise or perform the pilgrimage, no naked man would circumambulate the Holy House, and that whoever had a covenant with the Prophet of God — May God's peace and blessing be upon him — would have his covenant honored till its expiration, the unbelievers of the Arabian Peninsula realized that their idol worship would have to come to an end. They awoke to the fact that unless they themselves put an end to idolatry, they would eventually have to take up arms against God and His Prophet. This situation applied particularly to the southern regions of the Peninsula, al Yaman and Hadramawt, because al Hijaz and all the territories of the north had already entered into the new faith and stood under its protection.

Islam's Distinction between Paganism and the Religions of the Book

In the south, associationism and Christianity divided the land. As we have seen in the preceding chapter, most associationists announced their entry into God's religion and sent their delegations to Madinah to proclaim it. The Prophet accorded these delegations all the welcome possible,

458

thereby hastening the entrance of others and confirming the new converts in the faith. Muhammad's restitution to each prince of his princedom and to each leader of his leadership made all these new converts extremely keen to protect their new status. As for the People of the Book, whether Jews or Christians, the following verses from *Surah* "Al Tawbah," read by 'Ali on that momentous occasion had become known to them.

$$قَاتِلُواالَّذِينَ لَا يُؤْمِنُونَ بِاللهِ وَلَا بِالْيَوْمِ الْأَخِرِ وَلَا يُحَرِّمُونَ مَا حَرَّمَ اللهُ وَرَسُولُهُ وَلَا يَدِينُونَ دِينَ الْحَقِّ مِنَ الَّذِينَ أُوتُوا الْكِتَبَ حَتَّى يُعْطُوا الْجِزْيَةَ عَنْ يَدٍ وَهُمْ صَاغِرُونَ ٠$$

"Fight, therefore, those 'People of the Book' who do not believe either in God or in the Day of Judgment, who do not forbid that which God and His Prophet have forbidden, nor follow the religion of truth until they pay the *jizyah* and acknowledge their subjection. O Men who believe, many of the rabbis, priests and monks devour the wealth of the people by false means and turn men away from the true path of God. Many of them hoard gold and silver and do not spend it in the cause of God. To such as these will belong painful and strict punishment. Their punishment shall be a scorching fire, a fire branding their foreheads, sides and backs, and they will be told that such punishment is the reward for what they have hoarded, a taste of what they themselves have treasured."[1]

Faced with these verses from *Surah* "Al Tawbah" with which the whole Qur'anic revelation came to an end, many historians ask themselves whether or not the revelation of Muhammad — May God's peace and blessing be upon him — has not changed tone in regard to the People of the Book. Some western Orientalists even claim that these verses have put the People of the Book on a level with the unbelieving associationists; that after achieving victory over paganism with the assistance of Judaism and Christianity, as was demanded by the proclamation that Islam confirmed the religion of Jesus, Moses, Abraham and the earlier prophets, Muhammad had turned his wrath against the Jews who opposed him and fought them until they evacuated the Peninsula. During this time, so the claim runs, Muhammad pretended friendship with the Christians and recited verses which praised their genuine faith and friendliness, such as:

لَتَجِدَنَّ أَشَدَّ النَّاسِ عَدَاوَةً لِّلَّذِينَ ءَامَنُوا الْيَهُودَ وَالَّذِينَ أَشْرَكُوا وَلَتَجِدَنَّ أَقْرَبَهُم مَّوَدَّةً لِّلَّذِينَ

ءَامَنُوا الَّذِينَ قَالُوٓا إِنَّا نَصَارَىٰ ذَٰلِكَ بِأَنَّ مِنْهُمْ قِسِّيسِينَ وَرُهْبَانًا وَأَنَّهُمْ لَا يَسْتَكْبِرُونَ ۝

"You will find the Jews and the associationists more hostile to those who believe. You will find those who say 'We are Christians' the friendliest to those who believe, for many of them are monks and priests, and they are humble."2

But now, the claim continued, Muhammad has turned his wrath against Christianity and sought to destroy its adherents as he did those of Judaism before. Arguing from these premises, a number of Orientalists have blamed Muhammad for regarding Christianity on a level with unfaith. They invoke the fact that Christians had protected his followers when they took refuge in Abyssinia. They also invoke the facts that Muhammad had approved of the religion of the people of Najran and other Arab Christians and that he allowed them to follow their rituals of worship. Finally, the western Orientalists claim that it was this turnabout in the strategy of Muhammad which established the continuing hostility between Muslims and Christians. Their purpose is to impute to the Prophet a strategy which, they claim, made any reconciliation between the followers of Jesus and Muhammad very difficult, if not impossible.

On the face of it, this argument seems appealing and logical. Those to whom it is intended might even incline to see in it some if not all the truth. However, a careful investigation of the situation, context, and causes of revelation of the said verses leaves no reason for doubt that the attitude of Islam and Muhammad toward the scriptural religions was always one and the same. The Messiah, son of Mary, is of the spirit of God. He is God's word, given unto Mary. In his lifetime, the Messiah was a servant of God to whom God revealed the Book, whom He commissioned as a prophet, blessed, commanded to hold the prayers, and always to pay the *zakat*. From the beginning of Muhammad's prophethood to its end, the Qur'anic revelation maintained that God is One, that He was not born, that He did not give birth to anyone, and that None is like unto Him.

Such is the spirit of Islam. Such has been its foundation from the very first moment. And such will the spirit of Islam remain for all eternity. A delegation of the Christians of Najran went to the Prophet and argued with him in the matter of God as well as in the matter of Jesus' prophethood a long time before the revelation of *Surah* "Al Tawbah." They asked

Muhammad, "If Mary is the mother of Jesus, who was his father?" In this connection, the following verse was revealed:

"The example of Jesus is for God like that of Adam. He created him of clay and commanded him to be and he was. This is the truth from your Lord. Do not, therefore, have any doubt concerning it. Whosoever argues with you to the contrary now that certain knowledge has come to you, answer. 'Let us call our sons and yours, our women and yours, ourselves and yours to pray to God and seek His guidance. May His curse fall upon the liars.' This is the true knowledge and the true narrative; there is no God but God, and He is the Glorious, the All-Wise. But if they disagree, remember that God knows the propagators of falsehood. Say: 'O People of the Book, let us join together in upholding a noble principle common to both of us, namely, that we shall not worship any God but God, that we shall not associate aught with Him, and that we shall not take one another as lords besides God. If they disagree then tell them, 'Remember, as for us, we are indeed Muslims.'"[3]

In this *Surah* of "Al 'Imran," the text irrefutably indicts the People of the Book with discouraging the Muslims from believing in God and throwing obstacles in the path to Him. It asks them directly why they do not believe in this new revelation when it reaffirms the same truth which Jesus, Moses, and Abraham received from God, in its pristine purity, before it was tampered with and edited following the prejudices, ulterior motives, and vain desires of man. In many other *Surahs* of the Qur'an the same argument is repeated against the People of the Book. In *Surah* "Al 'Imran," for instance, as in the *Surah* "Al Ma'idah," God said:

لَقَدْ كَفَرَ الَّذِينَ قَالُوٓا إِنَّ اللّٰهَ هُوَ الْمَسِيحُ ابْنُ مَرْيَمَ وَقَالَ الْمَسِيحُ يٰبَنِىٓ إِسْرَآءِيلَ اعْبُدُوا اللّٰهَ رَبِّى وَرَبَّكُمْ إِنَّهُ مَنْ يُّشْرِكْ بِاللّٰهِ فَقَدْ حَرَّمَ اللّٰهُ عَلَيْهِ الْجَنَّةَ وَمَأْوٰىهُ النَّارُ وَمَا لِلظّٰلِمِينَ مِنْ أَنْصَارٍ لَقَدْ كَفَرَ الَّذِينَ قَالُوٓا إِنَّ اللّٰهَ ثَالِثُ ثَلٰثَةٍ وَمَا مِنْ إِلٰهٍ إِلَّآ إِلٰهٌ وَاحِدٌ وَإِنْ لَّمْ يَنْتَهُوا عَمَّا يَقُولُونَ لَيَمَسَّنَّ الَّذِينَ كَفَرُوا مِنْهُمْ عَذَابٌ أَلِيمٌ أَفَلَا يَتُوبُونَ إِلَى اللّٰهِ وَيَسْتَغْفِرُونَهُ وَاللّٰهُ غَفُورٌ رَّحِيمٌ مَا الْمَسِيحُ ابْنُ مَرْيَمَ إِلَّا رَسُولٌ قَدْ خَلَتْ مِنْ قَبْلِهِ الرُّسُلُ وَأُمُّهُ صِدِّيقَةٌ كَانَا يَأْكُلَانِ الطَّعَامَ انْظُرْ كَيْفَ نُبَيِّنُ لَهُمُ الْآيٰتِ ثُمَّ انْظُرْ أَنّٰى يُؤْفَكُونَ

"Those who claim that God is one of three have lied and committed unbelief. There is no God but God, the One. If they do not stop from propagating this lie, a severe punishment will fall upon them. But if they repent to God and seek His mercy, God is most pardoning and merciful. The Messiah, son of Mary, is only a prophet, one among many prophets who preceded him. His mother was a faithful believer but a human like him. Both ate worldly food. Is this not sufficient evidence to convince them? But see how they persist in going astray!"[4]

In the same *Surah*, God also says: "And when God asked Jesus, son of Mary, 'Did you tell the people to take you and your mother as two deities beside God?' Jesus answered, 'Praise be to God. How can I say that which is not true?'"[5] It was in the much earlier *Surah* "Al Ma'idah," not in "Al Tawbah," the last to be revealed, that the verse is to be found which the Christian historians use as evidence for their allegation that Muhammad turned toward Christianity following the change of his political fortunes. This is the verse, "You will find the Jews and the associationists more hostile to those who believe. You will find those who say 'We are Christians' the friendliest to those who believe, for many among them are monks and priests, and they are humble."[6] And yet, while they take this part of the *Surah* for evidence, they deliberately omit consideration of the evidence of its other parts.

On the other hand, the verses of *Surah* "Al Tawbah" which mention the People of the Book, do not discuss their faith in Jesus, the son of Mary. Rather, they discuss their association of other beings with God, their unjust economic exploitation of the people, and their hoarding of gold and silver. Islam undoubtedly regards such practices on the part of the People of the Book as violating the religion of Jesus. Therefore, Islam does well to criticize them as making legitimate that which God had forbidden and of being guilty of those practices which usually belong to those who believe neither in God nor in the Day of Judgment. Nonetheless, Islam was careful enough to remind them that their faith in God, despite all their evil and immoral practices, would intercede for them in God's judgment. It reassured them that their faith in God would lift them above the pagans and would enable them, even though they declare God to be one of three and tolerate that which God forbade, to get by with merely paying the *jizyah* and acknowledging subjection.

More Deputations to the Prophet

It was precisely this call, which was proclaimed by 'Ali at the pilgrimage led by Abu Bakr, that brought in its trail the conversion of the South Arabians. Their delegations then followed one another to Madinah as we have said earlier. Among these were the delegations of associationists as well as of People of the Book. The Prophet used to give the best welcome to anyone who sought him, and to reinstitute the princes and leaders in their positions of power upon conversion to Islam. Al Ash'ath ibn Qays led the delegation of Kindah which consisted of eighty horsemen. Seeking the Prophet, they entered the mosque clad in silken mantles, and with decorated eyes and faces. When the Prophet saw them in this condition, he said: "Have you not entered Islam?" They answered, "Certainly." Muhammad then retorted: "What is all this silk around your necks?" Immediately everyone of them tore his mantle to bits. Al Ash'ath said in apology to the Prophet: "O Prophet of God, we are noblemen, sons of noblemen. But so are you! You would, then, understand our will to self-distinction." The Prophet smiled and related the story to al 'Abbas ibn 'Abd al Muttalib and Rabi'ah ibn al Harith. Along with al Ash'ath there came Wa'il ibn Hujr, of Kindah, who was the ruler of the coastlands of Hadramawt. He, too, converted to Islam, was confirmed in his rulership and asked to collect the tithe from his citizens for transfer to the Muslim collectors. Mu'awiyah ibn Abu Sufyan was commanded to accompany Wa'il home. On the way, accustomed to behaving as royalty, Wa'il refused to let Mu'awiyah ride with him or even to lend him his sandals that he might protect his feet from the hot sand. He thought it sufficient condescension on his part to allow Mu'awiyah to walk in the shadow of his camel. Despite the violation of the egalitarianism and fraternity of Islam, Mu'awiyah acquiesced in order to help Wa'il and his people secure their new faith.

Arab Unity under the Banner of Islam

When Islam spread in Yaman, the Prophet sent Mu'adh to teach its people the ethic and law of the new faith. He advised Mu'adh, "Make things easy and do not raise obstacles. Reconcile and do not alienate. Some People of the Book will ask you, 'What is the key to Paradise?' Answer, 'It is to witness that there is no God but God; that He is alone and without associates!'" Mu'adh travelled to Yaman together with a number of early converts and tax collectors, all commissioned to teach the people and to judge between them by the law of God and His Prophet. As Islam spread from one corner of the Arabian Peninsula to another, its people from the extreme north to the extreme south became one *ummah*, unified under the banner of Muhammad, the Prophet of God — May God's peace and blessing be upon him! Everybody acknowledged one and the same religion, Islam; and all turned together to the worship of one God, without associates. Only twenty years before, the same people were hostile tribes, warring with one another, and robbing one another's property and wealth. Now that they all joined Islam's ranks, the country was cleansed of the abomination of paganism and became reconciled to live under the shadow of divine judgment. Thus, intertribal hostility was eradicated, and there was neither aggression nor injustice. Henceforth, no one was to draw his sword except to defend the greater country or to put an end to aggression against the religion of God.

Conversion of Arab Christians to Islam

A group of Christians from Najran opted to keep their faith and not to follow the example of Banu al Harith, the majority of whom had joined Islam. To these the Prophet sent Khalid ibn al Walid to preach to them the faith and to bring them into the *pax Islamica* that had just covered the Peninsula end to end. They responded favorably to his call and entered Islam. Khalid then arranged for a delegation of them to visit Madinah where the Prophet met them with friendly welcome. Another group from Yaman found it difficult to subject themselves to the dominion of Islam for the provincial reason that Islam arose in Hijaz rather than in their country. Since they had never been subjected to Hijaz, which had on many occasions been the object of military campaigns by the people of Yaman, the latter were too proud to submit. To them the Prophet sent 'Ali ibn Abu Talib to call them to Islam, but they attacked him. Tender of age though he was, and commanding no greater force than three hundred horsemen, 'Ali vanquished them. For a second time they regrouped their forces and fought. But again 'Ali surrounded them and broke their resistance. Finally, they submitted and converted to Islam in good faith. They listened to the teachings of Mu'adh and his companions. Their delegation to Madinah was the last one which the Prophet met before his death.

The Prophet Prepares for Pilgrimage

While 'Ali was preparing to return to Makkah, the Prophet was preparing to undertake the pilgrimage and advising his companions to do likewise. The month of Dhu al Qi'dah was almost at an end, to be followed by Dhu al Hijjah, the month of pilgrimage. Up until that time, the Prophet had not performed the pilgrimage ritual in full, though he had performed the lesser pilgrimage on two previous occasions. The ritual of the pilgrimage had to be established in its entirety so that the Muslims might learn and follow it. As soon as the people knew of the Prophet's intention and heard his call to march with him on pilgrimage, the whole Peninsula reverberated with the call, and thousands and thousands of people from all corners poured into Madinah. From every town and village, from every mountain and valley, from every plain and desert across the wide Peninsula, the people arrived to perform the pilgrimage. It was as if this vast expanse of land had all been illuminated by the dazzling light of God and His Holy Prophet. Around Madinah tents were set up to accommodate the new visitors, numbering 100,000 or more, who had risen up in response to the call of their Prophet, Muhammad the Prophet of God — May God's best blessing and peace be upon him. All these men came as brethren, in love and respect for one another, and united in the true bond of friendship and Islamic brotherhood, whereas but yesteryear they had been the most hostile of enemies. These thousands upon thousands of men crisscrossed the streets of Madinah, all manifesting the smiles of faith, the certainty of conviction, and the confidence and pride of true religion. Their convocation was an inspiring evidence of the victory of truth, of the wide reach of the light of God, and of the deep bond of truth and righteousness which had cemented them one to the other so that they stood like one great fortress.

The Muslims March for Pilgrimage

On the twenty-fifth of Dhu al Qi'dah of the year 10 A.H., the Prophet set forth toward Makkah accompanied by all his wives, each riding her own carriage. He was followed by a great multitude, numbering 90,000 according to some historians, 114,000 according to others. These men marched with consciences deeply moved by faith, with hearts full of joy and contentment at their intended accomplishment of pilgrimage to the holy sanctuary of God. They reached Dhu al Hulayfah at the end of the day and there they spent the night. On the following morning, the Prophet put himself into a sacral state and the Muslims followed his example. Everyone shed his clothes and put on two pieces of unsewn white cloth, the simplest of all garments. In this way, they expressed the absolute egalitarianism of Islam in its most eloquent and highest sense. Muhammad turned to God with all his heart and mind praying, "At your service, O God! At your service! You have no associates! At your service, O God! Praise be to God! Thanks be to God! At your service, O God! You have no associates! At your service, O God! You have no associates, O God! At your service, O God!" And all the Muslims repeated these words after him. Deserts, valleys, and mountains reverberated with this prayer. The sky itself reverberated with the call of those pious, believing, and worshipping souls. Thus the procession continued on its way to Makkah, its thousands and hundreds of thousands filling the air with the sound of this prayer. At every mosque on the way to Makkah, the procession would stop to pray, and the voices of the thousands would rise proclaiming the unity of God, their praise and blessing in anticipation of the great day of pilgrimage that awaited them. Everyone was impatient to reach the sanctuary of God that he revered and honored more than anything else in the world. Undoubtedly, the deserts, mountains, and valleys, the trees, birds and skies were moved by what they witnessed in this great call, the like of which they had never heard before! They and the Peninsula had been blessed by the advent of this illiterate Prophet, Muhammad, the Servant of God and His Apostle.

Desacralization after the 'Umrah or Lesser Pilgrimage

When the procession reached Sarif, midway between Makkah and Madinah, Muhammad said to his companions: "Those of you who do not have any sacrificial animals with them may perform the lesser pilgrimage. But those who do, must perform the complete ritual." The procession continued and reached Makkah on the fourth of Dhu al Hijjah. Upon arrival, the Prophet, followed by the Muslims, hastened to the Ka'bah. There, the Prophet went to the Black Stone and kissed it. Then he circumambulated the holy sanctuary seven times, the first three of which he did at a trotting pace, just as he had done in the lesser pilgrimage. He then proceeded to the Sanctuary of Ibrahim where he performed a prayer. Returning back to the Black Stone, he kissed it once more and then left the temple area for the Mount of al Safa, and from there performed the *Sa'y* between that mount and the mount of Marwah.[7] He then announced to the Pilgrims that whoever did not have an animal to sacrifice should now desacralize himself and bring his pilgrimage ritual to a close. Some pilgrims hesitated, and this angered the Prophet. He repeated his command. When he entered his tent, the anger visible on his face, 'A'ishah inquired about it. He answered, "How can I be otherwise when my commands are not obeyed?" As a visiting companion inquired again, adding, "Whoever angers the Prophet of God will taste of the fire," the Prophet said, "Is it not strange that I command the people and find them hesitant to obey? If it were permissible to come to pilgrimage without animals to sacrifice, I too would have been content to perform the lesser pilgrimage and desacralize at this moment." So relates Muslim.[8] When the news of the Prophet's anger reached the people, thousands of them terminated their pilgrimage regretfully. Even the wives of the Prophet, including his daughter Fatimah, did likewise. Only those people who had brought sacrificial animals with them kept themselves in the sacral state.

'Ali's Return from Yaman

While the Muslims were performing their pilgrimage, 'Ali returned from his campaign in Yaman. Before entering Makkah, and upon hearing that the Prophet of God was leading the pilgrimage, 'Ali put himself in a sacral state and wore the pilgrim garments. Upon finding that his wife Fatimah, had desacralized herself, he asked for an explanation. He was told that the Prophet had commanded that only lesser pilgrimage was permitted to those who did not bring their sacrificial animals with them. 'Ali went to the Prophet and there related to him the news of his campaign in Yaman. When he finished, the Prophet asked him to circumambulate the holy sanctuary and then to desacralize himself like the rest. 'Ali retorted: "Prophet of God, I have recited exactly the same prayers as you have." The Prophet said. "Even so, desacralize yourself as your companions have done." 'Ali rejoined again: "Prophet of God, when I put myself in the sacral state, I recited: 'O God, I intend to perform this pilgrimage in identically the same manner as Your Prophet, Servant, and Apostle Muhammad.'" The Prophet then asked 'Ali whether he had any sacrificial animals and, when 'Ali answered in the negative, Muhammad gave him some of his own. For this reason, 'Ali kept his sacral state and performed the ritual of pilgrimage in its complete form.

Performance of the Pilgrimage Ritual

On the eighth day of Dhu al Hijjah, the day of al Tarwiyah, Muhammad went to Mina and spent the day and night in that locality. There, he performed all the prayers incumbent during that period. The following day, Muhammad recited his dawn prayer and, at sunrise, proceeded on his camel, al Qaswa', to the Mount of 'Arafat, followed by all the pilgrims. As he ascended the mountain, he was surrounded by thousands of his companions reciting the *talbiyah* and the *takbir.*[9] The Prophet naturally heard their recitations but made no effort either to stop them or to encourage them. He commanded some of his companions to put up a tent for him on the east side of the mountain at a spot called Namirah. When the sun passed the zenith, he ordered his camel to be saddled, and rode on it until he reached the valley of 'Uranah.

The Prophet's Last Sermon

It was there that he, while sitting on his camel, delivered his sermon in a loud voice to his people. Rabi'ah ibn Umayyah ibn Khalaf repeated the sermon after him sentence by sentence. He began by praising God and thanking Him, and then turning to the people, he said:

"O Men, listen well to my words, for I do not know whether I shall meet you again on such an occasion in the future. O Men, your lives and your property shall be inviolate until you meet your Lord. The safety of your lives and of your property shall be as inviolate as this holy day and holy month. Remember that you will indeed meet your Lord, and that He will indeed reckon your deeds. Thus do I warn you. Whoever of you is keeping a trust of someone else shall return that trust to its rightful owner. All interest obligation shall henceforth be waived. Your capital, however, is yours to keep. You will neither inflict nor suffer inequity. God has judged that there shall be no interest and that all the interest due to 'Abbas ibn 'Abd al Muttalib shall henceforth be waived. Every right arising out of homicide in pre-Islamic days is henceforth waived. And the first such right that I waive is that arising from the murder of Rabj'ah ibn al Harith ibn 'Abd al Muttalib. O Men, the devil has lost all hope of ever being worshipped in this land of yours. Nevertheless, he still is anxious to determine the lesser of your deeds. Beware of him, therefore, for the safety of your religion. O Men, intercalation or tampering with the calendar is evidence of great unbelief and confirms the unbelievers in their misguidance. They indulge in it one year and forbid it the next in order to make permissible that which God forbade, and to forbid that which God has made permissible. The pattern according to which the time is reckoned is always the same. With God, the months are twelve in number. Four of them are holy. Three of these are successive and one occurs singly between the months of Jumada and Sha'ban. O Men, to you a right belongs with respect to your women and to your women a right with respect to you. It is your right that they not fraternize with anyone of whom you do not approve, as well as never to commit adultery. But if they do, then God has permitted you to isolate them within their homes and to chastise them without cruelty. But if they abide by your right, then to them belongs the right to be fed and clothed in kindness. Do treat your women well and be kind to them, for they are your partners and committed helpers. Remember that you have taken them as your wives and enjoyed their flesh only under God's trust and with His permission. Reason well, therefore, O Men, and ponder my words which I now convey to you. I am leaving you with the Book of God and the Sunnah of His Prophet. If you follow them, you will never go astray. O Men, hearken well to my words. Learn that every Muslim is a brother to every Muslim and that the Muslims constitute one brotherhood. Nothing shall be legitimate to a Muslim which belongs to a fellow Muslim unless it was given freely and willingly. Do not, therefore, do injustice to your own selves. O God, have I conveyed Your message?"

As the Prophet delivered his speech, Rabi'ah repeated it sentence by sentence and asked the people every now and then whether or not they had understood the Prophet's words and committed them to memory. In order to make sure that the people understood and remembered, the Prophet used to ask his crier to say: "The Prophet of God asks, 'Do you know which day is this?" The audience would answer, "Today is the day of the greater pilgrimage." The Prophet then would say, "Tell them that God has declared inviolate your lives and your property until the day you will meet your Lord; that he has made the safety of your property and of your lives as inviolate as this day." At the end of his speech, the Prophet asked, "O God, have I conveyed your message?" And the people answered from all corners, "Indeed so! God be witness."

When the Prophet finished his sermon, he dismounted and waited until noon, at which time he performed both the noon and the midafternoon prayers. He then mounted his camel and proceeded to al Sakharat where he recited to the people the concluding divine revelation: "Today I have completed for you your religion, and granted you the last of my blessings. Today I have accepted for you Islam as the religion."[10] When Abu Bakr heard this verse he realized that with the completion of the divine message, the Prophet's life was soon to come to a close.

The Prophet left 'Arafat and spent his night at Muzdalifah. In the morning, he visited first the sanctuary of al Mash'ar, and then Mina on the road to which he threw pebbles against the symbol of Satan. When he reached his tent, he sacrificed sixty-three camels, one for each year of his life. 'Ali sacrificed the rest of the animals which the Prophet had brought with him from Madinah. The Prophet then shaved his head and declared his pilgrimage completed. This pilgrimage is sometimes called "the Farewell Pilgrimage." Others have called it the "Pilgrimage of the Annunciation" and others, the "Pilgrimage of Islam." In truth, the Prophet's pilgrimage was all these at once. It was the "Farewell Pilgrimage" because Muhammad saw Makkah and the holy sanctuary for the last time. It was also the "Pilgrimage of Islam" because God completed His religion for the benefit of mankind and granted to them His total blessing. Finally, it was also the "Pilgrimage of the Annunciation" because the Prophet had completed his announcement and conveyance to the people of what he has been commanded by God to announce and to convey. Muhammad was truly only an announcer, a conveyor, and a warner sent to a people who see the truth and believe.

Sultan Hasan and Rifaʿi Mosques, Cairo, Egypt.

30

The Prophet's Sickness and Death

Effects of the "Farewell Pilgrimage"

The "Farewell Pilgrimage" completed, tens of thousands of pilgrims began their return home. Those who came from the desert returned to the desert; those who came from Tihamah returned hence, and those who came from the south, from Yaman, Hadramawt and neighboring territories, did likewise. The Prophet and his immediate companions set out in the direction of Madinah. When they reached it, they settled down confident that peace had covered the entire Peninsula. Henceforth, it was natural that Muhammad became preoccupied with the conditions of those countries under the dominion of Byzantium and Persia, especially al Sham, Egypt, and 'Iraq. Now that the people have converted to Islam in such large groups, that their delegations had already declared in Madinah their obedience and committed their peoples to serve under its banner and, finally, now that all the Arabs have united in this "Farewell Pilgrimage," the Arabian Peninsula became secure in its entirety. Indeed, there was no reason for any of the Arab kings and princes to withdraw or to violate loyalty to the Prophet or to his religion. Under no other regime did they enjoy more power and internal autonomy than under that which the unlettered Prophet had instituted. Badhan, the Persian governor of Yaman, was reinstated in his governorship as soon as he converted to Islam. In recognition of this, Badhan preserved the unity of Arabia and threw off the yoke of the Zoroastrian Persians. Whatever little rumblings took place in the Peninsula never came close to resembling rebellion, and they did not occupy the Prophet or raise in him any apprehension for the future. The dominion of the new religion had firmly spread over all parts of the Peninsula; all faces were turned to the living and eternal God, and all hearts truly believed in the One, the Almighty.

The Prophetic Pretenders

It was natural, therefore, that the pretenders to prophethood who arose at the time were not the object of anxiety or care on Muhammad's part. True, some of the tribes in the outlying distances hastened to listen to any pretender, especially after they had heard of the Prophet of God and of the success of his mission. Obviously, such tribes wished they had the same good fortune as the Prophet's tribe, Quraysh. Precisely because of their distance from Makkah and from the headquarters of the new religion, such tribes did not yet fully absorb the new religion. However, this new religion, this honest and candid call to God, struck its roots firmly everywhere else. To resist it would not be easy. The anecdotes of Muhammad's travails and sacrifices for the sake of his mission had already spread to the horizons, and everyone knew that none but Muhammad ibn 'Abdullah was capable of such sacrifice. Every false pretension, however, must sooner or later be exposed; and no pretender to prophethood can meet with any long lasting success. Tulayhah, for instance, the leader of Banu Asad and one of the greatest war heroes, a real lord of the desert, pretended that he, too, was a prophet and an apostle. He claimed that his true prophesying about the exact location of water when his people were lost in the desert, and almost perished from thirst, was the proof of his prophethood. But he remained afraid of contradicting Muhammad or withdrawing his loyalty to him as long as the Prophet lived. He therefore rebelled only after Muhammad's death. It was Ibn al Walid that led the Muslim forces in suppressing the rebellion of Tulayhah. Upon his defeat, Tulayhah once more joined the ranks of Islam and henceforth led a virtuous life. On the other hand, neither Musaylimah not al Aswad al 'Ansi fared any better than Tulayhah as long as the Prophet lived. The former sent to the Prophet — May God's blessing be upon Him — a message saying, "I, too, am a prophet like *you*. To us belongs half the earth, and to Quraysh belongs the other half, if Quraysh were only just." When Musaylimah's two messengers delivered this message of their master to Muhammad, the Prophet told them that, were it not for the conventional security granted to messengers, he would have ordered them executed. He then asked them to convey to Musaylimah the reply that Muhammad heard his message and realized its lies. The earth belongs to none but God, and God grants it to whomsoever He chooses among His worthy and righteous servants. Peace belongs to the right-guided."

As for al Aswad al 'Ansi, the Governor of Yaman after the death of Badhan, he began to practice magic and to call people to believe in him until he had achieved a measure of strength. Then he marched from the south toward Yaman and expelled Muhammad's governors from the territory. He marched on Najran and killed its governor, the son of Badhan who inherited the office from his father. Al Aswad then married the widow of the fallen ruler and brought the whole area under his dominion. All this, however, did not worry Muhammad nor did it call, in his judgment, for more than a word to his governors and agents in Yaman to pull al Aswad down. The Muslims of the area fulfilled the command of the Prophet by themselves, turned the tables on al Aswad and ended his regime. And it was his own wife who put an end to his life in vengeance for the blood of her first husband.

The Prophet's Concern for the Northern Front

Muhammad's care and preoccupation, therefore, were directed toward the north, not toward the south of Arabia. This was especially so following his return from the "Farewell Pilgrimage." In fact, ever since the campaign of Mu'tah, when the Muslims returned without conquest after the clever and strategic withdrawal of Khalid ibn al Walid, Muhammad had been giving to Byzantium a good portion of his thought and careful planning. He was convinced that Muslim power at the northern frontier with al Sham should be firmly established if those who had been evacuated from the Peninsula and who had emigrated to Palestine were not to return and attack again. It was in consequence of this care that Muhammad mobilized a very massive army when he heard that the Byzantines were about to advance on the northern frontier, and he himself led that army all the way to Tabuk. The Byzantines had withdrawn toward the interior upon hearing of the march of that army. This notwithstanding, Muhammad continued to plan for the day when the lords of Christendom who dominated the world through Byzantium might be stirred to attack in resentment against those who had brought Christianity to an end in Najran and other places in Arabia. Consequently, the Muslims did not stay long in Madinah following their return from the farewell Pilgrimage in Makkah. The Prophet had immediately ordered the mobilization of a large army and commanded it to march on al Sham. That is why he sent along with that army a number of the elders of Islam, the earliest Muhajirun, among whom were Abu Bakr and 'Umar. That is why he gave the command of the army to Usamah ibn Zayd ibn Harithah.

The Prophet's Counsel to Usamah

Usamah ibn Zayd, the commander of the army, was then a young man hardly twenty years of age. His appointment and precedence over the elders of Islam, the early Muhajirun, and greater companions of the Prophet, would have caused quite a stir among the people had it not been for everybody's genuine faith in the Prophet's judgment and calculation. By appointing him, the Prophet sought to place him in the same command in which his father fell in the campaign of Mu'tah. The Prophet had wanted to give Usamah cause for pride in victory tantamount to a reward for the martyrdom of his father. Moreover, such an appointment was sure to stir within the soul of the youth the greatest resolution, determination, and bravery. It was also meant as an example for the youths of Islam to carry the burden of great responsibility. Muhammad commanded Usamah and his army to enter the approaches of al Balqa' and al Darum in Palestine, in the vicinity of Mu'tah where his father had fallen. He also commanded him to fight the enemy in the early hours of dawn, to fight them fearlessly, and to shower them with fire. He also commanded him to surprise the enemy, never to let the news of his advance reach them beforehand. Once victory was achieved, Usamah was to return home quickly and not to extend his stay in those lands.

The Prophet's Illness

Usamah and his army set up their headquarters at al Jurf, in close proximity to Madinah, and there began their preparation for the long trip to Palestine. While they were getting ready, the Prophet of God fell ill and the seriousness of his ailment prevented their going forth. One may ask with surprise how the sickness of the Prophet of God could prevent an army from undertaking a campaign which he himself had ordered. One must remember, however, that for that army to go to al Sham, it had to cross wide deserts and empty places, a matter that was not at all easy and would take many long days. It was not easy for the Muslims, considering their great love for the Prophet, to leave Madinah while he suffered from grave illness. Those same men knew that the Prophet never suffered from any serious ailment. Nothing had adversely affected his health throughout this period except a brief lack of appetite in 6 A.H. falsely attributed to Jewish magic, and a little discomfort following his eating a bite of poisoned lamb in 7 A.H. Furthermore, the rhythm of his life and the logic of his teachings always protected him against disease. He always ate little and satisfied himself with the barest and simplest necessities. His clothes and his house were always perfectly clean, for Muhammad not only saw to it that the duties of ablutions were perfectly carried out at all times, but he even used to say: "Were it not for my fear of imposing hardship on my people, I would have made it a duty for them to brush their teeth five times a day." On the other hand, the ritual of prayer and daily exercise which Muhammad observed as well as his sense for economy in the pursuit of pleasure, his refrain from indulgences of all kinds, and his general unconcern for things of this world which always kept him at a distance from them, but in communion with cosmic life and the secrets of existence — all these aspects of his character protected him against disease and gave him good health. His strong natural construction and innate inclination to moral goodness consolidated his immunity against disease.

Now that he had fallen seriously ill, however, it was natural for his friends and companions to become concerned and anxious, fearing that the untold energies he spent during the last twenty years of life may have been begun to take effect upon him. Ever since he had proclaimed his prophethood in Makkah and begun to call men to worship God alone, to abandon the idols of the ancestors, Muhammad had met such great opposition and hardship that his companions had to flee to Abyssinia and he himself to the seclusion of the mountains in the outskirts of Makkah. His flight from Makkah to Madinah, following the covenant of 'Aqabah, took place under the most trying and dangerous of conditions. Muhammad did not know what awaited him in Madinah before he arrived there under cover of night. When he did arrive there, he immediately became the object of Jewish plotting and intrigue. After God gave him victory following all these trials and permitted men from all corners to join the new faith, Muhammad's duties multiplied to a tremendous extent. The keeping of the peace, the leadership of the community, the establishment of its institutions, the continuous wars he had to fight, and the attacks he had to repel would have broken the back of the strongest man.

What situation could have been more tragically trying than that in which Muhammad found himself at the Battle of Uhud when the Muslims ran away from their enemy and Muhammad ascended the hill alone pursued by Quraysh's soldiers; when, under a shower of enemy arrows and stones, he fell wounded, with his teeth broken? What position could be more frightening than that in which the Prophet found himself at the Battle of Hunayn when the Muslims fell back at dawn before their attacking enemies when so determined was their retreat that Abu Sufyan could say that "Only the sea could make them turn back again"; when in the midst of this retreating stream of people Muhammad held his ground and called unto the Muslims: "Where to? Where to? Come back! Come back to me!" until they returned and were victorious. Moreover, there was the burden of mission, the tremendous burden of revelation, the self-exhausting spiritual effort to keep in communion with the reality of the universe, with the supernal plenum — an effort the Prophet was reported to have described as more horrendous than the destiny of doom which befell Hud and other ancient civilizations. Muhammad's companions were witnesses to all this. They had seen him bear his burdens uprightly and with determination, never faltering. Now that he had fallen ill after such a splendid career, it was natural for them to want to postpone their march to al Sham for a while, until they could reassure themselves of God's disposition.

The Prophet's Visit to the Cemetery

In the meantime, another event took place which added to the companions' anxiety. At the beginning of his illness, Muhammad suffered from sleeplessness. On one night, as the days were long and hot and the nights short and breezy, Muhammad felt like going out of his house for a walk around the city. Only his servant, Abu Muwayhibah, accompanied him on this promenade. But where would he go? He went to Baqi' al Gharqad where all the cemeteries of the Muslims lay on the outskirts of Madinah. According to the reports, he stood between the graves of his fallen companions and addressed them in the following words: "Peace be upon you who are in these graves. Blessed are you in your present state to which you have emerged from the state in which the people live on earth. Subversive attacks are falling one after another like waves of darkness, each worse than the previous one." Abu Muwayhibah related that the Prophet had told him upon arrival at Baqi' al Gharqad: "I have been commanded to pray for those who lie in this terrain. Won't you come with me?" After praying for the dead buried in that cemetery, when it was time to return home, the Prophet approached Abu Muwayhibah and said to him: "O Abu Muwayhibah, I have been given the keys of this world and eternity in it, and now I am being offered Paradise, and meeting with my God. I am asked to choose between them." Abu Muwayhibah said: "What would I not give for your sake, O Master! Is it not possible to have both? Do take the keys of this world, eternity in it, as well as Paradise." Muhammad answered: "No, by God, O Abu Muwayhibah. I have chosen Paradise and meeting with my Lord."

Abu Muwayhibah must have reported what he had seen and heard. The Prophet began to complain from his sickness the morning following the night on which he had visited the cemetery of al Baqi'. It was then that the people became concerned and the army of Usamah did not move. True, the report of Abu Muwayhibah is doubted by many historians who believe that Muhammad's sickness could not have been the only reason that prevented the army from marching to al Sham, that another cause was the disappointment of many, including a number of elderly Muhajirun and Ansar, with respect to the leadership assigned to the army. They based their judgment on facts that are given in the sequel. Although we do not wish here to dispute their judgment concerning the report of Abu Muwayhibah, we do not find reason to justify their denial of the event altogether. Whatever the value of the report, it is not necessary to deny the event of the Prophet's visit to the cemetery of Baqi al Ghalqad, his prayer for its dead, or his realization that the hour of meeting with his Lord was soon to strike. In our age, science does not deny the possibility of communication between spirits. It subsumes such communication under the category of psychic phenomena. There have been many men endowed with strong and sensitive perception who knew that their hour was close, and many witnesses to this effect can be produced. Furthermore, communication between the living and the dead, the connection between the past and the present in a manner not limited by either space or time is today regarded as indubitable fact, although man's nature being what it is, it is not given for us to perceive its forms. There is hence no reason to deny the event of the Prophet's visit to the cemetery of Bail' as out of place considering Muhammad's spiritual and psychic power of communication with the realms of reality and his awareness of spiritual reality that surpasses that of ordinary men.

Muhammad's Congenial Mood

On the following morning, Muhammad found 'A'ishah, his wife, complaining of a headache and holding her head between her hands, murmuring, "O My head!" Having begun to feel pain, Muhammad answered, "But rather, O 'A'ishah, my own head!" However, the pain was not strong enough to put him to bed, to stop his daily work, or to prevent him from talking kindly to his wives and joking with them. As 'A'ishah continued to complain from her headache, Muhammad said to her: "It wouldn't be too bad after all, O 'A'ishah, if you were to die before me. For I would then pray for you and attend your funeral." But this only aroused jealousy in the youthful 'A'ishah, who answered: "Let that be the good fate of someone else besides me. By God, should that ever happen to me, your other wives would still be there to give you company." The Prophet smiled, but did not follow up the conversation because of an attack of pain. As soon as the pain subsided, he got up and visited with his wives just as he had always done. The pain returned with stronger force, however, so that Muhammad could not bear it any longer. He was in the quarters of Maymunah, his wife, when he found it necessary to call the members of his house and to ask all of them to attend to him in the quarters of 'A'ishah. His wives agreed to nurse him there. He moved out of Maymunah's quarters, his head wrapped, leaning on 'Ali ibn Abu Talib on one side and on al 'Abbas, his uncle, on the other. His legs could hardly carry him. He entered the quarters of 'A'ishah and there lay down.

Attacks of Fever

His fever increased in the first days of his sickness so that he felt as if he were on fire. When the attacks of fever subsided, the Prophet walked to the mosque to lead the prayers. He continued to do so for several days but felt too weak to talk to his companions or to listen to them. But he could hear their gossip about his appointment of a very young man to command the elder Muhajirun and Ansar in the coming campaign against al Sham. Despite the gradual deterioration of his health and the aggravation of his pain, he felt it necessary to address the people on that subject.

Sortie to the Mosque

One day he asked his wives and servants to pour on him seven goatskins of water from various wells. The water was brought from differ-

ent wells as he commanded and poured over him as he sat in a tub belonging to Hafsah. He then put on his clothes, wrapped his head, and went to
the mosque. Standing at the pulpit, he praised God, prayed for the martyrs of Uhud, and addressed the congregation in the following words: "O
Men, carry out the expedition under Usamah. Your complaint against his
generalship is of the same kind as your complaint against the generalship
of his father before him. By God, Usamah is as fit for the generalship as
was his father." Muhammad stopped for a while, and there was absolute
silence. He then resumed his address, saying: "Has he not made the better choice who, when given the option of taking this world, the other
world, or properly acquiescing in whatever is with God, chooses the last
alternative?" Muhammad fell silent again, and the people were absolutely
motionless. With his deep perception and sensitivity Abu Bakr realized
that Muhammad was here referring to himself. His loyalty to the Prophet
and profound feeling for his person overwhelmed Abu Bakr, who could
not hold back his tears. Deeply moved and crying, he said: "But we would
give our own lives and the lives of our children for you, O Muhammad!"
Fearing the spread of Abu Bakr's contagious affection among the congregation, Muhammad said softly: "O Abu Bakr!" He then commanded all
the gates of the mosque to be closed except the one which led to the quarters of Abu Bakr. When this was done, he said: "I do not know of anyone
whose companionship is preferable to me than yours. Of all the people of
the world, I would choose only Abu Bakr as a permanent friend and constant companion. His has been the friendship and fraternity of true faith!
And it will last until God brings us together again." Muhammad left the
pulpit to return to 'A'ishah's quarters. As he did, he turned to the people
and said: "O Muhajirun, be good to al Ansar. The Muslim community
increases every day, but the number of al Ansar remains the same. Al
Ansar have been my own people, my trustworthy people among whom I
have taken shelter. Be good to the virtuous among them, reward the pious,
and forgive the wrongdoers."

Muhammad proceeded to the house of 'A'ishah nearly exhausted by
the effort he had exerted. When a man is ill, suffering from high fever, to
get out of bed and go to the Mosque after having had to cool his body
with seven skins of water is hard enough. How much more exacerbating
must this brief outing have been for Muhammad when at the same time
he had to confront such momentous matters as Usamah's mobilized army
and the threatened fate of al Ansar as well as of the Arab *ummah*, newly
cemented together by the religion of Islam? The following day,

Muhammad tried to get out of bed and lead the prayers in the Mosque as usual. When he found his effort futile, he ordered that Abu Bakr lead the prayers in his place. 'A'ishah was anxious for her husband to lead the prayers himself. She thought that nothing would better allay the fears of the people than for them to see the Prophet resume his daily functions. She therefore apologized for her father, Abu Bakr, saying that his voice was too soft and that he would break down and cry whenever he recited the Qur'an. Realizing his incapacity to rise from bed, the Prophet ordered once again that Abu Bakr lead the prayers. When 'A'ishah insisted on her objection, the Prophet shouted in anger: "How obsessive are women! Order Abu Bakr to lead the prayers at once."

On another day, when Abu Bakr was absent, Bilal called the Muslims to prayer and invited 'Umar to lead them. As 'Umar's loud voice reached the ear of the Prophet next door, he took this as another flouting of his previous command. He said: "Where is Abu Bakr? God and the believers do not agree that Abu Bakr be not the leader." It was this incident that convinced the people that Muhammad has indeed appointed Abu Bakr as his successor, for leadership of the prayers was the foremost sign of succession to the Prophet.

The Prophet's Whisper to Fatimah

After this, the Prophet's sickness and pain increased. His fever was so high that it could be felt by his wives and servants upon touching the blankets which covered him. Fatimah, his daughter, whom he loved deeply as his only surviving offspring, visited him every day. Whenever she entered his room, the Prophet would cry, kiss her, and give her his own chair. One day when she entered the room, he greeted her saying, "Welcome, my daughter." But it was she who kissed him. He asked her to sit by him on his bed and whispered to her twice, first making her cry and then making her laugh. 'A'ishah sought to discover what was said; but Fatimah refused to give away what she took to be a secret. It was not until after he died that Fatimah divulged what he had then told her, namely, that he was to die of that same sickness — which caused her to cry — and that she would be the first member of his family to join him after death — which made her smile. In order to cool down his fever, Muhammad dipped his hand in a container by his bed, filled every now and then with cold water, and wiped his face. At times, the high fever gave him convulsions. Recovering from one of those attacks, he overheard his daughter,

Fatimah, say with deep sorrow: "Oh, the terrible pain my father is suffering!" At this Muhammad said, "Your father will suffer no more pain after this day," meaning that he was to meet his Lord before the day was over.

The Prophet's Wish to Write a Testament

Anxious to lighten his pain, his companions reminded him that he had counseled them not to complain when sick. He apologized to them, saying that his pains surpassed whatever any two of them could bear together. While under a strong attack of fever and surrounded by visitors, he asked that pen and ink and paper be brought. He said he would dictate something for his followers' benefit, assuring them that if they adhered to it, they would never go astray. Some of the people present thought that since the Prophet — May God's peace and blessing be upon him — was severely ill and since the Muslims already had the Qur'an, no further writing was necessary. It is related that that thought belonged to 'Umar. The people present disagreed among themselves, some wishing to bring writing materials and take down what the Prophet would dictate, and others thinking that any further writing besides that of the Book of God would be superfluous. Muhammad asked them all to leave, saying, "It does not become you to disagree in my presence." Ibn 'Abbas felt concerned that the people would lose something important if they did not hasten to bring the writing materials, whereas 'Umar held firmly to his judgment which he based upon God's own estimate of His Holy Book: "In this scripture, We have left out nothing."[1]

As the news of the deteriorating health of the Prophet spread, Usamah and a number of his aides left their encampment at al Jurf for Madinah seeking reassurance concerning the Prophet's health. Usamah entered the quarters of 'A'ishah unable to speak. But when Muhammad saw Usamah, he lifted his hands toward the sky before placing them on Usamah's shoulders, as a sign of prayer for him.

Members of the Prophet's household saw fit at this stage to give him some medicine which Asma', a relative of Maymunah, had learned to prepare during her stay in Abyssinia. Taking advantage of Muhammad's loss of consciousness, they poured the medicine into his mouth. When he came back to himself, he asked who had given him the medicine and why. His uncle, al 'Abbas, explained that they had prepared it and given it to him because they feared he had pleurisy. The Prophet said, "That is a disease which God would not inflict upon me." He then ordered everyone in the house except his uncle, al 'Abbas, to taste it. Even Maymunah, who was then fasting, was forced to taste it.

At the beginning of his illness, Muhammad had in his house seven Dinars; he feared he might die while some money was still in his possession. He therefore commanded his relatives to give the money away to the poor. However, their preoccupation with his sickness and constant attendance upon him, in addition to their concern for his deteriorating health, caused them to forget to execute his order. When he came to himself on Sunday, on the eve of the day of his death, he inquired whether they had fulfilled his order. 'A'ishah answered that the money was still in her possession. He asked her to bring it forth to put on the palm of his hand. He then said: "What spectacle is this of Muhammad, if he were to meet God in this condition?" The money was given forthwith to the poor.

Muhammad spent a peaceful night in which his fever seemed to subside. It was as if the medicine which his relatives had prepared for him had somewhat alleviated the disease. In the morning he was even able to go to the mosque although his head was still wrapped and he needed to lean on 'Ali ibn Abu Talib and al Fadl ibn al 'Abbas for support. Abu Bakr was leading the prayer at the time of Muhammad's entry into the mosque. As the Muslims saw the Prophet come in, they were so overjoyed at his recovery that they almost allowed their prayer to be interrupted. Abu Bakr raised his voice in the recitation signaling that the prayer must go on and not be interrupted. Muhammad was extremely pleased with what he saw, and Abu Bakr knew well that the people would not have been diverted from prayer by the arrival of any other man. As Muhammad came close to Abu Bakr to join in the prayer, the latter moved himself away from his position of leadership so that the Prophet might take over. Muhammad, however, pushed him back into place saying, "You lead." He sat beside Abu Bakr and prayed in a sitting position. When he finished, he joined the congregation and talked to them with a clear voice audible even outside the mosque. He said: "O Men, the fire is ready. Subversive attacks are advancing like the waves of darkness. By God, I shall not be held responsible for aught of this. I have never allowed anything but that which the Qur'an has made legitimate, and I have never forbidden aught which the Qur'an has not forbidden. God's curse is upon those who take graves for their mosques."[2]

Muslim Joy at the Prophet's Apparent Recovery

The Muslims were so overjoyed at the signs of recovery in the health of their Prophet that Usamah ibn Zayd even asked for permission to march on al Sham. Indeed, even Abu Bakr came forward to say: "O Prophet of God, it is evident that God has granted you His blessing and given you good health just as we all wished and prayed. I had promised the Daughter of Kharijah [meaning his wife] to spend the day with her. May I take leave of you?" The Prophet granted him leave, and Abu Bakr went to al Sunh on the outskirts of Madinah, where his wife resided. 'Umar and 'Ali returned to their business as usual. The Muslims dispersed in joy and happiness after their days of despondence over the news of Muhammad's illness. Muhammad returned to the quarters of 'A'ishah made happy by the happiness of his fellow Muslims who filled the mosque to see him and who anxiously awaited to hear of his news. But he felt quite weak. 'A'ishah helped her husband in with a heart full of awe and sympathy, wishing she could offer him her own life and energy to replace his waning strength.

The Interlude of Wakefulness before Death

The Prophet's visit to the mosque turned out to be only an interlude of wakefulness which precedes death. After he returned home, every minute saw further deterioration of his health. There was no doubt that he had only a few hours to live. How did he spend these last few hours of his life? What was his last vision? Did he spend those precious moments reviewing the career he had lived since God had commissioned him to prophethood and appointed him a guide to mankind? Did he recall the hardships he suffered, the joys he experienced, and the spiritual and military victories he achieved? Or did he spend his last moments praying to God and asking for mercy with all his soul and all his mind as he used to do throughout his life? Or was he too weak to review anything and too unconscious even to pray? The reports vary widely. Most reports tell that on that day, *i.e.,* June 8, 632 C.E., one of the hottest days in Arabia, Muhammad asked for a pitcher of cold water in which he dipped his hands and wiped his face. Most reports state that a man from the clan of Abu Bakr entered the quarters of 'A'ishah carrying a toothbrush in his hand. Muhammad looked at him in a way expressive of his desire to obtain the toothbrush. 'A'ishah took the toothbrush from her relative and worked it out until it became pliable and handed it over to Muhammad who used it to brush his teeth.

"Rather, God on High and Paradise"

The same reports also tell that as the agonies of death became stronger, the Prophet turned to God in prayer saying: "O, God, help me overcome the agonies of death." 'A'ishah reported that his head was in her lap during the last hour. She said, "The Prophet's head was getting heavier in my lap. I looked at his face and found that his eyes had become fixed. I heard him murmur, 'Rather, God on High and Paradise.' I said to him, 'By Him who sent you as a Prophet to teach the truth, you have been given the choice and you chose well.' The Prophet of God expired while his head was on my side between my lungs and my heart. It was my youth and inexperience that made me let him die in my lap. I then placed his head on the pillow and rose to bemoan my fate and to join the other women in our bereavement and sorrow."

Did Muhammad truly die? That is the question over which the Arabs differed greatly at the time, indeed so greatly that they almost came to blows. Thanks to God's will and care, the division was quickly stamped out and the religion of the Hanifs, God's true religion, emerged unscathed.

Interior of the Ulu Jami', Bursa, Turkey.

31

The Prophet's Burial

Muslim Shock at the News of Death

It was therefore in 'A'ishah's quarters, while his head lay in her lap that the Prophet — May God's peace and blessing be upon him — chose the company of God on High. When this happened, 'A'ishah laid his head down on a pillow and joined the other women of the house who rushed to her upon hearing the news and began to cry in bereavement and sorrow. The Muslims at the mosque were taken by surprise by the sudden noise. In the morning, they had seen the Prophet and were convinced his health was improving so much that Abu Bakr, it will be remembered, sought permission to go and visit his wife at al Sunh.

'Umar Belies the News

Upon hearing the news and hardly believing it, 'Umar returned quickly to the Prophet's quarters. Upon arrival, he went straight to Muhammad's bed, uncovered and looked at his face for a while. He perceived its motionlessness and deathlike appearance as a coma from which he believed Muhammad would soon emerge. Al Mughirah tried in vain to convince 'Umar of the painful fact. 'Umar, however, continued to believe firmly that Muhammad did not die. When al Mughirah insisted, 'Umar said to him in anger, "You lie." The two went to the mosque together while 'Umar was proclaiming at the top of his voice, "Some hypocrites are pretending that the Prophet of God — May God's peace and blessing be upon him — has died. By God I swear that he did not die: that he has gone to join his Lord, just as Moses went before. Moses absented himself from his people fourteen consecutive nights and returned to them after they had declared him dead. By God, the Prophet of God will return just as Moses returned. Any man who dares to perpetrate a false rumor such as Muhammad's death shall have his arms and legs cut off by this hand."

At the mosque, the Muslims heard these proclamations from 'Umar — they were shocked and stupefied. If Muhammad truly died, woe unto all those who saw him and heard him, who believed in him and in the God Who sent him a conveyor of true guidance and religion. Their bereavement would be so great that their hearts and minds would break asunder. If, on the other hand, it were true that Muhammad had not died but had gone to join his Lord, as 'Umar claimed, that was reason for an even greater shock. The Muslims should then await his return which, like that of Moses, would be all the more reason for wonder. The Muslim crowds sat around 'Umar and listened to him, inclined as they were to agree with him that the Prophet of God did not die. At any rate, they could not associate death with the man whom they had beheld in person only a few hours before and whose clear and resonant voice they had heard pray and invoke God's mercy and blessing. Moreover, they could not convince themselves that the friend whom God had chosen for the conveyance of His divine message, to whom all the Arabs had submitted, and to whom Chosroes and Heraclius were also soon to submit, could possibly die. They could not believe that a man could die who had shown such power as had shaken the world for twenty consecutive years and had produced the greatest spiritual storm of history. The women, however, were still beating their faces and crying at Muhammad's house, a sure sign that Muhammad had really died. Yet, here in the mosque, 'Umar was still proclaiming that Muhammad had not died; and that he had gone to join his Lord as Moses had done; that those who spoke of Muhammad's death were hypocrites who would suffer the cutting of their arms and necks by Muhammad upon his return. What would the Muslims believe? As they recovered from their severe shock, hope began to stir within them in consequence of 'Umar's claim that Muhammad was to return, and soon they almost believed their own wishes. Their wishful thinking had apparently painted for them the sky a beautiful blue.

Enter Abu Bakr

As they wavered between believing 'Umar or the indubitable meaning of the women's crying, Abu Bakr heard the news and returned from al Sunh. He looked through the door of the mosque and saw the Muslims being addressed by 'Umar, but he did not tarry there. He went straight to the quarters of 'A'ishah and asked for permission to enter. He was answered that there was no need that day for permission. He entered and found the Prophet laid down in a corner and covered with a striped cloth. He approached, uncovered the face and kissed it, saying, "How wholesome you are, whether alive or dead!" He then held the Prophet's head in his hands and looked closely at the face which showed no sign whatever of death's attack. Laying it down again, he said, "What would I not have sacrificed for you! The one death which God has decreed for you, as for any other man, to taste, you have now tasted. Henceforth, no death shall ever befall you." He covered the head with the striped cloth and went straight to the mosque where 'Umar was still proclaiming loudly that Muhammad had not died. The crowds made a way for him to the front, and as he came close to 'Umar he said to him: "Softly, O 'Umar! Keep silent!" But 'Umar would not stop talking and continued repeating the same claim. Abu Bakr rose and made a sign to the people that he wished to address them. No one could have dared impose himself upon the congregation in such manner except Abu Bakr, for he was the ever trustworthy friend of the Prophet, whom Muhammad would have chosen from among all men. Hence, it was natural that the people hastened to respond to his call and move away from 'Umar.

Muhammad Is Truly Dead

After praising and thanking God, Abu Bakr delivered the following brief address: "O Men, if you have been worshipping Muhammad, then know that Muhammad is dead. But if you have been worshipping God, then know that God is living and never dies." He then recited the Qur'anic verse,

وَمَا مُحَمَّدٌ إِلَّا رَسُولٌ قَدْ خَلَتْ مِن قَبْلِهِ الرُّسُلُ أَفَإِيْن مَّاتَ أَوْ قُتِلَ انقَلَبْتُمْ عَلَى أَعْقَابِكُمْ وَمَن يَنقَلِبْ عَلَى عَقِبَيْهِ فَلَن يَضُرَّ اللَّهَ شَيْئًا وَسَيَجْزِي اللَّهُ الشَّاكِرِينَ

"Muhammad is but a prophet before whom many prophets have come and gone. Should he die or be killed, will you abjure your faith? Know that whoever abjures his faith will cause no harm to God, but God will surely reward those who are grateful to him."[1]

Realizing that the people were withdrawing from him and going to Abu Bakr, 'Umar fell silent and listened to Abu Bakr's speech. Upon hearing Abu Bakr recite the Qur'anic verse, 'Umar fell to the ground. The certainty that the Prophet of God was truly dead shattered him. Beguiled by 'Umar's speech, the people listened to Abu Bakr's statement and to the Qur'anic verse as if it was given to them for the first time. They had forgotten that there was any such revelation. Abu Bakr's stark words dissipated all doubt and uncertainty. His Qur'anic quotation reassured the Muslims that their holding fast to God Who never dies would more than compensate for Muhammad's passing.

Further Thoughts on Muhammad's Death

Did 'Umar exaggerate when he convinced himself that Muhammad had not died, when he tried to cause the people to believe likewise? The answer must be in the negative. In like vein, men of science tell us that the sun will continue to rise in the morning until a certain day when it will explode and disappear. Does anyone of us accept such a claim without entertaining a doubt as to its validity and truth? Does not everyone of us ask himself, "How could the sun explode, disappear, and go away, the sun by whose light and warmth everything in the world lives? How could it explode and disappear and the world continue thereafter even for one day?" And yet, was the light of Muhammad any less brilliant than that of the sun or his warmth and power any less strong than those of the sun? The sun is source of much good. But was not Muhammad the source of as much and equal good? The sun stands in communion with all beings. But was not the soul of Muhammad equally in communion with all being? Does not his blessed memory still fill the whole universe with its grace and beauty? No wonder then that 'Umar was not convinced that Muhammad could have died, and in truth, in one sense Muhammad did not die and will not die.

Having seen him that morning when he went to the mosque and, like all other Muslims, having thought that the Prophet had recovered his health, Usamah ibn Zayd returned to al Jurf with those of his colleagues who had accompanied him to Madinah in search of reassuring news. He ordered the army to prepare to march to al Sham; but before the army proceeded forth, it heard the news of the Prophet's death. Usamah ordered the army to return to Madinah. He hung his command flag on the door of 'A'ishah's quarters and decided to wait until the Muslims recovered from their shock.

At Banu Sa'idah's Court

In fact, the Muslims were wondering which step to take. After hearing Abu Bakr and knowing for certain that Muhammad had died, they dispersed. Some of the al Ansar gathered around Sa'd ibn 'Ubadah in the courtyard of Banu Sa'idah. 'Ali ibn Abu Talib, al Zubayr ibn al 'Awwam, and Talhah ibn 'Ubaydullah gathered in the house of Fatimah; and al Muhajirun, together with the Usayd ibn Hudayr as well as Banu 'Abd al Ashhal, gathered around Abu Bakr. Soon a man came to Abu Bakr and 'Umar to inform them that al Ansar were gathering around Sa'd ibn 'Ubadah. The informant added that the two leaders should go out and reorganize Muslim leadership before the division of the Muslim community got any worse. Since the Prophet of God — May God's peace and blessing be upon him — was still laid out in his house and unburied, it was surely unbecoming that the Muslims begin to divide among themselves. 'Umar pleaded with Abu Bakr to go with him immediately to al Ansar and see what they were doing. On the way thither, they were met by two upright and trustworthy Ansar men who, when questioned, remarked that al Ansar were contemplating separatist ideas. When the two Ansar men questioned Abu Bakr and 'Umar in turn and learned from them that they were going to al Ansar's gathering, they advised them not to go but to try to settle the Muhajirun's own affairs. 'Umar was determined to go and Abu Bakr was not difficult to persuade on this point. They came to the courtyard of Banu Sa'idah and found that al Ansar had gathered around a man wrapped up in a blanket. 'Umar ibn al Khattab asked who the man was, and he was told that that was Sa'd ibn 'Ubadah suffering from a serious sickness. 'Umar and Abu Bakr, joined at this moment by a number of Muhajirun, took their seats in the assembly. Soon, a speaker rose and addressed al Ansar in the following words after praising God and thanking Him: "We are al Ansar — *i.e.,* the helpers of God and the army of Islam. You, the Muhajirun, are only a brigade in the army. Nonetheless, a group of you have gone to the extreme of seeking to deprive us of our natural leadership and to deny us our rights."

Actually, this complaint had always been on al Ansar's lips, even during the Prophet's lifetime. When 'Umar heard it being voiced again, he could hardly restrain himself. Indeed, he was ready to put an end to this situation once and for all by the sword, if needed. Fearing that harsh treatment might aggravate rather than improve matters, Abu Bakr held 'Umar back and asked him to act gently. He then turned to al Ansar, saying: "O men, we, the Muhajirun, were the first men to convert to Islam. We enjoy the noblest lineage and descendence. We are the most reputable and the best esteemed as well as the most numerous of any group in Arabia. Furthermore, we are the closest blood relatives of the Prophet. The Qur'an itself has given us preference. For it is God — May He be praised and blessed — Who said, 'First and foremost were al Muhajirun, then al Ansar, and then those who have followed these two groups in virtue and righteousness.'2 We were the first to emigrate for the sake of God, and you are literally 'al Ansar', i.e., the helpers. However, you are our brethren in religion, our partners in the fortunes of war, and our helpers against the enemy. All the good that you have claimed is truly yours, for you are the most worthy people of mankind. But the Arabs do not and will not recognize any sovereignty unless it belongs to the tribe of Quraysh. The princes shall be from among us, whereas your group will furnish the viziers." At this, a member of al Ansar became furious and said: "Rather am I, the experienced warrior! On my arm every verdict shall rest. And my verdict is that the people of Quraysh may have their prince as long as we, too, may have our own." Abu Bakr repeated his proposition that the princes of the Muslims must be of the Quraysh whereas their vizers must be of al Ansar. Taking the hand of 'Umar ibn al Khattab as well as that of Abu 'Ubaydah ibn al Jarrah, who were sitting on either side of him, Abu Bakr said, "Either one of these two men is acceptable to us as leader of the Muslim community. Choose whomsoever you please."

Nomination of Abu Bakr to the Caliphate

At that moment, all the men present began to talk at the same time, and the meeting itself was on the verge of disintegration. With his usual clear and loud voice, 'Umar said: "O Abu Bakr, stretch forth your hand and I will give you my oath of fealty. Did not the Prophet himself command you to lead the Muslims in prayer? You, therefore, are his successor.

We elect you to this position. In electing you, we are electing the best of all those whom the Prophet of God loved and trusted." 'Umar's words touched the hearts of the Muslims present, as they truly expressed the Prophet's will up to and including the last day of his life. On that day they had witnessed his insistence that Abu Bakr lead the prayer even in his presence. Thus, the difference between al Muhajirun and al Ansar was dissolved, and members of both camps came forward to give their oath of fealty.

Abu Bakr's Election

On the following day, as Abu Bakr took his place at the pulpit of the mosque, 'Umar ibn al Khattab rose before the congregation and said, after offering due praise to God: "Yesterday, I presented to you a novel idea. I drew it neither from the Book of God, nor from any memory I have of the Prophet of God. It just occurred to me that the Prophet of God would continue to lead us in this world forever and that he would survive us all. But now I know better. God has left us His Holy Book, the Repository of His Prophet's guidance. If we hold closely to it, God will surely guide us to the same felicity to which he guided His Prophet. God has consolidated you together under the leadership of the best man among you, of the companion of the Prophet of God — May God's peace and blessing be upon him — who was blessed by God with the honor of the Prophet's company in the cave when the Makkans were following in close pursuit. Rise and give him your oath of fealty." All the men rose and pledged their loyalty to Abu Bakr. That was the public bay'ah,[3] following the private bay'ah in the courtyard of Banu Sa'idah.

Inaugural Speech of the First "Rashidun" Caliph

Thereafter, Abu Bakr rose and delivered a speech which may be regarded as one of the most illustrious embodiments of wisdom and sound judgment. After thanking God and praising Him, Abu Bakr said:

"O Men! Here I have been assigned the job of being a ruler over you while I am not the best among you. If I do well in my job, help me. If I do wrong, redress me. Truthfulness is fidelity, and lying is treason. The weak shall be strong in my eyes until I restore to them their lost rights, and the strong shall be weak in my eye until I have restored the rights of the weak from them. No people give up fighting for the cause of God but God inflicts upon them abject subjection; and no people give themselves to lewdness but God envelops them with misery. Obey me as long as I obey God and His Prophet. But if I disobey God's command or His Prophet's, then no obedience is incumbent upon you. Rise to your prayer, that God may bless you."

The Quest for a Burial Site

Throughout the Muslims' disputing of the question of succession at the courtyard of Banu Sa'idah and in the mosque, the Prophet's remains were lying on his bed surrounded by his next of kin. After the election of Abu Bakr, the people came to the Prophet's house to prepare for his funeral and burial. There was disagreement as to where the Prophet was to be buried. Some Muhajirun advised that he ought to be buried in Makkah, his native town, in the proximity of his own relatives. Others advised that he ought to be buried in Jerusalem where the Prophets were buried before him. The latter was certainly a baffling view considering that Jerusalem was in the hands of the Byzantines, and the relations between them and the Muslims were most hostile, especially since the Mu'tah and Tabuk campaigns. Indeed, an army which the Prophet himself had mobilized and placed under the leadership of Usamah was supposed to fight them and avenge the Muslim defeat in those campaigns. At any rate, the proposals to bury the remains in Makkah or in Jerusalem were both rejected. The Muslims resolved to bury him in Madinah, the city which gave him shelter and assistance and which was the first one to raise the banner of Islam. Once this decision was made, they proceeded to look for a proper location for burial. Some advocated burial in the mosque where he used to address the people, preach the faith, and lead them in prayer. They thought that the most appropriate place was either the very spot of ground where the pulpit stood or the spot next to it. This opinion, however, did not meet with approval. 'A'ishah had related that in his last days, whenever his pain increased, the Prophet used to uncover his face to curse such people as had taken the grave of their prophets as places of worship. Abu Bakr solved the issue when he proclaimed that he had heard the Prophet say that prophets should be buried wherever they die. This opinion carried the day.

Preparing the Body for Burial

Washing the Prophet's body before burial was performed by his next of kin, by 'Ali ibn Abu Talib, al 'Abbas ibn 'Abd al Muttalib and his two sons, al Fadl and Qutham, as well as by Usamah ibn Zayd. Usamah ibn Zayd and Shuqran, the Prophet's client, poured the water while 'Ali washed the body, covered as it was by Muhammad's nightgown. It was decided that the Prophet's body should not, under any circumstance whatever, be fully exposed. As they performed their washing, contrary to what is usual in such cases, the body emitted beautiful smells, so that 'Ali said continually: "By God, what would I give for you! How sweet you are and how wholesome you are, both alive and dead!" Some western Orientalists sought to explain this fair scent emitted from the body of the Prophet by calling it the result of the perfume which he used so lavishly, remembering that he once declared it one of the good things he truly loved in this world. When the washing was completed, the Prophet's body was wrapped in three shrouds: two made in Suhar and the third in Hibarah in Yaman. When this operation was completed, the body was left where it was and the doors were flung open for the Muslims to enter from the mosque, to take a last look at their Prophet, and to pray for him.[4] Undoubtedly, they emerged deeply moved and conscious of their terrible bereavement.

The Funeral Prayer

The room was practically full when Abu Bakr and 'Umar entered the room and joined the Muslims in a funerary prayer for the Prophet. The prayer was performed without a leader. When it was over, Abu Bakr began to pray aloud, saying: "Peace, mercy, and blessings of God be upon you, O Prophet of God. We witness that the Prophet of God and His apostle conveyed the message entrusted to him by his Lord and that he exerted himself and fought in His cause until God gave victory to His religion. We equally witness that the Prophet of God and His apostle fully performed his promise and that he commanded us to worship none but God alone who has no associates." At the end of every phrase, the Muslims responded together, "Amen, Amen." When this prayer was complete, the men left and the women and children took turns taking a last look at the Prophet. One and all, every man, woman and child, emerged from that room torn with sorrow and crushed by a sense of bereavement for the loss of the Prophet of God, the Seal of His apostles. They were full of apprehension that some calamity might befall the religion of God in the future.

A Grave Moment of History

No man can today reconstruct this thirteen-centuries-old scene in his imagination without being filled with awe and reverence. The anguishing view of this body laid down in a corner of the room which was to become a grave the following day and which until the day before reverberated with Muhammad's vitality, mercy, and light, filled the hearts of the faithful mourners with apprehension. It could not have been otherwise. For, there lay the man who had called men to truth, to the path of righteousness and had struck for them the highest example of goodness, mercy, courage, chastity, purity, and justice. As the crowds of Muslims passed by his bier despondent, disheartened, and dispirited, every man, woman, and child among them saw in the body that lay motionless before him his own father, brother, friend, trustworthy companion, Prophet, and Apostle of God. To recall that hour is surely to reconstruct a pathetic scene. Even as he writes about it, this author is seized by the grip of its terror and can hardly overcome the consequent anguish.

Confusion of the Men of Little Faith

It was natural for the Muslims to be apprehensive of the future. Indeed, as soon as the news of the Prophet's death spread in Madinah and reached the Arab tribes in the surrounding area, Jews and Christians sprang to their feet, hypocrisy took a new lease on life, and the faith of many weak Arabs fell into confusion. The Makkans sought to abjure Islam, and they did so to the extent of instilling fear in 'Attab ibn Asid, their governor appointed by the Prophet to rule them. Suhayl ibn 'Amr, following the news of the Prophet's death, stood up in their midst and said: "The Prophet's death shall increase the power of Islam and strengthen it. Whoever attacks us or abjures our cause, we shall strike with the sword. O People of Makkah! you were the last to enter Islam. Do not, therefore, be the first to desert it. Have faith that God will bring you final victory just as the Prophet of God — May God's peace and blessing be upon him — has promised you." Only then did the Makkans change their minds.

The Prophet's Burial

The Arabs knew two ways of digging graves. The Makkans made their graves flat at the bottom while the Madinese made them curved. Abu 'Ubaydah ibn al Jarrah was the gravedigger for the Makkans, and Abu Talhah Zayd ibn Sahl was gravedigger for the Madinese. The Prophet's relatives could not choose between them. The Prophet's uncle, al 'Abbas, sent two men to call the two gravediggers for a consultation. Only one was found and could respond to the call, and that was Abu Talhah, the Madinese. He therefore was commissioned to dig a grave for the Prophet of God as he knew best. When evening came and the Muslims had taken leave of the body of their Prophet, Muhammad's relatives prepared for the burial. They waited until a quarter or a third of the night had passed before proceeding with the burial. In the grave, they spread out a red mantle that once belonged to the Prophet, and the men who had washed the body lowered it to its last repose. They built over it a bridge with bricks and then covered the grave with sand. 'A'ishah said: "We did not learn of the burial of the Prophet of God — May God's peace and blessing be upon him — until midnight or later"; and so did Fatimah report. The Prophet was buried on Tuesday night, 14th of Rabi' I, two days after his death, in the year 10 A.H.

'A'ishah and the Grave Room

'A'ishah lived thereafter in her quarters, next door to the Prophet's grave, contented with her proximity to this holy precinct. When Abu Bakr died, he was buried in the immediate vicinity of the Prophet's grave, as was 'Umar ibn al Khattab thereafter. It is related that 'A'ishah used to visit the grave room without veil until 'Umar was buried therein, i.e., during the time it contained only the grave of her father and husband. But after 'Umar's burial, she entered the room only when fully veiled.

Expediting Usamah's Army on Its March

As soon as the burial of the Prophet was completed, Abu Bakr commanded that the army of Usamah begin its march on al Sham in execution of the commandment the Prophet of God had issued in his last days. Some Muslims objected to this measure just as they had during the sickness of Muhammad. 'Umar joined the ranks of these objectors on the grounds that the Muslim forces ought not to be dispersed in this grave hour. Abu Bakr, however, did not hesitate to follow the commandment left unfulfilled by the Prophet at his death. He refused to give credit to those who counseled that an older and more experienced general in war than Usamah be appointed to lead that army. Al Jurf remained the rallying place for the army, and Usamah remained its leading general. Abu Bakr went out in person to see the army off on its march. It was there that Abu Bakr asked Usamah to absolve 'Umar ibn al Khattab from his duty to go forth in the army so that he might remain in Madinah in close proximity to Abu Bakr who needed his advice in his first days of administration. Twenty days after the army began its march northward, the Muslims launched their attack against al Balqa' and avenged the Muslims' setback in Mu'tah where Usamah's father fell under Byzantine arms. The war cry in that campaign was "O Victor! Give death to the enemy!" Thus Abu Bakr and Usamah fulfilled the commandment of the Prophet, and the army returned to Madinah victorious. Usamah was at its head, riding the very horse on which his father died at the Battle of Mu'tah, and carrying high the banner which the Prophet of God had entrusted to him in person.

Prophets Leave No Inheritance

After the death of the Prophet, his daughter Fatimah asked Abu Bakr to return to her the land the Prophet kept for himself at Fadak and Khaybar. Abu Bakr, however, answered her by quoting her father's words: "We, the Prophets, do not leave any inheritance for anyone. Whatever we do leave shall be given out in charity." Continuing with his own words, Abu Bakr said: "However, if it was the case that your father had made a grant to you of this property, then I shall certainly honor your word to this effect and fulfill for you his commandment." At this, Fatimah answered that her father had not made any such grant to her at all, but that Umm Ayman had informed her that that might have been Muhammad's purpose. Abu Bakr therefore resolved that the lands of Fadak and Khaybar should be kept by the public treasury of the Muslims as state domain.

Muhammad's Great Spiritual Legacy

Thus Muhammad left this world just as he had entered, without material shackles. His only inheritance left to mankind was the religion of truth and goodness. He had paved the ground and laid the foundation for the great civilization of Islam which had covered the world in the past and would cover the world in the future. It was a civilization in which *tawhid*, or the unitization of God, was the cornerstone; and an order in which the word of God and His commandments are always uppermost, while those of unfaith are nethermost. It was a civilization purged absolutely clean of all paganism and of all idolatrous forms and expressions, a civilization in which men were called upon to cooperate with one another for the good and moral felicity of all men, not for the benefit of any group or people. Muhammad left to this world the Book of God, a guidance and mercy to mankind, while the memory of his own life gave the highest and noblest example for man's emulation. One of the last sermons which the Prophet delivered to the people during his illness contained the following words: "O Men! If I have lashed the back of anyone, let him come forward and lash my back in return. If I have insulted anyone, let him come forth and take satisfaction of me. If I have dispossessed anyone of any wealth, let him come forth and seize his wealth from me. If there be any such men as these, let them come forth without fear of retaliation or hatred, for neither of these become of me." Only one man came forth to make a claim, that Muhammad owed him three dirhams; he was paid in full by Muhammad on his deathbed. The Prophet left this world an inheritance of a great spiritual legacy whose light continues to illumine the world and will continue to illumine the world until God completely fulfills His promise and gives victory to His religion over all the religions despite all unbelievers. May God's peace and blessing be upon Muhammad!

Conclusion
in Two Essays

1

Islamic Civilization as Depicted in the Qur'an

Islamic and Western Civilizations

Muhammad left a great spiritual legacy which enveloped the world in its light and guided man's civilization throughout many centuries, a legacy which will envelop the world again and guide man's civilization once more until the light of God has filled the universe. The legacy of Muhammad had such great effect in the past and will have great or greater effect in the future precisely because Muhammad established the religion of truth and laid the foundation of the only civilization which guarantees the happiness and felicity of man. The religion which Muhammad conveyed and the civilization which he established at his Lord's command for the benefit of mankind are inseparable from each other. Islamic civilization has been raised on a foundation of science and rationalism, and that is the same foundation on which western civilization of today is based. Moreover, Islam as a religion has based itself on personalist thinking and intentional logic. The relation between religion and its propositions on the one hand, and civilization and its foundation on the other, is binding and firm. Islam links metaphysical thought and personal feelings with the rules of logic and the precepts of science, with a bond that all Muslims must discover and grasp if they are to remain Muslims. From this aspect, the civilization of Islam is radically different from that of western civilization which dominates the world today. The two are different in their description of life as well as the foundation on which they base such

503

description. The difference between the two civilizations is so essential that they have developed in ways which are radically contradictory to each other.

The West and the Struggle between Church and State

The difference is due to a number of historical causes to which we have alluded in the prefaces to the first and second editions of this work. In western Christendom, the continuing struggle between the religious and secular powers, or — to use the contemporary idiom — between church and state, led to their separation and to the establishment of the state upon the denial of the power of the church. The struggle to which this will to power led has left deep effects upon the whole of western thought. The first of these effects was the separation of human feeling and reasoning from the logic of absolute reason and the findings of positive science based on sensory observation and evidence.

The Economic System as Foundation of Western Civilization

The victory of materialist thinking was largely due to the establishment of western civilization primarily upon an economic foundation. This situation led to the rise in the West of a number of world views which sought to place everything in the life of man and the world at the mercy of economic forces. Many an author in the West sought to explain the whole history of mankind — religious, esthetic, philosophic or scientific — in terms of the waves of progress or retrogression which constitute the economic history of the various peoples. Not only has this thinking pervaded historiography; it has even reached philosophy. A number of western philosophies have sought to found the laws and principles of morality on bases of pragmatism and utilitarianism. As a result of this fixation of thought in the West, all these theories, despite their perspicacity and originality, have been limited in scope to the realm of material benefits. In other words, all the laws of morality were based on a material foundation and in satisfaction of what was regarded as a necessary consequence of scientific research and evidence. As for the spiritual aspect, western civilization regarded it as purely individual, rationally incapable of being the object of any group consideration. From this followed the absolute freedom of belief which the West has sanctified. The West has honored the freedom of belief far more than it has the freedom of morals; and it has honored the freedom of morals far more than the freedom of economic activity. The latter it has tied hand and foot by public laws, and commanded that every western state and army prevent any violation of economic laws with all the power and coercive means at its disposal.

Incapacity of Western Civilization to Bring Happiness to Man

In this author's opinion, a civilization which founds itself upon economic activity and erects its moral system on that activity as a base, and yet gives no weight in public life to faith, is incapable of achieving for mankind the happiness that men seek. Indeed, a civilization which so regards human life is bound to bring upon mankind all the calamities which have befallen our world in the recent centuries. Under its aegis, any attempt to prevent war and to establish universal peace will prove futile and vain. As long as man's relation to man is based upon the loaf of bread and the struggle which man wages against his fellows in order to get it for himself, a struggle the success of which depends upon the animal power which each one of us can marshal for the purpose, it is indubitable that every man will watch for the best occasion to cheat his fellow out of his loaf of bread. Every man will regard his fellow man as his enemy rather than his brother; and personal morality will have nothing but the animal in us on which to stand. This is true though man's animality may remain hidden until need uncovers it, for only utility is consonant with such a moral foundation. Charity, altruism, love, brotherhood — in short, all the principles of nobler morality and the values of higher humanity — will forever pass over a consciousness disciplined by such a civilization just as water passes off the back of a duck.

The actualities of the contemporary world furnish empirical evidence for my claim. Competition and struggle are the first principles of the economic system and are the most salient characteristics of western civilization. This is the case regardless of whether the system is individualistic or socialistic. In the former, the worker competes with his fellow worker, the capitalist with his fellow capitalist, and worker and capitalist are committed enemies of each other. The devotees of this view regard struggle and competition as the forces of man's good and progress. They regard these forces as the source of motivation for the pursuit of perfection and the division of labor, as well as for a just criterion for the distribution of wealth. The socialist system, on the other hand, sees in the struggle between the classes a means to destroy those classes and bring the destiny

of society under control of the workers. This system is regarded by socialism as the necessary logic of nature. But as long as struggle and competition for wealth are the essence of life, and as long as class struggle is the
law of nature, then it is equally the law of nature that the nations of the
world struggle and prey upon one another in order to realize their purposes. Nationalism thus arose as a necessary consequence to this economic
anthropology. But if it is natural for the nations to struggle and compete
with one another for wealth, and if colonialism is a natural consequence
of this necessary system, how are wars ever to be avoided and how is peace
ever to be achieved? In this Christian twentieth century we have witnessed
sufficient evidence to convince anyone that a world founded upon such a
civilization may dream of, but never realize, peace. Because of it, peace will
forever be a false mirage and an impossible desideratum.

The Groundwork of Islamic Civilization

Unlike western civilization, the civilization of Islam is built upon a
spiritual base in which man is first and foremost called upon to recognize
ultimate reality and to realize his position in the world with regard to that
reality. Whenever man's consciousness of this relation reaches the point of
certainty and conviction, that conviction will demand of him ever to discipline himself, to cleanse his soul, and to nourish his heart as well as his
mind with the sublime principles of magnanimity, contentment, brotherhood, love, charity, and piety. On the basis of such principles man will
then organize his economic life. Such progression is the foundation of
Islamic civilization as the revelation of Muhammad conceived it. It is first
and foremost a spiritual civilization. In it, the spiritual order constitutes
the groundwork of the system of education, of personal and social morality. The principles constituting the moral order in turn constitute the
groundwork of the economic system. It is therefore not permissible in this
civilization that any moral principle be sacrificed for the sake of the economic system.

In this author's opinion, it is this conception peculiar to Islamic civilization that is capable of bringing mankind to a sure realization of happiness and felicity. Should it ever become firmly established in the minds
of men, and should it come to dominate this world as western civilization
has come to dominate it today, mankind will lead a different life. The current ideologies will be washed away, and nobler moral principles will take
over the solution of the chronic crises of the present world. In both East

and West, men have been trying to find solutions to these crises without anyone's realizing — not excluding the Muslims themselves — that Islam offers to them certain and guaranteed solutions. The western people are today groping for a new spiritual seriousness which might save them from the paganism in which they have allowed themselves to fall and from the worship of wealth which has been at the root of their misery and interminable wars. The western peoples are seeking to discover this new spiritual seriousness in the religions of India and the Far East, when it has been right here close to them all the time, established once and for all, and clearly elaborated in the Qur'an, as well as given its highest exemplification in the life and sayings of the Prophet Muhammad.

It is not my intention to predict here the role of Islamic civilization or to analyze its system. Such work would by itself occupy a volume of this size or even larger. But I do think it imperative to characterize that civilization in general now that I have pointed to the spiritual basis on which it stands. Therefore, I hope to give an idea of the nature of Muhammad's call and thereby to pave the road for further and more complete research and study.

No Competition between Church and State in Islam

Before I do this, however, it behooves me to point to the fact that the history of Islam has been free of any struggle between religious and secular authorities, that is, between church and state. This fact has protected Islamic history from the effects that struggle has left upon western thought. This salutary influence upon Islam and upon its history and thought is primarily due to the fact that it has never known anything called church or religious authority along the lines of Christianity. No Muslim, even if he should be a caliph, has any right to impose anything in the name of Islam. He can neither forgive nor punish any violation of such commandments imposed in the name of religion. Moreover, no Muslim may, even if he should be a caliph, impose upon the people anything other than that which God imposed in His Book. Indeed, in front of God, all Muslims are equal; none may be distinguished from the others except in virtue and piety. No ruler in Islam is entitled to the Muslim's obedience in a matter involving a violation of a divine commandment, or of that which has not been expressly commanded by God. We should recall here the inaugural speech of Abu Bakr following his election to the caliphate: "Obey me as long as I obey God and His Prophet. But if I disobey God's command or His Prophet's, then no obedience is incumbent upon you." Despite all the crass exercises of the will to political power and all the civil wars and rebellions which the history of the Islamic state has witnessed, the Muslims have remained true to this great personal freedom which their religion had established for them. Theirs has always been a freedom which assigned to reason the role of judge in everything, whether in religion or in the matter of conviction and faith itself. The Muslims have held strongly to this freedom even in the face of those kings and princes who claimed that they were the lieutenants of God on earth, not of His Prophet, and who wielded in their hands the keys of life and death. Witness the turbulent events during the reign of al Ma'mun when the issue was whether or not the Qur'an was created. The caliph believed one thing, but the Muslims differed from him despite the certainty of the punishment and wrath that awaited them.

Islam Makes Reason the Final Judge

Islam made reason the judge in everything, whether in religion or in conviction and faith itself. God said: "And the case of those who disbelieve is like that of a person who hears the sound of a call but who does not distinguish any word or idea. To talk to them is like talking to the deaf, dumb, and blind. Those who disbelieve simply do not use their reason and neither do they understand."[1] Commenting on this verse, Shaykh Muhammad 'Abduh wrote: "This verse clearly asserts that taqlid[2] without reason or guidance is the prerogative of the disbelievers, that man is not a convinced Muslim unless he has reasoned out his religion, known it in person, and become personally convinced of its truth and validity. Whoever, therefore, has been brought up so as to acquiesce without reason and to act without knowledge and wisdom — even though he may be virtuous — is not a convinced Muslim. Religious conviction does not have for its purpose the subjugation of man to the good as if he were an animal. Rather, its purpose is that man may, by the use of reason and the pursuit of knowledge, rise to the level where he will do the good because he fully knows that it is in itself good and acceptable to God, and avoid the evil because he fully knows its undesirable consequence and harm."

The foregoing claims of Shaykh Muhammad 'Abduh given in exegesis of this verse are all to be found in the Qur'an itself in a number of other verses. The Qur'an has called upon men to look into the universe and to discover its construction and structure. It commanded men to do so in the conviction that their investigation of the structure of the universe would lead them to the discovery of God as well as of His unicity — May He be adored! God — to Whom is the praise — says: "In the creation of heaven and earth, in the succession of day and night, in the phenomena of the ships sailing across the seas with goods "for the welfare of men, in the fall of rain water from heaven to quicken a dead earth, in populating the earth with all species of animals, in the ordering of winds and clouds between sky and earth — in all these there are signs and pieces of evidence for men who reason."[3] Further, God says:

وَ اٰيَةٌ لَّهُمُ الْاَرْضُ الْمَيْتَةُ ۚ اَحْيَيْنٰهَا وَ اَخْرَجْنَا مِنْهَا حَبًّا فَمِنْهُ يَأْكُلُوْنَ ۞ وَجَعَلْنَا فِيْهَا جَنّٰتٍ مِّنْ نَّخِيْلٍ وَّاَعْنَابٍ وَّفَجَّرْنَا فِيْهَا مِنَ الْعُيُوْنِ ۙ لِيَأْكُلُوْا مِنْ ثَمَرِهٖ ۙ وَمَا عَمِلَتْهُ اَيْدِيْهِمْ اَفَلَا يَشْكُرُوْنَ ۞ سُبْحٰنَ الَّذِيْ خَلَقَ الْاَزْوَاجَ كُلَّهَا مِمَّا تُنْۢبِتُ الْاَرْضُ وَمِنْ اَنْفُسِهِمْ وَمِمَّا لَا يَعْلَمُوْنَ ۞ وَاٰيَةٌ لَّهُمُ الَّيْلُ ۚ نَسْلَخُ مِنْهُ النَّهَارَ فَاِذَا هُمْ مُّظْلِمُوْنَ ۞ وَالشَّمْسُ تَجْرِيْ لِمُسْتَقَرٍّ لَّهَا ۚ ذٰلِكَ تَقْدِيْرُ الْعَزِيْزِ الْعَلِيْمِ ۞ وَالْقَمَرَ قَدَّرْنٰهُ مَنَازِلَ حَتّٰى عَادَ كَالْعُرْجُوْنِ الْقَدِيْمِ ۞ لَا الشَّمْسُ يَنْۢبَغِيْ لَهَآ اَنْ تُدْرِكَ الْقَمَرَ وَلَا الَّيْلُ سَابِقُ النَّهَارِ ۚ وَكُلٌّ فِيْ فَلَكٍ يَسْبَحُوْنَ ۞ وَاٰيَةٌ لَّهُمْ اَنَّا حَمَلْنَا ذُرِّيَّتَهُمْ فِي الْفُلْكِ الْمَشْحُوْنِ ۞ وَخَلَقْنَا لَهُمْ مِّنْ مِّثْلِهٖ مَا يَرْكَبُوْنَ ۞ وَاِنْ نَّشَأْ نُغْرِقْهُمْ فَلَا صَرِيْخَ لَهُمْ وَلَا هُمْ يُنْقَذُوْنَ ۙ اِلَّا رَحْمَةً مِّنَّا وَمَتَاعًا اِلٰى حِيْنٍ ۞

"Our signs and pieces of evidence which We have presented to man are the phenomena of a dead earth quickened and caused to give forth grain, gardens of date trees and vines, and fountains of fresh water with which We have covered the earth that man may eat and drink his fill. All these are not merely the work of man's hands; but will men not feel grateful? Will they not give thanks to God, saying, 'Praise be to God Who created from earth and from that which grows and remains hidden in the earth all the creatures that live in pairs, and all that they procreate of themselves.' Of our signs and evidence are the phenomena of night from which We cut off all light, causing man to stand in darkness; of the sun which runs in its orbit, an orbit well defined by the All-Knowing and Almighty; of the moon for which We have appointed various stages of growth and decline until it appears as an old shriveled tree branch. It is of Our signs and evidence that neither sun overtakes the moon nor night overtakes the day but that each runs in a well-defined and ordered course.

As further signs and clearer evidence, We have made it possible for laden ships to sail across the seas carrying men and their offspring. Were it not for divine providence, men would fall into the sea, no one would hear their cries, and they would perish. They are saved only by Our mercy. We wish them to enjoy their pleasures for a prescribed time."[4]

Indeed, the call to look into the universe to discover its laws and to arrive at the conviction that God is its creator is repeated a hundred times in the various *Surahs* of the Qur'an. All these Qur'anic invitations are directed to man's rational faculties in the expectation that he will consider, search for and discover the truth, so that his religious conviction might be rational and truly supported by the facts. The Qur'an constantly warns its readers not to adopt uncritically and blindly the ideas and principles of the forefathers, but to have faith in man's personal capacity to reach the truth.

The Power of *Iman*

Such is the nature of *iman,* or religious conviction, to which Islam has called. It has nothing to do with blind faith. Instead, it is involved with the conviction of the enlightened mind, the instructed reason which has considered and weighed the alternatives, pondered and reconsidered the evidence on all sides, researched and rediscovered and finally reached the certainty that God — May He be adored — is. Surely any man who considers the evidence with both heart and reason will be guided to religious conviction. Indeed, the more closely a man looks at the evidence, the longer he contemplates and the larger his scope of investigation becomes so that his awareness considers the whole of time, space, and all the eternally changing universes which they include, the more he will be convinced of his littleness *vis-a-vis* the well patterned, well-ordered, and well-governed worlds, of the shortcoming of his knowledge to grasp them or to enter him into meaningful relation to them without the assistance of a power surpassing his senses and reason, the more capable he will become of defining his place within the total realm of being. All this is the precondition of his entering into relation with the universe and of his encompassing with his consciousness and vision the whole of being. This enlarged vision is the strength given by religious conviction alone.

Iman in God

Iman, or religious conviction, then, is a spiritual intuition by which man's consciousness is filled whenever it seeks the universe and realizes that the infinity of space and time is unreachable, and whenever it seeks to encompass all being within itself, realizing that every species in existence lives, changes, and dies in accordance with laws and patterns, and that all existence realizes the divine pattern and fulfills the cosmic laws of its Lord and Creator. To look for God — May He be adored — as immanent in all existence and in contact with it, rather than as absolutely separate from it, is a futile search leading to error rather than to truth, harming rather than blessing the investigator. Moreover, it does not add to man's knowledge. Writers and philosophers have often exhausted themselves seeking evidence for God's immanence without avail, while others have sought to grasp the essence of the Creator Himself — all to no purpose. Some writers and philosophers have acknowledged that the success of such searches are forever impossible.

But if our reason falls short of achieving such knowledge, that very shortcoming can be the source of a greater realization, namely, the certain religious knowledge of God. This certitude of ours that God exists, that He knows, provides for, and governs everything, that He is the Creator, the Forgiver unto Whom everything returns, can also convince us that it cannot ever be possible for us to know the nature of God Himself. If to this day we do not understand the nature of electricity, even though our very eyes have seen its effects, nor the nature of ether, though we grant that its waves or quanta carry sound and light, how vain it is not to accept the existence of God when we constantly behold His original creations and effects, or to go about denying Him until we can know His very nature! God is transcendentally beyond anything anyone may say in description of Him. As a matter of fact, those who try to describe God under one form or another are precisely those whose consciousness is incapable of rising to the level requisite for grasping that which lies beyond human life. It is they who should be accused of seeking to measure being and the Creator of being with their own relative standards gathered from their own little knowledge of being. On the other hand, those who have true knowledge and wisdom will pause at these divine statements: "And when they ask you concerning the Spirit, answer, 'The Spirit belongs to God.' Given the little knowledge that you have, your minds must fall short of understanding its nature."[5] The consciousness of such men becomes filled with certitude and conviction regarding the Creator of the Spirit, the Maker of the whole universe. They do not allow themselves to become involved in futile and vain controversy.

Iman, the Basis of Islam

The Qur'an differentiates between conversion to Islam before or after such religious certitude and conviction. God says, "Some Arabs of the desert claimed that they have achieved religious conviction. Say, 'You have not achieved such conviction; you have been converted to Islam and have acquiesced in it, but religious certitude and conviction have not yet found their way to your heart and consciousness.'"[6] Such Islamization is an acquiescence arising from the call of ulterior motive, desire, fear, admiration, or reverence. It is not the acceptance by a consciousness which has understood and known full well that it has reached certitude and conviction. The subject of such Islamization has not been guided to his conviction through examination of the universe, grasping of its laws and patterns, and the movement of his thought from that knowledge to the recognition of the Creator of the universe. It is rather the acquiescence of a man in satisfaction of an ignoble desire or in blind imitation of his parents or community. Thus, religious conviction and certitude have not entered into his heart despite his acquiescence to Islam.

Many such Muslims exist who seek to cheat God and the true Muslims, but they succeed in cheating only themselves, little do they know. Their hearts are diseased, and their disease blinds their minds still further. Those men who convert to Islam without religious conviction but because of an ulterior motive, desire or fear, continue to have weak souls throughout their lives. Their faith remains doubtful, their commitment shaky, and their wills ever ready to submit to men upon command. On the other hand, those whose minds and hearts have reached conviction of God by means of investigation of the universe possess a genuine conviction which calls them to submit to God alone, to none other than Him. Neither do such men think of their Islam as a favor they have granted to anyone. "Rather, God grants you the favor of guiding you to religious conviction if only you are genuine."[7] Whoever, therefore, in conviction of God's existence and Lordship over the universe, opens himself to determination by Him alone, has reason neither to fear nor to grieve. Such men fear neither poverty nor humiliation in this world because religious certitude is the greatest wealth and the greatest glory. Glory does indeed belong to God and to the true believers who are contented and certain of their faith.

The soul which is happy and contented with such *iman* finds its fulfillment only in the search for the secrets of the world, the laws of the cosmos, and the pattern of the universe — all to the end that it may consolidate its communion with God. The means it employs for its search is scientific investigation, rational analysis, and consideration of all that is in creation. That is precisely what the Qur'an calls for and what the early Muslims practiced. That is the scientific method currently pursued in the West. The purpose of such pursuit, however, differs in Islam from western civilization. In the former, its purpose is to enable man to make the pattern of God in the universe the law and pattern of his own existence. In the latter, the purpose is to exploit the knowledge of cosmic laws for the material benefit of man. The foremost purpose of science in Islam is the achievement of firm and certain knowledge of God, a knowledge which strengthens man's conviction of Him — May He be adored — by its own comprehensiveness and certainty. Equally, it is a pursuit which seeks to achieve such better knowledge not for the individual alone but for the community as a whole. Spiritual perfection is not merely an individualistic matter, but rather the very foundation of the human community throughout the world. Islam therefore regards the pursuit of knowledge and understanding of the universe as a human duty, a duty incumbent upon all men as individuals as well as groups. Mankind must therefore seek this spiritual perfection even more conscientiously and systemically than it has sought to understand the nature of material things, and it ought to use the secrets of the material world and the laws and pattern of the universe as a means to attain spiritual perfection rather than as a means for achieving material mastery over things.

Divine Assistance to Discover the Pattern of the Universe

In order to attain this spiritual perfection, it is not sufficient to rely upon our own formal logic. Having reached the highest level possible through that logic, it is necessary to prepare our own hearts and minds for what lies beyond. This is possible by seeking God's assistance and by turning one's heart and soul toward the divine Being. By worshipping Him and asking for His assistance it is possible, once the highest levels of logic have been reached, to discover the secrets of the universe and the patterns of existence. This process is what is meant by communion with God, by gratitude for His blessings, and by prayer to Him for further guidance. God said:

وَإِذَا سَأَلَكَ عِبَادِى عَنِّى فَإِنِّى قَرِيبٌ أُجِيبُ دَعْوَةَ الدَّاعِ إِذَا دَعَانِ فَلْيَسْتَجِيبُوا لِى وَ
لْيُؤْمِنُوا بِى لَعَلَّهُمْ يَرْشُدُونَ

"And if My servants ask you of Me, tell them that I am near and that I respond to the caller who calls upon Me. Tell them then to pray to Me, to believe in Me. That is the way to wisdom."[8]

He also said: "Seek further assistance by patience and prayer. The latter overtaxes none but the irreverent and the proud. It is a force of genuine assistance for those who know that they will someday confront their Lord and that to Him they shall finally return."[9]

Nature of Islamic Prayer

Prayer, then, is communion with God in the certitude that He exists and is receptive to a solicitation for His assistance. Its purpose is not the bodily movements of kneeling and prostration nor the verbal recitation of the Qur'an, not the prescribed *takbir* and *ta'zim*.[10] Rather, it is meant to fill the soul with *iman* and the heart with reverence and recognition of God's holiness. Every element in the Muslim's prayer is designed to achieve this dual purpose. It is the worship of God for the sole sake of God, the recognition of God's face as the light of heaven and earth. He — May He be adored — said:

لَيْسَ الْبِرَّ أَنْ تُوَلُّوا وُجُوهَكُمْ قِبَلَ الْمَشْرِقِ وَالْمَغْرِبِ وَلَكِنَّ الْبِرَّ مَنْ آمَنَ بِاللَّهِ وَ
الْيَوْمِ الْآخِرِ وَالْمَلَائِكَةِ وَالْكِتَابِ وَالنَّبِيِّينَ وَآتَى الْمَالَ عَلَى حُبِّهِ ذَوِى الْقُرْبَى وَالْيَتَامَى
وَفِى الرِّقَابِ وَأَقَامَ الصَّلَاةَ وَآتَى الزَّكَاةَ وَالْمُوفُونَ بِعَهْدِهِمْ وَالْمَسَاكِينَ وَابْنَ السَّبِيلِ وَ
السَّائِلِينَ إِذَا عَاهَدُوا وَالصَّابِرِينَ فِى الْبَأْسَاءِ وَالضَّرَّاءِ وَحِينَ الْبَأْسِ أُولَئِكَ الَّذِينَ صَدَقُوا
وَأُولَئِكَ هُمُ الْمُتَّقُونَ

"Righteousness does not consist in your turning your faces toward east or west. Instead, it involves *iman* in God, in the Day of Judgment, in the Book, in the prophets, and spending of one's wealth out of love of Him for the welfare of the relative, the orphan, the deprived, the wayfarer, the poor, and for ransoming the captive. Righteousness also consists of the holding of prayer, the paying of *zakat*, the fulfillment of promises and covenants made, patience in good or ill, and steadfastness in war. Those who fulfill these values are the genuine in faith; they are the pious, the righteous."[11]

The man with genuine *iman*, therefore, is the man who turns with his whole heart to God in prayer, making God the witness of his own piety. It is he who implores His help in the fulfillment of the duties of life, solicits His guidance and blessing in his search for the secrets of the world and for the laws and pattern of the cosmos during his prayer as well as at any other time.

Hence, the Muslim is fully conscious of his insignificance before almighty God on high. We are capable of achieving such a view of the earth's insignificance when we ascend in an airplane a few thousand meters into the sky and begin to see the mountains, rivers, and cities as small marks upon a vast canvas. We see them delineated in front of our eyes as if they were mere lines on a map made out of paper. The earth looks flat; mountains and buildings lose their elevation, and wells and rivers their depression. The whole appears to be no more than patches of color moving and waving and intermingling with one another the higher we ascend into space. Our very earth is only a little planet among thousands of other heavenly bodies and systems, and these are only a very small pocket in the infinite magnitude of being. How small and little we therefore are! How weak and insignificant in relation to the Creator of all this being and to its Ruler and Provider whose very greatness stands beyond our grasp!

Equality before God

How worthy we are when we turn our heart to His sublime holiness and majesty, soliciting Him to strengthen us and guide us to the truth to realize the profound equality which characterizes all men in such weakness! How inevitable is then our realization of the absolute equality of mankind, an equality impervious to any amount of wealth or power achievable on earth, but deeply transformable by *iman* in God, by submission to Him, by righteousness, virtue, and piety! What a tremendous distance separates this kind of equality, this genuine equality before God, from equality before the law of man which western civilization has recently been professing so loudly! Indeed, western civilization is not far from denying equality before the law when its people deny the privileges of such equality to this or that group of men. How unlike each other are the two egalitarianisms! On the one hand is the equality before God, touched and held most concretely in the hour of prayer and reached by each man deliberately in the exercise of his own mind and free thought. On the other hand, we have an equality before the law, achieved in the struggle and competition for the acquisition of wealth. By definition, equality before the law does not rule out cheating, hypocrisy, and untruth; and it allows the culprit to escape the jurisdiction of the law if he is only creative enough to find ways and means of outwitting the legislator, the judge, or his own victim.

On the other hand, equality before God calls for genuine fraternity and brotherhood because it imposes upon all a realization of their fraternity in service to God and in the worship of the One Master. Such brotherhood is based on conscientious evaluation of the fact, free investigation, and critical research, all imposed by the Qur'an. Surely, no liberty, no equality, and no fraternity are greater than this one, where all men stand in front of God in one line prostrating their heads to Him, acknowledging His transcendence and unity, and kneeling and praying to Him without the slightest distinction between one and the other. No equality is greater than that which belongs to such a community whose every member actually seeks divine assistance in repentance and awe, asking for forgiveness and mercy, without any distinction whatever to differentiate the one from his fellowmen except his virtuous actions, his righteousness and piety. This kind of fraternity and equality purifies the hearts of men and cleanses them from the stain of matter. This condition alone guarantees happiness to mankind and leads it to certain knowledge of God's pattern in the world as long as God Himself is willing to lead men with His own light.

Nature of Islamic Fasting

Men are not all equal in their capacities to fulfill the piety and virtue which God has made incumbent upon them. Our bodies may weigh down our spirits so as to make them incapable of moving and rising toward

God. Our will to material need and welfare may overcome our humanity unless we keep up the exercise of our spirit and constantly turn to God in our prayers rather than being satisfied with the mechanical performance of kneeling, prostration, and recitation. Hence it is our duty wherever possible to stop all activities which tend to weigh us down, to shackle our spirit, or to give dominance to our material welfare over our humanity. Hence, Islam imposed fasting as a means for achieving virtue and piety. God has said: "O Men who believe, fasting has been imposed upon you as it has been imposed on those that have gone before you that you may achieve virtue and piety."[12] Piety, virtue, and righteousness are all equivalent. The righteous are those who are pious, who prove their *iman* in God on the Day of Judgment, and who, by following the angels, the Book and the prophets, fulfill the requisites of the above-mentioned verses.

But if the purpose of fasting is that the body may not weigh down the spirit and that matter may not overcome humanity, to abstain from food and drink from dawn till sunset and then to indulge in the enjoyment of all kinds of pleasures is surely to deny that purpose. Indulgence in pleasures is by itself immoral and vicious, regardless of whether it is preceded by fasting or not. The case is even worse if man fasts all day and then surrenders himself greedily to that of which he has been deprived. Such conduct is tantamount to bringing God to witness that the fast was not made in purification of the body and strengthening of humanity. Such a man does not fast in freedom, convinced of the advantage of fasting for his spiritual life, but in order to fulfill a duty, the meaning of which his mind is incapable of grasping. More likely, he regards fasting as a privation and a violation of the freedom which he will recapture at the end of the day. His case is not unlike that of the person who does not steal because the law forbids him to, not because he regards himself above stealing and denies it to himself as well as to others, in full exercise of his freedom.

Fasting Is Not Self-Privation

In fact, to regard fasting as privation, or as an attack upon man's liberty, is to misunderstand it and to make of it something utterly futile and vain. The truth is that fasting is a purification of the soul. It is demanded by reason and should be entered into freely if man is to recapture his freedom of willing and thinking which his material demands have denied or lessened. Once such freedom is gained, man may rise to the level of genuine *iman* in God. This is the purpose of the divine statement which fol-

lows the imposition of fasting upon men of faith of past or present, namely: "Fasting is to be performed on prescribed and numbered days. But if a
man is ill or suffers from the hardships of travel, fasting may be postponed
to other days. To those who are exempted from fasting because of hardship, the feeding of a poor man is imposed as expiation. At any rate, whoever willingly performs the good deed will be benefited. To fast is certainly better for you than not to fast, if only you had the wisdom to know."[13]

It may seem strange to claim that a person can recapture his freedom
of will and freedom of thinking if he should undertake to fast in deliberate pursuit of his spiritual welfare. But this strangeness is really the result
of a confusion which modern thought has brought to our idea of freedom.
Modern thought has pulled down the spiritual and psychic frontiers of
freedom, and preserved only its material frontiers whose guardianship and
protection it entrusted to the arms of the law. According to this modern
thinking, man is not free to attack the wealth of his neighbor nor his person, but he is free in all that pertains to his own person even if he were to
transgress the limits of reason or of morality.

The facts of life tell otherwise. They tell that man is the slave of habit;
that, for instance, man is accustomed to eat his food in the morning, at
noon, and in the evening. Therefore, his being asked to eat food only in
the morning and evening is considered an attack upon his freedom. The
truth is that it is only an attack upon his enslavement to his habit, so to
speak. Some men accustom themselves to smoking so heavily that they
can very well be said to have become the slaves of their habit. If they are
asked to spend an entire day without smoking, it will be regarded as an
attack upon their freedom, whereas in fact it is only an attack upon their
enslavement to their habit. Likewise, others have accustomed themselves
to drinking coffee or tea or other drinks at certain times. If they are asked
to change these times, it will be regarded as an attack upon their freedom.
But slavery to habit and custom is corruptive of the will, of the genuine
exercise of true freedom. Moreover, it is corruptive of sane thinking, for it
subjugates thinking to the material requirements to which the body has
become accustomed. That is why many people have had recourse to varying kinds of fasting which they observe at different intervals of the week
or the month. But God seeks no hardship for men. That is why He prescribed for them a definite number of days during which all men must fast
without distinction. That is why He allowed them to expiate for their failure to fast, and granted the sick and the traveler express permission to
postpone their fasting to other days.

The prescription of fasting for a definite number of days further consolidates the Muslim's feeling for and consciousness of equality with other men before God. This is the effect of complete abstinence from dawn to sunset undertaken not as physical but as spiritual exercise imposed equally on all. The same sense of equality is experienced in the communal fasting as that which communal prayer fosters so well. It is during their fast that the feeling of Muslim fraternity is at its greatest strength, for men are not then affected by the usual differences in enjoyment of the material goods of this life which separate them from one another. Fasting consolidates freedom, equality, and fraternity in man just as strongly as does prayer.

If we undertake fasting freely and in the consciousness that God's commandments can never differ from those of reason as long as it perceives the final purpose of life, we can appreciate how much fasting liberates us from the yoke of habit and contributes to the development of our will and capacity for freedom. We may remember that what man prescribes for himself with God's permission by way of spiritual and psychic limitations upon his own freedom in seeking to liberate himself from his habits and passions is the best guarantee for his reaching the highest levels of religious conviction. If, in matters of religion, *taqlid* constitutes no religious conviction at all but mere acquiescence to the proposed claim without conviction of its truth, *taqlid* in fasting is self-privation and a limitation of one's personal freedom, a totally different affair from that fasting which liberates man from the chains of habit and furnishes him with the greatest psychic nourishment and spiritual *élan*.

Nature of Islamic *Zakat*

Through prayer and fasting exercises which rest on a base of the widest and deepest possible scientific knowledge of the world, man may reach awareness of the pattern of the cosmos and a penetration of its secrets. In consequence, man may discover his place as well as that of his fellow men in the cosmos. His love for them and their love for him will increase with this realization. In service to God, they will cooperate with one another for the good and reinforce one another's piety; the strong will protect the weak, and the rich will share their bounty with the poor. But that is precisely the *zakat*. To do more than it requires is charity. The Qur'an joins *zakat* to prayer in many places. Some of the following verses have already been quoted: "But righteousness consists in being convinced

of the existence and unity of God, of the reality of the Day of Judgment,
of the angels, the Book, the Prophets; in giving of one's wealth lovingly to
the next of kin, the orphan, the destitute, the wayfarer, the poor, the slave;
and in holding the prayer and giving the *zakat*."[14] The Most High also
says: "Observe the prayer and remit the *zakat* and kneel with those who
pray."[15] Further, God — May He be adored — says: "Those believers
have done well and achieved felicity who hold their prayers with reverence, abstain from gossip, and complete their payment of *zakat*,"[16] etc.,
etc.

Concerning *zakat* and charity, the Qur'an talks at length, clearly and
emphatically. It has classified charity among the highest virtues deserving
of the greatest rewards; indeed, it has placed charity alongside the conviction of God, thus leading us to believe that the two are equal. Addressing
His angels regarding a man who violated the duty of charity, God said:

خُذُوهُ فَغُلُّوهُ ۞ ثُمَّ الْجَحِيمَ صَلُّوهُ ۞ ثُمَّ فِى سِلْسِلَةٍ ذَرْعُهَا سَبْعُونَ ذِرَاعًا فَاسْلُكُوهُ ۞ إِنَّهُ كَانَ لَا يُؤْمِنُ بِاللَّهِ الْعَظِيمِ ۞ وَلَا يَحُضُّ عَلَى طَعَامِ الْمِسْكِينِ ۞

"Take him away. Fetter him and cast him into the fire that he may
broil therein. Bind him in long and heavy chains that he may not move.
For he did not believe in God Almighty, nor did he urge the feeding of
the poor."[17]

Similarly, God said: "And give glad tidings to the humble, whose
hearts are filled with reverential fear whenever God is mentioned, who
patiently endure whatever befalls them, who observe the prayer and spend
of that which We have provided for them."[18] Further, God — May He
be blessed and adored — says: "Those who spend of their wealth at night
and during the day, in secret and in public, have their reward with God.
They have reason neither to fear nor to grieve."[19]

Islam and the Manners of Giving

Not satisfied with mentioning charity, nor with prescribing for it the
same reward as for faith in God and the observance of prayer, the Qur'an
furnishes norms for the manner of giving in charity. It says: "If you give
alms openly and to the public at large, it is good and you have done well.

But if you give it to the poor and you do so in secret, it is better for you."
God also says:

$$قَوْلٌ مَعْرُوفٌ وَمَغْفِرَةٌ خَيْرٌ مِنْ صَدَقَةٍ يَتْبَعُهَآ أَذًى وَاللهُ غَنِيٌّ حَلِيمٌ ۔$$
$$يَأَيُّهَا الَّذِينَ امَنُوا لَا تُبْطِلُوا اصَدَقَتِكُمْ بِالْمَنِّ وَالْاَذَى$$

"A word of kindness and an act of forgiveness are superior to an act of charity followed by injury or harm. God is self-sufficient and forbearing. O Men who believe, do not vitiate and annul your charitable deeds by taunting or injuring those to whom you give."[20]

God — May He be praised — specified the people who may be recipients of charity: "Rather, alms belong to the poor, the destitute, the protectors, those whose hearts need to be reconciled. They are for the freeing of slaves and debtors, for the cause of God, and for the wayfarers. To give alms is a duty imposed by God, the Omniscient, the All-Wise."[21]

Zakat as Act of Worship

Zakat and charity, therefore, constitute two of the major duties and pillars of Islam. It may be asked whether the performance of these duties is a matter of worship or merely of ethics and moral refinement. Without doubt the answer is worship. The believers are brethren; no man's iman is complete until he wishes for his neighbor that which he wishes for himself. The believers love one another by virtue of God's light and grace. The duties of zakat and charity are intimately related to this fraternal feeling. They are not pieces of moral sophistication nor elements of the Islamic theory of contracts. In Islam, that which pertains to brotherhood pertains equally to iman, or religious conviction of God; and all that pertains to iman is worship. That is why zakat is one of the five pillars of Islam, and why, after the death of the Prophet, Abu Bakr required the Muslims to pay it. When some Muslims failed to do so, the immediate successor of Muhammad regarded their failure as a fault of faith, a preference for wealth, and a violation of the spiritual system revealed in the Qur'an — in short, as abjuration of Islam itself. Hence, Abu Bakr conducted the Riddah War in order to confirm the establishment of the message of Islam in its totality, a message which has remained a cause for pride forever.

The Will To Wealth

To regard *zakat* and charity as duties essentially related to *iman, i.e.,* to faith as religious conviction of God, is to regard them as part of the spiritual system which ought to govern the civilization of the world. Such regard is, indeed, the highest wisdom which can guarantee happiness to man. The pursuit and acquisition of wealth, and its use as an instrument for the dominion of man over man, have always been and still are the cause of the misery of the world, of revolutions, and of wars. The worship of wealth was and still is the cause of the moral deterioration which has enveloped the world and of which human society continues to suffer. It is the acquisition, pursuit, and hoarding of wealth which has destroyed human fraternity and planted enmity between man and man. Were men to follow a higher vision and had they a nobler bent of mind, they would have realized that fraternity is more conducive to happiness than wealth, that to spend wealth on the needy is worthier with God and with men than the subjugation of men to its dominion. Were they truly convinced of God, they would realize this fraternity toward one another; and they would fulfill, as the least requirement of such a fraternity, the duties of rescuing the needy, assisting the deprived, and putting an end to the misery and suffering brought about by poverty and want. Granted, some highly civilized countries in our day do establish hospitals and communal buildings for rescuing the poor, for sheltering the homeless and assisting the deprived in the name of humanity and mercy. Still, were these constructions and communal services founded upon fraternal feeling and love in God for the neighbor as an expression of praise for His bounty, they would constitute nobler efforts and lead more truly to the happiness of all men. God said:

$$وَابْتَغِ فِيمَآ اٰتٰىكَ اللهُ الدَّارَ الْاٰخِرَةَ وَلَا تَنْسَ نَصِيبَكَ مِنَ الدُّنْيَا وَاَحْسِنْ كَمَآ اَحْسَنَ اللهُ اِلَيْكَ وَلَاتَبْغِ الْفَسَادَ فِى الْاَرْضِ ۖ اِنَّ اللهَ لَا يُحِبُّ الْمُفْسِدِيْنَ$$

"In all that God has provided for you, seek the higher value and do not forget to seek your share of this world. Do good as God has done good to you; and do not spread corruption in the world. God loves not the agent of corruption."[22]

Nature of Islamic Pilgrimage

Brotherhood reinforces men's love for one another. In Islam, it is not legitimate to limit the exercise of this love to the frontiers of one's homeland, nor even to one's race or continent. Fraternal love must have no spatial limits whatever. That is why Islam commands that men from all corners of the world know, defend, and fraternize with one another, that their love for one another in God may be strengthened and their conviction of God may be confirmed. The instrument proper for such exercise is the congregation of men from all corners of the earth in one place and for one purpose. The best locality for such a convocation is precisely the place where the light of this great love has broken through, namely God's sanctuary in Makkah. This assembly is the Islamic pilgrimage. As the believers gather and perform the rites of pilgrimage, it is their duty to lead such lives as would provide the most illustrious living example of conviction and faith in God and of a sincere openness to determination by His will. God — May He be praised — said: "Pilgrimage is during well-known months. Whoever performs the pilgrimage during these months shall engage in no gossip, corruption, vain controversy, or transgression. Everything you do is known to God. Equip yourself therefore with good deeds remembering that the best of deeds is piety. Fear Me, therefore, and fulfill My will, O Men of understanding."[23]

On this great and unique occasion when the believers perform the pilgrimage aiming at fraternizing with one another and thus strengthening their conviction of God, all distinctions between man and man must fall to the ground. All men must feel that they are equal before God, and all must turn their minds and hearts to Him in response to His call and fulfillment of His command. They should approach the pilgrimage fully convinced of His unicity and deeply grateful for His bounty. But what bounty and what felicity are greater than *iman* in God, the source of all good and all bounty? May He be adored! Before the light which such *iman* brings, all the worries and concerns of life dissolve; all its vanity, whether of wealth, children, political power or glory, utterly vanishes. By virtue of this light, man becomes capable of apprehending the truth, goodness, and beauty of this world, the eternal laws and immutable pattern on which the world is founded. It is this general convocation, namely the pilgrimage, that embodies the meaning of equality and brotherhood among all the believers and does so in the most comprehensive, clear, and sublime manner.

The Metaphysic of Morals in Islam

These are the fundamental principles of Islam and its duties as revealed to the Prophet Muhammad — May God's peace be upon him. They constitute the five pillars of Islam as the above-mentioned verses of the Qur'an show. They are the cornerstones of Islamic spiritual life. Now that these principles and duties have been enumerated, it is easy to infer from them the schemata of Islamic morality. These belong to a level so high, so sublime, that they have never been matched by any human civilization in any period of history. In this regard, the Qur'an has given rules and ideals of conduct which, if duly observed, fulfilled, and made to constitute the guiding principles of life, would enable man to attain moral perfection. These principles were not all recorded in the same chapter of the Qur'an but in many chapters. The reader has no sooner read a *surah* of the Qur'an than he feels himself elevated to the apex of moral advancement, an apex which had never been reached and will never be reached by any other civilization. Sufficient is the Qur'anic raising of the whole discipline of the soul on a spiritual foundation stemming from the conviction of God. Sufficient is the Qur'anic demand that mind and heart of man be nourished exclusively from this source and without regard either to material welfare or to any utilitarian value that might accrue from such conduct.

The Qur'anic Notion of the Perfect Man

In all ages and among all peoples, poets and writers, philosophers and dramatists have depicted the perfect man. Nonetheless, no picture of perfect man is to be found anywhere which dares compare with this sublime picture which the Qur'an has depicted in the *Surah* "al Isra'," though it constitutes only a small portion of the wisdom revealed by God to His Prophet. This *surah* by no means aims at giving a full description of the perfect man but only at reminding men of a fraction of the duties imposed upon them. God says:

وَقَضَى رَبُّكَ أَلَّا تَعْبُدُوا إِلَّا إِيَّاهُ وَبِالْوَالِدَيْنِ إِحْسَانًا إِمَّا يَبْلُغَنَّ عِنْدَكَ الْكِبَرَ أَحَدُ

هُمَا أَوْ كِلَاهُمَا فَلَا تَقُلْ لَهُمَا أُفٍّ وَلَا تَنْهَرْهُمَا وَقُلْ لَهُمَا قَوْلًا كَرِيمًا ۝ وَاخْفِضْ لَهُمَا

جَنَاحَ الذُّلِّ مِنَ الرَّحْمَةِ وَقُلْ رَبِّ ارْحَمْهُمَا كَمَا رَبَّيَانِي صَغِيرًا ۝ رَبُّكُمْ أَعْلَمُ بِمَا فِي نُفُوسِكُمْ

إِنْ تَكُونُوا صَالِحِينَ فَإِنَّهُ كَانَ لِلْأَوَّابِينَ غَفُورًا ۝ وَآتِ ذَا الْقُرْبَى حَقَّهُ وَالْمِسْكِينَ وَ

ابْنَ السَّبِيلِ وَلَا تُبَذِّرْ تَبْذِيرًا ۝ إِنَّ الْمُبَذِّرِينَ كَانُوا إِخْوَانَ الشَّيَاطِينِ وَكَانَ الشَّيْطَانُ

لِرَبِّهِ كَفُورًا ۝ وَإِمَّا تُعْرِضَنَّ عَنْهُمُ ابْتِغَاءَ رَحْمَةٍ مِنْ رَبِّكَ تَرْجُوهَا فَقُلْ لَهُمْ قَوْلًا

مَيْسُورًا ۝ وَلَا تَجْعَلْ يَدَكَ مَغْلُولَةً إِلَى عُنُقِكَ وَلَا تَبْسُطْهَا كُلَّ الْبَسْطِ فَتَقْعُدَ مَلُومًا مَحْسُورًا ۝

إِنَّ رَبَّكَ يَبْسُطُ الرِّزْقَ لِمَنْ يَشَاءُ وَيَقْدِرُ إِنَّهُ كَانَ بِعِبَادِهِ خَبِيرًا بَصِيرًا ۝ وَلَا تَقْتُلُوا

أَوْلَادَكُمْ خَشْيَةَ إِمْلَاقٍ نَحْنُ نَرْزُقُهُمْ وَإِيَّاكُمْ إِنَّ قَتْلَهُمْ كَانَ خِطْأً كَبِيرًا ۝ وَلَا

تَقْرَبُوا الزِّنَى إِنَّهُ كَانَ فَاحِشَةً وَسَاءَ سَبِيلًا ۝ وَلَا تَقْتُلُوا النَّفْسَ الَّتِي حَرَّمَ اللَّهُ إِلَّا بِالْحَقِّ

وَمَنْ قُتِلَ مَظْلُومًا فَقَدْ جَعَلْنَا لِوَلِيِّهِ سُلْطَانًا فَلَا يُسْرِفْ فِي الْقَتْلِ إِنَّهُ كَانَ مَنْصُورًا ۝

وَلَا تَقْرَبُوا مَالَ الْيَتِيمِ إِلَّا بِالَّتِي هِيَ أَحْسَنُ حَتَّى يَبْلُغَ أَشُدَّهُ وَأَوْفُوا بِالْعَهْدِ إِنَّ

الْعَهْدَ كَانَ مَسْئُولًا ۝ وَأَوْفُوا الْكَيْلَ إِذَا كِلْتُمْ وَزِنُوا بِالْقِسْطَاسِ الْمُسْتَقِيمِ ذَلِكَ خَيْرٌ

وَأَحْسَنُ تَأْوِيلًا ۝ وَلَا تَقْفُ مَا لَيْسَ لَكَ بِهِ عِلْمٌ إِنَّ السَّمْعَ وَالْبَصَرَ وَالْفُؤَادَ كُلُّ أُولَئِكَ

كَانَ عَنْهُ مَسْئُولًا ۝ وَلَا تَمْشِ فِي الْأَرْضِ مَرَحًا إِنَّكَ لَنْ تَخْرِقَ الْأَرْضَ وَلَنْ تَبْلُغَ الْجِبَالَ

طُولًا ۝ كُلُّ ذَلِكَ كَانَ سَيِّئُهُ عِنْدَ رَبِّكَ مَكْرُوهًا ۝

"Your Lord commands you to worship none but Him and to be kind to your parents. Should anyone of them be under your care until he reaches old age, do not say to him as much as 'Fie' and do not speak harshly to him but rather speak kindly. Humble yourself to your parents in love, and pray: 'May God have mercy on them as they nursed me when I was young.' Your Lord knows well that which is in your soul, especially whether or not you are truly virtuous. God forgives those who repent. Give the next of kin his due, as well as the poor and the wayfarer, but do not be a spendthrift. The spendthrifts are associates of the devil, and the latter is disobedient to God. Even if you have to avoid your parents on account of your fulfillment of God's call, give them a kind and compassionate explanation. Do not hold your hand back when it is time to give, nor give all you have so that you throw yourself in need. God spreads His bounty to whomsoever He wishes. He measures it carefully, for He cares for His servants and knows their need. Do not kill your children for fear of poverty. We shall provide for them as well as for you. Moreover, to kill them is a great misdeed. Do not commit adultery. It is an evil and its consequences are always bad. Do not kill any man — That is God's prohibition! — except after due process of law. To the heir of whoever is killed unjustly, a right of revenge is established. But he may not take that revenge wantonly, for his right shall be recognized. Do not touch the wealth of the orphan, unless it be to increase it. Be true to your covenants, for to covenant is a serious and responsible affair. Fill the measure when you measure, and when you weigh, weigh with the true weight; for that is better and more rewarding. Do not claim that of which you have no knowledge, and remember that as cognitive faculties, your hearing, sight, and heart were given to you for a responsible function. Do not walk around with impudence and false pride, for you will never measure up to the mountains of the earth. All these actions are evil and deemed undesirable by your Lord."[24]

What sublimity! What perfection! What magnanimity and purity! Everyone of the foregoing verses causes the reader to fall down in reverence and awe, combining as it does the moving appeal of moral value, the sublimity of expression, the beauty of form, the nobility of meaning, and the highest vividness of description. How I wish the occasion permitted an elaboration of this passage! But it does not, for to do justice to a passage even as short as the foregoing would require a whole volume.

The Qur'an on Self-Discipline

Indeed, even if we were to limit ourselves to a discussion of only a portion of what the Qur'an contains by way of self-discipline and morality, much more would be needed than a mere chapter of a book. Suffice it to say, therefore, that no writing has ever called man to do the good works and elevated the virtuous life as the Qur'an has done; that no book has elevated the human soul to the level to which the Qur'an has raised it; and that no book has emphasized virtue, mercy, fraternity and love, cooperation and harmony, charity and kindness, loyalty and trustworthiness, sincerity and good intention, justice and forgiveness, patience and forbearance, humility and submission, virtue and goodness, the commandment to good and the forbiddance of evil with as much power, persuasion, and sublimity as the Qur'an has done. No book has ever spoken against weakness and fear, favoritism and jealously, hatred and injustice, lying and libel, avarice and prodigality, false witness and perjury, aggression and corruption, cheating, treason, and all vice as profoundly and persuasively as the revelation which came to the Arab Prophet. The reader will find no *surah* in the Qur'an in which the call to virtue, the commandment to good, the forbiddance of evil, and the pursuit of perfection are not central. Every *surah* raises the reader to the highest level of moral awareness and tension. Let us mark well God's statement regarding tolerance: "Respond to the evil deed with a good one. . . . The good deed is certainly not the equivalent of the evil one. Repel the evil deed with the good one. Instantly, your enemy will be transformed into a warm friend."[25] This toleration to which the Qur'an calls, however, does not proceed from weakness but from magnanimity of spirit, a will to compete in good deeds and to avoid lowly ones. God says: "And if you are greeted, respond with a better greeting or, at least, with the same."[26] Further, God says: "And when you punish, inflict the same punishment as was meted out to you. But if you refrain out of patience, it is better for you."[27] All these verses clearly establish that the Islamic call to tolerance is at the same time a call to virtue unspoiled by any weakness. It is indeed the consequence of a self-transcendence that is pure and unalloyed.

Tolerance from strength and virtue, to which the Qur'an calls, is founded upon brotherhood which Islam places at the root of its civilization and which it holds to be absolutely universal. Islamic brotherhood integrates justice and mercy without weakness or sufferance. It arises from equality in right, goodness and virtue, unaffected by utilitarian advantage. Under its aegis, the Muslim prefers his fellows to himself even though they be far inferior to him. He fears God and none other; consequently, the Muslim is the model of pride, dignity, and self-respect. And yet he is the model of humility and modesty. He is truthful and fulfills a covenant once he has entered into it. He is as patient when tragedy strikes as when he receives good fortune and new power. Faced with calamity, he thinks, feels, and prays: "We are all God's, and to Him we shall all return." He never abases himself to anyone, and yet he has no false pride. God has protected him against avarice and stinginess when they are directed toward himself. He never reports falsely about God or about His servants; he never approves of adultery and always seeks to avoid transgression and crime. If he ever goes into a rage, he seeks God's mercy and forgiveness, sublimates his rage and fury, and forgives his offenders. He avoids suspicion, spying, and reporting secretly about his fellows. He does not violate the wealth of his fellows, nor allow the rulers to do so unjustly. He stands beyond jealousy, strategy, deceit, gossip, and every kind of misdemeanor.

Morality and Utilitarianism

These virtues and the ethical system which they constitute are all founded on the spiritual system revealed in the Qur'an which is essentially related to *iman* in God. As we have said earlier, this characteristic is the most important feature of Islamic morality. It guarantees the grasp of the human soul by these values and ideals, as well as saves that system from all corruption. Morality founded upon utility and mutual advantage is quickly corrupted as soon as the moral subject is convinced that his personal advantage does not suffer in consequence of his immorality. In such morality, it is most often the case that the subject is double-faced, showing an appearance different from what he holds deep within him. He would, for instance, seek to appear trustworthy while giving himself the right to use another's confidence as a means for increasing his advantage. He would seek to appear truthful but would not restrain from false pretense as long as this added to his advantage. A morality founded upon such standards falls down as the winds of temptation begin to blow. Its subject is often found pursuing ulterior motives and ever running after the satisfaction of his own prejudices.

This essential moral weakness is most conspicuous in our present-day world. How often have we heard of great scandals occurring in this or that part of the civilized world, scandals all traceable to the pursuit of wealth and power on the part of their subjects, and on the weakness of their will to possess true *iman* and noble morals. Many of these people who fall to the nethermost depths in morality and perpetrate the worst crimes have started out with high morals based upon utilitarianism. They regarded success in life as based upon the observance of these high morals; and so they observed them in order to succeed, not because moral practice is a necessary part of their personal path which they ought to follow even though it might incur serious disadvantage. Hence, when they realized that some deviation from moral uprightness did in fact bring forth a measure of success within the civilization of this age, they allowed themselves to swerve. Many of them have been able to keep their personal code of behavior hidden from the public and, therefore, have never been exposed to scandal. They continue to be respected and esteemed. Others, less adept, have been exposed and have fallen into scandalous involvements which often have ended in personal ruin or suicide.

To found morality on utility and advantage, therefore, is to expose it to eventual but certain calamity. On the other hand, to found it on a spiritual system such as the Qur'an has revealed is to guarantee its permanent strength, its moving appeal, and power to determine man's ethics. The intention behind a deed is itself the measure of its moral worth, the genuine rubbing stone against which it should be tested. The man who buys a lottery ticket designed to build a hospital does not buy it with the intention of doing good and being charitable but in pursuit of material gain. Such act is not moral. Likewise, the man who gives to the insistent beggar in order to rid himself of the nuisance caused, is not on a par with the man who gives to the poor who not only do not insist when they ask, but do not ask at all out of a deep sense of dignity, shame, and self-respect. Furthermore, the man who tells the truth to the judge in fear of the punishment the law metes out to perjurers is not equivalent to the man who tells the truth because he believes in the virtue of truthfulness. A system of morals based upon utility and mutual advantage therefore cannot have the strength of a morality which the subject believes to be essentially related to his human dignity and to his *iman* in God, a morality founded upon the spiritual system on which his *iman* in God is itself founded.

The Wisdom of Prohibition of Alcohol and Gambling in Islam

The Qur'an, seeking to preserve the jurisdiction of reason in morality, thus has kept morality immune to all that might vitiate its judgment in matters of faith or morals. Consequently, it has regarded alcohol and gambling as anathema, the inspiration of the devil. Even though they might bring some advantage in their wake, their crime and evil are greater than their advantage; hence, they ought to be avoided. Gambling, for instance, takes such possession of the mind of the gambler that its victim can think of nothing else and can make no other use of his time. It tempts him away from the fulfillment of any moral obligation. On the other hand, alcohol dissolves reason as well as wealth, to use the terms of 'Umar ibn al Khattab when he prayed that God might reveal His judgment in its regard. It is natural for the mind to err in its judgment when intoxicated; it is easy for the mind, once it has gone astray, to tolerate the pursuit of crime and evil instead of warning man against them.

The Qur'an and Science

The ethical system of the ideal state revealed in the Qur'an does not deprive man of the enjoyments of the good things of life, precisely because both privation and overindulgence may lead to the same consequences: neglect of the cosmos as a whole and of the pursuit of cosmic knowledge. The Islamic system strongly rejects man's total surrender to enjoyment of affluence and comfort even as it rejects his surrender to privation and abstinence in which he loses himself in subjective psychic pursuits. On the contrary, Islam seeks to make its people a community of the golden mean, to orient them toward pure virtue, to develop their knowledge of the cosmos, and to master all that it contains. The Qur'an continually speaks of the cosmos and of what it contains in a way directing us toward increasing our knowledge of it. It speaks about the new moons, about the sun and the moon, day and night, the earth and the creatures that roam over it, the sky and the stars which adorn it, the sea whose surface is crisscrossed with ships sailing in pursuit of God's bounty, of the animals we take as beasts of burden and others as ornaments, and of all that the earth contains for knowledge and art. In speaking about all these, the Qur'an asks man not only to look into them and study them but to enjoy their effects and to feel grateful to God for His bounty. With such discipline as the Qur'an has enjoined, and by following its insistent call to seek cosmic knowledge, man may fulfill his destiny. If he responds to the call of the Qur'an and fulfills its requisite rational contemplation of the cosmos, he bases his economic and social system upon solid and worthy foundations.

The Islamic Economic System

Were economic and social systems to be based upon such moral and spiritual foundations, man would be able both to achieve happiness and to put an end to human suffering and misery on earth. The high ethical principles which the Qur'an poses as the very content of its creed, as well as its faith, command men to remove any shortcoming or misery in the world which it is possible to remove. A person disciplined by these principles and gripped by their ethic will condemn selfish interests, the basis of present economic life and the source of misery for all mankind. That is why Islam categorically forbids charging interest for loans. God said, "Those who appropriate interest are like men possessed of the devil."[28] Further, the Qur'an says, "The interest which you impose seeking to increase your wealth will not bring about any increase in the sight of God. Rather, it is the *zakat* which you pay for the sake of God alone, that brings about such increase of your fortune."[29]

The Evils of the Interest System

The prohibition of interest is a basic principle of Islamic civilization. It guarantees and safeguards the happiness of mankind. In its least offensive sense, interest is a system which enables the unproductive man to share in the fruits of someone else's labor for no reason but that he lent him money. The argument advanced in its favor is that the money lent enabled the producer to produce his fruits and that without it, it would not have been possible for the producer to earn what he did. Even if this advantage were the only consequence of interest, it would not be justified. For, were the money lender capable of usufructing his money for himself, he would not have lent it to someone else. And were that money to remain in its coffer, it would not produce any fruits at all. Rather, it would probably be gradually consumed by its owner. If, therefore, the capitalist allows another man to usufruct his money, hoping thereby to win a share in its fruits, he should certainly be entitled to a share of the fruits — should there be such — rather than imposing a definite interest charge for his money. If the operation proves successful and economically profitable, the owner of the capital should receive the share agreed upon. If it should turn out to be a failure and a loss, however, then he, too, should share a proportionate part of the burden. On the other hand, to impose a definite interest charge for the use of capital regardless of whether or not the use of such capital has been productive is illegitimate exploitation.

It is futile to object here that capital is entitled to its rent because it is used like any other commodity, be it a piece of land or a mule, and that interest is really the equivalent of rent. The renting of movable and immovable property is vastly different from renting money; the latter may bring about mutual benefit and usufruct as well as pure exploitation and crime. Man does not rent a piece of land, a house, a beast of burden, or any immovable property except in order to use it to his advantage. Otherwise, he is insane, and his commitments are not responsible. It is otherwise with money. Money is for the most part lent for purposes of trade. But trade is always exposed to profit and loss. The renting of immovable or movable property is hardly ever exposed to loss except in rare, indeed exceptional, cases falling outside the realm of normal legislation. Where it does happen that the rent of movable or immovable property exposes the user to loss, the legislator usually intervenes between the landowner and the lessees in order to relieve such injustice and prevent exploitation by the landowner. Such has been the repeated practice of the world everywhere. On the bther hand, the imposition of a definite interest rate of seven or nine percent, more or less, is not affected by whether the usufruct of the money in question has realized a profit or a loss. Where "the result of the usufruct is a loss, to demand the interest is surely to commit a crime. It is on this account that hatred and immoral competition arise between men in place of fraternity and love. This source of misery is the primary cause of the repeated crises which the world community has been witnessing in recent times.

The foregoing is perhaps the least offensive description of interest. In other pictures the money lender is better compared to a wild beast rather than to anything human. Consider the case of the man who needs money for a purpose other than production. It is possible that a man may fall in need and seek financial assistance to feed himself and his family for an interval, pending his finding a job or his engaging in some productive activity. To come to the assistance of such a man is one of the first duties of humanity. This is precisely what the holy Qur'an demands. Is not the charging of interest in such cases a heinous crime, an offense deserving the same punishment as murder? And is it not a crime still more sinister to tempt those who are not shrewd in the management of their own affairs in order to get them to borrow money on interest and thereby rob them of the little wealth they possess? To tempt and to trap a man with interest is no less a crime than the lowliest theft. Surely it deserves the same if not greater punishment.

Interest and Colonialism

It was interest and the demand for the profit it entails to the lender which engulfed the world in all the calamities of colonialism. In most cases, colonialism began with a number of capitalists, whether individuals or corporations, lending money to the colonized at interest and infiltrating the colony's system with the aim of gaining control over its resources. When the borrowing people woke up and sought to liberate themselves from the money lender's clutches, the creditors appealed to their own governments to intervene and protect what then came to be called their national interest. The latter then arrived with their armies and fleets and imposed themselves as colonial powers seeking to protect the interests of their own citizens. The colonial power then imposed its rule, deprived the people of their liberty and began to control whatever God gave the people of His bounty in their own land. Their happiness thus vanished. Misery, suffering, and poverty engulfed them. Ignorance and misguidance stifled their minds. Their morals deteriorated and their *iman* became dissolute. They thus fell below the level of humanity and reached a degree of inferiority that no man believing in God would accept for himself. No man believing that God alone is worthy of worship will allow his fate to be so controlled by someone else as to bring about his own loss and suffering.

Colonialism is indeed the source of wars. It is the source of the misery which has befallen the whole of mankind in the present age. As long as interest is legitimate and real, as long as it is the basis of economic life and colonialism the dominant factor in international relations, there is no hope for the establishment of fraternity and love. Such a condition cannot be reached unless civilization is rebuilt upon the foundation which Islam has provided and which revelation has recorded in the Qur'an.

Islamic Socialism

The Qur'an also contains a system of socialism which has never yet been the object of research. It is a socialism which is not based on the competition of capital or class war, as the socialism of western civilization today. Rather it is based on moral principles guaranteeing fraternity between the classes and fostering mutual security and cooperation for the good and felicity of their members instead of crime and transgression. It is relatively easy to appreciate this Qur'anic socialism based upon brotherhood and institutionized in *zakat* and charity. It does not allow one class to dominate another or one group to impose its will upon another. The civilization depicted in the Qur'an knows no such dominion or imposition. It rests entirely upon genuine fraternity deriving from unswerving *iman* in God, a conviction which makes the recognition of God tantamount to giving to the poor and the deprived that which they need by way of nourishment, clothing, shelter, medicine, education, and upbringing, without even making them feel that they have been the object of charity.

Under this system, misery will vanish and men may hope God will complete His bounty and grant them the happiness they desire.

No Abolition of Private Property

Islamic socialism does not demand the annulment of private property, as is the case with western socialism. The facts are that even in Bolshevik Russia, as well as in any socialist country, the doing away with private property has not been fruitful. On the other hand, it goes without saying that all public utilities should become common property for the people. The definition of public utilities should be left for the state to conclude. As may be expected, men may disagree on such definition, as was the case in the first century of Islam. Some of the Prophet's companions demanded that all the creations of God should be included in the definition of public utilities. They regarded the land and all that it contained on a par with water and air, and thus not subject to becoming the property of anyone. They regarded every man as entitled to its fruits in proportion to his effort and capacity. Other companions saw the question differently. They deemed the land capable of becoming the property of individuals and, like the immovable properties, capable of being exchanged.

The Final Groundwork of Islamic Socialism

At any rate, one basic socialist principle that was agreed upon by all the Prophet's companions is passing today as a matter of course in the socialist countries of Europe: that every man *is* duty-bound to put to full use all his capacities for the sake of the community; and that *is* the duty of the community to guarantee to every individual all his basic needs. Every Muslim was entitled to draw from the public treasury all that was required to satisfy his survival needs and those of his family as long as he did not find work to do, or as long as the work he did was not sufficient to satisfy these wants. As long as morality is governed by the principles of the Qur'an, no one may tell a lie and claim that he is out of work when in reality he is just lazy and unwilling to exert himself. Nor will anyone claim falsely that his income is insufficient. In the first century of Islam, the caliphs and leaders of the Muslim community took it upon themselves to inspect the conditions of their subjects in order to insure themselves that no basic need remained unsatisfied.

Socialism Is Brotherhood

From this basic discussion, the reader will realize that the socialism of Islam is not a socialism of capital and distribution but one founded upon fraternity in the spiritual, moral, and economic spheres of life. If a person's *iman* is not regarded as complete until that person has wished for his fellow that which he wishes for himself, it can be deduced safely that no *iman* is complete unless its subject has urged the feeding of the hungry and has spent privately and publicly of what God has provided, with a view to serving the commonweal. The more altruistic a person becomes, the closer he comes to realizing internal peace and happiness. If God has so constituted men that some stand above others in capacities and achievements, and if God has given of his bounty differently to whomsoever He chooses, it is certain that there will be no end to evil in this world until the young respects the older, the older shows mercy to the younger, the richer gives to the poorer, and all have done so purely for the sake of God and in praise of Him as well as of His bounty.

It is not necessary in this connection to give the details of the laws of inheritance, of wills, of contracts, trade, and other areas of the Qur'anic economic system. Even the briefest reference to anyone of these topics, whether social or jurisprudential, would require many more chapters. It is sufficient to note that the contribution of Islam in anyone of these fields is still unsurpassed by any other kind of legislation. Indeed, one can only react with surprise when he considers some of the details of this Islamic contribution — e.g., the command always to write down one's contracts unless it be a case of irreversible trade; the arbitration of disputes between husband and wife by representatives of either party in order to avoid dissolution of the marriage; the commandment to reconcile any two disputing factions within the state and to all the Muslims to fight that faction which resists the efforts, judgment or instrument of reconciliation. One is surprised at the novelty of such provisions of Islamic law. And when compared with the provisions of other bodies of law, one invariably reaches the conclusion that that legislation is indeed the highest which has sought to fulfill the Qur'anic principles. It should, however, surprise no one — considering that the foregoing principles regarding interest and Islamic socialism are the bases of the Qur'anic economic system and that this legislation is the highest that has ever been reached by man in any period — that Islamic civilization is not only truly worthy of mankind but is also the only one that can guarantee man's happiness.

Probable Western Objections

After reading our presentation of the bases and structure of Qur'anic civilization, some western writers may deem them too utopian to be fulfilled by man and, hence, not destined to endure even when successfully realized. Such thinkers hold man to be motivated by fear and hope, prejudice and pressure, just like any other animal except that man adds to his equipment the faculty of speech. To expect humanity to follow a system such as that provided by Islam for civilization is either impossible or extremely difficult. The utmost that we may expect in ordering the life of human society is the regulation of human passion and greed and the orientation of human fear and hope from the economic aspect alone. What is beyond these desiderata is beyond the capacity of human society. The Islamic system, formulated by the Qur'an and described in this chapter, did not survive in Islamic history beyond the days of the Prophet and his immediate successors. This phenomenon constitutes for these thinkers further proof of the utopian nature of that system and its not having enveloped the world. They cite this failure to survive and to spread itself over the world as proof of its unfitness.

Refutation

To refute this claim, it is sufficient to note the acknowledgment of its adherents that the Islamic system was indeed realized during the period of the Prophet and that of his immediate successors. Muhammad was indeed the highest exemplar of that system and his application of it the highest instance of its feasibility. His immediate successors followed his example and carried his own application of it to perfection. Under the influence of various Israelitisms[30] and provincialisms,[31] that system was gradually dissolved by intrigue and corruption. Slowly but surely, men allowed material considerations to overrule the spiritual, and animal passion to elbow out the humane until mankind reached the situation of the present day in which it suffers from the most terrible miseries.

The Example of Muhammad

Muhammad's example was the best application of Islamic civilization as elaborated in the Qur'an. From this work, the reader may remember how the Prophet extended his fraternity to all men without distinction. In

Makkah, he regarded himself and his fellows absolutely on a par in poverty and suffering. Indeed, he assumed the greater share of privation and suffering for their sake. When he emigrated to Madinah, he established this fraternity between the Muhajirun and Ansar so firmly that he granted the privileges and obligations incumbent upon real blood relationship to all. In that period, the fraternity of believers was based upon mutual love and the common will to raise the foundations of the new civilization. It was fed and reinforced by a genuine *iman* in God, a faith and a conviction whose strength carried Muhammad to communion with God Himself — May He be adored. At the campaign of Badr, Muhammad called upon God to give him the promised victory and prayed to Him saying, that should the Muslims be defeated at Badr, God would not be worshipped in Arabia. This is strong evidence of that communion with the Divine. Indeed, many such stands which Muhammad took on other occasions point to his constant communion with God. These were moments other than those of revelation. It was this communion with the Divine based on his true *iman* in God which enabled Muhammad not to fear death but, indeed, to seek it. This was only as it should be, for the man of genuine conviction never fears death but welcomes it. Every life has a term, and death will reach its object wherever it may be. No man may escape. It was this conviction that enabled Muhammad to stand firmly on his ground when the Muslims ran away in panic at the outbreak of hostilities at Hunayn. When practically surrounded with death, Muhammad paid no attention to it and called his men to rally forth around him. It was this *iman* that made him give liberally without fear of poverty or privation and enabled him to do good to the orphan, the wayfarer, the deprived, and the suffering. In brief, it enabled him to rise to the highest pinnacle of every Qur'anic virtue. All this, as well as the Muslims' close observance of his example in the first period of their history, caused Islam to spread in the years immediately following the death of Muhammad and to establish itself by planting the seeds of Islamic civilization in every land. Finally, it was this *iman* that transformed corrupt and decadent peoples into strong and progressive states seeking knowledge and advancement, discovering the secrets of the universe, and developing creativity in every field of human endeavor. These same states can vie successfully even with the accomplishments of the modern age, the so-called 'Age of Light and Science,' an age so unsuccessful in bringing about happiness to mankind because of an *iman* weak in God and strong in matter.

The Misguided 'Ulama'

However, like any other civilization of Western Asia and Europe Islamic civilization was corrupted by the prejudices engendered by provincialism or Israelitism. This corruption is attributable to the fact that a number of 'ulama', who are normally expected to be the heirs of the Prophets, preferred power to the truth, worldly glory to virtue, and used their knowledge and leadership to misguide the community of the people and their young in the same way as do the 'ulama' of this age. Such 'ulama' however are the devil's associates. Upon them will fall the greatest responsibility on the Day of Judgment. It is the first duty of every modern 'alim, true to God and to his knowledge, to fight the misguiding 'ulama' and combat the evil propaganda they spread. If such 'ulama' have any kind of place in Christendom where the church and science have to fight each other and compete for power, they have utterly no place in the Islamic world where religion and science are close associates, where religion without science is deemed unbelief and ungodly, and where science without religion is deemed delusion. Had mankind entered into the civilization of Islam as the Qur'an depicts it, had the Mongols not destroyed its great centers, and had the insincere converts to Islam not taken their Islam as a means for subjecting the community of Muslims to their dominion, a dominion based on the opposite of Islamic fraternity, the world would have had a different destiny. Mankind would not have been subject to the miseries it finds itself under today.

Islamic Civilization and the Future

I am nonetheless certain that Qur'anic civilization will conquer the world if a group of 'ulama' rise today to call for it in a progressive, open, and scientific manner. This civilization addresses itself to both the heart and reason. It appeals to all men and to all people; no vested interests and no prejudices will be able to prevent their movement toward it. Nor is it required that such 'ulama' have any more than a genuine iman, and that they sincerely call men to God. Then will mankind find their happiness in this fraternity in God as they found it in the Prophet's time.

The accomplishments of the period of the Prophet and of that of his immediate successors constitute evidence for my claim, advanced in the preface to this work, that scientific research into the spiritual revolution which Muhammad initiated in this world will guide mankind to the new civilization toward, which it has been groping. There is no doubt whatever in this regard. Western men of knowledge object to this claim by deploring the spirit dominating Islamic civilization. On the basis of these objections, they accuse Islam of causing the decay and degradation of the Muslim peoples. The most important of these objections is the claim that the determinism of Islam weakens the will of its people, disables them from participating in the struggle for existence, and brings about their decadence and subjugation. To expose the falsity of this claim and other claims will be the purpose of the second essay in this conclusion.

2

Islamic Civilization and the Western Orientalists

Irving and Islamic Determinism

Washington Irving, one of the greatest writers the United States of America produced in the nineteenth century, is a real credit to his people. He has written a biography of the Arab Prophet in which the material is presented in an eloquent and captivating manner. Although his treatment is well taken at times, it is prejudiced at others. His book ends with a conclusion in which he presents the principles of Islam and what he has taken to be the historical sources of those principles. After mentioning *iman* in God, in His angels, Books, prophets, and the Day of Judgment, Washington Irving wrote:

"The sixth and last article of the Islam faith is PREDESTI-NATION, and on this Mahomet evidently reposed his chief dependence for the success of his military enterprises. He inculcated that every event had been predetermined by God, and written down in the eternal tablet previous to the creation of the world. That the destiny of every individual and the hour of his death were irrevocably fixed, and could neither be varied nor evaded by any effort of human sagacity or foresight. Under this persuasion the Moslems engaged in battle without risk; and, as death in battle was equivalent to martyrdom, and entitled them to an immediate admission into paradise, they had in either alternative, death or victory, a certainty of gain.

"This doctrine, according to which men by their own free will can neither avoid sin nor avert punishment, is considered by many Mussulmen as derogatory to the justice and clemency of God; and several sects have sprung up, who endeavor to soften and explain away this perplexing dogma; but the number of these doubters is small, and they are not considered orthodox.

"The doctrine of Predestination was one of those timely revelations to Mahomet that were almost miraculous from their seasonable occurrence. It took place immediately after the disastrous battle of Ohod, in which many of his followers, and among them his uncle Hamza, were slain. Then it was, in a moment of gloom and despondency, when his followers around him were disheartened, that he promulgated this law, telling them that every man must die at the appointed hour, whether in bed or in the field of battle. He declared, moreover, that the angel Gabriel had announced to him the reception of Hamza into the seventh heaven, with the title of Lion of God and of the Prophet. He added, as he contemplated the dead bodies, 'I am witness for these, and for all who have been slain for the cause of God, that they shall appear in glory at the resurrection, with their wounds brilliant as vermilion and odoriferous as musk.'

"What doctrine could have been devised more calculated to hurry forward, in a wild career of conquest, a set of ignorant and predatory soldiers, than assurance of booty if they survived, and paradise if they fell? It rendered almost irresistible the Moslem arms; but it likewise contained the poison that was to destroy their dominion. From the moment the successors of the Prophet ceased to be aggressors and conquerors, and sheathed the sword definitely, the doctrine of predestination began its baneful work. Enervated by peace, and the sensuality permitted by the Koran — which so distinctly separates its doctrine from the pure and self-denying religion of the Messiah — the Moslem regarded every reverse as preordained by Allah, and inevitable; to be borne stoically, since human exertion and foresight were vain. 'Help thyself and God will help thee,' was a precept never in force with the followers of Mahomet; and its reverse has been their fate. The crescent has waned before the cross, and exists in Europe, where it was once

so mighty, only by the suffrage, or rather the jealously of the great
Christian powers, probably ere long to furnish another illustration,
that 'they that take the sword shall perish with the sword.'"[1]

Falsity of Irving's Criticism

These are the words of Washington Irving. They are the words of a
man whose study fell short of grasping the spirit of Islam and of its civilization. Hence, his false interpretation of the problem of divine providence and predestination. Perhaps Irving had some excuse in that some of
the Islamic books which he may have read do in fact point in the direction of his interpretation. As for the Qur'an, the dictum "God helps them
that help themselves" is far too weak to be even comparable to its emphatic call for self-reliance, its thunderous warning that men will receive exactly what their deeds and intentions had earned for them. God said:

$$ قُلْ يَٰٓأَيُّهَا ٱلنَّاسُ قَدْ جَآءَكُمُ ٱلْحَقُّ مِن رَّبِّكُمْ فَمَنِ ٱهْتَدَىٰ فَإِنَّمَا يَهْتَدِى لِنَفْسِهِ ۖ وَمَن ضَلَّ فَإِنَّمَا يَضِلُّ عَلَيْهَا ۖ $$

"Say, O Men, the truth has come to you from your Lord. Whoever is
guided thereby is so to his own credit; whoever is not so guided is so to his
own discredit."

In another passage God said: "Whoever is guided by the truth will
earn the advantage thereof, and whoever goes astray will earn the disadvantage thereof. Do not extrapolate responsibility. No punishment is due
until a prophet has been duly sent and men have been duly warned; . . .
whoever seeks the advantage of the other world will receive the same and
more of it. Whoever seeks the advantage of this world will receive the
same, but he will have no share in the other. . . . God does not change the
conditions of a people until that people have changed their conditions by
themselves."[2]

The Qur'an and Determinism

It is, therefore, a clearly Qur'anic position that man's will and action
are the sole determinants of his worth, of his punishment or reward.

Emphatically, God has urged man to go forth into the world to seek its fruits and to enjoy them." He commanded self-exertion in His cause in very strong terms as may be seen from many verses quoted in this book. This is all irreconcilable with Irving's claim, which has been repeated by a number of other westerners, that Islam is a religion of lethargy and reliance, that it teaches its adherents that they can in no way influence whatever befalls them, whether good or evil, and hence that there is no point in their trying to do so. This claim argues that will and efficacy are exclusive prerogatives of God; that man's efforts come to naught when the divine decree orders otherwise; and that if it were decreed that somebody would become rich, strong, or a believer, this would surely come to pass without any effort or action on his part. The verses we have already cited all run counter to these claims.

It may also be possible that these western writers and thinkers attribute the lethargy and reliance of the Muslims in the recent period of their history to the Qur'anic verses which pertain to divine providence in the manner of the following: "No man may expire, except by permission of God and at a prefixed term. . . . every people has a term; so that whenever that term arrives, that people must fulfill that which is proper thereto at its time, neither before nor after it. . . . whatever calamity befalls the earth or your own persons is predetermined before it happens. Such determination is easy for God. . . . Say, 'Nothing shall befall us except that which God has predetermined for us. He is our Lord; and upon Him the believers will rely.'"[3] But if this is the line of their reasoning, then they have misunderstood the meanings of these verses and others like them. Misunderstanding these verses, they think Islam calls for resignation, whereas the Qur'an meant to stress the solid bond between God and His dedicated servants. The fact is that Islam is a religion which calls for exactly the opposite, for dynamism and personal initiative, self-exertion and sacrifice, self-respect and dignity, while it founds its civilization on brotherhood and mercy. Islam is the one religion which does so *par excellence!*

Scientific Determinism

As a matter of fact, these and like verses point to a scientific truth recognized by most western philosophers and men of science in which determinism is ascribed to the general pattern of the cosmos as a whole rather than to God, the Almighty and Omniscient. This view is narrower, more rigid, and less amenable to the good of mankind than the philosophic view deducible from the Qur'an, as we shall see in the sequel. Scientific determinism teaches that man has no freedom except in the narrowest and most insignificant fields and that this little freedom is relative and is evident only as a practical consequence of social needs, but not from any established scientific or philosophical reality. It is not a principle put a provision. For without some provision for freedom of choice, it would be impossible for society to find a basis for its legislation, for the regulations it imposes on all its members under threat of criminal and civil sanction. True, some men of science and jurisprudence do not regard punishment or sanction as based on either determinism or on freedom, and they explain punishment as a response on the part of society to the need for self-preservation, just as an individual would react for his own self-preservation. It is all one for society when it reacts in self-preservation, whether the individual criminal has been free or determined in the perpetration of his crime. Nonetheless, freedom of action is still the foundation for most jurists. Their evidence therefor is the principle that the person devoid of freedom and choice, such as the insane, the child, and the moron, are never judged as the conscious man who distinguishes between good and evil.

If we go beyond these practical considerations of legislation and jurisprudence to reach a scientific and philosophical principle, we are led to conclude in favor of determinism. No man, for instance, has any choice as to the period in which he is born, nor of the nation, community, environment, nor parents to whom he is born. Just as no man chooses his parents, no man chooses them as poor or rich, perfect or imperfect; neither has he chosen his sex nor the happenings which surround his life and determine it to any great extent. The French philosopher Hyppolite Taine expressed this view with the dictum, "Man is the product of his environment." Many philosophers and scientists have adopted this view, insisting that if it were possible to know the laws and secrets of human life to the same extent as we have discovered the laws of movement of the heavenly bodies, it would become possible to predict precisely the destiny of every man and nation, just as astronomers predict with precision an eclipse of the sun or of the moon.

All this notwithstanding, no one in the West or in the East has claimed that this determinist view prevents man from seeking success in life or the nations of the world from bringing themselves up to a position of affluence and prosperity. No one claims that this determinist view leads to the deterioration and decadence of the people who believe in it. This fact remains true in spite of the westerner's subscription to determinism as not being counteracted by such strong religious pronouncements as the Qur'anic verses quoted in this chapter, which assert that "Man acquires nothing but what he himself has earned; none of his deeds is lost and each will count on the Day of Judgment."[4] This point alone constitutes evidence that the western Orientalists' claim that determinism in Islam had led to the deterioration and decay of the Muslim peoples is nothing but a piece of sheer prejudice.

Rather, the determinism of Islam stresses far more than that of the West the need for self-exertion and personal initiative in the actualization of material and ethical values. Both systems are agreed that the cosmos has immutable patterns to which everything in the world is necessarily subject and that man is as subject to these patterns as is all of nature. Further, western determinism subjects man to determination by his environment and inheritance from his parents to such a degree that no escape from natural law is possible. It subjects man's will to this determination so that it is impossible for man to change himself. On the other hand, the Qur'an calls upon every man to govern his will by the judgment of reason and to orient it toward the ethical good. It teaches that even if the good has been predetermined to be the consequence of man's given endeavor, man cannot reach it haphazardly or without effort.

The Absolute Need for Deliberate Self-Change

God — May He be adored — said, "God does not change the conditions of a people until that people have changed their conditions by themselves."[5] It is hence within the capacity of men to think out and to ponder their course in life once God has guided them to their duties. God does this by means of His revealed Books, by His prophets — who show men the road of goodness and truth — or by calling men to look into the universe in order to grasp its laws and the will of God imperative therein, by stirring within them the innate will to know. Whoever believes that the final disposition is God's, and directs himself toward it, will not reach except that which God had predetermined for him. If, therefore, it has been predetermined for a man to fall on the battlefield of truth and goodness that God commanded us to realize, such man has no reason to fear. He and the like of him live with their Lord and enjoy His bounty. What philosophy of progress, advancement and self-exertion, and freedom of the will compares with this philosophy of Islam? Where in it is the lethargic reliance upon fate which Irving and his fellow Orientalists claim?

Tawakul, or lethargic reliance upon God, has nothing to do with *tawakkul,* or trust in God. Trust in God does not consist in man's lethargic immobility and lack of response to the commandment of his Lord but in the serious and active pursuit of that commandment. That is why God says, "And if you have resolved on a certain course, then put your trust *(tawakkul)* in God."[6] Resolution and will, therefore, must precede *tawakkul* or trust in God. Indeed, when a man does resolve to put his trust in God, he will surely reach his objective by God's grace. We may even say that if man seeks God's sake alone, if he fears Him alone, and if he follows His path alone, he will reach the good by reason of God's necessary pattern in the cosmos. This divine pattern, it must be remembered, is immutable and necessary. In his pursuit of the good, therefore, man must reach his objective since that is the pattern of God in the cosmos regardless of whether he survives his pursuit or perishes in the process. The good thus achieved by man is from God. The bad that he achieves is his own work, earned by following a path other than God's. The good is all in God's hands; evil and misguidance are both the inspiration of the devil and his handwork.

As for God's knowledge of all that happened in the world before its creation, the fact is that "Nothing, not even an atom in heaven and earth, or even anything smaller than that or bigger, escapes God's knowledge and attention. Everything is clearly laid out on the divine tablet.'" This statement simply means that God has provided for creation immutable patterns necessarily followed by everything which is or happens therein. And if, as we said earlier, scientists claim that positive science can predict the future of every individual and every nation with certainty if the secrets and laws of human life be known, just as it is possible to predict the eclipse of the sun or the moon, we should also admit that faith in God demands that we stand ever certain of His knowledge of everything before creation. An engineer who lays down a plan for a house or a palace and observes this plan in the erection of the building, knows how long the building will stand and what its various parts may suffer from exposure to the elements.

Likewise, economists claim that their knowledge of economic laws enables them to predict with certainty any future prosperity or crisis in the economic life of the world. Once such an assertion is granted, then there is all the more reason to say that God does indeed know everything big or small in this world and that to deny divine knowledge is unacceptable sophistry. Such knowledge of God, however, does not and need not prevent mea from planning their own course of action, from exerting themselves in the pursuit of truth and goodness, or from seeking to avoid misguidance. The knowledge of God is not open to man. But man will reach and know the truth at the end, however distant that end may seem today. God has taken upon Himself to show mercy. He accepts the repentance of His servants and is very forgiving. Since God's mercy envelops everything, man should not despair of receiving guidance to the truth and to the good as long as he constantly studies the universe and seeks to discover its laws. No man may despair of God's mercy, since his study of the cosmos will, in the final analysis, guide him to the path of God. But woe to him who denies his humanity, who is too proud to study the universe, and who fails to seek God's guidance! Such a man offends God and does not seek His face! Such a man has his heart and mind sealed! To him belongs hellfire and evil destiny!

Will then the western Orientalists see the loftiness of Islamic determinism and the wide scope it leaves open for human freedom of action? Will they realize the falsity of their claim that Islamic determinism demands self-immobilization, acceptance of humiliation, and satisfaction with submission to any but God? Certainly, Islamic determinism leaves the gate wide open for hope in God's mercy and forgiveness to anyone who repents and changes for better. What then becomes of their claim that Islamic determinism demands of the Muslim to regard whatever evil befalls him as an inscrutable divine decree that he must suffer in patience, however damaging or humiliating it may be? Such a claim stands at the farthest possible remove from Islamic determinism, which calls upon man always to exert himself in the pursuit of God's pleasure and to trust in God only after he has resolved upon a course of action. If man does not achieve the good today, he is commanded to keep on striving that he may achieve it on the morrow. He should fix his hope upon God that He may guide his path, accept his repentance, and forgive him. In this hope, man has the best impulsion to continue his search, his exertion and his pursuit, and will hence come nearer to realizing the utmost level of God's pleasure, the God Whom he worships, Whose help he asks for, and Who is the source of all guidance and unto Whom everything shall return.

The strength of thought which these noble teachings provide is tremendous, and the wide horizons they lay open before them are breathtaking. They regard man as sure to reach the good if, in his action, he seeks nothing but the face of God; and in case man is led astray by the devil, his repentance is acceptable to God as long as his reason and judgment over-whelm his passion and return him to the straight path. The straight path is itself the pattern of God in creation, a pattern discoverable by reason and heart through investigation of God's creation and constant self-exer-tion in the search for nature's laws. If, despite all this assurance, some men continue not to recognize God, to spread corruption on earth, and to remain blind to the values of brotherhood and immune to their moving appeal, they will sooner or later come to tragedy. Their fate, however, would only constitute God's didactic example to the rest of mankind. That is the justice of God and His mercy to all, which are not affected by the erring of the misguided few who finally receive that which their misdeeds had earned for them.

But, it may be asked: Since every man's hour is written already, why do men act when they know that death is lying in wait for them, that when their term comes, their fate will be fulfilled on the hour? Why do men think and search, exert themselves and work when some are prede-termined to happiness and felicity and others to suffering and misery? This is a repetition of the question which we have just answered. We are repeating it deliberately in order to raise another issue, namely that of man's last hour. That which God predetermined as man's last hour was indeed part of the pattern of the cosmos before there was even a cosmos, before God created the world by commanding it to be. This point is evi-denced in the divine statement, "God has taken upon Himself to show mercy."[8] This statement means that mercy is an attribute of God and hence part of the cosmic pattern, not an exertion of His will. God says that "We shall impose no punishment until We have sent a prophet."[9] If, therefore, a people have gone astray without God having sent them a prophet, the divine pattern prescribes that none of them shall suffer any punishment. God's knowledge of the effect of His pattern in the cosmos is evident to anyone who believes that God is the Creator of the cosmos. But if God does send a prophet to a certain people, and the cosmic pat-tern and God's will prescribe that some of them persist in going astray despite the call to wisdom and guidance, their evil is upon themselves and their suffering will be an example for the rest.

Misguidance Is Injustice to Oneself

It may not be claimed that those who persist in their misguidance have been punished or have suffered an injustice because their misguidance was predetermined for them. Such an assertion would be naive, not deceptive, because the least amount of reasoning leads to the conclusion that whoever goes astray does indeed do injustice to himself. To clarify this argument, it is sufficient for us to consider the example of the compassionate father of a child standing close to a fire. If the child seeks to touch the fire, the father moves him away from it, explaining that it would burn him otherwise. But if he brings his child close to the fire again, the father would do so under the assumption that his child's fingers being burnt will give him a direct sensation of fire, a realization which will persist in his memory throughout his life. Once the child becomes an adult and touches the fire, or throws himself into it, he surely deserves the burns thus inflicted. His father is not to blame, and no one would expect the father to stand between his grown son and the fire in order to stop such a happening. A similar case is that of the father who explains to his son the evils of alcohol and of gambling. If, after attaining maturity, the child violates the commandment of his father and suffers for it, his father may not be declared unjust toward him, even though it may have been within his capability to prevent his son by force from drinking or gambling. Indeed, it would even be the duty of his father not to interfere and prevent such violation if the son's violation provides a moral and example to his brethren and relatives. If one considers as relatives and brethren the hundreds and thousands who inhabit the cities where temptations necessarily abound, it is good and just that some violators do suffer the consequences of their deeds so that the moral health of the community may be preserved, however regretful their personal suffering may be to the community. This example is an elementary case of justice as we apprehend it in our human community. How stronger should it be when we consider the universe as a whole, the millions upon millions of creatures in infinite space and time! Whatever punishment may fall upon any individual or people as the result of their injustice is indeed just in the purview of that vast cosmic picture which our imagination can hardly represent.

Our Personal Ethical Ideals

If we impute injustice to a father who leaves his erring son to meet the consequences which have been predetermined for his misconduct, we should impute injustice to ourselves when we kill the flea in fear of its sting or in fear of contagion with the disease which it may carry and which may be calamitous to us as well as to the community in which we live.

Following that reasoning, we should not be surprised if injustice is imputed to ourselves when we break up and dissolve the stones in our liver or kidney in fear of the pain or discomfort which such stones bring, or when we cut off a member or organ of our body in fear of its disease spreading to the rest of the body and bringing about its death. If we do not kill the flea, break up the stone, or cut off the member or organ, and, in consequence, we suffer pain, contagion, calamity, or death, we blame only ourselves on the grounds that the road to cure was wide open.

But so is the road of repentance for the guilty. It is only the ignorant who submit to pain and misery in the belief that it has been predetermined for them. This kind of submission is nothing short of stupidity and naïveté on their part. But we do kill the flea, break and remove the stone, and cut off the sick organ and yet consider all this perfect justice when it is predetermined in the matter of the cosmos that the flea shall sting and thus carry contagion to man, that the stone shall disturb the organ and cause it to malfunction, that the sick organ shall communicate its sickness to the whole body and thus bring about death. How do we who make such judgments feel so certain of their validity and truth, and yet fail to recognize the implied limitation of justice to our own person and its non-extension to the human community as a whole? Indeed, how do we choose to ignore the cosmos as a whole, as it really is? To do so is an unjustified piece of idiocy and stupidity, a case of extreme narrow-mindedness and low intelligence.

Good Works Are Acts of Worship

And what is the flea, the stone, or man himself when compared to the large universe? Indeed, what is humanity itself in this regard? The universe is so great that our mind, incapable of imagining it, turns to such concepts as eternity, infinity, and the like in order to give us an incomplete picture of it, a picture as incomplete as our knowledge is little. Our knowledge is indeed limited, but despite its limitation, it is still great enough to guide us to the divine pattern in the universe, and to understand that divine pattern as orderly, immutable, and determined. God has given us faculties of knowledge, hearing, sight, and a heart that we may learn with them the creative work of His own hand and the patterns He has imbedded in the cosmos. Such knowledge is prerequisite to religious feeling and thinking. We must know God and know His work if we are to praise Him, to thank Him, and to do the good which He commands. To do the good in con-

viction or *iman* is the noblest form of worship that any rational creature
can offer to God.

Death, Conclusion, and Beginning of Life

As for death, it is the end of one life and the beginning of another.
Consequently, it is feared only by those who deny the other life or fear it
on account of their ill conduct in this life. Such men never wish for death
because they know what awaits them. Those who wish for death sincerely and fearlessly are the true believers, the truly convinced, and the doers
of good deeds in the world.

God — May He be adored — says:

الَّذِى خَلَقَ الْمَوْتَ وَالْحَيٰوةَ لِيَبْلُوَكُمْ اَيُّكُمْ اَحْسَنُ عَمَلًا ۚ وَهُوَ الْعَزِيزُ الْغَفُورُ ۙ

"He who created death as well as life that you may prove who of you
is the better in deed is the Almighty and the Merciful."[10]

Further, addressing His Prophet, He said — May He be praised —:
"No human has ever been granted everlasting life. If you will certainly die,
will they not? Every man shall taste of death, and the evil and good which
befall you are a trial for you. To earth will be your return."[11] Further, He
says: "Those unto whom the Torah has been revealed but who have not
observed its commandments are like a donkey carrying a load of books.
Wretched are the people who deny the revelations of God. God does not
guide the unjust in their injustice. Say, 'O Jews, if, as you pretend, you are
the friends of God and His elect of all mankind, wish for death that you
may prove your sincerity.' But they never wish for death, for rejoining their
Lord; and that is because they know that their arms have wrought evil and
injustice. God knows the unjust."[12] God also says, "It is He who termi-
nates your life by night, Who knows every violation you have committed
by day, Who will resurrect you after a prescribed term, return you to
Himself, and confront you with all the deeds that you have wrought on
earth."[13]

These verses are extremely emphatic in their rejection of the
Orientalists' claim that Islamic determinism implies immobilization and
unconcern for work and acquisition. God created life and death that men
may prove who among them is the better worker of deeds. The theater of

human achievement is this life; reward and punishment come after death. If men do not work, if they do not strike out into the earth and seek therein God's bounty, if they do not earn and hence do not give in charity of that which God has provided for them, nor perform any good to others, however little their means may be, they have disobeyed God. It is no excuse for them that they have nothing to give, for their duty is to go out and earn. Failure to perform one duty constitutes no justification of their failure to perform another. On the contrary, those who earn and give are the more righteous in God's sight and the more deserving of rewards in the other world. Through good and evil works God gives us the chance to prove ourselves. Upon us devolves the duty of rationally distinguishing between them. Not an atom's weight of good nor an atom's weight of evil done in this world will be lost on the Day of Judgment. If nothing befalls us except what has been predetermined by God, we should concern ourselves all the more to discern the good that we may realize it in the world. It makes no difference whatever whether God chooses to terminate our lives at the prime of youth, vitality, wisdom, and glory, or at old age when we become senile and lapse into childish ignorance. The measure of a life is certainly not the number of years one lives, but the good works which one does that nothing can obliterate. Those who die in the cause of God are alive with their Lord, and they are alive among us inasmuch as we continue to remember them. Many are the men who have written their names indelibly on history because they dedicated themselves to the good. Among us, surely, they are still alive, even though they may have died hundreds of years ago.

"And when their term arrives, men shall meet their death at its prescribed hour, neither before nor after."[14] This, indeed, is the truth. It alone accords with the pattern of the universe. Man has an hour which he cannot outlive, just as the sun and the moon have their terms and their eclipse always occurs according to law, without fail. It is more likely that man's awareness that his life will terminate will incite him to hasten the performance of good deeds and to exert all possible effort. Moreover, the fact that man does not know when his hour will strike will stir his anxiety enough to prepare for that eventuality. Everyday we witness new evidence that man's hour is determined and, when it strikes, inevitable. Some people die suddenly without apparent reason; others fall sick and fight for their lives for decades until they reach a decrepit old age. A number of medical men today claim that the agent which brings about man's death is innate to him and that the period this agent requires to achieve its objective would not be impossible to calculate if the agent itself could be isolated and identified — a problem of no little difficulty — though not impossible. God, who is omniscient, knows the hour of every man by reason of the immutable and eternal pattern he has imbedded in the cosmos as a whole.

Prophets Are Always Folkmen

It is the method of His mercy — May He be adored — that He will inflict no punishment until He has sent a prophet to guide men to the truth and to show them the path to the good. If God were to punish men for the injustices they commit, immediately upon their commission of them, no creature would be left alive on earth. But He defers judgment to a future but definite term in order to give them a chance to listen to the prophet, to follow his guidance, and to resist the appeal of lowly life. The prophets whom God has sent were neither royal nor wealthy. They belonged neither to the rank of the great and glorious nor to that of the men of science. Rather He has chosen His prophets from among the populace. Ibrahim was a carpenter, and so was his father. Jesus was a carpenter in Nazareth. Many others were shepherds, and so was the Seal and last of them, Muhammad — May God's peace and blessing be upon him. God chooses His prophets from among the populace in order to teach that the truth is not the exclusive monopoly of the rich or the strong but is available to whosoever seeks it for its own sake and for its own sake alone. The eternal truth is that man does not fulfill his *iman* until he has desired for his fellow man that which he has loved for himself, and has acted and lived in accordance with the principle. "The worthier among you in the sight of God is the more pious, the more virtuous. . . . Work and realize the good, for God will reckon your achievement" and you will be given exactly what you have earned.[15] The great truth is that God is, and that there is no God but He.

Death is the terminus of one life and the commencement of another. It is the terminus of this life and the beginning of the life beyond. We know but little about this life, namely, that which is accessible to our senses, that to which our reason leads us, and that which our intuitive faculties enable us to behold. As for the life beyond, we do not know anything about it except what God has revealed to us. Of the patterns of the cosmos, many are not given to us that are known to the Omniscient, the Great and Glorious God Who sees all. Sufficient unto us therefore is what

God related in His Holy Book concerning the life beyond. He told us that it is the House of Judgment, of Reward and Punishment. Let us then prepare ourselves in this life by our deeds and our resolution to take our affairs into our own hands. Let us put our trust in God and await His just reward. What lies beyond these considerations belongs to God alone.

After all this, will Washington Irving, and the Orientalists and non-Orientalists who follow in his footsteps, realize how deeply erroneous is their understanding of the determinism of Islam? Our foregoing discussion has been limited to what the Holy Qur'an has said on the matter. That is precisely because we do not wish to open a controversy by bringing in the opinions of the Sufis, the *mutakallimun*, the philosophers, and other Muslim schools. Irving is in deep error when he claims that divine judgment, providence, and man's final hour were all given in those Qur'anic passages that were revealed after the Battle of Uhud and the martyrdom of Hamzah. Actually, many of the verses that we have quoted in this discussion are Makkan and were revealed before the Hijrah and before any battles were fought by the Muslims. As a matter of fact, Irving and his like fall into error because they fail to give adequate scientific consideration to such an important and grave problem as determinism. They understand Islam under categories which accord with their Christian or Western inclinations and prejudices, and then they construct a patchwork of so-called evidence to prove their prejudice, thinking that they can really convince their readers and hoping that no one will take to task their argument and analyze their reasoning.

The Philosophic Value of Islamic Determinism

Had the Orientalists understood Islamic determinism in the manner we have described, they would have appreciated its philosophic worth and profound value. For Islamic determinism regards life in a manner coherent with the most advanced, precise, philosophical, and scientific theories which human thought has achieved in its long and progressive history. The Islamic philosophic idea is synthetic. It does not exclude scientific determinism, nor does it deny the world as will and idea or the doctrine of emergent evolution.[16] Rather, Islamic determinism includes all these views within its system as aspects of the pattern of the cosmos and life. This is not the place to elaborate this point in detail. Nonetheless, we shall try to state it as succinctly and as clearly as possible, hoping that the reader will agree that the greatness, comprehensiveness, and depth of this idea is comparable with any other theory known or discovered until now, and that it leaves the door wide open for any great advance human thought may achieve in the future.

Before we begin our brief statement, two observations are in order and should not be forgotten. First, it is not the intention of this author to contradict any Christian theory. The revelation of Jesus has been confirmed by Islam, as we have had many occasions to see in the course of this work. Islam sought to synthesize the prophecies and divine messages which had gone before and to provide for them a climax and a crowning. As the Gospel substantiates Jesus Christ's claim to his disciples, "Think not that I am come to destroy the law... I am not come to destroy but to fulfill,"[17] just so the Qur'an confirmed the Muslim's *iman* in Ibrahim, Moses, Jesus, and all the preceding prophets. Islam came as a synthesis of all the previous divine revelations, as a correction and reproof of all the tampering with scripture done by the followers of those prophets. The second point is that the philosophical theory deducible from the Qur'an has been discovered by others before but in a different Way than that which I am following in these pages. I have reached it in the way I have because I have opened myself to the guidance of the Qur'an and followed a modern scientific method. If God has guided me to the truth, to Him belongs the praise and the gratitude. And if I have missed the truth in some of my reasoning, then it is all the more cause to pray for my mistakes to be corrected by men of knowledge. But that too is to praise God and to be grateful for His blessing.

The first principle the Qur'an firmly establishes is that God has implanted in the universe immutable patterns and eternal laws. The universe does not only consist of our earth and all that is on it, nor is it limited to all that our senses can reach by way of stars and other heavenly bodies. The universe consists of all that God has created, whether sensory or non-sensory, past, present or future. If we only attempt to imagine God's creation, we will realize that our knowledge is indeed small. The space which stands between us and the stars of heaven, electricity which fills this space as well as our earth, the great vastness of space which separates us from the sun and the stars and other systems of heavenly bodies yet farther than the sun and separated from us by thousands of light years, and the infinity of space lying still beyond these which is beyond our imagination but known to God — all this runs according to changeless and immutable laws. All that we have scientifically known about creation is still very scant; in it the actual has been mixed up with the imaginary.

Indeed, the real component of our so-called knowledge is little by comparison with the fictitious. However, it constitutes all that we genuinely know of the universe and serves as foundation for what we call the laws of the universe and of life, and puts a critical brake on our overhasty will to generalize. If, for a moment, we were to lift this brake, our imagination would seek to encompass the whole and the result would be the greatest flowering of science fiction. Supposing, for instance, that the inhabitants of Mars were to build a broadcasting station of a force of one hundred million kilowatts in order to bring to us, the inhabitants of the earth, details of what was taking place on their planet and show it to us by means of television. Would it then be possible for man on earth to restrain his imagination, considering that Mars is not the most distant of the planets nor the most difficult with which to have communication?

Everything in this vast universe, of which we know so little, exerts some influence on our world and everything it contains. If anyone of these heavenly bodies were to change its course or structure in some measure, however little, the pattern of our universe would be equally affected by such a change, and our own short and insignificant life that is already determined by our environment would equally be affected. Naturally, our life is more deeply affected by the greater cosmic forces and changes; even so, in suffering their effects, we may achieve the good as well as its opposite. The final result is not only a function of the influences we suffer, but of our preparation for receiving such influences and our mastery of ourselves in disposing of their effects. Many an identical pattern has determined many people in different ways, propelling some to good, others to evil, with all the variant degrees between them. In this life, good and evil are the effects of a dialectical relation between the elements and factors of the cosmos and the human soul. Thus, both good and evil may be said to result from the immutable pattern of the cosmos and follow necessarily from its existence, just as the positive and the negative are necessary implications of the existence of electricity, and microbes and germs are necessary implications of human bodily life.

Nature of Good and Evil

Nothing, therefore, is evil in itself or good in itself but is so in relation to the purpose which it serves and the consequences which it brings about. What is sometimes regarded as evil may at other times be absolutely necessary, or absolutely good. Many of the devices that in war time serve to annihilate millions of humans and destroy man's greatest monuments may during peace furnish the greatest advantages. Dynamite, for instance, is absolutely necessary for the construction of tunnels, of railways, and for the discovery of mines and the realization of their priceless treasures. Even poison gas that hostile nations hurl at one another in the most shameful and calamitously irresponsible acts of war can be put to many advantageous uses during peace — such as the use of chlorine gas to purify water and to detect other harmful and dangerous gases. Men have always been tempted to think that some insects, birds, and animals are absolutely useless. Study and research have changed these prejudices by showing the good purpose each of these species serves. Indeed, some countries have even promulgated legislation for the protection of these species in appreciation of the service they render to mankind. The zoologists have observed that animals can live in peace with their environments as long as their environments do not interfere with the discharge of their natural functions and that they do not harm other creatures except in self-defense or under alien pressures.

Ethical Nature of Human Deeds

As for us humans, our deeds are likewise neither good nor evil in themselves but have value only with reference to the purpose that they serve and the consequence that they achieve. Is not homicide a crime and hence forbidden? Nonetheless, God says, "And do not kill anyone; for God has forbidden it, unless it be a case of right, and after due process of law."[18] Killing by right, therefore, is morally unassailable. God said, "In punishment, great value — indeed a whole life — may be realized, O Men of thought!"[19] The executioner who kills the condemned convict, the man who kills another in self-defense, the soldier who kills in defending his homeland, and the believer who kills resisting those who would force him to abjure his faith, all these are guilty of neither disobedience nor crime when they commit homicide. They are fulfilling a divine duty imposed upon them by God and are deserving of righteous merit. What is true of homicide may also be true of many other deeds of men, as far as good and evil are concerned. The scientist who discovers a destructive force and the technologist who produces the instruments with which to deliver it, whether for the purpose of defending the homeland or for peacetime use, indeed every human operation on earth — none of these is good or evil in itself, but only in reference to the purpose it seeks to realize and the actual consequence it brings about.

The Gateway of Repentance

Such is the will of God and His pattern for the universe. Since God created men with different endowments and hence with varying preparation for understanding this pattern, some men exhaust all their energies usufructing and exploiting the very spot of the environment in which they are born and in which they grow. Some men are endowed with technological skills, others are endowed with faculties necessary for the professions, the arts and the sciences — all of which together are necessary if man is to be guided to the divine pattern. Since knowledge of the divine pattern is absolutely necessary for man if he is to lead a life of righteousness, God has granted to some individuals the gift of prophethood. He has selected some to convey His message to men, to show them the good and the evil. To others, he has granted the faculties with which to pursue science and logic that they may, as heirs to the Prophet, guide mankind to what it ought to do and not to do. Moreover, God has endowed every man with the necessary intellectual and emotional faculties for understanding and grasping the teachings thus offered, for disciplining himself in truth and wisdom and fulfilling in life God's imperative: in short, for doing good and avoiding evil. If, all this notwithstanding, some men fail to understand and commit evil, and if the community punishes them for their misdeeds in order to safeguard itself against their harm, this need not hinder their repentance and return to the straight path. Whoever commits a misdeed in ignorance or weakness, corrects himself, changes his orientation, and returns to God obedient and repentant, God will surely forgive and accept. Hence, the criminal or author of any misdeed ought to learn from the wisdom of the past in order to purify himself; he ought to use this wisdom to enable himself to be rehabilitated. God, the Merciful and Forgiving, will accept his repentance.

This presentation of the moral issue of human life has the merit of synthesizing many philosophical views hitherto deemed beyond conciliation. It clearly recognizes a purposive, efficacious will in all that is. "All being," God says, "is such that if We desire any part of it to exist, We command it to be and it will be."[20] It regards the universe as inclusive of all that is perceivable by sense as well as that which is not so perceivable and as subject to immutable natural laws that, despite the limitation of our capacities, are still discoverable by rational effort, the more so the more we exert ourselves in their study and pursuit. Moreover, it regards the universe as one whose foundation is the good. Though evil is ubiquitous and oft seems to prevail, our view regards the constant victory of good over evil as constitutive of the universe's emergent evolution, the progressive perfection the world has so far achieved through its long history.

Man's Spiritual Development

The reader will recognize that our presentation assumes human progress toward perfection, and regards it as the ideal of the highest philosophical system possible. Furthermore, the Qur'an regards spiritual development as the central principle of God's creation of the earth and all that is in it. God created heaven and earth in six days, it asserts, and then rested on His throne. Were these six days equivalent to our days on earth? Or were they such that "One day with your Lord is like a thousand years of your reckoning?"[21] This is not the place to discuss whether such statements imply a theory of evolution, or whether the Qur'an regards evolution as the law of the cosmos. Further, it asserts that God created Adam and Eve and asked the angels to serve them and that all angels did so except Satan who was not moved by the fact that God had told Adam all the names. God said:

"'O Adam, reside with your wife in the Garden. Eat of such of its fruits as you wish, but do not come near this tree and thus be guilty of injustice.' Seeking to misguide them and to make them aware of their shame, Satan told them that God had forbidden them the fruit of that tree in order to prevent them from becoming angelic or eternal. He pledged to them that he only meant to give them good counsel. Thus, by deception he caused them to transgress. After they tasted of the fruit of the tree, their shame became manifest and they covered themselves with leaves. Their Lord called out to them: 'Have I not forbidden you the fruit of this tree and warned you of Satan's grave hostility to you?' They answered, 'O God, we have transgressed and thereby wronged ourselves. If You do not have mercy on us and forgive us, surely our fate will be that of the lost.' God said, 'Go forth! Some of you will henceforth be enemies of the others. On earth, you will have but a temporary abode. Therein you will spend your lives: you will

die and will be raised again.' O Men, We have provided for you
clothes and raiment with which to cover your bodies. But the raiment of piety and good deeds is far superior. This is another sign
and evidence from your Lord that you might remember and
observe. O Men, let not Satan deceive you anymore, as he succeeded in forcing your ancestors out of the Garden by seeking to
show them their shame. Satan and his legion keep a constant eye
upon you. You have no awareness of them. Their nature is to be
the friends and guides of those who have no faith and no conviction."[22]

Adam and Eve departed from the Garden, and their progeny became
hostile to one another. They strove and still strive the length of their lives.
The powers and faculties with which God had endowed them help them
in their effort, but they shall continue to struggle on earth until God's purpose is fulfilled.

Cruelty and prejudice, strife and competition characterize the first
attempts of human life on earth. God said:

"And relate to them the true story of the two sons of Adam.
Each one of them made an offering to God but only one was
accepted. The son whose offering was not accepted said to the
other, 'I shall kill you.' The other answered, 'God accepts the
offering only of those who are righteous. Should you attack and
kill me, I shall not attack you because I fear God, the Lord of the
Universe. If you do what you say, yours will be a double guilt —
that of being unrighteous in the first place and that of killing me
in the second. You will surely then deserve the right punishment
as all other unjust men, namely the fire.' Induced by his passion,
the son of Adam killed his brother and reaped the fate of the lost.
God then sent a raven which scratched into the ground, thereby
showing him how to bury the corpse of his brother. As he interred
his brother, remorse gripped him and he repented for what he had
done, realizing that he was not even as worthy as the raven who
had just taught him how to dispose of the dead. On this account
We have prescribed, as We did for the Children of Israel, that
whoever kills a man for a purpose other than self-defense or legitimate punishment for misdoing is as guilty as he who kills the
whole of mankind; and, likewise, that whoever saves a life has

saved the lives of all mankind. Repeatedly have Our messengers come to men with clear evidence of this, but many of them still perpetrate their injustice in the world."[23]

Jealousy, cruelty, resentment, and hostility are all amply evident in the story of this fratricide. The righteous victim, on the other hand, did not respond with forgiveness and pardon when his brother threatened to kill him. Rather, his response was that he wished to have him carry the double burden of his own misdeeds and of the murder he was contemplating and thus earn the punishment of hell. Undoubtedly, the man spoke in concert with human nature and its overwhelming inclination to seek to punish evil rather than magnanimously to forgive it.

The children of Adam multiplied and spread over the earth. God sent them prophets to remind and warn them of Him. But they persisted in going astray; their spiritual life was dead, and their minds utterly blocked to the truth. God sent Noah to call his people to the worship of the One God, and he warned them saying: "I fear for you the punishment of a painful death." But his people paid him little heed. Following Noah, many prophets came and many divine messages were conveyed, all calling to the worship of God alone. Gradually stagnation became the rule, and men's minds became utterly closed to the divine call. Indeed, they took the creatures of the world for Gods; and whenever a prophet was sent to them by their Lord, they either belied or killed him. Nonetheless, the stagnation of men was repeatedly shaken by prophets, sent from God, who planted good seeds. Although these were slow to grow, they were not without significant effects; for, is truth ever wholly lost? If men happen to be so vain as to avoid the message of truth or to ridicule its conveyor, they will still ponder that message when they are alone and consider what it says. At any rate, those who have apprehended the divine messages have always been few, and these few have often been guilty of false pride.

In ancient Egypt, the priesthood knew and believed the monotheistic truth, but they taught the people something else and multiplied for them their gods. They regarded this practice as necessary for safeguarding their authority and glory. So attached were they to their own powers that they opposed Moses and his brother Aaron's calling them to God and their seeking Pharaoh's permission for the Children of Israel to follow them. Further, the Qur'an relates the stories of the prophets who followed one another across the centuries while the great majorities of their people persisted in their misguidance. In the Qur'anic accounts of the prophets of the past, one significant point ought to be underlined. First, however, we must recall the history of Moses and Jesus and the subsequent history of Muhammad — May God's blessing be upon him.

The Judgment of Reason and Belief in Miracles

The point to be noted is the separation of, or what seems to be the discrepancy between, reason and its logique on one hand, and faith built upon acceptance of miracles and extraordinary events on the other. God confirmed everyone of His prophets with some miracle in order to enable him to win the confidence of his people. However, only a few men believed in their prophets or took them seriously. Men's minds were still too undeveloped to understand that God is the Creator of everything, that He is One, that He is the just Lord of the universe, and that there is no God but He. Before God chose to send Moses, the latter had run away from Egypt in fear and found security in the desert with the tribe of Midyan into which he also married. Before God permitted him to return, "He was called from the right side of the valley, from the blessed spot, out of the tree: 'O Moses, verily, I am God, Lord of the universe.' Moses was told to lay down his staff; but when he saw it move as if it were a serpent, he ran away without turning back. Again he was called to approach. He was ordered to search inside his garment, to shed away his fear, and compose himself. God then said to him: 'This is the judgment of your Lord which you will convey to Pharaoh and his government; namely, they have become a truly corrupt people.'"[24]

Pharaoh's magician priests did not respond favorably to Moses' call until his rod devoured all their rods. Only then did they prostrate themselves and declare their faith in God, the Lord of Aaron, and of Moses. Nonetheless, the Children of Israel persisted in their misguidance. Indeed, they even asked Moses to show them God with their own eyes; and as soon as he passed away, they returned to the worship of the calf. Following Moses, their prophets came to call them to God, but they killed them unjustly. When they did return to the worship of God, they expected a Messiah who would return to them a political kingdom and the material power with which to rule the world. This series of events is not so far removed from us that it remains lost in the darkness of early history. Barely twenty-five centuries old, this event clearly shows man's preference of selfishness over reason and his desire for material things over the things of spirit.

A few centuries later, Jesus, confirmed by God's holy spirit, came call-ing men to God. Since Jesus was a Jew, the Jews first thought of him as their Messiah and expected him to return to the Jews their lost kingdom in the promised land. The hardships they suffered under Roman rule had made them all the more anxious to achieve such a political kingdom. They waited, however, in order to find out more precisely what Jesus was about. Did Jesus appeal to the logic of reason alone? No. Rather, it was a miracle that opened the road to his persuasion of them. If the Christian stories are not mistaken, it was the miracle of transforming the water into wine at the wedding of Cana that first drew public attention to Jesus. Thereafter came the miracles of the loaves of bread and fishes, of curing the sick, and of resurrecting the dead that made it possible for him to teach the public by appealing to their hearts, feelings, and emotions. Reason and its logic played a very minor role in his teaching. Nonetheless, Jesus proved more successful than his predecessors. He had combined his appeal to feeling, mercy, forgiveness, and love with a call to God, devoid of critical evidence and rational proof. Whenever people suspected his cause, God permitted him to perform a new miracle and thus regain their loyalty and apprecia-tion. His miracles included the curing of the leper, giving sight to the blind and raising the dead. They produced such a strong appeal among his followers that some of them thought that he was the Son of God, and oth-ers that he was God incarnate coming to expiate the sins of men. This evi-dence clearly shows that men were not mature enough to comprehend by force of reason alone the supreme truth regarding the Creator — May He be adored — namely, that He is One, Eternal, Unbegotten and Unbegetting, and that nothing is like unto Him.

The Rational Sciences

Long before the times of Moses and Jesus, the science of ancient Egypt as well as its philosophy and law had passed to Greece and Rome, which had then spread their dominion. It was Egypt that contributed to Greek philosophy and literature their noblest ideas. The new rationalist awakening thus produced, warned and convinced the people that miracles constitute no argument at all. It was in consequence of this that Greek philosophy contributed to the multiplication of Christian doctrines and hence to sectarianism diversification in Egypt, Palestine and al Sham, as we had occasion to see earlier. But it was God's pattern that reason shall constitute the apogee of human life, as long as it is not composed of empty logic, not devoid of feeling and spirit, and as long as it marshals all these faculties in a synthesized effort to discover the secrets of the universe and achieve intimate knowledge of the cosmic pattern. Thus, it was decreed by God that soon the Prophet of Islam would rise to call men to the truth through reason, complemented by feeling and spirit, and that the one miracle of such a gnoseological synthesis should be the Holy Book revealed to His Prophet Muhammad. With Muhammad's revelation and teaching, God completed for men their religion and granted them His blessings. With it, He climaxed all prophethood, concluded all revelation, and sealed it. But all this took place only after the prophets' great and continuous effort and the messengers' guiding of mankind in its spiritual deportment until it could reach the height of the Islamic call to faith and conviction in one God alone.

To complement and buttress this new conviction in the Divine "Unicity," the duties discussed in the first part of this conclusion were instituted. All were designed to enable the believer to reach this pinnacle of vision. It is also man's duty always to strive after a vision of God's pattern in creation. That is what the Muslims strove to do in the early centuries of their history until they began to decline.

The arguments so far adduced refute the western Orientalists' interpretation of Islamic determinism and the Qur'anic position on fate and the last hour. They prove without a shadow of doubt that Islam is a religion of striving and activism in all the theaters of life — the spiritual, the scientific, the religious, and the worldly. They prove that God's immutable pattern in the cosmos is that man will get what his own deeds have earned for him and that God — May He be adored — will commit no injustice to anyone. Rather, it is men who commit injustice to themselves. Indeed, men do injustice to themselves when they think that they can achieve God's blessing through stagnation and inactivity, through *tawakul* or lazy dependence, disguised as *tawakkul* or trust in God.

Material Wealth and Children

Although these arguments have proved this point without a doubt, I am unable to overlook one other argument that I consider extremely important. It is the argument implied in the divine statement:

الْمَالُ وَالْبَنُونَ زِينَةُ الْحَيَوٰةِ الدُّنْيَا وَالْبٰقِيٰتُ الصّٰلِحٰتُ خَيْرٌ عِنْدَ رَبِّكَ ثَوَابًا وَخَيْرٌ أَمَلًا ۝

"Wealth and children are the ornaments and joy of this life; but the good deeds, imperishable as they are, weigh more with your Lord. They are indeed better, and provide a sound basis for greater hopes."[25]

Nothing in the world incites us to greater exertion, striving, and work than the acquisition of wealth. In its pursuit, most men spend the greatest part of their energies. Indeed, they often outdo themselves. One look at our modern world is sufficient to perceive the strenuous persistence, the hardships, the wars, the revolutions, and the disturbances that occur all for the sake of wealth. For its sake monarchies become republics, blood is shed, and men lay down their lives. So much for wealth. As for children, they are pieces of our flesh groping the earth in front of us! What hardship will we not gladly bear for their sake! What bitterness will not taste sweet as long as it leads to their security, health and happiness! Every hardship we encounter on the road to their happiness becomes easy; every conflict becomes harmony. And there are men who for the sake of wealth and children would do that which would otherwise be impossible. Indeed, some people are so committed to such a pursuit that they would sacrifice their own happiness and even their lives.

Wealth and children, therefore, do constitute "the joy and ornament" of this world. An ornament is nothing, however, by comparison to the essence. No one would sacrifice the essence for the sake of an ornament except the ignorant and the insane, vain women and deluded youths. Vain women would expose their health to danger that they might appear beautiful for a few hours or less; and deluded youths would squander their wealth that their companions may applaud and acclaim them as masters. Such people are no less mad than those who pursue wealth and children, the ornaments and joy of this life, at the cost of everything else. To repeat, wealth and children do constitute a joy and an ornament. But the essence of life is the doing of righteous deeds which are imperishable. It is for the sake of this imperishable righteousness that we ought to devote the greater part of our effort and striving.

The nobility of purpose served by the last quoted verse of Holy Scripture is truly arresting. What it purports to say is that if it is natural that man spend his effort and blood for the sake of an ornament, he should spend his whole soul and mind for the sake of the essence; that he should make the ornament subject to the essence and, finally, that he should dedicate his own life, his wealth, and his children to the pursuit of this essence which consists of righteous deeds. For the latter weigh more with God. Righteousness is the worthier ideal. Its merit is greater and its promise is nobler. It is the higher hope of mankind.

How did the thinking of Muslims change so radically from this sane, healthy, and clear logic to the very opposite? We referred to this question accidentally in the first part of this conclusion when we discussed the change that the Muslims underwent as result of being conquered by foreigners at the close of the 'Abbasi regime.

Shaykh Muhammad 'Abduh's Views

In the preface to the second edition we also mentioned how the government changed from being based upon consultation in the earliest period to a sheer contest of power during the Umawi period, and finally to rule by divine right during the 'Abbasi period. On this point, let us quote the late professor and leader, Shaykh Muhammad 'Abduh, who wrote in his book, *Al Islam wa al Nasraniyyah*, the following passage:

"The religion of Islam was once purely Arab. Science was once Greek and then became Arab too. Subsequently, one of the 'Abbasi caliphs committed a political mistake when he abused the tolerance of Islamic political theory. Suspecting that an army composed largely of Arabs might readily lend its support to a caliphal contender supporting the cause of 'Ali, he sought to build for himself an army of aliens, particularly of Turks and Daylams, whom he thought he could rule by his authority, win with his largesse, and keep loyal to him against all his enemies. Islamic law is tolerant enough to allow the Muslim ruler to take such measures, and it was on this account that Muslim society fell under dominion of foreign elements.

"Thus, an 'Abbasi caliph sought to secure himself on the caliphal throne and secure that throne for his progeny. He may have done well for himself and his children, but woe to him for what he did to his people and his religion. He increased the number of aliens in his army and appointed aliens to command it. But no sooner had he done so than these soldiers and their captains seized the upper hand, monopolized the political power, and subjected caliph, people, and state to their whims. These were still brutes not yet disciplined by Islam. Their hearts had not yet been sensitized to religious value. Rather, these frontiersmen came to the world of Islam with crudeness, ignorance, and injustice. Islam was for them a cover; little of it penetrated their consciousness, and only the superficial aspects of it influenced their thinking. Many of them even carried their own gods around with them but prayed with the Muslim masses in order to consolidate their power over them. Later, the world of Islam fell prey to the Tatars who held it in subjection for generations and who saw no other impediment to their sovereignty and power than knowledge which would make the people aware of the state of their masters and expose the immorality of their conduct. As a result, they became openly hostile to knowledge and to Islam itself, which promotes knowledge and requires its cultivation as an act of worship. As for knowledge, science, and wisdom, their cultivators were maltreated and most of them denied any assistance or subsidy. They encouraged their own protagonists to introduce themselves into the ranks of the men of knowledge, to wear their gowns, and pretend to belong to their circles. From this position, these protagonists began to teach in the name of religion such doctrines as would make knowledge hateful to the people and cause men to avoid striving for it. Their propaganda posed as piety, for they claimed that their new doctrines were designed but to safeguard the religion. They claimed that the religion was incomplete and they had set out to complete it; that it was diseased and they had set out to cure it; that it was floundering and they had set out to consolidate it; that it was about to collapse, and they had set out to rescue and support it.

"These newcomers to Islamic leadership wished to imitate some of the pageantry of pagans and Christians, and, therefore, they adopted some of their customs which were inconsistent with Islam. They convinced the ignorant masses that the new practices added glory and aggrandizement to the ritual of Islam. Demagogery is the resort of the unjust ruler. By recoursing to it, they instituted the celebrations with which we have been plagued. By prescribing the worship of saints and of their own leaders they divided the Muslim community, thus enabling it to fall into complacency and ignorance. They decided that the later generations may never question anything passed down by the former, and they defended this conservatism as a principle of faith precisely in order to freeze man's thinking and to stop deliberation.

Throughout the provinces of the Islamic world, they sent their mouthpieces and instructed them to teach such tales, stories, and reports as would convince the masses that public affairs were none of their concern, that all community and state affairs are the jurisdiction of the ruler alone, and that whoever interferes in the ruler's jurisdiction has overstepped the boundaries laid down by the religion. These mouthpieces also taught the masses that corruption, insecurity, hardship, and privation are not the responsibility of the rulers but the fulfillment of prophecies regarding the end of time; that it is futile to seek to change any state, any situation or verdict; that it is salutary to relinquish all responsibilities to God and the rulers, and that the Muslim is responsible only for the upkeep of himself and his immediate family. They found support for their claims in the letter of some prophetic, many spurious and fabricated, traditions which they were quick to exploit for their own purpose, interpreting them only in order to indoctrinate the people with their fictions and delusions. A whole army of such false teachers spread among the Muslims, and the puppet rulers in every province helped them to spread their poison. They misinterpreted the Islamic doctrine of divine decree so as to frustrate human will and to choke every striving for action. The peoples' ignorance of their religion, their naïveté, their inclination to the path of least resistance, and their desire to satisfy their passions persuaded the Muslims to accept those lethal superstitions and fables. As a result, the truth fell under the darkness of falsehood, and in the people's minds principles which diametrically contradicted their religion and ran counter to its precepts became the rule of the day and were accepted without hesitation.

"This policy of spreading the darkness of ignorance, injustice, and prejudice is responsible for the corruption of Islam, for mixing the Islamic with the unIslamic in an unholy concoction of faith and superstition. It robbed the Muslim of his will and of the hope which once prompted him to pierce the heavens. It caused him to imitate the despair of the non-Muslims. Most of what goes today under the name of Islam is not Islam at all. It may only have preserved the outer shell of the Islamic ritual of prayer, fasting, and pilgrimage, as well as some sayings which have been, however, perverted by allegorical interpretations. All these sinister accretions and superstitions that found their way into Islam brought about the stagnation that now passes under the name of religion. Accursed be that policy and its men for what they false- ly attribute to God and His religion. All that is today blamewor- thy among the Muslims is not of Islam. It is something else which falsely carries that name."[26]

Muslim Views in the Age of Decline

It was this situation, so well analyzed by Shaykh Muhammad 'Abduh, that led to the propagation among the Muslims of contradictory princi- ples which their authors claimed to be Islamic and falsely attributed to the Prophet. One of these principles is the doctrine of determinism which later Muslims interpreted in a way which runs counter to the Qur'anic spirit. In the foregoing pages, we have seen how the Qur'an understood that doctrine. Departing from that understanding, the advocates of those specious doctrines taught the virtues of surrender and stagnation. They preached that each man's life is not the result of striving and planning but is predetermined so that man cannot affect its outcome. Such is the false determinism which enables the western critics of Islam to impute to Islam that of which it is innocent. Another such principle is the contempt of matter and condemnation of its pursuit. This was the view of the Greek stoics which spread at certain periods among some Muslims despite its contradiction to the whole tenor of the Qur'anic message expressed in the command, "And do not forget to pursue your share of this world."[27]

Despite its contradiction of the Qur'an, this principle even produced a large body of literature in the 'Abbasi period and thereafter. The Qur'an in fact calls for the reasonable satisfaction of all wants. It does not toler- ate self-deprivation any more than it tolerates indulgence and license. And yet, Irving falsely supposes that Islam engulfed the Muslims in luxury, dis- tracted them from self-exertion in war and, indeed, brought the Muslim peoples to the state of decline in which they find themselves today.

Islam and Christianity: A Comparison

The American author contends that Christianity calls men to purity and charity and that it is, on this account, the opposite of what he thinks Islam is. This is not the place to compare Islam and Christianity on this point, because, fundamentally, the two religions are in agreement. Comparison in this manner would lead to futile controversy and to a prof-

itless competition between Christianity and Islam. However, I do wish to
observe that between Jesus — May God's blessing be upon him — and
Christianity, as far as this call to stoicism and asceticism is concerned,
there is a clear difference. Jesus was certainly no stoic. His first miracle was
the transformation of the water into wine at Cana where he was a guest.
Obviously, Jesus had not wished that the people go without drinking
wine. Neither did he turn down the invitation of the Pharisees to sit at
their lavish banquet, for he did not wish the people to deprive themselves
from enjoying the blessings of God. Likewise, Muhammad emphasized
the need for pursuing one's share of this world. On the other hand, it is
true that Jesus used to call the rich to give charitably to the poor and to
love the latter in good heart. In this, however, the Qur'an has given voice
to the greatest and most eloquent expression ever known to man. The
reader may recall that we have quoted from the Qur'an in connection with
the *zaktat* and *sadaqat* which we discussed earlier. Sufficient for us in reply
to Irving and his like to say that the Qur'an has called for charity, temperance, moderation, goodness, and love regarding everything.

"They That Take the Sword..."

There remains the last sentence of Washington Irving's statement. It
is that by which the West indicts us with that which it had better indict
itself namely, the sword. The crime is indeed that of the western world.
not ours. It is its stain of shame, the sinister seed which will finally destroy
its false pride and civilization. Irving says: "That the crescent has waned
before the cross, and exists in Europe where it was once so mighty, only
by the sufferance or rather the jealously of the great Christian powers,
probably ere long to furnish another illustration, that 'they that take the
sword shall perish with the sword.'"

"They that take the sword shall perish with the sword." This verse of
the New Testament Irving directs accusingly toward Islam in the name of
Christianity. How strange! Perhaps Irving might have had some excuse
had he hurled his accusation a hundred or so years ago when the imperialism of the West (as we like to call it) or of Christendom (as Irving likes
to call it) had not reached the terrible degree of greed and covetousness,
of conquest and aggression by the sword which it has reached today.
When Field Marshall Allenby captured Jerusalem in 1918 in the name of
the Allies, he made this terrible proclamation standing on the steps of the
Dome of the Rock: "Today the Crusades have come to an end." Doctor

Peterson Smith, in his book on the life of Jesus, wrote, "This capture of Jerusalem was indeed an eighth Crusade in which Christianity had finally achieved its purpose." And it may even be true to say that the capture of Jerusalem was not a purely Christian effort, but that it was equally the effort of the Jews, who used the Christians in order to realize the old diaspora dream of making the Land of Promise a national home for the Jews.

Islam Has Never Taken Anything by the Sword

"They that take the sword shall perish with the sword." If these words of the New Testament are true at all, and truly applied to any nation, they certainly apply today to the nations of Christian Europe more than any other. Islam did not take the sword and therefore will not be taken with the sword. Rather it is Christian Europe which has taken the sword throughout the modern period, and it is Christian Europe which gives itself utmost license in the enjoyment of pleasure and comfort which Irving falsely imputes to Islam and to the Muslims. Today, Christian Europe is playing exactly the same role which the Mongols and Tatars played in the past in relation to Islam. The latter had put on the appearance of Islam and conquered its territories without paying any heed to Islamic teaching at all. Jesus's judgment fell rightly upon them as they brought corruption and disintegration to their Muslim subjects. Indeed, Christian Europe stands today even more guilty than those Tatars and Mongols of the past. The countries which the latter conquered quickly entered into Islam as soon as they were able to see its simplicity and greatness. Europe, however, does not conquer in order to spread a faith, nor in order to spread a civilization. What it wants is to colonize; to this end it has made the Christian faith a tool and instrument. That is why the European missions never succeeded, for they were never sincere and their propaganda served ulterior motives. They did not meet with any success at all in the Muslim countries — and indeed they never will — because the greatness of Islam — its simplicity, its rational and scientific character — leave no room in the minds of its adherents for any alien religious propaganda at all.

"They that take the sword shall perish with the sword." That is true. If this dictum was once true of the late Muslims who conquered for the sake of conquest and colonization, not in self-defense nor in defense of the faith, it is all the more true of this Christian West which conquers and vanquishes the peoples of the earth in order to colonize and to exploit. As for the early Muslims, during the time of the Prophet and of his immediate successors, they did not conquer for the purpose of conquest and colonization but in defense of their faith when it was threatened by Quraysh, Arab tribes, Byzantines, and Persians. Throughout their conquests, they never imposed their religion on anyone, for it was a cardinal principal of their faith that "there shall be no coercion in religion."[28]

Forced by the needs of defense against persistent attack, the Muslims' conquests were never motivated by the will to colonize. The Prophet left the kings of Arabia and her princes on their thrones with their territories, economies, and political structures virtually untouched. In conquering, the Muslims sought the freedom to preach the faith. If the Islamic faith spread, it was simply because it of itself was strong by virtue of the truth which it proclaimed, the universalist nondiscrimination between Arab and non-Arab which it commanded and its adherents practiced, and the strict monotheism by which Islam enabled man to have no master except the one true God. It was because of these innate strengths of the Islamic faith that it spread throughout the earth, just as any genuine truth would spread. When the Tatar latecomers to Islam fought only for the purpose of conquest and took men by the sword, they, too, were soon taken by the sword. But Islam never took anything or anyone by the sword, and no one will take it by the sword. On the contrary, Islam conquered the minds, hearts, and consciences of the people by its innate strength. Consequently, the Muslim people have seen many governments, dictators, and tyrants, none of which has changed their faith and religion in the least. Today, Europe is still the ruler of the Muslim peoples and the tyrannic administrator of their affairs. But her tyranny will not change the Muslims' faith in God. And as she has taken the Muslims by the sword, she cannot and will not escape the destiny of being taken by the sword. Matthew's principle will once more prove true, but this time to mete out to Christian Europe her due.

The Muslim League of Nations

We have said that the Prophet reinstated the princes and kings to their thrones and kingdoms. Toward the end of the Prophet's life the Arabian Peninsula was truly a league of Arab-Islamic nations. None of them was a colony either of Makkah or of Yathrib. By virtue of their strong faith in God, the Arabs were all equal to one another before Him. They acted together like one man against anyone who was against them or sought to sway them away from their religious faith. Up to the age of decline, the Muslim peoples remained a league of nations, and the seat of the caliphate was the headquarters of their league. The caliphate never claimed for itself any authority over the Muslim spirit, nor did it ever monopolize knowledge and the search for enlightenment. No Muslim nation submitted to any spiritual authority except that of God. The Muslim capitals were all capitals of science, knowledge, art, and industry. This felicity continued until the Muslims changed their view of Islam, denied its noble principles, violated the brotherhood of the faithful, and forgot that man's faith is never complete until he has desired for his fellow man what he desires for himself. It was then that prejudice did its evil work and destructive contests for power tore up the Muslim brotherhood as the sword became sole judge. But whoever takes with the sword shall be taken by the sword.

After the 15th century, Christian Europe arose to a new life of the spirit which might have brought benefit to all mankind except for the corruption that had quickly found its way to it. Hence, Christianity began to split into many factions. It was in this relatively recent period of its rise that Christian Europe faced a Muslim World that had forgotten its Islam, and took it by the sword. Europe continued to take the Muslim people by the sword, and, indeed, made the sword the sole judge between it and the Muslim people. But when the sword rules, we can then bid farewell to reason, to science, to goodness, to love, to faith, and, indeed, to mankind and to humanity.

It is the rule of the world by the sword which is the cause of the spiritual and psychic crisis from which the world suffers and groans. Those countries which rule the world by the sword realized this unfortunate truth as a result of World War I. They thus sought to bring peace to the world, and, for this purpose, they established the League of Nations. The whole point of the League of Nations is summed up in this verse of the Qur'an:

وَإِن طَآئِفَتَانِ مِنَ الْمُؤْمِنِينَ اقْتَتَلُوا فَأَصْلِحُوا بَيْنَهُمَا فَإِن بَغَتْ إِحْدَىٰهُمَا عَلَى الْأُخْرَىٰ فَقَاتِلُوا الَّتِي تَبْغِي حَتَّىٰ تَفِيءَ إِلَىٰ أَمْرِ اللَّهِ فَإِن فَاءَتْ فَأَصْلِحُوا بَيْنَهُمَا بِالْعَدْلِ وَأَقْسِطُوا إِنَّ اللَّهَ يُحِبُّ الْمُقْسِطِينَ ۚ إِنَّمَا الْمُؤْمِنُونَ إِخْوَةٌ فَأَصْلِحُوا بَيْنَ أَخَوَيْكُمْ ۚ وَاتَّقُوا اللَّهَ لَعَلَّكُمْ تُرْحَمُونَ

"And if two factions of believers fight each other, reconcile them in peace. If, thereafter, one aggresses upon the other, then fight the aggressor until it returns to the command of God. If it heeds that command, reconcile that faction again with justice, for God loves justice and those who judge accordingly. The faithful are brothers of one another. Reconcile them therefore as brothers. Fear God that you may be shown mercy."[29]

The Spirit of World Peace Still Missing

Nonetheless, peace did not rule the world after World War I, for the foundation upon which the dominant civilization is based is that of colonialism, and colonialism is in turn based upon the competition of one nationalism against another and upon domination of the weak by the strong. It is the right of the vanquished people, indeed their first duty, to seek to destroy the yoke of the tyrant. Consequently, colonialism has bred and nurtured the germs of rebellion and war. As long as colonialism is the rule, peace will never be established and wars will be continuous. Colonizing or colonized, the nations of the world will continue to regard one another with suspicion and, in fact, to lie in wait for one another. How then can there be peace? Peace will come to this world only when men everywhere change that which is within themselves; that is to say, when they begin to believe truly in peace, when they base their world views upon peace, and when they agree with one another to defend peace against every attempt at disturbing it.

But all this will happen only when colonialism is no more the basis for world order, when the strong of the earth will regard it as their first duty to come to the assistance of the weak, when the affluent will give to the deprived, when the big will show mercy to the small, and when the more learned will teach the ignorant. Peace will indeed reign over the world when the dominant powers spread knowledge throughout the earth to the end of serving mankind rather than of exploiting them in the name of knowledge or industry or technology. When the whole world comes to believe in this principle and all men come to feel that the earth is their own homeland — that they are all brothers of one another, each of them wishing for his brothers that which he wishes for himself — then will clemency, tolerance and fellowship grow among them. Then will they address one another in a language different from that in which they speak today; they will trust one another though they may be separated by wide spaces. They will all do the good for the sake of God. Then and only then will hatred and resentment dissolve, truth be supreme, peace rule the world, and God be pleased with mankind, and mankind with Him.

World Peace Founded Only on Tolerance

God says:

اِنَّ الَّذِينَ اٰمَنُوْا وَالَّذِينَ هَادُوْا وَالنَّصٰرٰى وَالصّٰبِئِيْنَ مَنْ اٰمَنَ بِاللّٰهِ وَالْيَوْمِ الْاٰخِرِ وَ عَمِلَ صَالِحًا فَلَهُمْ اَجْرُهُمْ عِنْدَ رَبِّهِمْ وَلَا خَوْفٌ عَلَيْهِمْ وَلَا هُمْ يَحْزَنُوْنَ ۞

"Those who believe, and those who are Jews, Christians, Sabeans, all those who believe in God and in the Day of Judgment and do the good works, all of them have their merit with their Lord. They have no reason to fear nor will they grieve."[30]

Has the world known any tolerance wider than this? Whoever believes in God, in the Day of Judgment, and in doing good works will have his merits with his Lord. No difference separates the believer from those whom the Islamic call has not reached, whether Jews, Christians, or Sabeans.[31]

God — May He be adored — further says: "Of the people of the Book, some believe in God, in what has been revealed to you, and what has been revealed to them. These revere God and fear Him and do not exchange the revelations of God for a mean price. To them belongs their reward with their Lord. God is quick to take account."[32] How far is all this from our world dominated as it is by western civilization? How far is the tolerance of Islam from the national and religious fanaticisms of the West and all the wars and catastrophes which it has contributed to human history!

The Sublime Life of Muhammad

It is this high and noble spirit of tolerance that should dominate the world if the world is to live in peace and men are to live in happiness. It is this spirit that makes every study of the life of Muhammad, to whom God revealed these genuine truths, and of every scholarly study undertaken only for the sake of knowledge, capable of achieving a mastery of such

cosmic and spiritual principles as will guide humanity to the new civilization it seeks. Every deep research undertaken in such a study will expose
secrets many men believed for a long time to be forever closed to scientific investigations, but on which the investigations of psychology have shed
illuminating light. The life of Muhammad, as we have had occasion to see,
is a human life that realized in itself the highest ideals of which man is
capable. On this account, the Prophet's life constitutes a good example
and true guidance to whosoever wishes to reach human perfection
through faith and the work of virtue. What highness and nobility can
compare with that which made the life of Muhammad — even before his
commission to prophethood — the example of truthfulness, dignity and
trustworthiness, just as it made that life after the commission to prophethood one long poem of self-sacrifice in the cause of God — the cause of
truth and goodness, the final end of all prophethood? Muhammad
exposed his life to death many times; his people sought to tempt him with
wealth, sovereignty, and all things desired by men; but he resisted them all.
He remained the best of all men in nobility, ethical virtue, and dedication
to the cause of God.

   This human life of Muhammad attained exalted levels of vision and
nobility, of power and magnanimity such as no other life has realized. It
was a human life which kept itself in communion with the cosmos from
eternity to eternity, and with the Creator of the cosmos by His grace and
mercy. Were Muhammad not exactingly truthful in the conveyance of his
Lord's message, some thinkers throughout the centuries would have come
up with some evidence to this effect, and some principle taught by
Muhammad would have been exposed as untrue. But 1,350 years[33] have
passed while that which Muhammad conveyed from his Lord continues
to be the model of truth and genuine guidance. Sufficient is it to mention
in support of this that what God revealed to Muhammad, to the effect
that he was the last of the prophets and messengers of God, has never
been successfully overthrown by anybody else's claim to be a prophet and
a messenger of God. Throughout the world during all these centuries
many men have achieved the greatest possible heights of power and excellence in all aspects of life. None of them, however, has been given the gift
of prophethood, of conveying a message from God. Before Muhammad,
however, the prophets and the messengers were many, each of whom
warned his people that they had gone astray, and each one sought to bring
them back to the religion of truth. Yet none of them claimed that he was
sent to all men or that he was the last of the prophets. But Muhammad

made this claim which was revealed to him by God, and the centuries have proved his claim to be true. What Muhammad conveyed was no fabrication but a true report of a divine message meant to provide guidance and to bring mercy to all mankind.

In conclusion, let me say that the utmost purpose I have hoped my book to achieve is that it may have prepared the road for further researches and studies in these matters. Such researches and studies, we hope, will be wider in scope and deeper in insight than this book. In writing these pages, I have exerted all the effort of which I am capable and explored all the field that my vision could, with God's grace, encompass. God says:

لَا يُكَلِّفُ اللَّهُ نَفْسًا إِلَّا وُسْعَهَا لَهَا مَا كَسَبَتْ وَعَلَيْهَا مَا اكْتَسَبَتْ رَبَّنَا لَا تُؤَاخِذْنَا إِن نَّسِينَا أَوْ أَخْطَأْنَا رَبَّنَا وَلَا تَحْمِلْ عَلَيْنَا إِصْرًا كَمَا حَمَلْتَهُ عَلَى الَّذِينَ مِن قَبْلِنَا رَبَّنَا وَلَا تُحَمِّلْنَا مَا لَا طَاقَةَ لَنَا بِهِ وَاعْفُ عَنَّا وَاغْفِرْ لَنَا وَارْحَمْنَا أَنتَ مَوْلَانَا فَانصُرْنَا عَلَى الْقَوْمِ الْكَافِرِينَ ۝

"God only holds a man responsible to the extent of his capacity. He holds every man responsible for what he has done whether good or ill. O God! Grant to us that we may not forget, that we may not fall into error. O God! Grant to us that we may not have to bear the great burden of those who have gone before us. O God! Grant to us that we may not have to bear a burden beyond our capacity. Grant us Your forgiveness, and have mercy on us. You alone are our Lord and Master. Help us therefore to achieve victory over the Godless."[34]

Notes and References

Foreword

1. *'Ummah'* is not translatable into English. It "is not merely the 'nation' of the English language, nor *'La nation'* of post-revolution France and European nationalism. It adds to the utilitarian, practical connotation or the former, and the rationalistic idealistic meaning of the latter, the cosmological sense of being the eternal reality in which 'nations' in the foregoing senses may come and go, and the religio-axiological sense of being the real-existent substrate of divine will" (Faruqi, I. R., *On Arabism, 'Urubah and Religion,* Amsterdam: Djambatan, 1962, p. 15). —Tr.
2. *See* Preface to the First Edition, p. xl.
3. *Kalam* is the discipline of Islamic thought. The English concept of "theology" is inadequate because *kalam* includes logic, epistemology and metaphysics and is always presented as critical, not dogmatic, thought. "Philosophy" is equally inadequate on account of the confusion its use might imply, namely, the assumption that all there is to philosophical thought in Islam is the tradition which begins with al Kindi (d. 873 C.E.) and ends with ibn Rushd (d. 1198 C.E.). —Tr.
4. *Sunnah* means the example of the Prophet as normative concretization of the principles of Islam. — Tr.
5. *Mutakallimun* are those scholars who engage in *kalam.* —Tr.
6. *Isra'* refers to the night journey Muhammad undertook from Makkah to Jerusalem — whence he ascended to heaven — and back. — Tr.
7. *See* p. vli.
8. *See* p. ii.

Preface to First Edition

1. Al Sham or Diyar al Sham refers to the territories presently known as Lebanon, Syria, Palestine and Jordan. — Tr.
2. *I.e.*, China. — Tr.
3. *Zakat* means the sharing of one's legitimately earned wealth with the community. It is not equivalent to charity because it is levied under penalty of law, has a definite ratio to wealth and is, in Islam, institutionalized. It is not a "poor-tax" because its uses are not limited to those of the poor but extend to the general welfare of the community and state. — Tr.
4. In his book, Dr. Butler says that the name of this general was Khuriam, that "Shahrbaraz," "Shahrbaraz" and "Shirawazayh" by which this general has been known in other books are mistranscriptions of the Persian name "Shahr-Wazar," literally "the king's boar" and signifying as a title "great courage." A figurative representation of this title appeared on the seal of ancient Persia as well as of Armenia *(The Arab Conquest of Egypt,* p. 53.)
5. Qur'an, 30:1-7.
6. Qur'an, 5:82.
7. Qur'an, 3 :45-49.
8. Christian scholars have invariably attacked Islam on the ground that it has missed the nature of trinitarianism. They impute to the Qur'an and to Muhammad the charge of having misunderstood the trinity as consisting of Father, Mary and Jesus. *E.g.,* Gibb's statement that "the doctrine of the divine Sonship of Jesus is emphatically repudiated, in terms which betray the crassly anthropomorphic form in which it had been presented or presented itself to the Arabs. . . Mohammed had no direct knowledge of Christian doctrine" (Gibb, H. A. R., *Mohammedanism,* London: Oxford U. Press, 1954, p. 45). "A more serious confusion occurs, however, when Mary, the mother of Jesus, is admitted to the Trinity in the place of the Holy Spirit — Qur'an 5: 76-79, 116 (Donaldson, D. M., *Studies in Muslim Ethics,* London: S.P.C.K., 1953, p. 57). Like statements may be read in Guillaume, A., *Islam,* Edinburgh, Penguin paperback, 1956, p. 52-53; Cragg, K., *The Call of the Minaret,* New York: Oxford University Press paperback, 1964, p. 253; etc., etc. These charges are utterly groundless. The Qur'an certainly criticized and condemned trinitarianism — as in 5:171 ; 5:73; etc. It has certainly criticized and condemned the doctrine of *theotokos* or "mother of God" as in 5:75-79, 116. These are two distinct criticisms the Qur'an has directed at Christianity. But it has nowhere identified the persons of the trinity as consisting of God, the Father; Jesus, the son; and Mary, the mother. The Qur'anic position is simply that whoever and whatever the persons of the trinity may be, trinitarianism and theotokos are blasphemous compromises of divine trancendence and unity. Combining the two Qur'anic condemnations, some exegetes had regarded "The Mother of God" as part of "The Trinity." If this is a mistake,

it belongs to those exegetes, not to the Qur'an. Even so, it is not necessarily a mistake. The exegetes' works constitute evidence of the current tenets of faith of their contemporaries; and there is no apriori evidence that some Near Eastern Christians have not identified the Trinity in these terms. Indeed, there is but one small step from the Christian assertion that "the Logos took human nature to Himself in the womb of the Virgin Mary — that Godhead and Manhood were united in the Incarnate logos in one Person," to use Cyril's words, to the assertion that "theotokos" implies the unity of the mother with the embryo in her womb, and hence that the Incarnation creates a bond between mother & logos separable only in theory. (See for further detail F. J. Foakes Jackson, *The History of the Christian Church to C.E. 461*, London: George Allen & Unwin Ltd., 1st pub. 1891, rep. 1957, pp. 459 if.) This need not be a mistake; indeed it is quite probable that some Near Eastern Christians had held such a view, since in this, as well as in many other passages, the Qur'an is simply reporting what is being heard.

9. Arabic *mushrikun,* those who associated other gods with God. 10. Qur'an, 5:17-18.
11. Qur'an, 5:72-73.
12. Qur'an, 5:116-118.
13. Qur'an, 112:1-4.
14. Qur'an, 19:35.
15. Qur'an, 3:59.
16. Qur'an, 4:48.
17. Qur'an, 4:157-158.
18. Qur'an, 31:33.
19. Arabic *tawhid,* the Islamic doctrine of divine unity. The English "monotheism" is not specific enough and is applied to Christianity precisely where Islam would charge its inapplicability. Hence, our new term. — Tr.
20. Emil Dermenghem, *The Life of Mahomet,* translated by Arabella Yorke, New York: The Dial Press, 1930, pp. 119-121.
21. Theosophy is a doctrine founded by Madame Plawatzki, of the U.S.A., and derived from the religions of India, from Buddhism and Brahmanism especially. It is also called "religion of wisdom." A society embracing this new faith was founded in America and Madame Plawatzki has been its president. Branches of this society have arisen in many European countries. As soon as the founder passed away, the Theosophic Society divided into three main groups. However, they all believe in the unity of being and of life and observe a kind of Sufi discipline aimed at reaching Nirvana of Buddhism. Such a state is reached only when the subject achieves, by means of discipline and exercise, a total separation of the spirit from the concerns of material life and when the soul rises to such heights of holiness and purity that it joins the spirits on high. Theosophy also calls for universal fraternity among mankind,

an order in which race, language and all other impediments would dissolve away.

22. One of the sources of Islamic law. Creative interpretation of the principles and precepts of Islam. — Tr.

23. According to Webster, where it is spelled "ulema," "a body of scholars trained in Moslem religion and law," or "sometimes, erroneously, a Moslem learned man or theologian." — Tr.

24. Rational conviction of religious truth, possibly only as a category of critical natural theology such as Islam provides. Colloquially convertible with "faith." — Tr.

25. Dr. Haykal is here referring to France's expulsion of the Jesuit, Dominican, Franciscan, and other missionary orders. — Tr.

Preface to Second Edition

1. Qur'an, 61:6.
2. *Ibid.*
3. Dr. Haykal translated this term so as to mean "recitation" rather than "composition," in conformity with the Islamic position. — Tr.
4. Sir William Muir, *The Life of Mahomet*, London: Smith, Elder and Company, 1878, pp. 551-562.
5. *See* p. 355.
6. Qur'an, 33:56.
7. 1574-1624 C.E., great grammarian, court clerk, and qadi who lived in Safad, Saida, Beirut and Jerusalem.
8. Arabic *"adab al Qur'an."*
9. Qur'an, 16:103.
10. Qur'an, 53:19-20.
11. Literally "hypocrite;" as a special name it applied to the Zoroastrians and Manichaeans who pretended to embrace Islam but remained true to their old gods. — Tr.
12. The Law of Islam.
13. *See* p. x.
14. *Al Maniir,* May 3, 1935, p. 793.
15. Qur'an, 17:90-93.
16. Qur'an, 6:109-111.
17. Qur'an, 26:43-48.
18. *See* pp. 50-51.
19. *See* pp. 285-289.
20. *The Sahih of Muslim*, Istanbul, 1332 A.H., Vol. VII, p. 60.
21. Rule of consultation, or consent. Presently used as equivalent to representative government or democratic rule.

22. The Shu'ubiyyah movement (hence the adjective shu'ubi) comprehends all the fissiparous tendencies of the non-Arab Muslims in the Islamic Empire. The movement was begun in the Umawi period predominantly by Persians, but it came to include many other national, ethnic, cultural and religious minorities. The movement fomented the rebellion which brought the Umawi dynasty and period to an end, but it was itself dissipated with the triumph of Islam and the Arabic language in the succeeding two centuries.

23. Qur'an,15:9.

24. Qur'an, 60:40.

Chapter 1

1. As in the Qur'anic verse: "As to their saying, 'We did kill the Messiah, Jesus, Son of Mary, the Apostle of God;' whereas they slew him not, nor crucified him, but it was made to appear to them as if they did. Those who differ therein are certainly in a state of doubt about it. They have no definite knowledge thereof but only follow a conjecture. None of them knows for sure that he was killed. Rather, God raised him unto Himself. God is Mighty and Wise." 4:156-7. — Tr.

2. The term "al Rum" used in pre-Islamic (Qur'an, 30:2) times, as well as later, refers to Rome, the Roman Empire and the East Roman Empire or Byzantium. Arab historians say "Roman" when they mean "Byzantine." — Tr.

3. 476 C.E.

4. *Heeren's Researches: Africa*, Vol. I, p. 23, quoted by Muir, *op. cit.*, pp. ii-iii.

5. Perhaps the author meant the Euphrates, for it is hard to see why a westbound caravan should travel alongside the Tigris. — Tr.

6. The narrow plain alongside the East coast of the Red Sea, separating the latter from the Hijaz mountain chain and the desert beyond. — Tr.

7. Qur'an, 85: 5-9.

8. This fact is confirmed by most historians in a number of works of history and reference. It is confirmed by the *Encyclopredia Britannica* and the *Historian's History of the World*. In his book, *The Life of Muhammad*, Dermenghem accepts it as true. Al Tabari reports from Hisham ibn Muhammad that when the Yamani Christians solicited the Negus's assistance against Dhu Nuwas, informed him of what the Jewish King did to the Christians and showed him a partially burnt Evangel, the Negus said: "My men are many but I have no ships. I shall write to the Byzantine Emperor to send me ships with which to carry the men over to Yaman." The Negus wrote to the Byzantine Emperor and sent him the partially burned Evangel. The Emperor responded by sending many ships. Al Tabari adds: "Hisham ibn Muhammad claims that when the ships arrived, the Negus sent his army therein and landed

them on the shores of Mandib" (Al Tabari, ibn Jarir, *Tarikh al Rusul wa al Muluk*, Cairo: Al Matba'ah al Husayniyyah, Vol. II, pp. 106,108).

9. Literally, "the man with the cut lip."

10. Some historians give a different explanation of the conquest of Yaman by Abyssinia. They claim that trade moved along connected links between Abyssinia, Yaman, and Hijaz; that Abyssinia then had a large commercial fleet operating on the shores of the Red Sea. The Byzantines were anxious to conquer Yaman in order to reap some of its produce and wealth. Anxious to conquer Yaman for Byzantium, Aelius Gallus, Governor of Egypt, equipped and prepared the army on the shore of the Red Sea, sent it to Yaman, and occupied Najran. The Yamanis put up a stiff resistance and were helped by the epidemic which ravaged the expeditionary force and compelled a withdrawal to Egypt. A number of other attempts to conquer Yaman were made by the Byzantines, but none of them succeeded. It was this long history of conflict which opened the eyes of the Negus and prompted him to avenge his fellow Christians against the Yamani Jews; it also explains why he prepared the army of Aryat, sent it to conquer Yaman (525 C.E.). — Tr. The Abyssinians ruled the country until the Persians forced them out of the Peninsula.

11. Al Sham refers to the lands otherwise known as Syria, Lebanon, Palestine, and Jordan. — Tr.

Chapter 2

1. Qur'an, 21 :62-63

2. Qur'an, 6 :76-79.

3. Haykal here reports a typical case of Israelitism in the Muslim tradition. With little variation the story of Genesis had passed into Muslim legends through Jewish converts to Islam. — Tr.

4. Genesis 22:2 also calls Isaac Abraham's "only son," thus corroborating the claim and making the Bible's declaration of Isaac as the sacrificial son a very likely emendation of the Biblical text. — Tr.

5. Unfortunately, Haykal has not shown how this implication follows from the claim in favor of Isma'il. — Tr.

6. Qur'an, 37:102-107.

7. Qur'an, 3 :96-97.

8. Qur'an, 2: 125-127.

9. Qur'an, 11 :53.

10. Qur'an, 17:15.

11. For definitions of these terms, *see* pp. 31-32.

12. *Ibid.*

13. The author is using the pre-Islamic and Islamic names of the same city interchangeably. Pre-Islamic "Yathrib" had, upon the Prophet's emigration thereto and the establishment therein of the first Islamic polity, become "Madinah al Nabi" (literally, the city of the Prophet) and "Madinah" for short. — Tr.
14. Qur'an, 105:1-5.
15. Literally, "man with a book or scripture," following the Qur'anic appellation for Jews and Christians, "People of the Book," or "scripturists."
16. *"Sidanah"* is synonymous to *"hijabah."* For a definition of this and *"siqayah,"* see pp. 31-32.

Chapter 3

1. Quran, 94:1-3.
2. "Most Arab among you" (Arabic, *"a'rabukum")* could well have been rendered "most eloquent among you." To be an Arab, or "to arabize" means to speak forth eloquently in Arabic, without stammering or grammatical mistakes, and with literary beauty. *'Urubah* or Arabness is always something which admits of many degrees, the more Arab being always the man in better command of the Arabic language, Arabic diction, style, letters and all forms of literary beauty. Ya'rub, (literally, "he arabizes" or "speaks eloquent Arabic") was the name of the first Arab King, whom legend declares to be the first to have spoken in Arabic. As far as history goes, the Arabs have regarded the desert Arabic purer and more classical and beautiful than that of the towns; the tribes were graded in *'Urubah* according to their racial purity as means for the preservation of the purity of Arabic. Hence, the Prophet's statement. — Tr.
3. Waraqah ibn Nawfal was a *hanif* (an ethical monotheist of pre-Islamic times). He was the relation of the Prophet's wife, Khadijah, from whom she sought advice regarding Muhammad's reports about revelation. *(See p. 77.)*
4. A village located between Madinah and Jahfah, twenty-three miles south of Madinah.
5. Qur'an, 93 :6-7.
6. At the yearly market of 'Ukaz (near Makkah), held during the holy months, poets from all tribes competed with one another in poetry. They recited their compositions in public and the greatest was given the prize of having his composition written down and "hung" on the walls of the Ka'bah. According to al Mufaddal (d. 189 A.H./805 C.E.), Imru' al Qays (d. 560 C.E.), Zuhayr (d. 635 C.E.), al Nabighah (d. 604 C.E.), al A'sha (d. 612 C.E.), Labid (d. 645 C.E.), 'Amr ibn Kulthum (d. 565 C.E.) and Tarafah (d. 565 C.E.) were authors of the greatest poems of pre-Islamic days, accorded this special honor. Hence, their name *"al mu'allaqat,"* literally "the hanging poems." Other early historians of Arabic literature claimed that the *mu'allaqat* were

eight, adding to the seven above-mentioned a poem of 'Antarah. Other pre-Islamic and early Islamic (up to 50 A.H./672 C.E.) poems, numbering 42 in all, were divided into six groups of seven poems each — the whole of pre-Islamic poetry adding up to seven groups of seven poems each — arranged according to their literary merit, poetic eloquence and force. They included: *al mujamharat* by 'Ubayd, 'Antarah, 'Adiyy, Bishr and Umayyah, *al muntaqayat* (literally, "the selected poems") by al Musayyib, al Muraqqash, al Mutalammis, 'Urwah, al 'Muhalhil, Durayd and al Mutanakhkhil; *al mudhahhabat* (literally, "The golden poems," or "written in gold") by Hassan ibn Rawahah, Malik, Qays ibn al Khatim, Uhayhah, Abu Qays ibn al Aslat and 'Amr ibn Umru' al Qays; *al mashubat* (literally, "the poems touched by Islam as well as pre-Islamic unbelief"), *al malhamat* (literally, "the epic poems"). For further details, see any literary history of the Arabs, or Muhammad 'Abd al Mun'im Khafaji, *al Hayah al Adabiyyah fi al 'Asr al Jahili,* Cairo: Maktabat al Husayn al Tijariyyah, 1368/1949. — Tr.
7. Literally, "the immoral war." — Tr.
8. Quss ibn Sa'idah al Iyadi, Archbishop of Najran.
9. Literally, "the alliance for charity." — Tr.

Chapter 4

1. Most of the scholars who have investigated the geneological descendents of Muhammad and his family agree that the sons of the Prophet — may God's peace and blessing be upon him — given him by Khadijah were two: al Qasim and 'Abdullah, who was also called "the pure" and "the good." It has also been reported that his sons were three or even four.
2. Title given to each of the wives of the Prophet.
3. *See* p. 97.
4. Qur'an, 29:7-8.
5. Qur'an, 96:1-5.

Chapter 5

1. Qur'an, 73 :1-7.
2. Qur'an, 93 :1-11.
3. Arabic *"mawla,"* the person standing under protection. This was the position of the manumitted slave. — Tr.
4. Unfortunately, in this as in many other cases, Haykal has quoted the author and placed his words between quotation marks but has not indicated the source. — Tr.
5. Qur'an, 26 :214-216; 15-94.

6. Qur'an, 111 :1-3.
7. Qur'an, 102 :1-8.
8. Qur'an, 7:188.
9. Qur'an, 79:24.
10. Qur'an, 99: 7-8.
11. Qur'an, 32.
12. Qur'an, 19 :29-33.

Chapter 6

1. Qur'an, 53 :19-20.
2. Qur'an, 17:73-75.
3. Non-Muslims concealing their unbelief, falsely pretending that they are members of the ummah; mostly Zoroastrians and Manichaeans. — Tr.
4. Qur'an, 22: 52-53.
5. Qur'an, 17: 73-75; *see* p. 106.
6. Qur'an, 22 :52-53; *see* p. 107.
7. "Muhammad saw some of his Lord's greatest signs. Would you consider, after al Lat and al 'Uzza, Manat, the third goddess? But would you give God the females and keep for yourselves the males? That is indeed an unjust division. But they are all mere names which you and your ancestors have named and for which God gave no authority. In this claim of yours you followed naught but conjecture and your own wishful thinking, while true guidance has arrived to you from your Lord" (Qur'an, 53: 18-23).
8. Literally, unitization of God or conviction of His unity, transcendence and absolute uniqueness. Often the term applies to Islam as a whole, to Islamic theology and to monotheism. — Tr.

Chapter 7

1. Qur'an, 16:103.
2. Qur'an, 80 :1-16.
3. Qur'an, 49: 14.
4. Qur'an, 43:31-32.
5. Qur'an, 80:33-42.
6. Qur'an, 70: 8-18.
7. Qur'an, 69 :18-37.
8. Qur'an, 50:30; 4:56.

Chapter 8

1. Qur'an, 17: 73-75.
2. *Al Isra'* means the night journey the Prophet was reported to have taken from Makkah to al Masjid al Aqsa, the distant mosque, or Jerusalem. *Al Mi'raj* means the Prophet's ascension to heaven and his visit to paradise and hell, later to serve as model for Dante's *La Divina Comedia.* See M. Asin Palacios, *La escatologia musulmana en la Divina Comedia,* Madrid, 1919; 2nd edition, Madrid, 1943. — Tr.
3. Qur'an, 17: 60.
4. Emile Dermenghem, *The Life of Mahomet,* New York: Lincoln MacVeagh, 1930, pp. 132-135.
5. Qur'an, 18:110.
6. Qur'an, 4: 48.
7. The Arabic text has "spiritual" at both poles of the comparison, which I assume to be a misprint. — Tr.
8. *Al Siddiq, i.e.,* he who believes the truth to be true. — Tr.

Chapter 9

1. Qur'an, 41 :34.
2. Literally, "the helpers," the name given by Muhammad to the first Muslims of Madinah who gave assistance to the cause at the time of its greatest peril. Later on, the name was to apply to all the Muslims of Madinah in contrast to al Muhajirun — literally, "the emigrants" — applied to those Muslims of Makkah who emigrated before or after the Prophet to Madinah. — Tr.
3. See note 2, *supra.*

Chapter 10

1. E. Dermenghem, *op. cit.,* p. 149.
2. Qur'an, 8:30; 9:40.
3. The word is originally the Greek *"drachme,"* a silver coin of varying value. — Tr.
4. Six and a half miles south of the city. — Tr.

Chapter 11

1. Qur'an, 22 :39.
2. Qur'an, 8 :39.

3. The allusion here is to Constantine who began to show favors toward Christianity in 312 C.E. and decreed the Edict of Toleration in 313. He supported both paganism as well as Christianity. To the end of his life he bore the title of *pontifex maximus*, being the chief priest of the pagan state cult and classed among the gods by the Roman Senate. He was not baptized until the latter part of his life. — Tr.
4. Qur'an, 2 :194.
5. Qur'an, 2: 179.
6. A dish made out of layers of bread often topped with meat, rice, and soaked with gravy. — Tr.
7. Qur'an, 2:57; 28:77.
8. Qur'an, 112:1-3.
9. *I.e.*, al Aws and al Khazraj.
10. Qur'an, 2: 87-89.
11. Qur'an, 2 :245.
12. Qur'an, 3 :181.
13. Qur'an, 5 :49-50.
14. Qur'an, 2 :144.
15. Qur'an, 2: 142-143.
16. Qur'an, 2 :136.
17. Qur'an, 3:64.

Chapter 12

1. A *dinar* is a golden coin, equivalent to twenty silver *dirhims*. — Tr.
2. *Munafiqun*, literally, the pretenders; applied to the insincere idolaters who joined the ranks of Islam for ulterior motives. — Tr.
3. Qur'an, 2:190.
4. Qur'an, 2 :217.
5. Matthew, 10 :34.
6. Qur'an, 2 :256, 190.
7. Matthew, 17:20.

Chapter 13

1. Qur'an,8:7.
2. Qur'an, 8: 65, 8: 66.
3. Qur'an, 8:12, 17.
4. Qur'an, 8:41.
5. Qur'an, 21 :67; 14 :36.
6. Qur'an, 5 :118.

7. Qur'an, 71 :26; 10:88.
8. Qur'an, 8 :67.
9. *Ibid.*

Chapter 15

1. The locality halfway between Makkah and Madinah on the coastal route.
2. The Qur'an called the insincere Muslims *"munafiqun"* or pretenders. — Tr.
3. Qur'an, 56 :25-26.
4. According to another version, it was Sa'd ibn Abu Waqqas that was so attracted.
5. Qur'an, 16:126-127.
6. Significantly, this is the same question which Western Islamicist Wilfred Cantwell Smith thinks confutes Muslims in modern times because of its novelty. See his *Islam in Modern History,* Princeton, New Jersey, Princeton University Press, 1957, ch. II, where he argues that the view that Islam's movement in history is God-willed and God-incepted — such as Islam holds — leads in case of frustration, loss or defeat, to the absurdity either that God's will is being frustrated or that the movement in question is not God-willed. Smith omits here to consider that the unfolding of God's will in history is, in Islam, not the working of blind necessity but that of free men whose responsible decisions are the very stuff of divine will, so that defeat or victory are attributable to them rather than to God. It was this moralism of the Muslims that saved them after their defeat at Uhud and at the hands of Crusaders and Tatars in the Middle Ages. And it is likely to save them, too, after their defeat by an imperialist West in modern times. — Tr.

Chapter 16

1. Qur'an, 59: 5.
2. Qur'an, 59 :11-13.
3. Qur'an, 59: 22-24.
4. Qur'an, 3 :168-75.

Chapter 17

1. Qur'an, 33: 37.
2. Title attributed to all wives of the Prophet. — Tr.
3. Qur'an, 4 :3.
4. Qur'an, 4:129.
5. Qur'an, 49: 13.

6. Qur'an, 33 :36.
7. Qur'an, 33 :4.
8. Qur'an,33:37.
9. *Ibid.*

Chapter 18

1. Qur'an, 4 :51-52.
2. Qur'an, 33: 10-13.

Chapter 19

1. Qur'an, 5: 3.
2. John, 8:7.
3. Qur'an, 33 :58-62.
4. Qur'an, 24 :30-31.
5. Qur'an, 33:53.
6. Qur'an, 33 :32-33.
7. Qur'an, 63 :7-8.
8. Qur'an, 24:11, 16-17.
9. Qur'an, 24:4.

Chapter 20

1. Qur'an, 2 :217.
2. Qur'an, 8: 34-36.
3. Pilgrimage to the Sanctuary of Makkah at a time other than that prescribed for it by custom and the Qur'an. — Tr.
4. A group of strong bowmen from Arabia — i.e. Abyssinians — so called for their dark complexion. Another possible explanation for their name is that it refers to Hubshi, a mountain south of Makkah.
5. Qur'an, 48:18.
6. It was customary for the pilgrim in pre-Islamic Arabia to shave his head as evidence of desacralization after a complete performance of the religious function of pilgrimage. When the performance of the religious function had been interrupted or anyone of its rituals for some reason missed, the pilgrim would only cut his hair short rather than shave it. He thereby gave evidence of his awareness that his religious function had not been completely fulfilled and of the need to repeat the same function in the following season. — Tr.
7. Qur'an, 48:1-30.
8. Qur'an, 60 :10.

Chapter 21

1. *See* p. 355.
2. Qur'an, 2 :219.
3. Qur'an, 4: 43.
4. Qur'an, 5:90-91.
5. Qur'an, 5 :93.
6. Recognizing that there has been a large variety of views regarding the vow-eling and meaning of the term *"al arisiyyin,"* the author appended a footnote in which he preferred its meaning as "subjects." This view was based on the *Nihayat* of Ibn al Athir and other dictionaries of the Arabic language, q.v. *Rum.* Another meaning of the term, which does not at all seem improbable, is "Arians." In this case the Prophet would seem to be giving Heraclius the alternative of accepting the monotheism of Islam or of remaining a trinitar-ian Christian. In the latter case, the emperor would fall under a new indict-ment of heresy regarding the truth of Jesus Christ which Islam was teaching in consonance with Arianism. — Tr.
7. Qur'an, 48 :15.
8. Not personally, but as chief of state. — Tr.
9. The old city of Emessa in Syria.
10. That is, Hagia Sophia. — Tr.
11. The year in question was 7 A.H./629 C.E. — Tr.

Chapter 22

1. Two hills outside of Makkah, between which Hagar ran a number of times to and fro in search of water for her thirsty son, Isma'il. It was part of the pre-Islamic pilgrimage as well as the Islamic pilgrimage to Makkah to reenact this anxious running between these two hilts and thereby pay tribute to Isma'il, the common ancestor, founder of Makkah and co-builder of the Ka'bah with his father, Ibrahim. — Tr.

Chapter 23

1. Qur'an, 60:1.
2. Some biographers relate that al 'Abbas met the Muslim army at Rabigh. Others assert that al 'Abbas had reached Madinah before Muhammad resolved to march against Makkah, that he converted to Islam in Madinah and accompanied the Muslim army on its march. This latter view, however, is refuted by the historians as a fabrication injected into the biography of Muhammad in order to please the 'Abbasi rulers during whose reign the biographies of the Prophet were first written down. The refutation of the his-

torians is confirmed by the fact that if the claim were true, al Abbas, as the last notable of Makkah to join the ranks of Islam, would have been the first to be visited by Abu Sufyan for the purpose of extending the Treaty of Hudaybiyah. It would seem that despite his defense of his nephew when the latter was at Makkah, al ʿAbbas did not join Islam. Al ʿAbbas was a Makkan tradesman and, like all other tradesmen of the city, feared the disastrous consequences Islam would bring to his business.

3. Qurʾan, 96: 1-5.
4. Qurʾan, 49: 13.
5. Qurʾan, 17: 81.
6. *I.e.,* Makkah. — Tr.

Chapter 25

1. Qurʾan, 9 :25-28.

Chapter 26

1. As in the *Sahih* of Muslim. In the account of Tabari there is no mention of a wife of ʿUmar by this name. In *Ruh al Maʾani* of Allusi, the same statement by ʿUmar names "The daughter of Zayd" instead.
2. Qurʾan, 30: 28-29.
3. Qurʾan, 30 :1-5.

Chapter 27

1. *See* pp. 31-32.
2. *I.e.,* "the tax of the tenth," levied on the Muslims' annual incomes at the rate of 10%. — Tr.
3. *I.e.,* income tax levied on the annual incomes of non-Muslims at varying rates not exceeding 10%. — Tr.
4. Qurʾan, 9 :81-82.
5. Qurʾan, 9 :49.
6. Qurʾan, 9: 117-118.

Chapter 28

1. Qurʾan, 9: 1-36.
2. The *surah* in question is Qurʾan 9. It is known by either of the two titles "Al Tawbah" (repentence) and "Baraʾah" (absolution). — Tr.

Chapter 29

1. Qur'an, 9 :29, 34-35.
2. Qur'an, 5:82.
3. Qur'an. 3: 59-64.
4. Qur'an, 5 :73-75.
5. Qur'an, 5 :11.
6. Qur'an, 5 :82.
7. *I.e.,* running to and fro between the two mountains. This part of the pilgrim-age ritual is a re-creation of Hagar's desperate running on the same plain in search of water for her son Isma'il. — Tr.
8. Muslim ibn al Hajjaj, 817-865 C.E., compiler of the *Sahih,* the second canonical collection of *Hadith.* — Tr.
9. The invocations which include either "At your service, O Lord" or "God is Great" as dominant theme. — Tr.
10. Qur'an, 5:4.

Chapter 30

1. Qur'an, 6 :38. There can be little doubt that this story is a fabrication of later times, specifically, of the eighth century C.E./second century A.H., when at the height of the *hadith* movement, controversy arose as to the place of *hadith* in the framework of Islamic Law and ideas. It is not likely that Muhammad's closest and most trusted companions or the members of his house would have refused to fulfill a wish their Prophet was making on his death bed. Nor is it likely that the Prophet's *Sunnah* would have constituted a problem at all, or one necessitating such hard contradiction between the written and the oral traditions. — Tr.
2. Here again, there can be little doubt of the spuriousness of this report. It is evidently anachronistic and must have come from a much later time than the Prophet's. Firstly, it is not possible that the Prophet had such a low and pes-simistic esteem of his time. At his death the Prophet stood at the height of power, having welded Arabia into one powerful unity, strong enough to ven-ture beyond its borders. No Arab tribe or person was strong enough to wage "subversive attacks" against the Islamic polity. Secondly, no justification could be adduced for the Prophet's public defense of himself because he was under serious attack from no one. No one in his senses could have accused the Prophet of violating the legislation of the Qur'an. Thirdly, no Muslims had at that time built mausoleums for anyone, including the Prophet, and no one had used grave-sites or cemeteries as mosques. The Prophet's condem-nation is hence pointless. Granted, then, that this *hadith* was not the Prophet's but that of later Muslims, it becomes a source of historical infor-

mation about its time. Only the late Umawi and early 'Abbasi times could have presented "subversive attacks" against the regime in power; only then could some caliphs have been indicted for violating the Qur'anic legislation; and only then, if not even much later, did Muslims begin the practice of building mausoleum-mosques mostly under Sufi and Persian inspiration. — Tr.

Chapter 31

1. Qur'an, 3:144.
2. Qur'an, 9:100.
3. In Islamic political theory, *"bay'ah"* means the investment of the caliph with political authority. It consists of a "private" and "public" investment. The former amounts to nomination of the caliph by a number of supporters; the latter to confirmation of the private *bay'ah* by the electorate at large. It is only when the two *bay'ahs* have taken place and have been accepted by the caliph that he is said to have legitimately acceded to the caliphate. — Tr.
4. The reader may be thrown off by this usage of "pray upon" instead of the commonplace "pray for." In the Muslim practice nobody "prays for" the Prophet in the sense that one prays for a departed loved one. Prayer upon the Prophet is much more formal and is commanded by the Qur'an (33:56). "It is a main part of Muslim worship to use the Qur'anic "pray upon" in invoking God's blessing upon His Prophet. — Tr.

Essay 1 of Conclusion

1. Qur'an, 2:171.
2. Imitation of the ancestors, conservatism. — Tr.
3. Qur'an, 2: 164
4. Qur'an, 36: 33-44.
5. Qur'an, 17: 85.
6. Qur'an, 49 :14.
7. Qur'an, 49 :17.
8. Qur'an, 2: 186.
9. Qur'an, 2 :45-46.
10. The reference is here to the phrases, *Allahu Akbar* (God is Greatest) and *Subhana Rabbi al 'Azim* (Praise to my Lord Almighty) repeated many times in the course of the Islamic prayer.
11. Qur'an, 2: 177.
12. Qur'an, 2: 183.
13. Qur'an, 2 :184.

14. Qur'an, 2:277.
15. Qur'an, 2 :43.
16. Qur'an, 23 :1-4.
17. Qur'an, 69 :30-34.
18. Qur'an, 22: 34-35.
19. Qur'an, 2 :274.
20. Qur'an, 2: 271, 263-64.
21. Qur'an, 9 :60.
22. Qur'an, 28: 77.
23. Qur'an, 2:197.
24. Qur'an, 17 :23-38.
25. Qur'an, 23-96; 41 :34.
26. Qur'an, 4:86.
27. Qur'an, 16:126.
28. Qur'an, 2 :275.
29. Qur'an, 30 :39.
30. An "Israelitism" is usually a spurious interpretation of, or a fabricated addition to, an Islamic religious text, the Qur'an being naturally excluded. While most "Israelitisms" had to do with Islamic doctrine, tradition, and semitic history, their purpose was always to subvert the faith from within. They are supposed to be the work of Jews of the first two centuries who ostensibly converted to Islam but who nursed for it the strongest hatred. — Tr.
31. Provincialism, or "shu'ubiyyah," is the name given by Muslim historians to every centrifugal movement in the Islamic empire, such as Persian nationalism, Turkish nationalism, Coptic nationalism, etc. — Tr.

Essay 2 of Conclusion

1. Washington Irving, *Mahomet and His Successors,* Philadelphia, J. B. Lippincott and Co., 1871, Vol. I, pp. 360-362.
2. Qur'an, 10:108; 17:15; 42:20; 13:11.
3. Qur'an, 3:145; 7:34; 57:22; 9:51.
4. Qur'an, 53 :40
5. Qur'an, 13:11.
6. Qur'an, 3 :159.
7. Qur'an, 34:3.
8. Qur'an, 7: 12.
9. Qur'an, 17 :15.
10. Qur'an, 6:2.
11. Qur'an, 21 :34-35.
12. Qur'an, 62 :5-7.
13. Qur'an, 6:60.

14. Qur'an, 7:13.
15. Qur'an, 49 :13; 4 :106. The author does not quote these words in the manner proper to Qur'anic words, but uses them as his own — a perfectly permissive literary feature in Arabic. The last part of the sentence not included within quotation marks sounds Qur'anic in construction and phrasing, but it is not of the Qur'an. — Tr.
16. "Scientific Determinism," "The World as Will and Idea," and "Emergent Evolution" are philosophic systems advanced by the positivist philosophers, Schopenhauer and Henri Bergson.
17. Matthew, 5:17.
18. Qur'an, 6:151; 17:33.
19. Qur'an, 2 :179.
20. Qur'an, 16 :40.
21. Qur'an, 22 :47.
22. Qur'an, 7 :19-27.
23. Qur'an, 6: 27-32.
24. Qur'an, 28 :30-32.
25. Qur'an, 18:46.
26. Muhammad 'Abduh, *Al Islam wa al Nasraniyyah Ma'a al 'Ilm wa al Madaniyyah,* Cairo, n.d., pp. 122-125.
27. Qur'an, 28-77.
28. Qur'an, 2 :256.
29. Qur'an, 49 :9-10.
30. Qur'an, 2 :62.
31. Commenting on this verse, al Tabari wrote in his exegesis: "'Those who believe' refers to the people who believed in the Prophet of God.' 'The Jews' refers to those who gave themselves this name as a derivation from their statement, 'We have returned to You,' that is, 'we have repented.' 'The Christians,' are the followers of Jesus. They were called by this name — *nasara* — in derivation from the name, Nazareth, the village of Jesus in Palestine. According to another view, the derivation was one of Jesus' statements, 'And who are my helpers — *ansar* — in God?' 'The Sabeans' are, according to one view, those who worship the angels. According to another view, the Sabeans were a people who believed that there is no God but God but had neither scripture nor prophet. Their religion may be characterized by no other statement except that there is no God but God. According to a third view, the Sabeans were a people without religion." Al Tabari explained the verse as follows: "Those who believe in God and in the reality of resurrection after death, in the Day of Judgment, who do the good works in obedience to God — such men have their merit with their Lord; that is, they have the merit earned by their good works. As for the statements 'they have no reason to fear' and 'neither shall they grieve,' the meaning which God — May He be adored — intended is that those people have no reason to fear any of the

terrors of the Day of Judgment, nor will they grieve for all the good things of the world which they left behind when they come to know all the bliss which God has reserved for them in Paradise." Following these comments, al Tabari mentioned that this verse was revealed in reference to those Christians who guided Salman al Farisi and converted him to their religion, announcing to him that an Arab prophet would come forth and asking Salman to verify the identity of such prophet with given signs and to follow him if he could find him. After Salman converted to Islam, he told the Prophet about those Christians, and the Prophet replied: "O Salman, those people belong to Hell." Salman was grieved, and on this account, God revealed the verse: "Those who believe, the Christians, etc." According to another view, God had revoked this verse with another verse, namely, "Whoever seeks another religion besides Islam, it will not be accepted of him" (Qur'an 3:85). However, al Tabari adds: "What we have mentioned at the beginning is the closer to the commonsense meaning of the revelation because God-May He be praised-could not have restricted merit for the good works and faith to some of His creatures rather than to others. The predicate of the verse therefore belongs to every subject mentioned therein, including the Muslims." A confirmation of this view of al Tabari is that it may be said in regard to the verse, "Whoever seeks another religion besides Islam, it will not be accepted of him." It applies to those ,Muslims who seek another religion besides Islam, after they have been born into Islam or come to believe in it. As to those who are born in another religion, and those whom the Islamic call has not reached without falsification, their case will be like that of those who have gone before the advent of Muhammad and his prophethood, and who have not come to know of his message as it is and without falsification. (See further Ibn Jarir al Tabari, *Kitab al Tafsir,* Vol. 1, pp. 253-57.)

32. Qur'an 3:199.
33. The current year is Islam's one thousand, three hundred, eighty-seventh year, A.H. — Tr.
34. Qur'an 2 :286.

Supplementary Readings in the English Language on the Life of the Prophet

Abu'l-Fadl, Mirza (ed. and tr.). *Muhammad in the Hadees,* or *Sayings of the Prophet Mohammad.* Allahabad: Abbas Manzil Library, 195-.

Ahmad, Fazl. *Muhammad, the Holy Prophet,* "Heroes of Islam Series." Lahore: Ashraf, 1960.

Ahmad, Syed Khan Bahadur. *Essays of the Life of Mohammed and Subjects Subsidiary Thereto.,* Vol. I. London: Trubner, 1870.

Ali, Muhammad. *The Living Thoughts of the Prophet Muhammad.* London: Cassell, 1947.

———. *Muhammad and Christ.* Madras: S.P.C.K. Press, 1921.

———. *Muhammad the Prophet.* Lahore: Ahmadiyya Anjuman-i-Isha'at-I-Islam, 1933.

Ali, Syed Ameer. *A Critical Examinatian of the Life and Teachings of Mohammed.* London: William, 1873.

———. *The Spirit of Islam, A History of the Evolution and Ideals of Islam with a Life of the Prophet.* Amplified and revised ed.; London: Chattos and Windus, 1964.

Amin, Muhammad (ed.). *The Sayings of Prophet Muhammad.* Lahore: Lion Press, 1960.

———. *Wisdom of Prophet Muhammad.* Lahore: Lion Press, 1960.

Andrae, Tor. *Mohammed: The Man and His Faith,* translated by Theophil Menzel. New York: Barnes and Noble, 1957.

Azzam, Abdel Rahman. *The Eternal Message of Muhammad,* translated from the Arabic by Caesar E. Farah, with an introduction by Vincent Sheean. New York: Devin-Adair Co., 1964.

Bodley, Ronald Victor Courtenay. *The Messenger: The Life of Muhammed.* Garden City, New York: Doubleday and Co., Inc., 1946.

Bosworth-Smith, R. *Mohammed and Mohammedanism.* London: Murray, 1889.

Bush, Rev. George. *The Life of Mohammed; Founder of the Religion of Islam, and of the Empire of the Saracens.* New York: J. & J. Harper, 1830.

Carlyle, Thomas. *On Heroes, Hero-Worship, and the Heroic in History* (lecture II). London: J. Fraser, 1841, and various other editions.

Draz, Muhammad 'Abd Allah. "Muhammad" in *Islam, The Straight Path,* ed. by Kenneth W. Morgan. New York: The Ronald Press, 1958.

Draycott, Gladys M. *Mohomet Founder of Islam.* New York: Dodd, Mead and Co., 1916.

Essad Bey. *Mohammed: A Biography,* translated by Helmut L. Ripperger. New York and Toronto: Longmans, Green and Co., 1936.

Foster, H. Frank. "An Autobiography of Mohammed," *The Moslem World,* XXVI (1936),130-152.

Galwash, A. A. "The Life of Prophet Mohammad," *The Religion of Islam.* 5th ed.; Cairo: Imprimerie Misr, 1958.

al Ghazzali, Abu Hamid Muhammad. *Ihya' 'Ulum al Din,* Book XX, edited and translated by L. Zolondek. Leiden: E. J. Brill, 1963.

Gibb, H. A. R. *Mohammedanism, An Historical Survey.* London: Oxford University Press, 1953.

Glubb, Sir John Bagot. *The Life and Times of Muhammad.* London: Hodder and Stoughton, and New York: Stein and Day, 1970.

Guillaume, Alfred. *New Light on the Life of Muhammad.* Manchester: Manchester University Press, 1960.

Gulick, Robert. *Muhammad, the Educator.* Lahore: Institute of Islamic Culture, 1953.

Hakim, Khalifa Abdul. *The Prophet and His Message.* Lahore: Institute Of Islamic Culture, 1972.

Hamadeh, Muhammad Maher. "Muhammad the Prophet: A Selected Bibliography." Unpublished Ph.D. dissertation, Michigan University, 1965.

Hashmi, Rahm Ali. *Mohammad, the Benefactor of Humanity,* translation and condensation of the Urdu *Mohsin-e-insaniyat* by Naeem Siddiqi. Delhi: Board of Islamic Publications, 1971.

Hilliard, Frederick Hadaway. *The Buddha, the Prophet, and the Christ.* London and New York: G. Allen and Unwin and Macmillan, 1956.

Hosain, Saiyid Safdar. *The Early History of Islam: An Impartial Review of the Early Islamic Period Compiled from Authentic Sources.* Karachi: Mushtaq Ali K. Laddhani, 1971.

Husain, Athar. *Prophet Muhammad and His Mission.* Bombay and New York: Asia Publishing House, 1967.

Ibn Hisham, 'Abd al-Malik. *The Life of Muhammad: A Translation of ibn Ishaq's Sirat Rasul Allah.* London and New York: Oxford University Press, 1955.

Ibn Sa'd, Muhammad. *Kitab al-Tabaqat al Kabir,* translated by S. Moinul Haq assisted by H. K. Ghazanfar. Karachi: Pakistan Historical Society, 1967.

Imamuddin, S. M. *A Political History of Muslims: Prophet and Pious Caliphs.* Dacca: Najmah, 1967.

Iqbal, Afzal. *Diplomacy in Islam: An Essay on the Art of Negotiations as Conceived and Developed by the Prophet of Islam.* Lahore: Institute of Islamic Culture, 1962.

Irving, Washington. *Life of Mahomet.* London: J. M. Dent and Sons, and New York: E. P. Dutton and Co., 1911.

———. *Mahomet and His Successors,* edited by Henry A. Pochmann and E. N. Feltskog. Madison: University of Wisconsin Press, 1970.

Jeffery, Arthur. *Islam: Muhammad and His Religion.* New York: Liberal Arts Press, 1958.

Johnstone, P. DeLacy. *Muhammad and His Power.* New York: Charles Scribner's Sons, 1901.

Khan, Inamullah. *Maxims of Mohummud.* Karachi: Umma Pub. House, 1965.

Lane-Poole, Stanley. *The Prophet and Islam,* abridged from 1879 edition. Lahore: National Book Society, 1964.

Liu Chai-Lien. *The Arabian Prophet: A Life of Mohammed from Chinese and Arabic Sources,* translated by Isaac Mason. Shanghai: Commercial Press, Ltd., 1921.

Margoliouth, D. S. *Mohammed and the Rise of Islam.* London: G. P. Putnam's Sons, 1905.

Merrick, J. L. (tr.). *Life and Religion of Mohammed as Contained in the Sheeah Traditions of the Hyat-ul-Kuloob.* Boston: Phillips, 1850.

Mohy-ud-Din, Ata. *The Arabian Prophet: His Message and Achievements.* Karachi: Ferozsons, 1955.

Muir, Sir William. *The Life of Mohammad from Original Sources,* a new and revised edition by T. H. Weir. Edinburgh: J. Grant, 1923.

Nadvi, Muzzaffar Uddin. *An Easy History of the Prophet of Islam.* Lahore: M. Ashraf, 1954.

Pike, Edgar Royston. *Mohammed, Prophet of the Religion of Islam.* 2nd ed.; London: Weidenfeld, 1968.

Rahnama, Zayn al 'Abidin. *Payambar: The Messenger,* translated by L. P. Elwell-Sutton. Lahore: Sh. M. Ashraf, 1964-65.

Rodinson, Maxime. *Mohammed,* translated by Anne Carter. New York: Pantheon Books, 1971.

Sarwar, Hafiz Ghulam. *Muhammad the Holy Prophet.* Lahore: Sh. Muhammad Ashraf, 1964.

Shibli Numani, Muhammad. *'Allamah Shibli's Sirat al-Nabi*, translated by Fazlur Rahman. Karachi: Pakistan Historical Society, 1970.

Siddiqui, Abdul Hameed. *The Life of Muhammad*. Lahore: Islamic Publications, 1969.

Smith, Reginald Bosworth. *Mohammed and Mohammedanism*, lectures delivered at the Royal Institution of Great Britain in 1874. London: Smith, Elder and Co., 1874.

Sprenger, Aloys. *Life of Mohammad from Original Sources*. Allahabad, 1851.

Stobart, James William Hampson. *Islam and Its Founder*. London: Society for Promoting Christian Knowledge; and New York: Pott, Young, and Co., 1877.

Suhrawardy, Sir Abdullah al-Mamun. *The Sayings of Muhammad*. London: J. Murray, 1954.

Wahab, Syed Abdul. *The Shadowless Prophet of Islam: Being a Treatise on the Spiritual Aspect of the Prophet's Life and Spiritualism of Islam as Taught by Him*. Lahore: Sh. Muhammad Ashraf, 1962.

Waheeduddin Fakir, Syed. *The Benefactor*, translation of *Mohsin-e-Azam and Mohsanin*, English text revised by Faiz Ahmed Faiz. Karachi: Lion Art Press, 1964.

Watt, William Montgomery. *Muhammad at Mecca*. Oxford: Clarendon Press, 1960.

———. *Muhammad at Medina*. Oxford: Clarendon Press, 1966.

———. *Muhammad: Prophet and Statesman*. London: Oxford University Press, 1961.

Wessels, Antonie. *A Modern Arabic Biography of Muhammad: A Critical Study of Muhammad Husayn Haykal's Hayat Muhammad*. Leiden: E. J. Brill, 1972.

Widengren, George. *Muhammad, the Apostle of God, and His Ascension*. Uppsala: Lundequistska Bokhandeln, 1955.

Index of Proper Names

Midyan (tribe), 562

Mikha'il (the angel), 423

Mikraz ibn Hafs, 231

Mina, 21, 152, 170, 445, 468, 470

al Miqdad ibn 'Amr, 213, 225

al Mi'raj, 133, 136-39

Mis'ar ibn Rukhaylah, 292

Mistah, (by ibn Athathah), 326

Moab, see Ma'ab

Moghuls, lxxxvii

Mohamet, xxxvii, See also Mahomet

Mongols, 538, 571

Montesquieu, xxxvii

Morocco, xxviii, 99, 373

Mosaic religion, xxxvii, 9, 87, 123, See also Judaism

Moseilama, lix, See also Musaylimah

Moses, Masa (the prophet), xxxi, lxxxii, 2, 51, 54, 67, 73-74, 82, 87, 94, 134-35, 135, 144, 174, 186, 189, 213, 228, 277, 287, 459, 461, 488, 555, 561-63

Moslem(s), see Muslim(s)

Mosque, the, lxxxii, 90, 139, 188, 203-4, 221, 328-29, 405, 413, 447, See also the Ka'bah

Mosque of Madinah, 385, 428, 441

"Mother of the Faithful," ('A'ishah), lxxvi, 63

"Mothers of the Believers," 322, 421-22

Mount Hira', cave of, 66, 75

Mount al Safa, xv, 24-25, 44, 80, 82, 97-98, 196, 368, 395, 466

Mount Sinai, 134, 138

Mount Uhud, 246

Mu'adh ibn 'Afra', 164

Mu'adh ibn 'Amr ibn al Jamah, 221

Mu'adh ibn Jabal, lxxxii, 358, 412-13

Mu'allaqat, 51-52

Mu'awiyah, lxxxvi, 133, 360, 410, 463

Mudad ibn 'Amu ibn al Harith, 24, 29, 34

Mudhahhabat, 51

al Mughirah ibn 'Abdullah al Makhzumi, 34-35, 61

al Mughirah ibn Shu'bah, 336, 441, 443

Muhaddithun, 69

al Muhajirun, 154, 168-69, 171-75, 184-85, 187, 191-92, 195-202, 212, 247, 269, 271, 282, 306, 316-18, 323, 329, 332, 349, 366, 369, 380, 386, 388, 390-391, 399, 402, 409, 412-13, 435, 475, 478-80, 491-94, 537

Muhammad ibn Maslamah, 267-68, 356, 366, 431

Muharram, 44

Muir, Sir William (author of *The Life of Muhammad*), xlv, lvii, lxiv, 25-26, 46, 102, 326

Mundhir ibn 'Amr, 265

Mu'nis ibn Fadalah, 246

Munyah, 57

Murad (tribe), 455

Murarah ibn al Rabi', 435

al Muraysi', 316, 318

Mus'ab ibn 'Umayr, 148, 162, 225

Musaylimah ibn Habib (al Kadhdhab), 455, 473-74

Muslim (the compiler of Hadith), 418, 467

Muslim(s), ix-xii, xv, xvii, xxii, xxiv, xxvii-xxxii, xxxv-xxxvi, xxxviii-xli, xliii-xlviii, liv-lvii, lxiv-lxvi, lxviii-lxxx, lxxxii-lxxxvii, lxxxix, 11, 16-17, 22, 25, 36, 46-48, 63, 79, 82, 84, 86, 89-95, 97-98, 100-104, 108-110, 125-26, 129, 132, 139-40, 142, 146, 148-50, 152-56, 162-64, 168-80, 183-87, 190-92, 194-207, 209-31, 234-44, 246-74, 277-83, 289-90, 290, 292-307, 310-11, 313-21, 325, 327-35, 337-48, 351-61, 363-72, 376-97, 399-410, 412, 414-16, 418, 422-25, 427-32, 434-42, 444-46, 449-50, 453-55, 458, 460-61, 463, 465-67, 469, 473-74, 476-77, 480-84, 487-98, 503, 507-8, 512-15, 519, 521, 527, 534, 535, 537-38, 543, 545, 547, 554-55, 564, 566-69, 571-73

-Jewish, 174

of Madinah, 234, 239-40, 357, 381

Makkan, 149, 367